POSTINDUSTRIAL

1945	1950	1955	1960	1965	1970	1975	1980	1985	1990	1995	2000	2003	2005	2008

1954
Brown v. Board of Education

1965
Watts riot

Rodney King arrest and LA riot

Colin Powell Sec. of State

Univ. of Mich. AA cases

Condoleezza Rice becomes Sec. of State; Hurricane Katrina

Barack Obama elected president of the United States

← CIVIL RIGHTS MOVEMENT → ← URBAN UNDERCLASS → ← INCREASING CLASS DIFFERENTIATION →

Termination

1972
Trail of Broken Treaties

1975
CERT

1988
Federal legislation legalizes reservation gambling

Number of Indians exceeds 4 million

Revenue from gaming in reservations reaches $25 billion

RED POWER AND PANTRIBALISM

DEVELOPMENT OF RESERVATIONS AND ASSIMILATION

DEVELOPMENT OF RESERVATIONS AND GAMBLING

Zoot Suit Riots

Operation Wetback

Cuban immigration

CHICANISMO

N E W   I M M I G R A T I O N

P O L I C Y

Marielitos

Proposition 187 in California

NAFTA passed

2004
Hispanic Americans become largest minority group

2005
President Bush proposes Guest Worker Program

2007
Demonstrations against proposed changes in immigration policy in many cities

INCREASE IN IMMIGRATION, URBAN POVERTY, ETHNIC ENCLAVES, ASSIMILATION

Token immigration from China

1982
Vincent Chin murder

2001
Hate crimes against Arab and Asian Americans following 9/11 attacks

INCREASE IN IMMIGRATION, URBAN POVERTY, ETHNIC ENCLAVES, ASSIMILATION

ETHNIC REVIVAL

World War II

———— ASSIMILATION ————→

FLUID COMPETITIVE

Improve your grade

and get more out of the course by using our

Student Study Site!

www.pineforge.com/healey5e

For every chapter, you will find

- Self-quizzes
- E-flashcards for all key terms in the text
- Revised Internet research projects
- *This American Life* radio program links and related discussion questions
- PBS *Frontline* television program links and related discussion questions
- "Learning From SAGE Journal Articles" features that incorporate three to four SAGE journal articles as well as two to three corresponding critical thinking questions

2010/2011 UPDATE

FIFTH EDITION

Race, Ethnicity, Gender, and Class

Only when lions have historians will hunters cease to be heroes.

African Proverb

Not everything that is faced can be changed, but nothing can be changed until it is faced.

James Baldwin

2010/2011 UPDATE

FIFTH EDITION
Race, Ethnicity, Gender, and Class
The Sociology of Group Conflict and Change

Joseph F. Healey
Christopher Newport University

⑤SAGE | PINE FORGE

Los Angeles | London | New Delhi
Singapore | Washington DC

For information:

Pine Forge Press
An Imprint of SAGE Publications, Inc.
2455 Teller Road
Thousand Oaks, California 91320
E-mail: order@sagepub.com

SAGE Publications India Pvt. Ltd.
B 1/I 1 Mohan Cooperative Industrial Area
Mathura Road, New Delhi 110 044
India

SAGE Publications Ltd.
1 Oliver's Yard
55 City Road
London EC1Y 1SP
United Kingdom

SAGE Publications Asia-Pacific Pte. Ltd.
33 Pekin Street #02-01
Far East Square
Singapore 048763

Printed in Canada

Library of Congress Cataloging-in-Publication Data

Healey, Joseph F.
Race, ethnicity, gender, and class : the sociology of group conflict and change / Joseph F. Healey.—5th ed., 2010-2011 update
    p. cm.
Includes bibliographical references and index.
ISBN 978-1-4129-9058-5 (pbk. : acid-free paper)
    1. Minorities—United States. 2. Ethnicity—United States. 3. Racism—United States. 4. Group identity—United States. 5. Social conflict—United States. 6. United States—Race relations. 7. United States—Ethnic relations. 8. United States—Social conditions. I. Title.

E184.A1H415 2011
305.800973—dc22   2010021206

This book is printed on acid-free paper.

10   11   12   13   14   10   9   8   7   6   5   4   3   2   1

Acquisitions Editor:	David Repetto
Editorial Assistant:	Maggie Stanley
Production Editors:	Astrid Virding and Laureen Gleason
Copy Editor:	Carla Freeman
Typesetter:	C&M Digitals (P) Ltd.
Proofreader:	Scott Oney
Indexer:	Molly Hall
Cover Designer:	Gail Buschman
Marketing Manager:	Erica DeLuca

Contents

3 Prejudice and Discrimination 107

4 The Development of Dominant-Minority Group Relations in Preindustrial America: The Origins of Slavery   163

5 Industrialization and Dominant-Minority Relations: From Slavery to Segregation and the Coming of Postindustrial Society   201

PART 3 Understanding Dominant-Minority Relations in the United States Today

PART 4   Challenges for the Present and the Future

10 New Americans, Assimilation, and Old Challenges   461

Preface

Of all the challenges confronting the United States today, those relating to minority groups continue to be among the most urgent and the most daunting. Discrimination and racial inequality are part of our national heritage and—along with equality, freedom, and justice—prejudice and racism are among our oldest values. Minority group issues penetrate every aspect of society, and virtually every item on the national agenda—welfare and health care reform, crime and punishment, safety in the streets, the future of the family, even defense spending, foreign policy, and the war on terrorism—has some connection with dominant-minority relations.

These issues will not be resolved easily or quickly. Feelings are intense, and controversy and bitter debate often swamp dispassionate analysis and calm reason. As a society, we have little hope of resolving these dilemmas unless we confront them openly and honestly; they will not disappear, and they will not resolve themselves.

This textbook contributes to the ongoing discussion by presenting information, raising questions, and probing issues. My intent is to help students increase their fund of information, improve their understanding of the issues, and clarify their thinking regarding matters of race and ethnicity. This text has been written for undergraduate students—sociology majors and nonmajors alike. It makes minimal assumptions about students' knowledge of history or sociological concepts, and the material is presented in a way that students will find accessible and coherent.

For example, a unified set of themes and concepts is used throughout the text. The analysis is consistent and continuous, even as multiple perspectives and various points of view are examined. The bulk of the conceptual framework is introduced in the first five chapters. These concepts and analytical themes are then used in a series of case studies of minority groups in contemporary America and are also used to investigate group relations in various societies around the globe. In the final chapter, main points and themes are summarized and reviewed, the analysis is brought to a conclusion, and some speculations are made regarding the future.

The analysis is in the tradition of conflict theory, but this text does not aspire to be a comprehensive statement of that tradition. Other perspectives are introduced and applied, but no attempt is made to give equal attention to all current sociological paradigms. The text does not try to explain everything, nor does it attempt to include all possible analytical points of view. Rather, the goals are (a) to present the sociology of minority group relations in a way that students will find understandable as well as intellectually challenging and (b) to deal with the issues and tell the stories behind the issues in a textbook that is both highly readable and a demonstration of the power and importance of thinking sociologically.

Although the text maintains a unified analytical perspective, students are also exposed to a wide variety of perspectives on a number of different levels. For example, clashing points of view are presented in the "Current Debates" at the end of chapters. The debates focus on an issue taken from the chapter but present the views of scholars and analysts from a variety of disciplines and viewpoints. Without detracting from the continuity of the main analysis, these debates reinforce the idea that no one has all the answers (or for that matter, all the questions). The debates can be used to stimulate discussion, bring additional perspectives to the classroom, and suggest topics for further research.

In addition, every chapter (except the last) includes at least one "Narrative Portrait" recounting the personal experiences and thoughts of a wide variety of people: immigrants, minority group members, journalists, sociologists, racists, and slaves, among others. These excerpts reinforce the analysis dramatically, memorably, and personally and are integrated into the flow of the chapters. Also, the experiences of minority groups and the realities of prejudice, racism, and discrimination are documented with photos throughout the text. Several photo essays are also included.

This text also explores the diversity of experiences within each minority group, particularly gender differences. Too often, minority groups (and the dominant group, for that matter) are seen by nonmembers as single, undifferentiated entities. The text acknowledges the variety of experiences within each group and, in particular, explores differences in the experiences of minority group males and females. The analysis explores the ways in which gender differences cut across ethnic and racial differences and stresses that these sources of inequality and injustice are independent of each other. Solving one set of problems (e.g., prejudice and racial discrimination) will not automatically or directly solve the other (e.g., sexism and gender inequalities).

This text focuses on the experiences of minority groups in the United States, but a considerable amount of comparative, cross-national material has also been included. A series of boxed inserts called "Comparative Focus" explores group relations in other societies.

Finally, this text stresses the ways in which American minority groups are inseparable from American society. The relative success of this society is due no less to the contributions of minority groups than to those of the dominant group. The nature of the minority group experience has changed as the larger society has changed, and to understand America's minority groups is to understand some elemental truths about America. To raise the issues of race and ethnicity is to ask what it means, and what it has meant, to be an American.

Changes in This Edition

Many changes have been made in this edition, most of them designed to decrease length and sharpen focus. Needless to say, research findings and all data have been updated. In particular, this edition relies on the 2006 American Community Survey of the U.S. Bureau of the Census for the latest background information on America's minority groups.

- The material on prejudice and discrimination has been combined into a single chapter with more emphasis on the sociological perspective.
- The cross-national materials have been moved into the individual chapters and incorporated in the flow of the analysis. The separate chapter on dominant-minority relations around the globe has been eliminated.

RACE, ETHNICITY, GENDER, AND CLASS

- The chapter on "New Americans" has been shortened by moving most new immigrant groups into the case study chapters. That is, the smaller Hispanic groups are now covered in Chapter 8 and the smaller Asian groups in Chapter 9. This allows Chapter 10 to be more focused on recent immigrants and immigration issues in general.

- The separate chapter on white ethnic groups has been eliminated, and much of the material has been moved to Chapter 2 ("Assimilation and Pluralism"). This has the advantage of reducing some redundancy and introducing a model of successful assimilation against which the experiences of groups in Part 3 can be compared. Also, this change creates an opportunity, early in the text, to demonstrate to many white, dominant group students that exclusion and rejection, prejudice and discrimination were important realities for their recent ancestors.

- Many of the selections in the "Current Debates" have been updated, and some new topics have been added.

- An Appendix comparing the status of all groups covered in this text on a number of variables has been added. The Appendix also presents some information on gender differences within the groups. The information for these graphs comes from the 2006 American Community Survey of the U.S. Bureau of the Census.

- Many maps and other graphics have been added to increase the visual appeal of the text and to convey information in a more easily comprehensible way.

- A new type of graph displaying the distribution of income for groups, not just the averages, has been added to the case study chapters.

- A section on the racial and gender implications of Hurricane Katrina has been added to Chapter 1.

All textbooks, even those with a single author's name on the title page, are profoundly collaborative efforts. This book has been shaped by almost 40 years of teaching minority relations and by the thoughts and reactions of hundreds of students. My approach to this subject has grown from years of "field testing" ideas, concepts, theories, and research and constant monitoring of what seemed to help the students make sense of the world they live in. I acknowledge and thank my students for their myriad contributions.

When I was a student, I had the good fortune of learning from faculty members who were both accomplished scholars and exceptionally dedicated teachers. Each of them contributed to my interest in and commitment to sociology, but two stand out in my memory as mentors and intellectual role models: Professors Edwin H. Rhyne and Charles S. Green. Dr. Rhyne encouraged me as a young scholar and quite literally introduced me to the world of ideas and the life of the mind. Later in my career, Dr. Green showed me what it means to be a professional scholar, a sociologist, and a teacher. Their influence on my life was profound, and I thank them deeply.

I am no less indebted to my colleagues Stephanie Byrd, Cheri Chambers, Robert Durel, Michael Lewis, Marcus Griffin, Mai Lan Gustafsson, Marion Manton, Lea Pellett, Eduardo Perez, Virginia Purtle, and Linda Waldron of Christopher Newport University. They have been unflagging in their support of this project, and I thank them for their academic, logistical, and intellectual assistance. I would also like to thank the incomparable Mrs. Iris Price of Christopher Newport University for her indispensable help and support. I thank Ben Penner of Pine Forge Press for his invaluable assistance in the preparation of this manuscript and Steve Rutter, formerly of Pine Forge Press, for his help in the development of this project.

This text has benefited in innumerable ways from the reactions and criticisms of a group of reviewers who proved remarkably insightful about the subject matter and about the challenges of college teaching. I can no longer even estimate the number of points in the process of writing and research where the comments of the reviewers led to significant improvements in scholarship, clarity, and more meaningful treatments of the subject. The shortcomings that remain are, of course, my responsibility, but whatever quality this text has is a direct result of the insights and expertise of these reviewers. I thank the following people:

First Edition Reviewers

Audwin Anderson, *University of South Alabama*
Donna Barnes, *University of Wyoming*
Norma Burgess, *Syracuse University*
Steven Cornell, *University of California, San Diego*
Gerry R. Cox, *Fort Hays State University*
Kevin Delaney, *Temple University*
Raul Fernandez, *University of California, Irvine*
Timothy Fiedler, *Carroll College*
Ramona Ford, *Southwest Texas State University*
Joni Fraser, *University of California, Davis*
Nicole Grant, *Ball State University*
Anne Hastings, *University of North Carolina, Chapel Hill*
Michael Hodge, *Georgia State University*
Ray Hutchison, *University of Wisconsin, Green Bay*
Joseph J. Leon, *California State Polytechnic University, Pomona*
Seymour Leventman, *Boston College*
Wendy Ng, *San Jose State University*
Carol Poll, *Fashion Institute of Technology*
Dennis Rome, *Indiana University*
Gerald Rosen, *California State University, Fullerton*
Ellen Rosengarten, *Sinclair Community College*
A. Seals, *Kentucky State University*
Charles Smith, *Florida A&M*
Susan Takata, *University of Wisconsin, Parkside*
Joyce Tang, *City University of New York, Queens College*
Maura I. Toro-Morn, *Illinois State University*
Diana Torrez, *University of Texas, Arlington*
Robert Williams, *Jackson State University*
Min Zhou, *University of California, Los Angeles*

Second Edition Reviewers

JoAnn DeFiore, *University of Washington*
Jeremy Hein, *University of Wisconsin, Eau Claire*
Linda Green, *Normandale Community College*
David Matsuda, *Chabot College*

Victor M. Rodriguez, *Concordia University*
Craig Watkins, *University of Texas, Austin*
Norma Wilcox, *Wright State University*
Luis Zanartu, *Sacramento City College*
Min Zhou, *University of California, Los Angeles*

Third Edition Reviewers

Rick Baldoz, *University of Hawaii, Manoa*
Jan Fiola, *Minnesota State University, Moorhead*
David Lopez, *California State University, Northridge*
Peggy Lovell, *University of Pittsburgh*
Gonzalo Santos, *California State University, Bakersfield*
Carol Ward, *Brigham Young University*

Fourth Edition Reviewers

Herman DeBose, *California State University, Northridge*
Abby Ferber, *University of Colorado, Colorado Springs*
Celestino Fernandez, *University of Arizona*
Samuel Leizear, *West Virginia University*
Gregory J. Rosenboom, *University of Nebraska/Nebraska Wesleyan University*
Peggy A. Shifflett, *Radford University*
Debbie Storrs, *University of Idaho*
Carol Ward, *Brigham Young University*
Norma Wilcox, *Wright State University*
Earl Wright, *University of Central Florida*

Fifth Edition Reviewers

Sharon Allen, *University of South Dakota*
Cathy Beighey, *Aims Community College*
Wendy H. Dishman, *Santa Monica College*
Bruce K. Friesen, *University of Tampa*
Susan E. Mannon, *Utah State University*
David McBride, *Pennsylvania State University*
Pam Brown Schachter, *Marymount College, Palos Verdes*
John Stone, *Boston University*
Merwyn L. Strate, *Purdue University*
Leigh A. Willis, *The University of Georgia*

About the Author

Joseph F. Healey is Professor of Sociology at Christopher Newport University in Virginia. He received his PhD in sociology and anthropology from the University of Virginia. An experienced, innovative teacher of numerous race and ethnicity courses, he has written articles on minority groups, the sociology of sport, social movements, and violence, and he is also the author of *Statistics: A Tool for Social Research* (8th ed., 2008).

About the Publisher

Pine Forge Press is an educational publisher, dedicated to publishing innovative books and software throughout the social sciences. On this and any other publications, we welcome your comments and suggestions.

Please call or write us at

Pine Forge Press
An Imprint of SAGE Publications, Inc.
2455 Teller Road
Thousand Oaks, CA 91320
(800) 818-7243
E-mail: order@sagepub.com

Visit our Web site, your direct link to a multitude of online resources:
http://www.pineforge.com

Bonus Introductory Chapter

The Election of President Barack Obama

If there is anyone out there who still doubts that America is a place where all things are possible, who still wonders if the dream of our founders is alive in our times, who still questions the power of our democracy, tonight is your answer.

—President-Elect Barack Obama
November 4, 2008

Despite the bitter cold, more than a million people filled the National Mall. They came to celebrate, to participate, to witness a turning point in history. Millions more around the nation and around the globe watched on television and on the Internet as Barack Hussein Obama took the oath of office and became the 44th president of the United States. To many, the ceremony marked the end of an era and a final, decisive rejection of American racism, injustice, and unfairness. For many, hope and optimism surged: If it was possible for a person of color to rise to the highest office in the United States, the most powerful position in the world, what else was possible? What *couldn't* be achieved? Barriers and limitations melted away, obstacles and impediments crumbled, and, at least for a time, people everywhere felt their horizons stretch and their goals expand. Had the United States finally fulfilled its promise and become what it had often proclaimed itself to be: the last, best hope for the world—a bastion of decency and fairness in a world filled with injustice, oppression, and despair?

People will be discussing and debating this inauguration for generations, and, of course, only time will permit final judgments and assessments. Was this truly the dawning of a new day? Or was the significance of the day overblown? What did the triumph of President Obama mean for the day-to-day lives of black Americans and other minority groups? Did it truly alter their life chances and the prospects of their children? Racism and the structures that perpetuate inequality have been powerful and resilient features of American life since colonial days:

For many people, the election of Barack Obama was an event of great significance, far exceeding the mere passing of authority from one president or party to the next. To capture some of these perceptions and emotions, I asked several friends to recount their reactions to President Obama's inauguration. These memories come from people who vary in race, age, and experience, but they are NOT a random or representative sample of U.S. society. All were watching intently on Inauguration Day, all voted for Obama, and all saw the events as momentous. The memories vary in details, but note how they frame the event in very personal terms and how they all link the inauguration to the flow of their own lives, often reaching back to childhood for perspective and context. Also, note the euphoria and sense of awe the respondents commonly express: Clearly, through their eyes, we are watching a very fundamental and positive change in the nation and the world.

Were we mistaking the triumph of one man for the dissolution of the systems of white privilege and minority group disadvantage?

What can we learn by focusing the concepts and perspectives developed in this text on the election of President Barack Obama? At the end of Chapter 6 of this volume, I point out that the situation of African Americans today can be seen as either a glass half full or half empty. The same metaphor can be applied to President Obama's triumph: Should we stress the progress marked by this historic election and rejoice in the ability of U.S. society to grow and remake itself? Or should we stress the challenges that remain for American minority groups, especially those that are afflicted by urban poverty and systematically excluded from the mainstream? Does Obama's election verify that the glass is growing fuller, or does it throw the half-empty glass into starker relief? Is this truly a breakthrough or merely a distraction from the grim realities of everyday racism and disenfranchisement? Can it be both?

A Post-Racial Society?

Some have appraised the Obama victory as evidence that the United States has become *post-racial.* What could this term mean? Different people attach different meanings to the word, so let's begin by sorting out some common interpretations.

The most positive interpretation—the strongest meaning of post-racial—is that the forces of prejudice, racism, and discrimination have been canceled out ("The glass is growing rapidly fuller"). A post-racial society, by this definition, can be described in the words of Dr. Martin Luther King Jr.'s famous "I Have a Dream" speech in 1963: In such a society, all are judged by the content of their character, not by the color of their skin. According to this interpretation, President Obama's election signifies the end of prejudgment (or prejudice) based on skin color or ethnicity (and also religion and gender?) and the disappearance (or at least drastic reduction) of the gaps between dominant and minority groups in income, education, occupational profiles, political power, and other dimensions of equality.

A second interpretation of post-racial, somewhat weaker but still quite positive, stresses the diminishing power of racial identity in society: In a post-racial United States of this type, people's lives and perceptions are much less constricted or determined by their race (for an example of this view, see Hsu, 2009). While racial inequality may continue, multiculturalism and tolerance rule the day, and race is no more important in everyday life than a multitude of other lifestyle and cultural differences, including religion, political ideology, education, occupation, musical preferences, and hundreds of others. In this view, the all-embracing color line established during slavery and perpetuated during segregation has been blurred and is now negotiable. Americans are freer than ever to manufacture their own identities and lifestyles, to change them as they see fit, or, indeed, to completely abandon them if they so choose. The argument that racial identity has become an individual choice—not unilaterally imposed by the larger society—is reminiscent of the concept of "symbolic ethnicity" for white ethnic groups, discussed in Chapter 2. This view is also compatible with many trends discussed throughout this text: the growing diversity of our society, the decline of the white numerical majority, and the increasing number of mixed-race individuals. Can people of color choose to be as racial or nonracial as they want to be?

A third perspective sees the term post-racial as empty rhetoric, a mistaken or greatly exaggerated interpretation of the significance of Obama's victory. This view ("The glass is still half empty") stresses the continuing racial gaps and the power of anti-black prejudice, even if disguised in more subtle terms: The United States remains a racist society and a bastion of white privilege and supremacy, and the success of one man means little or nothing for the millions trapped by poverty and institutionalized discrimination and marginalized on the edge of mainstream society. At first glance, this view seems most consistent with the hypotheses and concepts emphasized throughout the text of this book and would seem to urge that claims of the demise of racism and racial inequality be treated with a strong dose of skepticism.

Of course, there are many other ways to view Obama's election, and the truth—always complex and subtle—may well lie in some mixture of these three views. Nevertheless, let's take a look at the election and changing U.S. society and see which of the three interpretations, if any, is most supported by the evidence.

Was Race a Factor in Obama's Election?

If the strongest interpretation of post-racial is accurate, and President Obama's election signaled the demise of racism in U.S. society, his campaign and his support base should have been nonracial. Were they?

Practical Politics and an Early Victory

Any politician seeking office in a pluralistic, diverse society must rely on coalitions of blocs of voters for victory. This is especially true for minority candidates. To have a chance at

Bob

Bob is a sociologist and an African American. Born in 1935, he has a very personal acquaintance with the indignities of second-class citizenship. As a young man, he was involved in active resistance to Jim Crow and participated in sit-ins, demonstrations, and protests and also worked for the civil rights commission in his state. He was one of the first 100,000 supporters of Obama, and during the campaign, he edited a blog devoted to "Black and Progressive Sociologists for Obama."

The world has changed!!! On January 20, 2009, the world . . . has been stood on its head!! A "colonized minority" is now president of the world's most powerful nation. To say that electing an African American, Barack Obama, to the presidency of the United States is historic is almost trite. His election was historic, but it was more than that. The inauguration of Barack Obama . . . is not as much about the past as it is the future. The leader of the so-called free world is a person of African descent. The face of America has changed. There is no turning back. Barack Obama is just the first black president of the United States. There will be women presidents. There will be presidents of color who are not black. America has changed. Before our very eyes, America is being transformed for a future very different from its past.

With an African American as the Democratic Party nominee, the presidential election of 2008 became a referendum on white nationalism. As a dialectical reaction to the post–World War II liberalism (that included . . . the civil rights and anti–Vietnam War movements), the presidency of Ronald Reagan and the "Reagan Revolution" . . . [marked the beginning of] almost 30 years of anti–civil rights conservative hegemony. The election of Obama overturns an era [defined by] white nationalism. . . . Like Reagan's, Obama's presidency will be transformative . . . away from a conservatism rooted in a "southern strategy" toward a more inclusive progressivism.

The essence of white nationalism is . . . to promote the interests of . . . the "white nation." The whole history of Americans of African descent has been a struggle to be citizens of a nation [in whose history and development] they played a central role . . . America's intent from slavery through Manifest Destiny was to make America white and deny citizenship to its former chattel. The Naturalization and Citizen Act of 1790 made it clear than only whites could be citizens. Continuing through the Dred Scott case in the 1850s and Jim Crow into the 1950s, only whites had full citizenship rights. While 53% of whites did not vote for Obama, a new majority has been formed. That new majority is composed of whites who do not share the ideology of white nationalism, African Americans, Latinos, Asians, and the "new immigrants." Like the "Reagan Revolution's" economic policies, its social policies of intolerance are being rejected, as well.

Barack Obama's election to the presidency of the United States means that he, a black man, is America's citizen numero uno. As such, his election manifests a reality that African Americans are in fact full-fledged Americans. At the inauguration, you could see in the faces of the multitude of African Americans in attendance as they waved American flags, shouted cheers, and shed tears of joy (!), we are now American citizens. By electing Obama president at the ballot box, America has recognized that black people are indeed citizens.

the polls, it was necessary for Obama to reach people everywhere, not just in the black community or in minority neighborhoods. From the start, he sought to construct a winning coalition by emphasizing the issues about which Americans are most concerned: the economy, the war in Iraq, health care, and national policy on energy and the environment, among others. He did not focus on "black" issues (e.g., civil rights or racism in the criminal justice system), and his strategy was to discuss issues of race "only in the context of other issues" (Ifill, 2009, p. 53). The campaign strategy aimed to avoid associations that presented Obama as "the black candidate" and instead to promote him as a viable, competent candidate who happened to be black.

The power of this strategy and Obama's ability to attract the support of large numbers of white voters were demonstrated in Iowa, the first state test in the race for the Democratic nomination for president. Iowa is only 7% black, but Obama attracted nearly 40% of the voters in the statewide caucuses, a huge boost to the campaign and a clear demonstration of his appeal to a broad coalition of voters. While he had to fight for literally every vote following his victory in Iowa and lost several primaries to chief rival Hillary Clinton, this early triumph sent a clear signal of his broad appeal and his ability to attract support from across the electorate, a fact that seems consistent with the idea that his campaign signaled the coming of a post-racial era.

A New Generation

Obama's campaign heralded the rise of a new generation of black politicians. The older generation—men and women now in their 70s, 80s, or long deceased—had cleared the way in the southern civil rights movement, voter registration drives, campaigns to raise the awareness of Americans about racial inequality, and continuing efforts to keep the issues of racial justice at the forefront of the public consciousness. The older generation—including Jesse Jackson and Al Sharpton, both of whom had run for the Democratic presidential nomination in past campaigns—had forced the larger society to dismantle the Jim Crow system, make at least a formal commitment to racial equality, and enfranchise the black community. They campaigned as black Americans first and foremost and kept up the pressure to make racial equality a reality, not just a formal commitment. They succeeded in erasing many racial barriers, and their efforts created the opportunity for the next generation of African American politicians to enter the mainstream.

Barack Obama is the most prominent member of the younger generation of black leadership. Others include Governor Deval Patrick of Massachusetts and Mayor Cory Booker of Newark, New Jersey. These younger African American leaders are not "race men"; they are pragmatic, flexible, less ideological in their positions, and even willing to challenge their elders when they see fit. For example, several (including Obama) support charter schools as one strategy for dealing with the woeful state of inner-city education, a position that is anathema to members of the older generation who view the charter school movement as a strategy to avoid racial integration (Ifill, 2009, pp. 127–128).

Consistent with the idea of an emerging post-racial America, Obama was born in 1961 and grew up in Hawaii and Indonesia, far removed from the realities of Jim Crow segregation and the legacy of systemic, state-sponsored racial inequality. Obama was not the first choice of the old-line black leadership (who tended to favor Hillary Clinton) and, in fact, was the target of some decidedly negative remarks from Jesse Jackson (Weisman, 2008, p. A4). What Obama presented to the American public was not the passion and fire of racial rhetoric, but an image of competence, articulate integrity, and the promise of change. While he is, of course, aware of the debt his generation owes to the civil rights pioneers, his message to the electorate in 2008 urged the need to move forward on issues that affect *all* Americans.

Bill

Bill is a white American who grew up in the civil rights era. He is an educator, engineer, and musician who recently retired after nearly 3 decades as a college president.

A black-and-white metal advertising button now yellowed by almost a half century leans against my computer. In the center of the button, two hands—one black, one white—grasp each other. Around the handshake, the text reads, "March on Washington for Jobs & Freedom August 28, 1963."

Through four-and-a-half decades, this button has adorned my guitar case, my clothes, and . . . my desk. With the kind of zeal accessible only to idealistic youth, I first pinned on this button as a prelude to my senior year in . . . high school. But, I did not attend the march. I did not see it on television. I did not hear Dr. King's "I Have A Dream" speech on radio.

August 28 was my father's birthday. He would not suffer, on that day or any other day, a son to march with "those people." The concept of "those people" was an indispensable part of his southern legacy. His construct of a just America was anchored in the text of *Plessy v. Ferguson.* He understood that the doctrine of separate-but-equal would eventually end as the law of the land and took considerable comfort in believing that the change would not happen during his lifetime. Constant alarms filled my young ears that the social fabric of the country would be rent beyond recognition and that the United States would decline because of the rise of the Negro. The message was clear, unwavering, and to me both archaic and offensive.

In the presence of company mixed by age, gender, and race, I wore the 46-year-old button while we watched . . . Barack Hussein Obama take the oath to faithfully execute the office of president of the United States. That button is only 2 years the junior of Mr. Obama. Wearing it made me feel that the portion of the country that sought civil rights had not merely endured a long, ugly struggle, but had prevailed over the power of privilege.

Throughout the . . . inaugural address, my thoughts sprinted across the paradoxes and closure the event brought. My father's admonition that the rise of part of our society would devastate the entire society was laid to waste now that a black man was president. The White House, first occupied by the antislavery president John Adams, was now home to an African American. For the first time in its history, the political will of the United States had rejected the false principle that American society can function only as a zero-sum game in which the privileged are gatekeepers to power.

Although that historic badge and its wearer will forever remain virgins to the event the one proclaimed and the other sought to attend, recalling why I have preserved that button for nearly half a century permitted me to watch the ceremony with the kind of zeal accessible only to idealistic youth. I was engulfed by a sense of hope and the feeling that, after all, good will arise from the struggle that permitted Mr. Obama to seek and to secure the presidency.

Race and the Campaign

What role did race play in the 2008 campaign? In recent decades, consistent with the rise of the more muted and subtle forms of prejudice, racial issues and racism in political campaigns have been communicated through code words, not blatant attacks. The playing of the race card can be exemplified by the infamous Willy Horton ads run in the 1988 presidential contest between candidates George H. W. Bush and Michael Dukakis, then governor of Massachusetts. Horton, a black man, had been convicted of murder but came to be released from a Massachusetts prison through a weekend furlough program that had been established during Dukakis's term as governor. Horton proceeded to embark on a crime spree and committed several felonies, including assault and rape, before being apprehended again. The ads were used to paint the liberal

Dukakis as soft on crime and punishment, not tough enough to be entrusted with the leadership of the nation. Meanwhile, the not-so-subtle subtext of the ads portrayed the traditional stereotype of the menacing black male, violent, out of control, and a threat to white women.

Similar attempts were made to brand Obama as a soft-hearted liberal who was weak on issues of crime, law and order, and national defense, all common political code signifying race and racism. The most notable of these episodes stemmed from Obama's link to the flamboyant, outspoken Reverend Jeremiah Wright, pastor of the Chicago church attended by Obama. In the spring of 2008, a video of Reverend Wright surfaced and was replayed endlessly on the cable news channels and the Internet (see YouTube at http://www.youtube.com/watch?v=9hPR5jnjtLo). In the video, Pastor Wright roundly condemns U.S. society for its treatment of black Americans and urges his followers not to sing "God Bless America" but "God Damn America" for its killing of innocents and repression and mistreatment of blacks. Wright argued that the September 11, 2001, attacks had been provoked by the United States' own aggression abroad—including the World War II bombings of Nagasaki and Hiroshima—and he condemned U.S. support of "state terrorism" against Palestinians and black South Africans (Ross & El-Buri, 2008).

Wright's remarks derailed the Obama campaign staff for weeks as they sought a way to defuse the issue. The danger, from the standpoint of the Obama camp, was that the Wright video would be used to drive a wedge between the candidate and his white supporters by emphasizing his racial identity and activating the anti-black prejudice that lies beneath the surface of American society. Just as Willie Horton was used to brand Governor Dukakis as a soft-hearted liberal, Jeremiah Wright might be used to brand Obama and raise those ancient American cultural perceptions associating race with incompetence.

After considerable confusion and mixed messages from his campaign, Obama finally dissociated himself from Wright and addressed the underlying issues in an elegant, carefully crafted speech on race and America. Obama acknowledged both America's racist past and the continuing importance of racism in the present (in terms suggestive of the concept of "past-in-present" discrimination introduced in Chapter 5). He argued that Wright's view of America was distorted and that the pastor's error was that he had "elevated what is wrong with America above all that we know is right with America" (Obama, 2008). Contrary to those who argue for the diminishing importance of race, Obama stated that U.S. society has been "stuck in a racial stalemate for years" and that he did not believe that "we can get beyond our racial divisions in a single election cycle, or with a single candidacy." But, he argued, "We can move beyond our old racial wounds, and . . . in fact we have no choice if we are to continue on the path to a more perfect union." Finally, he argued that Wright's mistake was speaking as if the United States were static and incapable of change: "What we know—what we have seen—is that this America can change. This is the true genius of this nation."

The speech put the Obama campaign back on track and put the furor over Pastor Wright in the past. It also made clear that Obama himself, the supposed harbinger of a new racial age, had no illusions about the waning strength of racism or the sudden emergence of a new age of racial justice and fairness.

The issue of race continued to lurk in the near background. Indeed, as many have remarked, it would be naive to think that a person of color could run for the highest office in the land without raising racial concerns in the minds of Americans. Although there were

Gwen

Gwen is a professor of social work. She grew up in a southern state during the days of segregation and rose, through her own efforts and determination, to her present status. She remembers well the all-black high school she attended, and this provides a context for appreciating the inauguration ceremony.

Words cannot begin to express the emotions that I felt on January 20, 2009. The anticipation and waiting for 12:00 p.m. on this historic day was a humbling experience. As I sat in my office watching TV with two of my students, witnessing this experience was surreal and beyond my wildest imagination. I felt as if I was having an "out-of-body experience," and I was carried back through time. . . . My mind floated back through my life's journey . . . and the tears uncontrollably flowed down my cheeks. The tears that I shed were tears of sadness, joy, happiness, humility, love, hope, forgiveness, and gratitude. The mixed emotions were so overwhelming.

As a young black girl growing up on a farm . . . during the 1950s and 1960s when segregation was at its peak, believing that a black man would hold the highest office in the nation was not something that would have even been . . . a dream. On the other hand, I remember vividly the dedication and commitment of my great-grandparents, parents, teachers, neighbors, and basically the entire community working and fighting for our voting and civil rights. . . . Forty years later, because of my ancestors and the many, many other unsung heroes who challenged the oppressive nature of those who felt superior, we were given encouragement and hope.

As I watched Barack Obama take his oath as the president of this great nation on this historic day, the tears of sadness that rolled down my cheeks were in memory of my ancestors who struggled to pave the way for this day and were not able to see the fruits of their labor. However, I was also joyful and happy that I was alive to witness this day and now . . . believing [and] knowing that there is hope and insurmountable possibilities for future generations. At the same time, I was able to feel a sense of forgiveness for all those who fought against social and economic justice for all humankind, regardless of race, color or creed, and gratitude to those who stood up to do what was morally right. This historic moment would not have been possible without all races and ethnicities coming together for change.

persistent tendencies to see Obama as something other than a "true American"—including rumors that he was Muslim, that a "fist bump" he exchanged with his wife was a signal to terrorists, and that he consorted with political radicals and revolutionaries—the campaign managed to stay on track and defuse or deflect the rumors. Ultimately, the image that Obama was a worthy candidate who happened to be black (rather than a black candidate who might be worthy) triumphed at the polls on election day.

Race and Support for Obama

How did Obama supporters break down along racial lines? In many ways, the election reflects the increasing diversity of U.S. society. For the first time in history, in 2008, white voters made up less than 75% of the electorate—a dramatic decline since 1976, when 90% of voters were white, and a clear reflection of the changing composition of our population (see Chapter 1, Exhibit 1.1). Black Americans constituted 13% of all voters, up from 11% in 2004 and, unlike the past, proportional to their share of the total population. The Hispanic vote had also increased, but by only 1 point, to 9% of the electorate, still far below their relative share of the total population (ABC News, 2008).

Obama supporters reflected the emerging, more diverse America: 61% white, 23% black, and 11% Hispanic. In contrast, John McCain's supporters were 90% white (ABC News, 2008). Obama's support was broad based, and he pulled a larger percentage of voters from every category and subcategory of the electorate, except those age 65 and over, than had John Kerry, the Democratic candidate for president in 2004 (see Exhibit P.1).

There clearly are racial dimensions to Obama's support, but his backers came from every faction in society, including conservatives and Republicans. His campaign was perhaps especially notable for its ability to mobilize younger voters: up a whopping 12% from 2004.

Was the Election Post-Racial?

What can we conclude? The strongest meaning of post-racial might apply to some aspects of the election, including the fact that Obama drew support from a broad cross-section of Americans. On the other hand, the continuing power of race on American society lay just beneath the surface and manifested itself in episodes such as the furor over Reverend Wright's remarks and the persistent tendency to see Obama as an "other," not quite a "true American." It seems reasonable to conclude that the campaign and the election itself were more consistent with some mixture of the other two interpretations. Race was not the paramount issue (as it might have been in years past), but the campaign was waged in a society that had not outgrown the traditions of race, racial inequality, and racism.

A New Racial Order or Same Old Racial Perceptions?

Barack Obama has been consistently identified as "African American" and "black" throughout the campaign, during the inauguration, and still today. In the context of American traditions of race and racism, what do these labels signify?

First of all, as discussed in Chapter 1, the racial labels used in everyday American life are socially as well as biologically based. They were created in a particular historical context and during certain economic and political struggles between groups, and they reflect the realities of those conflicts. American cultural understandings of the differences between blacks and whites were formed during the time of slavery and attempted to rationalize the system by asserting the categorical inferiority of Africans. Racial distinctions were perpetuated during segregation de jure and institutionalized in a variety of ways, including the "One-Drop Rule": Any trace of African ancestry—even a single drop of blood—identified a person as black, inferior, and subject to all the restrictions reserved for racial subordinates in the Jim Crow regime. Although contemporary perceptions of race may be moving away from these rigid traditions, it seems that many Americans continue to perceive race largely

Support for Obama in 2008 and Changes in Support for the Democratic Candidate Since 2004

	Obama (%)	McCain (%)	Democrat Gains/Losses, 2004–2008 (percentage points)
Total	52	46	+4
Race/Ethnic Group			
White	43	55	+2
Black	95	4	+7
Hispanic	66	32	+13
Age Group			
18–29	66	32	+12
30–44	52	46	+6
45–64	49	49	+2
65+	45	53	–2
Income Group			
Less than $50,000	60	38	+5
$50,000–$99,999	49	49	+5
$100,000+	49	50	+8
Party Affiliation			
Republican	9	89	+3
Democrat	89	10	0
Independent	52	44	+3
Political Ideology			
Conservative	20	78	+5
Moderate	60	39	+6
Liberal	88	10	+3
Residence			
Urban	63	35	+9
Suburban	50	48	+3
Rural	45	53	+3

SOURCE: Pew Research Center (2008). Based on exit polls.

RACE, ETHNICITY, GENDER, AND CLASS

Matt

Matt is white, a journalist, and a veteran of 3 years in Ukraine with the Peace Corps.

Growing up, I always wondered what it was like to be alive during the time of John F. Kennedy or Abraham Lincoln, and what I might have felt had I heard one of them give a speech. Like any American, I yearned for an American leader who would inspire my entire generation, plus those that followed.

But Kennedy died 17 years before I was born. Abraham Lincoln had been dead for 115 years. With the recent crop of politicians fading fast, I had nearly given up hope, until I shook the hand of Barack Obama.

It was August 2008, just a day or two before Obama was to accept the Democratic nomination in Denver. I was working as a newspaper reporter in Montana, and I broke the news that Obama would be making a fifth trip to our state.

I angled to get close to the man—not as a fan, but as a journalist. I wanted to see him up close, because with him, I felt that history was being written a little early. I worked for days to get details on his visit. I even trailed an advance Secret Service team that was checking out possible venues.

But I struck out, it seemed. I was able to cover his rally . . . but only from the press bleachers in the back. Then came a call that Obama would be dropping in on a house full of supporters to watch the convention that night. I jumped up from my seat at a bush league baseball game and raced to the house with my wife, a Ukrainian whom I'd met while serving in the Peace Corps.

We couldn't get in the house, but we waited across the street for Obama to emerge. Cars whizzed by with no idea why a crowd had gathered in front of a little brown duplex. Eventually, Obama came out the garage door. By then, a crowd of 30 had gathered, and they began cheering. Obama waded into the road as his security stopped traffic. He walked over and grabbed my hand first, and then my wife's. Then everyone else's. It was over in seconds.

My wife was elated. And this certainly wasn't Ukraine, where political cynicism overwhelms all else. She didn't want to wash her hand.

"Maybe I'm the first Ukrainian to have shaken his hand!" she said.

Two months later, on election night, I stood among a crowd of reporters and editors in front of the TV. At exactly 9 p.m., they called the election for Obama. Looking at the newsroom eyeballs fixed on the screen, I saw a motley crowd of liberals, conservatives, libertarians, and who-knows-what-else. They all had one thing in common: They watched silently. No one cheered—that's not kosher in a newsroom—but I sensed that everyone would remember that moment forever. I don't remember other election moments, but I won't forget 9 p.m. on election night 2008.

as a matter of skin color and to believe that everyone belongs, unambiguously, to one and only one race.

The racial labeling of President Obama as black or African American is quite consistent with these long, deep traditions of American racism. This is especially the case since the labels do not apply to him literally, at least as the terms are usually understood. He is not descended from American slaves nor did he have relatives in the United States prior to the immigration of his father in 1959, from Kenya. To be sure, President Obama is both African and American, but he is not "African American." His father was "black," but his mother was "white," and, like many Americans, his European roots can be traced to a variety of locales, including Ireland.

In one way, consistent with the second view of a "post-racial" United States, President Obama, along with other prominent mixed race individuals, such as Tiger Woods and Halle

Berry, may well serve as an icon for an emerging era of changed consciousness about race: His mixed-race background and the fact that he does not fit into the traditional rigid categories challenge—in a very prominent way—the usefulness and validity of those categories. Although only 2% of the population in the 2000 U.S. Census chose to identify themselves with more than one race, some project that as much as 20% of the population will identify as "mixed" by 2050.

On the other hand, the very persistence of racial labeling as applied to President Obama suggests that we have not yet made the transition to a new racial consciousness and have not rejected the racist simplicities of past generations. Seeing and labeling Obama as black or African American—as a member of a clearly defined and delimited group—allows people to avoid the ambiguities of mixed race or thinking in new ways about the color line that has existed at the core of our society for so long. As one newspaper columnist remarked, "In general, Barack Hussein Obama brings us face-to-face with the discomfort our society feels with this idea of difference" (Iwaela, 2008, p. A-23). Labeling Obama as black or African American sustains the place of race in American life as a fundamental characteristic by which to differentiate and identify people. It also continues the perception that only "others" (non-whites) have race—after all, other prominent politicians and Obama's opponents in the election were not routinely labeled "white."

Reactions in Black and White

How did Americans view the campaign and election of President Obama? Consistent with the multicultural, diverse, complicated society we are, reactions were extremely variable and ranged from exhilaration and euphoria to deep despair. Although many people from all walks of life saw the election as positive, reactions and perceptions clearly broke down along racial lines, as they have in the past.

Black Americans were much more enthusiastic about the election and optimistic about the future than were whites. According to one CNN poll conducted just before Obama's inauguration, nearly 70% of black Americans reported that they believed that Dr. King's vision for America—as a society in which people are judged by the content of their character, not the color of their skin—had been achieved (CNN, 2009). Only 46% of white respondents agreed. The percentage of both groups had risen since March 2008, when only 34% of blacks and 35% of whites agreed that Dr. King's goal had been achieved. The January poll is possibly the only survey in U.S. history showing black Americans as being more favorable about race relations than whites and more optimistic about the future. More typical would be the poll reported in Chapter 1, in Exhibit 1.2, which shows greater pessimism among blacks. It seems that the CNN poll reflected the euphoria and exhilaration of the moment, not a realistic or objective appraisal of American race relations.

Other, more personal reactions are presented in the "Eyewitness to History" inserts scattered throughout this Bonus Introductory Chapter. These accounts come from a variety of Obama supporters, and judging by their intensity, it seems clear that the events of January 20,

Judi

Judi lives in West Virginia. She is white, and her husband is African American. She says that she and her husband "have walked the path for equality for over 40 years. We have walked in silence and let our lives show folks how love and respect for each other shine as our light." Judi and her husband were on the National Mall for the inauguration.

On January 20, 2009, [my husband, a friend], and myself were standing on the mall with folks from all walks of life, listening to President-Elect Obama take his oath. I watched my husband's face...fill with so much emotion. I could witness his sorrow, sadness (his mother, father, grandparents, and other family members who have passed over to the next life), the mistreatment of his family and [his] experience. Rejoicing and humbling as his soul was cleansed. An African American spiritual came in my mind: "Hush, hush someone is calling my name." His ancestors were jumping for joy as an African American was taking the oath as the 44th president of the United States of America. The pain, suffering from the past generations; their offspring are climbing the mountain top.

2009, will take a very prominent place in the collective memory of this society. The respondents see the election in the context of their own lives and struggles and commonly express not only enthusiasm and optimism, but the sense that the society has been transformed, even revolutionized. They would not mistake this presidency for the coming of a completely post-racial America, but they would agree that the United States has turned a corner and that, in the words of one, "There is no going back."

Have Racial Gaps Decreased?

Perhaps the crucial test of the power of race in American society lies in the size of the racial gaps documented in Chapter 6: On many dimensions, there is a large difference between blacks and whites. In a truly post-racial society, these gaps would be nonexistent, or at least diminishing over time. An overview of the facts presented in Chapter 6 shows a closing of the racial gap in some areas. For example, Exhibit 6.9 shows a dramatic narrowing of the racial gap in high school education and some narrowing in college education (although the falling percentage of college-educated black males in the most recent year is certainly cause for alarm). On other dimensions, the picture is more mixed, although a determined optimist could perhaps argue that the racial gap is narrowing in some ways. For example, Exhibits 6.3, 6.11, and 6.12 may be seen as indicating some narrowing of the economic gap in income and poverty levels, at least over the long run.

We can update some of these figures using data that became available since this edition originally went to press. The most recent data presented in Chapter 6 came from 2005, but new data from 2007 were recently made available by the U.S. Census Bureau. Before looking at the information, it should be noted that variables such as these do not change very rapidly and we should not expect dramatic differences in just a 2-year time period.

Exhibit P.2 shows an improvement in black median household income relative to whites between 2005 and 2007, but no change in levels of poverty. Although the picture is somewhat mixed (and at least the gaps didn't grow any larger), there continues to be a large economic gap between black and white households, families, and children.

Exhibit P.3 presents a grimmer picture. The values in the body of the table are the percentages of each race/gender group relative to white males. Contrary to the narrowing of the income gap for households displayed in Exhibit P.2, black male and female and white female full-time, year-round workers all lost ground relative to white males between 2005 and 2007. In 2005, for example, black male workers earned 78% of what white male workers earned. This percentage fell 2 points by 2007. This is not a huge drop, and since this data comes from random samples rather than the entire population, there is some margin for error in the values. Nonetheless, these trends are not reassuring to those who have argued for the coming of a post-racial society.

We do not know what has happened to the racial gaps since 2007 as the economy soured and rates of unemployment rose. However, as I point out in Chapter 6, racial minorities have a more tenuous grasp on prosperity and affluence even in the best of times, and it would not be unreasonable to speculate that the burden of the recent recession has harmed blacks more than whites.

Exhibit P.3 also shows a widening in the educational gap, especially for black males. Black and white females held their relative positions on level of high school education, but both black males and black females fell in terms of college education. These are ominous trends for the future economic prospects of the black community.

Exhibit P.2 **Gaps Between Blacks and Whites, 2005 and 2007**

Variable	Year	Whites	Blacks	Blacks Compared With Whites
Median household income	2005	$50,784	$30,858	60.7%
	2007	$53,714	$34,001	63.3%
Families in poverty	2005	7.6%	22.8%	3.0 times higher
	2007	7.0%	21.3%	3.0 times higher
Children in poverty	2005	13.8%	35.2%	2.6 times higher
	2007	13.3%	34.5%	2.6 times higher

SOURCE: U.S. Census Bureau (2009). Blacks and whites alone.

RACE, ETHNICITY, GENDER, AND CLASS

Exhibit P.3 Racial Gaps, 2005 and 2007: Race/Gender Categories as a Percentage of White Males

Race/Gender	Percentage of Median Income, Full-Time, Year-Round Workers		Percentage of Population 25 and Older With a High School Degree		Percentage of Population 25 and Older With a College Degree	
	2005	2007	2005	2007	2005	2007
Black males	78	76	95	92	55	52
White females	78	75	101	101	91	93
Black females	70	66	95	95	64	61

SOURCE: U.S. Census Bureau (2009). Blacks and whites alone.

Eyewitnesses to History: *On the Mall 2*

Theresa

Theresa is white and part owner of a business that specializes in fund-raising, mostly for liberal causes. She is a long-time political junkie, activist, and observer who made the journey to the National Mall on inauguration day with her family.

We [got to the mall] around 9 a.m. and settled on the World War II monument as our site. . . . No further walking, but the downside was that the cold definitely started settling in. . . . We had a great view of the JumboTron. I was so impressed at how quiet people were. . . .

The people near us included a group of [African American] high school girls. . . . I got that little slice of understanding of what it meant to them to see an African American becoming president. They were so excited and wanted to know who all the other people up on the dais were. It was like a door opening up for them. [It was] very exciting to see that happen for them. They were definitely the highlight.

[They also made] me realize just how old I am. I could name all the old politicians with no trouble, but when the camera would show one of the many celebs, they had to tell me who they were.

Now we are home listening to all the stories on the news and reading the newspaper articles. They are capturing the day very well. The speeches, the music, the people, the excitement, the general sense of unity and goodwill. It was absolutely worth the frozen toes.

I felt like I was observing a life-changing (I hope) experience for other people, not so much for myself. Euphoria is a dangerous mental state, and I'm careful of it. Yet, I know that without that sense of belief in your own ability to effect a change, we all lose. I really loved seeing those young girls become interested in the political process. If young people are not willing to invest, we are totally screwed. [Those girls] owned that day. Those powerful people up on that stage were all of a sudden people that those girls wanted to know something about.

Here is what I'm realizing now (several weeks after the inauguration). I might have said, "It was the most important event of my lifetime." Then, I remember a lot of us saying that after the 9–11 attacks, and how we all came together. But that was unifying out of fear, because we realized we could not control what happened next.

In some ways, January 20, 2009, was the antidote to 9–11. People felt like they themselves made something good happen and unified around hope and empowerment. I'll take that any day.

Eileen

Eileen is a sociologist specializing in American race relations. She is white, and her husband is black. They have two children. Following are some excerpts from a letter she wrote a letter to President Obama the day after the inauguration.

Dear President Obama:

I am writing to thank you for deciding to run for president, for restoring my hope and optimism in the American political process, and for allowing a moment to happen that I never thought would be possible in my lifetime. I write you from the perspective of a white mother of two biracial children, from the vantage point of a race relations sociologist, and as a onetime political activist and community organizer who hadn't done door-to-door canvassing for close to a decade until your campaign reinspired me.

I'm not one of those people who had never voted or been politically active. . . . I've shown up to the polls every year, sometimes more than once a year for primaries and special elections, since I turned 18. . . . But the more I've participated, the more jaded I've become. . . . I had become habituated to the majority going on with their plans to leave people out/leave people behind. . . . The comfort in marching/protesting/speaking out had simply been the companionship of like-minded others and the knowledge that I had done my best to do my part, since a real political "win" seemed increasingly rare. Although I had not realized it until now, I think I had come to expect that my hopes and dreams would remain in the margins, and never in the mainstream of the political process. [For example], in 2004, I [supported] Kucinich in the Democratic primaries—the only antiwar candidate, the only anti–death penalty candidate, the only one supporting gay marriage, universal health care—and of course, he only got like 1% of the vote. I am used to my ideals for this country being way in the margins but sticking by them anyway. At least I could say I didn't stand idly by. . . .

Then, pregnant with my second biracial child, you announced you'd be running for president. A few weeks after your announcement, I found out I would be having a boy. And anyone in my field knows all the statistics on young black men. As my daughter thrived at the head of her class, now I would be entering a whole new world. . . . For my son, things would be different. Believe it or not, jaded as I had become, I could honestly tell myself that things would be different for my son, as I followed a man named Barack Obama.

[During the Bush years], it was all about war and terror and getting tough on terrorists, and "You're either with us or you're with the terrorists" unilateralism. When your platform was about working together with other nations, and extended a friendly olive branch to our so-called enemies, I couldn't help but listen. And when I went to vote in the primaries, . . . it was . . . becoming clear that this time, I wasn't just going to the primaries to "make a statement" before the real candidate won and eclipsed my ideal. This time my ideal also just might become a winner!

I've never sat glued to the TV for hours as election results came in, because the person I wanted was usually out of the running. . . . I've never watched an inauguration, because by then it was a done deal. . . . But after years and years of teaching my undergraduates to peel off their white denial, to realize that racism still matters, to realize that the U.S. has been covering up and smoothing over its racism for too long—I had to watch your inauguration. I had to savor this moment, of the U.S. actually doing something in race that it could be proud of, for once in its life! Well, for the first time in its life. And now we can all actually envision that there could be more times to come. . . .

Of course, as all the progressives say, "Time will tell" if the power structure really is such that you can put all these ideals into being. . . . But merely for giving us a vision of the possible, and for allowing us all to be a part of something greater than ourselves, and for giving me hope that my son's life will be different from those who came before him, I am eternally grateful. Thank you.

In other areas of social life—residential and school segregation, and the continuing high rates of imprisonment for young black males—the differences between blacks and whites documented in Chapter 6 continue to verify the power of the Blauner hypothesis (introduced in Chapter 3): Minority groups created by colonization and conquest will face stronger, more persistent racism and resistance than groups created by immigration; the degree of inequality will be greater; and the struggle for liberation and equality will be lengthier.

Conclusion

Which of the three versions of the interpretation for "post-racial" seems most viable in the light of the information presented here? The strongest, most positive view—the vision of a society in which racial equality has been achieved—is clearly wrong. The truth perhaps lies in some mixture of the two other views: While race may be losing some of its historic power to shape our perceptions and control our lives and may be becoming a more "voluntary" identity, our society continues to be deeply divided by race.

What does President Obama's victory mean in terms of the issues raised in this text? Although a truly post-racial society remains a distant dream, this momentous event does show that in 2008—in circumstances dominated by severe economic woes, an unpopular war, and the failed presidency of George W. Bush—the United States was ready to turn for leadership to an exceptionally articulate and charismatic man who happened to be "black." For a person of color to become the president of the United States is an extraordinary event, the significance of which will shape this society (and the world) for decades to come. It is a great thing, momentous and earthshaking. But it is not everything.

References

ABC News. 2008. "Exit Polls: Storm of Voter Dissatisfaction Lifts Obama to Historic Win." Retrieved March 12, 2009, from http://abcnews.go.com/print?id=6189129

CNN. 2009. "Most Blacks Say MLK's Vision Is Fulfilled, Poll Finds." Retrieved March 12, 2009, from http://www.cnn.com/2009/POLITICS/01/19/king.poll

Hsu, Hua. 2009. "The End of White America?" *The Atlantic*. Retrieved March 12, 2009, from http://www.theatlantic.com/doc/print/200901/end-of-whiteness

Ifill, Gwen. 2009. *The Breakthrough*. New York: Doubleday.

Iwaela, Uzodinma. 2008. "Race Still Matters." *Los Angeles Times*, January 23, p. A-23.

Obama, Barack. 2008. Transcript of Speech. *The New York Times*. Retrieved April 17, 2009, from http://www.nytimes.com/2008/03/18/us/politics/18text-obama.html

Pew Research Center. 2008. "Inside Obama's Sweeping Victory." Retrieved April 17, 2009, from http://pewresearch.org/pubs/1023/exit-poll-analysis-2008

Ross, Brian, and Rehab El-Buri. 2008. "Obama's Pastor: God Damn America, U.S. to Blame for 9/11." Retrieved March 12, 2009, from http://abcnews.go.com/blotter/story?id=4443788

U.S. Census Bureau. 2009. *American Community Surveys 2005 and 2007*. Retrieved April 17, 2009, from http://factfinder.census.gov/servlet/DatasetMainPageServlet?_program=ACS&_submenuId=&_lang=en&_ts=

Weisman, Jonathan. 2008. "Rev. Jackson Apologizes to Obama." *The Washington Post*, July 10, p. A4.

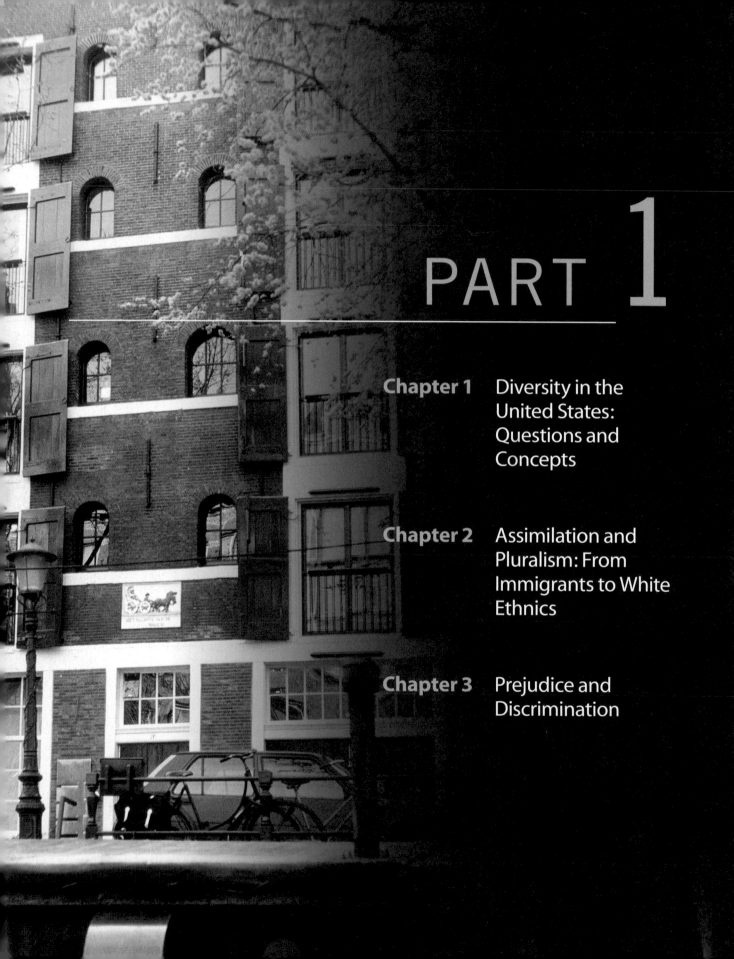

PART 1

An Introduction to the Study of Minority Groups in the United States

The United States is a nation of groups as well as individuals. These groups vary along a number of dimensions, including size, wealth, education, race, culture, religion, and language. Some of these groups have been part of American society since colonial days, and others have formed in the past few years.

How should all these groups relate to one another? Who should be considered American? Should we preserve the multitude of cultural heritages and languages that currently exists and stress our diversity? Should we encourage everyone to adopt Anglo-American culture and strive to become more similar and unified? Should we emphasize our similarities or celebrate our differences? Is it possible to do both?

Questions of unity and diversity are among the most pressing to face the United States today. In this text, we analyze these and many other questions. Our goal is to develop a broader, more informed understanding of the past and present forces that have created and sustained the groups that compose U.S. society.

What Is Public Sociology?

Many sociologists have called for a more "public sociology," a sociology that is engaged in the community, the society, and the world. Although not all sociologists would endorse a call for activism and involvement, the study of American race relations will, for many people, stimulate an impulse to address social problems directly and personally. To facilitate that involvement, we have developed a number of projects for students that will lead them into their communities and provide them with the possibility of making a positive difference in the lives of others. The projects will be presented in the introductions to the parts of this book, and each will be keyed to the material covered in the chapters that follow. The assignments, as stated here, should be regarded as outlines and suggestions, and it is quite likely that participants will have to improvise and respond to unanticipated challenges as they arise. Nonetheless, these assignments will allow students to bridge the (sometimes large) gap between the classroom and the community and to develop and practice their own public sociology. Each assignment could be the basis for a semester-long project for individual students or teams of students.

The first two public sociology assignments will lead students to confront diversity in their communities through two different avenues: schools and soup kitchens. In Assignment 1, it is very likely that students will discover that diversity is increasing in the local school system at a rate that reflects the national trends discussed in Chapter 1 and presented in Exhibit 1.1.

The challenges of educating a diverse population are analyzed at various places throughout the text, including the Current Debate at the end of Chapter 2.

Assignment 2 addresses homelessness, a condition that affects all groups, not just minorities. However, the realities of institutional discrimination (see Exhibit 1.5) and the legacies of American racism and inequality mean that minority groups are likely to be overrepresented in the soup kitchen, along with other more vulnerable populations: women and children and recent immigrants. We explore these patterns of poverty throughout the text and especially in the case studies presented in Part 3 of this text.

The next two assignments connect students to both exponents and victims of prejudice and discrimination. Assignment 3 focuses on hate groups. Although they are largely on the fringes of mainstream society, these groups are vivid reminders of the persistence of racism in our society. An overview of these groups is presented at the end of Chapter 3. Assignment 4 focuses on one of the many targets of hate groups (and the casual rejection of everyday Americans throughout society): recent immigrants in general and Arab Americans in particular. Prejudice and discrimination against these groups is covered in a number of places in Chapter 3, including the sections on the scapegoat hypothesis, social distance scales, and hate crimes.

Public Sociology Assignments

Marcus Griffin

Assignment 1:
Revealing Diversity in the United States in Your Local School

The United States is inherently diverse despite the domination of one or more groups over others. The diversity can be seen in ethnic composition, national origin, religious affiliation, and gendered behavior. However, this diversity is not always obvious, nor are its historical roots apparent. In this assignment, you will choose a local school and, working with its staff, take the lead in creating a 20-year portrait of diversity. The school may use this information to assess how well it has addressed its multicultural education needs.

Step 1

Locate a school in your community. It may be public, private, or religious but should be at least 20 years old.

Step 2

Create your draft research design. You will want to decide what diversity variables you think will be important for an accurate picture of your community and the school it serves. All categories, such as Asian, White, Hispanic, and so on, include a great deal of diversity within them. If, for example, there is a large Latino population locally, perhaps you will want to discern the diversity within the larger ethnic category (for example, Puerto Rican, Cuban, Mexican, Brazilian) to create a more accurate portrait.

Once you know your variables, decide where you will get data to explore them. Local information is often made more compelling when compared with another data set, so you may want to get data on your variables from the U.S. Bureau of the Census or your particular state's databook (a compilation of census and vital statistics available through the state's official Web site). After preliminary exploration of data, you will be ready to discuss the project with a school.

Step 3

Meet with the school principal or other appropriate administrator to discuss your interest in conducting this assignment. Review your research design and rationale together and modify according to input. A key aspect of this research is that officials at the school should agree that there is a need for the diversity portrait and participate as key stakeholders.

If the school does not agree, you will need to decide whether another school would provide a better subject population, and you may need to approach the school district administrator (in a public system) for suggestions on likely candidates. Once you find a school that understands the need and accepts the terms, you will work with school staff to locate enrollment records and begin compiling your data.

Step 4

As you compile your data, you will begin packaging it in an easily understood portrait. Programs such as Microsoft Excel can present clear and accessible tables and charts of data showing ethnic and gender (or your other variables) enrollment trends for the 20-year study period. Periodically meet with your stakeholders to review the growing findings or areas of difficulty and obtain feedback, revising data collection methods and presentation as needed until you complete data collection and charting for the chosen variables.

Step 5

Review all of your charts and tables of data. Consider the patterns you see among the data and the gaps that reveal themselves. Now write an executive summary describing these patterns and gaps and the overall portrait of diversity at the school for the past 20 years. Include in your report each of your charts with brief (one- or two-paragraph) summaries of what they seem to mean.

Step 6

Present your findings to the school staff, providing them with electronic copies of all data files and charts and one master hard copy. You have now provided them with the necessary data to begin assessing how to best address the multicultural education needs of their student body. Thank them for allowing you to work with them and ask them to share with you in the future the curriculum innovations they implement as a result of the data.

Step 7

Congratulate yourself for hard work well-done!

NOTE: This project was inspired by the fine demographic work conducted by Susan M. Cheng and T. Linh Ho. Their publication, though much larger in scope than your final report, may help you to visualize your project.

SOURCE: Cheng, Susan M., & Ho, T. Linh. (2003). *A Portrait of Race and Ethnicity in Hawaii: An Analysis of Social and Economic Outcomes of Hawaii's People*. Honolulu, HI: Pacific American Research Center. Retrieved April 15, 2005, from http://www.thepaf.org/Research/Portrait_I.pdf

Assignment 2:
Diversity in a Soup Kitchen

The homeless population in the United States is often an invisible population. Many people pretend not to see such individuals on the streets asking for loose change, offering to work for food, or simply sitting quietly reading the newspaper in the local public library on a cold winter day. Nonetheless, the homeless are an important population to understand because they are the most vulnerable in many ways to cutbacks in social services. This assignment is designed to help a soup kitchen better understand the diversity of social backgrounds their patrons bring to the table.

Step 1

Locate one or more soup kitchens serving the homeless and contact their representatives, asking whether you may make an appointment with them to discuss a school research project. Many soup kitchens are run by religious organizations, maybe even by one with which you participate, and may be approached through a ministry liaison. This will be your choice. When you meet the ministry staff or other representatives, discuss your interest in conducting a series of oral histories and interviews with homeless patrons. Share with them your basic research design (as described here) and explore the potential to better understand the diversity of cultural backgrounds the homeless bring to the soup kitchen. Try to discover whether such information is welcome and valued as a means to provide an environment that is not culturally alien and is more than a place to get a warm meal and be safe for an evening, among other things. Be open to changing aspects of your research design to meet the soup kitchen's particular needs and interests.

Step 2

Set up a schedule to volunteer at the soup kitchen. To better understand the perspective of those serving the homeless, one should walk a mile in their shoes, so to speak. Volunteer at the soup kitchen regularly for a minimum of 3 weeks to get a feel for the rhythm of the facility, discern patterns among the behaviors of the patrons, and get to know a few of the patrons while serving them from the food line, wiping down tables afterward, and chatting casually with those remaining behind. To successfully get to know others, one must build rapport and share a bit of oneself, and wiping tables, sweeping floors, and otherwise not staying behind the food service counter is critical to this end.

Step 3

After volunteering regularly for a minimum of 3 weeks, you will probably know a few of the patrons by name, and they will know you. Now is the time to design a survey instrument to get general background information on the soup kitchen's clientele. Write a survey form that asks questions about life history and vital statistics. Questions may include the following:

- Are you married, divorced, widowed, or single?
- Do you have any children?
- How old are you?
- How long have you lived in this town?
- What town did you last live in?
- What is your ethnic background?
- Who was your last employer, and how long were you employed with them?
- How long have you been homeless?

Discuss your survey with the soup kitchen staff and solicit feedback and input on its design. To be useful to them, it must include information they can use that you may not have thought of.

Step 4

Conduct a pretest of your survey instrument. Before conducting interviews with a fairly large number of informants, conducting a pretest on a small sample is usually a good idea. Approach the few (four to six individuals at most) patrons that you have gotten to know over the past weeks and ask them whether you may interview them. Explain what you are doing as a student and how you hope the information may help the soup kitchen best serve its visitors. Assuming they agree, administer your survey. Review your results reflectively to discern questions that seem irrelevant and include questions in the revised survey to tap information you did not think of initially. Share the revised survey with the soup kitchen staff, revising as needed.

Step 5

Administer your survey to as many patrons as possible, but do not include the initial sample used for the pretest. You may get other staff to assist you if they are able and willing. Compile your responses using a spreadsheet software program such as Microsoft Excel. You will need to think creatively to discover the patterns that are likely to exist in your data. Such patterns may involve amount of time homeless, general proximity of last residence, ethnic composition, gender, age, or marital status. Part of the wonder of social science is discovering the patterns, so spend some time perusing the data rather than giving them a cursory overview.

Step 6

Conduct oral history interviews. By this point, you will have been a regular volunteer for approximately 6 weeks at the soup kitchen, and you will know several patrons by name and a fair amount of information about the clientele as a whole. Now is the time to explore the depth of the population with a small sample of oral histories. Oral histories of any worth generally require a fair amount of rapport with an informant, so your best bet is to approach the patrons you first interviewed for the pretest. Ask them whether you may obtain an oral history from them and, assuming they agree, begin. The first stage is to get a general portrait of their lives in their own words. Your informant should lead the conversation with you providing encouragement—focus on active listening. This should be followed by questions derived from the patterns you discovered in your survey in Step 5, and in this conversation, you are in the lead.

Step 7

Organize your two kinds of data: quantitative survey and qualitative personal history. Review the two sets, exploring the patterns and meanings that emerge. Write an executive summary of approximately six pages that describes and explains the patterns in your data. Share this with the soup kitchen staff. This data may be useful in ensuring that their community outreach activities are targeted efficiently and giving them baseline information on their clientele's backgrounds. Ask the staff to share with you in the future the changes they make based on the data you collected.

Step 8

Congratulate yourself for rewarding work well-done, and do not forget to occasionally visit the soup kitchen: You are likely to brighten the day of the informants you once served.

Assignment 3:
Local Hate Groups

The United States is marred by a history of hate. Unfortunately, this hatred is not a thing of the past. In this assignment, you will work for the local chapter of the National Association for the Advancement of Colored People (NAACP) or Anti-Discrimination League or some other advocacy group by providing the organization with background research on hate groups within the area. Hate groups include those referred to as Black Separatist, Neo-Nazi, Racist Skinhead, Ku Klux Klan, and Neo-Confederate. Research on these and other groups may benefit the organization by providing their personnel and clients with quick "hot sheets" that can be referred to when problems arise or when considering who might be disruptive during an advocacy event.

Step 1

Contact the local chapter of the NAACP, Anti-Discrimination League, or other advocacy group. Discuss with the organization's representative the assignment you would like to conduct and explore how it may serve the group's needs.

Step 2

Review the organization's records of any hate groups it has had previous experience with and write descriptive summaries of each, including political orientation, hate ideology, location, number of members, known hate crimes committed and alleged, and leadership contact information.

Step 3

Go online and view the Southern Poverty Law Center's Web site, http://www.splcenter.org, and use the organization's data resources to locate hate groups in your area or region. As a courtesy, send an e-mail to notify the Law Center of your project and ask how it would prefer to be referenced in your research for having provided data. You may want to ask about suggestions for your project and other sources of data.

Step 4

Write summaries of the information you have about each hate group in your area, including (if you have not already recorded this information in Step 2) political orientation, hate ideology, location, number of members, known hate crimes committed and alleged, and leadership contact information. If any information is available on how the group has been successfully dealt with, be sure to include that and other pertinent information.

Step 5

Share your summaries with your client group staff and solicit their help in making it even better. You will need to think of questions to ask the staff regarding how to create a custom fit between available information and information needs. These documents will ideally be dynamic and updated regularly to maintain currency and usefulness, and you will want their initial structure to reflect that potential.

Step 6

Modify your "hot sheets" according to the feedback you get from your client and share the final results with staff. Ask them to let you know how the data are used and whether particular hot sheets are instrumental in dealing with a hate group's activities.

Step 7

Congratulate yourself for hard work well-done!

Assignment 4:
Cultural Brokerage and Arab Americans

The United States is home to more than a million new immigrants a year. Among these immigrants are Arabs from a variety of ethnic and religious backgrounds. Included in this group are doctors, lawyers, farmers, merchants, and laborers seeking better lives for their families, as well as refugees fleeing war-torn homelands and persecution. Many Arab Americans face strong discrimination in the United States because of ignorance and fear surrounding terrorism and the ongoing conflict in Iraq. This assignment is designed to facilitate better understanding between Arab Americans (immigrant or otherwise) and the communities they live and work within.

Step 1

Contact a local mosque or Arab American community center and meet with the staff. Discuss with them your interest in working for them as part of a school assignment on cultural brokerage. Assuming they agree that there is a need for such information and image management, proceed to Step 2. If they do not feel there is such a need, solicit their suggestions about which communities do, in fact, have such a need, and start over at one of these locations.

Step 2

Develop a demographic description of the Arab American community using available records, such as census bureau records. With the help of the staff at the community center or mosque, develop a survey to augment the information available from public records. Be sure to include questions regarding the history of immigration and include information such as where community members emigrated from, how long they have been in the United States, and how long they have been in the local community. Count the number of men, women, and children and the ages of each. List occupations, general income brackets, and home ownership, from which you can estimate income and property tax contributions. Place these data into a spreadsheet, using a program such as Microsoft Excel, and create a simple series of charts to visually represent this data. This data will help create a picture of what the Arab American community contributes to the local economy and well-being of the town or city.

Step 3

Using the community center staff as liaisons, solicit individual interviews to obtain a cultural collage of the Arab American community. This interview can be open-ended and general. You could ask your interviewees about the values that are important to them as Arab Americans and to their community and how these values might conflict with U.S. culture. Your conversation might also cover other aspects of culture, including cuisine, popular culture and entertainment, religious practices, gender roles, or any other topic that arises during the course of the conversation. In these interviews, allow your informant some freedom to guide the session and provide information that he or she feels is important to convey. If you are not able to interview one of the genders due to cultural prohibitions, solicit help from the center's staff in getting an appropriate person to conduct the other interviews to ensure you do not end up with a collage that leaves out, for example, women's experiences and lives.

Step 4

Using your creativity, combine the forms of data you collected and processed into a series of brochures and computer-based presentations that paint a portrait of the Arab community, using programs such as Microsoft PowerPoint or Apple Keynote. If you are proficient at creating Web pages, consider putting together the material you collected into Web site form.

Step 5

With these files prepared, present the information to the community center staff and clientele to obtain vital feedback. Based on their suggestions, modify your material to best meet their concerns and interests.

Step 6

Submit your final draft materials to the community center and congratulate yourself for hard work well-done! Be sure to occasionally stop by the center and inquire about how members of the community are doing. You will probably have made several friends who not only contribute to the community but enrich your life as well!

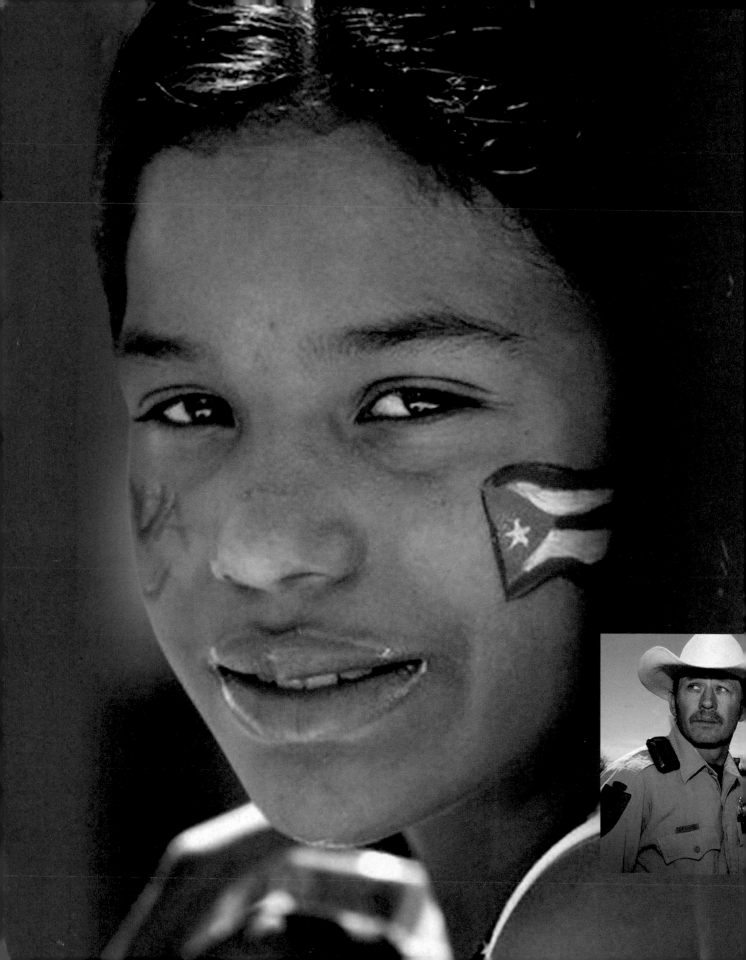

Diversity in the United States

CHAPTER 1

Questions and Concepts

What does it mean to be an American? Is the United States splintering into separate racial and ethnic groups? Is there a limit to the amount of diversity we can tolerate? Should the number of immigrants entering the United States be reduced? Should Spanish become an official second language? Should multiculturalism be a part of the public school curriculum? Should Black History Month be celebrated by everyone?

Questions like these are crucial, but they are not new. They have been debated in one form or another over and over in our past, and continuing controversies about race, immigration, and language suggest that these questions are far from settled. We are a nation of immigrants, and we have been arguing, often passionately, about exclusion and inclusion and unity and diversity since the infancy of American society. Every member of our society is in some sense an immigrant or the descendant of immigrants. Even Native Americans "immigrated" to this continent, albeit thousands of years ago. We are all from someplace else, with roots in another part of the globe. Some came here in chains; others came on ocean liners, on 747s, or on foot. Some arrived last week, and others have had family here for centuries. Each wave of newcomers has in some way altered the social landscape of the United States. As many have observed, American society is continually becoming and permanently unfinished.

Our immigrant heritage and cultural diversity have made us a nation of both groups and individuals. Some of us feel intensely connected to the groups to which we belong and identify closely with our heritage. For others, the group connection is tenuous and distant. Either way, our group memberships influence our lives and perceptions. They help to shape who we are and how we fit into the larger society.

Six American Stories

To illustrate the influences of our connections with others who share our heritage, consider the life stories of six Americans. Each represents millions of others, and each exemplifies a part of what it means to be an American.

Kim Park is a 24-year-old immigrant from Korea. He arrived in New York City about 3 years ago to work in his uncle's grocery store. Kim typically works a 14-hour shift every day, 7 days a week. His duties include stocking and cleaning, and he operates the register when necessary. He is also learning how to do the bookkeeping. Instead of wages, Kim receives room and board and some spending money.

Kim is outgoing and gregarious. His English is improving rapidly, and he practices it whenever possible. He has twice enrolled in English language classes, but the demands of his job prevented him from completing the courses. On a third occasion, he was turned away because the course was already filled and there was no money to hire additional teachers. Eventually, Kim wants to become a U.S. citizen, bring his siblings to America, get married and start a family, and take over the store when his uncle retires. The store is located in a neighborhood that is changing in ethnic composition. Many different minority groups have called this neighborhood home over the years. During the late 1950s, the area was almost exclusively Jewish. The Jewish residents have since died or moved out, and they were followed by a mixture of African Americans, Puerto Ricans, and Asians.

Not far from Kim's store is the apartment building where Shirley Umphlett spent much of her childhood. In search of work, her family moved to New York from Alabama in the 1920s. Both her grandfather and father were construction workers, but because most labor unions and employers discriminated against African Americans, they had limited access to the better-paying, more stable jobs and were often unemployed. Shirley's mother worked as a housekeeper in a large downtown hotel to help meet family expenses. Shirley did well in school, attended college on scholarship, and is now a successful executive with a multinational corporation. She is in her 40s, is married with two children, and is career oriented and ambitious. At the same time, she is committed to helping other African Americans and poor Americans. She and her spouse are volunteers in several community action programs and maintain memberships in three national organizations that serve and represent African Americans.

Shirley's two children attend public school. One of their teachers is Mary Ann O'Brien, a fourth-generation Irish Catholic. Mary Ann's great-grandparents were born in Ireland and came to New York as young adults in the 1880s. Her great-grandfather found work on the docks, and her great-grandmother worked as a housekeeper before her marriage. They had 7 children and 23 grandchildren. Mary Ann keeps in touch with more than 50 of her cousins, most of whom live within an hour of New York City. Each successive generation of Mary Ann's family tended to do a little better educationally and occupationally. Mary Ann's father was a fireman, and her sister is a lawyer. Mary Ann does not think much about her Irish ancestry. She does attend Mass regularly, mostly because she likes the ritual and the connection with tradition. She has a vague interest in Ireland and admits she goes a little crazy on St. Patrick's Day, but otherwise her energies are completely focused on her family and her job.

In one of her fourth-grade classes, Mary Ann took a liking to a young Native American student named George Snyder. George was born on a reservation in upstate New York, but his family moved to the city when he was a baby. The unemployment rate on the reservation often exceeded 50%, and George's father thought that the city would offer a better chance for work. Mary Ann and George kept in touch after he left elementary school, and George stopped by occasionally for a chat. Then, when George was in high school, his father was laid off, and the family returned to the reservation. Shortly thereafter, George became rebellious, and his grades began to slip. He was arrested for shoplifting and later for selling drugs, spent some time in a state correctional facility, and never finished school. The last time Mary Ann saw him, she tried to persuade him to return to school but got nowhere. She pointed out that he was still young and told him that there were many things he could do in the future, that life was full of opportunities. He responded, "What's the use? I'm an Indian with a record—I've got no future."

George's parole officer is Hector Gonzalez. Hector's parents came to the United States from Mexico. Every year, they crossed the border to join the stream of agricultural migrant laborers and then returned to their village in Mexico at the end of the season. With the help of a cousin, Hector's father eventually got a job as a cabdriver in New York City, where Hector was raised. Hector's mother never learned much English but worked occasionally in a garment factory located in her neighborhood. Hector thinks of himself as American but is very interested in his parents' home village back in Mexico, where most of his extended family still lives. Hector is bilingual and has visited the village several times. His grandmother still lives there, and he calls her once a month.

Hector worked his way through college in 7 years. After 10 years as a parole officer, he is becoming increasingly burned out and discouraged, especially about young men like George. There are no jobs in the city, no real opportunities. What's the point of working with these guys if all they have the chance to do is hustle dope?

Hector rents an apartment in a building owned by a corporation headed by William Buford III. The Bufords have been a part of New York's high society for generations. The family invests the bulk of its fortune in real estate and owns land and buildings throughout the New York metropolitan area. The Bufords have a three-story luxury townhouse in Manhattan but rarely go into town, preferring to spend their time on their rural Connecticut estate. William Buford attended the finest private schools and graduated from Harvard University. At age 57, he is semi-retired, plays golf twice a week, vacations in Europe, and employs a staff of five to care for himself and his family. He has little interest in the history of his family but knows that his ancestors came to America from England. Family legend has it that a distant relative played an important role in the Revolutionary War, but no one has ever bothered to investigate this claim.

These six individuals belong to groups that vary along some of the most consequential dimensions within our society—ethnicity, race, social class, gender, and religion—and their lives have been shaped by these affiliations (some more than others, of course). Similarly, our group memberships affect the ways others perceive us, the opportunities available to us, the way we think about ourselves, and our view of American society and the larger world. They affect our perception of what it means to be American.

The Increasing Variety of American Minority Groups

Our group memberships also shape the choices we make in the voting booth and in other areas of social life. We face important decisions that will affect our lives and the lives of countless millions, and we need to contemplate these choices systematically and thoroughly. We also need to be aware that members of different groups will evaluate these decisions in different ways. The issues will be filtered through the screens of divergent experiences, group histories, and present situations. The debates over which direction our society should take are unlikely to be meaningful or even mutually intelligible without some understanding of the variety of ways of being American.

These choices about the future of our society are especially urgent because the diversity of U.S. society is increasing dramatically, largely due to high rates of immigration. Since the 1960s, the number of immigrants arriving in the United States each year has tripled and includes groups from all over the globe (U.S. Department of Homeland Security, 2005).

Can our society deal successfully with this diversity of cultures, languages, and races? Concerns about increasing diversity are compounded by other long-standing minority issues and grievances that remain unresolved. For example, charts and graphs presented in Part 3 of this text show persistent gaps in income, poverty rates, and other measures of affluence and equality between minority groups and national norms. In fact, in many ways, the problems of African Americans, Native Americans, Hispanic Americans, and Asian Americans today are just as formidable as they were a generation ago.

As one way of gauging the dimensions of diversity in our nation, consider the changing makeup of U.S. society. Exhibit 1.1 presents the percentage of the total U.S. population in each of five groups. Before examining the data in the exhibit, consider the groups themselves and the labels used to designate them. All of these categories are arbitrary; none of these groups have clear or unambiguous boundaries. Two people within any of these categories might be as different from each other as any two people selected from different categories. The

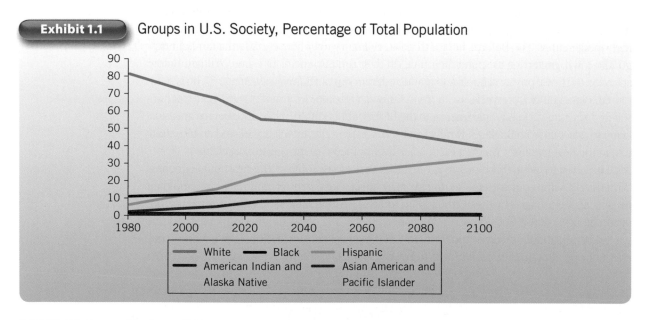

Exhibit 1.1 Groups in U.S. Society, Percentage of Total Population

SOURCE: U.S. Bureau of the Census (2000c).

NOTE:

"Whites" are non-Hispanics only.

"Blacks" are non-Hispanics only.

"Hispanics" may be of any race.

people included in a category may share some general physical or cultural traits, but they will also vary by social class, religion, and gender as well as in thousands of other ways. People classified as "Asian and Pacific Islander" represent scores of different national and linguistic backgrounds (Japanese, Samoans, Vietnamese, Pakistanis, and so forth), and "American Indian or Alaska Native" includes people from hundreds of different tribal groups. The racial and ethnic categories, as stated in Exhibit 1.1, frequently appear in government reports and in the professional literature of the social sciences, but they are arbitrary and should never be mistaken for unchanging or "natural" divisions between people.

Exhibit 1.1 reports the actual relative sizes of the groups for 1980 and 2000 and the projected or estimated relative sizes for the remainder of the 21st century. Note how the increasing diversity of U.S. society is reflected in the declining numerical predominance of non-Hispanic whites, who are projected to fall to less than half of the population shortly after the middle of the century. Several states (Texas, California, Hawaii, and New Mexico) are already "majority-minority," and this will be true of the entire nation within several decades.

African Americans and American Indians are projected to remain stable in their relative size, but Hispanic Americans and Asian Americans and Pacific Islanders will grow dramatically. Asian and Pacific Islander groups made up only 2% of the population in 1980 but will grow to over 10% by midcentury and reach the 13% mark (equal in size to African Americans) by the end of the century. The most dramatic growth, however, will be for Hispanic American groups. Hispanic Americans became the largest minority group in 2002, surpassing African Americans, and will grow to 25% of the population by midcentury and to almost a third of the population by the end of the century.

The projections into the future are merely educated guesses, but they presage profound change for the United States. As this century unfolds, our society will grow more diverse racially, culturally, and linguistically. The United States will become less white, less European, and more like the world as a whole. Some see these changes as threats to traditional white middle-class American values and lifestyles. Others see them as providing an opportunity for other equally attractive and legitimate value systems and lifestyles to emerge.

Even though the categories in Exhibit 1.1 are broad, they still provide no place for a number of groups. For example, where should we place Arab Americans and recent immigrants from Africa? Although these groups are relatively small in size (about 1 million people each), there is no clear place for them in Exhibit 1.1. Should Arab Americans be classified as "Asian"? Should recent immigrants from Africa be placed in the same category as African Americans? Of course, there is no particular need to have a category for every single group, but we should recognize that classification schemes like the one used in this exhibit (and in many other contexts) have limited utility and application.

A further problem with the type of classification schemes used in Exhibit 1.1 will become increasingly apparent in the years to come: There are no categories for the growing number of mixed-race individuals. The number of "mixed" Americans is relatively small today, about 2% of the population in 2006 (U.S. Bureau of the Census, 2007a), but is likely to increase rapidly because of the growing number of marriages across group lines. The number of these marriages has increased more than 10 times over since 1960 and tripled between 1980 and 2005 (U.S. Bureau of the Census, 2007b, p. 52). Obviously, the greater the number of mixed marriages, the greater the number of mixed Americans: One study estimates that 21% of the population will claim membership in this category by 2050 (Smith & Edmonston, 1997, p. 119).

What kind of society are we becoming? What should it mean to be American? In the past, opportunity and success have been far more available to white Anglo-Saxon Protestant males than to members of other groups. Most of us, even the favored males such as William Buford III, would agree that this definition of American is far too narrow, but how inclusive should the definition be? Should we stress unity or celebrate diversity? How wide can the limits be stretched before national unity is threatened? How narrow can they be before the desire to preserve cultural and linguistic diversity is unjustly and unnecessarily stifled?

These first few paragraphs have raised a lot of questions. The purpose of this book is to help you develop some answers and some thoughtful, informed positions on these issues. You should be aware from the beginning that the questions addressed here are complex and that the answers we seek are not obvious or easy. Indeed, there is no guarantee that we as a society will be able or willing to resolve all the problems of intergroup relations in the United States. However, we will never make progress in this area unless we confront the issues honestly and with an accurate base of knowledge and understanding. Certainly, these issues will not resolve themselves or disappear if they are ignored.

In the course of our investigation, we will rely on sociology and other social sciences for concepts, theory, and information. Chapters 1 to 3 introduce and define many of the ideas that will guide our investigation. Part 2 explores how relations between the dominant group and minority groups have evolved in American society. Part 3 analyzes the current situation of U.S. minority groups. In Part 4, the final section of the book, we explore many of the challenges and issues facing our society (and the world) and see what conclusions we can glean from our investigations and how they might shape the future.

What Is a Minority Group?

Before we can begin to sort out the issues, we need common definitions and a common vocabulary for discussion. We begin with the term **minority group**.[1] Taken literally, the mathematical connotation of this term is a bit misleading because it implies that minority groups are small. In reality, a minority group can be quite large and can even be a numerical majority of the population. Women, for example, are sometimes considered to be a separate minority group, but they form a numerical majority in the U.S. population. In South Africa, as in many nations created by European colonization, whites are a numerical minority (less than 30% of the population), but despite recent changes, they remain the most powerful and affluent group.

Minority status has more to do with the distribution of resources and power than with simple numbers. The definition of minority group used in this book is based on Wagley and Harris (1958). According to this definition, a minority group has five characteristics:

1. The members of the group experience a pattern of disadvantage or inequality.
2. The members of the group share a visible trait or characteristic that differentiates them from other groups.
3. The minority group is a self-conscious social unit.
4. Membership in the group is usually determined at birth.
5. Members tend to marry within the group.

We will examine each of the defining characteristics here, and a bit later, we will return to examine the first two—inequality and visibility—in greater detail, because they are the most important characteristics of minority groups.

The first and most important defining characteristic of a minority group is inequality, that is, some pattern of disability and disadvantage. The nature of the disability and the degree of disadvantage are variable and can range from exploitation, slavery, and genocide to slight irritants, such as a lack of desks for left-handed students or a policy of racial exclusion at an expensive country club. (Note, however, that you might not agree that the irritant is slight if you are a left-handed student awkwardly taking notes at a right-handed desk or if you are a golf aficionado who happens to be African American.)

Whatever its scope or severity, whether it extends to wealth, jobs, housing, political power, police protection, or health care, the pattern of disadvantage is the key characteristic of a minority group. Because the group has less of what is valued by society, the term **subordinate group** is sometimes used instead of minority group. The pattern of disadvantage is the result of the actions of another group, often in the distant past, that benefits from and tries to sustain the unequal arrangement. This group can be called the **core group** or the **dominant group**. The latter term is used most frequently in this book because it reflects the patterns of inequality and the power realities of minority group status.

The second defining characteristic of a minority group is some visible trait or characteristic that sets members of the group apart and that the dominant group holds in low esteem. The trait can be cultural (language, religion, speech patterns, or dress styles), physical (skin color, stature, or facial features), or both. Groups that are defined primarily by their cultural characteristics are called **ethnic minority groups**. Examples of such groups are Irish Americans and Jewish Americans. Groups defined primarily by their physical characteristics are **racial minority groups**, such as African Americans or Native Americans. Note that these categories can overlap. So-called ethnic groups may have (or may be thought to have) distinguishing physical characteristics (for example, the stereotypical Irish red hair or Jewish nose), and racial groups commonly have (or are thought to have) cultural traits that differ from the dominant group (for example, differences in dialect, religious values, or cuisine).

These distinguishing traits set boundaries and separate people into distinct groups. The traits are outward signs that identify minority group members and help to maintain the patterns of disadvantage. The dominant group has (or at one time, had) sufficient power to create the distinction between groups and thus solidify a higher position for itself. These markers of group membership are crucial: Without these visible signs, it would be difficult or impossible to identify who was in which group, and the system of minority group oppression would soon collapse.[2]

It is important to realize that the characteristics that mark the boundaries between groups usually are not significant in and of themselves. They are selected for their visibility and convenience, and objectively, they may be quite trivial and unimportant. For example, scientists have concluded that skin color and other so-called racial traits have little scientific, evolutionary, medical, or biological importance. As we shall see, skin color is an important marker of group membership in our society because it was selected during a complex and lengthy historical process, not because it has any inherent significance. These markers become important because we attribute significance to them.

A third characteristic of minority groups is that they are self-conscious social units, aware of their differentiation from the dominant group and of their shared disabilities. This shared social status can provide the basis for strong intragroup bonds and a sense of solidarity and can lead to views of the world that are quite different from those of the dominant group and other minority groups. For example, public opinion polls frequently show vast differences between dominant and minority groups in their views of the seriousness and extent of discrimination in American society. Exhibit 1.2 shows persistent and sizable gaps in the percentage of nationally representative samples of whites, Hispanics, and blacks who agree that "racial minorities have equal job opportunities." As would be expected, given their different histories, experiences, and locations in the social structure, blacks have the most negative view of racial equality, followed by Hispanic respondents. In 2006, 17% of black respondents versus 53% of white respondents agreed that job opportunities are equal for all races, a difference of 36%.

A fourth characteristic of minority groups is that in general, membership is an **ascribed status**, or a status that is acquired at birth. The traits that identify minority group membership typically cannot be easily changed, and minority group status is usually involuntary and for life.

Finally, minority group members tend to marry within their own groups. This pattern can be voluntary, or the dominant group can dictate it. In fact, interracial marriages were illegal in many states. Laws against **miscegenation** were declared unconstitutional only 40 years ago, in the late 1960s, by the U.S. Supreme Court (Bell, 1992).

This is a lengthy definition, but note how inclusive it is. Although it encompasses "traditional" minority groups such as African Americans and Native Americans, it also could be applied to other groups (with perhaps a little stretching). For instance, women arguably fit the first four criteria and can be analyzed with many of the same concepts and ideas that guide the analysis of other minority groups. Also, gay, lesbian, and transgendered Americans; Americans with disabilities; left-handed Americans; the aged; and very short, very tall, or very

Exhibit 1.2 Percentage of Whites, Blacks, and Hispanics Agreeing That Racial Minorities Have Equal Job Opportunities as Whites

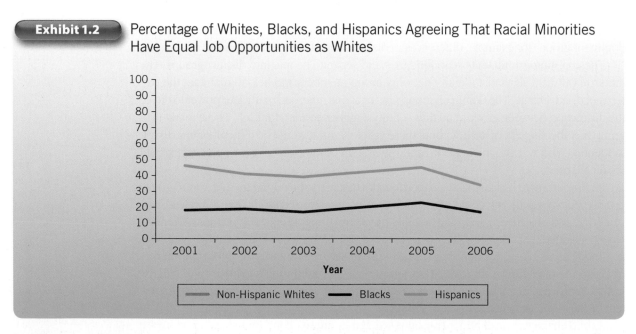

SOURCE: Gallup Poll (2006).

obese Americans could fit the definition of minority group without much difficulty. Although we should not be whimsical or capricious about matters of definition, it is important to note that the analyses developed in this book can be applied more generally than you might realize at first and may lead to some fresh insights about a wide variety of groups and people.

The Pattern of Inequality

As I mentioned earlier, the most important defining characteristic of minority group status is inequality. As documented in later chapters, minority group membership can affect access to jobs, education, wealth, health care, and housing. It is associated with a lower (often much lower) proportional share of valued goods and services and more limited (often much more limited) opportunities for upward mobility.

Stratification, or the unequal distribution of valued goods and services, is a basic feature of society. Every human society, except perhaps the simplest hunter-gatherer societies, is stratified to some degree; that is, the resources of the society are distributed so that some get more and others less of whatever is valued. Societies are divided into horizontal layers (or strata), often called **social classes**, which differ from one another by the amount of resources they command. Many criteria (such as education, age, gender, and talent) may affect a person's social class position and his or her access to goods and services. Minority group membership is one of these criteria, and it has had a powerful impact on the distribution of resources in the United States and many other societies.

This section begins with a brief consideration of theories about the nature and important dimensions of stratification. It then focuses on how minority group status relates to stratification. During the discussion, I identify several concepts and themes used throughout this book.

Photo 1.1

Karl Marx (1818–1883) was one of the founders of sociology and the author of The Communist Manifesto.

© Bettmann/Corbis.

Theoretical Perspectives

Sociology and the other social sciences have been concerned with stratification and human inequality since the formation of the discipline in the 19th century. An early and important contributor to our understanding of the nature and significance of social inequality was Karl Marx, a noted social philosopher. Half a century later, a sociologist named Max Weber, a central figure in the development of the discipline, critiqued and elaborated on Marx's view of social inequality. Here, we will also consider the views of Gerhard Lenski, a contemporary sociologist whose ideas about the influence of economic and technological development on social stratification have considerable relevance when comparing societies and understanding the evolution of intergroup relations.

Karl Marx. Although best known as the father of modern Communism, Karl Marx was also the primary architect of a political, economic, and social philosophy that has played a major role in world affairs for over 150 years. Marxism is a complex theory of history and social change in which inequality is a central concept and concern.

Marx believed in social class as econ'c security.
2 classes: Elites, and workers

Marx argued that the most important source of inequality in society was the system of economic production. More specifically, he focused on the **means of production**, or the materials, tools, resources, and organizations by which the society produces and distributes goods and services. In an agricultural society, the means of production include land, draft animals, and plows. In an industrial society, the means of production include factories, commercial enterprises, banks, and transportation systems, such as railroads.

All societies include two main social classes that struggle over the means of production. One class owns or controls the means of production, and in the case of an industrial society, Marx called this elite or ruling class the **bourgeoisie**. The other class is the working class, or the **proletariat**. Marx believed that conflict between these classes was inevitable and that the ultimate result of this class struggle would be the victory of the working class, followed by the creation of a utopian society without exploitation, coercion, or inequality: in other words, a classless society.

Marxism has been extensively revised and updated over the past century and a half. Still, modern social science owes a great deal to Marx's views on inequality and his insights on class struggle and social conflict. As you shall see, Marxism remains an important body of work and a rich source of insight into group relations in industrial society.

Max Weber.

One of Marx's major critics was Max Weber, a German sociologist who did most of his work around the turn of the 20th century. Weber thought that Marx's view of inequality was too narrow. Whereas Marx saw social class as a matter of economic position or relationship to the means of production, Weber noted that inequality was more complex than this and included dimensions other than just the economic. Individuals could be members of the elite in some ways but not in others. For example, an aristocratic family that has fallen on hard financial times might belong to the elite in terms of family lineage but not in terms of wealth. To use a more contemporary example, a major figure in the illegal drug trade could enjoy substantial wealth but be held in low esteem otherwise.

Weber expanded on Marx's view of inequality by identifying three separate stratification systems. First, economic inequality is based on ownership or control of property, wealth, and income. This is similar to Marx's concept of class, and, in fact, Weber used the term *class* to identify this form of inequality.

A second system of stratification revolves around differences in **prestige** between groups, or the amount of honor, esteem, or respect given to us by others. Class position is one factor that affects the amount of prestige enjoyed by a person. Other factors might include family lineage, athletic ability, and physical appearance. In the United States and other societies, prestige is affected by the groups to which people belong, and members of minority groups typically receive less prestige than members of the dominant group. The difference between prestige and class can be illustrated by Shirley Umphlett, one of the six Americans introduced earlier. As a minority group member with an economically rewarding career, she is ranked higher on one dimension of stratification (class or control of property, wealth, and income) but lower on another (status or amount of prestige).

Weber's third stratification system is based on **power**, or the ability to influence others, have an impact on the decision-making process of society, and pursue and protect one's self-interest and achieve one's goals. One source of power is a person's standing in politically active organizations, such as labor unions or pressure groups, which lobby state and federal legislatures. Some politically active groups have access to great wealth and can use their riches to promote their causes. Other groups may rely more on their size and their ability to mobilize large demonstrations to achieve their goals. Political groups and the people they represent vary in their abilities to affect the political process and control decision making; that is, they vary in the amount of power they can mobilize.

Typically, these three dimensions of stratification go together: Wealthy, prestigious groups will be more powerful (more likely to achieve their goals or protect their self-interest) than low-income groups or groups with little prestige. It is important to realize, however, that power is a separate dimension: Even very impoverished groups have sometimes found ways to express their concerns and pursue their goals.

Gerhard Lenski.

Gerhard Lenski is a contemporary sociologist who follows Weber and distinguishes between class (or property), prestige, and power. Lenski expands on Weber's ideas, however, by analyzing stratification in the context of societal evolution or the **level of development** of a society (Nolan & Lenski, 2004). He argues that the nature of inequality (the degree of inequality or the specific criteria affecting a group's position) is closely related to **subsistence technology**, the means by which the society satisfies basic needs such as hunger and thirst. A preindustrial agricultural society relies on human and animal labor to generate the calories necessary to sustain life. Inequality in this type of society centers on control of land and labor because they are the most important means of production at that level of development.

In a modern industrial society, however, land ownership is not as crucial as ownership of manufacturing and commercial enterprises. At the industrial level of development, control of capital is more important than control of land, and the nature of inequality will change accordingly.

The United States and other societies have recently entered still another stage of development, often referred to as postindustrial society. In this type of society, economic growth is powered by developments in new technology, computer-related fields, information processing, and scientific research. It seems fairly safe to speculate that economic success in the postindustrial era will be closely related to specialized knowledge, familiarity with new technologies, and education in general (Chirot, 1994, p. 88; see also Bell, 1973).

These changes in subsistence technology, from agriculture to industrialization to the "information society," alter the stratification system. As the sources of wealth, success, and power change, so do the relationships between minority and dominant groups. For example, the shift to an information based, "hi-tech," postindustrial society means that the advantages conferred by higher levels of education will be magnified and that groups that have less access to schooling are likely to fall even lower in the stratification system.

Minority Group
Status and Stratification

Patricia Hill-Collins is an important contemporary contributor to the ongoing attempts by American social scientists to analyze minority-dominant relations.

The theoretical perspectives we have just reviewed raise three important points about the connections between minority group status and stratification. First, as already noted, minority group status affects access to wealth and income, prestige, and power. A society in which minority groups systematically receive less of these valued goods is stratified at least partly by race and ethnicity. In the United States, minority group status has been and continues to be one of the most important and powerful determinants of life chances, health and wealth, and success. These patterns of inequality are documented and explored in Part 3, but even casual observation of U.S. society will reveal that minority groups control proportionately fewer resources and that minority group status and stratification are intimately and complexly intertwined.

Second, although social classes and minority groups form correlated, they are separate social realities. The degree to which one is dependent on the other varies from group to group. Mary Ann O'Brien, the Irish American schoolteacher introduced at the beginning of this chapter, belongs to a group that today enjoys considerable **social mobility** or easy access to opportunities, even though the Irish faced considerable discrimination in the past. Although her ethnicity may not matter much these days, her gender can still be an extremely consequential factor in shaping her life chances. Many studies document the persistence of inequality in American society for all women and especially for minority women (e.g., see Browne, 1999; DeNavas-Walt, Proctor, & Lee, 2006).

Because social classes and minority groups form different dimensions, they can vary independently. Some minority group members can be successful economically, wield great political power, or enjoy high prestige even though the vast majority of their group languishes in poverty and powerlessness. Each minority group is internally divided by systems of inequality based on class, status, or power, and in the same way, members of the same social class may be separated by ethnic or racial differences.

The third point concerning the connections between stratification and minority groups brings us back to group conflict. Dominant-minority group relationships are created by struggle over the control of valued goods and services. Minority group structures (such as slavery) emerge so that the dominant group can control commodities such as land or labor, maintain its position in the stratification system, or eliminate a perceived threat to its well-being. Struggles over property, wealth, prestige, and power lie at the heart of every dominant-minority relationship. Karl Marx believed that all aspects of society and culture were shaped to benefit the elite or ruling class and sustain the economic system that underlies its privileged position. The treatment of minority groups throughout American history provides a good deal of evidence to support Marx's point.

In this section, we focus on the second defining characteristic of minority groups: the visible traits that denote membership. The boundaries between dominant and minority groups have been established along a wide variety of lines, including religion, language, and occupation. Here we consider race and gender, two of the more physical and permanent—and thus more socially visible—markers of group membership.

Race

In the past, **race** has been widely misunderstood. The false ideas and exaggerated importance attached to race have not been mere errors of logic, subject to debate and refutation. At various times and places, they have been associated with some of the greatest tragedies in human history: massive exploitation and mistreatment, slavery, and **genocide**. Many myths about race survive in the present, although perhaps in diluted or muted form, and it is important to cultivate an accurate understanding of the concept (although the scientific knowledge that has accumulated about race is no guarantee that the concept will not be used to instigate or justify further tragedies in the future).

Thanks to advances in the sciences of genetics, biology, and physical anthropology, we know more about what race is and, more important, what race it is not. We cannot address all of the confusion in these few pages, but we can establish a basic framework and use the latest scientific research to dispel some of the myths.

Race and Human Evolution.
Our species first appeared in East Africa about 100,000 year ago. Our ancient ancestors were hunters and gatherers who slowly wandered away from their ancestral regions in search of food and other resources. Over the next 90,000 years, our ancestors slowly wandered across the entire globe, first to what is now the Middle East and then to Asia, Europe, Australia, and North and South America.

Human "racial" differences evolved during this period of dispersion, as our ancestors adapted, physically as well as culturally, to different environments and ecological conditions. For example, consider skin color, the most visible "racial" characteristic. Skin color is derived from a pigment called melanin. In areas with intense sunlight, at or near the equator, melanin screens out the ultraviolet rays of the sun that cause sunburn and, more significantly, protects against skin cancer. Thus, higher levels of melanin and darker skin colors are found in peoples who are adapted to equatorial ecologies.

In peoples adapted to areas with less intense sunlight, the amount of melanin is lower, and skin color is lighter. The lower concentration of melanin may also be an adaptation to a particular ecology. It maximizes the synthesis of vitamin D, which is important for the absorption of calcium and protection against disorders such as rickets. Thus, the skin color (amount of melanin) of any group balances the need for vitamin D and the need to protect against ultraviolet rays.

The map in Exhibit 1.3 shows the distribution of skin color prior to the mass population movements of the past several centuries. Note the rough correlation between skin color

Exhibit 1.3   The Distribution of Skin Color

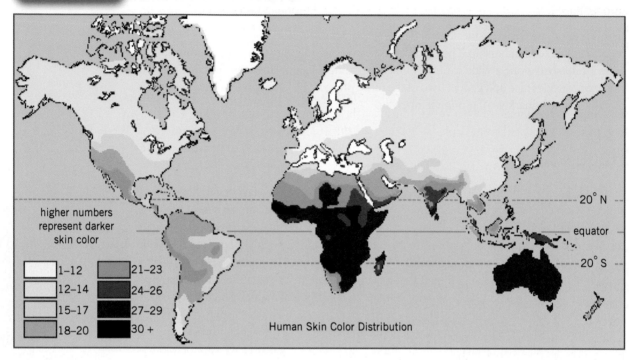

higher numbers
represent darker
skin color

1–12	21–23
12–14	24–26
15–17	27–29
18–20	30 +

Human Skin Color Distribution

20° N

equator

20° S

SOURCE: O'Neil, Dennis (n.d.).

NOTE: Data for native populations collected by R. Biasutti prior to 1940.

and proximity to the equator: Peoples with darker skin color were generally found within 20 degrees of the equator, while peoples with lighter skin were found primarily in the Northern Hemisphere, in locales distant from tropical sunlight. Note also that our oldest ancestors were adapted to the equatorial sun of Africa. This almost certainly means that they were dark skinned (had a high concentration of melanin) and that lighter skin colors are the more recent adaptation.

The period of dispersion and differentiation began to come to a close about 10,000 years ago when some of our hunting-and-gathering ancestors developed a new subsistence technology and settled down in permanent agricultural villages. Over the centuries, some of these settlements grew into larger societies and kingdoms and empires that conquered and absorbed neighboring societies, some of which differed culturally, linguistically, and racially from each other. The great agricultural empires of the past—Roman, Egyptian, Chinese, Aztec—united different peoples, reversed the process of dispersion and differentiation, and began a phase of consolidation and merging of human cultures and genetics. Over the next 10,000 years, human genes have been intermixed and spread around the globe, eliminating any "pure" races (if such ever existed). The differentiation created during the 90,000 years of dispersion was swamped by the consolidation that continues in the present. In our society, consolidation manifests itself in the increasing numbers of mixed-race people, but similar patterns are common across the globe and throughout more recent human history. The consolidation phase accelerated beginning about 500 years ago with the expansion of European power, which resulted in the exploration and conquest of much of the rest of the world.

Race and Western Traditions.

The U.S. concept of race has it origins in Western Europe. Race became a matter of concern in the Western European tradition beginning in the 1400s, when Europeans, aided by breakthroughs in navigation and ship design, began to travel to Africa, Asia, and eventually North and South America. They came into continuous contact with the peoples of these continents and became more aware of and curious about the physical differences they saw. Europeans also conquered, colonized, and sometimes destroyed the peoples and cultures they encountered. From the beginning, the European awareness of the differences between the races was linked to notions of inferior and superior (conquered vs. conquering) peoples. For centuries, the European tradition has been to see race in this political and military context and to intermix biological and physical variation with judgments about the relative merits of the various races. Racist thinking was used to justify military conquest, genocide, exploitation, and slavery. The toxic form of racism that bloomed during the expansion of European power continues to haunt the world today.

Race and Biology.

While Europeans used race primarily to denigrate, reject, and exclude nonwhites, there were also attempts to apply the principles of scientific research to the concept. These investigations focused on the construction of typologies or taxonomies, systems of classification that were intended to provide a category for every race and every person. Some of these typologies were quite elaborate and included scores of races and subraces. For example, the "Caucasian" race was often subdivided into Nordics (blond, fair-skinned Northern Europeans), Mediterraneans (dark-haired Southern Europeans), and Alpines (those falling between the first two categories).

One major limitation of these systems of classification is that the dividing lines between the so-called racial groups are arbitrary and blurred. There is no clear or definite point where, for example, "black" skin color stops and "white" skin color begins. The characteristics used to define race blend imperceptibly into each other, and one racial trait (skin color) can be blended with others (e.g., hair texture) in an infinite variety of ways. A given individual might have a skin color that is associated with one race, the hair texture of a second, the nasal shape of a third, and so forth. Even the most elaborate racial typologies could not handle the fact that many individuals fit into more than one category or none at all. Although people undeniably vary in their physical appearance, these differences do not sort themselves out in a way that permits us to divide people up like species of animals: The differences between the so-called human races are not at all like the differences between elephants and butterflies. The ambiguous and continuous nature of racial characteristics makes it impossible to establish categories that have clear, nonarbitrary boundaries.

The children in Photos 1.5-1.7, an Inuit boy, a Masai girl from Kenya, and an American boy, suggest the enormous range of variation in human physical appearance. Only some of the differences between people are perceived to be "racial" and used to create minority groups.

Over the past several decades, dramatic advances in the science of genetics have provided additional information and new insights into race that continue to refute many racial myths and further undermine the validity of racial typologies. Perhaps the most important single finding of modern research is that genetic variation within the "traditional" racial groups is greater than the variation between those groups (American Sociological Association, 2003). In other words, any two randomly selected members of, say, the "black" race are likely to vary genetically from each other at least as much as they do from a randomly selected member of the "white" race. No single finding could be more destructive of traditional racial categories, which are, after all, supposed to place people into homogeneous groupings.

The Social Construction of Race.
Despite its very limited scientific usefulness, race continues to animate intergroup relations in the United States and around the world. It continues to be socially important and a significant way of differentiating among people. Race, along with gender, is one of the first things people notice about one another. In the United States, we still tend to see race as a simple, unambiguous matter of skin color alone and to judge everyone as belonging to one and only one group, ignoring the realities of multiple ancestry and ambiguous classification.

How can such an unimportant scientific concept retain its relevance? Because of the way it developed, Western concepts of race have a social as well as a biological or scientific dimension. To sociologists, race is a **social construction**, and its meaning has been created and sustained not by science, but by historical, social, and political processes (see Omi & Winant, 1986; Smedley, 1999). In other words, race is largely a matter of social definitions and traditions, and our understandings of race are based on social convention, not science. Race remains important not because of objective realities, but because of the widespread, shared social perception that it is important.

The arbitrary, subjective nature of race does not lessen its importance for those who must grapple with it on an everyday basis, especially for members of racial minority groups. Consider the thoughts of one "mixed race" individual in the following Narrative Portrait.

Gender

You have already seen that minority groups can be internally divided by social class and other factors. An additional source of differentiation is gender. Like race, gender has both a biological and a social component and can be a highly visible and convenient way of judging and sorting people. From birth, the biological differences between the sexes form the basis for different **gender roles**, or societal expectations about proper behavior, attitudes, and personality traits. In virtually all societies, including those at the advanced industrial stage, adult work roles tend to be separated by gender, and boys and girls are socialized differently in preparation for these roles. In hunter-gatherer societies, for example, boys typically train for the role of hunter, whereas girls learn the skills necessary for successful harvesting of vegetables, fruit, and other foodstuffs. In advanced industrial societies, girls tend to learn nurturing skills that will help them take primary responsibility for the well-being of family and community members, and boys learn aggressiveness, which is considered necessary for their expected roles as leaders, combatants, and providers in a highly competitive society.

Text continued on p. 31

Racial Identity and the Sociological Imagination

*A*t 4 weeks of age, Deirdre Royster was adopted by a black family living in the suburbs of Washington, D.C. Royster's biological mother was white, and her biological father was black. Although she was light skinned and could easily pass for white, she was, in the racial thinking of the day, black, not "mixed." She grew up in a middle-class, mostly black neighborhood and attended schools with diverse student bodies and was often able to form friendships across racial and ethnic lines. However, she became aware of her dual identity early on: "I knew, as early as first grade, that in school I was white and at home I was black."

Royster was able to accommodate comfortably to the multiple racial worlds she lived in for much of her childhood but gradually began to puzzle over the meaning of race in the larger society and for her personally. In the passage below, she describes how her concerns led her to explore her own identity and probe and question the racial realities that surrounded her. People of mixed-race backgrounds may feel that they are marginal in the larger society: members of two (or more) groups but not fully accepted or completely at home in either. Marginality can be uncomfortable, but it can also stimulate a questioning, critical attitude toward the taken-for-granted realities of both communities. In Royster's case, this analytical journey eventually led her to the discipline of sociology as an undergraduate major and, ultimately, as a profession. She is now an award-winning instructor and a professor of sociology at the College of William and Mary. Her first book, Race and the Invisible Hand *(see Chapter 6)*, won the Oliver C. Cox award from the American Sociological Association in 2004.

White Like Me Black Me

Deirdre Royster

I live in a body that is routinely assumed to belong to a white person, so I enjoy the privilege of not appearing suspect to landlords, bankers, shopkeepers, police officers, and lots of other institutional representatives. People generally view me as an ordinary white person or a white ethnic person, like an Italian or Greek, and this is especially the case when I'm with my white spouse. When I'm alone, some see me more exotically as a Latina, Indian, or Middle Eastern woman, but only once in a while does a person guess that I am mixed or black, my actual backgrounds. My appearance or phenotype is white or nonblack, but my self-conception and interpretive lenses are black. Looking as I do, people from many racial and ethnic backgrounds are friendly and open toward me. Many from unique ethnic backgrounds are curious about whether we share an ethnicity, while many whites seem to just find mine a pleasant and uncomplicated presence to be around. As a result of this comfort zone, in everyday encounters, I've been privy to private racial talk: talk that is sometimes critical of another group, more often than not blacks, but that is only uttered among those the speaker considers an insider. Private racial talk sometimes reveals hidden prejudices that . . . structure life negatively for those who are racially vulnerable. But sometimes private racial talk allows individuals to check how they have interpreted racial experiences or other stimuli with a trusted other who can provide an alternative point of view. So, private racial talk can contribute to deepening our society's racial difficulties, but also to easing them. I've been a fly-on-the-wall in the midst of both types of racial talk, and living as a racial chameleon probably led me to study sociology, a social science that sheds light on the historical and contemporary experiences of different groups in society.

Sociological insights have helped me to understand the nature of prejudicial attitudes, but also that getting rid of prejudicial attitudes, hard as that has been and continues to be, will not eliminate patterns of racial inequalities that have accumulated over hundreds of years. Our paradoxical beginning as a "democratic" republic that institutionalized white supremacy haunts us today, as it has every generation of Americans, including the country's first forebears. We sense that those early social, political, economic, and cultural choices—that some of the forebears argued were unacceptable trade-offs—live on somehow in the present, but our ethos as a young and dynamic society that sees itself as always improving, moving forward, and growing, makes us reticent to gauge more deeply the continuing price of earlier mistakes. While we are generally aware that some groups enjoyed a newfound freedom and opportunity on these shores while other groups found un-freedom and blocked opportunity, we typically don't know any group's experiences as well as our own group's (which we might not know well either), and we know very little about the full spectrum of difficulties that faced (and face) the most vulnerable groups. In our best moments as a society, we express a common and undifferentiated language of pride and admiration for every vulnerable group's ingenuity, hard labor, and tenacity in overcoming the specific set of obstacles they faced in the United States. What we seem to lack is a common language of anguish for the vulnerabilities that remain, vulnerabilities that are racially concentrated and that could be addressed as earlier groups' vulnerabilities were addressed. As a sociologist, my aim is not just to share my personal experience of privilege as a phenotypical white person and vulnerability as a self-conscious black person, but also to unveil the hidden nature of rewarding and punishing systems that influence the life chances of Americans across the color spectrum. . . . My story . . . tells a far larger story of privilege and vulnerability about which many Americans are sadly, and unacceptably, unaware. We have many important decisions to make as citizens in this democracy; I hope [my thoughts] will provide useful perspectives to consider as we try to make informed choices about which policies and practices might best address the racial conditions we wish to change.

SOURCE: Royster, Deirdre (2007). *White Like Me Black Me*. Unpublished manuscript.

The Blending of America: Mixed Race

It has been projected that over the next several decades, as American society becomes more culturally and linguistically diverse, the population of the United States will also look like the rest of the globe, that is, less white. As the population becomes more ethnically diverse, it also seems to be becoming more racially "mixed." In my own lifetime, the marriage of Italians and Slavs, even when both bride and groom were Roman Catholic, was looked upon somewhat as a "mixed marriage," and marriages between Jews and Gentiles were extremely unusual. Historically the most problematic forms of social integration or blending have been racial.

For example, socially created racial categories like black and white (as well as even more arbitrary human colors of "yellow" for Asian and "red" for Indigenous Americans), despite the lack of a scientifically biological basis, were seen as fixed. The hierarchy of racism argued that just one drop of black blood would essentially contaminate an otherwise apparently "white" and allegedly also superior person. In fact, marriages between arbitrarily defined white and nonwhite races were illegal in many states. Following are a number of 19th-century illustrations that cast racial mixing, or miscegenation, as sinister and threatening to society.

© Bettmann/CORBIS.

© CORBIS.

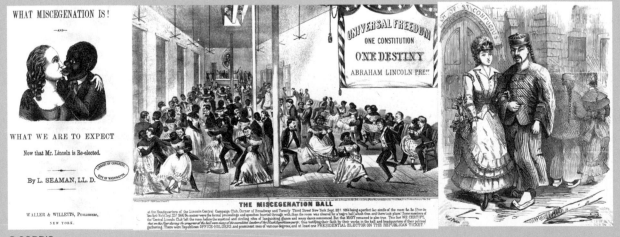

© CORBIS.

AP Photo.

© Bettmann/CORBIS.

Photo by Jerome Krase.

© Underwood & Underwood/CORBIS.

Jack Johnson (pictured at right) was the first African American heavyweight champion. There was a campaign of hatred and bigotry waged against him by whites who wished to regain the heavyweight title and who also resented his interracial relationships with women.

After his first interracial marriage and his defeat of several white hopefuls, Johnson was convicted in 1913 under contrived circumstances for violation of a federal law, the Mann Act.

Popular media reflected and in some cases helped the movement in the United States for racial equality. Films such as "Guess Who's Coming to Dinner?" (1967; see below), which starred Sidney Poitier, presented the issue of interracial marriage, once a virtually taboo subject in mass media, in a humorous way.

The opening of Hollywood for black movie stars ironically led to the decline of "race" films; a notable artistic and commercial industry of black writers, producers, directors, and actors which had resulted from segregation and discrimination.

Having stars like Sidney Poitier in leading roles side-by-side with white men and (once even more unthinkable) women have greatly enhanced the American movie industry.

Racially mixed gatherings and residential neighborhood integration continued to be unusual in the 1970s even after the many successes of the Civil Rights Movement. Organizations such as "National Neighbors" worked to bring groups together in successfully integrating neighborhoods.

AP Photo/Laura Rauch.   Photo by Jerome Krase.   AP Photo/Dom Furore, Golf Digest.

Karen Krase and friends at Prospect-Lefferts-Gardens Neighborhood Association gathering, photo by Jerome Krase

Although it might seem that we have come a long way since the days when miscegenation was illegal, both interracial dating and interracial marriage continue to evoke hostility and, in too many cases, violence as well.

But things are changing. Perhaps the strongest indication of the belated acceptance of interracial mixing in the United States today is the fact that some of the most celebrated idols of beauty and athletics could be called "Blended Americans." Moreover, many of our newest immigrants and migrants to America are in one way or another "mixed," such as European-, Indigenous-, and African-blended Latinos. Other groups, such as those from South Asia as well as the Middle and Near East, also challenge the old racial categories.

Photo by William Thomas Cain/Getty Images   AP Photo.

Gender roles and relationships vary across time and from society to society, but gender and inequality have usually been closely related, and men typically claim more property, prestige, and power. Exhibit 1.4 provides some perspective on the variation in gender inequality across the globe. The map shows the distribution of a statistic called the gender development index, which measures the amount of inequality between men and women across a range of variables, including education, health, and income. As you can see, gender equality is generally highest in the more developed, industrialized nations of North America and Western Europe and lowest in the less developed, more agricultural nations of sub-Saharan Africa.

Despite their high scores on gender equality, the societies of Western Europe and the United States have strong traditions of **patriarchy**, or male dominance. In a patriarchal society, men have more control over the economy and more access to leadership roles in religion, politics, and other institutions. In these societies, women possess many characteristics of a minority group (namely, a pattern of disadvantage based on group membership marked by a physical stigma). Thus, women could be, and in many ways should be, treated as a separate minority group.

In this book, however, rather than discussing women as a separate group, I will focus on the divergent experiences of men and women within each minority group. This approach will permit us to analyze the ways in which race, ethnicity, gender, and class combine, overlap, and crosscut each other to form a "matrix of domination" (Hill-Collins, 1991, pp. 225–227). We will consider how the interests and experiences of females of different groups and classes coincide with and diverge from each other and from the men in their groups. For example, on some issues, African American females might have interests identical to white females and

Exhibit 1.4   Map of Gender Development Index Scores

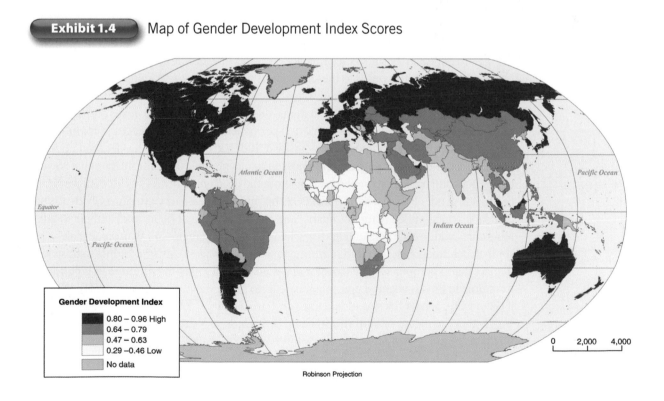

Gender Development Index

- 0.80 – 0.96 High
- 0.64 – 0.79
- 0.47 – 0.63
- 0.29 – 0.46 Low
- No data

Robinson Projection

opposed to African American males. On other issues, the constellations of interests might be reversed. As you shall see, the experience of minority group membership varies by gender, and the way gender is experienced is not the same for every group.

History generally has been and is written from the standpoint of the "winners," that is, those in power. The voices of minority groups have generally been repressed, ignored, forgotten, or trivialized. Much of the history of slavery in America, for instance, has been told from the viewpoint of the slave owners. Slaves were kept illiterate by law and had few mechanisms for recording their thoughts or experiences. A more balanced and accurate picture of slavery began to emerge only in the past few decades, when scholars began to dig beneath the written records and memoirs of the slave owners and reconstruct the experiences of African Americans from nonwritten materials such as oral traditions and the physical artifacts left by the slaves.

However, our understanding of the experiences of minority groups is often based almost entirely on the experiences of minority group males alone, and the experiences of minority group females are much less well-known and documented. If the voices of minority groups have been hushed, those of female minority group members have been virtually silenced. One of the important trends in contemporary scholarship is to adjust this skewed focus and systematically incorporate gender as a factor in the minority group experience (Espiritu, 1997; Zinn & Dill, 1994).

Are Gender Roles Learned or Genetic? The huge majority of social scientists regard race as a social construction formulated in certain historical circumstances (such as the era of European colonialism) when it was needed to help justify the unequal treatment of nonwhite groups. What about gender? Is it also merely a social creation designed by men to rationalize their higher status, or do the commonly observed gender differences (e.g., men tend to be more aggressive, women more nurturing) have biological causes that are stronger and more controlling than those supposedly associated with race? Are men and women different because of nature (differences in biology and genetic inheritance) or because of nurture (differences in expectations and experience for boys and girls during childhood socialization)?

Needless to say, responses to these questions vary both in the scientific community and in the society at large. On one hand, some believe that the behavioral differences between males and females are the results of "natural" differences between the sexes and are "hardwired" in our genetic code just as surely and permanently as the differences in reproductive organs. Others (including most sociologists) argue that gender roles are learned and that the commonly observed gender differences in adults are the results of the fact that society tracks boys and girls in different directions from the moment of birth and discourages "inappropriate" gender behaviors. Proponents of the "nurture" point of view cite as evidence the malleable, open-ended nature of infants and the great range of behavioral and personality repertoires within each gender (e.g., some females are more aggressive than some males, and some males are more tender and nurturing than some females). Also, according to this view, the fact that "appropriate" behaviors for males and females vary from culture to culture and from time to time is taken as proof that there is no biological basis for gender roles, because if there were, gender roles would be fixed and permanent.

Neither the nature or nurture approach, by itself, is very useful. Modern research shows that biology and genetic inheritance (nature) and socialization experiences (nurture) work together in a variety of ways, some exquisitely subtle, to produce adult personality and the commonly observed gender differences (see Udry, 2000). Furthermore, the evidence is accumulating that the social environment, not genes and hormones, is the key to understanding gender role socialization (Booth, Granger, Mazur, & Kivligham, 2006, pp. 167–191). Where does that leave us? Current research shows that biology and genetics play a role but that adult gender roles are largely the result of the social expectations attached to biological sex. Gender is a social construction, like race, when it is treated as a categorical, fixed difference and then used to deny opportunity and equality to women.

Key Concepts in Dominant-Minority Relations

Whenever sensitive issues such as dominant-minority group relations are raised, the discussion turns to (or on) matters of prejudice and discrimination. We will be very much concerned with these subjects in this book, so we need to clarify what we mean by these terms. This section introduces and defines four concepts that will help you understand dominant-minority relations in the United States.

The book addresses how individuals from different groups interact, as well as relations among groups. Thus, we need to distinguish between what is true for individuals (the psychological level of analysis) and what is true for groups or society as a whole (the sociological level of analysis). Beyond that, we must attempt to trace the connections between the two levels of analysis.

We also need to make a further distinction on both the individual and the group levels. At the individual level, what people think and feel about other groups and how they actually behave toward members of those groups may differ. A person might express negative feelings about a group in private but deal fairly with members of the group in face-to-face interactions. Groups and entire societies may display this same kind of inconsistency. A society may express support for equality in its official documents or formal codes of law and simultaneously treat minority groups in unfair and destructive ways. An example of this kind of inconsistency is the contrast between the commitment to equality stated in the Declaration of Independence ("All men are created equal") and the actual treatment of black slaves, Anglo-American women, and Native Americans at that time.

At the individual level, social scientists refer to the "thinking/feeling" part of this dichotomy as prejudice and the "doing" part as discrimination. At the group level, the term *ideological racism* describes the "thinking/feeling" dimension and institutional discrimination describes the "doing" dimension. Exhibit 1.5 depicts the differences among these four concepts.

Prejudice

Prejudice is the tendency of an individual to think about other groups in negative ways, to attach negative emotions to those groups, and to prejudge individuals on the basis of their group memberships. Individual prejudice has two aspects: the cognitive, or thinking, aspect and the affective, or feeling, part. A prejudiced person thinks about other groups in terms of **stereotypes (cognitive prejudice)**, generalizations that are thought to apply to group members. Examples of familiar stereotypes include notions such as "Women are emotional," "Jews are stingy," "Blacks are lazy," "The Irish are drunks," and "Germans are authoritarian." A prejudiced

Exhibit 1.5 Four Concepts in Dominant-Minority Relations

Dimension	Individual	Group or Societal
Thinking/feeling	Prejudice	Ideological racism
Doing	Discrimination	Institutional discrimination

person also experiences negative emotional responses to other groups, **affective prejudice**, including contempt, disgust, arrogance, and hatred. People vary in their levels of prejudice, and levels of prejudice vary in the same person from one time to another and from one group to another. We can say that a person is prejudiced to the extent that he or she uses stereotypes in his or her thinking about other groups or has negative emotional reactions to other groups.

Generally, the two dimensions of prejudice are highly correlated with each other. However, they are also distinct and separate aspects of prejudice and can vary independently. One person may think entirely in stereotypes but feel no particular negative emotional response to any group. Another person may feel a very strong aversion toward a group but be unable to articulate a clear or detailed stereotype of that group.

Discrimination

Discrimination is defined as the unequal treatment of a person or persons based on group membership. An example of discrimination is an employer who decides not to hire an individual because he or she is African American (or Puerto Rican, Jewish, Chinese, etc.). If the unequal treatment is based on the group membership of the individual, the act is discriminatory.

Just as the cognitive and affective aspects of prejudice can be independent, discrimination and prejudice do not necessarily occur together. Even highly prejudiced individuals may not act on their negative thoughts or feelings. In social settings regulated by strong egalitarian codes or laws (for example, restaurants and other public facilities), people who are highly bigoted in their private thoughts and feelings may abide by the codes in their public roles.

On the other hand, social situations in which prejudice is strongly approved and supported might evoke discrimination in otherwise unprejudiced individuals. In the southern United States during the height of segregation or in South Africa during the period of state-sanctioned racial inequality, it was usual and customary for whites to treat blacks in discriminatory ways. Regardless of a person's actual level of prejudice, he or she faced strong social pressure to conform to the official patterns of racial superiority and participate in acts of discrimination.

Ideological Racism

Ideological racism, a belief system that asserts that a particular group is inferior, is the group or societal equivalent of individual prejudice. These ideas and beliefs are used to legitimize or rationalize the inferior status of minority groups and are incorporated into the culture of a society and passed on from generation to generation during socialization.

Because it is a part of the cultural heritage, ideological racism exists apart from the individuals who inhabit the society at a specific time (Andersen, 1993, p. 75; See & Wilson, 1988, p. 227). An example of a racist ideology is the elaborate system of beliefs and ideas that attempted to justify slavery in the American South. The exploitation of slaves was "explained" in terms of the innate racial inferiority of blacks and the superiority of whites.

Distinguishing between individual prejudice and societal racist ideologies naturally leads to a consideration of the relationship between these two phenomena. We will explore this relationship in later chapters, but for now I can make what is probably an obvious point: People socialized into societies with strong racist ideologies are very likely to absorb racist ideas and be highly prejudiced. It should not surprise us that a high level of personal prejudice existed among whites in the antebellum American South or in other highly racist societies, such as South Africa. At the same time, we need to remember that ideological racism and individual prejudice are different things with different causes and different locations in society. Racism is not a prerequisite for prejudice; prejudice may exist even in the absence of an ideology of racism.

Institutional Discrimination

The final concept is the societal equivalent of individual discrimination. **Institutional discrimination** refers to a pattern of unequal treatment based on group membership that is built into the daily operations of society, whether or not it is consciously intended. The public schools, the criminal justice system, and political and economic institutions can operate in ways that put members of some groups at a disadvantage.

Institutional discrimination can be obvious and overt. For many years following the Civil War, African Americans in the American South were prevented from voting by practices such as poll taxes and rigged literacy tests. For nearly a century, well into the 1960s, elections and elected offices in the South were confined to whites only. The purpose of this blatant pattern of institutional discrimination was widely understood by African American and white southerners alike: It existed to disenfranchise the African American community and keep it politically powerless.

At other times, institutional discrimination may operate more subtly and without conscious intent. If public schools use aptitude tests that are biased in favor of the dominant group, decisions about who does and who does not take college preparatory courses may be made on racist grounds, even if everyone involved sincerely believes that they are merely applying objective criteria in a rational way. If a decision-making process has unequal consequences for dominant and minority groups, institutional discrimination may well be at work.

Note that although a particular discriminatory policy may be implemented and enforced by individuals, the policy is more appropriately thought of as an aspect of the operation of the institution as a whole. Election officials in the South during segregation did not and public school administrators today do not have to be personally prejudiced themselves to implement these discriminatory policies.

However, a major thesis of this book is that both racist ideologies and institutional discrimination are created to sustain the positions of dominant and minority groups in the stratification system. The relative advantage of the dominant group is maintained from day to day by widespread institutional discrimination. Members of the dominant group who are socialized into communities with strong racist ideologies and a great deal of institutional discrimination are likely to be personally prejudiced and to routinely practice acts of individual discrimination. The respective positions of dominant and minority groups are preserved over time through the mutually reinforcing patterns of prejudice, **racism**, and discrimination on both individual and institutional levels. Institutional discrimination is but one way in which members of a minority group can be denied access to valued goods and services, opportunities, and rights (such as voting). That is, institutional discrimination helps to sustain and reinforce the unequal positions of racial and ethnic groups in the stratification system.

Applying Concepts

Intersecting Inequalities, Racism, and Hurricane Katrina

In late August 2005, there was plenty of warning that a monster storm was approaching the Gulf Coast and threatening the city of New Orleans. People did what they could to protect themselves and their property, and many boarded up their houses and evacuated or moved to shelters. But there is little a person can do in the face of the 120 mph winds and storm surge of a Category 3 hurricane (See Exhibit 1.6).

When Katrina made landfall on the morning of August 29, its winds were felt along a 200-mile stretch of the Gulf Coast. The storm affected almost 6 million people and killed over 1,800 (Gabe, Falk, & McCarthy, 2005). Katrina obliterated houses, stores, shopping malls, hospitals, and entire towns. When the cost of all the damage was finally totaled up, many months later, Katrina became the most expensive natural disaster in U.S. history.

Exhibit 1.6   Hurricane Katrina

© NASA/Corbis.

The city of New Orleans was heavily damaged by the storm, but the real problems began when the levee system failed the day after Katrina passed, flooding virtually the entire city. The combination of hurricane winds and floodwaters nearly annihilated New Orleans, wrecked its infrastructure, killed over 700 of its citizens, and displaced almost the entire population. The city ceased to function and may never again be home for hundreds of thousands of its former residents or return to its status as one of America's premier cities and tourist attractions.

In the days and weeks that followed Katrina, the disaster of late August was compounded by the massive failure of the governmental relief response. Americans watched in horror as the people of New Orleans cried out for help—any kind of help—and the government (especially the Federal Emergency Management Agency, or FEMA) failed to rescue people and provide food, water, or safe shelter. The people of New Orleans were victimized twice, first by the storm and the flooding and then by the colossal ineptitude of the governmental response.

What relevance could Hurricane Katrina have for the concerns of this text? Aren't natural disasters—earthquakes, tornados, floods, and tsunamis as well as hurricanes—blind to race,

ethnicity, class, and gender? Even though hurricanes don't care who lies in their path, they do not affect everyone equally, and class, race, ethnicity, and gender are prime factors in determining who becomes a victim and who walks away unscathed. At the time of the disaster, television reports gave the impression that Katrina's victims in New Orleans were poor, black, and disproportionately female, and research since has confirmed the accuracy of this impression. For example, a 2006 Gallup Poll reported that 53% of black residents of New Orleans had lost everything versus only 19% of white residents (Lavelle & Feagin, 2006, p. 60).[3] Exhibit 1.7 superimposes two maps: One shows the damaged neighborhoods (cross-hatched yellow sections) and the other shows the percentage of each neighborhood that is black. The city of New Orleans is in the upper part of the map, outlined in red. Clearly, the damage was widespread and affected nearly everyone; rich and poor, black and white. However, the map shows that virtually every predominantly black New Orleans neighborhood suffered from the storm and the flooding.

Why did these racial and class differentials develop? What could explain the multiple victimizations of the poor black citizens of New Orleans? Was it simply prejudice and racism? Was it because, in the famous words of rapper Kanye West, "George Bush just doesn't care about black people" (Moraes, 2005, p. C1)? Or were more subtle and less visible forces at work? The underlying principles that explain the racial and class pattern of victimization are consistent with many of the themes of this text, and we will take some time now to begin to explore them, apply them to the disaster in New Orleans, and preview their importance in chapters to come.

Exhibit 1.7   New Orleans Neighborhoods: Racial Composition and Damage

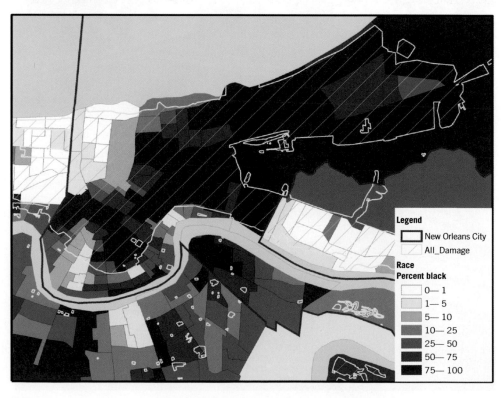

SOURCE: Logan, John (n.d.). *The Impact of Katrina: Race and Class in Storm-Damaged Neighborhoods.*

The first point we can make is that vulnerability to natural (and many man-made) disasters is closely related to social class and minority group status. Hurricanes don't seek out specific groups, but people with fewer resources (a defining characteristic of a minority group) are more vulnerable to the initial catastrophe and less able to recover in its aftermath. Consider, for example, the ability to evacuate in the hours before the storm struck. Who got out, and who was left behind to face the fury of the storm and the flooding? A general evacuation order was issued for the city, but twice as many poor whites as poor blacks (83% vs. 40%) had access to cars to help them escape (Lavelle & Feagin, 2006, p. 59).

A consideration of vulnerability leads to a deeper issue: Why was such a large percentage of the vulnerable population of New Orleans both poor and black? Let's start with a basic sociological profile of the city prior to the storm. Blacks were a majority of the population of New Orleans, but, as I pointed out earlier in this chapter, minority groups are defined by the distribution of resources, power, wealth, and opportunity, not by relative numbers. New Orleans was 67% black when the hurricane hit, but, to consider only one dimension of minority group status, blacks had much higher rates of poverty and much lower incomes, as demonstrated in Exhibit 1.8. Five summary statistics are presented in Exhibit 1.8 for the year 2000, the date of the last census. Note that median income for blacks was less than half that of whites and was especially low (for both blacks and whites) for female-headed households. Also, 20% of black families lived on yearly incomes of less than $10,000, while only 4% of white families did the same. These income patterns are consistent with racial differences in poverty. Nearly 30% of the black families in New Orleans lived in poverty, almost 5 times as many as white families. Female-headed households of both races were more likely to be poor, but nearly half of black, female-headed families lived in poverty, a rate 2½ times that of white, female-headed households.

These simple statistics clearly demonstrate the greater economic vulnerability of black New Orleans, but how can we account for these huge racial differences? We can begin with a consideration of some of the themes of this text:

- The situation of a minority group in the present is a result of their experiences in the past.
- Minority groups are created in response to the fundamental forces shaping the larger society, especially the subsistence technology.
- Minority-dominant group relations change as the larger society evolves and develops.

Exhibit 1.8 Racial Differentials in Poverty and Income in New Orleans City, 2000

	Blacks	Whites
Median income, all families*	$26,110	$54,008
Median income, female-headed households	$15,684	$28,941
Percentage of all families with incomes less than $10,000	20.0%	4.0%
Percentage of all families with incomes below the poverty line	29.8%	6.0%
Percentage of all female-headed households with incomes below the poverty line	46.8%	17.9%

SOURCE: U.S. Bureau of the Census (2000f).

*Median income is the income that divides a group in half: Half earns more than this figure, and half earns less.

We will explore these themes in the chapters to come, but we can point to the centuries of racial oppression and exclusion, institutional discrimination, and racism that preceded the arrival of Katrina as one powerful explanation for the gaps displayed in Exhibit 1.8. Present-day racial inequalities began centuries ago, during the days of slavery (see Chapter 4), when the preindustrial agricultural technology of the day stimulated the demand for slave labor. In the era before labor-saving machines were developed to do the bulk of farmwork, the elite groups that dominated southern society developed slavery to supply a large, highly controlled labor force. Slavery ended in 1865 but was quickly followed by a system of race relations called **de jure segregation** (see Chapter 5), in which state and local laws were used to continue the powerlessness and economic disadvantages of blacks and to perpetuate their economic and political control by whites. Racial inequality was massive during this era and included separate and distinctly lower positions for blacks in housing, schooling, jobs, and access to political power. To cite only one example of the racial oppression characteristic of segregation, the state of Louisiana passed an amendment to the state constitution in 1898 that effectively denied the right to vote to the black community. African Americans were deprived of their most fundamental political resource and their ability to use the political institution to protect their self-interests.

The formal, legal barriers to equality were abolished as a result of the civil rights revolution of 1960s (see Chapter 6), only four decades ago. While progress toward racial equality has been made since that time—at least nationally—we must remember that we, as a society, are only two generations removed from a system that required racial inequality by law and by custom. Furthermore, class inequalities have been hardening throughout the nation over the past several decades as the United States moves into the postindustrial era (see Chapter 5).

The experiences of black Americans during slavery and de jure segregation varied by class (e.g., house slaves vs. field hands) and by gender. I explore some of these differences in chapters to come, but one dimension of continuing gender differences within the system of racial oppression is reflected in Exhibit 1.8. Minority group females are the most vulnerable and oppressed segment of the society on many dimensions. Continuing sexism combined with racism often results in black females having the lowest positions in the job market. Also, joblessness for minority males is common, leaving women with the responsibility for the care of the children and other family members. Combined, these forces lead to high rates of female-centered households and, ultimately, to women being vastly overrepresented in shelters after Katrina passed (Strolovitch, Warren, & Frymer, 2006).

The status of the black community in New Orleans in the early 21st century was the product of centuries-long processes of institutional discrimination, exclusion, and oppression. The differences in financial resources and social class status documented in Exhibit 1.8 weren't created overnight, and they will not disappear without a concerted struggle, even under the most favorable economic conditions. In modern, postindustrial society, we should note, the key to financial security and upward mobility is education, and access to quality schooling also varies by race. Some of the differences in educational achievement are presented in Exhibit 1.9. The New Orleans school system was in poor shape before Katrina and is now in absolute shambles, a reality that is likely to reinforce the lower educational levels of the black community for years to come.

The situation of poor blacks in New Orleans took centuries to create and reflects how recently blacks were formerly and legally excluded from the opportunity structure of the

Exhibit 1.9 Racial Differentials in Educational Attainment in New Orleans City, 2000

	Blacks	Whites
Percentage 25 years of age and older who are high school graduates or higher	67.6%	83.6%
College graduates or higher	12.7%	27.4%
Percentage 18–24 years of age with less than a high school degree		
Males	40.1%	26.0%
Females	28.6%	19.0%

SOURCE: U.S. Bureau of the Census (2000f).

larger society. As Senator Barack Obama famously remarked at the time of the disaster, the poor black people of New Orleans were "abandoned long before the hurricane" (Ivey, 2005).

A Global Perspective

In the chapters that follow, we will focus on developing a number of concepts and theories and applying those ideas to the minority groups of the United States. However, it is important to expand our perspective beyond the experiences of just a single nation. Just as you would not accept an interview with a single person as an adequate test of a psychological theory, you should not accept the experiences of a single nation as proof for the sociological perspective developed in this text. Thus, we will take time, throughout this text, to apply our ideas to other societies, other historical eras, and a variety of non-American minority groups. If the ideas and concepts developed in this text can help us make sense of these other situations, we will have some assurance that they have general applicability and that the dynamics of intergroup relations in the United States are not unique.

Photo 1.10

In an era of rapid globalization, it is crucial to develop a perspective that reaches beyond the United States.

© Will & Deni McIntyre/Corbis.

CURRENT DEBATES

Race and Sports

How real is race? Is it a matter of biology and genes and evolution or purely a social construction arising from specific historical circumstances, such as American slavery? Does knowing people's race tell us anything important about them? Does it give any useful information about their character, their medical profiles, their trustworthiness, their willingness to work hard, or their intelligence? Does race play a role in shaping a person's character or his or her potential for success in school or on the job?

This debate about the significance of race and the broader question of "nature versus nurture" has been going on in one form or another for a very long time. One version of the debate has centered on the relationship between intelligence and race. One side of the debate argues that biological or genetic differences make some races more capable than other races. Most scientists reject this argument and maintain that there is no meaningful connection between race and mental aptitude (for the latest round of arguments in this debate, see Herrnstein & Murray, 1994; Jacoby & Glauberman, 1995).

Another manifestation of this debate centers on the relationship between race and sport. The fact is that contrary to their general status as members of a minority group, African Americans dominate several different sports in the United States today. For example, African Americans are heavily overrepresented at the highest levels of achievement in basketball, football, track and field, and, to a lesser extent, several other sports. Although African Americans are less than 13% of the population, they are more than 73% of professional basketball players and two thirds of professional football players (Lapchick, 2006, pp. 23, 48). African Americans are more prominent among professional athletes—and especially among the very elite—than in virtually any other sphere of American life. Furthermore, the phenomenon is worldwide:

In international track, athletes of African descent dominate both sprinting and long-distance running events.

Why is this so? Has race played a role in establishing this pattern? Are people of African descent "naturally" better athletes? Are there social, cultural, and environmental forces at work here that produce this extraordinary dominance? One thing we do know, after so many decades of debate on this topic, is that there is no easy choice between nature and nurture; virtually every scholar agrees that explanations must include both genetic heritage and experience.

Journalist Jon Entine (2000) has argued that the dominance of black athletes in some sports is more biological: "Elite athletes who trace most or all of their ancestry to Africa are by and large better than the competition" (p. 4). Although Entine agrees that the racial performance gap in sports is partly due to cultural and environmental conditions (nurture), he argues that blacks are better athletes mainly because of a superior genetic heritage. The genetic differences are slight, but they are "crucial in competitions in which a fraction of a second separates the gold medalist from the also-ran" (p. 4). Specifically, blacks of West African heritage (which would include African Americans, whose ancestors were taken as slaves mostly from this area) have a number of physiological traits that give them a decisive advantage in sprinting, leaping, and quick, explosive movements. These traits, in Entine's view, explain the dominance of blacks in certain sports (sprinting, basketball) and in certain positions (wide receiver in football) that capitalize on these abilities. Athletes of East African descent, on the other hand, inherit a set of abilities that give them greater endurance and lung capacity, traits that, according to Entine, explain the dominance of East Africans (Kenyans, for example) in long-distance races on the international and

Olympic levels. In the excerpt that follows, Entine summarizes what he sees as the biological advantage of black athletes.

Writer Kenan Malik (2000) argues that Entine's position is based on an arbitrary and uncritical view of race. He raises several questions and probes the weaknesses of some widespread assumptions about race.

The Dominance of Black Athletes Is Genetic

JON ENTINE

Since the first known studies of differences between black and white athletes in 1928, the data have been remarkably consistent: In most sports, African-descended athletes have the capacity to do better with their raw skills than whites. Let's summarize the physical and physiological differences known to date. Blacks with West African ancestry generally have relatively less subcutaneous fat on arms and legs and proportionally more lean body and muscle mass . . . bigger, more developed musculature in general, a longer arm span, faster patellar tendon reflex, greater body density, a higher percentage of fast-twitch muscles and more anaerobic enzymes, which can translate into more explosive energy. Relative advantages in these physiological and biomechanical characteristics are a gold mine for athletes who compete in . . . football, basketball, and sprinting. . . .

East Africa produces some of the world's best aerobic athletes because of a variety of bio-physiological attributes. Blacks from this region . . . have more energy-producing enzymes in the muscles and an apparent ability to process oxygen more efficiently, resulting in less susceptibility to fatigue; they have a slighter body profile and a larger lung capacity than whites or West Africans, which translates into greater endurance.

White athletes appear to have a physique between . . . West Africans and East Africans. They have more endurance but less explosive running and jumping ability than West Africans; they tend to be quicker than East Africans but have less endurance.

SOURCE: Entine, Jon. (2000). *Taboo: Why Black Athletes Dominate Sports and Why We're Afraid to Talk About It,* pp. 268–269. New York: Public Affairs.

The Argument for Genetic Differences Is Deeply Flawed

KENAN MALIK

What lies behind black domination of sport? The traditional liberal answer points the finger at social factors. Black people, so the argument goes, have been driven into sport because racism has excluded them from most areas of employment. Racism also makes blacks hungrier than whites for success. . . . Journalist Jon Entine dismisses [this] environmentalist theory of black athletic prowess as "political correctness." . . .

The liberal consensus, Entine argues, has served only to disguise the truth about the black domination of sport—which is that black people are built to run and jump. . . . [Entine and others argue] that it's time we put away our fears of talking about racial differences and face up to the facts of genetic diversity.

The view that black sportsmen and women have a natural superiority rests on the evidence of physiological research, largely into two groups of athletes: East African long-distance runners and West African sprinters.

East Africa, and Kenya in particular, is the powerhouse of middle- and long-distance running . . . . [R]esearch suggests that the secret of such spectacular success lies in superior biology. Athletes of West African descent—and that includes most African Americans . . . have, on the other hand, a physique that is suited to . . . sprinting and jumping.

For Entine, such . . . differences demonstrate the natural superiority of black athletes. For Entine's critics, . . . the very search for such differences betrays a racist outlook. . . . The . . . problem with the "blacks are born to run" thesis is . . . that it is factually incorrect. . . . It is certainly possible to divide humanity into a number of races...according to skin colour and body form. However, it is also possible to do it many other ways—using, for instance, blood group, lactose tolerance, sickle cell, or any other genetic trait. Genetically, each would be as valid a criterion as skin colour. The distribution of one physical or genetic characteristic is not necessarily the same as that of another.... The current division of the world into black, white, [and] Asian races is, in other words, as rooted in social convention as in genetics.

Entine rejects such criticisms as mere "semantics," but his own argument shows why it is not so. According to Entine, East Africans are naturally superior at endurance sports, West Africans at sprinting and jumping, and "whites fall somewhere in the middle." But if East and West Africans are at either end of a genetic spectrum of athletic ability, why consider them to be part of a single race, and one that is distinct from whites? Only because, conventionally, we use skin colour as the criterion of racial difference....

Not only are genetic notions of population differences distinct from political concepts of race, but the physiology of human differences is not easy to interpret in sporting terms. Jon Entine suggests that West Africans have relatively slender calves compared to whites, and that this helps their sprinting ability. It is difficult to see how, because muscle power increases with cross-sectional area; smaller calves should make it harder, not easier, to excel in explosive sprinting events....

It is true that athletes of West African descent living in North America, Western Europe and the Caribbean dominate many sports. But contemporary West Africans do not. This is the opposite of what one should expect if athletic ability were predominantly determined by genetics. In the United States, considerable intermixing between black and white has meant that the African American population embodies, on average, roughly 30 percent of genes from populations of European descent. Hence, African Americans should be poorer athletes than West Africans. The reverse is true.

What all this suggests is that the relationship between sport, culture and genetics is much more complex than either liberal anti-racists or conservatives such as Entine...will allow. Athletic talent is at least in part inherited, and there are undoubted genetic differences between regional populations.... There is no reason to assume that all populations have physical characteristics equally suited to every athletic activity. But are blacks naturally better athletes than whites? Not necessarily. After all, how many African Pygmies have you ever seen climbing on to the winners' rostrum?

SOURCE: Malik, Kenan. (2000). "Yes, Nature Does Help to Explain African Sporting Success. If You Think That's Racist, Your Idea of Race Is Wrong." *New Statesman,* September 18, pp. 13–18.

Debate Questions to Consider

1. Is Entine using the social or biological definition of race? Is it racist to argue that blacks are "naturally" gifted? Is it appropriate for scientists to pursue the issue raised by Entine?

2. How strong are Malik's arguments? What does he mean when he questions the practice of grouping East and West Africans into the same race? What larger point is he making when he notes the absence of West Africans and Pygmies from the highest levels of sports competition?

3. If Entine is wrong, what social and environmental arguments might explain black dominance in sports? What is Malik implying when he says that these relationships are "more complex" than is commonly recognized?

Main Points

- The United States faces enormous problems in dominant-minority relationships. Although many historic grievances of minority groups remain unresolved, our society is becoming increasingly diverse.

- The United States is a nation of immigrants, and many different groups and cultures are represented in its population.

- A minority group has five defining characteristics: a pattern of disadvantage, identification by some visible mark, awareness of its disadvantaged status, a membership determined at birth, and a tendency to marry within the group.

- A stratification system has three different dimensions (class, prestige, and power), and the nature of inequality in a society varies by its level of development. Minority groups and social class are correlated in numerous and complex ways.

- Race is a criterion widely used to identify minority group members. As a biological concept, race has been largely abandoned, but as a social category, race maintains a powerful influence on the way we think about one another.

- Minority groups are internally differentiated by social class, age, region of residence, and many other variables. In this book, I focus on gender as a source of variation within minority groups.

- Four crucial concepts for analyzing dominant-minority relations are prejudice, discrimination, ideological racism, and institutional discrimination.

- The public sociology assignments presented in the Introduction to Part 1 give you several opportunities to apply some of the concepts presented in this chapter. Studying diversity in a local school or in a soup kitchen will bring you face-to-face with the increasing diversity of U.S. society as well as some of the realities of inequality, discrimination, and racism.

Study Site on the Web

Don't forget the interactive quizzes and other resources and learning aids at www.pineforge .com/healeystudy5.

For Further Reading

Allport, Gordon. (1954). *The Nature of Prejudice*. Reading, MA: Addison-Wesley.

   The classic work on individual prejudice.

Baca Zinn, Maxine, & Dill, Bonnie Thornton. (1994). *Women of Color in U.S. Society*. Philadelphia: Temple University Press.

   A wide-ranging collection of articles examining the intersecting forces of race, class, and gender in the United States.

Feagin, Joseph. (2001). *Racist America*. New York: Routledge.

> *A passionate analysis of the pervasiveness of racism and anti-black prejudice in America.*

New York Times. (2001). *How Race Is Lived in America*. New York: New York Times Books.

> *An in-depth look at the continuing importance of race in American life conducted by correspondents of the New York Times. Based on the Pulitzer-Prize-winning television documentary.*

Omi, Michael, & Winant, Howard. (1986). *Racial Formation in the United States From the 1960s to the 1980s*. New York: Routledge & Kegan Paul.

> *An adept analysis of the social and political uses of race.*

Smedley, Audrey. (1999). *Race in North America: Origin and Evolution of a Worldview*. Boulder, CO: Westview Press.

> *An analysis of the origins of the American view of race.*

Takaki, Ronald. (1993). *A Different Mirror: A History of Multicultural America*. Boston: Little, Brown.

> *A highly readable look at minority groups and cultural diversity in American life.*

Questions for Review and Study

1. What kind of society should the United States strive to become? In your view, does the increasing diversity of American society represent a threat or an opportunity? Should we acknowledge and celebrate our differences, or should we strive for more unity and conformity? What possible dangers and opportunities are inherent in increasing diversity? What are the advantages and disadvantages of stressing unity and conformity?

2. What groups should be considered "minorities"? Using each of the five criteria included in the definition presented in this chapter, should gay and lesbian Americans be considered a minority group? How about left-handed people or people who are very overweight? Explain and justify your answers.

3. What is a social construction? How do race and gender differ in this regard? What does it mean to say "Gender becomes a social construction—like race—when it is treated as an unchanging, fixed difference and then used to deny opportunity and equality to women"?

4. Define and explain each of the terms in Exhibit 1.5. Cite an example of each from your own experiences. How does "ideological racism" differ from prejudice? Which concept is more sociological? Why? How does institutional discrimination differ from discrimination? Which concept is more sociological? Why?

A. Updating Data on Diversity

Update Exhibit 1.1, "Groups in U.S. Society." Visit the Web site of the U.S. Bureau of the Census (http://www.census.gov) to get the latest estimates on the sizes of minority groups in the United States. Good places to begin the search for data include "Minority Links," "Statistical Abstract," and the list at "Subjects A to Z."

B. How Does the U.S. Government Define Race?

In this chapter, I stressed the point that race is at least as much a social construction as a biological reality. Does the federal government see race as a biological reality or a social convention? Search the U.S. Bureau of the Census Web site for information on the federal definition of race. How was a person's race defined in the 2000 census? How does this differ from previous censuses? Who determines a person's race, the government or the person filling out the census form? Is this treatment of race based on a biological approach or a more arbitrary social perspective? Given the goals of the census (e.g., to accurately count the number and types of people in the U.S. population), is this a reasonable approach to classifying race? Why or why not?

Notes

1. Boldface terms in the text are defined in the Glossary at the end of the book.
2. A partial exception to this generalization, the Buraku in Japan, is covered in Chapter 9.
3. These percentages are almost certainly gross underestimates, as the poll taker contacted only people with active New Orleans phone numbers.

Assimilation and Pluralism

CHAPTER 2

From Immigrants to White Ethnics

This chapter continues to look at the ways in which ethnic and racial groups in the United States relate to each other. Two concepts, assimilation and pluralism, are at the core of the discussion. Each includes a variety of possible group relations and pathways along which group relations might develop.

Assimilation is a process in which formerly distinct and separate groups come to share a common culture and merge together socially. As a society undergoes assimilation, differences among groups decrease. Pluralism, on the other hand, exists when groups maintain their individual identities. In a pluralistic society, groups remain separate, and their cultural and social differences persist over time.

In some ways, assimilation and pluralism are contrary processes, but they are not mutually exclusive. They may occur together in a variety of combinations within a particular society or group. Some groups in a society may be assimilating as others are maintaining (or even increasing) their differences. As we shall see in Part 3, virtually every minority group in the United States has, at any given time, some members who are assimilating and others who are preserving or reviving traditional cultures. Some Native Americans, for example, are pluralistic. They live on or near reservations, are strongly connected to their heritage, and speak their native language. Other Native Americans are very much assimilated into the dominant society: They live in urban areas, speak English only, and know relatively little about their traditional cultures.

Both assimilation and pluralism are important forces in the everyday lives of Native Americans and most other minority groups.

American sociologists have been very concerned with these processes, especially assimilation. This concern was stimulated by the massive immigration from Europe to the United States that occurred between the 1820s and the 1920s. Over 31 million people crossed the Atlantic during this time, and a great deal of energy has been devoted to documenting, describing, and understanding the experiences of these immigrants and their descendants. These efforts have resulted in the development of a rich and complex literature that I will refer to as the "traditional" perspective on how newcomers are incorporated in U.S. society.

This chapter begins with a consideration of the traditional perspective on both assimilation and pluralism and a brief examination of several other possible group relationships. The concepts and theories of the traditional perspective are then applied to European immigrants and their descendants, and we develop a model of American assimilation based on these experiences. This model will be used in our analysis of other minority groups throughout the text and especially in Part 3.

A particularly important issue is whether the theories, concepts, and models based on the first mass immigration to the United States (from the 1820s to the 1920s) apply to the second (post-1965) mass immigration. The newest arrivals differ in many ways from those who came earlier, and ideas and theories based on the earlier experiences will not necessarily apply to the present. We will briefly note some of the issues in this chapter and explore them in more detail in the case study chapters in Part 3.

Finally, at the end of this chapter, I briefly consider the implications of these first two chapters for the exploration of intergroup relations. By the end of this chapter, you will be familiar with many of the concepts that will guide us throughout this text as we examine the variety of possible dominant-minority group situations and the directions our society (and the groups within it) can take.

Assimilation

We begin with assimilation because the emphasis in U.S. group relations has historically been on this goal rather than on pluralism. This section presents some of the most important sociological theories and concepts that have been used to describe and analyze the assimilation of the 19th-century immigrants from Europe.

Types of Assimilation

Assimilation is a general term for a process that can follow a number of different pathways. One form of assimilation is expressed in the metaphor of the "**melting pot**," a process in which different groups come together and contribute in roughly equal amounts to create a common culture and a new, unique society. People often think of the American experience of assimilation in terms of the melting pot. This view stresses the ways in which diverse peoples helped to construct U.S. society and made contributions to American culture. The melting-pot metaphor sees assimilation as benign and egalitarian, a process that emphasizes sharing and inclusion.

Although it is a powerful image in our society, the melting pot is not an accurate description of how assimilation actually proceeded for American minority groups (Abrahamson,

Photo 2.1

Assimilation happens on many levels, including food. In this photo, a New York deli offers food from several ethnic traditions (Jewish, Italian, and Middle Eastern) brought together in a distinctly American venue.

© 2008 Jupiterimages Corporation.

1980, pp. 152–154). Some groups—especially the racial minority groups—have been largely excluded from the "melting" process. Furthermore, the melting-pot brew has had a distinctly Anglocentric flavor: "For better or worse, the white Anglo-Saxon Protestant tradition was for two centuries—and in crucial respects still is—the dominant influence on American culture and society" (Schlesinger, 1992, p. 28). Contrary to the melting-pot image, assimilation in the United States generally has been a coercive and largely one-sided process better described by the terms **Americanization** or **Anglo-conformity**. Rather than an equal sharing of elements and a gradual blending of diverse peoples, assimilation in the United States was designed to maintain the predominance of the English language and the British-type institutional patterns created during the early years of American society.

Under Anglo-conformity, immigrant and minority groups are expected to adapt to Anglo-American culture as a precondition to acceptance and access to better jobs, education, and other opportunities. Assimilation has meant that minority groups have had to give up their traditions and adopt Anglo-American culture. To be sure, many groups and individuals were (and continue to be) eager to undergo Anglo-conformity, even if it meant losing much or all of their heritage. For other groups, Americanization created conflict, anxiety, demoralization, and resentment. We assess these varied reactions in our examination of America's minority groups in Part 3.

The "Traditional" Perspective on Assimilation: Theories and Concepts

American sociologists have developed a rich body of theories and concepts based on the assimilation experiences of the immigrants who came from Europe from the 1820s to the 1920s, and we shall refer to this body of work as the traditional perspective on assimilation. As you will see, the scholars working in this tradition have made invaluable contributions, and their thinking is impressively complex and comprehensive. This does not mean, of course, that they have exhausted the possibilities or answered (or asked) all the questions. Theorists working in the pluralist tradition and contemporary scholars studying the experiences of more recent immigrants have questioned many aspects of traditional assimilation theory and have made a number of important contributions of their own.

Robert Park.
Many theories of assimilation are grounded in the work of Robert Park. He was one of a group of scholars who had a major hand in establishing sociology as a discipline in the United States in the 1920s and 1930s. Park felt that intergroup relations go through a predictable set of phases that he called a "**race relations cycle**." When groups first come into contact (through immigration, conquest, etc.), relations are conflictual and competitive. Eventually, however, the process, or cycle, moves toward assimilation, or the "interpenetration and fusion" of groups (Park & Burgess, 1924, p. 735).

Park argued further that assimilation is inevitable in a democratic and industrial society. In a political system based on democracy, fairness, and impartial justice, all groups will eventually secure equal treatment under the law. In an industrial economy, people tend to be judged on rational grounds—that is, on the basis of their abilities and talents—and not by ethnicity or race. Park believed that as American society continued to modernize, urbanize, and industrialize, ethnic and racial groups would gradually lose their importance. The boundaries between groups would eventually dissolve, and a more "rational" and unified society would emerge (see also Geschwender, 1978, pp. 19–32; Hirschman, 1983).

Social scientists have examined, analyzed, and criticized Park's conclusions for nearly 80 years. One frequently voiced criticism is that he did not specify a time frame for the completion of assimilation, and therefore his idea that assimilation is "inevitable" cannot be tested. Until the exact point in time when assimilation is deemed complete, we will not know whether the theory is wrong or whether we just have not waited long enough.

Photo 2.2

These children are at Gordon's structural assimilation (secondary sector) stage.

© Owen Franken/Corbis.

An additional criticism of Park's theory is that he does not describe the nature of the assimilation process in much detail. How would assimilation proceed? How would everyday life change? Which aspects of the group would change first?

Milton Gordon. To clarify some of the issues left unresolved by Park, we turn to the works of sociologist Milton Gordon, who made a major contribution to theories of assimilation in his book *Assimilation in American Life* (1964). Gordon broke down the overall process of assimilation into seven subprocesses; we will focus on the first three. Before considering these phases of assimilation, we need to consider some new concepts and terms.

Gordon makes a distinction between the cultural and the structural components of society. **Culture** encompasses all aspects of the way of life associated with a group of people. It includes language, religious beliefs, customs and rules of etiquette, and the values and ideas people use to organize their lives and interpret their existence. The **social structure**, or structural components of a society, includes networks of social relationships, groups, organizations, stratification systems, communities, and families. The social structure organizes the work of the society and connects individuals to one another and to the larger society.

It is common in sociology to separate the social structure into primary and secondary sectors. The **primary sector** includes interpersonal relationships that are intimate and personal, such as families and groups of friends. Groups in the primary sector are small. The **secondary sector** consists of groups and organizations that are more public, task oriented, and impersonal. Organizations in the secondary sector are often very large and include businesses, factories, schools and colleges, and bureaucracies.

Now we can examine Gordon's earliest stages of assimilation, which are summarized in Exhibit 2.1.

Exhibit 2.1 Gordon's Stages of Assimilation

Stage	Process
1. Acculturation (cultural assimilation)	The group learns the culture, language, and value system of the dominant group.
2. Integration (structural assimilation)	
a. At the second level	Members of the group enter the public institutions and organizations of the dominant society.
b. At the primary level	Members of the group enter the cliques, clubs, and friendship groups of the dominant society.
3. Intermarriage (marital assimilation)	Members of the group intermarry with members of the dominant group on a large-scale basis.

SOURCE: Adapted from Gordon (1964, p. 71). Reprinted by permission of Oxford University Press, Inc.

1. **Cultural Assimilation, or Acculturation**. Members of the minority group learn the culture of the dominant group. For groups that immigrate to the United States, acculturation to the dominant Anglo-American culture may include (as necessary) learning the English language, changing eating habits, adopting new value systems, and altering the spelling of the family surname.

2. **Structural Assimilation, or Integration**. The minority group enters the social structure of the larger society. Integration typically begins in the secondary sector and gradually moves into the primary sector. That is, before people can form friendships with members of other groups (integration into the primary sector), they must first become acquaintances. The initial contact between groups often occurs in public institutions such as schools and workplaces (integration into the secondary sector). The greater their integration into the secondary sector, the more nearly equal the minority group will be to the dominant group in income, education, and occupational prestige. Once a group has entered the institutions and public sectors of the larger society, according to Gordon, integration into the primary sector and the other stages of assimilation will follow inevitably (although not necessarily quickly). Measures of integration into the primary sector include the extent to which people have acquaintances, close friends, or neighbors from other groups.

3. **Marital Assimilation, or Intermarriage**. When integration into the primary sector becomes substantial, the basis for Gordon's third stage of assimilation is established. People are most likely to select spouses from among their primary relations, and thus, in Gordon's view, primary structural integration typically precedes intermarriage.

Gordon argued that acculturation was a prerequisite for integration. Given the stress on Anglo-conformity, a member of an immigrant or minority group would not be able to compete for jobs or other opportunities in the secondary sector of the social structure until he or she had learned the dominant group's culture. Gordon recognized, however, that successful acculturation does not automatically ensure that a group will begin the integration phase. The dominant group may still exclude the minority group from its institutions and limit the opportunities available to the group. Gordon argued that "acculturation without integration" (or Americanization without equality) is a common situation in the United States for many minority groups, especially the racial minority groups.

In Gordon's theory, movement from acculturation to integration is the crucial step in the assimilation process. Once that step is taken, all the other subprocesses will occur inevitably, although movement through the stages can be very slow. Gordon's idea that assimilation runs a certain course in a certain order echoes Park's conclusion regarding the inevitability of the process.

More than 40 years after Gordon published his analysis of assimilation, some of his conclusions have been called into question. For example, the individual subprocesses of assimilation that Gordon saw as linked in a certain order are often found to occur independently of one another (Yinger, 1985, p. 154). A group may integrate before acculturating or combine the subprocesses in other ways. Also, many researchers no longer think of the process of assimilation as necessarily linear or one-way (Greeley, 1974). Groups (or segments thereof) may "reverse direction" and become less assimilated over time, revive their traditional cultures, relearn their old language, or revitalize ethnic organizations or associations.

Nonetheless, Gordon's overall model continues to guide our understanding of the process of assimilation, to the point that a large part of the research agenda for contemporary studies of immigrants involves assessment of the extent to which their experiences can be described in Gordon's terms (Alba & Nee, 1997). In fact, Gordon's model will provide a major organizational framework for the case study chapters presented in Part 3 of this text.

Human Capital Theory. Why did some European immigrant groups acculturate and integrate more rapidly than others? Although not a theory of assimilation per se, **human capital theory** offers one possible answer to this question. This theory argues that status attainment, or the level of success achieved by an individual in society, is a direct result of educational levels, personal values and skills, and other individual characteristics and abilities. Education is seen as an investment in human capital, not unlike the investment a business might make in machinery or new technology. The greater the investment in a person's human capital, the higher the probability of success. Blau and Duncan (1967), in their pioneering statement of status attainment theory, found that even the relative advantage conferred by having a high-status father is largely mediated through education. In other words, high levels of affluence and occupational prestige are not so much a result of being born into a privileged status as they are the result of the superior education that affluence makes possible.

Why did some immigrant groups achieve upward mobility more rapidly than others? Human capital theory answers questions such as these in terms of the resources and cultural characteristics of the members of the groups, especially their levels of education and familiarity with English. Success is seen as a direct result of individual effort and the wise investment of personal resources. People or groups who fail have not tried hard enough, have not made the right kinds of educational investments, or have values or habits that limit their ability to compete.

More than most sociological theories, human capital theory is quite consistent with traditional American culture and values. Both tend to see success as an individual phenomenon, a reward for hard work, sustained effort, and good character. Both tend to assume that success is equally available to all and that the larger society is open and neutral in its distribution of rewards and opportunity. Both tend to see assimilation as a highly desirable, benign process that blends diverse peoples and cultures into a strong, unified whole. Thus, people or groups that resist Americanization or question its benefits are seen as threatening or illegitimate.

On one level, human capital theory is an important theory of success and upward mobility, and we will on occasion use the theory to analyze the experiences of minority and immigrant groups. On another level, the theory is so resonant with American "commonsensical" views of success and failure that we may tend to use it uncritically.

A final judgment on the validity of the theory will be more appropriately made at the end of the text, but you should be aware of the major limitations of the theory from the beginning. First of all, as an explanation of minority group experience, human capital theory is not so much "wrong" as it is incomplete. In other words, it does not take account of all the factors that affect mobility and assimilation. Second, as we shall see, the assumption that U.S. society is equally open and fair to all groups is simply wrong. We will point out other strengths and limitations of this perspective as we move through the text.

Pluralism

Sociological discussions of pluralism often begin with a consideration of the work of Horace Kallen. In articles published in the Nation magazine in 1915, Kallen argued that people

should not have to surrender their culture and traditions to become full participants in American society. He rejected the Anglo-conformist, assimilationist model and contended that the existence of separate ethnic groups, even with separate cultures, religions, and languages, was consistent with democracy and other core American values. In Gordon's terms, Kallen believed that integration and equality were possible without extensive acculturation and that American society could be a federation of diverse groups, a mosaic of harmonious and interdependent cultures and peoples (Kallen, 1915a, 1915b; see also Abrahamson, 1980; Gleason, 1980).

Assimilation has been such a powerful theme in U.S. history that in the decades following the publication of Kallen's analysis, support for pluralism remained somewhat marginalized. In more recent decades, however, interest in pluralism and ethnic diversity has increased, in part because the assimilation predicted by Park (and implicit in the conventional wisdom of many Americans) has not fully materialized. Perhaps we simply have not waited long enough, but as the 21st century unfolds, distinctions among the racial minority groups in our society show few signs of disappearing, and, in fact, some members of these groups are questioning the very desirability of assimilation. Also, more surprising perhaps, is that white ethnicity maintains a stubborn persistence, although it continues to change in form and decrease in strength.

An additional reason for the growing interest in pluralism, no doubt, is the everyday reality of the increasing diversity of U.S. society, as reflected in Exhibit 1.1. Controversies over issues such as "English-only" policies, bilingual education, and welfare rights for immigrants are common and often bitter. Many Americans feel that diversity or pluralism has exceeded acceptable limits and that the unity of the nation is at risk (for example, visit http://www.us-english.org/, the home page of a group that advocates for English-only legislation).

Finally, interest in pluralism and ethnicity in general has been stimulated by developments around the globe. Several nation-states have disintegrated into smaller units based on language, culture, race, and ethnicity. Recent events in India, the Middle East, Eastern Europe, the former U.S.S.R., Canada, and Africa, just to mention a few, have provided dramatic and often tragic evidence of how ethnic identities and enmities can persist across decades or even centuries of submergence and suppression in larger national units.

In contemporary debates, discussions of diversity and pluralism are often couched in the language of **multiculturalism**, a general term for a variety of programs and ideas that stress mutual respect for all groups and for the multiple heritages that have shaped the United States. Some aspects of multiculturalism are controversial and have evoked strong opposition. In many ways, however, these debates merely echo a recurring argument about

Photo 2.5

The United States incorporates a wide variety of traditions and peoples including Jewish, Amish, and Cuban Americans.

© Carlos Barria/Reuters/Corbis.

the character of American society, a debate that will be revisited throughout this text.

Types of Pluralism

We can distinguish various types of pluralism by using some of the concepts introduced in the discussion of assimilation. **Cultural pluralism** exists when groups have not acculturated and each maintains its own identity. The groups might speak different languages, practice different religions, and have different value systems. The groups are part of the same society and might even live in adjacent areas, but in some ways, they live in different worlds. Many Native Americans are culturally pluralistic, maintaining their traditional languages and cultures and living on isolated reservations. The Amish, a religious community sometimes called the Pennsylvania Dutch, are also a culturally pluralistic group. They are committed to a way of life organized around farming, and they maintain a culture and an institutional life that is separate from the dominant culture (see Hostetler, 1980; Kephart & Zellner, 1994; Kraybill & Bowman, 2001).

Following Gordon's subprocesses, a second type of pluralism exists when a group has acculturated but not integrated. That is, the group has adopted the Anglo-American culture but does not have full and equal access to the institutions of the larger society. In this situation, called **structural pluralism**, cultural differences are minimal, but the groups occupy different locations in the social structure. The groups may speak with the same accent, eat the same food, pursue the same goals, and subscribe to the same values, but they may also maintain separate organizational systems, including different churches, clubs, schools, and neighborhoods. Under structural pluralism, groups practice a common culture but do so in different places and with minimal interaction across group boundaries. An example of structural pluralism can be found on any Sunday morning in the Christian churches of the United States. Not only are local parishes separated by denomination, they are also often identified with specific ethnic groups or races. What happens in the various churches—the rituals, expressions of faith, statements of core values and beliefs—is similar and expresses a common, shared culture. Structurally, however, this common culture is expressed in separate buildings and by separate congregations.

A third type of pluralism reverses the order of Gordon's first two phases: integration without acculturation. This situation is exemplified by a group that has had some material success (measured by wealth or income, for example) but has not become Americanized (learned English, adopted American values and norms, etc.). Some immigrant groups have found niches in American society in which they can survive and occasionally prosper economically without acculturating very much.

Photo 2.6

Many American cities have Chinatowns, ethnic enclaves that have provided safe havens for Chinese immigrants for a century and a half. The photo shows Chinatown in San Francisco, one of the oldest Chinatowns.

© Klaus Hackenberg/zefa/Corbis.

Two different situations can be used to illustrate this pattern. An **enclave minority** establishes its own neighborhood and relies on a set of interconnected businesses, each of which is usually small in scope, for its economic survival. Some of these businesses serve the group, whereas others serve the larger society. The Cuban American community in South Florida and Chinatowns in many larger American cities are examples of ethnic enclaves. A similar pattern of adjustment, the **middleman minority**, also relies on small shops and retail firms, but the businesses are more dispersed throughout a large area rather than concentrated in a specific locale. Some Chinese American communities fit this second pattern, as do Korean American greengroceries and Indian-American-owned motels (Portes & Manning, 1986). These types of minority groups are discussed further in Part 3.

The economic success of enclave and middleman minorities is partly due to the strong ties of cooperation and mutual aid within their groups. The ties are based, in turn, on cultural bonds that would weaken if acculturation took place. In contrast with Gordon's idea that acculturation is a prerequisite to integration, whatever success these groups enjoy is due in part to the fact that they have not Americanized. Kim Park, whom we met in the first chapter, is willing to work in his uncle's grocery store for room and board and the opportunity to learn the business. His willingness to forgo a salary and subordinate his individual needs to the needs of the group reflects the strength of his relationship to family and kin. At various times and places, Jewish, Chinese, Japanese, Korean, and Cuban Americans have been enclave or middleman minorities (see Bonacich & Modell, 1980; Kitano & Daniels, 2001).

The situation of enclave and middleman minorities, integration without acculturation, can be considered either a type of pluralism (emphasizing the absence of acculturation) or a type of assimilation (emphasizing a high level of economic equality). Keep in mind that assimilation and pluralism are not opposites but can occur in a variety of combinations. It is best to think of acculturation, integration, and the other stages of assimilation (or pluralism) as independent processes.

Other Group Relationships

This book concentrates on assimilation and pluralism, but there are, of course, other possible group relationships and goals. Two commonly noted goals for minority groups are separatism and revolution (Wirth, 1945). The goal of separatism is for the group to sever all ties (political, cultural, and geographic) with the larger society. Thus, separatism goes well beyond pluralism. Native Americans have expressed both separatist and pluralist goals, and separatism has also been pursued by some African American organizations, such as the Black Muslims. In the contemporary world, there are separatist movements among groups in French Canada, Scotland, Chechnya, Cyprus, southern Mexico, Hawaii, and scores of other places.

A minority group promoting **revolution** seeks to switch places with the dominant group and become the ruling elite or create a new social order, perhaps in alliance with members of the dominant group. Although revolutionary activity can be found among some American minority groups (e.g., the Black Panthers), this goal has been relatively rare for minority groups in the United States. Revolutionary minority groups are more commonly found in situations such as those in colonial Africa, in which one nation conquered and controlled another racially or culturally different nation.

The dominant group may also pursue goals other than assimilation and pluralism, including forced migration or expulsion, extermination or genocide, and continued subjugation of the minority group. Chinese immigrants were the victims of a policy of expulsion, beginning in the 1880s, when the Chinese Exclusion Act (1882) closed the door on further immigration and concerted efforts were made to encourage those in the country to leave (see Chapter 9). Native Americans have also been the victims of expulsion. In 1830, all tribes living east of the Mississippi were forced to migrate to a new territory in the West (see Chapter 4). The most infamous example of genocide is the Holocaust in Nazi Germany, during which 6 million Jews were murdered. The dominant group pursues "continued subjugation" when, as with slavery in the antebellum South, it attempts to maintain a powerless and exploited position for the minority group. A dominant group may simultaneously pursue different policies with different minority groups and may, of course, change policies over time.

From Immigrants to White Ethnics

In this section, we will explore the experiences of the minority groups that stimulated the development of the traditional perspective. A massive immigration from Europe began in the 1820s, and over the next century, millions of people made the journey from the Old World to the New. They came from every corner of the continent: Ireland, Greece, Germany, Italy, Poland, Portugal, Ukraine, Russia, and scores of other nations and provinces. They came as young men and women seeking jobs, as families fleeing religious persecution, as political radicals fleeing the police, as farmers seeking land and a fresh start, and as paupers barely able to scrape together the

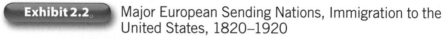

Exhibit 2.2   Major European Sending Nations, Immigration to the United States, 1820–1920

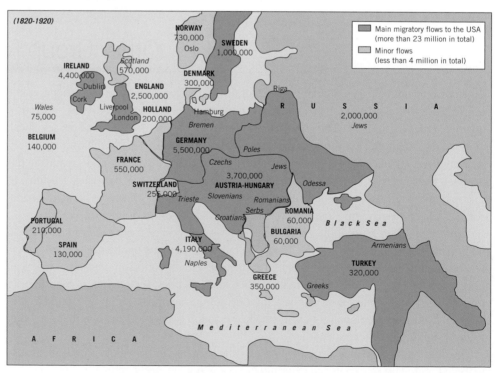

cost of the passage. They came as immigrants, became minority groups upon their arrival, experienced discrimination and prejudice in all its forms, went through all the varieties and stages of assimilation and pluralism, and eventually merged into the society that had rejected them so viciously upon their arrival. Exhibit 2.2 shows the major European sending nations.

This first mass wave of immigrants shaped the United States in countless ways. When the immigration started in the 1820s, the United States was not yet 50 years old, an agricultural nation clustered along the East Coast. The nation was just coming into contact with Mexicans in the Southwest, immigration from China had not begun, slavery was flourishing in the South, and conflict with American Indians was intense and brutal. When the immigration ended in the 1920s, the population of the United States had increased from fewer than 10 million to more than 100 million, and the society had industrialized, become a world power, and stretched from coast to coast, with colonies in the Pacific and the Caribbean.

It was no coincidence that European immigration, American industrialization, and the rise to global prominence occurred simultaneously. These changes were intimately interlinked, the mutual causes and effects of each other. Industrialization fueled the growth of U.S. military and political power, and the industrial machinery of the nation depended heavily on the flow of labor from Europe. By World War I, for example, 25% of the nation's total labor force was foreign-born, and more than half of the workforce in New York, Detroit, and Chicago consisted of immigrant men. Immigrants were the majority of the workers in many important sectors of the economy, including coal mining, steel manufacturing, the garment industry, and meatpacking (Martin & Midgley, 1999, p. 15; Steinberg, 1981, p. 36).

In the sections that follow, we explore the experiences of these groups, beginning with forces that caused them to leave Europe and come to the United States and ending with an assessment of their present status in American society.

Industrialization and Immigration

What forces stimulated this mass movement of people? Like any complex phenomenon, immigration from Europe had a multitude of causes, but underlying the process was a massive and fundamental shift in subsistence technology: the **Industrial Revolution**. I mentioned the importance of subsistence technology in Chapter 1. Dominant-minority relations are intimately related to the system a society uses to satisfy its basic needs, and they change as that system changes. The immigrants were pushed out of Europe as industrial technology wrecked the traditional agricultural way of life, and they were drawn to the United States by the jobs created by the spread of the very same technology. We will consider the impact of this fundamental transformation of social structure and culture in some detail.

Industrialization began in England in the mid-1700s, spread to other parts of Northern and Western Europe and then, in the 19th century, to Eastern and Southern Europe. As it rolled across the continent, the Industrial Revolution replaced people and animal power with machines and new forms of energy (steam, coal, and eventually oil), causing an exponential increase in the productive capacity of society. At the dawn of the Industrial Revolution, most Europeans lived in small, rural villages and survived by traditional farming practices that had changed very little over the centuries. The work of production was **labor-intensive** or done by hand or with the aid of draft animals. Productivity was low, and the tasks of food production and survival required the efforts of virtually the entire family working ceaselessly throughout the year.

Industrialization destroyed this traditional way of life as it introduced new technology, machines, and new sources of energy to the tasks of production. The new technology was **capital-intensive** or dependent on machine power, and it reduced the need for human labor in rural areas as it modernized agriculture. Also, farmland was consolidated into larger and larger tracts for the sake of efficiency, further decreasing the need for human laborers. At the same time, even as survival in the rapidly changing rural economy became more difficult, the rural population began to grow.

In response, peasants began to leave their home villages and move toward urban areas. Factories were being built in or near the cities, opening up opportunities for employment. The urban population tended to increase faster than the job supply, however, and many migrants had to move on. Many of these former peasants responded to opportunities available in the New World, especially in the United States, where the abundance of farmland on the frontier kept people moving out of the cities and away from the East Coast, thereby sustaining a fairly constant demand for labor in the very areas that were easiest for Europeans to reach. As industrialization took hold on both continents, the population movement to European cities and then to North America eventually grew to become the largest in human history (so far).

The timing of immigration from Europe followed the timing of industrialization. The first waves of immigrants, often called the "**Old Immigration**," came from Northern and Western Europe in the 1820s. A second wave, the "**New Immigration**," began arriving from Southern and Eastern Europe in the 1880s. Exhibit 2.3 shows both waves and the rates of legal immigration up to 2006. Note that the "new" immigration was much more voluminous than the "old"

Exhibit 2.3 Legal Immigration to the United States, 1820–2006

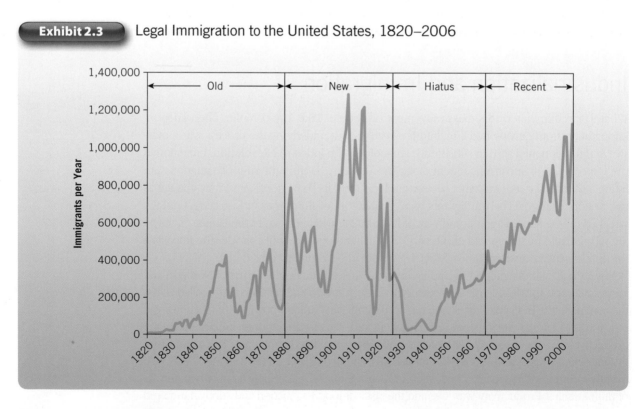

SOURCE: U.S. Department of Homeland Security (2007).

and that the number of immigrants declined drastically after the 1920s. We will explore the reasons for this decline later in this chapter and discuss in detail the more recent (post-1965) increase in immigration in Chapters 8 through 10.

European Origins and Conditions of Entry

The immigrants from Europe varied from each other in innumerable ways. They followed a variety of pathways into the United States, and their experiences were shaped by their cultural and class characteristics, their countries of origin, and the timing of their arrival. Some groups encountered much more resistance than others, and different groups played different roles in the industrialization and urbanization of America. To discuss these diverse patterns systematically, I distinguish three subgroups of European immigrants: Protestants from Northern and Western Europe, the largely Catholic immigrant laborers from Ireland and from Southern and Eastern Europe, and Jewish immigrants from Eastern Europe. We look at these subgroups in roughly the order of their arrival. In later sections, we will consider other sociological variables (social class, gender) that further differentiated these groups.

Northern and Western Protestant Europeans.
Northern and Western European immigrants included English, Germans, Norwegians, Swedes, Welsh, French, Dutch, and Danes. These groups were similar to the dominant group in their racial and religious characteristics and also shared many cultural values with the host society, including the Protestant Ethic—which stressed hard work, success, and individualism—and support for the

Photo 2.7

Until the Industrial Revolution, virtually the entire population of Europe lived in the countryside. This village scene depicts the crowds gathered on market day.

principles of democratic government. These similarities eased their acceptance into a society that was highly intolerant of religious and racial differences until well into the 20th century, and these immigrant groups generally experienced a lower degree of ethnocentric rejection and racist disparagement than did the Irish and immigrants from Southern and Eastern Europe.

Northern and Western European immigrants came from nations that were just as developed as the United States. Thus, these immigrants tended to be more skilled and educated than other immigrant groups, and they often brought money and other resources with which to secure a comfortable place for themselves in their new society. Many settled in the sparsely populated Midwest and in other frontier areas, where they farmed the fertile land that had become available after the conquest and removal of American Indians and Mexican Americans (see Chapter 4). By dispersing throughout the midsection of the country, they lowered their visibility and their degree of competition with dominant group members. Two brief case studies, first Norwegians and then Germans, outline the experiences of these groups.

Immigrants From Norway. Norway had a small population base, and immigration from this Scandinavian nation was never sizable in absolute numbers. However, "America Fever" struck here as it did elsewhere in Europe, and on a per capita basis, Norway sent more immigrants to the United States before 1890 than any European nation except Ireland (Chan, 1990, p. 41).

The first Norwegian immigrants were moderately prosperous farmers searching for cheap land. They found abundant acreage in upper-Midwest states, such as Minnesota and Wisconsin, and then found that the local labor supply was too small to effectively cultivate the available land. Many turned to their homeland for assistance and used their relatives and friends to create networks and recruit a labor force. Thus, chains of communication and migration linking Norway to the Northern Plains were established, supplying immigrants to these areas for decades (Chan, 1990, p. 41). Today, a strong Scandinavian heritage is still evident in the farms, towns, and cities of the upper Midwest.

Immigrants From Germany. The stream of immigration from Germany was much larger than that from Norway, and German Americans left their mark on the economy, the political structure, and the cultural life of their new land. In the last half of the 19th century, at least 25% of the immigrants each year were German (Conzen, 1980, p. 406), and today more Americans (about 15%) trace their ancestries to Germany than to any other country (Brittingham & de la Cruz, 2004).

The German immigrants who arrived earlier in the 1800s moved into the newly opened farmland and the rapidly growing cities of the Midwest, as had many Scandinavians. By 1850, large German communities could be found in Milwaukee, St. Louis, and other midwestern cities (Conzen, 1980, p. 413). Some German immigrants followed the transatlantic route of the cotton trade between Europe and the southern United States and entered through the port of New Orleans, moving from there to the Midwest and Southwest.

German immigrants arriving later in the century were more likely to settle in urban areas, in part because fertile land was less available. Many of the city-bound German immigrants were skilled workers and artisans, and others found work as laborers in the rapidly expanding industrial sector. The double penetration of German immigrants into the rural economy and the higher sectors of the urban economy is reflected by the fact that by 1870, most employed German Americans were involved in skilled labor (37%) or farming (25%) (Conzen, 1980, p. 413).

German immigrants took relatively high occupational positions in the U.S. labor force, and their sons and daughters were able to translate that relative affluence into economic mobility.

By the dawn of the 20th century, large numbers of second-generation German Americans were finding their way into white-collar and professional careers. Within a few generations, German Americans had achieved parity with national norms in education, income, and occupational prestige.

Assimilation Patterns. By and large, assimilation for Norwegian, German, and other Protestant immigrants from Northern and Western Europe was consistent with the traditional views discussed earlier in this chapter. Although members of these groups felt the sting of rejection, prejudice, and discrimination, their movement from acculturation to integration and equality was relatively smooth, especially when compared with the experiences of racial minority groups. Their relative success and high degree of assimilation is suggested in Exhibits 2.6 and 2.7, presented later in this chapter.

Immigrant Laborers From Ireland and Southern and Eastern Europe.

The relative ease of assimilation for Northern and Western Europeans contrasts sharply with the experiences of non-Protestant, less-educated and less-skilled immigrants. These "immigrant laborers" came in two waves. The Irish were part of the Old Immigration that began in the 1820s, but the bulk of this group—Italians, Poles, Russians, Hungarians, Greeks, Serbs, Ukrainians, Slovaks, Bulgarians, and scores of other Southern and Eastern European groups—made up the New Immigration that began in the 1880s. Most of the immigrants in these nationality groups (like many recent immigrants to the United States) were peasants or unskilled laborers, with few resources other than their willingness to work. They came from rural, village-oriented cultures in which family and kin took precedence over individual needs or desires. Family life for them tended to be autocratic and male dominated, and children were expected to subordinate their personal desires and to work for the good of the family as a whole. Arranged marriages were common. This cultural background was less consistent with the industrializing, capitalistic, individualistic, Protestant, Anglo-American culture of the United States and was a major reason that these immigrant laborers experienced a higher level of rejection and discrimination than the immigrants from Northern and Western Europe.

The immigrant laborers were much less likely to enter the rural economy than were the Northern and Western European immigrants. Much of the better frontier land had already been claimed by the time most new immigrant groups began to arrive, and a large number of them had been permanently soured on farming by the oppressive and exploitative agrarian economies from which they were trying to escape. They settled in the cities of the industrializing Northeast and found work in plants, mills, mines, and factories. They supplied the armies of laborers needed to power the Industrial Revolution in the United States, although their view of this process was generally from the bottom looking up. They arrived during the decades in which the American industrial and urban infrastructure was being constructed. They built roads, canals, and railroads, as well as the buildings that housed the machinery of industrialization. For example, the first tunnels of the New York City subway system were dug, largely by hand, by laborers from Italy. Other immigrants found work in the coal fields of Pennsylvania and West Virginia and the steel mills of Pittsburgh, and they flocked by the millions to the factories of the Northeast.

Like other low-skill immigrant groups, these newcomers took jobs in which strength and stamina were more important than literacy or skilled craftsmanship. In fact, the minimum level of skills required for employment actually declined as industrialization proceeded

Hester Street, circa 1900, was one of the main streets in the Lower East Side of New York City, the most famous American Jewish neighborhood.

© Bettmann/CORBIS.

through its early phases. To keep wages low and take advantage of what seemed like an inexhaustible supply of cheap labor, industrialists and factory owners developed technologies and machines that required few skills and little knowledge of English to operate. As mechanization proceeded, unskilled workers replaced skilled workers in the workforce. Not infrequently, women and children replaced men because they could be hired for lower wages (Steinberg, 1981, p. 35).

Eventually, as the generations passed, the prejudice, systematic discrimination, and other barriers to upward mobility for the immigrant laborer groups weakened, and their descendants began to rise out of the working class. Although the first and second generations of these groups were largely limited to jobs at the unskilled or semiskilled level, the third and later generations rose in the American social class system. As Exhibits 2.6 and 2.7 show (later in this chapter), the descendants of the immigrant laborers achieved parity with national norms by the latter half of the 20th century.

Eastern European Jewish Immigrants and the Ethnic Enclave.

Jewish immigrants from Russia and other parts of Eastern Europe followed a third pathway into U.S. society. These immigrants were a part of the New Immigration and began arriving in the 1880s. Unlike the immigrant laborer groups, who were generally economic refugees and included many young, single males, Eastern European Jews were fleeing religious persecution and arrived as family units intending to settle permanently and become citizens. They settled in the urban areas of the Northeast and Midwest. New York City was the most common destination, and the Lower East Side became the best-known Jewish American neighborhood. By 1920, about 60% of all Jewish Americans lived in the urban areas between Boston and Philadelphia, with almost 50% living in New York City alone. Another 30% lived in the urban areas of the Midwest, particularly in Chicago (Goren, 1980, p. 581).

In Russia and other parts of Eastern Europe, Jews had been barred from agrarian occupations and had come to rely on the urban economy for their livelihoods. When they immigrated to the United States, they brought these urban skills and job experiences with them. For example, almost two thirds of the immigrant Jewish men had been tailors and other skilled laborers in Eastern Europe (Goren, 1980, p. 581). In the rapidly industrializing U.S. economy of the early 20th century, they were able to use these skills to find work.

Other Jewish immigrants joined the urban working class and took manual labor and unskilled jobs in the industrial sector (Morawska, 1990, p. 202). The garment industry in particular became the lifeblood of the Jewish community and provided jobs to about one third of all Eastern European Jews residing in the major cities (Goren, 1980, p. 582). Women as well as men were involved in the garment industry. Jewish women, like the women of more recent immigrant laborer groups, found ways to combine their jobs and their domestic responsibilities. As young girls, they worked in factories and sweatshops, and after marriage, they did the same work at home, sewing precut garments together or doing other piecework such as wrapping cigars or making artificial flowers, often assisted by their children (Amott & Matthaei, 1991, p. 115).

Unlike most European immigrant groups, Jewish Americans became heavily involved in commerce and often found ways to start their own businesses and become self-employed. Drawing on their experience in the old country, many started businesses and small independent enterprises and developed an enclave economy. The Jewish neighborhoods were densely populated and provided a ready market for services of all kinds. Some Jewish immigrants became street peddlers or started bakeries, butcher and candy shops, or any number of other retail enterprises.

Capitalizing on their residential concentration and close proximity, Jewish immigrants created dense networks of commercial, financial, and social cooperation. The Jewish American enclave survived because of the cohesiveness of the group; the willingness of wives, children, and other relatives to work for little or no monetary compensation; and the commercial savvy of the early immigrants. Also, a large pool of cheap labor and sources of credit and other financial services were available within the community. The Jewish American enclave grew and provided a livelihood for many of the children and grandchildren of the immigrants (Portes & Manning, 1986, pp. 51–52). As has been the case with other enclave groups that we will discuss in future chapters, including Chinese Americans and Cuban Americans, economic advancement preceded extensive acculturation, and Jewish Americans made significant strides toward economic equality before they became fluent in English or were otherwise Americanized.

One obvious way in which an enclave immigrant group can improve its position is to develop an educated and acculturated second generation. The Americanized, English-speaking children of the immigrants used their greater familiarity with the dominant society and their language facility to help preserve and expand the family enterprise. Furthermore, as the second generation appeared, the American public school system was expanding, and education through the college level was free or inexpensive in New York City and other cities (Steinberg, 1981, pp. 128–138). There was also a strong push for the second and third generations to enter professions, and as Jewish Americans excelled in school, resistance to and discrimination against them increased. By the 1920s, many elite colleges and universities, such as Dartmouth, had established quotas that limited the number of Jewish students they would admit (Dinnerstein, 1977, p. 228). These quotas were not abolished until after World War II.

The enclave economy and the Jewish neighborhoods established by the immigrants proved to be an effective base from which to integrate into American society. The descendants of the Eastern European Jewish immigrants moved out of the ethnic neighborhoods years ago, and their positions in the economy—their pushcarts, stores, and jobs in the garment industry—have been taken over by more recent immigrants. When they left the enclave economy, many second- and third-generation Eastern European Jews did not enter the mainstream occupational structure at the bottom, as the immigrant laborer groups tended to do. They used the resources generated by the entrepreneurship of the early generations to gain access to prestigious and advantaged social class positions (Portes & Manning, 1986, p. 53). Studies show that Jewish Americans today, as a group, surpass national averages in income, levels of education, and occupational prestige (Sklare, 1971, pp. 60–69; see also Cohen, 1985; Massarik & Chenkin, 1973). The relatively higher status of Russian Americans shown in Exhibits 2.6 and 2.7 (later in this chapter) is due in part to the fact that many Jewish Americans are of Russian descent.

Chains of Immigration

All of the immigrant groups tended to follow "chains" established and maintained by the members of their groups. Some versions of the traditional assimilation perspective (especially human capital theory) treat immigration and status attainment as purely individual (psychological) matters. To the contrary, scholars have demonstrated that immigration to the United States was in large measure a group (sociological) phenomenon. Immigrant chains stretched across the oceans and were held together by the ties of kinship, language, religion, culture, and a sense of common peoplehood (Bodnar, 1985; Tilly, 1990). The networks supplied information, money for passage, family news, and job offers.

Here is how chain immigration worked (and continues to work today): Someone from a village in, say, Poland, would make it to the United States. The successful immigrant would send word to the home village, perhaps by hiring a letter writer. Along with news and stories of his adventures, he would send his address. Within months, another immigrant from the village, perhaps a brother or other relative, would show up at the address of the original immigrant. After his months of experience in the new society, the original immigrant could lend assistance, provide a place to sleep, help with job hunting, and orient the newcomer to the area.

Before long, others would arrive from the village in need of the same sort of introduction to the mysteries of America. The compatriots would tend to settle close to one another, in the same building or on the same block. Soon, entire neighborhoods were filled with people from a certain village, province, or region. In these ethnic enclaves, the old language was spoken and the old ways observed. Businesses were started, churches or synagogues were founded, families were begun, and mutual aid societies and other organizations were formed. There was safety in numbers and comfort and security in a familiar, if transplanted, set of traditions and customs.

Immigrants often responded to U.S. society by attempting to re-create as much of their old world as possible. Partly to avoid the harsher forms of rejection and discrimination and partly to band together for solidarity and mutual support, immigrants created their own miniature social worlds within the bustling metropolises of the industrializing Northeast and the West Coast. These Little Italys, Little Warsaws, Little Irelands, Greektowns, Chinatowns, and Little Tokyos were safe havens that insulated the immigrants from the larger society and allowed them to establish bonds with one another, organize a group life, pursue their own group interests, and have some control over the pace of their adjustment to American culture. For some groups and in some areas, the ethnic subcommunity was a short-lived phenomenon. For others (the Jewish enclave discussed earlier, for example), the neighborhood became the dominant structure of their lives, and the networks continued to function long after their arrival in the United States.

The Campaign Against Immigration: Prejudice, Racism, and Discrimination

Today, it may be hard to conceive of the bitterness and intensity of the prejudice that greeted the Irish, Italians, Poles, Jews, and other new immigrant groups. Even as they were becoming an indispensable segment of the American workforce, they were castigated, ridiculed, attacked, and disparaged. The Irish were the first immigrant laborers to arrive and thus the first to feel this intense prejudice and discrimination. Campaigns against immigrants were waged, Irish neighborhoods were attacked by mobs, and Roman Catholic churches and convents were burned. Some employers blatantly refused to hire the Irish, often advertising their ethnic preferences with signs that read "No Irish Need Apply." Until later arriving groups pushed them up, the Irish were mired at the bottom of the job market. Indeed, at one time they were referred to as the "niggers of Boston" (Blessing, 1980; Potter, 1973; Shannon, 1964).

Other groups felt the same sting of rejection as they arrived. Italian immigrants were particularly likely to be the victims of violent attacks, one of the most vicious of which took place

in New Orleans in 1891. The city's police chief was assassinated, and rumors of Italian involvement in the murder were rampant. Hundreds of Italians were arrested, and 9 were brought to trial. All were acquitted. Anti-Italian sentiment was running so high, however, that a mob lynched 11 Italians while police and city officials did nothing (Higham, 1963).

Anti-Catholicism. Much of the prejudice against the Irish and the new immigrants was expressed as anti-Catholicism. Prior to the mid-19th century, Anglo-American society had been almost exclusively Protestant. Catholicism, with its celibate clergy, Latin masses, and cloistered nuns, seemed alien, exotic, and threatening. The growth of Catholicism, especially because it was associated with non-Anglo immigrants, raised fears that the Protestant religions would lose status. There were even rumors that the Pope was planning to move the Vatican to America and organize a takeover of the U.S. government.

Although Catholics were often stereotyped as single groups, they also varied along a number of dimensions. For example, the Catholic faith as practiced in Ireland differed significantly from that practiced in Italy, Poland, and other countries. Catholic immigrant groups often established their own parishes, with priests who could speak the old language. These cultural and national differences often separated Catholic groups, despite their common faith (Herberg, 1960).

Discrimination against ethnic groups extended far beyond the job market, as illustrated by this anti-Semitic sign.

Anti-Semitism. Jews from Russia and Eastern Europe faced intense prejudice and racism (or anti-Semitism) as they began arriving in large numbers in the 1880s. Biased sentiments and negative stereotypes of Jews have been a part of Western tradition for centuries and, in fact, have been stronger and more vicious in Europe than in the United States. For nearly two millennia, European Jews have been chastised and persecuted as the "killers of Christ" and stereotyped as materialistic moneylenders and crafty businessmen. The stereotype that links Jews and moneylending has its origins in the fact that in premodern Europe, Catholics were forbidden by the church to engage in usury (charging interest for loans). Jews were under no such restriction, and they filled the gap thus created in the economy. The ultimate episode in the long history of European anti-Semitism was, of course, the Nazi Holocaust, in which six million Jews died. European anti-Semitism did not end with the demise of the Nazi regime, and it remains a prominent concern throughout Europe and Russia.

Before the mass immigration of Eastern European Jews began in the late 19th century, anti-Semitism in the United States was relatively mild, perhaps because the group was so small. As the immigration continued, anti-Jewish prejudice increased in intensity and viciousness, fostering the view of Jews as cunning but dishonest merchants. In the late 19th century, Jews began to be banned from social clubs and the boardrooms of businesses and other organizations. Summer resorts began posting notices: "We prefer not to entertain Hebrews" (Goren, 1980, p. 585).

By the 1920s and 1930s, anti-Semitism had become quite prominent among American prejudices and was being preached by the Ku Klux Klan and other extreme racist groups. Also, because many of the political radicals and labor leaders of the time were Jewish immigrants, anti-Semitism became fused with a fear of Communism and other anticapitalist doctrines. Some prominent Americans espoused anti-Semitic views, among them Henry Ford, the founder of Ford Motor Company; Charles Lindbergh, the aviator who was the first to fly solo across the Atlantic; and Father Charles Coughlin, a Catholic priest with a popular radio show (Selzer, 1972).

Anti-Semitism reached a peak before World War II and tapered off in the decades following the war, but as we shall see in Chapter 3, it remains part of U.S. society (Anti-Defamation League, 2000). Anti-Semitism also has a prominent place in the ideologies of a variety of extremist groups that have emerged in recent years, including "skinheads" and various contemporary incarnations of the Ku Klux Klan. Some of this targeting of Jews seems to increase during economic recession and may be related to the stereotypical view of Jewish Americans as extremely prosperous and materialistic.

A Successful Exclusion.
The prejudice and racism directed against the immigrants also found expression in organized, widespread efforts to stop the flow of immigration. A variety of anti-immigrant organizations appeared almost as soon as the mass European immigration started in the 1820s. The strength of these campaigns waxed and waned, largely in harmony with the strength of the economy and the size of the job supply. Anti-immigrant sentiment increased in intensity, and the strength of its organized expressions increased during hard times and depressions and tended to soften when the economy improved. The campaign ultimately triumphed with the passage of the National Origins Act in 1924. This act drastically reduced the overall number of immigrants that would be admitted each year. The effectiveness of the numerical restrictions is clearly apparent in Exhibit 2.3.

The National Origins Act established a quota system that limited the number of immigrants that would be accepted each year from each sending nation, a system that was openly racist. For example, the size of the quota for European nations was based on the proportional representation of each nationality in the United States as of 1890. This year was chosen because it predated the bulk of the New Immigration and gave the most generous quotas to Northern and Western European nations. Immigration from Western Hemisphere nations was not directly affected by this legislation, but immigration from Asian nations was banned altogether. At this time, almost all parts of Africa were still the colonial possessions of various European nations and received no separate quotas. In other words, the quota for immigrants from Africa was zero.

The result was that the quota system allocated nearly 70% of the available immigration slots to the nations of Northern and Western Europe, despite the fact that immigration from those areas had largely ended by the 1920s. The National Origins Act was very effective, and by the time the Great Depression took hold of the American economy, immigration had dropped to the lowest level in a century. The National Origins Act remained in effect until 1965.

Patterns of Assimilation

In this section, we will explore some of the common patterns in the process of assimilation followed by European immigrants and their descendants. These patterns have been well established by research conducted in the traditional perspective and are consistent with the model of assimilation developed by Gordon. They include assimilation by generation, ethnic succession, and structural mobility. We discuss each separately in this section.

The Importance of Generations

People today—social scientists, politicians, and ordinary citizens—often fail to recognize the time and effort it takes for a group to become completely Americanized. For most European immigrant groups, the process took generations, and it was the grandchildren or the great-grandchildren (or even great-great-grandchildren) of the immigrants who finally completed acculturation and integration. Mass immigration from Europe ended in the 1920s, but the assimilation of some European ethnic groups was not completed until late in the 20th century.

Here is a rough summary of how assimilation proceeded for these European immigrants: The first generation, the actual immigrants, settled in ethnic neighborhoods, such as "Little Italy" in New York City, and made only limited movement toward acculturation and integration. They focused their energies on the network of family and social relationships encompassed within their own groups. Of course, many of them—most often the men—had to leave their neighborhoods for work and other reasons, and these excursions required some familiarity with the larger society. Some English had to be learned, and taking a job outside the neighborhood is, almost by definition, a form of integration. Nonetheless, the first generation lived and died largely within the context of the "old country," which had been re-created within the new.

The second generation, or the children of the immigrants, found themselves in a position of psychological or social marginality: They were partly ethnic and partly American but full members of neither group. They were born in America but in households and neighborhoods that were ethnic, not American. They learned the old language first and were socialized in the old ways. As they entered childhood, however, they entered the public schools, where they were socialized into the Anglo-American culture.

Very often, the world the second generation learned about at school conflicted with the world they inhabited at home. For example, the old country family values often expected children to subordinate their self-interests to the interests of their elders and of the family as a whole. Marriages were arranged by parents, or at least were heavily influenced by and subject to their approval. Needless to say, these expectations conflicted sharply with American ideas about individualism and romantic love. Differences of this sort often caused painful conflict between the ethnic first generation and their Americanized children.

As the second generation progressed toward adulthood, they tended to move out of the old neighborhoods. Their geographic mobility was often motivated by social mobility. They were much more acculturated than their parents, spoke English fluently, and enjoyed a wider range of occupational choices and opportunities. Discriminatory policies in education, housing, and the job market sometimes limited them, but they were upwardly mobile, and in their pursuit of jobs and careers, they left behind the ethnic subcommunity and many of the customs of their parents.

The members of the third generation, or the grandchildren of the immigrants, were typically born and raised in nonethnic settings. English was their first (and often their only) language, and their values and perceptions were thoroughly American. Although family and kinship ties with grandparents and the old neighborhood often remained strong, ethnicity for this generation was a relatively minor part of their daily realities and their self-images. Visits on weekends and holidays and family rituals revolving around the cycles of birth, marriage, and death—these activities might have connected the third generation to the world of their ancestors, but in terms of their everyday lives, they were American, not ethnic.

The pattern of assimilation by generation progressed as follows:

- The first generation began the process and was at least slightly acculturated and integrated.

- The second generation was very acculturated and highly integrated (at least into the secondary sectors of the society).

- The third generation finished the acculturation process and enjoyed high levels of integration at both the secondary and the primary levels.

Exhibit 2.4 illustrates these patterns in terms of the structural assimilation of Italian Americans. The educational and occupational characteristics of this group converge with those of white Anglo-Saxon Protestants (WASPs) as the generations change. For example, the percentage of Italian Americans with some college shows a gap of more than 20 points between the first and second generations and WASPs. Italians of the third and fourth generations, though, are virtually identical to WASPs on this measure of integration in the secondary sector. The other differences between Italians and WASPs shrink in a similar fashion from generation to generation.

The first five measures of educational and occupational attainment in Exhibit 2.4 illustrate the generational pattern of integration (structural assimilation). The last comparison measures marital assimilation, or intermarriage. It displays the percentage of males of "unmixed," or 100%, Italian heritage who married females outside the Italian community. Note once more the tendency for integration, now at the primary level, to increase across the generations. The huge majority of first-generation males married within their group (only 21.9% married non-Italians). By the third generation, 67.3% of the males were marrying non-Italians.

Of course, this model of step-by-step, linear assimilation by generation fits some groups better than others. For example, immigrants from Northern and Western Europe (except for the Irish) were generally more similar, racially and culturally, to the dominant group and tended to be more educated and skilled. They experienced relatively easier acceptance and tended to complete the assimilation process in three generations or less. In contrast, immigrants from Ireland and from Southern and Eastern Europe were mostly uneducated, unskilled peasants who were more likely to join the huge army of industrial labor that manned the factories, mines, and mills. These groups were more likely to

	Exhibit 2.4	Some Comparisons Between Italians and WASPs

	WASPs*	Generation		
		First	Second	Third and Fourth
Percentage with some college	42.4	19.0	19.4	41.7
Average years of education	12.6	9.0	11.1	13.4
Percentage white collar	34.7	20.0	22.5	28.8
Percentage blue collar	37.9	65.0	53.9	39.0
Average occupational prestige	42.5	34.3	36.8	42.5
Percentage of "unmixed" Italian males marrying non-Italian females		21.9	51.4	67.3

SOURCE: Adapted from Alba (1985), Tables 5-3, 5-4, and 6-2. Data are originally from the NORC *General Social Surveys* (1975–1980) and the *Current Population Survey* (U.S. Bureau of the Census, 1979). Copyright © 1985 Richard D. Alba.

*White Anglo-Saxon Protestants (WASPs) were not separated by generation, and some of the differences between groups may be the result of factors such as age. That is, older WASPs may have levels of education more comparable to first-generation Italian Americans than WASPs as a whole.

remain at the bottom of the American class structure for generations and to have risen to middle-class prosperity only in the recent past. As mentioned earlier, Eastern European Jews formed an enclave and followed a distinctly different pathway of assimilation, using the enclave as a springboard to launch the second and third generations into the larger society (although their movements were circumscribed by widespread anti-Semitic sentiments and policies).

It is important to keep this generational pattern in mind when examining immigration to the United States today. It is common for contemporary newcomers (especially Hispanics) to be criticized for their "slow" pace of assimilation, but their "progress" takes on a new aspect when viewed in the light of the generational time frame for assimilation followed by European immigrants. Especially with modern forms of transportation, immigration can be very fast. Assimilation, on the other hand, is by nature slow.

Ethnic Succession

A second factor that shaped the assimilation experience is captured in the concept of **ethnic succession**, or the myriad ways in which European ethnic groups unintentionally affected each other's position in the social class structure of the larger society. The overall pattern was that each European immigrant group tended to be pushed to higher social class levels and more favorable economic situations by the groups that arrived after them. As more experienced groups became upwardly mobile and began to move out of the neighborhoods that served as their "ports of entry," they were often replaced by a new group of immigrants who would begin the process all over again. Some neighborhoods in the cities of the Northeast served as the ethnic neighborhood—the first safe haven in the new society—for a variety of successive groups. Some neighborhoods continue to fill this role today.

This process can be understood in terms of the second stage of Gordon's model: integration at the secondary level (see Exhibit 2.1) or entry into the public institutions and organizations of the larger society. Three pathways of integration tended to be most important for European immigrants: politics, labor unions, and the church. We will cover each in turn, illustrating with the Irish, the first immigrant laborers to arrive in large numbers, but the general patterns apply to all white ethnic groups.

Politics.
The Irish tended to follow the Northern and Western Europeans in the job market and social class structure and were, in turn, followed by the wave of new immigrants. In many urban areas of the Northeast, the moved into the neighborhoods and took jobs left behind by German laborers. After a period of acculturation and adjustment, the Irish began to create their own connections with the mainstream society and improve their economic and social positions. They were replaced in their neighborhoods and at the bottom of the occupational structure by Italians, Poles, and other immigrant groups arriving after them.

As the years passed and the Irish gained more experience, they began to forge more links to the larger society, and, in particular, they allied themselves with the Democratic Party and helped to construct the political machines that came to dominate many city governments in the 19th and 20th centuries. Machine politicians were often corrupt and even criminal, regularly subverting the election process, bribing city and state officials, using city budgets to fill the pockets of the political bosses and their cronies, and passing out public jobs as payoffs for favors and faithful service. Although not exactly models of good government, the political machines performed a number of valuable social services for their constituents and loyal followers. Machine politicians, such as Boss Tweed of Tammany Hall in New York City, could find jobs, provide food and clothing for the destitute, aid victims of fires and other calamities, and intervene in the criminal and civil courts.

Much of the power of the urban political machines derived from their control of the city payroll. The leaders of the machines used municipal jobs and the city budget as part of a "spoils" system (as in "to the winner go the spoils") and as rewards for their supporters and allies. The faithful Irish party worker might be rewarded for service to the machine with a job in the police department (thus the stereotypical Irish cop) or some other agency. Private businessmen might be rewarded with lucrative contracts to supply services or perform other city business.

The political machines served as engines of economic opportunity and linked Irish Americans to a central and important institution of the dominant society. Using the resources controlled by local government as a power base, the Irish (and other immigrant groups after them) began to integrate themselves into the larger society and carve out a place in the mainstream structures of American society, as illustrated in the following Narrative Portrait.

Ethnicity, Prejudice, and the Irish Political Machine

*D*avid Gray grew up a Welsh Protestant in the city of Scranton, Pennsylvania, during the 1930s and 1940s. At that time, this coal-mining town was split along ethnic lines, and Gray (1991) recounts in this memoir his gradual socialization into the realities of in-groups and out-groups. He also describes how Scranton's Irish Catholic community responded to the Great Depression and how they used the local political machine to protect their own. Gray reflects on the consequences of these experiences for his own personal prejudices and sense of social distance.

Gray eventually left Scranton and earned a PhD in sociology. He became a college professor and an accomplished and respected sociologist. Among his many admiring students was the author of this textbook, who grew up in Scranton's Irish Catholic community a generation after Gray.

Shadow of the Past

David Gray

C. Wright Mills (an American sociologist) [stressed] the intimate relationship of "history, social structure, and biography." Though he did not say so directly, the logic of Mills' position would surely indicate that, for self-knowledge, no biography is more important than one's own. Born within a social context not of our own making, subject to social forces we did not create, in retrospect, we attempt to understand. . . .

Personally, then, I did not ask to be born Welsh Protestant in Scranton, Pennsylvania. No more than Eddie Gilroy, with whom I attended . . . school, asked to be born Irish Catholic. But there we both were in the heart of the anthracite coal region . . . during the years of the Great Depression. . . . We were friends, good friends. During recess and after 3:00 p.m., he played second base and I played shortstop in the shrunken, dirt diamond in the schoolyard. . . . We thought we made a good double-play combination and, beyond the baseball field, we respected and liked each other as well.

But, there was something wrong with Eddie Gilroy. At age ten I didn't know exactly what it was. He didn't make many errors and we often shared whatever pennies we had . . . at the corner candy store. Still, there was something wrong with him—vague, general, apart from real experience, but true all the same.

His fundamental defect came into sharper focus at the age of twelve. Sunday movies had just arrived in Scranton and . . . I wanted to go with Eddie and Johnny Pesavento [but] I couldn't.

"Why?"

"Because Protestants don't go to the movies on Sunday—nor play cards, football, or baseball."

"How come Eddie and Johnny can go?"

"They're Catholic."

No one quite used the word "immoral" but . . . anyone who attended Sunday movies was certainly close to sinful. And the implication was clear: If Catholics did such bad things on Sunday, they surely did a lot of bad things on other days as well.

No matter, then, that Gilroy might sacrifice for even a Protestant runner to go to second, or let you borrow his glove, or share his candy. . . . His Catholicism permeated his being, . . . muting his individual qualities. Eddie wasn't the point, his Catholicism was.

[The] deeply held beliefs . . . of the adult world were visited upon the young. Most often subtly . . . but persistently and effectively, little Welsh Protestant boys and girls learned that Catholics were somehow the enemy. . . .

Unfortunately, from their vantage point, the Welsh of Scranton were not the only ones in town. While they had come to the coal regions in large numbers, others, in even larger numbers, had come also. Irish, Italian, Polish, German, many from eastern European countries, fewer who were Jewish—all constituted Scranton's ethnic portion of broader 19th-century immigrant waves. With [some] obvious exceptions, most were Catholic.

In this communal setting—a very ethnically and religiously distinct one—the Great Depression arrived with particular force. [The region suffered from massive unemployment and began to lose population as people left in search of work elsewhere.] The coal industry, upon which the economy of Northeastern Pennsylvania essentially rested, was gone. The private sector, initially hard-hit, did not recover [until after the 1960s]. The public sector consequently became the primary possibility for often meager, by no means high-paying jobs.

And the Irish, their political talents augmented by the fact that they were the largest single ethnic group in town, controlled political power. Allied with others of Catholic faith, the Irish did their best to take care of their religiously affiliated, politically important, own.

In Scranton's political life, the intimate relationship of religion, politics, and economics was clear for all to see. The mayor was Jimmy Hanlon, . . . the political boss, Mickey Lawlor, . . . McNulty ran the post office, and Judge Hoban the courts. From the mayor's office to trash collectors, with policemen, foremen, school teachers, truant officers, and dog catchers in between, the public payroll included the names of O'Neill, Hennigan, Lydon, Kennedy, Walsh, Gerrity, and O'Hoolihan. As the depression persisted, Welsh Protestants came to know (with reason but also as an act of faith) that Lewis, Griffiths, and Williams need not apply.

Pale shades of contemporary Northern Ireland, but with political power reversed. No shots were fired, perhaps because American democratic traditions compel accommodation and compromise. Nonetheless, among the Welsh, the general feeling of resentment on more than one occasion was punctuated with: "Those goddam Irish Catholics."

Whatever may have been true in pre-depression years, however tolerant or intolerant individuals may have been, . . . that Welsh sentiment was not at all limited to individuals guilty of irrational prejudice. It was communally shared. Jobs, homes, and lives were at stake, and religious affiliation was relevant to them all. Irish Catholic political power was a fact from which Welsh Protestant resentment followed. Prejudice there certainly was deeply felt, poignantly articulated, subjectively often going beyond what facts would justify and, unfortunately, communicated to the young. . . .

The public sector was vulnerable to Irish Catholic control. The Welsh knew that. The private sector (banks, small businesses) simultaneously retained a diminished but tightened, now more consciously Protestant, ownership and/or control. Though the musically inclined Welsh never composed it, their regional battle hymn surely was: If Irish politicians were using their political power to control what they could, it was essential for Protestants to protect what they privately had.

SOURCE: Gray, David J. (1991). "Shadow of the Past: The Rise and Fall of Prejudice in an American City." *American Journal of Economics and Sociology,* 50.33–39.

Labor Unions. The labor movement provided a second link between the Irish, other European immigrant groups, and the larger society. Although virtually all white ethnic groups had a hand in the creation and eventual success of the movement, many of the founders and early leaders were Irish. For example, Terence Powderly, an Irish Catholic, founded one of the first U.S. labor unions, and in the early years of the 20th century, about one third of union leaders were Irish, and more than 50 national unions had Irish presidents (Bodnar, 1985, p. 111; Brody, 1980, p. 615).

As the labor movement grew in strength and gradually acquired legitimacy, the leaders of the movement also gained status, power, and other resources, while the rank-and-file membership gained job security, increased wages, and better fringe benefits. The labor movement provided another channel through which resources, power, status, and jobs flowed to the white ethnic groups.

Because of the way in which jobs were organized in industrializing America, union work typically required communication and cooperation across ethnic lines. The American workforce at the turn of the 20th century was multiethnic and multilingual, and union leaders had to coordinate and mobilize the efforts of many different language and cultural groups to represent the interest of the workers as a social class. Thus, labor union leaders became important intermediaries between the larger society and European immigrant groups.

Women were also heavily involved in the labor movement. Immigrant women were among the most exploited segments of the labor force, and they were involved in some of the most significant events in American labor history. For example, one of the first victories of the union movement occurred in New York City in 1909. The Uprising of the 20,000 was a massive strike of mostly Jewish and Italian women (many in their teens) against the

Photo 2.11

Labor unions sometimes mixed ethnic groups. Note that the signs of these strikers are in Hebrew as well as English.

© CORBIS.

garment industry. The strike lasted 4 months despite attacks by thugs hired by the bosses and abuses by the police and the courts. The strikers eventually won recognition of the union from many employers, a reversal of a wage decrease, and a reduction in the 56- to 59-hour week they were expected to work (Goren, 1980, p. 584).

One of the great tragedies in the history of labor relations in the United States also involved European immigrant women. In 1911, a fire swept through the Triangle Shirtwaist Company, a garment industry shop located on the 10th floor of a building in New York City. The fire spread rapidly, and the few escape routes were quickly cut off. About 140 young immigrant girls died, and many chose to leap to their deaths rather than be consumed by the flames. The disaster outraged the public, and the funerals of the victims were attended by more than a quarter of a million people. The incident fueled a drive for reform and improvement of work conditions and safety regulations (Amott & Matthaei, 1991, pp. 114–116; see also Schoener, 1967).

European immigrant women also filled leadership roles in the labor movement and served as presidents and in other offices, although usually in female-dominated unions. One of the most colorful union activists was Mother Jones, an Irish immigrant who worked tirelessly to organize miners:

> Until she was nearly one hundred years old, Mother Jones was where the danger was greatest—crossing militia lines, spending weeks in damp prisons, incurring the wrath of governors, presidents, and coal operators—she helped to organize the United Mine Workers with the only tools she felt she needed: "convictions and a voice." (Forner, 1980, p. 281)

Women workers often faced opposition from men as well as from employers. The major unions were not only racially discriminatory but also hostile to organizing women. For example, women laundry workers in San Francisco at the start of the 20th century were required to live in dormitories and work from 6 a.m. until midnight. When they applied to the international laundry workers union for a charter, they were blocked by the male members. They eventually went on strike and won the right to an 8-hour workday in 1912 (Amott & Matthaei, 1991, p. 117).

Religion. A third avenue of mobility for the Irish and other white ethnic groups was provided by religious institutions. The Irish were the first large group of Catholic immigrants and were thus in a favorable position to eventually dominate the church's administrative structure. The Catholic priesthood became largely Irish, and as they were promoted through the hierarchy, these priests became bishops and cardinals. The Catholic faith was practiced in different ways in different nations. As other Catholic immigrant groups began to arrive, conflict within the Irish-dominated church increased. Both Italian and Polish Catholic immigrants demanded their own parishes in which they could speak their own languages and celebrate their own customs and festivals. Dissatisfaction was so intense that some Polish Catholics broke with Rome and formed a separate Polish National Catholic Church (Lopata, 1976, p. 49).

The other Catholic immigrant groups eventually began to supply priests and other religious functionaries and to occupy leadership positions within the church. Although the church continued to be disproportionately influenced by the Irish, other white ethnic groups also used the Catholic Church as part of their power base for gaining acceptance and integration into the larger society.

Other Pathways. Besides party politics, the union movement, and religion, European immigrant groups forged other not-so-legitimate pathways of upward mobility. One alternative to legitimate success was offered by crime, a pathway that has been used by every ethnic group to some extent. Crime became particularly lucrative and attractive when Prohibition, the attempt to eliminate all alcohol use in the United States, went into effect in the 1920s. The criminalization of liquor failed to lower the demand, and Prohibition created a golden economic opportunity for those willing to take the risks involved in manufacturing and supplying alcohol to the American public.

Italian Americans headed many of the criminal organizations that took advantage of Prohibition. Criminal leaders and organizations with roots in Sicily, a region with a long history of secret antiestablishment societies, were especially important (Alba, 1985, pp. 62–64). The connection between organized crime, Prohibition, and Italian Americans is well-known, but it is not so widely recognized that ethnic succession operated in organized crime as it did in the legitimate opportunity structures. The Irish and Germans had been involved in organized crime for decades before the 1920s, and the Italians competed with these established gangsters and with Jewish crime syndicates for control of bootlegging and other criminal enterprises. The pattern of ethnic succession continued after the repeal of Prohibition, and members of groups newer to urban areas, including African Americans, Jamaicans, and Hispanic Americans, have recently challenged the Italian-dominated criminal "families."

Ethnic succession can also be observed in the institution of sports. Since the beginning of the 20th century, sports have offered a pathway to success and affluence that has attracted countless millions of young men. Success in many sports requires little in the way of formal credentials, education, or English fluency, and sports have been particularly appealing to the young men in minority groups that have few resources or opportunities.

For example, at the turn of the century, the Irish dominated the sport of boxing, but boxers from the Italian American community and other new immigrant groups eventually replaced them. Each successive wave of boxers reflected the concentration of a particular ethnic group at the bottom of the class structure. The succession of minority groups continues to this day, with boxing now dominated by African American and Latino fighters (Rader, 1983, pp. 87–106). A similar progression, or "layering," of ethnic and racial groups can be observed in other sports and in the entertainment industry.

The institutions of American society, both legitimate and illegal, reflect the relative positions of minority groups at a particular moment in time. Just a few generations ago, European immigrant groups dominated both crime and sports because they were blocked from legitimate opportunities. Now, the colonized racial minority groups still excluded from the mainstream job market and mired in the urban underclass are supplying disproportionate numbers of young people to these alternative opportunity structures.

Continuing Industrialization and Structural Mobility

We have already mentioned that dominant-minority relations tend to change along with changes in subsistence technology, and we can find an example of this process in the history of the European immigrant groups across the 20th century. Industrialization is a continuous process, and as it proceeded, the nature of work in America evolved and changed and created opportunities for upward mobility for the white ethnic groups. One important form of upward mobility throughout the 20th century, called **structural mobility**, resulted more from changes in the structure of the economy and the labor market than from any individual effort or desire to "get ahead."

Structural mobility is the result of the continuing mechanization and automation of the workplace. As machines replaced people in the workforce, the supply of manual, blue-collar jobs that had provided employment for so many first- and second-generation European immigrant laborers dwindled. At the same time, the supply of white-collar jobs increased, but access to the better jobs depended heavily on educational credentials. For white ethnic groups, a high school education became much more available in the 1930s, and college and university programs began to expand rapidly in the late 1940s, spurred in large part by the educational benefits made available to World War II veterans. Each generation of white ethnics, especially those born after 1925, was significantly more educated than its parents, and many were able to translate that increased human capital into upward mobility in the mainstream job market (Morawska, 1990, pp. 212–213).

The descendants of European immigrants became upwardly mobile not only because of their ambitions and efforts but also because of the changing location of jobs and the progressively greater opportunities for education available to them. Of course, the pace and timing of this upward movement was highly variable from group to group and place to place. Ethnic succession continued to operate, and the descendants of the most recent immigrants from Europe (Italians and Poles, for example) tended to be the last to benefit from the general upgrading in education and the job market. Still, structural mobility is one of the keys to the eventual successful integration of all white ethnic groups that is displayed in Exhibits 2.6 and 2.7 (later in this chapter). During these same years, the racial minority groups, particularly African Americans, were excluded from the dominant group's educational system and from the opportunity to compete for better jobs.

Variations in Assimilation

In the previous section, we discussed patterns that were common to European immigrants and their descendants. Now we address some of the sources of variation and diversity in assimilation, a complex process that is never exactly the same for any two groups. Sociologists have paid particular attention to the way that degree of similarity, religion, social class, and gender shaped the overall assimilation of the descendants of the mass European immigration. They have also investigated the way in which immigrants' reasons for coming to this country have affected the experiences of different groups.

Degree of Similarity

Since the dominant group consisted largely of Protestants with ethnic origins in Northern and Western Europe and especially in England, it is not surprising to learn that the degree of resistance, prejudice, and discrimination encountered by the different European immigrant groups varied in part by the degree to which they differed from these dominant groups. The most significant differences related to religion, language, cultural values, and, for some groups, physical characteristics. Thus, Protestant immigrants from Northern and Western Europe experienced less resistance than the English-speaking Catholic Irish, who in turn were accepted more readily than the new immigrants, who were both non–English speaking and overwhelmingly non-Protestant.

The preferences of the dominant group correspond roughly to the arrival times of the immigrants. The most similar groups immigrated earliest, and the least similar tended to be the last to arrive. Because of this coincidence, resistance to any one group of immigrants tended to fade as new groups arrived. For example, anti-German prejudice and discrimination never became particularly vicious or widespread (except during the heat of the World Wars), because the Irish began arriving in large numbers at about the same time. Concerns about the German immigrants were swamped by the fear that the Catholic Irish could never be assimilated. Then, as the 19th century drew to a close, immigrants from Southern and Eastern Europe—even more different from the dominant group—began to arrive and made concerns about the Irish seem trivial.

In addition, the New Immigration was far more voluminous than the Old Immigration (see Exhibit 2.3). Southern and Eastern Europeans arrived in record numbers in the early 20th century, and the sheer volume of the immigration raised fears that American cities and institutions would be swamped by hordes of what were seen as racially inferior, unassimilable immigrants (a fear with strong echoes in the present).

Thus, a preference hierarchy was formed in American culture that privileged Northern and Western Europeans over Southern and Eastern Europeans and Protestants over Catholics and Jews. These rankings reflect the ease with which the groups have been assimilated and made their way into the larger society. This hierarchy of ethnic preference is still a part of American prejudice, as we shall see in Chapter 3, although it is much more muted today than in the heyday of immigration.

Religion

A major differentiating factor in the experiences of the European immigrant groups, recognized by Gordon and other students of American assimilation, was religion. Protestant, Catholic, and Jewish immigrants lived in different neighborhoods, occupied different niches in the workforce, formed separate networks of affiliation and groups, and chose their marriage partners from different pools of people.

One important study that documented the importance of religion for European immigrants and their descendants (and also reinforced the importance of generations) was conducted by sociologist Ruby Jo Kennedy (1944). She studied intermarriage patterns in New Haven, Connecticut, over a 70-year period ending in the 1940s and found that the immigrant generation chose marriage partners from a pool whose boundaries were marked by ethnicity and religion. For example, Irish Catholics married other Irish Catholics, Italian Catholics married Italian Catholics, Irish Protestants married Irish Protestants, and so forth across all the ethnic and religious divisions she studied.

The pool of marriage partners for the children and grandchildren of the immigrants continued to be bounded by religion but not so much by ethnicity. Thus, later generations of Irish Catholics continued to marry other Catholics but were less likely to marry other Irish. As assimilation proceeded, ethnic group boundaries faded (or "melted"), but religious boundaries did not. Kennedy described this phenomenon as a **triple melting pot**: a pattern of structural assimilation within each of the three religious denominations (Kennedy, 1944, 1952).

Will Herberg (1960), another important student of American assimilation, also explored the connection between religion and ethnicity. Writing in the 1950s, he noted that the pressures of acculturation did not affect all aspects of ethnicity equally. European immigrants and their descendants were strongly encouraged to learn English, but they were not so pressured to change their religious beliefs. Very often, their religious faith was the strongest connection between later generations and their immigrant ancestors. The American tradition of religious tolerance allowed the descendants of the European immigrants to preserve this tie to their roots without being seen as "un-American." As a result, the Protestant, Catholic, and Jewish faiths eventually came to occupy roughly equal degrees of legitimacy in American society.

Thus, for the descendants of the European immigrants, religion became a vehicle through which their ethnicity could be expressed. For many members of this group, religion and ethnicity were fused, and ethnic traditions and identities came to have a religious expression. For example, Mary Ann O'Brien, the Irish American schoolteacher introduced in Chapter 1, attends Mass partly as a family matter and partly as a religious devotion. She does not know much about the Irish culture of her immigrant ancestors or about the adjustments and changes they had to make to survive in the United States. What she does know is that they were Catholic and that by observing the rituals of the church in the present, she is honoring her connections to the past. It is not just that she is Irish-Catholic-American but that—for her and millions of others—being Catholic is part of being Irish in America.

Social Class

Social class is a central feature of social structure, and it is not surprising that it affected the European immigrant groups in a number of ways. First, social class combined with religion to shape the social world of the descendants of the European immigrants. In fact, Gordon (1964) concluded that U.S. society in the 1960s actually incorporated not three, but four melting pots (one for each of the major ethnic/religious groups and one for black Americans), each of which were internally subdivided by social class. In his view, the most significant structural unit within American society was the ethclass, defined by the intersection of the religious, ethnic, and social class boundaries (e.g., working-class Catholic, upper-class Protestant, etc.). Thus, people were not "simply American," but tended to identify with, associate with, and choose their spouses from within their ethclasses.

Second, social class affected structural integration. The huge majority of the post-1880s European immigrants were working class, and because they "entered U.S. society at the bottom of the economic ladder, and . . . stayed close to that level for the next half century, ethnic history has been essentially working class history" (Morawska, 1990, p. 215; see also

Bodnar, 1985). For generations, many groups of Eastern and Southern European immigrants did not acculturate to middle-class American culture, but to an urban working-class, blue-collar set of lifestyles and values. Even today, ethnicity for many groups remains interconnected with social class factors, and a familiar stereotype of white ethnicity is the hard-hat construction worker.

Gender

Anyone who wants to learn about the experience of immigration will find a huge body of literature incorporating every imaginable discipline and genre. The great bulk of this material, however, concerns the immigrant experience in general or focuses specifically on male immigrants. The experiences of female immigrants have been much less recorded and hence far less accessible. Many immigrant women came from cultures with strong patriarchal traditions, and they had much less access to leadership roles, education, and prestigious, high-paying occupations. As is the case with women of virtually all minority groups, the voices of immigrant women have been muted. The research that has been done, however, documents that immigrant women played multiple roles both during immigration and during the assimilation process. As would be expected in patriarchal societies, the roles of wife and mother were central, but immigrant women were involved in myriad other activities as well.

In general, male immigrants tended to precede women, and it was common for the males to send for the women only after they had secured lodging, jobs, and a certain level of stability. However, women immigrants' experiences were quite varied, often depending on the economic situation and cultural traditions of their home societies. In some cases, women were not only prominent among the "first wave" of immigrants but also began the process of acculturation and integration. During the 19th century, for example, a high percentage of Irish immigrants were young single women. They came to America seeking jobs and often wound up employed in domestic work, a role that permitted them to live "respectably" in a family setting. In 1850, about 75% of all employed Irish immigrant women in New York City worked as servants, and the rest were employed in textile mills and factories. As late as 1920, 81% of employed Irish-born women in the United States worked as domestics. Factory work was the second most prevalent form of employment (Blessing, 1980; see also Steinberg, 1981).

Because the economic situation of immigrant families was typically precarious, it was common for women to be involved in wage labor. The type and location of the work varied from group to group. Whereas Irish women were concentrated in domestic work and factories and mills, this was rare for Italian women. Italian culture had strong norms of patriarchy, and "one of the culture's strongest prohibitions was directed against contact between women and male strangers" (Alba, 1985, p. 53). Thus, acceptable work situations for Italian women were likely to involve tasks that could be done at home: doing laundry, taking in boarders, and doing piecework for the garment industry. Italian women who worked outside the home were likely to find themselves in single-sex settings among other immigrant women. Thus, women immigrants from Italy tended to be far less acculturated and integrated than those from Ireland.

Eastern European Jewish women represent a third pattern of assimilation. They were refugees from religious persecution, and most came with their husbands and children in intact family units. According to Steinberg (1981), "Few were independent bread-winners, and when they did work, they usually found employment in the . . . garment industry. Often they worked in small shops as family members" (p. 161).

Generally, immigrant women, like working-class women in general, were expected to work until they married, after which time it was expected that their husbands would support them and their children. In many cases, however, immigrant men could not earn enough to support their families, and their wives and children were required by necessity to contribute to the family budget. Immigrant wives sometimes continued to work outside the home, or they found other ways to make money. They took in boarders, did laundry or sewing, tended gardens, and were involved in myriad other activities that permitted them to contribute to the family budget and still stay home and attend to family and child-rearing responsibilities. A 1911 report on Southern and Eastern European households found that about half kept lodgers and that the income from this activity amounted to about 25% of the husbands' wages. Children also contributed to the family income by taking after-school and summertime jobs (Morawska, 1990, pp. 211–212). Compared with the men, immigrant women were more closely connected to home and family, less likely to learn to read or speak English or otherwise acculturate, and significantly more influential in preserving the heritage of their groups.

When they sought employment outside the home, they found opportunities in the industrial sector and in clerical and sales work, occupations that were quickly stereotyped as "women's work." Women were seen as working only to supplement the family treasury, and this assumption was used to justify a lower wage scale. Evans (1989) reports that in the late 1800s, "Whether in factories, offices, or private homes . . . women's wages were about half of those of men" (p. 135).

Sojourners

Some versions of the traditional perspective and the "taken-for-granted" views of many Americans assume that assimilation is desirable and therefore desired. However, immigrant groups from Europe were highly variable in their interest in Americanization, a factor that greatly shaped their experiences.

Some groups were very committed to Americanization. Eastern European Jews, for example, came to America because of religious persecution and planned to make America their home from the beginning. They left their homeland in fear for their lives and had no plans and no possibility of returning. They intended to stay, for they had nowhere else to go. (The nation of Israel was not founded until 1948.) These immigrants committed themselves to learning English, becoming citizens, and familiarizing themselves with their new society as quickly as possible.

Other immigrants had no intention of becoming American citizens and therefore had little interest in Americanization. These **sojourners**, or "birds of passage," were oriented to the old country and intended to return once they had accumulated enough capital to be successful in their home villages or provinces. Because immigration records are not very detailed, it is difficult to assess the exact numbers of immigrants who returned to the old country (see Wyman, 1993). We do know, for example, that a large percentage of Italian immigrants were sojourners. It is estimated that although 3.8 million Italians landed in the United States between 1899 and 1924, around 2.1 million departed during the same interval (Nelli, 1980, p. 547).

The Descendants of the Immigrants Today

Geographical Distribution

Exhibit 2.5 shows the geographical distribution of 15 racial and ethnic groups across the United States. The map displays the single largest group in each county. There is a lot of detail in the map, but for our purposes, we will focus on some of the groups mentioned in this chapter, including Norwegian, German, Irish, and Italian Americans (the Jewish population is too small to appear on this map).

First of all, the single largest ancestry group is German American, and this is reflected on the map in Exhibit 2.5 by the predominance of light blue from Pennsylvania to California. Note also how the map reflects the original settlement areas for this group, especially in the Midwest and East Texas. Likewise, Norwegian Americans (light green) are numerically dominant in some sections of the upper Midwest (e.g., Northwestern Minnesota and northern North Dakota), along with Finnish Americans (green), another Scandinavian group. Irish Americans (dark purple) and Italian Americans (dark blue) are also concentrated in their original areas of settlement, with the Irish in Massachusetts and Italians more concentrated around New York City.

Thus, almost a century after the end of mass immigration from Europe, the descendants of the immigrants have not wandered far from their ancestral locales. Of course, the map shows that the same point could be made for other groups, including blacks (concentrated in the "black belt" across the states of the old Confederacy), Mexican Americans

Exhibit 2.5 Ancestry With Largest Population in Each County, 2000

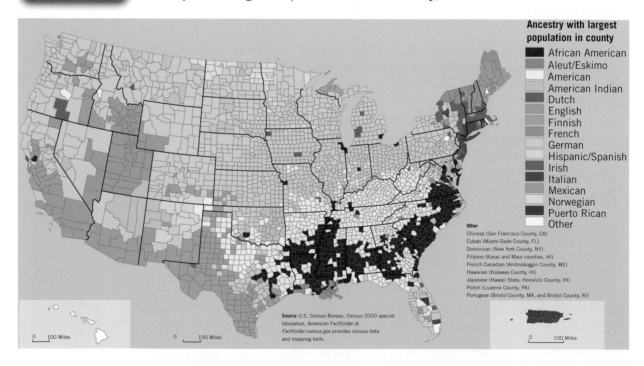

Ancestry with largest population in county
- African American
- Aleut/Eskimo
- American
- American Indian
- Dutch
- English
- Finnish
- French
- German
- Hispanic/Spanish
- Irish
- Italian
- Mexican
- Norwegian
- Puerto Rican
- Other

Other
Chinese (San Francisco County, CA)
Cuban (Miami-Dade County, FL)
Dominican (New York County, NY)
Filipino (Kauai and Maui counties, HI)
French Canadian (Androskoggin County, ME)
Hawaiian (Kalawao County, HI)
Japanese (Hawaii State; Honolulu County, HI)
Polish (Luzerne County, PA)
Portugese (Bristol County, MA, and Bristol County, RI)

Source U.S. Census Bureau, Census 2000 special tabulation. American Factfinder at *Factfinder.census.gov* provides census data and mapping tools.

0 100 Miles

SOURCE: U.S. Bureau of the Census (2004a).

(concentrated along the southern border from Texas to California), and Native Americans (their concentration in the upper Midwest, eastern Oklahoma, and the Southwest reflects the locations of the reservations into which they were forced after the end of the Indian wars).

Given all that has changed in American society over the past century—industrialization, population growth, urbanization, and massive mobility—the stable location of white ethnics (and other ethnic and racial groups) seems remarkable. Why aren't people distributed more randomly across the nation's landscape?

The stability is somewhat easier to explain for some groups. African Americans, Mexican Americans, and American Indians have been limited in their geographic as well as their social mobility by institutionalized discrimination, racism, and limited resources. We will examine the power of these constraints in detail in later chapters.

For white ethnics, on the other hand, the power of exclusion and rejection waned as the generations passed and the descendants of the immigrants assimilated and integrated. Their current locations are perhaps more a reflection of the idea (introduced in Chapter 1) that the United States is a nation of groups as well as individuals. Our group memberships, especially family and kin, exert a powerful influence on our decisions about where to live and work and, despite the transience and mobility of modern American life, can keep people connected to their relatives, the old neighborhood, their ethnic roots, and the sites of their ancestors' struggles.

Integration and Equality

Perhaps the most important point, for our purposes, about white ethnic groups (the descendants of the European immigrants) is that they are today on the verge of being completely assimilated. Even the groups that were the most despised and rejected in earlier years are acculturated, integrated, and thoroughly intermarried.

To illustrate this point, consider Exhibits 2.6 and 2.7, which illustrate the degree of integration and equality of a variety of white ethnic groups as long ago as 1990. The exhibits display data for 9 of the more than 60 white ethnic groups that people mentioned when asked to define their ancestries. The groups include the 2 largest white ethnic groups (German and Irish Americans) and 7 more chosen to represent a range of geographic regions of origin and times of immigration (U.S. Bureau of the Census, 2008).

The graphs show that by 1990, all 9 of the groups selected were at or above national norms ("all persons") for all measures of equality. There is some variation among the groups, of course, but all exceeded the national averages for both high school and college education and for median income. Also, Exhibit 2.7 shows that all 9 groups had dramatically lower poverty rates (see the line in the graph and refer to the right-hand axis for values), usually less than half the national average. The bars in Exhibit 2.7 show median household income (refer to the left-hand axis for values). All 9 groups exceed the national average, some—Russians, for example, many of whom are Jewish—by a considerable margin. (See the Appendix for 2006 information on the relative standing of some white ethnic groups.)

In other areas, the evidence for assimilation and equality is also persuasive. For example, the distinct ethnic neighborhoods that these groups created in American cities (Little Italy, Greektown, Little Warsaw, etc.) have faded away or been taken over by other groups, and the rate of intermarriage between members of different white ethnic groups is quite high. For example, based on data from the 1990 census, about 56% of all married whites have spouses whose ethnic backgrounds do not match their own (Alba, 1995, pp. 13–14).

Exhibit 2.6 Educational Attainment for Selected White Ethnic Groups, 1990

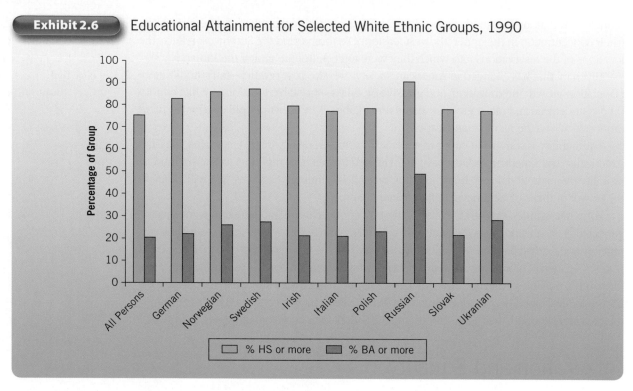

SOURCE: U.S. Bureau of the Census (2008).

Exhibit 2.7 Median Household Income and Percentage of Families Living in Poverty for Selected White Ethnic Groups, 1990

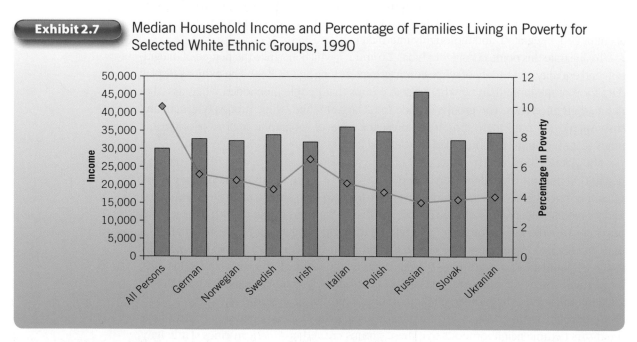

SOURCE: U.S. Bureau of the Census (2008).

NOTE:

Bars = Median Income (Left Axis)

Line = Percentage in Poverty (Right Axis)

The Twilight of White Ethnicity?[1]

Absorption into the American mainstream was neither linear nor continuous for the descendants of European immigrants. Over the generations, white ethnic identity sporadically reasserted itself in many ways, two of which are especially notable. First, there was a tendency for later generations to be more interested in their ancestry and ethnicity than were earlier generations. Marcus Hansen (1952) captured this phenomenon in his principle of third-generation interest: "What the second generation tries to forget, the third generation tries to remember" (p. 495). Hansen observed that the children of immigrants tended to minimize or de-emphasize ("forget") their ethnicity to avoid the prejudice and intolerance of the larger society and compete on more favorable terms for jobs and other opportunities. As they became adults and started families of their own, the second generation tended to raise their children in nonethnic settings, with English as their first and only language.

By the time the third generation reached adulthood, especially the "new" immigrant groups that arrived last, the larger society had become more tolerant of white ethnicity and diversity, and having little to risk, the third generation tried to reconnect with its grandparents and roots. These descendants wanted to remember their ethnic heritage and understand it as part of their personal identities, their sense of who they were and where they belonged in the larger society. Thus, interest in the "old ways" and the strength of the identification with the ancestral group was often stronger in the more Americanized third generation than in the more ethnic second. Ironically, of course, the grandchildren of the immigrants could not recover much of the richness and detail of their heritage because their parents had spent their lives trying to forget it. Nonetheless, the desire of the third generation to reconnect with its ancestry and recover its ethnicity shows that assimilation is not a simple, one-dimensional, or linear process. This process of ethnic recovery in later generations is illustrated in the biography of Mary Ann, the Irish Catholic introduced in Chapter 1, who attends Mass in part because she feels that the rituals connect her with her ancestors.

In addition to this generational pattern, the strength of white ethnic identity also responded to the changing context of American society and the activities of other groups. For example, in the late 1960s and early 1970s, there was a notable increase in the visibility of and interest in white ethnic heritage, an upsurge often referred to as the **ethnic revival**. The revival manifested itself in a variety of ways. Some people became more interested in their families' genealogical roots, and others increased their participation in ethnic festivals, traditions, and organizations. The "white ethnic vote" became a factor in local, state, and national politics, and appearances at the churches, meeting halls, and neighborhoods associated with white ethnic groups became almost mandatory for candidates for office. Demonstrations and festivals celebrating white ethnic heritages were organized, and buttons and bumper stickers proclaiming the ancestry of everyone from Irish to Italians were widely displayed. The revival was also endorsed by politicians, editorialists, and intellectuals (e.g., see Novak, 1973), reinforcing the movement and giving it additional legitimacy.

The ethnic revival may have been partly fueled, à la Hansen's principle, by the desire to reconnect with ancestral roots, even though most groups were well beyond their third generations by the 1960s. More likely, the revival was a reaction to the increase in pluralistic sentiment in the society in general and by the pluralistic, even separatist assertions of other groups that marked the decade. Virtually every minority group generated a protest movement (Black Power, Red Power, Chicanismo, etc.) and proclaimed a recommitment to its own heritage and to the authenticity of its own culture and experience. The visibility of these movements for cultural pluralism among racial minority groups helped make it more acceptable for European Americans to express their own ethnicity and heritage.

Besides the general tenor of the times, the resurgence of white ethnicity had some political and economic dimensions that bring us back to issues of inequality and competition for resources. In the 1960s, a white ethnic urban working class made up largely of Irish and Southern and Eastern European groups still remained in the neighborhoods of the industrial Northeast and Midwest and still continued to breathe life into the old networks and traditions (see Glazer & Moynihan, 1970; Greeley, 1974). At the same time that cultural pluralism was coming to be seen as more legitimate, this ethnic working class was feeling increasingly threatened by minority groups of color. In the industrial cities, it was not unusual for white ethnic neighborhoods to adjoin black and Hispanic neighborhoods, putting these groups in direct competition for housing, jobs, and other resources.

Many members of the white ethnic working class saw racial minority groups as inferior and perceived the advances being made by these groups as unfair, unjust, and threatening. They also reacted to what they saw as special treatment and attention being accorded on the basis of race, such as school busing and affirmative action. They had problems of their own (the declining number of good, unionized jobs; inadequate schooling; and deteriorating city services) and felt that their problems were being given lower priority and less legitimacy because they were white. The revived sense of ethnicity in the urban working-class neighborhoods was in large part a way of resisting racial reform and expressing resentment for the racial minority groups. Thus, among its many other causes and forms, the revival of white ethnicity that began in the 1960s was fueled by competition for resources and opportunities. As we have seen throughout this text, such competition commonly leads to increased prejudice and a heightened sense of cohesion among group members.

White Ethnicity in the 21st Century

As the conflicts of the 1960s and 1970s faded and white ethnic groups continued to leave the old neighborhoods and rise in the class structure, the strength of white ethnic identity resumed its slow demise. Today, several more generations removed from the tumultuous 1960s, white ethnic identity has become increasingly nebulous and largely voluntary. It is often described as **symbolic ethnicity** or as an aspect of self-identity that symbolizes one's roots in the "old country" but otherwise is minor. The descendants of the European immigrants feel vaguely connected to their ancestors, but this part of their identities does not affect their lifestyles, circles of friends and neighbors, job prospects, eating habits, or other everyday routines (Gans, 1979; Lieberson & Waters, 1988). For the descendants of the European immigrants today, ethnicity is an increasingly minor part of their identities that is expressed only occasionally or sporadically. For example, they might join in ethnic or religious festivals (e.g., St. Patrick's Day for Irish Americans, Columbus Day for Italian Americans), but these activities are seasonal or otherwise peripheral to their lives and self-images. The descendants of the European immigrants have choices, in stark contrast with their ancestors, members of racial minority groups, and recent immigrants: They can stress their ethnicity, ignore it completely, or maintain any degree of ethnic identity they choose. Many people have ancestors in more than one ethnic group and may change their sense of affiliation over time, sometimes emphasizing one group's traditions and sometimes another's (Waters, 1990).

In fact, white ethnic identity has become so ephemeral that it may be on the verge of disappearing altogether. For example, based on a series of in-depth interviews with white Americans from various regions of the nation, Gallagher (2001) found a sense of ethnicity so weak that it did not even rise to the level of "symbolic." His respondents were the products of ancestral lines so thoroughly intermixed and intermarried that any trace of a unique heritage from a particular group was completely lost. They had virtually no knowledge of the experiences of their immigrant ancestors or of the life and cultures of the ethnic communities they had inhabited, and for many, their ethnic ancestries were no more meaningful to them than their states of birth. Their lack of interest in and information about their ethnic heritage was so complete that it led Gallagher to propose an addendum to Hansen's principle: "What the grandson wished to remember, the great-granddaughter has never been told."

At the same time that more specific white ethnic identities are disappearing, they are also evolving into new shapes and forms. In the view of many analysts, a new identity is developing that merges the various "hyphenated" ethnic identities (German American, Polish American, etc.) into a single, generalized "European American" identity based on race and a common history of immigration and assimilation. This new identity reinforces the racial lines of separation that run through contemporary society, but it does more than simply mark group boundaries. Embedded in this emerging identity is an understanding, often deeply flawed, of how the white immigrant groups succeeded and assimilated in the past and a view, often deeply ideological, of how the racial minority groups should behave in the present. These understandings are encapsulated in "immigrant tales": legends that stress heroic individual effort and grim determination as key ingredients leading to success in the old days. These tales feature impoverished, victimized immigrant ancestors who survived and made a place for themselves and their children by working hard, saving their money, and otherwise exemplifying the virtues of the Protestant Ethic and American individualism. They stress the idea that past generations became successful despite the brutal hostility of the dominant group and with no government intervention, and they equate the historical difficulties faced by immigrants from Europe with those suffered by racial minority groups (slavery, segregation, attempted genocide, etc.). They strongly imply— and sometimes blatantly assert—that the latter groups could succeed in America by simply following the example set by the former (Alba, 1990; Gallagher, 2001).

These accounts mix versions of human capital theory and traditional views of assimilation with prejudice and racism. Without denying or trivializing the resolve and fortitude of European immigrants, equating their experiences and levels of disadvantage with those of African Americans, American Indians, and Mexican Americans is widely off the mark, as we shall see in the remainder of this text. These views support an attitude of disdain and lack of sympathy for the multiple dilemmas faced today by the racial minority groups and by many contemporary immigrants. They permit a more subtle expression of prejudice and racism and allow whites to use these highly distorted views of their immigrant ancestors as a rhetorical device to express a host of race-based grievances without appearing racist (Gallagher, 2001). Alba (1990) concludes as follows:

> The thrust of the [emerging] European American identity is to defend the individualistic view of the American system, because it portrays the system as open to those who are willing to work hard and pull themselves out of poverty and discrimination. Recent research suggests that it is precisely this individualism that prevents many whites from sympathizing with the need for African Americans and other minorities to receive affirmative action in order to overcome institutional barriers to their advancement. (p. 317)

What can we conclude? The generations-long journey from immigrant to white ethnic to European American seems to be drawing to a close. The separate ethnic identities are merging into a larger sense of "whiteness" that unites descendants of the immigrants with the dominant group and provides a rhetorical device for expressing disdain for other groups, especially African Americans.

Contemporary Immigrants: Does the Traditional Perspective Apply?

How relevant is the traditional perspective based on the experiences of European immigrants and their descendants for understanding more recent immigrants? This is a key issue facing social scientists, government policymakers, and the general public today. Will contemporary immigrants duplicate the experiences of earlier groups? Will they acculturate before they integrate? Will religion, social class, and race be important forces in their lives? Will they take as many as three (or more) generations to assimilate? What will their patterns of intermarriage look like? Will they achieve socioeconomic parity with the dominant group? When? How?

Sociologists (as well as the general public and policymakers) are split in their answers to these questions. Some social scientists believe that the "traditional" perspective on assimilation does not apply and that the experiences of contemporary immigrant groups will differ greatly from those of European immigrants. They believe that assimilation today is fragmented or **segmented** and will have a number of different outcomes. Although some contemporary immigrant groups may integrate into the middle-class mainstream, others will find themselves permanently mired in the impoverished, alienated, and marginalized segments of racial minority groups. Still others may form close-knit enclaves based on their traditional cultures and become successful in the United States by resisting the forces of acculturation (Portes & Rumbaut, 2001, p. 45).

In stark contrast, other theorists believe that the traditional perspective on assimilation is still relevant and that contemporary immigrant groups will follow the established pathways of mobility and assimilation. Of course, the process will be variable from group to group and place to place, but even the groups that are today the most impoverished and marginalized will, in time, move into mainstream society.

How will the debate be resolved? We cannot say at the moment, but we can point out that this debate is reminiscent of the critique of Park's theory of assimilation. In both cases, the argument is partly about time: Even the most impoverished and segmented groups may find their way into the economic mainstream eventually, at some unspecified time in the future. There are also other levels of meaning in the debate, however, related to one's perception of the nature of modern U.S. society. Is U.S. society today growing more tolerant of diversity, more open and equal? If so, this would seem to favor the traditionalist perspective. If not, this trend would clearly favor those who argue for the segmented-assimilation hypothesis. Although we will not resolve this argument in this text, we will use the debate between the traditional and segmented views on assimilation as a very useful framework as we consider the experiences of these groups (see Chapters 8, 9, and 10).

Implications for Examining Dominant-Minority Relations

Chapters 1 and 2 have introduced many of the terms, concepts, and themes that form the core of the rest of this text. Although the connections between the concepts are not simple, some key points can be made to summarize these chapters and anticipate the material to come.

First, minority group status has much more to do with power and the distribution of resources than with simple numbers or the percentage of the population in any particular category. We saw this notion expressed in Chapter 1 in the definition of *minority group* and in our exploration of inequality. The themes of inequality and differentials in status were also covered in our discussion of prejudice, racism, and discrimination. To understand minority relations, we must examine some very basic realities of human society: inequalities in wealth, prestige, and the distribution of power. To discuss changes in minority group status, we must be prepared to discuss changes in the way society does business, makes decisions, and distributes income, jobs, health care, and opportunity.

A second area that we will focus on in the rest of the book is the question of how our society should develop. Assimilation and pluralism, with all their variations, define two broad directions. Each has been extensively examined and discussed by social scientists, by leaders and decision makers in American society, and by ordinary people from all groups and walks of life. The analysis and evaluation of these two broad directions is a thread running throughout this book.

Assimilation, Then and Now

Mario Puzo and Luis Rodriguez are both sons of immigrants, but they grew up in two very different Americas. Puzo, best known as the author of The Godfather, *grew up in the Italian American community, and his memoir of life in New York City in the 1930s illustrates some of the patterns that are at the heart of Gordon's theory of assimilation. Writing in the 1970s, Puzo remembers the days of his boyhood and his certainty that he would escape the poverty that surrounded him. Note also his view of (and gratitude for) an America that gave people (or at least white people) the opportunity to rise above the circumstances of their birth.*

Rodriguez paints a rather different picture of U.S. society. He grew up in the Los Angeles area in the 1950s and 1960s and was a veteran of gang warfare by the time he reached high school. His memoir, Always Running: La Vida Loca (1993), illustrates the realities of segmented assimilation for contemporary immigrants. In this extract, he describes how his high school prepared Mexican American students for life. Contrast his despair with Puzo's gratitude. Which sector of American society is Rodriguez being prepared to enter?

Choosing a Dream: Italians in Hell's Kitchen

Mario Puzo

In the summertime, I was one of the great Tenth Avenue athletes, but in the wintertime I became a sissy. I read books. At a very early age I discovered libraries. . . . My mother always looked at all this reading with a fishy Latin eye. She saw no profit in it, but since all her children were great readers, she was a good enough general to know she could not fight so pervasive an insubordination. And there may have been some envy. If she had been able to, she would have been the greatest reader of all.

My direct ancestors for a thousand years have most probably been illiterate. Italy, the golden land, . . . so majestic in its language and cultural treasures . . . has never cared for its poor people. My father and mother were both illiterates. Both grew up on rocky, hilly farms in the countryside adjoining Naples. . . . My mother was told that the family could not afford the traditional family gift of linens when she married, and it was this that decided her to emigrate to America. . . . My mother never heard of Michelangelo; the great deeds of the Caesars had not reached her ears. She never heard the great music of her native land. She could not sign her name.

And so it was hard for my mother to believe that her son could become an artist. After all, her one dream in coming to America had been to earn her daily bread, a wild dream in itself. And looking back, she was dead right. Her son an artist? To this day she shakes her head. I shake mine with her. America may be a Fascistic, warmongering, racially prejudiced country today. It may deserve the hatred of its revolutionary young. But what a miracle it once was!

What has happened here has never happened in any other country in any other time. The poor, who have been poor for centuries ... whose children had inherited their poverty, their illiteracy, their hopelessness, achieved some economic dignity and freedom. You didn't get it for nothing, you had to pay a price in tears, in suffering, but why not? And some even became artists.

SOURCE: Puzo, Mario (1993). "Choosing a Dream: Italians in Hell's Kitchen." In W. Brown & A. Ling (Eds.), *Visions of America,* pp. 56–57. New York: Persea. Reprinted by permission of Donadio & Olson, Inc. Copyright © 1993 Mario Puzo.

Always Running: La Vida Loca

Luis Rodriguez

Mark Keppel High School was a Depression-era structure with a brick and art deco facade and small, army-type bungalows in the back. Friction filled its hallways. The Anglo and Asian upper-class students from Monterey Park and Alhambra attended the school. They were tracked into the "A" classes; they were in the school clubs; they were the varsity team members and lettermen. They were the pep squad and cheerleaders.

But the school also took in the people from the Hills and surrounding community who somehow made it past junior high. They were mostly Mexican, in the "C" track (what were called the "stupid" classes). Only a few of these students participated in school government, in sports, or in the various clubs.

The school had two principal languages. Two skin tones and two cultures. It revolved around class differences. The white and Asian kids ... were from professional, two-car households with watered lawns and trimmed trees. The laboring class, the sons and daughters of service workers, janitors, and factory hands lived in and around the Hills (or a section of Monterey Park called "Poor Side"). The school separated these two groups by levels of education: The professional-class kids were provided with college-preparatory classes; the blue-collar students were pushed into "industrial arts." ...

If you came from the Hills, you were labeled from the start. I'd walk into the counselor's office and looks of disdain greeted me—one meant for a criminal, alien, to be feared. Already a thug. It was harder to defy this expectation than just accept it and fall into the trappings. It was a jacket I could try to take off, but they kept putting it back on. The first hint of trouble and the preconceptions proved true. So why not be an outlaw? Why not make it our own?

SOURCE: Rodriguez, Luis (1993). *Always Running: La Vida Loca,* pp. 83–84. New York: Touchstone Books.

Immigration, Emigration, and Ireland

Immigrating and adjusting to a new society are among the most wrenching, exciting, disconcerting, exhilarating, and heartbreaking of human experiences. Immigrants have recorded these feelings, along with the adventures and experiences that sparked them, in every possible media, including letters, memoirs, poems, photos, stories, movies, jokes, and music. These immigrant tales recount the traumas of leaving home, dealing with a new language and customs, coping with rejection and discrimination, and thousands of other experiences. The most poignant of these stories express the sadness of parting from family and friends, perhaps forever.

Peter Jones captured some of these feelings in his song *Kilkelly*, based on letters written nearly 150 years earlier by an Irish father to his immigrant son—Jones's great-grandfather—in the United States. Each verse of the song paraphrases a letter and includes news of the family and community left behind and also expresses, in simple but powerful language, the deep sadness of separation and the longing for reunion:

> Kilkelly, Ireland, 18 and 90, my dear and loving son John
>
> I guess that I must be close on to eighty,
>
> it's thirty years since you're gone.
>
> Because of all of the money you send me,
>
> I'm still living out on my own.
>
> Michael has built himself a fine house
>
> and Brigid's daughters have grown.
>
> Thank you for sending your family picture,
>
> they're lovely young women and men.
>
> You say that you might even come for a visit,
>
> what joy to see you again.[2]

It is particularly appropriate to use an Irish song to illustrate the sorrows of immigration. Just as the United States has been a major receiver of immigrants for the last 200 years, Ireland has been a major supplier. Mass immigration from Ireland began with the potato famines of the 1840s and continued through the end of the 20th century, motivated by continuing hard times, political unrest, and unemployment. The sadness of Peter Jones's ancestors was repeated over and over as the youth of Ireland left for jobs in Great Britain, the United States, and hundreds of other places, never expecting to return. This mass immigration cut the 1840 Irish population of 7 million in half, and today, the population is still only about 4 million.

History rarely runs in straight lines, however. Today, after nearly 200 years of supplying immigrants, Ireland (along with other nations of Northern and Western Europe) has become a consumer. As illustrated in Exhibit 2.8, the number of newcomers entering Ireland increased more than 4 times over between 1987 and 2006, to almost 90,000, and the number of people leaving decreased dramatically, to less than 20,000. These numbers are minuscule compared with the volume of immigrants received by the United States each year, but the percentage of Ireland's population that consists of immigrants (13.8%) is actually greater than the comparable percentage in the United States (12.8%) ("Immigrants as a Percentage of State Population," n.d.).

What explains the switch from immigration to emigration? The answers are not hard to find. After decades of unemployment and depression, the Irish economy entered a boom phase in the early 1990s. Spurred by investments from multinational corporations and the benefits of joining the European Economic Union, the Irish economy and the job supply have grown rapidly. The unemployment rate was less than 5% in 2006, and Ireland ranks 137th lowest out of 181 nations on this statistic ("Unemployment Rate," n.d.).

Irish nationals who left Ireland to find work are now returning in large numbers, and people from Europe and other parts of the globe are also arriving. In addition, Ireland is receiving refugees and people seeking asylum. In 2006, for example, roughly 23% of immigrants were of Irish origin, 64% were from the United Kingdom or other nations of the European Union, and 13% were from "the rest of the world," a category that includes the Middle East, Nigeria, and various "trouble spots" around the globe (Central Statistics Office, Ireland, 2006). The immigration is changing the racial

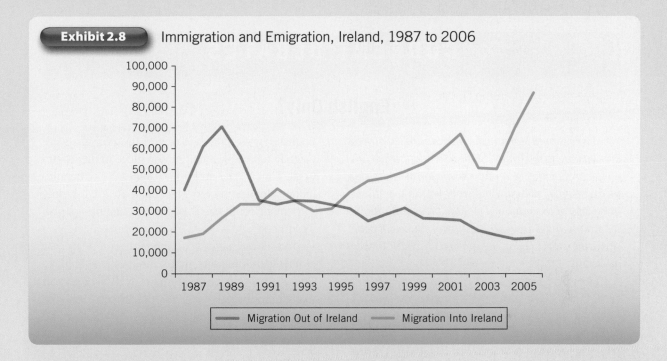

Exhibit 2.8 Immigration and Emigration, Ireland, 1987 to 2006

Migration Out of Ireland — Migration Into Ireland

composition of Irish society. Although still a small minority of the total population, the number of Irish residents of African descent has increased by a factor of 7 since 1996, from less than 5,000 to over 35,000. Also, the number of Irish of Asian descent increased by a factor of 6, from about 8,000 to almost 47,000. Both groups are about 1% of the total population.

What awaits these newcomers when they arrive on the Emerald Isle? Will they be subjected to the Irish version of "Anglo-conformity"? Will Irish society become a melting pot? Will Gordon's ideas about assimilation be applicable to their experiences? Will their assimilation be segmented? Will the Irish, such immigrants themselves, be especially understanding and sympathetic to the traumas faced by the newcomers?

Although many Irish are very sympathetic to the immigrants and refugees, others have responded with racist sentiments and demands for exclusion, reactions that ironically echo the rejection Irish immigrants in the United States experienced in the 19th century. Irish radio and TV talk shows commonly discuss issues of immigration and assimilation and frequently evoke prejudiced statements from the audience, and there are also reports of racism and discrimination.

The rejection of non-Irish newcomers was manifested in the passage of the "Citizenship Amendment"

to the Irish Constitution, which was overwhelmingly supported (80% in favor) by the Irish electorate in June 2004. Prior to the passage of the amendment, any baby born in Ireland had the right to claim Irish citizenship. The amendment denied the right of citizenship to any baby that did not have at least one Irish parent and was widely interpreted as a hostile rejection of immigrants (see Fanning, 2003). One poll suggested that people supported the amendment because they believed that there were simply too many immigrants in Ireland (Neissen, Schibel, & Thompson, 2005).

Like the United States, Ireland finds itself dealing with diversity and debating what kind of society it should become. It is too early to tell whether the Irish experience will parallel America's or whether the sociological concepts presented in this chapter will prove useful in analyzing the Irish immigrant experience. We can be sure, however, that the experience of the immigrants in Ireland will be laced with plentiful doses of the loneliness and longing experienced by Peter Jones's ancestors. Times have changed, but today's immigrants will yearn for Abuja, Riga, or Baku with the same melancholy experienced by previous waves of immigrants yearning for Kilkelly, Dublin, or Galway. Who knows what songs and poems will come from this?

English Only?

What role should learning English take in the process of adjusting to the United States? Should English language proficiency be a prerequisite for full inclusion in the society? Should English be made the official language of the nation? Does the present multiplicity of languages represent a danger for social cohesion and unity? Following are two reactions to these questions.

The first excerpt is from Mauro Mujica (2003), the chairman of U.S. English, Inc. (http://www.us-english.org/inc/), an immigrant himself and a passionate advocate for the unifying power of a single national language. His organization opposes efforts to recognize Spanish as an official second language (in part because of the expense and confusion that would ensue if all government documents, election ballots, street signs, etc., were published in both English and Spanish) and most forms of bilingual education. He is particularly concerned with stressing that the primary beneficiaries of learning English will be the immigrants.

An opposing point of view is presented by Andrew Hartman (2005), who argues that the "English Only" movement is a subtle but powerful form of American racism. He specifically attacks U.S. English, the organization chaired by Mujica, and attempts to expose its bias and refute its positions.

English Only Will Speed the Assimilation of Immigrants

MAURO MUJICA

[During my 11 years as chairman] of U.S. ENGLISH … I have encountered many myths about official

English legislation. … A few of these myths were recently repeated in an opinion piece in the Contra Costa Times. [The author] … writes, " … the anti-bilingual education movement and the English-only movement could easily be labeled an anti-Spanish movement."

In that one sentence, [the author] repeats two of the most ridiculous myths about official English. There are other distortions as well. These will likely come up as Congress debates HR 997, the English Language Unity Act of 2003, which would make English the official language of the United States. …

Here are five of the most common myths about official English and the realities behind them.

Myth No. 1: Official English Is Anti-Immigrant. Declaring English the official language benefits all Americans, but it benefits immigrants most of all. Immigrants who speak English earn more money, do better in school and have more career options than those who do not.

As an immigrant from Chile, I can testify that English proficiency is the most important gift we can give to newcomers. In fact, polls show that 70% of Hispanics and 85% of all immigrants support making English the official language of the United States. Learning English is the key to assimilating into the mainstream of American society. That is why our organization, U.S. ENGLISH, Inc., advocates for English immersion classes for immigrant students and adults.

Myth No. 2: Official English Is "English Only." Many far-left opponents of official English, such as the ACLU, refer to our legislation as "English Only." Official English simply requires that government conduct its business in English. It does not dictate what language must be spoken in the home, during conversations, cultural celebrations or religious ceremonies. It does not prohibit the teaching of foreign languages. It does not affect private businesses or the services offered by them. In addition, HR 997 makes exceptions for emergency situations.

Myth No. 3: Today's Immigrants Are Learning English Just Like the Immigrants of Old.

The United States has a rapidly growing population of people—often native born—who are not proficient in English. The 2000 Census found that 21.3 million Americans (8% of the population) are classified as "limited English proficient," a 52% increase from 1990, and more than double the 1980 total. More than 5.6 million of these people were born in the United States. In states like California, 20% of the population is not proficient in English.

The Census also reports that 4.5 million American households are linguistically isolated, meaning that no one in the household older than age 14 can speak English. These numbers indicate that the American assimilation process is broken. If not fixed, we will see our own "American Quebec" in the Southwestern United States and perhaps other areas of the country.

Myth No. 4: The Founding Fathers Rejected Making English the Official Language. English has been the language of our nation from its earliest days. In 1789, 90% of our nation's non-slave inhabitants were of English descent. Any notion that they would have chosen another language or used precious resources on printing documents in multiple languages lacks common sense.

The issue of an official language was never discussed at the Constitutional Convention as the topic was not controversial enough to be debated. Even the Dutch colonies had been under English rule for more than a century. Contrary to popular belief, Congress never voted on a proposal to make German the official language. This myth is probably based on a 1794 bill to translate some documents into German (it was defeated).

Myth No. 5: In a Global Culture, an Official Language Is Anachronistic. Ninety-two percent of the world's countries (178 of 193) have at least one official language. English is the sole official language in 31 nations and has an official status in 20 other nations, including India, Singapore, the Philippines, Samoa and Nigeria.

There has never been a language so widely spread in so short a time as English. It is the lingua franca of the modern world as much as Latin was the common tongue of the Roman Empire. Roughly one quarter of the world's population is already fluent or competent in English and this number grows by the day.

English is the global language of business, communications, higher education, diplomacy, aviation, the Internet, science, popular music, entertainment and international travel. Immigrants who don't know English not only lose out in the American economy, but also in the global economy.

These are just some of the myths that must be corrected if we are to have a debate on a coherent language policy. This policy should be built on fact, not myth. Multilingual government is a disaster for American unity and results in billions of dollars in unnecessary government spending. We need only to look at Canada to see the problems that multilingualism can bring. HR 997 could be our last best chance to stop this process and we cannot let distortions about official English sidetrack this legislation.

SOURCE: Mujica, Mauro (2003). "Official English Legislation: Myths and Realities." *Human Events*, 59:24.

The English-Only Movement Is Racist

ANDREW HARTMAN

The English-only movement has its roots in the historical racism and white supremacy of the United States. This does not mean, however, that it can be understood in the same way as overtly racist movements. Those who support the English-only movement, including many liberals, do not understand it to be racist. But that does not discount racism as a root of the movement; rather, it demands a more complex analysis of U.S. racism. . . .

English-only supporters claim that English-only legislation and pedagogy will empower rather than victimize non-English-speakers. . . . To them, English is a "common bond" that allows people of diverse backgrounds to overcome differences and reach mutual understanding—a theory particularly seductive to liberals. Unfortunately, the English-only movement's non-racist claims are seriously undermined by their systematic attacks on bilingual education. If English acquisition were indeed their mission, the English-only movement would not partake in these attacks [since bilingual education has been shown by research to be the most effective way to learn English.]

The ideology of the English-only movement is constructed upon a well-worn national mythology [that sees] bilingualism as a menace to American civilization. . . . For many Americans, the symbolism of the English language has become a form of civic religiosity in much the same vein as the flag. . . .

While proponents of the English-only movement commonly invoke the original institutions of the American nation and its surrounding mythology, opponents of the movement have fertile grounds for a historical rebuttal. The Constitution makes no mention of language. The new American elite of the revolution . . . did not seek a national policy on language. . . . The new nation welcomed hundreds of thousands of refugees from the French Revolution and did not try to force English upon them. An English-only nation was not the original . . . goal.

The framers' views on language, however, are less important than their doctrines of freedom. Before a citizenry comes to identify the English language with freedom, it must embrace freedom itself as something more than an abstract myth. A population sold on this myth is one of the primary achievements of the American nationalist program; freedom is assumed as self-evident in the United States. The English-only rhetoric in relation to the immigrant experience underlies these assumptions, for it is assumed that immigrants who learn English and assimilate to American mainstream culture will share in the mythical freedom enjoyed by all U.S. citizens. . . .

Underlying the message of immigrant opportunity following language acquisition is the long-standing myth of the melting pot. . . . Although scholars who recognized the distinct, and often conflicting, experiences that constitute American immigrant history have largely discredited this absurd image, the English-only movement testifies to its continuing influence. Through the lens of this fraudulent ideology, the downside of the American melting pot (loss of language and culture) is more than made up for by the upside (social mobility). . . . In fact, [however], mastery of English is not an accurate predictor of social mobility among the Latino population. Surprisingly, Latinos who speak only English fare worse economically than those who speak no English. Spanish language skills offer Latinos a cultural, social and economic community. Latinos who lose the benefits of the Spanish-speaking community do not gain reciprocal rewards from the American English-speaking community. . . .

If English acquisition and resulting assimilation do not necessarily produce social mobility, why does this mythology persist? How can it justify the English-only movement? Why does the English-only movement garner huge support and continue to push for legislative change? In order to answer these important questions, it is necessary to delve beyond the rhetoric of the

English-only movement and examine its racist roots. . . .

The first order in understanding the English-only movement is to understand the organization known as "U.S. English." U.S. English claims it does not maintain a racist, anti-immigrant agenda. Many of its original supporters were people of color or immigrants. . . . However, . . . U.S. English has had close ties to the anti-immigrant organization Federation for American Immigration Reform (FAIR) and has been financed by the Pioneer Fund, a racist organization that promotes the use of eugenics. . . .

Jefferson, Franklin and their ilk were interested in extending their humanism to those they considered the civilized few, not those defined as "inferior in body and mind." . . . [In] the American Enlightenment, all who stood in the way of progress were doomed to extinction. American Indians represented the savage, who by definition obstructed the path of civilization and progress. The democratic ideals of the United States . . . forced the Indians to either assimilate or die. . . . The path of assimilation required the American colonial power to embark on a program of linguistic oppression.

In the United States, . . . the language of the powerful is the language sought by those wishing to ascend into "civilization." The better one speaks "standard" English in the United States, the more likely one is to be elevated in American society. The speaker of "standard" English is then able to assume the role of a "civilized" being. . . . The colonial model of language as oppression follows: The colonizer uses language to assimilate and control the colonized; the colonized strive to speak the language of the colonizer and develop an inferiority complex to the extent that they fall short. The English-only movement embodies the colonial model of language as oppression.

The psychological inferiority of non-whites in a colonial society—the U.S. included—is reinforced by the standardization of language. . . . For the English-only movement, Spanish . . . has . . . become the language of the savage, of the "wetback" illegally crossing the Rio Grande hoping to steal American jobs. It is the language of brown-skinned and hungry children growing up along a militarized border—militarized in order to block the paths of these millions of needy seeking to "sponge" off American civilization. . . .

Most white Americans can operate from an advantageous social position granted them by their "standard" English language skills. White Americans learn to enjoy this advantage and seek to maintain it. The English-only movement recognizes the disadvantages of those who do not speak "standard" English. This rift in the population creates a fertile breeding ground for the English-only movement. . . . Groups perceived to be different from one another are left to fight for scraps, thus forming harmful divisions. The English-only movement, although supported by many . . . representatives of American capitalism, is not an intentional stratification program. But its end result is the formation of harmful divisions. The English-only movement is, in this respect, a form of social control.

We must resist the English-only movement, which reflects the . . . hegemony of capitalism. The English-only movement needs to be denounced as racist. We must recognize the purpose of this movement as the immobilization of immigrants—particularly non-white immigrants—through harmful divisions and damaging policies. A concern for social justice requires us to reject it.

SOURCE: Hartman, Andrew (2005). "Language as Oppression: The English-Only Movement in the United States." *Poverty & Race*, 14:1–8.

Debate Questions to Consider

1. What assumptions are these authors making about the role of language in the process of assimilation? Can a group adjust successfully to U.S. society without learning English? What stage of Gordon's model of assimilation are they discussing?

2. What reaction might other groups (recent immigrants, African Americans, Native Americans, white ethnics) have to making Spanish an official second language? What stakes would they have in this policy issue?

3. As you think about the issue of bilingualism and multilingualism, see whether you can identify some social class aspects. Which economic classes would benefit from an English-only policy? Which economic classes are hurt? How? Why?

4. Mujica argues that English is a global language and that non-English speakers are handicapped not only in the United States but also in the global economy. Hartman argues that English-only is a thin disguise for racism and a veiled effort to maintain the supremacy of the dominant group. To clarify the debate, list the points of each author side by side. Which argument seems more credible?

5. Should Spanish be made an official second language? Would this threaten societal unity, as Mujica argues? Or would rejecting it be simply an expression of the dominant group's disdain for the "savage wetbacks" that have entered the United States illegally, as argued by Hartman? Review this debate after you have finished this text to see whether your perceptions of the arguments have changed.

Main Points

- Assimilation and pluralism are two broad pathways of development for intergroup relations. Assimilation and pluralism are in some ways contrary processes but may appear together in a variety of combinations.

- Two types of assimilation are the melting pot and Anglo-conformity. The latter has historically been the dominant value in the United States.

- Gordon theorized that assimilation occurs through a series of stages, with integration being the crucial stage. In his view, it is common for American minority groups, especially racial minority groups, to be acculturated but not integrated. Once a group has begun to integrate, all other stages will follow in order.

- In the past few decades, there has been increased interest in pluralism. There are three types of pluralistic situations: cultural, or full, pluralism; structural pluralism; and enclave, or middleman, minority groups.

- According to many scholars, white ethnic groups survived decades of assimilation, albeit in altered forms. New ethnic (and racial) minority groups continue to appear, and old ones change form and function as society changes. As the 21st century unfolds, however, white ethnicity may well be fading in salience for most people, except perhaps as a context for criticizing other groups.

- In the United States today, assimilation may be segmented and have outcomes other than equality with and acceptance into the middle class.

- Several opportunities for extending the concepts and issues discussed in this chapter are presented in the public sociology assignments included in the introduction to Part 1. If you choose to do research in your local schools, for example, you will find that the schools are grappling with issues of immigration, assimilation, language diversity, Americanization, and pluralism every day. If you choose to investigate one of your local soup kitchens, it is extremely likely that you will find recent immigrants among the clientele, people and families wrestling at a very personal level with barriers created by language differences, low levels of human capital, discrimination, racism, and a host of other problems discussed in this chapter.

Study Site on the Web

Don't forget the interactive quizzes and other resources and learning aids at www.pineforge .com/healeystudy5.

For Further Reading

Alba, Richard. (1990). *Ethnic Identity: The Transformation of White America*. New Haven, CT: Yale University Press.

A useful analysis of the changing meanings of ethnic identity for the descendants of European immigrants.

Alba, Richard, & Nee, Victor. (2003). *Remaking the American Mainstream: Assimilation and Contemporary Immigration*. Cambridge, MA: Harvard University Press.

Bean, Frank, & Stevens, Gillian. (2003). *America's Newcomers and the Dynamics of Diversity* New York: Russell Sage.

Two recent works that argue that the "traditional" model of assimilation remains viable.

Foner, Nancy. (2005). *In a New Land: A Comparative View of Immigration*. New York: NYU Press.

A masterful analysis of immigration across time and space.

Gordon, Milton. (1964). *Assimilation in American Life*. New York: Oxford University Press.

Herberg, Will. (1960). *Protestant-Catholic-Jew: An Essay in American Religious Sociology*. New York: Anchor.

Two classic works of scholarship on assimilation, religion, and white ethnic groups.

Perlman, Joel. (2005). *Italians Then, Mexicans Now.* New York: Russell Sage.

  A detailed, intriguing, and rigorous comparison of immigrant groups from two different eras.

Portes, Alejandro, & Rumbaut, Richard. (2001). *Ethnicities: Children of Immigrants in America.* New York: Russell Sage Foundation.

Portes, Alejandro, & Rumbaut, Rubén (2001). *Legacies: The Story of the Immigrant Second Generation.* Berkeley: University of California Press.

Zhou, Min, & Bankston, Carl. (1998). *Growing Up American: How Vietnamese Children Adapt to Life in the United States.* New York: Russell Sage.

  Three outstanding works analyzing the new immigrants and the concept of segmented assimilation.

Questions for Review and Study

1. Summarize Gordon's model of assimilation. Identify and explain each stage and how the stages are linked together. Explain Exhibit 2.4 in terms of Gordon's model.

2. "Human capital theory is not so much wrong as it is incomplete." Explain this statement. What does the theory leave out? What questionable assumptions does it make?

3. What are the major dimensions along which the experience of assimilation varies? Explain how and why the experience of assimilation can vary.

4. Define pluralism and explain the ways in which it differs from assimilation. Why has interest in pluralism increased? Explain the difference between and cite examples of structural and cultural pluralism. Describe enclave minority groups in terms of pluralism and in terms of Gordon's model of assimilation. How have contemporary theorists added to the concept of pluralism?

5. Define and explain segmented assimilation and explain how it differs from Gordon's model. What evidence is there that assimilation for recent immigrants is not segmented? What is the significance of this debate for the future of U.S. society? For other minority groups (e.g., African Americans)? For the immigrants themselves?

6. Do American theories and understandings of assimilation apply to the case of Ireland?

Internet Research Project

Update and supplement the debate on language and assimilation presented at the end of the chapter. You might begin with the Web sites of prominent national newspapers, such as the *New York Times* or *Washington Post*, and search for relevant items within them or perhaps do a general search on the Internet itself, using key terms such as "English first" or "language diversity." Search for a variety of opinions and, to the extent that they are relevant, analyze the data you find in terms of Gordon's model of assimilation and the concepts of Americanization, the melting pot, acculturation, integration, pluralism, and human capital theory.

Notes

1. This phrase comes from Alba (1990).
2. Copyright © Green Linnet Music 1983. Used with permission.

Prejudice and Discrimination

CHAPTER 3

What causes prejudice and discrimination? Why do some people regard members of other groups with contempt, hostility, and even hatred? Why do people sometimes exclude, fear, and attack outsiders? What is the source of these negative attitudes and behaviors? American social scientists have been pursuing these issues for many decades, and we will explore their conclusions in this chapter.

Prejudice (as you learned in Chapter 1) is the tendency of individuals to think and feel in negative ways about members of other groups. Discrimination, on the other hand, is actual, overt, individual behavior. Although these concepts are obviously related, they do not always occur together or have a causal relationship. Exhibit 3.1 presents four possible combinations of prejudice

and discrimination in individuals. In two cases, the relationship between prejudice and discrimination is consistent. The "all-weather liberal" is not prejudiced and does not discriminate, whereas the "all-weather bigot" is prejudiced and does discriminate. The other two combinations, however, are inconsistent. The "fair-weather liberal" discriminates without prejudice, whereas the "timid bigot" is prejudiced but does not discriminate. These inconsistencies between attitudes and behavior are not uncommon and may be caused by a variety of social pressures, including the desire to conform to the expectations of others. They illustrate the fact that prejudice and discrimination can be independent of each other. Most of the material in this chapter is focused more on prejudice than on discrimination, but we will address the relationship between the two concepts on several occasions.

Exhibit 3.1 Four Relationships Between Prejudice and Discrimination in Individuals

	Does Not Discriminate	Does Discriminate
Unprejudiced	Unprejudiced nondiscriminator (all-weather liberal)	Unprejudiced discriminator (fair-weather liberal)
Prejudiced	Prejudiced nondiscriminator (timid bigot)	Prejudiced discriminator (all-weather bigot)

SOURCE: Adapted from Merton (1968).

Photo 3.1

Prejudice and discrimination can be subtle and discrete or open, dramatic, and violent.

© AP Images.

Prejudice

American social scientists of all disciplines have made prejudice a primary concern and have produced literally thousands of articles and books on the topic. They have approached the subject from a variety of theoretical perspectives and have asked many different questions. One firm conclusion that has emerged is that prejudice is not a single, unitary phenomenon. It has a variety of possible causes (some more psychological and individual, others more sociological and cultural) and can present itself in a variety of forms (some blatant and vicious, others subtle and indirect). No single theory has emerged that can explain prejudice in its entirety. One way to approach this complex subject is by examining the two main dimensions of prejudice.

The Affective Dimension

Individual prejudice is partly a set of feelings or emotions that people attach to groups, including their own. The emotions can run a wide gamut from mild to extremely intense. At one extreme, we might find a genteel expression of disparagement, such as "I don't care much for Italians." At the other, we might find the dreadful rage that accompanies a lynching or other hate crime. What makes these emotions part of prejudice is their generalized association with an entire group, often in the complete absence of any actual experience with group members, and their element of *pre*-judgment (which is, after all, the literal meaning of *prejudice*).

There are a number of psychological and social-psychological research traditions that focus on the emotional or affective aspect of prejudice. Here, we will briefly examine two of these theories: the **scapegoat hypothesis** and the theory of the authoritarian personality.

The Scapegoat Hypothesis.
This theory links prejudice to feelings of frustration and aggression. People sometimes deal with personal failure or disappointment by expressing their anger against a substitute target (or scapegoat), not against the object or person that actually caused their frustration. For example, someone who has been demoted at work might attack his or her spouse rather than the boss, or a student who received a low grade on a test might "take it out" on a pet rather than on the professor. Generally speaking, the substitute targets (spouses or pets) will be less powerful than the actual cause of the frustration and may serve as a "safe" alternative to attacking bosses or professors. Minority groups can make excellent substitute targets because they, by definition, control fewer power resources. In other words, minority groups are often selected as the recipients of anger and aggression that, for whatever reason, cannot be directed at the actual cause of a person's frustration. When released against a minority group, displaced aggression is expressed as or accompanied by prejudice.

Many researchers have produced scapegoating against minority groups in laboratory settings. In a typical experiment, subjects are purposely frustrated, perhaps by being asked to complete a task that the researchers have made sure is impossible. Then, the subjects are offered the opportunity to release their anger as prejudice, sometimes by completing a survey that measures their feelings about various minority groups. Many people respond to this situation with increased feelings of rejection and disparagement against other groups (see Berkowitz, 1978; Dollard, Miller, Doob, Mowrer, & Sears, 1939; Miller & Bugleski, 1948).

Outside the laboratory, the scapegoat theory has been proposed as an explanation for a variety of political, social, and economic events. For example, the theory has been applied to the rise of the Nazi Party in Germany in the 1930s. At that time, Germany was trying to cope with its defeat in World War I, a powerful economic recession, rampant unemployment, and horrific inflation. According to this line of analysis, the success of the extremely racist, violently anti-Semitic Nazi party was in part a result of its ability to capture and direct these intense frustrations against Jews and other minorities (see Dollard et al., 1939). Along the same analytical lines, Hovland and Sears (1940) argued that the rate of lynching of African Americans in the South between 1882 and 1930 was correlated with fluctuations in cotton prices. Lynchings generally increased during hard times when the price of cotton was low and (presumably) frustrations were more widespread (for a different, more sociological view, see Beck & Clark, 2002, and Beck & Tolnay, 1990). Finally, scapegoating has been implicated in many hate crimes in the United States, including seemingly random attacks on Middle Easterners following the terrorist attacks of September 11, 2001. We will return to the topic of hate crimes at the end of this chapter.

The Theory of the Authoritarian Personality. This theory links prejudice to early childhood experiences and personality structure and argues that prejudice is produced by stern, highly punitive styles of parenting. On the surface, the children of authoritarian families respect and love their parents. Internally, however, they resent and fear their severe and distant parents. They can't admit that they feel negatively toward their parents, so, instead, they express their fear and anger as prejudice against minority groups. Thus, the prejudice of persons with authoritarian personalities provides them with a way of coping with their conflicted feelings for their parents.

The tradition of research on the authoritarian personality theory stretches back to before World War II and is supported by experiments and research projects that demonstrate a link between family structure, childhood experience, and prejudice (Adorno, Frenkel-Brunswick, Levinson, & Sanford, 1950). However, this theory—and other psychological theories—has been widely criticized for focusing solely on the internal dynamics of personality and not taking sufficient account of the social settings in which an individual is acting. Some individuals do use prejudice as a tool for handling their personality problems, but to fully understand prejudice, we need to see its connections with social structure, social class, and the context and history of group relations. The theory of the authoritarian personality is not "wrong" so much as it is incomplete. The sociological perspective, as we shall see, takes a broader approach and incorporates the social world in which the individual acts.

The Cognitive Dimension: Stereotypes

In this section, we address the cognitive dimension of prejudice or the ways we think about other groups. *Stereotypes* are generalizations about groups of people that are exaggerated, overly simplistic, and resistant to disproof (Pettigrew, 1980, p. 822; see also Jones, 1997, pp. 164–202). Stereotypes stress a few traits and assume that these characteristics apply to all members of the group, regardless of individual characteristics. Highly prejudiced people will maintain their stereotypical views even in the face of massive evidence that their views are wrong.

Virtually all Americans share a common set of images of the prominent ethnic, racial, and religious groups that make up U.S. society. These images include notions such as "Asians are clannish," "Jews are miserly," or "Blacks are musical." People who are low on prejudice are familiar with these images but pay little attention to them, and they do not use them to actually judge the worth of others. People who are more prejudiced will use the stereotypes widely, attribute them to all members of particular group, make sweeping judgments about the worth of others, and even commit acts of violence based solely on the group identity of another person.

For the prejudiced individual, stereotypes are an important set of cognitive categories. Once a stereotype is learned, it can shape perceptions to the point that the individual pays attention only to information that confirms that stereotype. **Selective perception**, the tendency to see only what one expects to see, can reinforce and strengthen stereotypes to the point that the highly prejudiced individual simply does not accept evidence that challenges his or her views. Thus, these overgeneralizations can become closed perceptual systems that screen out contrary information and absorb only the sensory impressions that ratify the original bias.

The Content of American Stereotypes.

A series of studies with Princeton University undergraduates provides some interesting perspectives on the content of American stereotypes. Students were given a list of personality traits and asked to check those that applied to a number of different groups. The study was done first in 1933 and then repeated in 1951 and 1967 (Karlins, Coffman, & Walters, 1969). It is unusual to have comparable data covering such a long period of time, which makes these studies significant despite the fact that Princeton undergraduates are hardly a representative sample of American public opinion. Exhibit 3.2 lists the traits most commonly mentioned for four of the groups in the 1933 study and charts their changes over time.

Several elements of these data are worth noting. First, the two different types of stereotypes we previously discussed can be found in these results. Jews are seen as successful ("industrious," "intelligent") but pushy ("grasping," "mercenary"), whereas African Americans

Exhibit 3.2 Changes in Stereotypes Expressed by Princeton Undergraduates

(Percentage Identifying Trait With Ethnic Group)							
English	1933	1951	1967	**Italians**	1933	1951	1967
Sportsmanlike	53	21	22	Artistic	53	28	30
Artistic	46	29	23	Impulsive	44	19	28
Conventional	34	25	19	Passionate	37	25	19
Tradition loving	31	42	21	Quick tempered	35	15	28
Conservative	30	22	53	Musical	32	22	9
Jews				**African Americans**			
Shrewd	79	47	30	Superstitious	84	41	13
Mercenary	49	28	15	Lazy	75	31	26
Industrious	48	29	33	Happy-go-lucky	38	17	27
Grasping	34	17	17	Ignorant	38	24	11
Intelligent	29	37	37	Musical	26	33	47

SOURCE: Karlins, Coffman, & Walters (1969). Copyright © 1969 by the American Psychological Association. Adapted with permission.

are seen as inferior ("lazy," "ignorant"). Second, the study shows that the willingness to stereotype seems to decline over the years. Princeton undergraduates in 1951 and 1967 were less willing to attach labels to entire groups than in 1933 (although there was no particular decline between 1951 and 1967).

Third, although muted, the willingness to stereotype still existed in 1967. For example, about 30% still saw Jews as being "shrewd" and Italians as "impulsive" and "quick tempered." In fact, the attribution of some traits (the English as conservative, African Americans as musical) actually increased in the years between 1933 and 1967.

Similar studies of stereotypical thinking have been conducted on other campuses in more recent years. Clark and Person (1982) measured white stereotypes of African Americans among undergraduates at two southeastern universities in the early 1980s. They found some continuity in the content of the stereotypes from earlier studies but also found that their subjects were more likely to characterize African Americans as having seemingly positive traits such as "loyal to family" (Clark & Person, 1982). In contrast, a 1993 study conducted by Wood and Chesser found that white students at a large midwestern university had more negative stereotypes of African Americans. The top five most common traits selected by the sample were uniformly negative and included "loud," "aggressive," and "lazy" (Wood & Chesser, 1994). This finding was echoed in a 1995 study at the University of Wisconsin that replicated the three Princeton University tests. Three of the top five most commonly selected traits for African Americans were similar to those selected by Princeton undergraduates: "rhythmic" (vs. "musical"), "low in intelligence" (vs. "ignorant"), and "lazy," and two were new, "athletic" and "poor" (Devine & Elliot, 1995).

We should stress that these studies are very limited by time and place and are not necessarily consistent with the attitudes of Americans in general. Perhaps the most significant thing about this line of research is that when asked to characterize entire groups of people, the subjects—even highly educated college students—did so.

Types of Stereotypes and Dominant-Minority Relations. Stereotypes are, by

definition, exaggerated overgeneralizations. At some level, though, even the most simplistic and derogatory stereotype can reflect some of the realities of dominant-minority group relationships. The content of a stereotype flows from the actual relationship between dominant and minority groups and is often one important way in which the dominant group tries to justify or rationalize that relationship.

For example, Pettigrew (1980) and others have pointed out two general stereotypes of minority groups. The first attributes extreme inferiority (e.g., laziness, irresponsibility, or lack of intelligence) to minority group members and tends to be found in situations (such as slavery) in which a minority group is being heavily exploited and held in an impoverished and powerless status by the dominant group. This type of stereotype is a rationalization that helps to justify dominant group policies of control, discrimination, or exclusion.

The second type of stereotype is found when power and status differentials are less extreme, particularly when the minority group has succeeded in gaining some control over resources, has experienced some upward mobility, and has had some success in school and business. In this situation, credulity would be stretched too far to label the group "inferior," so their relative success is viewed in negative terms: They are seen as *too* smart, *too* materialistic, *too* crafty, *too* sly, or *too* ambitious (Pettigrew, 1980, p. 823; see also Simpson & Yinger, 1985, p. 101).

You should also realize that stereotypes and prejudice can exist apart from any need to rationalize or justify dominant-group advantage. Research shows that some individuals will readily stereotype groups about which they have little or no information. In fact, some individuals will express prejudice against groups that do not even exist! In one test, respondents were asked how closely they would associate with "Daniereans, Pireneans, and Wallonians"—all fictitious groups. A number of white respondents apparently reacted to the "foreign" sound of the names, rejected these three groups, and indicated that they would treat them about the same as other minority groups (Hartley, 1946). Clearly, the negative judgments about these groups were not made on the basis of personal experience or a need to rationalize some system such as slavery. The subjects were exhibiting a generalized tendency to reject minority groups of all sorts.

Cognitive and Affective Dimensions of Stereotypes

Remember that individual prejudice has an affective dimension in addition to the cognitive. Robert Merton (1968), a prominent American sociologist, makes this distinction between dimensions dramatically. Merton analyzed stereotypical perceptions of Abraham Lincoln, Jews, and Japanese. In the following passage, he argues that the three "stereotypes" are identical in content but vastly different in emotional shading:

> The very same behavior undergoes a complete change of evaluation in its transition from the in-group Abe Lincoln to the out-group Abe Cohen or Abe Kurokawa. Did Lincoln work far into the night? This testifies that he was industrious, resolute, perseverant, and eager to realize his capacities to the full. Do the out-group Jews or Japanese keep these same hours? This only bears witness to their sweatshop mentality, their ruthless undercutting of American standards, their unfair competitive practices. Is the in-group hero frugal, thrifty, and sparing? Then the out-group villain is stingy, miserly, and penny-pinching. All honor is due to the in-group Abe for his having been smart, shrewd and intelligent, and, by the same token, all contempt is owing the out-group Abes for their being sharp, cunning, crafty, and too clever by far. (p. 482)

The stereotype of all three Abes is identical; what varies is the affect, or the emotional tone, reflected in the descriptive terms. Thus, the same stereotype evokes different emotional responses for different groups or in different individuals.

Intersections of Race, Gender, and Class

The affective and cognitive dimensions of prejudice vary not only by race and ethnicity but also by gender and class, the major axes that define minority group experience. For example, the stereotypes and feelings attached to black males differ from those attached to black females, and feelings about lower-class Mexican Americans may vary dramatically from those attributed to upper-class members of the same group. Some of this variation

was captured in a study that asked white students at Arizona State University about their perceptions of women (Weitz & Gordon, 1993). Sharp distinctions were found between "women in general" (a label that, to the students, apparently signified white women) and African American women in particular. When asked to select traits for "American women in general," the responses were overwhelmingly positive and included "intelligent," "sensitive," and "attractive." Of the 10 most commonly selected traits, only 2 ("materialistic" and "emotional") might have had some negative connotations. The students selected very different terms to describe African American women. The single most commonly selected trait was "loud," and only 22% of the sample saw African American women as "intelligent." Of the 10 most commonly selected traits, 5 (e.g., "talkative," "stubborn") seemed to have at least some negative affect attached to them.

A study by sociologist Edward Morris further illustrates how race, gender, and class can intersect in shaping feelings and thoughts of other groups (Morris, 2005). He studied an urban high school and focused on how various types of students were perceived and disciplined by school administrators and faculty. Morris found that consistent with the notion of a "matrix of domination" mentioned in Chapter 1, stereotypes varied "not just through gender, or just through race, or just through class, but through all of these at once" (p. 44). For example, black boys were seen by school administrators and faculty as "too" masculine, extremely aggressive, and dangerous and in need of careful watching. Black girls, in contrast, were seen as not feminine enough, too loud and aggressive, and in need of being molded into more compliant and deferential females. Other groups in the school—Latinas, Asian males, white males and females—were also the objects of clear sets of stereotypes and feelings and tended to be subjected to forms of discipline that, ultimately, tended to reproduce the systems of inequality in the larger society.

Prejudice is a complex phenomenon with multiple causes and manifestations. In this section, we will focus on a macrosociological approach and examine theories that stress the causes of prejudice that are related to culture, social structure, and group relationships.

The Role of Group Competition

Every form of prejudice—even the most ancient—started at some specific point in history. If we go back far enough in time, we can find a moment that predates anti-black prejudice, **anti-Semitism**, negative stereotypes about Native Americans or Hispanic Americans, or antipathy against Asian Americans. What sorts of conditions create prejudice?

The one common factor that seems to account for the origin of all prejudices is competition between groups—some episode in which one group successfully dominates, takes resources from, or eliminates a threat from some other group. The successful group becomes the dominant group, and the other group becomes the minority group.

Why is group competition associated with the emergence of prejudice? Typically, prejudice is more a result of the competition than a cause. Its role is to help mobilize emotional energy for the contest; justify rejection and attack; and rationalize the structures of domination, such as slavery or segregation, that result from the competition. Groups react to the competition and to the threat presented by other groups with antipathy and stereotypes about the "enemy" group. Prejudice emerges from the heat of the contest but then can solidify and persist for years (even centuries) after the end of the conflict.

Robber's Cave. The relationship between prejudice and competition has been demonstrated in a variety of settings and situations ranging from labor strikes to international war to social psychology labs. In the chapters to come, we will examine the role of prejudice during the creation of slavery in North America, as a reaction to periods of high immigration, and as an accompaniment to myriad forms of group competition. Here, to illustrate our central point about competition and prejudice, we will examine a classic experiment from the sociological literature. The Robber's Cave experiment was conducted in the 1950s at a summer camp for 11- and 12-year-old boys.

The camp director, social psychologist Muzafer Sherif, divided the campers into two groups, the Rattlers and the Eagles (Sherif, Harvey, White, Hood, & Sherif, 1961). The groups lived in different cabins, and the staff continually pitted them against each other in a wide range of activities. Games, sports, and even housekeeping chores were set up on a competitive basis. As the competition intensified, the groups developed and expressed negative feelings (prejudice) against each other. Competition and prejudicial feelings grew quite intense and were manifested in episodes of name-calling and raids on the "enemy" group.

Sherif attempted to reduce the harsh feelings he had created by bringing the campers together in various pleasant situations featuring food, movies, and other treats. But the rival groups only used these opportunities to express their enmity. Sherif then came up with some activities that required the members of the rival groups to work cooperatively with each other. For example, the researchers deliberately sabotaged some plumbing to create an emergency that required the efforts of everyone to resolve. As a result of these cooperative activities, intergroup "prejudice" declined, and eventually, friendships were formed across groups.

In the Robber's Cave experiment, as in many actual group relationships, prejudice (negative feelings and stereotypes about other campers) arose to help mobilize feelings and to justify rejection and attacks, both verbal and physical, against the out-group. When group competition was reduced, the levels of prejudice abated and eventually disappeared, again demonstrating that prejudice is caused by competition, not the other way around.

Although the Robber's Cave experiment illustrates our central point, we must be cautious in generalizing from these results. The experiment was conducted in an artificial environment with young boys (all white) who had no previous acquaintance with each other and no history of grievances or animosity. Thus, these results may be only partially generalizable to group conflicts in the real world. Nonetheless, Robber's Cave illustrates a fundamental connection between group competition and prejudice that we will observe repeatedly in the chapters to come. Competition and the desire to protect resources and status and to defend against threats from other groups are the primary motivations for the construction of traditions of prejudice and structures of inequality that benefit the dominant group.

Theoretical Perspectives on Group Competition and Prejudice Power/Conflict Models

Many theorists have examined the dynamics of group competition and the results for prejudice and discrimination. Here we examine two of the most influential sociological perspectives on this topic.

Marxist Analysis. In Chapter 1, Marxism was discussed as a theory of social inequality. One of the tenets of Marxism is that the elites who control the means of production in a society also control the ideas and intellectual activity of the society. Ideologies and belief systems are shaped to support the dominance of the elites, and these ideologies and belief systems change when new elites come into control: "What else does the history of ideas prove, than that intellectual production changes in character in proportion as material production is changed? The ruling ideas of each age have been the ideas of its ruling class" (Marx & Engels, 1848/1967, p. 102).

Elite classes who subordinate or exploit a minority group will develop and institutionalize ideologies to justify or "explain" the arrangement. The history of the United States (and many other nations) includes numerous situations in which prejudice was used to help sustain the control of elite classes. For example, slave owners in the South used anti-black prejudice to attempt to control perceptions and justify the exploitation of the slaves. If it were commonly believed that blacks were inferior and too irresponsible to care for themselves, the constraints of slavery would seem less oppressive and unjust. People who did not benefit directly from slavery might not oppose the institution if they accepted the idea of black inferiority.

The slave owners also attempted to use Christianity to "brainwash" the slaves into accepting their powerless status. The exposure of slaves to religion was carefully controlled and emphasized those aspects of Christianity that stress the virtues of meekness and humility and promise rewards—but only in heaven. Thus, religion was used to stress obedience and to focus the attention of the slaves on the next life, not on the misery and injustice of this life.

In a more industrial example, the history of the United States for the past 150 years is replete with instances of struggle between the capitalists who control the means of production (factories, mills, mines, banks, etc.) and workers. Early in the 20th century, it was common for industrialists to try to weaken labor unions by splitting the working class along racial lines. The greater the extent to which black and white workers fought each other, the less likely there would be a unified uprising against the capitalist class. The capitalist class controlled the racially mixed working class by following a strategy of "divide and conquer" (Cox, 1948; Reich, 1986).

Split Labor Market Theory. This theory agrees with the Marxist idea that prejudice and racist ideologies serve the interest of a specific class, but it identifies a different beneficiary. In split labor market theory, there are three actors in the economic sector of an industrial society. First are the elites, the capitalists who own the means of production. The other two groups are segments of the working class. The labor market is divided (or split) into higher-priced labor and cheaper labor. It is in the economic self-interest of the capitalist class to use cheaper labor whenever possible. Recent immigrants and minority groups often fill the role of cheaper labor.

Higher-priced labor (usually consisting of members of the dominant group) will attempt to exclude cheaper labor from the marketplace whenever it can. Such efforts include barring minority groups from labor unions, violent attacks on minority group communities, support for discriminatory laws, and efforts to exclude groups from the United States entirely. Prejudice is used by higher-priced labor to arouse and mobilize opposition to the cheaper labor pool represented by the minority group. The economic nature of the competition and the economic self-interests of higher-priced labor are obscured by appeals to racial or cultural unity against the "threat" represented by the minority group. The major beneficiary of prejudice is not the capitalist class, but the more powerful elements of the working class (Bonacich, 1972; Bonacich & Modell, 1980).

Summary and Limitations.
Marxism and **split labor market theory** share the conclusion that prejudice begins as a side issue in a struggle to control or expand a group's share of scarce resources. The primary beneficiary of prejudice is sometimes the elite class (e.g., capitalists or plantation owners) and sometimes another segment of the dominant group (higher-priced labor). In general, though, these perspectives agree that prejudice exists because someone or some group gains by it.

While these points of view are persuasive and can help us understand why prejudice originates in the first place, we must also recognize that they cannot account for prejudice in all its forms. No theory can explain everything, especially something as complex as prejudice. The origins of prejudice can be found in culture, **socialization**, family structure, and personality development, as well as in politics and economics. As the authoritarian personality theory reminds us, prejudice can have important psychological and social functions independent of group power relationships.

To illustrate these limitations, consider an analysis of attitudes toward immigrants. Consistent with the idea that prejudice is stimulated by group competition, Burns and Gimpel (2000) found that opposition to immigration is greater when times are hard and people feel economically threatened. However, they also found that anti-immigration prejudice cannot be explained by economics alone and that it persists even when economic conditions improve, a finding consistent with the idea that prejudice is shaped by cultural and personality factors in addition to conflict over scarce resources.

How and Why Does Prejudice Persist Through Time?

Prejudice originates in group competition of some sort but often outlives the conditions of its creation. It can persist, full-blown and intense, long after the episode that sparked it has faded from memory. How does prejudice persist through time?

The Vicious Cycle

In his classic analysis of American race relations, *An American Dilemma* (1944/1962), Swedish economist Gunnar Myrdal proposed the idea that prejudice is perpetuated through time by a self-fulfilling prophecy or a **vicious cycle**, as illustrated in Exhibit 3.3. The dominant group uses its power to force the minority group into an inferior status, such as slavery, as shown in the diagram in Area 1. Partly to motivate the construction of a system of racial stratification and partly to justify its existence, individual prejudice and racist belief systems are invented and accepted by the dominant group, as shown in Area 2. Individual prejudices are reinforced by the everyday observation of the inferior status of the minority group. The fact that the minority group is impoverished, enslaved, or otherwise exploited confirms and strengthens the attribution of inferiority. The belief in inferiority motivates further discrimination and unequal treatment, as shown in Area 3 of the diagram, which reinforces the inferior status, which validates the prejudice and racism, which justifies further discrimination, and so on. Over a few generations, a stable, internally reinforced system of racial inferiority becomes an integral, unremarkable, and (at least for the dominant group) accepted part of everyday life.

Culture is conservative, and once created, prejudice will be sustained over time just like any set of attitudes, values, and beliefs. Future generations will learn prejudice in the same way and for the same reasons that they learn any other aspect of their culture. Thus, prejudice and racism come to us through our cultural heritage as a package of stereotypes, emotions, and ideas. We learn which groups are "good" and which are "bad" in the same way we learn table manners and religious beliefs (Pettigrew, 1958, 1971, p. 137; Simpson & Yinger, 1985, pp. 107, 108). When prejudice is part of the cultural heritage, individuals learn

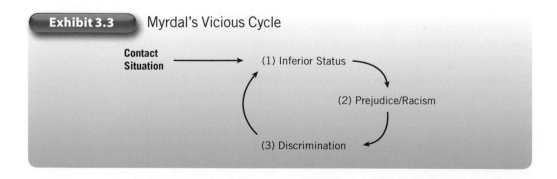

Exhibit 3.3 Myrdal's Vicious Cycle

to think and feel negatively toward other groups as a routine part of socialization. Much of the prejudice expressed by Americans—and the people of many other societies—is the normal result of typical socialization in families, communities, and societies that are, to some degree, racist. Given our long history of intense racial and ethnic exploitation, it is not surprising that Americans continue to manifest antipathy toward and stereotypical ideas about other groups.

Prejudice in Children

The idea that prejudice is learned during socialization is reinforced by studies of the development of prejudice in children. Research generally shows that people are born without bias and have to be taught whom to like and dislike. Children become aware of group differences (e.g., black vs. white) at a very early age. By age 3 or younger, they recognize the significance and the permanence of racial groups and can accurately classify people on the basis of skin color and other cues (Brown, 1995, pp. 121–136; Katz, 1976, p. 126). Once the racial or group categories are mentally established, the child begins the process of learning the "proper" attitudes and stereotypes to associate with the various groups, and both affective and cognitive prejudice begin to grow at an early age.

It is important to note that children can acquire prejudice even when parents and other caregivers do not teach it overtly or directly. Adults control the socialization process and valuable resources (food, shelter, praise), and children are motivated to seek their approval and conform to their expectations (at least in the early years). There are strong pressures on the child to learn and internalize the perceptions of the older generation, and even a casual comment or an overheard remark can establish or reinforce negative beliefs or feelings about members of other groups (Ashmore & DelBoca, 1976). Children need not be directly instructed about presumed minority group characteristics; it is often said that racial attitudes are "caught and not taught."

A somewhat different line of research on the development of prejudice argues that children are actively engaged in their learning and that their levels of prejudice reflect their changing intellectual capabilities. Children as young as 5 to 6 months old can make some simple distinctions (e.g., by gender or race) between categories of people. The fact that this capability emerges so early in life suggests that it is not simply a response to adult teaching. "Adults use categories to simplify and make sense of their environment; apparently children do the same" (Brown, 1995, p. 126). Gross, simplistic distinctions between people may help very young children organize and understand the world around them. The need for such primitive categorizations may decline as the child becomes more experienced in life and more sophisticated in his or her thinking. Doyle and Aboud (1995), for example, found that prejudice was highest for younger children and actually decreased between kindergarten and the third grade. The decline was related to increased awareness of racial similarities (as well as differences) and diverse perspectives on race (see also Black-Gutman & Hickson, 1996; Brown, 1995, pp. 149–159; Powlishta, Serbin, Doyle, & White, 1994; Van Ausdale & Feagin, 2001). Thus, changing levels of prejudice in children may reflect an interaction between children's changing mental capacities and their environment rather than a simple or straightforward learning of racist cultural beliefs or values.

Social Distance Scales: The Cultural Dimensions of Prejudice

Further evidence for the cultural nature of prejudice is provided by research on the concept of **social distance**, which is related to prejudice but is not quite the same thing. Social distance is the degree of intimacy that a person is willing to accept in his or her relations with members of other groups. On this scale, the most intimate relationship is close kinship, and the most distant is exclusion from the country. The Seven Degrees of Social Distance, as specified by Emory Bogardus (1933), the inventor of the scale, are as follows:

1. To close kinship by marriage

2. To my club as personal chums

3. To my street as neighbors

4. To employment in my occupation

5. To citizenship in my country

6. As visitors only to my country

7. Would exclude from my country

Research using social distance scales demonstrates that Americans rank other groups in similar ways across time and space. The consistency indicates a common frame of reference or set of perceptions, a continuity of vision possible only if perceptions have been standardized by socialization in a common culture.

Exhibit 3.4 presents some results of seven administrations of the scale to samples of Americans from 1926 to 2001. The groups are listed by the rank order of their scores for 1926. In that year, the sample expressed the least social distance from the English and the most distance from Asian Indians. Whereas the average social distance score for the English was 1.02, indicating virtually no sense of distance, the average score for Indians was 3.91, indicating a distance between "to employment in my occupation" and "to my street as neighbors."

Note, first of all, the stability in the rankings. The actual scores (not shown) generally decrease from decade to decade, indicating less social distance and presumably a decline in prejudice over the years. The group rankings, however, tend to be the same year after year. This stability is clearly displayed in the bottom row of the table, which shows correlations between the group rankings for each year and the 1926 ranking. If any of the lists of scores had been identical, the statistic in this row would have shown its maximum value of 1.00. Although they weaken over time, the actual correlations approach the maximum value of 1.00 and indicate that the rank order of the groups from year to year is substantially the same. Considering the changes that society experienced between 1926 and 2001 (the Great Depression; World War II, the Korean War, Vietnam, and the cold war with the U.S.S.R.; the civil rights movement; the resumption of large-scale immigration, etc.), this overall continuity in group rankings is remarkable.

Second, note the nature of the ranking: Groups with origins in Northern and Western Europe are ranked highest, followed by groups from Southern and Eastern Europe, with racial

Exhibit 3.4 Rank on Social Distance of Selected Groups, 1926–2001

Group	1926	1946	1956	1966	1977	1993	2001
English	1	3	3	2	2	2	4
American Whites	2	1	1	1	1	—	1
Canadians	3	2	2	3	3	—	3
Irish	5	4	5	5	7	1	5
Germans	7	10	8	10	11	10	8
Norwegians	10	7	10	7	12	8	—
Russians	13	13	24	24	29	13	20
Italians	14	16	12	8	5	3	2
Poles	15	14	13	16	18	12	14
American Indians	18	20	18	18	10	16	12
Jews	19	19	16	15	15	15	11
Mexicans	21	24	28	28	26	18	25
Japanese	22	30	26	25	25	19	22
Filipinos	23	23	21	21	24	—	16
African Americans	24	29	27	29	17	17	9
Turks	25	25	23	26	28	22	—
Chinese	26	21	25	22	23	20	17
Koreans	27	27	30	27	30	21	24
Asian Indians	28	28	29	30	27	—	26
Vietnamese	—	—	—	—	—	—	28
Muslims	—	—	—	—	—	—	29
Arabs	—	—	—	—	—	—	30
Mean (all scores)	2.14	2.12	2.08	1.92	1.93	1.43	1.44
Range	2.85	2.57	1.75	1.56	1.38	1.07	0.87
Total Number of Groups Included	28	30	30	30	30	24	30
Correlation With 1926 Rankings	—	.95	.93	.90	.84	.92	.76

SOURCE: 1926 through 1977: Smith & Dempsey (1983, p. 588); 1993: Kleg & Yamamoto (1998; 2001), Parrillo (2003).

NOTE: Values in the table are ranks for that year. To conserve space, some groups and ranks have been eliminated.

Key:

Red = Northern and Western Europeans

Blue = Southern and Eastern Europeans

Black = "nonwhites"

minorities near the bottom. These preferences reflect the relative status of these groups in the U.S. hierarchy of racial and ethnic groups which, in turn, reflect the timing of immigration and the perceived "degree of difference" with the dominant group (see Chapter 2). The rankings also reflect the relative amount of exploitation and prejudice directed at each group over the course of U.S. history.

Although these patterns of social distance scores support the general point that prejudice is cultural, this body of research has some important limitations. The respondents were generally college students from a variety of campuses, not representative samples of the population, and the differences in actual scores from group to group are sometimes very small. Still, the stability of the patterns cannot be ignored: The top groups are always Northern European, Poles and Jews are always ranked in the middle third, and Koreans and Japanese always fall in the bottom third. African Americans and American Indians were also ranked toward the bottom until the most recent rankings.

Finally, note how the relative positions of some groups change with international and domestic relations. For example, both Japanese and Germans fell in the rankings at the end of World War II (1946). Comparing 1966 with 1946, Russians fell and Japanese rose, reflecting changing patterns of alliance and enmity in the global system of societies. The dramatic rise of Native Americans and African Americans since the 1966 ranking may reflect declining levels of overt prejudice in American society. In 2001, the scale was administered in the weeks following the terrorist attacks on September 11, and the low ranking of Arabs reflects the societal reaction toward those traumatic events.

How do we explain the fact that group rankings generally are so stable from the 1920s to 2001? The stability strongly suggests that Americans view the various groups through the same culturally shaped lens. A sense of social distance, a perception of some groups as "higher" or "better" than others, is part of the cultural package of intergroup prejudices we acquire from socialization into American society. The social distance patterns illustrate the power of culture to shape individual perceptions and preferences and attest to the fundamentally racist nature of American culture.

The power of culture to shape our perceptions is illustrated in Narrative Portrait 1 in this chapter.

Situational Influences

As a final point in our consideration of the persistence of prejudice, we should note the importance of the social situation in which attitudes are expressed and behavior occurs. What people think and what they do is not always the same. Even intense prejudice may not translate into discriminatory behavior, and discrimination is not always accompanied by prejudice (refer back to Exhibit 3.1).

One of the earliest demonstrations of the difference between what people think and feel (prejudice) and what they actually do (discrimination) was provided by sociologist Robert LaPiere (1934). In the 1930s, he escorted a Chinese couple on a tour of the United States. At that time, Chinese and other Asians were the victims of widespread discrimination and exclusion, and anti-Chinese prejudice was quite high, as demonstrated by the scores in Exhibit 3.4. However, LaPiere and his companions dined in restaurants and stayed in hotels without incident for the entire trip and experienced discrimination only once.

Six months later, LaPiere wrote to every establishment the group had patronized and inquired about reservations. He indicated that some of the party were Chinese and asked if that would be a problem. Of those establishments that replied (about half), 92% said that they would not serve Chinese and would be unable to accommodate the party.

Why the difference? Although not a definitive or particularly sophisticated method of data gathering (for example, there was no way to tell whether the correspondents were the same persons LaPiere and his associates had dealt with in person), this episode exemplifies the difference between saying and doing and the importance of taking the situation into account. On LaPiere's original visit, anti-Asian prejudice may well have been present but was not expressed, to avoid making a scene. In a different situation, the more distant interaction of written correspondence, the restaurant and hotel staffs may have allowed their prejudice to be expressed in open discrimination because the potential for embarrassment was much less.

The situation a person is in shapes the relationship between prejudice and discrimination. In highly prejudiced communities or groups, the pressure to conform may cause relatively unprejudiced individuals to discriminate. For example, if an ethnic or racial or gender joke is told in a group of friends or relatives, all might join in the laughter. Even a completely unprejudiced person might crack a smile or register a slight giggle to avoid embarrassing or offending the person who told the joke.

On the other hand, situations in which there are strong norms of equal and fair treatment may stifle the tendency of even the most bigoted individual to discriminate. For example, if a community vigorously enforces antidiscrimination laws, even the most prejudiced merchant might refrain from treating minority group customers unequally. Highly prejudiced individuals may not discriminate so they can "do business" (or at least avoid penalties or sanctions) in an environment in which discrimination is not tolerated or is too costly.

Summary and Limitations

The theories and perspectives examined in this section help us understand how prejudice can persist through time. Prejudice becomes a part of the culture of a society and is passed along to succeeding generations along with other values, norms, and information.

Although cultural causes of prejudice are obviously important, considering only cultural factors may lead us to the mistaken belief that all members of the same society have similar levels of prejudice. On the contrary, no two people have the same socialization experiences or develop exactly the same prejudices (or any other attitude, for that matter). Differences in family structure, parenting style, school experiences, attitudes of peers, and a host of other factors affect the development of an individual's personality and attitude.

Furthermore, socialization is not a passive process; we are not neutral recipients of a culture that is simply forced down our throats. Our individuality, intelligence, and curiosity affect the nature and content of our socialization experiences. Even close siblings may have very different experiences and, consequently, different levels of prejudice. People raised in extremely prejudicial settings may moderate their attitudes as a result of experiences later in life, just as those raised in nonprejudiced settings may develop stronger biases as time passes.

The development of prejudice is further complicated by the fact that in the United States, we also learn egalitarian norms and values as we are socialized. Gunnar Myrdal was referring to this contrast when he titled his landmark study of race relations in the United States *An*

The Cultural Sources of Prejudice

In The Crazy Ladies of Pearl Street, *best-selling novelist Trevanian (2005) recounts his experiences growing up Irish Catholic in a poor neighborhood in Albany, New York, in the 1930s. In the passage below, he recounts how his mother, Ruby LaPointe, decided to apply for public assistance after her husband had abandoned them. Trevanian, then a boy of 8, advises her to enlist the assistance of Mr. Kane, the local grocer who has already extended them credit to buy food and other essentials. The young Trevanian sees Mr. Kane as kindly and full of good humor. His mother focuses on another part of his identity: Mr. Kane is Jewish, and this dominates how she sees him.*

For the author, his mother is powerful, even heroic. She was the central character of his childhood, and he recounts in his memoir how she coped with daily disasters and rebounded from setback after setback, always determined to care for her children properly. She is also, as demonstrated in this passage, a product of her culture and her upbringing. She inherited a set of attitudes, images, and emotions about other groups and especially about Jews. Note her ability to see Mr. Kane and other Jews negatively: No matter what he says or does, her stereotypes are reinforced. Her view of Mr. Kane exemplifies how selective perception can sift through evidence and experience and turn positives into negatives.

The Crazy Ladies of Pearl Street

Trevanian

Here's how things were: We were marooned on this slum street in this strange city where we didn't know anybody and nobody gave a damn about us, and we had only a little more than five bucks to our name. But we weren't beaten. Not by a damn sight. Nobody beats Ruby Lucille LaPointe! No, sir! . . . Her pride had never let her seek public assistance, and it burned her up to have to do so now, but she . . . couldn't let pride stand in the way of us kids having food on the table. There must be agencies and people that she could turn to, just until we were on our feet again. First she'd contact them and ask them for help . . . make them help us, goddammit! Then she'd look for work as a waitress. . . . But first, she had to find out the addresses of the welfare agencies. If only she knew someone she could ask about things like this.

"What about Mr. Kane?" I suggested.

"The grocery man? Oh, I don't know. I don't think we want any more favors from his sort."

" . . . His sort?"

She shrugged.

"But he's nice," I said. "And smart, too."

She thought about that for a moment. She didn't like being beholden to strangers, but . . . Oh, all right, she'd go over to thank him for giving us credit. That was just common courtesy. And maybe while she was there she'd . . . "You know, come to think of it, this Mr. Kane of yours just might help us out because if he doesn't, we won't be able to pay what we owe him. You can only count on these people if there's something in it for them."

"He'd help us anyway. He's nice." . . .

She often said, and honestly believed, that she was not prejudiced—well, except in the case of Italian mobsters and drunken Irish loafers and stupid Poles and snooty Yankee Protestants, but then who wasn't? Among the cultural scars left by her early years in convent school was a stereotypical view of "the people who slew Jesus." "On the other hand," she said, always wanting to be fair, "I served some very nice Jewish people in Lake George Restaurant last season. They always chose my station. Real good tippers. But then they had to be, didn't they? To make up for things."

I accompanied her across the street, and Mr. Kane spent half the morning looking up the appropriate welfare agencies and using the pay phone at the back of his shop to call people and make appointments for my mother. . . . I looked up at my mother to give her an "I told you he was nice" look, and I was surprised to see tears standing in her eyes. . . . She confessed [to Mr. Kane] that she didn't know what she would do if somebody didn't help her. . . .

She thanked him for his help, but now there was a chill in her tone. I could tell that she was ashamed of having broken down before this stranger. As we crossed the street back to [the apartment] she told me that I must always be careful with these people.

"But Mr. Kane was just trying to be . . ."

"They have a way of worming things out of you."

"He wasn't worming any—"

"You just be careful what you tell them, and that's final. Period!"

Later that month, when we were able to begin paying something against our slate, my mother felt vindicated in her mistrust of "these people." She discovered that Mr. Kane had charged her a nickel for each call he made on her behalf. I explained that this was only fair because he had put a nickel into the slot for each call, but she waved this aside, saying she was sure he made a little something on each call. Why else would he have a phone taking up space in his shop? No, they work every angle, these people. . . .

SOURCE: Trevanian (2005). *The Crazy Ladies of Pearl Street,* pp. 31–33. New York: Crown Books. Copyright © 2005 by Trevanian. Used by permission of Crown Publishers, a division of Random House, Inc.

American Dilemma. We learn norms of fairness and justice along with norms that condone or even demand unequal treatment based on group membership. Typically, people develop more than one attitude about other groups, and these multiple attitudes are not set in concrete. They can change from time to time and place to place, depending on the situation and a variety of other variables. The same point could be made about other attitudes besides prejudice; people have an array of attitudes, beliefs, and values about any particular subject, and some of them are mutually contradictory.

Recent Trends in Prejudice

Is prejudice declining in the United States? We will consider two answers to the question. First, we will focus on what we will call "traditional" prejudice: the blatant, overt feelings and ideas that have characterized American prejudice virtually from the birth of the nation. Surveys and public opinion polls show that this type of prejudice is losing strength. We also examine some possible causes of the decline in traditional prejudice.

Second, we will deal with a body of research that argues that prejudice is not so much declining as it is changing in form. Blatant prejudice has become "politically incorrect," and people have responded by developing more subtle, less obvious (but still very consequential) ways to express their antipathy for other groups.

Traditional Prejudice: Changing Attitudes, Rising Education, and Increasing Contact

Research has left little doubt that traditional prejudice in the United States is declining. We have already seen evidence of a decline in the research conducted at Princeton University that demonstrated that the willingness to stereotype minority groups had declined over a 35-year period. Also, there has been a decline in social distance scale scores since the 1920s, indicating less perceived social distance between groups and (presumably) less prejudice.

Further evidence of declining prejudice comes from public opinion polls. Surveys measuring prejudice have been administered to representative samples of U.S. citizens since the early 1940s, and these polls document a consistent decrease in support for prejudicial statements, as the data in Exhibit 3.5 indicate.

In 1942, the huge majority—a little more than 70%—of white Americans thought that black and white children should attend different schools. Forty years later, in 1982, support for separate schools had dropped to less than 10%. Similarly, support for the right of white people to maintain separate neighborhoods declined from 65% in 1942 to 18% in the early 1990s. In more recent decades, the percentage of white respondents who support laws against interracial marriage decreased from almost 40% in the early 1970s to about 10% in 2002, and the percentage that believe that blacks are inferior fell from 26% to 8% between the early 1970s and 2006.

The overall trend is unmistakable: There has been a dramatic decline in support for prejudiced statements since World War II. In the early 1940s, most white Americans supported prejudiced views. In recent times, only a small minority expresses such views.

Exhibit 3.5 Declining Traditional Prejudice in the United States, 1942–2006 (White Americans Only)

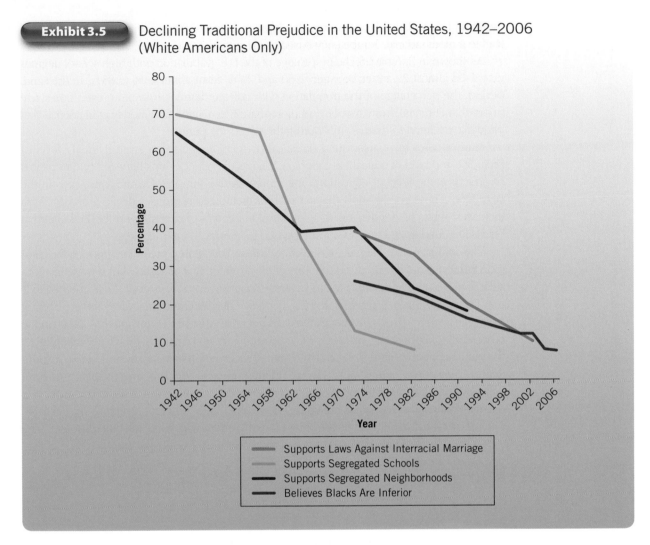

SOURCE: 1942, 1956, 1963: Hyman & Sheatsley (1964); 1972–2006: National Opinion Research Council (1972–2007).

NOTE: Results are accurate to within 3 or 4 percentage points.

Of course, these polls also show that prejudice has not vanished. A percentage of the white population continues to endorse highly prejudicial sentiments and opinions. Remember also that the polls show only what people *say* they feel and think, which might be different from what they truly believe. What changes in the larger society might explain the decline in traditional prejudice?

Education. One possible cause of declining prejudice is that Americans have become much more educated during the time period covered in Exhibit 3.5. Education has frequently been singled out as the most effective cure for prejudice and discrimination. Education, like travel, is said to "broaden one's perspective" and encourage a more sophisticated view of human affairs. People with higher levels of education are more likely to view other people in terms of their competence and abilities and not in terms of physical or ethnic characteristics. In some theories of assimilation (see Chapter 2), education is one of the modernizing forces that will lead to a more rational, competency-based social system.

As shown in Exhibit 3.6, the percentage of the U.S. population with high school degrees increased almost 2½ times between 1950 and 2005, from about 34% to 85%. In the same period, the percentage of the population with college degrees rose at an even faster rate (more than 4 times), from about 6% to more than 27%. Could it be merely coincidental that prejudice declined so dramatically during the same time period?

Many studies have also found statistical correlations between an individual's level of prejudice and level of education. Exhibit 3.7 shows the relationships between two measures of prejudice and level of education for a representative sample of white Americans in the year 2006. These graphs show that support for prejudiced responses declines as education increases. White respondents with less education express greater support for the belief that blacks are inferior, and they are more opposed to interracial intermarriage.

The correlation between increased education and decreased prejudice supports the common wisdom that education is the enemy of (and antidote to) prejudice, but we need to consider some caveats and qualifications before we come to any conclusions. First, correlation is not the same thing as causation, and just because education and prejudice change together over time and are statistically associated does not prove that one is causing the change in the other. Perhaps people are still highly prejudiced and are simply hiding their true feelings from the public opinion pollsters. Second, the limited set of possible responses offered to respondents (for example, "agree" or "disagree") might not record the full range, subtlety, or complexity of people's feelings. People typically have many attitudes about a subject, especially one as emotionally charged as prejudice. As we have seen, different situations may activate different sets of attitudes, and public opinion surveys may evoke more tolerant responses. The

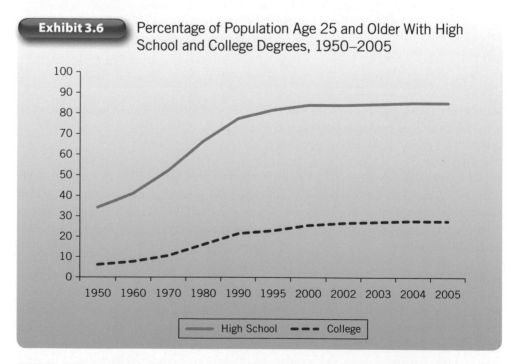

Exhibit 3.6 Percentage of Population Age 25 and Older With High School and College Degrees, 1950–2005

SOURCE: 1950: U.S. Bureau of the Census (1997); 1960–2005: U.S. Bureau of the Census (2007a, p. 143).

INTRODUCTION TO THE STUDY OF MINORITY GROUPS

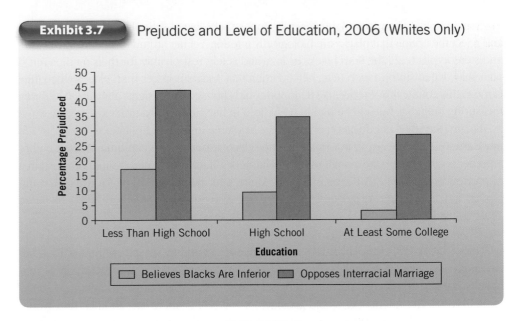

Exhibit 3.7   Prejudice and Level of Education, 2006 (Whites Only)

SOURCE: National Opinion Research Council (1972–2007).

more educated are particularly likely to be aware of the "correct" responses and more likely to express socially acceptable opinions. The bottom line is that it is hard to determine how much of the apparent reduction in prejudice has been genuine and how much of it is due to conformity to the prevailing and fashionable attitudes of the day (see Jackman, 1978, 1981; Jackman & Muha, 1984; Smith & Seelbach, 1987; Weil, 1985).

As I have suggested, part of the problem here may lie in the way questions are asked in surveys. Open-ended interviews, in which people are able to express themselves in more detail and in their own words, result in a somewhat different picture of American prejudice. In this format, a general topic is presented to respondents, who are then encouraged to speak their mind and not simply select "agree" or "disagree." For example, Gallagher (2001), whose study was mentioned in Chapter 2, conducted in-depth, open-ended interviews. Although respondents were not asked directly about their prejudices, their true feelings for other groups often emerged in the conversation. Consider the responses of Shannon, a white female, when she was asked why she believed that blacks see racial inequality in situations in which she does not:

> I think that the black people have a very hard time accepting that they are not suc-
> ceeding because they don't want to work, when they could work and they could
> succeed just like—I mean look at all the black people who have succeeded in this
> world—even in this country—how can they say that we're like, suppressing them in
> any way. I mean look at all the ways you can succeed. I think that they are blaming
> the wrong people and I think that the Korean and the Chinese, I don't think they do
> that.... I mean when we came to this country no one had anything—I mean they
> [Asians] had less than the blacks when they came over to this country, way less. And
> look at where this country has come. They [blacks] can work just as hard and suc-
> ceed way above their expectations if they just stopped and looked at themselves.
> (Gallagher, 2001)

Someone like Shannon might sincerely oppose segregated schools and neighborhoods and reject the notion that blacks are biologically inferior. Yet her attitudes mix negative views and stereotypes (e.g., she sees blacks as lazy and solely responsible for their own poverty) with selective misinformation (e.g., her assertion that Asians had less than blacks when they came to this country). Someone like Shannon could choose all the "right" answers to a survey measuring prejudice but still be highly prejudiced in her views and attitudes.

Finally, the effect of education on prejudice has some important limitations. People evade unpleasant or disconcerting information, and selective perception can limit or even nullify arguments contrary to one's point of view. Thus, even highly educated people can sustain a racist view of the world. For example, David Duke, a former leader of the Ku Klux Klan and a politician, holds a master's degree in history (see also Selznik & Steinberg, 1969; Stember, 1961; Williams, 1964).

Contact Between Groups. Like education, contact and increased communication between groups have often been suggested as remedies for prejudice, misunderstandings, and hostile race and ethnic relations. A generic statement of this point of view might read something like this: "If only people would get together and really talk to one another, they would see that we're all the same, all human beings with hopes and dreams," and so on, and so forth. Such sentiments are common, and a number of organizations at all levels of society are devoted to opening and sustaining a dialogue between groups. How effective are such efforts? Does increased contact reduce prejudice? If so, under what conditions?

First of all, contact between groups is not, in and of itself, an immediate or automatic antidote for prejudice. Contact can have a variety of outcomes and can either reduce or increase prejudice, depending on the nature of the situation. When contact occurs under conditions in which groups have unequal status, such as during American slavery or segregation, prejudice

Photo 3.3

Contact across group lines in the classroom can fulfill all four conditions of the contact hypothesis.

© Ron Chapple Stock/Corbis.

is likely to be reinforced, not reduced. On the other hand, certain forms of intergroup contact do seem to reduce prejudice.

One theory that addresses the relationship between contact and prejudice is the **equal status contact hypothesis**. This theory specifies the conditions under which intergroup contact can reduce prejudice: *Intergroup contact will tend to reduce prejudice when four conditions are filled: The groups must have (a) equal status and (b) common goals and must (c) interact intensively in noncompetitive, cooperative tasks and (d) have the active endorsement of authority figures* (Pettigrew, 1998, pp. 66–67). Each of the four conditions is crucial to the reduction of prejudice.

1. *Equal Status.* Only in situations in which all groups have equal resources and prestige are people likely to view one another as individuals, not as representatives of their respective groups. When the people involved in intergroup contacts are unequal in status, they are more likely to sustain or even intensify their prejudice. During slavery, for example, there was a high volume of contact across racial lines because of the nature of agricultural work. These interactions between blacks and whites were conducted in a context of massive inequality, however, and the contact did not encourage (to say the least) an honest and open sharing of views. Under the system of segregation that followed slavery, the frequency of interracial contact actually declined as blacks and whites were separated into unequal communities. By World War II, segregation was so complete that whites and blacks hardly saw each other except in situations in which blacks were clearly lower in status (Woodward, 1974, p. 118).

2. *Common Goals.* The most effective contact situations for reducing prejudice are those in which members of different groups come together in a single group with a common goal. Examples of such settings include athletic teams working for victories; study groups of students helping each other prepare for tests; and community groups organized to build a playground, combat crime, raise money for cancer research, and so forth.

3. *Intergroup Cooperation and Intensive Interaction.* If contact is to reduce prejudice, it must occur in an atmosphere free from threat or competition between groups. When intergroup contact is motivated by competition for scarce resources, prejudice tends to increase and may even be accompanied by hatred and violence. Recall the Robber's Cave experiment and the levels of prejudice that were manufactured in that situation. If contact is to have a moderating effect on attitudes, it must occur in a setting where there is nothing at stake, no real (or imagined) resource that might be allocated differently as a result of the contact. If people are bound together by cooperative behavior across group lines and are motivated to achieve a common goal, they are much more likely to come to regard one another as individuals, not as caricatures or stereotypical representatives of their groups.

Furthermore, the contact has to be more than superficial. The situation must last for a significant length of time, and the participants must be fully involved. Standing next to each other at a bus stop or eating at adjoining tables in a restaurant does not meet this criterion; people of different groups must deal with each other face-to-face and on a personal level.

4. *Support of Authority, Law, or Custom.* The greater the extent to which contact takes place with strong support from authority figures (politicians, teachers, ministers, etc.) and is supported by moral codes and values, the more likely it is to have a positive impact on intergroup attitudes.

One of the most persuasive and interesting illustrations of the contact hypothesis is the Robber's Cave experiment, discussed earlier in this chapter (Sherif et al., 1961). As you recall, rival groups of campers were placed in competitive situations and became prejudiced as a result. It was not until the researchers created some situations in which the rival groups had to actively cooperate to achieve some common goals that prejudice began to decline. Contact, in and of itself, did not affect intergroup attitudes. Only contact that required the goal-oriented cooperation of equals in status reduced the prejudice that the staff had created through competition.

The Robber's Cave experiment provides dramatic support for the contact hypothesis, but we must be cautious in evaluating this evidence. The experiment was conducted in a "pristine" environment in which the campers had no prior acquaintance with one another and brought no backlog of grievances and no traditions of prejudice to the situation. The study illustrates and supports the contact hypothesis but cannot prove the theory. For additional evidence, we turn to everyday life and more realistic intergroup contact situations.

In another classic study, Deutsch and Collins (1951) studied the anti-black prejudices of white residents of public housing projects. This study is significant because Deutsch and Collins were able to eliminate the problem of self-selection. In other studies, participation in the contact situation is typically voluntary. The people who volunteer for experiments in interracial contacts are usually not very prejudiced in the first place or at least are more open to change. Thus, any change in prejudice might be due to the characteristics of the people involved, not to the contact situation itself. By contrast, in the Deutsch and Collins study, some of the white participants were randomly assigned to live close to black families. The participants had no control over their living arrangement and thus were not self-selected for lower prejudice or openness to change.

A total of four public housing projects were studied. In two of the projects, black and white families were assigned to separate buildings or areas. In the remaining two, dwelling units were assigned regardless of race, and black and white families lived next to one another. As a result of proximity, the white subjects in these two housing projects had higher rates of contact with their black neighbors than did the white families assigned to "segregated" units.

The researchers interviewed the mothers of the white families and found that those living in the integrated projects were less racially prejudiced and much more likely to interact with their African American neighbors than those living in the segregated setting. Deutsch and Collins (1951) concluded that the higher volume of interracial contact had led to lower prejudice.

More recent studies have been based on surveys administered to large, representative samples of black and white Americans and have generally supported the contact hypothesis. Sigelman and Welch (1993), for example, report that the professional research literature is generally consistent with the predictions of the contact hypothesis (Sigelman & Welch, 1993, p. 793). (For more on the contact hypothesis, see Aberson, Shoemaker, & Tomolillo, 2004; Damico & Sparks, 1986; Dixon, 2006; Dixon & Rosenbaum, 2004; Ellison & Powers, 1994; Forbes, 1997; Katz & Taylor, 1988; Miller & Brewer, 1984; Pettigrew, 1998; Powers & Ellison, 1995; Smith, 1994; Wittig & Grant-Thompson, 1998; Yancey, 1999, 2007).

Recent Trends in Intergroup Contact.

Since the 1950s, concerted attempts have been made to reduce discrimination against minority groups in virtually every American social institution. In Gordon's (1964) terms, these efforts increased structural assimilation or integration (see Chapter 2) and provided opportunities for dominant and minority group members to associate with one another. Compared with the days of slavery and segregation, there is considerably more contact across group lines today in schools and colleges, workplaces, neighborhoods, and social gatherings.

Some of this increased contact has reduced prejudice. In other instances, contact situations that seem on paper to be likely to reduce prejudice have had no effect or have actually made matters worse. For example, schools and universities across the country have been officially integrated for decades, but these situations do not always lead to increased acceptance and the growth of friendships across group boundaries. The groups involved—whites, African Americans, Latinos, Asians, or Native Americans—sometimes organize themselves in a way that minimizes face-to-face interaction and contact across the social dividing lines. To illustrate, you need only visit the cafeteria of many university campuses during mealtime and observe how the seating pattern follows group lines. (For a view of intraracial interactions on racially diverse campuses, see Cowan, 2005).

The contact hypothesis offers a possible explanation for this pattern of separation within integration. The student body in many schools and colleges is organized along lines that meet some, but not all, of the conditions necessary for a contact situation to lower prejudice. Even when students from the various racial and ethnic groups are roughly equal in status, they do not engage in many cooperative activities that cross group lines. Classrooms themselves are typically competitive and individualistic; students compete for grades and recognition on a one-by-one basis. Cooperation among students (either within or across groups) is not required and is not, in fact, particularly encouraged. The group separation and the lack of opportunities for cooperation often extend beyond the classroom into clubs, sports, and other activities (for an application of the contact hypothesis to high school sports teams, see Brown, Brown, Jackson, Sellers, & Manuel, 2003).

The separation might be reduced and positive contacts increased by encouraging cooperative activities between members of different groups—for example, by imitating the plumbing "emergency" fabricated during the Robber's Cave experiment. One successful attempt to increase cooperation and positive contact was made using a cooperative learning technique called the **jigsaw method** (Aronson & Gonzalez, 1988).

In this experiment, the students in a fifth-grade class were divided into groups. A certain learning task was divided into separate parts, like a jigsaw puzzle. Researchers ensured that each jigsaw group included both dominant and minority group children. Each student in the jigsaw group was responsible for learning one part of the lesson and then teaching his or her piece to the other students. Everyone was tested on all of the pieces, not just his or her own. Each study group needed to make sure that everyone had all of the information necessary to pass the test. This goal could be achieved only through the cooperation of all members of the group.

Unlike typical classroom activities, the jigsaw method satisfies all the characteristics for a positive contact experience: Students of equal status are engaged in a cooperative project in which mutual interdependence is essential for the success of all. As Aronson and Gonzalez point out, the students do not need to be idealistic, altruistic, or motivated by a commitment

The Contact Hypothesis and European Prejudice

Much of the research on the contact hypothesis has been conducted in the United States. How will the theory fare in other societies? Rather well,

according to sociologist Lauren McLaren (2003). Professor McLaren used data from representative samples of citizens drawn from 17 European societies to study anti-immigrant sentiment.

As has the United States, European nations have experienced a sharp increase in immigration over the past decades, and there is considerable concern about

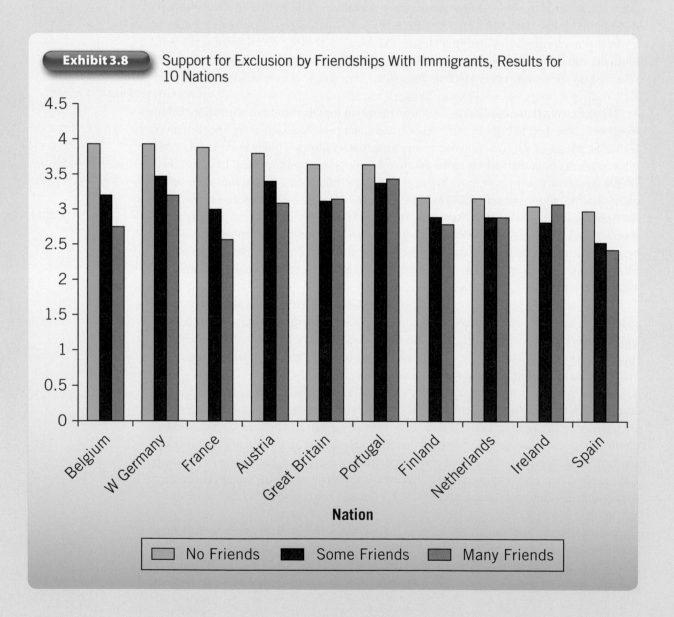

Exhibit 3.8 Support for Exclusion by Friendships With Immigrants, Results for 10 Nations

Nation

☐ No Friends   ■ Some Friends   ▨ Many Friends

the impact of these newcomers. Some Europeans wish to exclude immigrants completely, while others want to help newcomers find their way into their new societies. What social factors might explain these varying responses?

One possibility is that people with greater equal status contacts with immigrants will be more tolerant and less likely to support expulsion. Another possibility is that Europeans who feel the most threatened by immigrants will be the most supportive of exclusion, an idea consistent with theories that link prejudice to group competition. Professor McLaren considered both of these possibilities and used statistical techniques to assess which explanation is more powerful.

Attitudes toward legal immigrants were measured on a 5-point scale that ranged from very open and positive views ("Legal immigrants should be allowed to naturalize") to very negative views ("Immigrants should all be sent back to where they came from"). The higher the score on this scale, the more negative the view.

Equal status contact was measured by a question about whether the respondent had "no, some, or many" friends among immigrant groups, and feelings of threat were measured by two sets of items, one measuring perceived threat to "personal life circumstances" (losing one's job, for example) and one measuring broader threats to the society (e.g., the perception that immigrants increase the unemployment rate) and culture (the view that immigrant religions threaten "our way of life") (McLaren, 2003, p. 919).

McLaren found significant differences in support for expulsion by the number of immigrant friends in 16 of the 17 nations tested (the exception was Greece). Some illustrative results for 10 of the 17 nations are shown in Exhibit 3.8. For each nation, the average score for the respondents with "no friends" (the green bar in Exhibit 3.8) was higher than the average score for respondents with "some friends" (blue bar), and the latter score was generally higher than the score for people with "many friends" (orange bar). This pattern is very (but not perfectly) consistent with the predictions of the equal status contact hypothesis.

Professor McLaren also found that support for expulsion increased with the sense of threat felt by the respondent. Which was stronger, sense of threat or degree of contact? Contact still reduced support for exclusion even among those who felt a high level of threat, and the two factors had roughly equal strength in predicting support for expulsion. Thus, our confidence in the equal status contact hypothesis is increased by its strong performance in a non-U.S. arena.

to racial justice for this method to work. Rather, the students are motivated by pure self-interest; without the help of every member of their group, they cannot pass the test (Aronson & Gonzalez, 1988, p. 307).

As we would expect under true equal status contact, the results of the jigsaw method included reductions in prejudice (Aronson & Gonzalez, 1988, p. 307; see also Aronson & Patnoe, 1997).

Limitations of the Contact Hypothesis. The contact hypothesis is supported by evidence from a variety of sources. However, it would be a mistake to conclude that all that is necessary to further reduce prejudice is to contrive more equal status contact situations. In many cases, the reduction in prejudice resulting from contact is situation specific; that is, the changed attitudes in one situation (e.g., the workplace) do not necessarily generalize to other situations (e.g., neighborhoods). Both prejudice and discrimination are situational, and stereotypes can be astonishingly resilient perceptual categories. Nonetheless, although this strategy is not a panacea, equal status cooperative contact does seem to have an effect in reducing prejudice and discrimination.

Modern Racism

A number of scholars reject the idea that prejudice in the United States has declined and argue that it is simply changing forms. They have been investigating new forms of prejudice variously called **symbolic**, **color-blind**, or **modern racism**. Whatever the label, this form of prejudice is a more subtle, complex, and indirect way of expressing negative feelings toward minority groups and opposition to change in dominant-minority relations (see Bobo, 1988, 2001; Bonilla-Silva, 2001, 2006; Kinder & Sears, 1981; Kluegel & Smith, 1982; McConahy, 1986; Sears, 1988).

People affected by modern racism have negative feelings (the affective aspect of prejudice) toward minority groups but reject the idea of genetic or biological inferiority and do not think in terms of the traditional stereotypes. Instead, their prejudicial feelings are expressed indirectly and subtly. The attitudes that define modern racism tend to be consistent with some tenets of the traditional assimilation perspective discussed in Chapter 2, especially human capital theory and the "Protestant Ethic": the traditional American value system that stresses individual responsibility and the importance of hard work. Specifically, modern racism assumes the following:

- There is no longer any serious or important racial, ethnic, or religious discrimination in American society.
- Any remaining racial or ethnic inequality is the fault of members of the minority group, who simply are not working hard enough.
- Demands for preferential treatment or affirmative action for minorities are unjustified.
- Minority groups (especially African Americans) have already gotten more than they deserve (Sears & Henry, 2003).

Modern racism tends to "blame the victim" and place the responsibility for change and improvements on the minority groups, not on the larger society.

To illustrate the difference between traditional and modern racism, consider the results of a recent public opinion survey administered to a representative sample of Americans (National Opinion Research Council, 1972–2007). Respondents were asked to choose from among four explanations of why black people, on the average, have "worse jobs, income, and housing than white people." Respondents could choose as many explanations as they wanted.

One explanation, consistent with traditional or overt anti-black prejudice, attributes racial inequality to the genetic or biological inferiority of African Americans ("The differences are mainly because blacks have less inborn ability to learn"). Only 8% of the white respondents chose this explanation. A second explanation attributes continuing racial inequality to discrimination and a third to the lack of opportunity for an education. Of white respondents, 31% chose the former, and 44% chose the latter.

A fourth explanation, consistent with modern racism (and with the views of Shannon, whose interview was quoted earlier), attributes racial inequality to a lack of effort by African Americans ("The differences are because most blacks just don't have the motivation or willpower to pull themselves up out of poverty"). Of the white respondents, 50% chose this explanation, the most popular of the four.

Thus, the survey found support for the idea that racial inequality was the result of discrimination and lack of educational opportunities, views that are consistent with the analysis presented in this book, and relatively little support for traditional anti-black prejudice based on genetic or biological stereotypes. However, the single most widely endorsed explanation was that the root of the problem of continuing racial inequality lies in the African American community, not the society as a whole. Modern racism asserts that African Americans could solve their problems themselves but are not willing to do so.

What makes this view an expression of prejudice? Besides blaming the victim, it deflects attention away from centuries of oppression and continuing institutional discrimination in modern society. It stereotypes African Americans and encourages the expression of negative attitudes against them (but without invoking the traditional image of innate inferiority).

Researchers have consistently found that modern racism is correlated with opposition to policies and programs intended to reduce racial inequality (Bobo, 2001, p. 292). In the survey summarized earlier, for example, respondents who blamed continuing racial inequality on the lack of motivation or willpower of blacks—the "modern racists"—were the least likely to support government help for African Americans and affirmative action programs. In fact, as Exhibit 3.9 shows, the modern racists were less supportive of these programs than were the traditional racists (those who chose the "inborn ability" explanation)!

In the view of many researchers, modern racism has taken the place of traditional or overt prejudice. If this view is correct, the "report card" on progress in the reduction of racial hostility in the United States must be rather mixed. On one hand, we should not understate the importance of the fading of blatant, overt prejudice. On the other hand, we cannot ignore the evidence that anti-black prejudice has changed in form rather than declined in degree.

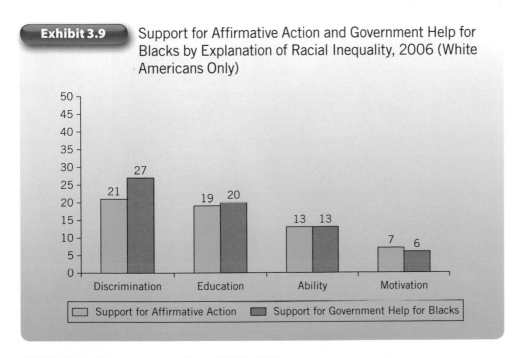

Exhibit 3.9 Support for Affirmative Action and Government Help for Blacks by Explanation of Racial Inequality, 2006 (White Americans Only)

SOURCE: National Opinion Research Council (1972–2007).

Subtle and diffuse prejudice is probably preferable to the blunt and vicious variety, but it should not be mistaken for its demise. In fact, there is considerable reason to believe that "old-fashioned," blatant racism lives on and in some ways is thriving. This possibility is considered in the last section of this chapter.

Has Sexism Modernized?

Has sexism, like racism, evolved into more "modern" (more subtle and indirect) forms? A number of researchers have been investigating this possibility and have found substantial similarities between modern racism and sexism. Also, they have compiled evidence that modern sexism is related to lack of support for (or interest in) women's rights, gender equality, and "women's issues" (e.g., sexual harassment).

Modern sexism, in parallel to modern racism, asserts that

- there is no longer any serious discrimination against women,
- women (specifically, feminists) are pushing their agenda too hard, and
- programs such as affirmative action are unwarranted and give women unfair advantages over men (Swim & Cohen, 1997, p. 105; Swim, Mallett, & Stangor, 2004; Tougas, Rupert, & Joly, 1995, p. 843).

The modern sexist, as does the modern racist, has negative feelings but expresses them indirectly and symbolically. The old-fashioned sexist believes that gender inequality is natural and even desirable; the modern sexist denies the existence of sexual discrimination and inequality and trivializes or dismisses the concerns of women. Modern sexism is harder to detect and measure, in part because it is often expressed in the language of equality and fairness. For example, the modern sexist might express opposition to affirmative action programs for women by arguing that such programs are unfair to men rather than by invoking notions of female inferiority or incompetence (Beaton, Tougas, & Joly, 1996).

Before considering modern sexism further, we should pause to address the assertion that gender inequality is a thing of the past in U.S. society. In the chapters to come, we will present evidence that documents the lower (often, much lower) status of female minority group members. Here, we will compare the overall status of all men and women in the U.S., but because of space considerations, we will consider only inequalities of income. Exhibit 3.10 shows median income for full-time, year-round workers of both sexes and documents a persistent, though shrinking, gender gap. In 1955, women earned about 65% of what men earned. In the years following, this percentage actually declined and then began to rise in the 1980s. By 2005, the gender gap in income had shrunk, but women were still earning only about 79% of what men earned. Contrary to the assertion that the United States has achieved gender equality, these results document the persistence of a substantial (though declining) gender gap in income.

Exhibit 3.10   Income for Full-Time, Year-Round Workers by Gender, 1955–2005 (in 2005 Dollars per Year)

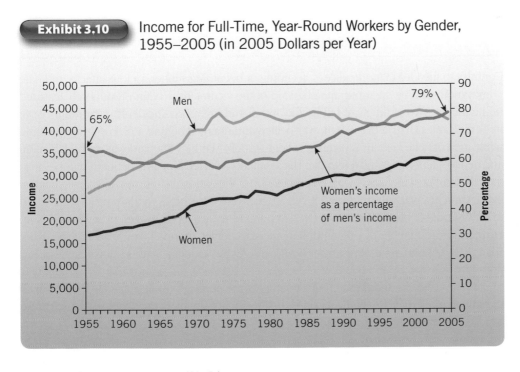

SOURCE: U.S. Bureau of the Census (2007c).

Why do women continue to earn less than men do? This is a complex question that would require the analysis of many factors (e.g., the changing American economy and the career choices made by men and women) to answer fully. However, research findings suggest that modern sexism is one important factor in the continued maintenance of gender inequality. The studies indicate that modern sexists are less likely to perceive instances of sexist discrimination and more likely to dismiss complaints of sexism as trivial (for example, see Barreto & Ellemers, 2005; Cameron, 2001; Swim et al., 2004). Also, modern sexists were less likely to identify instances of sexist discrimination and more likely to use sexist language. Another study (Swim & Cohen, 1997) examined reactions to several situations involving charges of sexual harassment (e.g., an offer to trade career assistance for sexual favors and a work situation in which male employees displayed sexually explicit photos or made sexual comments to female employees). The subjects in the study, all male, were asked to judge the seriousness of these various scenarios. Subjects who scored higher on modern sexism were less likely to classify the incidents as sexual harassment, had less sympathy for victims, were more likely to see the female victims as overreacting, and were less likely to recommend harsh punishments for perpetrators.

Modern sexism shapes perceptions and attitudes, desensitizes people to the damage that can be caused by sexually hostile work environments, and predisposes them to be unsympathetic to programs designed to reduce gender inequality. Thus, gender attitudes appear to be becoming "modernized" along with racial prejudice. Gender inequality remains a pervasive reality in modern American society and is perpetuated in part by attitudes of modern sexism that allow people to express opposition to the changing role of women without appearing to be blatantly or overtly sexist.

Hate Crimes

Contrary to the idea that prejudice is declining or becoming subtler, vicious attacks and hate crimes motivated by the group membership of the victims have been prominently featured in the media. Two of the most publicized and disturbing recent incidents occurred in 1998. In Texas, James Byrd, a black man, was beaten and dragged behind a pickup truck by three white men until he died. In Wyoming, college student Matthew Shepard was robbed, beaten, and tied to a fence post and left to die. His assailants selected him as a victim in part because they thought he was gay. Other hate crimes across the nation include assaults, arson against black churches, vandalism of Jewish synagogues, cross burnings, nooses prominently tied to office doors of black university professors, and other acts of intimidation and harassment. Furthermore, a number of violent, openly racist extremist groups—skinheads, the Ku Klux Klan (KKK), White Aryan Resistance (WAR), and Aryan Nations—have achieved widespread notoriety.

Do these attacks and these groups contradict the public opinion polls? Do they balance the shift to modern racism with an opposite shift to blatant, violent racism? What causes these attacks? What are the implications?

As we will see in chapters to come, racial violence, hate crimes, and extremist racist groups are hardly new to the United States. Violence between whites and nonwhites began in the earliest days of this society (e.g., conflicts with Native Americans, the kidnapping and enslavement of Africans) and has continued, in one form or another, to the present. Contemporary racist attacks and hate crimes, in all their manifestations, have deep roots in the American past.

Also, racist and extremist groups are no strangers to American history. The KKK, for example, was founded almost 150 years ago, shortly after the Civil War, and has since played a significant role in local and state politics and in everyday life at various times and places—and not just in the South. During the turbulent 1920s, the Klan reached what was probably the height of its popularity. It had a membership in the millions and was said to openly control many U.S. senators, governors, and local politicians.

Photo 3.5

Many modern hate groups maintain a presence on the Internet and offer merchandise, such as this T-shirt, in addition to their views.

© Les Stone/Sygma/Corbis.

Are hate crimes increasing or decreasing? It's difficult to answer this question, though the FBI has been collecting and compiling information on hate crimes for over a decade. Not all localities report these incidents or classify them in the same way, and perhaps more important, not all hate crimes are reported. Thus, the actual volume of hate crimes may be many times greater than the "official" rate compiled by the FBI (for a recent analysis, see Fears, 2007a).

Keeping these sharp limitations in mind, here is some of what is known. Exhibit 3.11 reports the breakdown of hate crimes in 2006 and shows that most incidents were motivated by race. In the great majority (66%) of these racial cases, blacks were the target group. Most of the religious incidents (66%) involved Jewish victims, and most of the anti-ethnic attacks were against Hispanics (59%). The great majority (63%) of the attacks motivated by the sexual orientation of the victims were directed against male homosexuals (FBI, 2007).

Exhibit 3.12 shows the number of hate crimes by the group membership of victims for a 10-year period. In all four cases, the number of crimes has decreased at least slightly, and especially so for racially motivated incidents. However, because our information on these crimes is so partial and untrustworthy, it is best not to make any hard-and-fast conclusions.

Hate crimes and hate groups are not limited to a particular region. The Southern Poverty Law Center (SPLC) tracks hate groups and hate crimes around the nation and estimates that there were 751 hate groups (defined as groups that "have beliefs or practices that attack or malign an entire class of people, typically for their immutable characteristics") active in the United States in 2006 (SPLC, 2007). These groups include the KKK, various skinhead and white power groups, and black groups such as the Nation of Islam. The SPLC maintains a map at its Web site showing the location of the known hate groups (see Exhibit 3.13). The map shows that although the greatest concentration is in the Southeast, Texas, and California, hate groups are spread across the nation and can be found in all but two states (North and South Dakota).

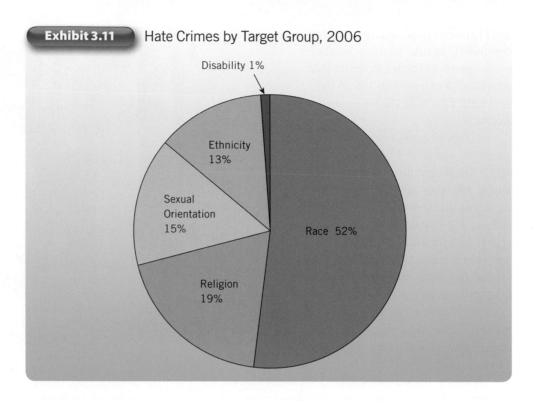

Exhibit 3.11 Hate Crimes by Target Group, 2006

Disability 1%

Ethnicity 13%

Sexual Orientation 15%

Religion 19%

Race 52%

SOURCE: FBI (2007).

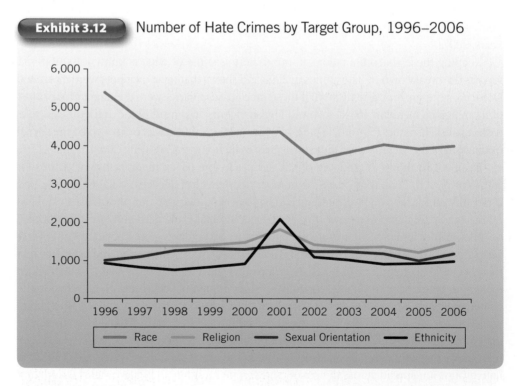

Exhibit 3.12 Number of Hate Crimes by Target Group, 1996–2006

Race   Religion   Sexual Orientation   Ethnicity

SOURCE: FBI (2007).

Exhibit 3.13 Distribution of Hate Groups

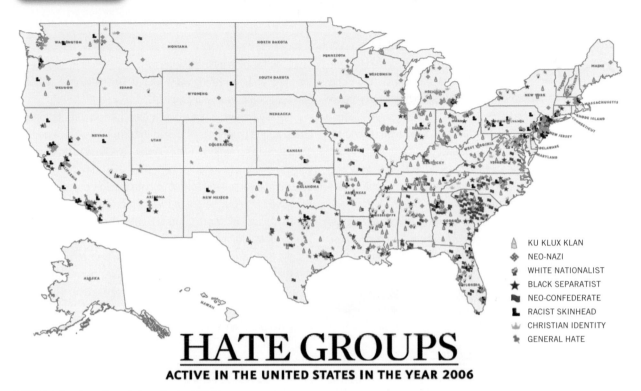

KU KLUX KLAN
NEO-NAZI
WHITE NATIONALIST
BLACK SEPARATIST
NEO-CONFEDERATE
RACIST SKINHEAD
CHRISTIAN IDENTITY
GENERAL HATE

HATE GROUPS
ACTIVE IN THE UNITED STATES IN THE YEAR 2006

SOURCE: Southern Poverty Law Center (2007).

Photo 3.6

This lynching took place in the central square of a town in Indiana in 1930.

© Bettmann/Corbis.

The Dynamics of Racial Hatred

C. P. Ellis was born in North Carolina in the 1930s to a poor white family. When his father passed away, he had to drop out of the eighth grade and take the first in a long line of hard, poorly paid jobs. The frustration of trying to support himself and his family finally motivated him to join the KKK. During the 1950s and 1960s, he became deeply involved in Klan activity and participated in many confrontations with the civil rights movement, some of them verging on violence. Eventually, however, his involvement led him to an unexpected metamorphosis. How many different theories of prejudice from Chapter 3 can be applied to Ellis's memoir (as transcribed by Studs Terkel, 1992)?

The Making (and Unmaking) of a Klansman

C. P. Ellis

All my life, I had work, never a day without work, worked all the overtime I could get and still could not survive financially. I began to say there's somethin' wrong with this country. . . .

They say to abide by the law, go to church, do right and live for the Lord, and everything will work out. But it didn't work out. It just kept gettin' worse and worse.

I really began to get bitter. I didn't know who to blame. I tried to find somebody. I began to blame it on black people. I had to hate somebody. Hatin' America is hard to do because you can't see it to hate it. You gotta have something to look at. The natural person for me to hate would be black people, because my father before me was a member of the Klan.

[A group of men I knew] said they were with the Klan. . . . Would I be interested? Boy, that was an opportunity I really looked forward to! To be part of somethin'! I joined the Klan, went from member to chaplain, from chaplain to vice-president, from vice-president to president. The title is exalted cyclops. . . .

It disturbs me when people . . . are so critical of individual Klansmen. The majority of 'em are low-income whites. People who really don't have a part in something. They have been shut out as well as blacks. Some are not very well educated either. Just like myself. . . .

Maybe they've had a bitter experience in this life and they had to hate somebody. So the natural person to hate would be the black person. He's beginnin' to come up, he's beginnin' to learn to read and start votin' and run for political office. Here are white people who are supposed to be superior to them, and we're shut out. . . .

This was the time when the civil rights movement was really beginnin' to peak. The blacks were beginnin' to demonstrate and picket downtown stores. I never will forget some black lady I hated with a purple passion. Ann Atwater. Every time I'd go downtown, she'd be leadin' a boycott. How I hated—pardon the expression, I don't use it much now—how I just hated that black nigger. . . . Her and I had some pretty close confrontations. . . .

[A series of meetings was organized to attempt to reconcile blacks and whites and focus on problems in the schools. Ellis, as a representative of the Klan, was invited to attend. He went reluctantly but gradually became committed to the peacemaking efforts.] The third night, after they elected all the committees, they went to elect [co-chairpersons. Ellis was nominated] . . . and, of all things, they nominated Ann Atwater, the big old fat black gal that I just hated with a purple passion, as co-chairman. . . . Finally, I agreed to accept it, 'cause at that point, I was tired of fightin', either for survival or against black people or against Jews or against Catholics. . . . A Klansman and a militant black woman, co-chairmen of a school committee. It was impossible. . . .

[Both Ellis and Atwater experienced intense pressure from their respective constituencies to dissolve their relationship.] One day, Ann and I went back to school and we sat down. We began to talk and just reflect. . . . I began to see, here we are, two people from the far ends of the fence, havin' identical problems, except her bein' black and me bein' white. From that moment on, I tell ya, that gal and I worked together good. I began to love that girl, really.

SOURCE: Terkel, Studs (1992). *Race,* pp. 271–276. New York: New Press.

What causes hate crimes and extremist groups? One possible explanation for at least some hate crimes is that they are fueled by perceived threats, frustration and fear, and anger and scapegoating. Some white Americans believe that minority groups are threatening their position in the society and making unfair progress at their expense. They feel threatened by what they perceive to be an undeserved rise in the status of minority groups and fear that they may lose their jobs, incomes, neighborhoods, and schools to what they see as "inferior" groups.

Given the nature of American history, it is logical to suppose that the white Americans who feel most threatened and angriest would be those toward the bottom of the stratification system: lower-class and working-class whites. It seems significant, for example, that the three murderers of James Byrd were unemployed ex-convicts with low levels of education and few prospects for economic success (at least in the conventional economy). On a broader scale, there is evidence that males from these classes commit the bulk of the hate crimes and are the primary sources of membership for the extremist racist groups (Schafer & Navarro, 2004). In the eyes of the perpetrators, attacks on minorities may represent attempts to preserve status and privilege. These ideas are illustrated in Narrative Portrait 2 in this chapter.

The connection between social class and hate crimes might also reflect some broad structural changes in the economy. The United States has been shifting from an industrial, manufacturing economy to a postindustrial, information-processing economy since the mid-20th century. We will examine this transition in depth in later chapters, but here, we will note that this economic change has meant a decline in the supply of secure, well-paying, blue-collar jobs. Many manufacturing jobs have been lost to other nations with cheaper workforces; others have been lost to automation and mechanization. The tensions resulting from the decline in desirable employment opportunities for people with lower levels of education have been exacerbated by industry downsizing, increasing inequality in the class structure, and rising costs of living. These economic forces have squeezed the middle and lower ranges of the dominant group's class system, creating considerable pressure and frustration, some of which may be expressed by scapegoating directed at immigrants and minority groups.

The idea that many hate crimes involve scapegoating is also supported by the spontaneous, unplanned, and highly emotional nature of these crimes. Consider how these themes of economic dislocation and scapegoating are illustrated in the murder of Vincent Chin, a frequently cited example of an American hate crime. Chin, who was Chinese American, was enjoying a final bachelor fling in a bar in a working-class Detroit neighborhood in June 1982 when he was confronted by two drunken autoworkers who blamed Japanese auto companies for their unemployment. Making no distinction between Chinese and Japanese (or American and Japanese), the autoworkers attacked and murdered Chin with a baseball bat. Apparently, any Asian would have served as a scapegoat for their resentment and anger (Levin & McDevitt, 1993, p. 58; see also U.S. Commission on Civil Rights, 1992, pp. 25–26).

Several studies also support the idea that hate crimes are motivated at least in part by scapegoating. One study found that at the state level, the rate of hate crimes increased as unemployment rose and as the percentage of the population between 15 and 19 years old increased. Also, the rate fell as average wages rose (Medoff, 1999, p. 970; see also Jacobs & Wood, 1999). Another study, based on county-level data gathered in South Carolina, found a correlation between white-on-black hate crimes and economic competition (D'Alessio,

Stolzenberg, & Eitle, 2002). Finally, Arab Americans were victimized by a rash of violent attacks after September 11, 2001 (Ibish, 2003). These patterns are exactly what one would expect if the perpetrators of hate crimes tended to be young men motivated by a sense of threat and economic distress.

The Sociology of Prejudice

The sociological approach to prejudice stresses several points. Prejudice has its origins in competition between groups, and it is more a result of that competition than a cause. It is created at a certain time in history to help mobilize feelings and emotional energy for competition and to rationalize the consignment of a group to minority status. It then is absorbed into the cultural heritage and is passed on to later generations as part of their taken-for-granted world, where it helps to shape their perceptions and reinforce the very group inferiority that was its original cause.

Some additional conclusions and qualifications about prejudice should be noted:

1. Changes in the social environment, rising levels of education, or changing forms of intergroup contact will have relatively little impact on some types of prejudice. Prejudice that is caused by scapegoating or authoritarian personality structures, for example, is motivated by processes internal to the individual and may not respond to changes in the environment. It may be difficult to reduce these types of prejudice and impossible to eliminate them altogether. A more realistic goal might be to discourage their open expression. The greater the extent to which culture, authority figures, and social situations discourage prejudice, the more likely it will be that even people with strong personality needs for prejudice can be turned into prejudiced nondiscriminators, or "timid bigots" (see Exhibit 3.1).

2. Culture-based or "traditional" prejudice can be just as vicious and extreme as personality-based prejudice. This type of prejudice differs not in intensity, but in the extent to which it is resistant to change. A person who has learned to be prejudiced should be more open to change than the authoritarian personality and more responsive to education and contact with members of other groups. To create more "all-weather liberals," situations that encourage or reward prejudice and discrimination must be minimized, and public opinion, the views of community and societal leaders, and the legal code must all promote tolerance. The reduction in overt prejudice over the past five or six decades, documented in Exhibit 3.5, is probably mainly due to a decline in traditional prejudice sparked in large part by antidiscrimination laws and the protests of minority groups.

3. Intergroup conflict produces vicious, even lethal, prejudice and discrimination, but the problems here are inequality and scarce resources, not prejudice. Intergroup rivalries are more likely to be provoked by inequities in the distribution of resources and opportunities than by stereotypes or negative attitudes. Even the most concerted attacks on individual prejudice cannot by themselves eliminate this source of prejudice. Group conflicts and the prejudices they stimulate will continue as long as society is stratified along the lines of race, ethnicity, and gender. Efforts to decrease hostile attitudes without also reducing inequality and exploitative relationships treat the symptoms rather than the disease.

4. Reducing prejudice will not necessarily change the situation of minority groups. The fundamental problems of minority group status are inequality and systems of institutional discrimination and privilege that sustain the advantages of the dominant group. Dominant group prejudice is *a* problem, but it is not *the* problem. Reducing prejudice will not, by itself, eliminate minority group poverty or unemployment or end institutional discrimination in schools or in the criminal justice system.

5. Individual prejudice and discrimination are not the same as racism and institutional discrimination (see Chapter 1), and any one of these variables can change independently of the others. Thus, we should not confuse the recent reductions in overt individual prejudice with the resolution of American minority group problems. Prejudice is only part of the problem and, in many ways, not the most important part.

These points are reflected in some key trends of the past several decades: Ethnic and racial inequalities persist (and may even be increasing) despite the declines in overt prejudice. The verbal rejection of extreme or overt prejudice has been replaced by the subtleties of modern racism combined with an unwillingness to examine the social, political, and economic forces that sustain minority group inequality and institutional discrimination. Unless there are significant changes in the structure of the economy and the distribution of opportunities, we may have reached the limits of tolerance in America.

CURRENT DEBATES

Racial Profiling and Prejudice

Racial profiling is discrimination based on a stereotypical judgment of a person's group membership. The issue has been phrased most commonly in terms of relations between the police and African Americans (e.g., being stopped for "driving while black") but affects most minority groups (e.g., discriminatory treatment of Middle Easterners by airport security personnel). Is racial profiling motivated by prejudice and stereotypical thinking, or is it a reasonable practice based on objective information about the relative threats presented by different groups in society? Are there any circumstances under which it is reasonable to treat people based on their group memberships?

To what extent is racial profiling a matter of taking sensible precautions, and to what extent is it racist oppression?

The selections below present very different answers to these questions. Prosise and Johnson (2004) argue that racial profiling is racial discrimination motivated by stereotypes and reinforced by popular culture in general and by "reality" TV cop shows in particular. Taylor and Whitney (2002), on the other hand, argue that racial profiling—specifically, police behavior toward African Americans—is justified by the relatively higher rate of crime in the African American community.

Racial Profiling Is Motivated by Prejudice and Reinforced by Reality Cop Shows on Television

THEODORE PROSISE AND ANN JOHNSON

For different reasons, "Reality TV" programming has captured the attention of television executives, public audiences, and media scholars.... The media's portrayal of law enforcement and crime tells public audiences about such things as "good and evil," heroes and villains, "morality," and it suggests appropriate societal responses to crime and social problems.... The reality TV [shows] that deal with... crime [blur the line between fact and fiction]... and... may influence how audiences view themselves and their society.

The focus of this study concerns two prominent crime-based reality programs: *Cops* and *World's Wildest Police Videos (WWPV),* both of which boast of representing the reality of police-suspect interaction.... The edited segments in *Cops* and *WWPV,* accompanied by narratives and interviews, present audiences with short dramatic engagements between law enforcement officials and citizen-suspects. These videotaped interactions intend... to present... the encounters between these characters as "real" rather than fictional.

Both programs are very popular, and... because the programs offer audiences the "reality" of police work, scholars... should consider what the programs present to viewers. Based upon our... analysis of these programs,... we argue that... they serve as justification for controversial police practices. Particularly troublesome, the [shows]... may serve as an implicit justification for the controversial practice of racial profiling....

Most clearly, reality crime programming reinforces certain "myths" of crime and crime fighting in America.... Central elements of the media's dissemination of crime mythology involve characterizations of police and criminals. Specifically, a central myth of crime in American society concerns those types of citizens who are perceived to be criminals:... lower-class minority males... and in particular African Americans. [This can foster] a fear of crime associated with minority males... [and these] depictions further racism by bolstering audiences' conceptual link between minorities and crime.

Reality TV typically portrays crime as a threat to citizens that results from the pathology of individual criminals—not from the social and environmental conditions within which citizen-suspects are situated.... [T]he suspected criminals [are] portrayed as "dangerous people who are beyond social control."... Thus, the solution to such a social problem is to apprehend and arrest the individual criminal.... By promoting a fear of crime and the image that minorities are responsible for most crime, these reality programs may serve as justification for harsher penalties and even police aggression toward citizen-suspects....

The vignettes [depicted on these shows] share key elements. To begin, a clear moral distinction exists between the heroic police and dangerous citizen-suspects. In *Cops,* for example, one officer comments that "we" are out here to "get the bad guy" and "fight crime." Officers describe their work as "doing our good deed."... [C]riminals are "beyond insane," and the well-trained police must use many means, both standard and improvised, to combat them.... Whereas police are humanized through the use of actual names and portrayed as courageous defenders against the hordes of the criminally insane, the voice of the citizen-suspects is given little credibility.... Police work is also portrayed as exciting, a result of the menace of those who would antagonize the police. Officers in *Cops* explain that the street is "a madhouse, and that keeps you going." The life out here is much different than his memories of life on the street of his middle class upbringing, opines one officer.... Law enforcers are in total control and always in the right....

In general, these programs work to legitimize police actions, even controversial police practices. For example, the celebration of police competence combined with their aggressive behaviors sends a message that . . . aggression by police [is] legitimate, given the intense danger suspects pose to the public. . . . Of significant concern, these programs justify the practice of racial profiling implicitly through the depiction of pretextual stops [where officers pull over motorists for a minor traffic violation or a "routine traffic stop" with the expectation that they will find evidence of a more serious crime.] Such profiling has recently become a major concern and public controversy. Studies drawing on victim testimony, police records, and court records reveal patterns of racial profiling from San Diego to New Jersey. . . . Representative John Conyer Jr. (Dem.-Michigan) maintains that "race-based traffic stops turn driving, one of our most ordinary and fundamental American activities, into an experience fraught with danger and risk for people of color." . . . Although African Americans comprise less than one-sixth of the population in the United States, they make up almost three-fourths of all routine traffic stops. . . .

Our argument . . . rests on the depiction of pretextual stops as an effective method of law enforcement. . . . Pretextual stops provide officers with a great deal of discretion, allowing them to act on a hunch or their intuition to determine who to tail, pursue, stop, and interrogate. Race and suspicion may be tangled in officers' minds. . . .

Because the programs under study here show only successful stops, searches, seizures, and arrests, and many of these suspects are minority males, the programming sends a clear but disturbing message: stopping minority drivers or pedestrians when police notice minor traffic infractions or anomalies in behavior, such as possessing out of state plates, or because they are "acting squirrelly," or because they are "acting suspicious or something," is appropriate because it invariably leads to incarceration of serious criminals. . . . Racial profiling is legitimated through the celebration of the intuitive capacities of law enforcement officers.

SOURCE: Prosise, Theodore O., & Johnson, Ann (2004). "Law Enforcement and Crime on Cops and World's Wildest Police Videos: Anecdotal Form and the Justification of Racial Profiling." *Western Journal of Communication,* 68(1):72–92.

Racial Profiling Is Rational and Justified by Differential Crime Rates

JARED TAYLOR AND GLAYDE WHITNEY

One of the strangest phenomena in contemporary criminology is the treatment of race and ethnicity. On the one hand there is a long history of academic attention to differences among racial and ethnic groups in involvement in various sorts of criminality. . . . On the other hand, there appears to be media and political pressure to avoid acknowledgement of the differences and possible consequences of the differences. . . . [R]eports which criticize the practice of racial profiling and criticize the "belief" that there may be race differences in criminality get wide media coverage [but] other reports that deal with the actual incidence of crimes as related to race get short shrift. . . .

Different racial groups in the United States commit crimes at different rates. . . . The data show a consistent pattern: Blacks are arrested at dramatically higher rates than other racial groups. . . . The popular conception of crime in America is correct: rates are much higher among blacks than among whites or other groups.

[Do these data] . . . reflect police bias rather than genuine group differences in crime rates? Police actually have very little discretion in whom they arrest for violent crimes. Except for murder victims, most people can tell the police the race of an assailant. If a victim says she was mugged by a white man, the police cannot very well arrest a black man even if they want to. . . . [I]f racist white police were unfairly arresting non-whites we would expect arrest rates for

Asians to be higher than those for whites. Instead, they are lower for almost every kind of crime.

Many people resist the idea that different racial groups have substantially different rates of violent crime. However, there are several group differences in crime rates that virtually everyone accepts and, indeed, takes for granted. Men in their late teens and 20s, for example, are much more prone to violence than men beyond their 50s. . . . Likewise, virtually no one disputes the reason for higher arrest rates for men than for women: Men commit more violent crime than women. . . . This is the case for racial groups as well: Asians are arrested at lower rates than whites because they commit fewer crimes; blacks and Hispanics are arrested at higher rates because they commit more crimes. . . . The multiples of black v. white arrest rates are very close to the multiples of male v. female arrest rates, suggesting that blacks are as much more dangerous than whites as men are more dangerous than women.

What does this mean? Most people . . . have an intuitive understanding that men are more violent and dangerous than women. If someone in unfamiliar circumstances is approached by a group of strange men she feels more uneasy than if she is approached by an otherwise similar group of strange women. No one would suggest that this differential uneasiness is "prejudice." It is common sense, born out by the objective reality that men are more dangerous than women.

In fact, it is just as reasonable to feel more uneasy when approached by blacks than by otherwise similar whites; the difference in danger as reflected by arrest rates is virtually the same. It is rational to fear blacks more than whites, just as it is rational to fear men more than women. Whatever additional precautions a person would take [that] are justified because a potential assailant was male rather than female are, from a statistical point of view, equally justified if a potential assailant is black rather than white. . . .

There is now much controversy about so-called "racial profiling" by the police, that is, the practice of questioning blacks in disproportionate numbers in the expectation that they are more likely than people of other races to be criminals. . . . "Racial" profiling is just as rational and productive as "age" or "sex" profiling. Police would be wasting their time if they stopped and questioned as many little old ladies as they do young black men. It is the job of the police to catch criminals, and they know from experience who is likely to be an offender. Americans who do not question the wisdom of police officers who notice a possible suspect's age and sex should not be surprised to learn those officers also notice race.

SOURCE: Taylor, Jared, & Whitney, Glayde (2002). "Racial Profiling: Is There an Empirical Basis?" *Mankind Quarterly*, 42:285–313.

Debate Questions to Consider

1. This chapter mentions several different causes of prejudice, including personality structures, culture or tradition, and group competition. Which type of prejudice are Prosise and Johnson discussing? How do you know? How serious is this form of prejudice? Can television really have much of an effect on level of prejudice? Are these TV shows isolated events, or are they part of a larger pattern in the U.S. culture of racial prejudice? How could you research this topic further?

2. Taylor and Whitney argue that racial profiling is justified—a point of view that might be regarded as evidence that the authors are prejudiced. Would such a charge be justified? Why or why not?

3. Are Taylor and Whitney referring to all types of crime when they say that blacks have higher crime rates? What types of crime are higher in the white community? How would inclusion of such crimes change their argument, if at all? What gender and class dimensions are implicit in their argument?

4. If you were the police chief of your town, what specific guidelines could you use to differentiate between prejudiced racial profiling and legitimate policing? What would you tell your officers not to do when they are on patrol?

Main Points

- Prejudice is the tendency to think and feel negatively about the members of other groups. Discrimination refers to negative acts of behavior motivated by a person's group membership. Prejudice has at least two dimensions: the cognitive and the affective.

- Prejudice takes multiple forms and can have a variety of causes, and no one theory can account for the entirety of the phenomenon. However, all forms of prejudice seem to have their origins in group conflict over scarce resources.

- Once created, prejudice can become part of culture, handed down across the generations by socialization and reinforced by the everyday realities of minority group inequalities. The likelihood that prejudice or discrimination will be expressed depends heavily on the situation the individual is in.

- Traditional, overt forms of prejudice have lost strength in U.S. society over the past several decades. This decline in prejudice may be the result of higher levels of education and greater equal status contact across group lines.

- Contrary to the idea that prejudice is decreasing, many researchers argue that it is merely changing form. Modern racism combines subtle intergroup antipathy with low support for programs that address the situations of minority groups. Sexism also appears to be modernizing.

- Hate crimes and hate groups are a continuing reminder that the most vicious forms of prejudice and discrimination have not disappeared from U.S. society. These acts may be linked to scapegoating and the perception of less-educated young males that their position is threatened by the undeserved increase in the status of American minority groups.

- The concepts and theories developed in this chapter can be applied in a variety of ways in the public sociology assignments presented in the introduction to Part 2. If you explore the dynamics of local hate groups, for example, what theories of prejudice might be most applicable? You will probably find that all theories have some application, but some might seem more relevant.

- If you do public sociology Assignment 2, you will probably find an opportunity to apply the material in this chapter on stereotypes. For example, do anti-Arab stereotypes stress inferiority? Are these stereotypes more comparable to traditional American stereotypes of African Americans or Jews?

Study Site on the Web

Don't forget the interactive quizzes and other resources and learning aids at www.pineforge.com/healeystudy5.

For Further Reading

Allport, Gordon. (1954). *The Nature of Prejudice.* Reading, MA: Addison-Wesley.

   A classic work in the field. A comprehensive summary of theory and research.

Brown, Rupert. (1995). *Prejudice: Its Social Psychology.* Cambridge, MA: Blackwell.

   A comprehensive review of the literature.

Bonacich, Edna, & Modell, John. (1980). *The Economic Basis of Ethnic Solidarity: Small Business in the Japanese American Community.* Berkeley: University of California Press.

   Split labor market theory applied to the Japanese American community.

Bonilla-Silva, Eduardo. (2006). *Racism Without Racists: Color-Blind Racism and the Persistence of Racial Inequality in the United States* (2nd ed.). Lanham, MD: Rowman & Littlefield.

   One of the most important treatments of modern (or "color-blind") racism

Levin, Jack, & McDevitt, Jack. (2002). *Hate Crimes Revisited: America's War on Those Who Are Different.* Boulder, CO: Westview Press.

   An important sociological analysis of hate crimes.

Feagin, Joe, & O'Brien, Eileen. (2004). *White Men on Race: Power, Privilege, and the Shaping of Cultural Consciousness.* Boston: Beacon Press.

   An analysis of the sometimes subtle expression of racial sentiment among elite white males.

Yancey, George. (2007). *Interracial Contact and Social Change.* Boulder, CO: Lynne Rienner.

   A thin volume that presents a comprehensive and largely positive assessment of the contact hypothesis.

Questions for Review and Study

1.   Distinguish between prejudice and discrimination and explain clear examples of both. Explain the different dimensions of prejudice and differentiate between them. What are stereotypes? What forms do stereotypes take? How are stereotypes formed and maintained?

2.   Explain the various causes of prejudice, including the theoretical perspectives presented in this chapter. Explain and *evaluate* the research evidence that has been presented. Which theories seem most credible in terms of evidence? Why? Try to think of an incident—from your own experience, the news, or popular culture—that illustrates each theory.

3. How does prejudice persist through time? What are children taught about other groups? What were you taught by your parents? How did this compare with what you learned from friends? How would your socialization experience have changed if you had been raised in another group? Have your views been changed by education or intergroup contact? How?

4. Is prejudice really decreasing, or are the negative emotions and attitudes changing into modern racism? What evidence is most persuasive in leading you to your conclusion? Why?

5. Interpret the information presented in Exhibit 3.9. Does this exhibit support the notion that modern racism is an important cause of resistance to racial change? How?

6. What forms of prejudice are involved in hate crimes? What are the roles of group competition and scapegoating? Develop an explanation for hate crimes based on these connections.

Internet Research Project

A. Test Your Individual Level of Racial Prejudice

Follow the links to the Race Implicit Association Test (https://implicit.harvard.edu/implicit/demo/) and try some of the other tests as well. Be sure to explore the site and learn more about the test before signing off. What type of prejudice (personality based, culture based, or prejudice based on group competition) does the Implicit Association Test measure? Do you feel that the test produced valid results in your case?

B. Is American Prejudice Continuing to Decline?

Go to the home page for the Gallup Polls (http://www.gallup.com) and search for poll results measuring prejudice. You might search using the key words "prejudice" or "African American." Compare your results with those presented in this chapter. Can you determine whether your results support the idea that racial intolerance in the United States is declining? How?

As an alternative, search the Internet for relevant survey results using key words such as "prejudice," "race relations," and "survey." Make sure that the information you find is from a reputable source before placing any trust in the results.

C. Search the Internet for Web Sites of White Extremist or Racist Groups

Two addresses with links to other sites are http://www.stormfront.org and http://www.kkk .com. Describe and analyze the content of the Web sites you visit and link the material to this chapter. What type of prejudice (personality based, culture based, or prejudice that results from group competition) is displayed on these sites? Do these Web sites contradict the idea that U.S. prejudice is declining?

As an alternative, visit the Web site of the Southern Poverty Law Center (http://www .splcenter.org). They track hate group activity around the nation, and the Web site offers a variety of valuable information.

(CAUTION: The contents of these sites may be offensive to you or to others. Please use discretion in completing this assignment.)

PART 2

The Evolution of Dominant-Minority Relations in the United States

The chapters in Part 2 explore several questions: Why do some groups become minorities? How and why do dominant-minority relations change over time? These questions are more than casual or merely academic. Understanding the dynamics that created and sustained prejudice, racism, discrimination, and inequality in the past will build understanding about group relations in the present and future, and such understanding is crucial if we are ever to deal effectively with these problems.

Both chapters in Part 2 use African Americans as the primary case study. Chapter 4 focuses on the preindustrial United States and the creation of slavery but also considers the fate of American Indians and Mexican Americans during the same time period. Chapter 5 analyzes the changes in group relations that were caused by the Industrial Revolution and focuses on the shift from slavery to segregation for African Americans and their migration out of the South. Throughout the 20th century, industrial technology continued to evolve and shape American society and group relationships. We begin to explore the consequences of these changes in Chapter 5, and we continue the investigation in the case studies of contemporary minority groups in Part 3.

The concepts introduced in Part 1 are used throughout Chapters 4 and 5, and some very important new concepts and theories are introduced as well. By the end of Part 2, you will be familiar with virtually the entire conceptual framework that will guide us through the remainder of this text.

A Note on the Morality and the History of Minority Relations in America: Guilt, Blame, Understanding, and Communication

Very often, when people confront the kind of material presented in the next few chapters, they react on a personal level. Some might feel a sense of guilt for America's less-than-wholesome history of group relations. Others might respond with anger about the injustice and unfairness that remains in American society. Still others might respond with denial or indifference and might argue that the events discussed in Chapters 4 and 5 are so distant in time that they have no importance or meaning today.

These reactions—guilt, anger, denial, and indifference—are common, and I ask you to consider them. First, the awful things I will discuss did happen, and they were done largely by members of a particular racial and ethnic group: white Europeans and their descendants in America. No amount of denial, distancing, or disassociation can make these facts go away. African Americans, American Indians, Mexican Americans, and other groups were victims, and they paid a terrible price for the early growth and success of white American society.

Second, the successful domination and exploitation of these groups was made easier by the cooperation of members of each of the minority groups. The slave trade relied on agents and slavers who were black Africans; some American Indians aided and abetted the cause of white society, and some Mexicans helped to cheat other Mexicans. There is plenty of guilt to go around, and European Americans do not have a monopoly on greed, bigotry, or viciousness. Indeed, some white southerners opposed slavery and fought for the abolition of the "peculiar institution." Many of the ideas and values on which the United States was founded (justice, equality, liberty) had their origins in European intellectual traditions, and minority group protest has often involved little more than insisting that the nation live up to these ideals. Segments of the white community were appalled at the treatment of American Indians and Mexicans. Some members of the dominant group devoted (and sometimes gave) their lives to end oppression, bigotry, and racial stratification.

My point is to urge you to avoid, insofar as is possible, a "good-guy/bad-guy" approach to this subject matter. Guilt, anger, denial, and indifference are common reactions to this material, but these emotions do little to advance understanding, and often they impede communication between members of different groups. I believe that an understanding of America's racial past is vitally important for understanding the present. Historical background provides a perspective for viewing the present and allows us to identify important concepts and principles that we can use to disentangle the intergroup complexities surrounding us.

The goal of the chapters to come is not to make you feel any particular emotion. I will try to present the often ugly facts neutrally and without extraneous editorializing. As scholars, your goal should be to absorb the material, understand the principles, and

apply them to your own life and the society around you—not to indulge yourself in elaborate moral denunciations of American society, develop apologies for the past, or deny the realities of what happened. By dealing objectively with this material, we can begin to liberate our perspectives and build an understanding of the realities of American society and American minority groups.

About the Public Sociology Assignments

The public sociology assignments in Part 2 focus on two controversial issues. Affirmative action, as a tool for combating modern institutional discrimination and increasing diversity on campus and in the workplace, is covered at the end of Chapter 5. How exactly has affirmative action worked on your campus? Has it increased diversity? This assignment will provide you with answers to these questions.

The second assignment takes up the topic of "self-segregation" of racial and ethnic groups on campus. How prevalent is this phenomenon on your campus? What social processes lead students to sort themselves out by group? This assignment connects to the equal status contact hypothesis (Chapter 3) and to a number of ideas presented in this part, including the Noel and Blauner hypotheses (Chapter 4).

Public Sociology Assignments

Marcus Griffin

Assignment 1
Employment and Achieving the American Dream

Much of U.S. immigration history is characterized by people coming to the United States in the hope of achieving economic and social success. This story of immigrants going from rags to riches is often referred to as the "American Dream" and the United States itself as the "Land of Opportunity." Is this dream really possible for the average person (immigrant or otherwise), or is it only for white males generally? This assignment is designed to answer this question by exploring affirmative action at your school or a large corporation.

Step 1

Review the suggested resource at the end of this assignment or conduct a literature review on equal employment opportunity and affirmative action (EEO/AA) issues prior to meeting with the company or school program director so that you are best able to articulate your project and be an informed listener. Your school is required to remain in compliance with a variety of federal and state laws, plus any directions the board of regents or visitors mandate. A passing familiarity with these compliance issues will enable you to productively discuss the project with the director.

Step 2

Meet with your university or college's EEO/AA director to discuss your interest in studying the school's staff diversity over the past 20 years. The basic question you will propose to answer is whether or not historical inequalities among ethnic groups and genders have declined during the past 20 years at your institution. If you are at a very large university (which as a whole would require a scope of work beyond this assignment), you may want to limit your study to a particular college or school, such as the College of Engineering, Arts and Letters, or School of Business. The college that oversees your major course of study is a good place to start, in this case, and you will probably want to speak initially with the dean. You may alternatively choose to conduct this research in a relatively large corporation instead of your college or university and follow the same steps.

Step 3

Using data your institution provides, chart the number of staff in each racial or ethnic group for the past 20 years. Chart the number of male and female staff in each racial ethnic category. As you go through each year's data, group individuals according to professional status (e.g., professor, secretary, janitor, and so on).

Step 4

Compare your institution with other entities. A good source of professorial staffing data is the American Association of University Professors at http://www.aaup.org. Your institution may have their Annual Report on the Economic Status of the Profession. This report can be mined for excellent data. Another source of general income data according to ethnic or racial grouping and according to gender is the U.S. Census Bureau at http://www.census.gov. You will want to obtain data from both the 2000 and 1990 decennial censuses. A good place to start is the Census Bureau's Historical Census Reports, whose most current URL may be obtained by entering the name on the Census Home Page search field.

Step 5

Compare the data trends you obtained for your institution, universities nationwide, and the U.S. population as a whole. Your object is to try to decide whether affirmative action and equal employment opportunity laws are creating a trend toward reduced inequalities among historically advantaged and disadvantaged populations.

Step 6

Present your data in spreadsheet and chart form with accompanying summary descriptions and analyses of the data to the EEO/AA director and his or her chief academic officer (this may be a dean, provost, or chancellor). Ask them to inform you of any initiatives implemented to improve the recruitment, retention, and promotion of historically disadvantaged populations as a result of your study.

Step 7

Congratulate yourself for hard work well-done!

Suggested Resource

Vander Waerdt, Lois. 1997. *Affirmative Action in Higher Education: A Source Book* (3rd ed.). St. Louis, MO: Employment Partnership.

Assignment 2
Ethnic Self-Segregation in College

Many schools are characterized by the tendency for ethnic groups, like other groups, to self-segregate. This can be observed in dining halls, the student center, residence halls, and classrooms. The social risk of this phenomenon is that people are not given the opportunity to discover the rich diversity their classmates bring to campus. Individuals who do not experience much contact with minority groups will fail to learn the common ground they share. The end result is often the perpetuation of ethnocentrism, increased competition, and eventual differentials in power among students. Following the Noel hypothesis outlined in Part 3, these conditions lead to some form of ethnic or racial stratification (social inequality), not just in society at large but within the college or university itself.

This assignment is designed as a group research project for approximately five students, who will gauge the degree of self-segregation in the college or university and determine its social implications. The research design is primarily unobtrusive.

Step 1

Form your research team and divide the labor according to individual interest and ability. The basis of your group's research design is unobtrusive observation of group clustering in a variety of social environments. These environments are likely to include dining facilities, the student center or union, residence halls, classrooms, and the library. You may, of course, choose other places to observe people based on your own experience. One member of the team should request student demographic data from the admissions office or dean of students office to construct a series of numbers-based diversity profiles of the student body.

Step 2

Over a 2-week period, go to your chosen or assigned location(s) and observe how people congregate. Take notes on your observations, including ethnic similarity or difference, gender, age, behavior and mannerisms of individuals and groups, and other characteristics you determine are noteworthy. Be sure to go to your locations at different times of the day and to continuously observe for at least 1 hour at a time. You should have approximately 10 hours of observation recorded for each location.

Step 3

As a group, review your notes and look for patterns in the way people group themselves, separate themselves from others, and behave. The student who compiles the demographic data should present his or her charts and insight to the group regarding what is institutionally known about the student body.

Step 4

Brainstorm questions that might be asked of individuals in a personal interview. The following are a few questions that might be asked, but your group should collectively decide the final questions to ask based on the unique insight derived from the observations and demographic data.

- How do you define your ethnic identity?
- How do you define other students' ethnic identities?
- Are there school clubs or activities that promote ethnic segregation or blending?
- In your experience, do students use their ethnic consciousness to self-segregate?

Step 5

Conduct three or four interviews per researcher. Be sure to take note of material your informants provide you with, and raise questions not initially considered that may present themselves.

Step 6

Gather as a group and share the results of your interviews with each other. Explore the patterns in the responses and particularly cogent responses to get a better understanding of how the informants perceive ethnic stratification, consciousness, and segregation.

Step 7

Collaboratively write the results of your group research. The paper should contain an executive summary; discussion of methods; discussion of observation, demographic, and interview data; and conclusion regarding the prevalence and character of self-segregation at your college or university.

Step 8

Present a copy of your paper and data to the dean of students and ask that he or she share with each researcher any policy changes that might result from the research.

Step 9

Do not forget to congratulate yourself for socially sensitive work well-done, and the next time you are at the dining facility, consider eating with someone or some group you have not joined before. It's likely that you will no longer be surprised at how much you have in common now that you have conducted this research.

The Development of Dominant-Minority Group Relations in Preindustrial America

CHAPTER 4

The Origins of Slavery

From the first settlements in the 1600s until the 19th century, most people living in what was to become the United States relied directly on farming for food, shelter, and other necessities of life. In an agricultural society, land and labor are central concerns, and the struggle to control these resources led directly to the creation of minority group status for three groups: African Americans, American Indians, and Mexican Americans. Why did the colonists create slavery? Why were Africans enslaved but not American Indians or Europeans? Why did American Indians lose their land and most of their population by the 1890s? How did the Mexican population in the Southwest become "Mexican Americans"? How did the experience of becoming a subordinated minority group vary by gender?

In this chapter, the concepts introduced in Part 1 will be used to answer these questions. Some new ideas and theories will also be introduced, and by the end of the chapter, we will have developed a theoretical model of the process that leads to the creation of a minority group. The creation of black slavery in colonial America, arguably the single most significant event in the early years of this nation, will be used to illustrate the process of minority group creation. We will also consider the subordination of American Indians and Mexican Americans—two more historical events of great significance—as additional case studies. We will follow the experiences of African Americans through the days of segregation (Chapter 5) and into the contemporary era (Chapter 6). The story of the development of minority group status for American Indians and Mexican Americans will be picked up again in Chapters 7 and 8, respectively.

Two broad themes underlie this chapter and, indeed, the remainder of the text:

1. The nature of dominant-minority group relations at any point in time is largely a function of the characteristics of the society as a whole. The situation of a minority group will reflect the realities of everyday social life and particularly the subsistence technology (the means by which the society satisfies basic needs such as food and shelter). As explained by Gerhard Lenski (see Chapter 1), the subsistence technology of a society acts as a foundation, shaping and affecting every other aspect of the social structure, including minority group relations.

2. The contact situation—the conditions under which groups first come together—is the single most significant factor in the creation of minority group status. The nature of the contact situation has long-lasting consequences for the minority group and the extent of racial or ethnic stratification, the levels of racism and prejudice, the possibilities for assimilation and pluralism, and virtually every other aspect of the dominant-minority relationship.

The Origins of Slavery in America

By the beginning of the 1600s, Spanish explorers had conquered much of Central and South America, and the influx of gold, silver, and other riches from the New World had made Spain a powerful nation. Following Spain's lead, England proceeded to establish its presence in the Western Hemisphere, but its efforts at colonization were more modest than those of Spain. By the early 1600s, only two small colonies had been established: Plymouth, settled by pious Protestant families, and Jamestown, populated primarily by males seeking their fortunes.

By 1619, the British colony at Jamestown, Virginia, had survived for more than a decade. The residents of the settlement had fought with the local natives and struggled continuously to eke out a living from the land. Starvation, disease, and death were frequent visitors, and the future of the enterprise continued to be in doubt.

In August of that year, a Dutch ship arrived. The master of the ship needed provisions and offered to trade his only cargo: about 20 black Africans. Many of the details of this transaction have been lost, and we probably will never know exactly how these people came to be chained in the hold of a ship. Regardless, this brief episode was a landmark event in the formation of what would become the United States. In combination with the strained relations between the English settlers and American Indians, the presence of these first few Africans

SLAVERS REVENGING THEIR LOSSES.

David Livingstone, *The Last Journals of David Livingstone, in Central Africa, From 1865 to His Death,* edited by Horace Waller (London: John Murray, 1874, p. 62; New York, Harper & Bros., 1875, p. 58).

Photo 4.1 & 4.2

Slaves to provide labor for American plantations were kidnapped from their villages in Africa and marched to the sea, a journey that sometimes covered hundreds of miles. They were loaded aboard slave ships and packed tightly below decks. The "Middle Passage" across the Atlantic could take months.

Scene in the Hold of the "Blood-stained Gloria." (Middle Passage.)

Richard Drake, *Revelations of a Slave Smuggler* (New York: Robert M. Dewitt, 1860, p. 28). Library of Congress, Prints and Photographs Division, LC-USZ62-30818.

raised an issue that has never been fully resolved: How should different groups in this society relate to each other?

The colonists at Jamestown had no ready answer. In 1619, England and its colonies did not practice slavery, so these first Africans were probably incorporated into colonial society

Exhibit 4.1   The African Diaspora

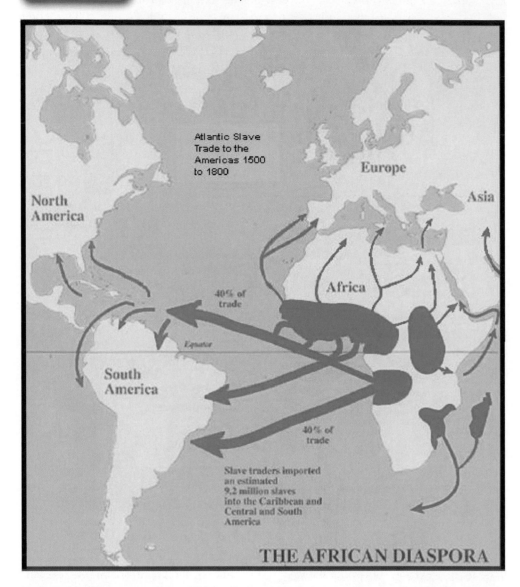

SOURCE: "The African Diaspora." (n.d.). Slave Trade and African American Ancestry. Retrieved December 4, 2007, from http://www.homestead.com/wysinger/mapofafricadiaspora.html.

NOTE: The size of the arrows is proportional to the number of slaves. Note that the bulk went to South America and that there were also flows to Europe and Asia.

as **indentured servants**, contract laborers who are obligated to serve a master for a specific number of years. At the end of the indenture, or contract, the servant became a free citizen. The colonies depended heavily on indentured servants from the British Isles for labor, and this status apparently provided a convenient way of defining the newcomers from Africa, who were, after all, treated as commodities and exchanged for food and water.

The position of African indentured servants in the colonies remained ambiguous for several decades. American slavery evolved gradually and in small steps; in fact, there was little demand for African labor during the years following 1619. By 1625, there still were only 23 blacks in Virginia, and that number had increased to perhaps 300 by midcentury (Franklin & Moss, 1994, p. 57). In the decades before the dawn of slavery, we know that some African indentured servants did become free citizens. Some became successful farmers and land-owners and, like their white neighbors, purchased African and white indentured servants themselves (Smedley, 1999, p. 97). By the 1650s, however, many African Americans (and their offspring) were being treated as the property of others, or in other words, as slaves (Morgan, 1975, p. 154).

It was not until the 1660s that the first laws defining slavery were enacted. In the century that followed, hundreds of additional laws were passed to clarify and formalize the status of Africans in colonial America. By the 1750s, slavery had been clearly defined in law and in custom, and the idea that a person could own another person—not just the labor or the energy or the work of a person, but the actual person—had been thoroughly institutionalized.

What caused slavery? The gradual evolution and low demand for indentured servants from Africa suggest that slavery was not somehow inevitable or preordained. Why did the colonists deliberately create this repressive system? Why did they reach out all the way to Africa for their slaves? If they wanted to create a slave system, why didn't they enslave the American Indians nearby or the white indentured servants already present in the colonies?

The Labor Supply Problem

American colonists of the 1600s saw slavery as a solution to several problems they faced. The business of the colonies was agriculture, and farmwork at this time was **labor-intensive**, performed almost entirely by hand. The Industrial Revolution was two centuries in the future, and there were few machines or labor-saving devices available to ease the everyday burden of work. A successful harvest depended largely on human effort.

As colonial society grew and developed, a specific form of agricultural production began to emerge. The **plantation system** was based on cultivating and exporting crops such as sugar, tobacco, and rice on large tracts of land using a large, cheap labor force. Profit margins tended to be small, so planters sought to stabilize their incomes by farming in volume and keeping the costs of production as low as possible. Profits in the labor-intensive plantation system could be maximized if a large, disciplined, and cheap workforce could be maintained by the landowners (Curtin, 1990; Morgan, 1975).

At about the same time the plantation system began to emerge, the supply of white inden-tured servants from the British Isles began to dwindle. Furthermore, the white indentured servants who did come to the colonies had to be released from their indenture every few years. Land was available, and these newly freed citizens tended to strike out on their own. Thus, landowners who relied on white indentured servants had to deal with high turnover rates in their workforces and faced a continually uncertain supply of labor.

Attempts to solve the labor supply problem by using American Indians failed. The tribes closest to the colonies were sometimes exploited for manpower. However, by

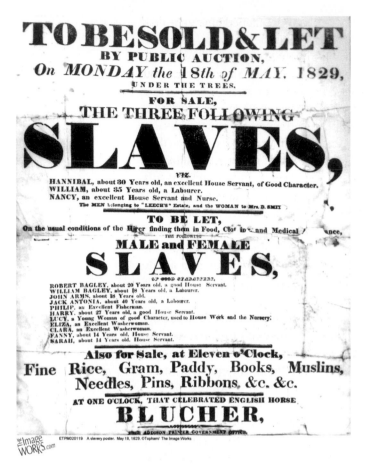

the time the plantation system had evolved, the local tribes had dwindled in numbers as a result of warfare and disease. Other Indian nations across the continent retained enough power to resist enslavement, and it was relatively easy for American Indians to escape back to their kinfolk.

This left black Africans as a potential source of manpower. The slave trade from Africa to the Spanish and Portuguese colonies of South America was firmly established by the mid-1600s and could be expanded to fill the needs of the British colonies as well. The colonists came to see slaves imported from Africa as the most logical, cost-effective way to solve their vexing shortage of labor. The colonists created slavery to cultivate their lands and generate profits, status, and success. The paradox at the core of U.S. society had been established: The construction of a social system devoted to freedom and individual liberty "in the New World was made possible only by the revival of an institution of naked tyranny foresworn for centuries in the Old" (Lacy, 1972, p. 22).

Photo 4.3

Slaves were regarded as commodities to be bought and sold.

© Topham/The Image Works.

The Contact Situation

The conditions under which groups first come into contact determine the immediate fate of the minority group and shape intergroup relations for years to come. We discussed the role of group competition in creating prejudice in Chapter 3. Here, I expand on some these ideas by introducing two theories that will serve as analytical guides in understanding the contact situation.

The Noel Hypothesis.
Sociologist Donald Noel (1968) identifies three features of the contact situation that in combination lead to some form of inequality between groups. The **Noel hypothesis** states: *If two or more groups come together in a contact situation characterized by ethnocentrism, competition, and a differential in power, then some form of racial or ethnic stratification will result* (p. 163; italics added). If the contact situation has all three characteristics, some dominant-minority group structure will be created.

Noel's first characteristic, **ethnocentrism**, is the tendency to judge other groups, societies, or lifestyles by the standards of one's own culture. Ethnocentrism is probably a universal component of human society, and some degree of ethnocentrism is essential to the maintenance of social solidarity and cohesion. Without some minimal level of pride in and loyalty to one's own society and cultural traditions, there would be no particular reason to observe the norms and laws, honor the sacred symbols, or cooperate with others in doing the daily work of society.

Regardless of its importance, ethnocentrism can have negative consequences. At its worst, it can lead to the view that other cultures and peoples are not just different, but inferior. At the very least, ethnocentrism creates a social boundary line that members of the groups involved will recognize and observe. When ethnocentrism exists in any degree, people will tend to sort themselves out along group lines and identify characteristics that differentiate "us" from "them."

Competition is a struggle over a scarce commodity. As we saw in Chapter 3, competition between groups often leads to harsh negative feelings (prejudice) and hostile actions (discrimination). In competitive contact situations, the victorious group becomes the dominant group, and the losers become the minority group. The competition may center on land, labor, jobs, housing, educational opportunities, political office, or anything else that is mutually desired by both groups or that one group has and the other group wants. Competition provides the eventual dominant group with the motivation to establish superiority. The dominant group serves its own interests by ending the competition and exploiting, controlling, eliminating, or otherwise dominating the minority group.

The third feature of the contact situation is a **differential in power** between the groups. Power, as you recall from Chapter 1, is the ability of a group to achieve its goals even in the face of opposition from other groups. The amount of power commanded by a group is a function of three factors. First, the size of the group can make a difference, and all other things being equal, larger groups are more powerful. Second, in addition to raw numbers, the degree of organization, discipline, and the quality of group leadership can make a difference in the ability of a group to pursue its goals. A third component of power is resources: anything that can be used to help the group achieve its goals. Depending on the context, resources might include anything from land to information to money. The greater the number and variety of resources at the disposal of a group, the greater that group's potential ability to dominate other groups. Thus, a larger, better-organized group with more resources at its disposal will generally be able to impose its will on smaller, less-well-organized groups with fewer resources. The Noel hypothesis is diagrammed in Exhibit 4.2.

Exhibit 4.2 A Model of the Establishment of Minority Group Status

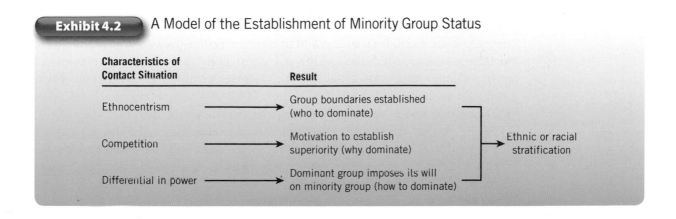

Characteristics of Contact Situation	Result	
Ethnocentrism	Group boundaries established (who to dominate)	
Competition	Motivation to establish superiority (why dominate)	Ethnic or racial stratification
Differential in power	Dominant group imposes its will on minority group (how to dominate)	

Note the respective functions of each of the three factors in shaping the contact situation and the emergence of inequality. If ethnocentrism is present, the groups will recognize their differences and maintain their boundaries. If competition is also present, the group that eventually dominates will attempt to maximize its share of scarce commodities by controlling or subordinating the group that eventually becomes the "minority" group. The differential in power allows the dominant group to succeed in establishing a superior position. Ethnocentrism tells the dominant group whom to dominate, competition tells the dominant group why it should establish a structure of dominance, and power is how the dominant group's will is imposed on the minority group.

The Noel hypothesis can be applied to the creation of minority groups in a variety of situations. We will also use the model to analyze changes in dominant-minority structures over time.

The Blauner Hypothesis.

The contact situation has also been analyzed by sociologist Robert Blauner, in his book *Racial Oppression in America* (1972). Blauner identifies two different initial relationships—colonization and immigration—and hypothesizes that *minority groups created by colonization will experience more intense prejudice, racism, and discrimination than those created by immigration. Furthermore, the disadvantaged status of colonized groups will persist longer and be more difficult to overcome than the disadvantaged status faced by groups created by immigration.*

Colonized minority groups, such as African Americans, are forced into minority status by the superior military and political power of the dominant group. At the time of contact with the dominant group, colonized groups are subjected to massive inequalities and attacks on their cultures. They are assigned to positions, such as slave status, from which any form of assimilation is extremely difficult and perhaps even forbidden by the dominant group. Frequently, members of the minority group are identified by highly visible racial or physical characteristics that maintain and reinforce the oppressive system. Thus, minority groups created by colonization experience harsher and more persistent rejection and oppression than groups created by immigration.

Immigrant minority groups are at least in part voluntary participants in the host society. That is, although the decision to immigrate may be motivated by extreme pressures, such as famine or political persecution, immigrant groups have at least some control over their destinations and their positions in the host society. As a result, they do not occupy positions that are as markedly inferior as those of colonized groups. They retain enough internal organization and resources to pursue their own self-interests, and they commonly experience more rapid acceptance and easier movement to equality. The boundaries between groups are not so rigidly maintained, especially when the groups are racially similar. In discussing European immigrant groups, for example, Blauner (1972) states that entering into American society

> involved a degree of choice and self-direction that was for the most part denied to people of color. Voluntary immigration made it more likely that … European … ethnic groups would identify with America and see the host culture as a positive opportunity. (p. 56)

Acculturation and, particularly, integration were significantly more possible for European immigrant groups than for the groups formed under conquest or colonization.

Blauner stresses that the initial differences between colonized and immigrant minority groups have consequences that persist long after the original contact. For example, based on measures of equality—or integration into the secondary sector, the second step in Gordon's model of assimilation (see Chapter 2)—such as average income, years of education, and unemployment rate, descendants of European immigrants are equal with national norms today (see Chapter 2 for specific data). In contrast, descendants of colonized and conquered groups (e.g., African Americans) are, on the average, below the national norms on virtually all measures of equality and integration (see Chapters 6–9 for specific data).

Blauner's two types of minority groups lie at opposite ends of a continuum, but there are intermediate positions between the extremes. Enclave and middleman minorities (see Chapter 2) often originate as immigrant groups who bring some resources and thus have more opportunities than colonized minority groups to carve out places for themselves in the host society. Unlike European groups, however, many of these minorities are also racially distinguishable, and certain kinds of opportunities may be closed to them. For instance, U.S. citizenship was expressly forbidden to immigrants from China until World War II. Federal laws restricted the entrance of Chinese immigrants, and state and local laws restricted their opportunities for education, jobs, and housing. For these and other reasons, the Asian immigrant experience cannot be equated with European immigrant patterns (Blauner, 1972, p. 55). Because they combine characteristics of both the colonized and the immigrant minority group experience, we can predict that in terms of equality, enclave and middleman minority groups will occupy an intermediate status between the more assimilated white ethnic groups and the colonized racial minorities.

Blauner's typology has proven to be an extremely useful conceptual tool for the analysis of U.S. dominant-minority relations, and it is used extensively throughout this text. In fact, the case studies that compose Part 3 of this text are arranged in approximate order from groups created by colonization to those created by immigration. Of course, it is difficult to measure such things as the extent of colonization objectively or precisely, and the exact order of the groups is somewhat arbitrary.

The Creation of Slavery in the United States

The Noel hypothesis helps explain why colonists enslaved black Africans instead of white indentured servants or American Indians. First, all three groups were the objects of ethnocentric feelings on the part of the elite groups that dominated colonial society. Black Africans and American Indians were perceived as being different on religious as well as racial grounds. Many white indentured servants were Irish Catholics, criminals, or paupers. They not only occupied a lowly status in society, but were perceived as different from the British Protestants who dominated colonial society.

Second, competition of some sort existed between the colonists and all three groups. The competition with American Indians was direct and focused on control of land. Competition with indentured servants, white and black, was more indirect; these groups were the labor force that the landowners needed to work on their plantations and become successful in the New World.

Noel's third variable, differential in power, is the key variable that explains why Africans were enslaved instead of the other groups. During the first several decades of colonial history,

	Three Causal Factors		
Potential Sources of Labor	**Ethnocentrism**	**Competition**	**Differential in Power**
White indentured servants	Yes	Yes	No
American Indians	Yes	Yes	No
Black indentured servants	Yes	Yes	Yes

Exhibit 4.3 The Noel Hypothesis Applied to the Origins of Slavery

the balance of power between the colonists and American Indians was relatively even and, in fact, often favored American Indians (Lurie, 1982, pp. 131–133). The colonists were outnumbered, and their muskets and cannons were only marginally more effective than bows and spears. The American Indian tribes were well-organized social units capable of sustaining resistance to and mounting reprisals against the colonists, and it took centuries for the nascent United States to finally defeat American Indians militarily.

White indentured servants, on the one hand, had the advantage of being preferred over black indentured servants (Noel, 1968, p. 168). Their greater desirability gave them bargaining power and the ability to negotiate better treatment and more lenient terms than black indentured servants. If the planters had attempted to enslave white indentured servants, this source of labor would have dwindled even more rapidly.

Africans, on the other hand, had become indentured servants by force and coercion. In Blauner's terms, they were a colonized group that did not freely choose to enter the British colonies. Thus, they had no bargaining power. Unlike American Indians, they had no nearby relatives, no knowledge of the countryside, and no safe havens to which to escape. Exhibit 4.3 summarizes the impact of these three factors on the three potential sources of labor in colonial America.

Paternalistic Relations

Recall the first theme stated at the beginning of this chapter: The nature of intergroup relationships will reflect the characteristics of the larger society. The most important and profitable unit of economic production in the colonial South was the plantation, and the region was dominated by a small group of wealthy landowners. A society with a small elite class and a plantation-based economy will often develop a form of minority relations called **paternalism** (van den Berghe, 1967; Wilson, 1973). The key features of paternalism are vast power differentials and huge inequalities between dominant and minority groups, elaborate and repressive systems of control over the minority group, castelike barriers between groups, elaborate and highly stylized codes of behavior and communication between groups, and low rates of overt conflict. Each of these characteristics will be considered in turn.

As slavery evolved in the colonies, the dominant group shaped the system to fit its needs. To solidify control of the labor of their slaves, the plantation elite designed and enacted an elaborate system of laws and customs that gave masters nearly total legal power over slaves. In these laws, slaves were defined as **chattel**, or personal property, rather than as persons, and they were accorded no civil or political rights. Slaves could not own property, sign contracts, bring lawsuits, or even testify in court (except against another slave). The masters were given the legal authority to determine almost every aspect of a slave's life, including work schedules, living arrangements, diets, and even names (Elkins, 1959; Franklin & Moss, 1994; Genovese, 1974; Jordan, 1968; Stampp, 1956).

The law permitted the master to determine the type and severity of punishment for misbehavior. Slaves were forbidden by law to read or write, and marriages between slaves were not legally recognized. Masters could separate husbands from wives and parents from children if it suited them. Slaves had little formal decision-making ability or control over their lives or the lives of their loved ones.

In colonial America, slavery became synonymous with race. Race, slavery, inferiority, and powerlessness became intertwined in ways that, according to many analysts, still affect the ways black and white Americans think about one another (Hacker, 1992). Slavery was a **caste system**, or closed stratification system. In a caste system, there is no mobility between social positions, and the social class you are born into (your ascribed status) is permanent. Slave status was for life and was passed on to any children a slave might have. Whites, no matter what they did, could not become slaves.

Interaction between members of the dominant and minority groups in a paternalistic system is governed by a rigid, strictly enforced code of etiquette. Slaves were expected to show deference and humility and visibly display their lower status when interacting with whites. These rigid behavioral codes made it possible for blacks and whites to work together, sometimes intimately, sometimes for their entire lives, without threatening the power and status differentials inherent in the system. Plantation and farmwork required close and frequent contact between blacks and whites, and status differentials were maintained socially rather than physically.

The frequent but unequal interactions allowed the elites to maintain a pseudotolerance, an attitude of benevolent despotism, toward their slaves. Their prejudice and racism were often expressed as positive emotions of affection for their black slaves. The attitude of the planters toward their slaves was often paternalistic and even genteel (Wilson, 1973, pp. 52–55).

For their part, black slaves often could not hate their owners as much as they hated the system that constrained them. The system defined slaves as pieces of property owned by their masters—yet they were, undeniably, human beings. Thus, slavery was founded, at its heart, on a contradiction.

> The master learned to treat his slaves both as property and as men and women, the slaves learned to express and affirm their humanity even while they were constrained in much of their lives to accept their status as chattel. (Parish, 1989, p. 1)

The powerlessness of slaves made it difficult for them to openly reject or resist the system. Slaves had few ways in which they could directly challenge the institution of slavery or their position in it. Open defiance was ineffective and could result in punishment or even death. In general, masters would not be prosecuted for physically abusing their slaves.

One of the few slave revolts that occurred in the United States illustrates both the futility of overt challenge and the degree of repression built into the system. In 1831, in Southampton County, Virginia, a slave named Nat Turner led an uprising during which 57 whites were killed. The revolt was starting to spread when the state militia met and routed the growing slave army. More than 100 slaves died in the armed encounter, and Nat Turner and 13 others were later executed. Slave owners and white southerners in general were greatly alarmed by the uprising and consequently tightened the system of control over slaves, making it even more repressive (Franklin & Moss, 1994, p. 147). Ironically, the result of Nat Turner's attempt to lead slaves to freedom was greater oppression and control by the dominant group.

Others were more successful in resisting the system. Runaway slaves were a constant problem for slave owners, especially in the states bordering the free states of the North. The difficulty of escape and the low likelihood of successfully reaching the North did not deter thousands from attempting the feat, some of them repeatedly. Many runaway slaves received help from the Underground Railroad, an informal network of safe houses supported by African Americans and whites involved in **abolitionism**, the movement to abolish slavery. These escapes created colorful legends and heroic figures, including Frederick Douglass, Sojourner Truth, and Harriet Tubman. Narrative Portrait 1 in this chapter presents the experiences of two ex-slaves who eventually escaped to the North.

Besides running away and open rebellion, slaves used the forms of resistance most readily available to them: sabotage, intentional carelessness, dragging their feet, and work slowdowns. As historian Peter Parish (1989) points out, it is difficult to separate "a natural desire to avoid hard work [from a] conscious decision to protest or resist" (p. 73), and much of this behavior may fall more into the category of noncooperation than of deliberate political rebellion. Nonetheless, these behaviors were widespread and document the rejection of the system by its victims.

On an everyday basis, the slaves managed their lives and families as best they could. Most slaves were neither docile victims nor unyielding rebels. As the institution of slavery developed, a distinct African American experience accumulated, and traditions of resistance and accommodation developed side by side. Most slaves worked to create a world for themselves within the confines and restraints of the plantation system, avoiding the more vicious repression as much as possible while attending to their own needs and those of their families. An African American culture was forged in response to the realities of slavery and was manifested in folklore, music, religion, family and kinship structures, and other aspects of everyday life (Blassingame, 1972; Genovese, 1974; Gutman, 1976).

The Dimensions of Minority Group Status

The situation of African Americans under slavery can be more completely described by applying some of the concepts developed in Part 1.

Power, Inequality, and Institutional Discrimination.

The key concepts for understanding the creation of slavery are power, inequality, and institutional discrimination. The plantation elite used its greater power resources to consign black Africans to an inferior status. The system of racial inequality was implemented and reinforced by institutionalized discrimination and became a central aspect of everyday life in the antebellum South. The legal and political institutions of colonial society were shaped to benefit the landowners and give them almost total control over their slaves.

Prejudice and Racism.

What about the attitudes and feelings of the people involved? What was the role of personal prejudice? How and why did the ideology of anti-black racism start? As we discussed in Chapter 3, individual prejudice and ideological racism are not so important as *causes* of the creation of minority group status but are more the *results* of systems of racial inequality (Jordan, 1968, p. 80; Smedley, 1999, pp. 94–111). The colonists did not enslave black indentured servants because they were prejudiced or because they disliked blacks or thought them inferior. The decision to enslave black Africans was an attempt to resolve a labor supply problem. The primary roles of prejudice and racism in the creation of minority group status are to rationalize and "explain" the emerging system of racial and ethnic advantage (Wilson, 1973, pp. 76–78).

Prejudice and racism help to mobilize support for the creation of minority group status and to stabilize the system as it emerges. Prejudice and racism can provide convenient and convincing justifications for exploitation. They can help insulate a system like slavery from questioning and criticism and make it appear reasonable and even desirable. Thus, the intensity, strength, and popularity of anti-black southern racism actually reached its height almost 200 years after slavery began to emerge. During the early 1800s, the American abolitionist movement brought slavery under heavy attack, and in response, the ideology of anti-black racism was strengthened (Wilson, 1973, p. 79). The greater the opposition to a system of racial stratification or the greater the magnitude of the exploitation, the greater the need of the beneficiaries and their apologists to justify, rationalize, and explain.

Once created, dominant group prejudice and racism become widespread and common ways of thinking about the minority group. In the case of colonial slavery, anti-black beliefs and feelings became part of the standard package of knowledge, understanding, and truths shared by members of the dominant group. As the decades wore on and the institution of slavery solidified, prejudice and racism were passed on from generation to generation. For succeeding generations, anti-black prejudice became just another piece of information and perspective on the world learned during socialization. Anti-black prejudice and racism began as part of an attempt to control the labor of black indentured servants, became embedded in early American culture, and were established as integral parts of the socialization process for succeeding generations (see Myrdal's "vicious cycle" in Chapter 3).

These conceptual relationships are presented in Exhibit 4.4. Racial inequality arises from the contact situation, as specified in the Noel hypothesis. As the dominant-minority relationship begins to take shape, prejudice and racism develop as rationalizations. Over time, a vicious

A Slave's Life

The memoirs of two escaped slaves, Henry Bibb and Harriet Jacobs, illustrate some of the features of southern slavery. Bibb was married and had a child when he escaped to the North, where he spent the rest of his life working for the abolition of slavery. The passage printed here gives an overview of his early life and expresses his commitment to freedom and his family. He also describes some of the abuses he and his family suffered under the reign of a particularly cruel master. Bibb was unable to rescue his daughter from slavery and agonizes over leaving her in bondage.

Harriet Jacobs grew up as a slave in Edenton, North Carolina, and in this excerpt, she recounts some of her experiences, especially the sexual harassment she suffered at the hand of her master. Her narrative illustrates the dynamics of power and sex in the "peculiar institution" and the very limited options she had for defending herself from the advances of her master. She eventually escaped from slavery by hiding in her grandmother's house for nearly 17 years and then making her way to the North.

Narrative of the Life and Adventures of Henry Bibb

Henry Bibb

I was born May 1815, of a slave mother, in Shelby County, Kentucky, and was claimed as the property of David White. I was brought up . . . or, more correctly speaking, I was flogged up; for where I should have received moral, mental, and religious instruction, I received stripes without number, the object of which was to degrade and keep me in subordination. . . . The first time I was separated from my mother, I was young and small. . . . I was. . . hired out to labor for various persons and all my wages were expended for the education of [my master's daughter]. It was then I first commenced seeing and feeling that I was a wretched slave, compelled to work under the lash without wages, and often without clothes to hide my nakedness. . . .

All that I heard about liberty and freedom . . . I never forgot. Among other good trades I learned the art of running away to perfection. I made a regular business of it, and never gave it up, until I had broken the bands of slavery, and landed myself safely in Canada, where I was regarded as a man, and not a thing.

[Bibb describes his childhood and adolescence, his early attempts to escape to the North, and his marriage to Malinda.] Not many months [later] Malinda made me a father. The dear little daughter was called Mary Frances. She was nurtured and caressed by her mother and father. . . . Malinda's business was to labor out in the field the greater part of her time, and there was no one to take care of poor little Frances. . . . She was left at the house to creep under the feet of an unmerciful old mistress, Mrs. Gatewood (the owner's wife). I recollect that [we] came in from the field one day and poor little Frances came creeping to her mother smiling, but with large tear drops standing in her dear little eyes. . . . Her little face was bruised black with the whole print of Mrs. Gatewood's hand. . . . Who can imagine the feelings of a mother and father, when looking upon their infant child whipped and tortured with impunity, and they placed in a situation where they could afford it no protection? But we were all claimed and held as property; the father and mother were slaves!

On this same plantation, I was compelled to stand and see my wife shamefully scourged and abused by her master; and the manner in which this was done was so violent and inhuman that I despair in finding decent language to describe the bloody act of cruelty. My happiness or pleasure was all blasted; for it was sometimes a pleasure to be with my little family even in slavery. I loved them as my wife and child. Little Frances was a pretty child; she was quiet, playful, bright, and interesting. . . . But I could never look upon the dear child without being filled with sorrow and fearful apprehensions, of being separated by slaveholders, because she was a slave, regarded as property. . . . But Oh! When I remember that my daughter, my only child, is still there, . . . it is too much to bear. If ever there was any one act of my life as a slave, that I have to lament over, it is that of being a father and a husband to slaves. I have the satisfaction of knowing that I am the father of only one slave. She is bone of my bone, and flesh of my flesh; poor unfortunate child. She was the first and shall be the last slave that ever I will father, for chains and slavery on this earth.

SOURCE: Osofsky, Gilbert (1969). *Puttin' On Ole Massa,* pp. 54–65, 80–81. New York: Harper & Row.

Life as a Slave Girl

Harriet Jacobs

During the first years of my service in Dr. Flint's family, I was accustomed to share some indulgences with the children of my mistress. Though this seemed to me no more than right, I was grateful for it, and tried to merit the kindness by the faithful discharge of my duties. But I now entered on my fifteenth year—a sad epoch in the life of a slave girl. My master began to whisper foul words in my ear. Young as I was, I could not remain ignorant of their import. I tried to treat them with indifference or contempt. The master's age, my extreme youth, and the fear that misconduct would be reported to my grandmother made me bear this treatment for many months.

He was a crafty man, and resorted to many means to accomplish his purposes. Sometimes he had stormy, terrific ways, that made his victims tremble; sometimes he assumed a gentleness that he thought must surely subdue. Of the two, I preferred his stormy moods, although they left me trembling. He tried his utmost to corrupt the pure principles my grandmother had instilled. He peopled my young mind with unclean images, such as only a vile monster could think of. I turned from him with disgust and hatred. But he was my master. I was compelled to live under the same roof with him, where I saw a man forty years my senior daily violating the most sacred commandments of nature. He told me I was his property; that I must be subject to his will in all things. My soul revolted against the mean tyranny. But where could I turn for protection? No matter whether the slave girl be as black as ebony or as fair as her mistress. In either case, there is no shadow of law to protect her from insult, from violence, or even from death; all these are inflicted by fiends who bear the shape of men. The mistress, who ought to protect the helpless victim, has no other feelings towards her but those of jealousy and rage. The degradation, the wrongs, the vices that grow out of slavery, are more than I can describe. They are greater than you would willingly believe. Surely, if you credited on half the truths that are told you concerning the helpless millions suffering in this cruel bondage, you at the north would not help tighten the yoke. You surely would refuse to do for the master, on your own soil, the mean and cruel work which trained bloodhounds and the lowest class of whites do for him at the south.

SOURCE: Jacobs, Harriet (1987). *Incidents in the Life of a Slave Girl, Written by Herself* (Jean Yellin, Ed.), pp. 27–31. Cambridge, MA: Harvard University Press.

Reprinted by the permission of the publishers from INCIDENTS IN THE LIFE OF A SLAVE GIRL: WRITTEN BY HERSELF by Harriet Jacobs, edited and with an Introduction by Jean Fagan Yellin, pp. 27–31, Cambridge, MA: Harvard University Press, Copyright © 1987, 2000 by the President and Fellows of Harvard College.

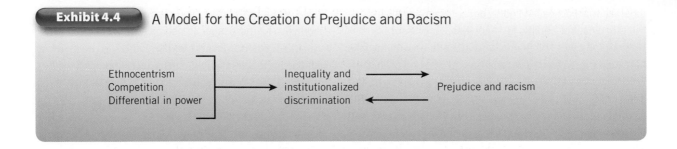

Exhibit 4.4 A Model for the Creation of Prejudice and Racism

Ethnocentrism
Competition
Differential in power → Inequality and institutionalized discrimination → Prejudice and racism

cycle develops as prejudice and racism reinforce the pattern of inequality between groups, which was the cause of prejudice and racism in the first place. Thus, the Blauner hypothesis states, the subordination of colonized minority groups is perpetuated through time.

Assimilation. There is an enormous literature on American slavery, and research on the nature and meaning of the system continues to this day. Many issues remain unsettled, however, and one of the more controversial, consequential, and interesting of these concerns the effect of slavery on the slaves.

Apologists for the system of slavery and some historians of the South writing early in the 20th century accepted the rationalizations inherent in anti-black prejudice and argued that slavery was actually beneficial for black Africans. According to this view, British-American slavery operated as a "school for civilization" (Phillips, 1918) that rescued savages from the jungles of Africa and exposed them to Christianity and Western civilization. Some argued that slavery was benevolent because it protected slaves from the evils and exploitation of the factory system of the industrial North. These racist views were most popular a century ago, early in the development of the social sciences. Since that time, scholars have established a number of facts (e.g., Western Africa, the area from which most slaves came, had been the site of a number of powerful, advanced civilizations) that make this view untenable by anyone but the most dedicated racist thinkers.

At the opposite extreme, slavery has been compared with Nazi concentration camps and likened to a "perverted patriarchy" that brainwashed, emasculated, and dehumanized slaves, stripping them of their heritage and culture. Historian Stanley Elkins provocatively argued this interpretation, now widely regarded as overstated, in his book *Slavery: A Problem in American Institutional and Intellectual Life* (1959). Although his conclusions might be overdrawn, Elkins's argument and evidence are important for any exploration of the nature of American slavery. In fact, much of the scholarship on slavery since the publication of Elkins's book has been an attempt to refute or at least modify the points he made.

Still a third view of the impact of slavery maintains that through all the horror and abuse of enslavement, slaves retained a sense of self and a firm anchor in their African traditions. This point of view stresses the importance of kinship, religion, and culture in helping African Americans cope and has been presented most poignantly in Alex Haley's semifictional family history *Roots,* but it is also represented in the scholarly literature on slavery since Elkins (see Blassingame, 1972; Genovese, 1974).

The debate over the impact of slavery continues (see the Current Debates section at the end of this chapter), and we cannot hope to resolve the issues here. However, it is clear that African Americans, in Blauner's terms, were a "colonized" minority group who were extensively—and coercively—acculturated. Language acculturation began on the slave ships, where different tribal and language groups were mixed together to inhibit communication and lower the potential for resistance and revolt (Mannix, 1962).

The plantation elite and their agents needed to communicate with their workforce and insisted on using English. Within a generation or two, African language use died out. Some scholars argue that some African words and language patterns persist to the present day, but even if this is true, the significance of this survival is trivial compared with the coerced adoption of English. To the extent that culture depends on language, Africans under slavery experienced massive acculturation.

Acculturation through slavery was clearly a process that was forced on African Americans. Because they were a colonized minority group and unwilling participants in the system, they had little choice but to adjust to the conditions established by the plantation elite as best they could. Their traditional culture was suppressed, and their choices for adjustment to the system were sharply constrained. Black slaves developed new cultural forms and social relationships, but they did so in a situation with few options or choices (Blauner, 1972, p. 66). The extent to which any African cultural elements survived the institution of slavery is a matter of some controversy, but given the power differentials inherent in the system, African Americans had few choices regarding their manner of adjustment.

Gender Relations.
Southern agrarian society developed into a complex social system stratified by race and gender as well as by class. The plantation elite, small in number but wealthy and politically powerful, was at the top of the structure. Most whites in the South were small farmers, and relatively few of them owned slaves. In 1860, for example, only 25% of all southern whites owned slaves (Franklin & Moss, 1994, p. 123).

The principal line of differentiation in the antebellum South was, of course, race, which was largely synonymous with slave versus nonslave status. Each of the racial groups was, in turn, stratified by gender. White women were subordinate to the males of the plantation elite, and the slave community echoed the patriarchal pattern of southern society, except that the degree of gender inequality among blacks was sharply truncated by the fact that slaves had little autonomy and few resources. At the bottom of the system were African American female slaves. Minority women are generally in double jeopardy, oppressed through their gender as well as their race. For black female slaves, the constraints were triple: "Black in a white society, slave in a free society, women in a society ruled by men, female slaves had the least formal power and were perhaps the most vulnerable group of antebellum America" (White, 1985, p. 15).

The race and gender roles of the day idealized southern white women and placed them on a pedestal. A romanticized conception of femininity was quite inconsistent with the roles women slaves were required to play. Besides domestic roles, female slaves also worked in the fields and did their share of the hardest, most physically demanding, least "feminine" farmwork. Southern ideas about feminine fragility and daintiness were quickly abandoned when they interfered with work and the profit to be made from slave labor (Amott & Matthaei, 1991, p. 146).

Reflecting their vulnerability and powerlessness, women slaves were sometimes used to breed more slaves to sell. They were raped and otherwise abused by the males of the dominant group. John Blassingame (1972) expresses their vulnerability to sexual victimization:

Many white men considered every slave cabin a house of ill-fame. Often through "gifts" but usually by force, white overseers and planters obtained the sexual favors of black women. Generally speaking, the women were literally forced to offer themselves "willingly" and receive a trinket for their compliance rather than a flogging for their refusal. (p. 83)

Note the power relationships implicit in this passage: Female slaves had little choice but to feign willing submission to their white owners.

The routines of work and everyday life differed for male and female slaves. Although they sometimes worked with the men, especially during harvest time, women more often worked in sex-segregated groups organized around domestic as well as farm chores. In addition to working in the fields, they attended the births and cared for the children of both races, cooked and cleaned, wove cloth and sewed clothes, and did the laundry. The women often worked longer hours than the men, doing housework and other chores long after the men retired (Robertson, 1996, p. 21; White, 1985, p. 122).

The group-oriented nature of their tasks gave female slaves an opportunity to develop same-sex bonds and relationships. Women cooperated in their chores, in caring for their children, in the maintenance of their quarters, and in myriad other domestic and family chores. These networks and interpersonal bonds could be used to resist the system. For example, slave women sometimes induced abortions rather than bring more children into bondage. They often controlled the role of midwife and were able to effectively deceive slave owners and disguise the abortions as miscarriages (White, 1985, pp. 125–126). The networks of relationships among the female slaves provided mutual aid and support for everyday problems, solace and companionship during the travails of a vulnerable and exploited existence, and some ability to buffer and resist the influence and power of the slave owners (Andersen, 1993, pp. 164–165).

Slaves in the American system were brutally repressed and exploited, but females were even more subordinated than males. Also, their oppression and exclusion sharply differentiated female slaves from white females. The white "Southern Belle," chaste, untouchable, and unremittingly virtuous, had little in common with African American women under slavery.

The Creation of Minority Status for American Indians and Mexican Americans

Two other groups became minorities during the preindustrial period. In this section, we will review the dynamics of these processes and make some comparisons with African Americans. As you will see, both the Noel and Blauner hypotheses provide some extremely useful insights into these experiences.

American Indians

As Europeans began to penetrate the New World, they encountered hundreds of societies that had lived on this land for thousands of years. American Indian societies were highly variable in culture, language, size, and subsistence technology. Some were small, nomadic hunter-gatherer bands, whereas others were more developed societies in which people lived in settled villages and tended large gardens. Regardless of their exact nature, the inexorable advance of white society eventually devastated them all. Contact began in the East and established a pattern of conflict and defeat for American Indians that continued until the last of the tribes were finally defeated in the late 1800s. The continual expansion of white society into the West allowed many settlers to fulfill their dreams of economic self-sufficiency, but American Indians, who lost not only their lives and their land but also much of their traditional way of life, paid an incalculable price.

An important and widely unrecognized point about American Indians is that there is no such thing as the American Indian. Rather, there were—and are—hundreds of different tribes or nations, each with its own language, culture, home territory, and unique history. There are, of course, similarities from tribe to tribe, but there are also vast differences between, for example, the forest-dwelling tribes of Virginia, who lived in longhouses and cultivated gardens, and the nomadic Plains tribes, who relied on hunting to satisfy their needs. Each tribe was and remains a unique blend of language, values, and social structure. Because of space constraints, we will not always be able to take all these differences into account. Nonetheless, it is important to be aware of the diversity and sensitive to the variety of peoples and histories subsumed within the general category of American Indian.

A second important point is that many American Indian tribes no longer exist or are vastly diminished in size. When Jamestown was established in 1607, it is estimated that there were anywhere from 1 million to more than 10 million American Indians living in what became the United States. By 1890, when the Indian Wars finally ended, the number of American Indians had fallen to fewer than 250,000. By the end of the nearly 300-year long "contact situation," American Indian populations had declined by 75% or more (Wax, 1971, p. 17; see also McNickle, 1973).

Very little of this population loss was due directly to warfare and battle casualties. The greatest part was caused by European diseases brought over by the colonists and by the destruction of the food supplies on which American Indian societies relied. American Indians died by the thousands from measles, influenza, smallpox, cholera, tuberculosis, and a variety of other infectious diseases (Wax, 1971, p. 17; see also Oswalt & Neely, 1996; Snipp, 1989). Traditional hunting grounds and garden plots were taken over by the expanding American society, and game such as the buffalo was slaughtered to the point of extinction. The result of the contact situation for American Indians very nearly approached genocide.

American Indians and the Noel and Blauner Hypotheses.
We have already used the Noel hypothesis to analyze why American Indians were not enslaved during the colonial era. Their competition with whites centered on land, not labor, and the Indian nations were often successful in resisting domination (at least temporarily). As American society spread to the West, competition over land continued, and the growing power, superior technology, and greater resource base of the dominant group gradually pushed American Indians to near extinction.

Various attempts were made to control the persistent warfare, the most important of which occurred before independence from Great Britain. In 1763, the British Crown ruled that the various tribes were to be considered "sovereign nations with inalienable rights to their land" (see Lurie, 1982; McNickle, 1973; Wax, 1971). In other words, each tribe was to be treated as a nation-state, like France or Russia, and the colonists could not simply expropriate tribal lands. Rather, negotiations had to take place, and treaties of agreement had to be signed by all affected parties. The tribes had to be compensated for any loss of land.

This policy was often ignored but was continued by the newborn federal government after the American Revolution. The principle of sovereignty is important because it established a unique relationship between the federal government and American Indians. The fact that white society ignored the policy and regularly broke the treaties gives American Indians legal claims against the federal government that are also unique.

East of the Mississippi River, the period of open conflict was brought to a close by the Indian Removal Act of 1830, which dictated a policy of forced emigration to the tribes. The law required all eastern tribes to move to new lands west of the Mississippi. Some of the affected tribes went without resistance, others fought, and still others fled to Canada rather than move to the new territory. Regardless, the Indian Removal Act "solved" the Indian problem in the East. The relative scarcity of American Indians in the eastern United States continues to the present, and the majority of American Indians live in the western two thirds of the nation.

In the West, the grim story of competition for land accompanied by rising hostility and aggression repeated itself. Wars were fought, buffalo were killed, territory was expropriated, atrocities were committed on both sides, and the fate of the tribes became more and more certain. By 1890, the greater power and resources of white society had defeated the Indian nations. All of the great warrior chiefs were dead or in prison, and almost all American Indians were living on reservations controlled by agencies of the federal government. The reservations consisted of land set aside for the tribes by the government during treaty negotiations. Often, these lands were not the traditional homelands and were hundreds or even thousands of miles away from what the tribe considered to be "home." It is not surprising that the reservations were usually on undesirable, often worthless land.

The 1890s mark a low point in American Indian history, a time of great demoralization and sadness. The tribes had to find a way to adapt to reservation life and new forms of subordination to the federal government. Although elements of the tribal way of life have survived, the tribes were impoverished and without resources and had little ability to pursue their own interests.

American Indians, in Blauner's terms, were a colonized minority group who faced high levels of prejudice, racism, and discrimination. Like African Americans, they were controlled by paternalistic systems (the reservations) and in a variety of ways were coercively acculturated. Furthermore, according to Blauner, the negative consequences of colonized minority group status will persist long after the contact situation has been resolved. As we will see in Chapter 8, there is a great deal of evidence to support this prediction.

Gender Relations. In the centuries before contact with Europeans, American Indian societies distributed resources and power in a wide variety of ways. At one extreme, some American Indian societies were highly stratified, and many practiced various forms of slavery. Others stressed equality, sharing of resources, and respect for the autonomy and dignity of each individual, including women and children (Amott & Matthaei, 1991, p. 33). American Indian societies were generally patriarchal and followed a strict gender-based division of labor, but this did not necessarily mean that women were subordinate. In many tribes, women held positions of great responsibility and controlled the wealth. For example, among the Iroquois (a large and powerful federation of tribes located in the Northeast), women controlled the land and the harvest, arranged marriages, supervised the children, and were responsible for the appointment of tribal leaders and decisions about peace and war (Oswalt & Neely, 1996, pp. 404–405). It was not unusual for women in many tribes to play key roles in religion, politics, warfare, and the economy. Some women even became highly respected warriors and chiefs (Amott & Matthaei, 1991, p. 36).

Gender relations were affected in a variety of ways during the prolonged contact period. In some cases, the relative status and power of women rose. For example, the women of the Navajo tribe (located mainly in what is now Arizona and New Mexico) were traditionally responsible for the care of herd animals and livestock. When the Spanish introduced sheep and goats into the region, the importance of this sector of the subsistence economy increased, and the power and status of women grew along with it.

In other cases, women were affected adversely. The women of the tribes of the Great Plains, for example, suffered a dramatic loss as a result of contact. The sexual division of labor in these tribes was that women were responsible for gardening, whereas men handled the hunting. When horses were introduced from Europe, the productivity of the male hunters was greatly increased. As their economic importance increased, males became more dominant and women lost status and power. Women in the Cherokee nation—a large tribe whose original homelands were in the Southeast—similarly lost considerable status and power under the pressure to assimilate. Traditionally, Cherokee land was cultivated, controlled, and passed down from generation to generation by the women. This matrilineal pattern was abandoned in favor of the European pattern of male ownership when the Cherokee attempted (futilely, as it turned out) to acculturate and avoid relocation under the Indian Removal Act of 1830 (Evans, 1989, pp. 12–18).

Summary. By the end of the contact period, the surviving American Indian tribes were impoverished, powerless, and clearly subordinate to white society and the federal government. Like African Americans, American Indians were sharply differentiated from the dominant group by race, and, in many cases, the tribes were internally stratified by gender. As was the case with African American slaves, the degree of gender inequality within the tribes was limited by their overall lack of autonomy and resources.

Hawaii

In 1788, while American Indians and whites continued their centuries-long struggle, white Europeans first made contact with the indigenous people of Hawaii. The contact situation and the system of group relations that evolved on the island nation provide an interesting and instructive contrast with the history of American Indians.

In Hawaii, contact was not immediately followed by conquest and colonization. Early relations between Europeans and Hawaiians were organized around trade and commerce, not competition over the control of land or labor. Also, Hawaiian society was large and highly developed, and it had sufficient military strength to protect itself from the relatively few Europeans who came to the islands in the early days. Thus, two of the three conditions stated in the Noel hypothesis for the emergence of a dominant-minority situation were not present in the early days of European-Hawaiian contact, and, consistent with the hypothesis, overt structures of conquest or dominance did not emerge until decades after first contact.

Contact with Europeans did bring other consequences, of course, including smallpox and other diseases to which native Hawaiians had no immunity. Death rates began to rise, and the population of native Hawaiians, which numbered about 300,000 in 1788, fell to less than 60,000 a century later (Kitano & Daniels, 1995, p. 137). White Europeans gradually turned the land to commercial agriculture, and by the mid-1800s, white planters had established large sugar plantations, an enterprise that is extremely labor-intensive and that has often been associated with systems of enforced labor and slavery (Curtin, 1990). By that time, however, there were not enough native Hawaiians to fill the demand for labor, and the planters began to recruit abroad, mostly in China, Portugal, Japan, Korea, Puerto Rico, and the Philippines. Native Hawaiians continued to shrink in numbers and were gradually pushed off their land and to the margins of the emerging society.

The white plantation owners came to dominate the island economy and political structure. Other groups, however, were not excluded from secondary structural assimilation. Laws banning entire groups from public institutions or practices such as school segregation are unknown in Hawaiian history. Americans of Japanese ancestry, for example, are very powerful in politics and have produced many of the leading Hawaiian politicians. Most other groups have taken advantage of the relative openness of Hawaiian society and have carved out niches for themselves in the institutional structure.

In the area of primary structural assimilation, rates of intermarriage among the various groups are much higher than on the mainland, reflecting an openness to intimacy across group lines that has characterized Hawaii since first contact. In particular, Native Hawaiians have intermarried freely with other groups (Kitano & Daniels, 1995, pp. 138–139).

Unlike the mainland society, Hawaii has no history of the most blatant and oppressive forms of group domination, racism, and legalized discrimination. Still, all is not perfect in this reputed racial paradise, and there is evidence of continuing ethnic and racial stratification, as well as prejudice and discrimination. In particular, Native Hawaiians today retain their minority group status. The group is quite small and numbers about 150,000, an increase from the historic lows of the

Photo 4.6

A male dancer prepares for the Hula. Many elements of traditional Hawaiian culture survived the contact period.

© Richard A. Cooke/Corbis.

19th century but still only about 12% of the state's population and a tiny minority of U.S. population.

On the other hand, Native Hawaiians compare favorably with both American Indians and black Americans in terms of education, income, and poverty (see Exhibit 4.6). This relatively higher status today is consistent with both the Noel and Blauner hypotheses: They were not subjected to the harsh conditions (slavery, segregation, near genocide, and massive institutional discrimination) of the other two groups. Although they compare favorably to the two colonized and conquered groups, Native Hawaiians tend to be the poorest of the various ethnic and racial groups on the island, and a protest movement of Native Hawaiians that stresses self-determination and the return of illegally taken land has been in existence since at least the 1960s.

Exhibit 4.5 Map of the Hawaiian Islands

Exhibit 4.6 Native Hawaiians Compared With Total Population, Black Americans, and American Indians, 2006

Indicator	Group			
	Total U.S. Population	Native Hawaiians	Black Americans	American Indians
High school graduate	84.1%	87.2%	79.6%	79.9%
College graduate	27.0%	14.1%	17.1%	15.7%
Median household income	$48,451	$50,877	$32,465	$36,011
Families in poverty	9.8%	12.4%	21.4%	19.2%

SOURCE: U.S. Bureau of the Census (2007a).

Mexican Americans

As the population of the United States increased and spread across the continent, contact with Mexicans inevitably occurred. Spanish explorers and settlers had lived in what is now the southwestern United States long before the wave of American settlers broke across this region. For example, Santa Fe, New Mexico, was founded in 1598, nearly a decade before Jamestown. As late as the 1820s, Mexicans and American Indians were almost the sole residents of the region.

In the early 1800s, four areas of Mexican settlement had developed, roughly corresponding to what was to become Texas, California, New Mexico, and Arizona. These areas were sparsely settled, and most Mexicans lived in what was to become New Mexico (Cortes, 1980,

p. 701). The economy of the regions was based on farming and herding. Most people lived in villages and small towns or on ranches and farms. Social and political life was organized around family and the Catholic Church and tended to be dominated by an elite class of wealthy landowners.

Texas. Some of the first effects of U.S. expansion to the West were felt in Texas early in the 1800s. Mexico was no military match for its neighbor to the north, and the farmland of East Texas was a tempting resource for the cotton-growing interests in the American South. Anglo-Americans began to immigrate to Texas in sizable numbers in the 1820s, and by 1835, they outnumbered Mexicans 6 to 1. The attempts by the Mexican government to control these immigrants were clumsy and ineffective and eventually precipitated a successful revolution by the Anglo-Americans, with some Mexicans also joining the rebels. At this point in time, competition between Anglos and Texans of Mexican descent (called *Tejanos*) was muted by the abundance of land and opportunity in the area. Population density was low, fertile land was readily available for all, and the "general tone of the time was that of inter-cultural cooperation" (Alvarez, 1973, p. 922).

Photo 4.7

A Mexican woman working in an onion field. Mexican labor has been vital for the development of the Southwest.

© Corbis.

Competition between Anglo-Texans and Tejanos became increasingly intense. When the United States annexed Texas in the 1840s, full-scale war broke out and Mexico was defeated. Under the Treaty of Guadalupe Hidalgo in 1848, Mexico ceded much of the Southwest to the United States. In the Gadsden Purchase of 1853, the United States acquired the remainder of the territory that now composes the southwestern United States. As a result of these treaties, the Mexican population of this region had become, without moving an inch from their traditional villages and farms, both a conquered people and a minority group.

Following the war, intergroup relations continued to sour, and the political and legal rights of the Tejano community were often ignored in the hunger for land. Increasingly impoverished and powerless, the Tejanos had few resources with which to resist the growth of Anglo-American domination. They were badly outnumbered and stigmatized by the recent Mexican military defeat. Land that had once been Mexican increasingly came under Anglo control, and widespread violence and lynching reinforced the growth of Anglo dominance (Moquin & Van Doren, 1971, p. 253).

California. In California, the Gold Rush of 1849 spurred a massive population movement from the East. Early relations between Anglos and *Californios* (native Mexicans in the state) had been relatively cordial, forming the basis for a multiethnic, bilingual state. The rapid growth of an Anglo majority after statehood in 1850 doomed these efforts, however, and the Californios, like the Tejanos, lost their land and political power.

Laws were passed encouraging Anglos to settle on land traditionally held by Californios. In such situations, the burden was placed on the Mexican American landowners to show that their deeds were valid. The Californios protested the seizure of their land but found it difficult to argue their cases in the English-speaking, Anglo-controlled court system. By the mid-1850s, a massive transfer of land to Anglo-American hands had taken place in California (Mirandé, 1985, pp. 20–21; see also Pitt, 1970).

Other laws passed in the 1850s made it increasingly difficult for Californios to retain their property and power as Anglo-Americans became the dominant group as well as the majority of the population. The area's Mexican heritage was suppressed and eliminated from public life and institutions such as schools and local government. For example, in 1855, California repealed a requirement in the state constitution that all laws be published in Spanish as well as English (Cortes, 1980, p. 706). Anglo-Americans used violence, biased laws, discrimination, and other means to exploit and repress Californios, and the new wealth generated by gold mining flowed into Anglo hands.

Arizona and New Mexico.
The Anglo immigration into Arizona and New Mexico was less voluminous than that into Texas and California, and both states retained Mexican numerical majorities for a number of decades. In Arizona, most of the Mexican population were immigrants themselves, seeking work on farms, on ranches, in the mines, and on railroads. The economic and political structures of the state quickly came under the control of the Anglo population.

Only in New Mexico did Mexican Americans retain some political power and economic clout, mostly because of the relatively large size of the group and their skill in mobilizing for political activity. New Mexico did not become a state until 1912, and Mexican Americans continued to play a prominent role in governmental affairs even after statehood (Cortes, 1980, p. 706).

Thus, the contact situation for Mexican Americans was highly variable by region. Although some areas were affected more rapidly and more completely than others, the ultimate result was the creation of minority group status for Mexican Americans (Acuna, 1999; Alvarez, 1973; McLemore, 1973; McWilliams, 1961; Moore, 1970; Stoddard, 1973).

Mexican Americans and the Noel and Blauner Hypotheses.
The causal model we have applied to the origins of slavery and the domination of American Indians also provides a way of explaining the development of minority group status for Mexican Americans. Ethnocentrism was clearly present from the very first contact between Anglo immigrants and Mexicans. Many American migrants to the Southwest brought with them the prejudices and racism they had acquired with regard to African Americans and American Indians. In fact, many of the settlers who moved into Texas came directly from the South in search of new lands for the cultivation of cotton. They readily transferred their prejudiced views to at least the poorer Mexicans, who were stereotyped as lazy and shiftless (McLemore, 1973, p. 664). The visibility of group boundaries was heightened and reinforced by physical and religious differences. Mexicans were "racially" a mixture of Spaniards and American Indians, and the differences in skin color and other physical characteristics provided a convenient marker of group membership. In addition, the vast majority of Mexicans were Roman Catholic, whereas the vast majority of Anglo-Americans were Protestant.

Competition for land began with the first contact between the groups. However, for many years, population density was low in the Southwest, and the competition did not immediately or always erupt into violent domination and expropriation. Nonetheless, the loss of land and power for Mexican Americans was inexorable, although variable in speed.

The size of the power differential between the groups was variable and partly explains why domination was established faster in some places than others. In both Texas and California, the subordination of the Mexican American population followed quickly after a rapid influx of Anglos and the military defeat of Mexico. Anglo-Americans used their superior numbers and military power to acquire control of the political and economic structures and expropriate the resources of the Mexican American community. In New Mexico, the groups were more evenly matched in size, and Mexican Americans were able to retain a measure of power for decades.

Unlike the case of American Indians, however, the labor as well as the land of the Mexicans was coveted. On cotton plantations, ranches, and farms, and in mining and railroad construction, Mexican Americans became a vital source of inexpensive labor. During times of high demand, this labor force was supplemented by workers who were encouraged to emigrate from Mexico. When demand for workers decreased, these laborers were forced back to Mexico. Thus began a pattern of labor flow that continues to the present.

As in the case of African Americans and American Indians, the contact period clearly established a colonized status for Mexican Americans in all areas of the Southwest. Their culture and language were suppressed even as their property rights were abrogated and their status lowered. In countless ways, they, too, were subjected to coercive acculturation. For example, California banned the use of Spanish in public schools, and bullfighting and other Mexican sports and recreational activities were severely restricted (Moore, 1970, p. 19; Pitt, 1970). In contrast to African Americans, however, Mexican Americans were in close proximity to their homeland and maintained close ties with villages and families. Constant movement across the border with Mexico kept the Spanish language and much of the Mexican heritage alive in the Southwest. Nonetheless, 19th-century Mexican Americans fit Blauner's category of a colonized minority group, and the suppression of their culture was part of the process by which the dominant culture was established.

Anglo-American economic interests benefited enormously from the conquest of the Southwest and the colonization of the Mexican people. Growers and other businessmen came to rely on the cheap labor provided by Mexican Americans and immigrant and day laborers from Mexico. The region grew in affluence and productivity, but Mexican Americans were now outsiders in their own land and did not share in the prosperity. In the land grab of the 1800s and the conquest of the indigenous Mexican population lies one of the roots of Mexican American relations with the dominant U.S. society today.

Gender Relations.
Prior to the arrival of Anglo-Americans, Mexican society in the Southwest was patriarchal and maintained a clear gender-based division of labor. These characteristics tended to persist after the conquest and the creation of minority group status.

Most Mexican Americans lived in small villages or on large ranches and farms. The women devoted their energies to the family, child rearing, and household tasks. As Mexican Americans were reduced to a landless labor force, women along with men suffered the economic devastation that accompanied military conquest by a foreign power. The kinds of jobs available to the men (mining, seasonal farmwork, railroad construction) often required them to be away from home for extended periods of time, and women, by default, began to take over the economic and other tasks traditionally performed by males.

Poverty and economic insecurity placed the family structures under considerable strain. Traditional cultural understandings about male dominance and patriarchy became moot when the men were absent for long periods of time and the decision-making power of Mexican American women increased. Also, women were often forced to work outside the household for the family to survive economically. The economics of conquest led to increased matriarchy and more working mothers (Becerra, 1988, p. 149).

For Mexican American women, the consequences of contact were variable even though the ultimate result was a loss of status within the context of the conquest and colonization of the group as a whole. Like black female slaves, Mexican American women became the most vulnerable part of the social system.

Comparing Minority Groups

American Indians and black slaves were the victims of the explosive growth of European power in the Western Hemisphere that began with Columbus's voyage in 1492. Europeans needed labor to fuel the plantations of the mid-17th-century American colonies and settled on slaves from Africa as the most logical, cost-effective means of resolving their labor supply problems. Black Africans had a commodity the colonists coveted (labor), and the colonists subsequently constructed a system to control and exploit this commodity.

To satisfy the demand for land created by the stream of European immigrants to North America, the threat represented by American Indians had to be eliminated. Once their land was expropriated, American Indians ceased to be of much concern. The only valuable resource they possessed—their land—was under the control of white society by 1890, and American Indians were thought to be unsuitable as a source of labor.

Mexico, like the United States, had been colonized by a European power, in this case, Spain. In the early 1800s, the Mexican communities in the Southwest were a series of outpost settlements, remote and difficult to defend. Through warfare and a variety of other aggressive means, Mexican citizens living in this area were conquered and became an exploited minority group

African Americans, American Indians, and Mexican Americans, in their separate ways, became involuntary players in the growth and development of European and, later, American economic and political power. None of these groups had much choice in their respective fates; all three were overpowered and relegated to an inferior, subordinate status. Many views of assimilation (such as the "melting pot" metaphor discussed in Chapter 2) have little relevance to these situations. These minority groups had little control over their destinies, their degree of acculturation, or even their survival as groups. These three groups were coercively acculturated in the context of paternalistic relations in an agrarian economy. Meaningful integration (structural assimilation) was not a real possibility, especially for African Americans and American Indians. In Milton Gordon's (1964) terms (see Chapter 2), we might characterize these situations as "acculturation without integration" or structural pluralism. Given the grim realities described in this chapter, Gordon's terms seem a little antiseptic, and Blauner's concept of colonized minority groups seems far more descriptive.

Mexico, Canada, and the United States

In this chapter, we argued that dominant-minority relations are profoundly shaped by the contact situation and by the characteristics of the groups involved (especially their subsistence technologies). We saw how these factors shaped relations with Native Americans and Mexican Americans and how they led British colonists to create a system of slavery to control the labor of African Americans. How do the experiences of the Spanish and the French in the Western Hemisphere compare with those of the British in what became the United States? What roles did the contact situation and subsistence technology play in the development of group relations in these two neighbors of the United States?[1]

The Spanish were the first of the three European nations to invade the Western Hemisphere, and they conquered much of what is now Central and South America about a century before Jamestown was founded. Their first encounter with an American Indian society occurred in 1521, when they defeated the Aztec Empire, located in what is now central Mexico. Aztec society was large, highly organized, and complex. It was ruled by an emperor and included scores of different societies, each with its own language and identity, which had been conquered by the fiercely warlike Aztecs. The bulk of the population of the empire consisted of peasants or agricultural laborers who farmed small plots of land owned by members of the elite classes, to whom they paid rents. Peasants are a fundamental part of any labor-intensive, preindustrial agrarian society and were just as common in Spain as they were among the Aztecs.

When the Spanish defeated the Aztecs, they destroyed their cities, their temples, and their leadership (the emperor, the nobility, priests, etc.). They did not destroy the Aztec social structure; rather, they absorbed it and used it for their own benefit. For example, the Aztec Empire had financed its central government by collecting taxes and rents from citizens and tribute from conquered tribes. The Spanish simply grafted their own tax collection system onto this structure and diverted the flow from the Aztec elite classes (which they had, at any rate, destroyed) to themselves (Russell, 1994, pp. 29–30).

The Spanish tendency to absorb rather than destroy operated at many levels. For example, Aztec peasants became Spanish (and then Mexican) peasants, occupying roughly the same role in the new society that they had in the old, save for paying their rents to different landlords. There was also extensive interbreeding between the Spanish and the conquered tribes of Mexico, but again, unlike the situation in the English colonies, the Spanish recognized the resultant racial diversity and developed an elaborate system for classifying people by race. They recognized as many as 56 racial groups, including whites, **mestizos** (mixed European-Indian), and mulattoes (mixed European-African) (Russell, 1994, p. 35). The society that emerged was highly race conscious, and race was highly correlated with social class: The elite classes were white, and the lower classes were nonwhite. However, the large-scale intermarriage and the official recognition of mixed-race peoples did establish the foundation for a racially mixed society. Today, the huge majority of the Mexican population is mestizo, although there remains a very strong correlation between race and class, and the elite positions in the society tend to be monopolized by people of "purer" European ancestry.

The French began to colonize Canada at about the same time the English established their colonies further south. The dominant economic enterprise in the early days was not farming, but trapping and the fur trade. The French developed a lucrative trade in this area by allying themselves with some American Indian tribes. The Indians produced the furs and traded them to the French, who, in turn, sold them on the world market. Like the Spanish in Mexico, the French in Canada tended to link to and absorb Native American social structures. There was also a significant amount of intermarriage between the French and Native Americans, resulting in a mixed-race group, called *Métis,* who had their own identities and, indeed, their own settlements along the Canadian frontier (Russell, 1994, p. 39).

Note the profound differences in these three contact situations between Europeans and Native Americans. The Spanish confronted a large, well-organized social system and found it expeditious to adapt Aztec practices to their own benefit. The French developed an economy that required cooperation with at least some of the Native American tribes they encountered, and they, too, found benefits in adaptation. The tribes encountered by the English were much smaller and much less developed than the Aztecs, and there was no particular reason for the English to adapt to or absorb these social structures. Furthermore, because the business of the English colonies was agriculture (not trapping), the competition at the heart of the contact situation was for land, and American Indians were seen as rivals for control of that most valuable resource. Thus, the English tended to confront and exclude American Indians, keeping them on the outside of their emerging society and building strong boundaries between their own "civilized" world and the "savages" that surrounded them. The Spanish and French colonists had to adapt their societies to fit with American Indians, but the English faced no such restraints. They could create their institutions and design their social structure to suit themselves (Russell, 1994, p. 30).

As we have seen, one of the institutions created in the English colonies was slavery based on African labor. Slavery was also practiced in New Spain (Mexico) and New France (Canada), but the institution evolved in very different ways in those colonies and never assumed the importance that it did in the United States. Why? As you might suspect, the answer has a lot to do with the nature of the contact situation. Like the English colonists, both the Spanish and French attempted large-scale agricultural enterprises that might have created a demand for imported slave labor. In the case of New Spain, however, there was a ready supply of Native American peasants available to fill the role played by blacks in the

English colonies. Although Africans became a part of the admixture that shaped modern Mexico racially and socially, demand for black slaves never matched that of the English colonies. Similarly, in Canada, slaves from Africa were sometimes used, but farmers there tended to rely on the flow of labor from France to fill their agricultural needs. The British opted for slave labor from Africa over indentured labor from Europe, and the French made the opposite decision.

Another difference between the three European nations that helps to explain the divergent development of group relations is their relative level of modernization. Compared with England, Spain and France were more traditional and feudalistic in their cultures and social structures. Among other things, this meant that they had to shape their agricultural enterprises in the New World around the ancient social relations between peasants and landlords they brought from the Old World. Thus, the Spanish and French colonists were limited in their actions by these ancient customs, traditions, and understandings. Such old-fashioned institutions were much weaker in England, and thus the English colonists were much freer to design their social structure to suit their own needs. Whereas the Spanish and French had to shape their colonial societies to fit both American Indian social patterns and European traditions, the English could improvise and attend only to their own needs and desires. The closed, complex, and repressive institution of American slavery—designed and crafted from scratch in the New World—was one result.

Finally, we should note that many of the modern racial characteristics of these three neighboring societies were foreshadowed in their colonial origins (for example, the greater concentration of African Americans in the United States and the more racially intermixed population of Mexico). The differences run much deeper than race alone, of course, and include differences in class structure and relative levels of industrialization and affluence. For our purposes, however, this brief comparison of the origins of dominant-minority relations underscores the importance of the contact situation in shaping group relations for centuries to come.

How Did Slavery Affect the Origins of African American Culture?

A debate over the impact of slavery on African American culture began in the 1960s and continues to the present day. Stanley Elkins, in his 1959 book Slavery: A Problem in American Institutional and Intellectual Life, *laid down the terms of the debate. Elkins concluded that African American culture in the United States was created in response to the repressive plantation system and in the context of brutalization, total control of the slaves by their owners, and dehumanization. He argued that black culture was "made in America," but in an abnormal, even pathological social setting. The plantation was a sick society that dominated and infantilized black slaves. The dominant reality for slaves—and the only significant other person in their lives—was the master. Elkins described the system as a "perverted patriarchy" that psychologically forced the slaves to identify with their oppressors and to absorb the racist values at the core of the structure.*

Elkins's book has been called "a work of great intellectual audacity, based on a methodology which has little connection with conventional historical research and arriving at conclusions which were challenging or outrageous, according to one's point of view" (Parish, 1989, p. 7). The book stimulated an enormous amount of controversy and research on the impact of slavery and the origins of African American culture. This body of research developed new sources of evidence and new perspectives and generally concluded that African American culture is a combination of elements, some from the traditional cultures of Africa and others fabricated on the plantation. The selection that follows the one by Elkins, from the work of historian William Piersen,

illustrates this argument and focuses on West African and African American family customs.

A third view is presented in an excerpt from the writings of Deborah Gray White. She argues that most scholarly work on slavery is written from the perspective of the male slave only, to the point of excluding the female experience. In the passage from her 1985 book Ar'n't I a Woman? Female Slaves in the Plantation South, *she also addresses the problems of research in the area of minority group females and summarizes some of what has been learned from recent scholarship on the impact of slavery.*

All three of these views are consistent with Blauner's idea that the cultures of colonized minority groups are attacked and that the groups are forcibly acculturated. Elkins's argument is the most extreme in that it sees African American culture as fabricated entirely in response to the demands of enslavement and the fearful, all-powerful figure of the master.

Slavery Created African American Culture

STANLEY ELKINS

Both [the Nazi concentration camps and the American slave plantations] were closed systems from which all standards based on prior connections had been effectively detached. A working adjustment to either system required a childlike conformity, a limited choice of "significant other." Cruelty per se cannot be considered the primary key to this; of far greater importance was the simple "closedness" of the system, in which all lines of authority descended from the master and in which alternative social bases that might have supported alternative standards were systematically suppressed. The individual, consequently, for his very psychic security, had to picture his master in some way as the "good father," even when, as in the concentration camp, it made no sense at all.

For the Negro child, in particular, the plantation offered no really satisfactory father image other than the master. The "real" father was virtually without authority over his child, since discipline, parental responsibility, and control of rewards and punishments all rested in other hands; the slave father could not even protect the mother of his children.

From the master's viewpoint, slaves had been defined in law as property, and the master's power over his property must be absolute. . . . Absolute power for him meant absolute dependency for the slave—the dependency not of the developing child but of the perpetual child. For the master, the role most aptly fitting such a relationship would naturally be that of father.

SOURCE: Elkins, Stanley (1959). *Slavery: A Problem in American Institutional and Intellectual Life*, pp. 130–131. New York: Universal Library.

African American Culture Was Created by an Interplay of Elements From Africa and America

WILLIAM D. PIERSEN

In the colonial environment, . . . [African and European] traditions were fused. . . . The result was an unprecedented and unintended new multicultural American way of life. . . .

[Africans] had little choice [but this] adjustment was not as difficult . . . as we might suppose: the cultures of Africa and Europe were both dominated by the rhythms and sensibilities of a premodern, agricultural way of life shaped more by folk religion than by science, and domestic responsibilities were relatively similar on both continents. . . .

One of the greatest sacrifices that faced the new African Americans was the loss of the extended families that had structured most social relationships in Africa. . . . [African marriage customs were usually polygynous (permitting more than one wife) and patrilineal (tracing ancestry through the male side).] With marriage, most African Americans seem . . . to have settled quickly into Euro-American style, monogamous nuclear families that trace inheritance bilaterally through the lines of both parents. Nonetheless, colonial naming choices show the continuing importance of African ideas of kinship among African Americans, for black children were more commonly . . . named after recently deceased relatives, a practice rooted in the African belief of rebirth across generations. . . .

African Americans . . . tried to rebuild as best they could the social cohesion once provided by the now missing extended families of Africa. [They] tried to duplicate some of the kinship . . . functions . . . by forging close relationships with their countrymen and shipmates from the Middle Passage. . . . [Many] treated both the blacks and whites that lived with them . . . as a kind of artificial kin. . . .

In North America many white colonials soon gave up traditional European village residence patterns to move out individually on the land, but African Americans, when they had the choice, generally preferred to stay together. . . . Such communalism [was] a reflection of the value that Africans and African Americans put on collective living.

In West Africa kin groups gathered in their housing together in large compounds that featured centralized open spaces devoted to social functions and collective recreation. Husbands and wives within the compounds usually had their own separate family quarters. . . . In colonial

African American housing the old ways were maintained. . . . [In early-18th-century Virginia] most slaves lived in clusterings of more than 10 people. In these quarters, black social life was centered not on the interior of the small dark sleeping structures but outside on the common space devoted to social functions.

SOURCE: Piersen, William D. (1996). *From Africa to America: African American History From the Colonial Era to the Early Republic, 1526–1790*. New York: Twayne.

The Experiences of Female Slaves Have Been Under-researched and Under-reported

DEBORAH GRAY WHITE

Stanley Elkins began [the debate] by alleging that the American slave master had such absolute power and authority over the bondsman that the slave was reduced to childlike dependency. "Sambo," Elkins argued, was more than a product of Southern fantasy. He could not be dismissed as a "stereotype." . . .

Elkins' thesis had a profound effect upon the research and writing of the history of slavery. The direction that the research took, however, was in large part predetermined because Elkins' slavery defined the parameters of the debate. In a very subtle way these parameters had more to do with the nature of male slavery than with female slavery. . . .

John Blassingame's *The Slave Community* is a classic but much of it deals with male status. For instance, Blassingame stressed the fact that many masters recognized the male as the head of the family. He observed that during courtship, men flattered women and exaggerated their prowess. There was, however, little discussion of the reciprocal activities of slave women. Blassingame also described how slave men gained status in the family and slave community, but did not do the same for women. . . .

The reality of slave life gives us reason to suspect that we do black women a disservice when we rob them of a history that placed them at the side of their men in their race's struggle for freedom. The present study takes a look at slave women and argues that they were not submissive, subordinate, or prudish and they were not expected to be so. Women had different roles from those of men and they also had a great deal in common with their African foremothers, who held positions not inferior but complementary to those of men. . . .

Source material on the general nature of slavery exists in abundance, but it is very difficult to find source material about slave women in particular. Slave women are everywhere, yet nowhere. . . .

The source problem is directly related to what was and still is the black woman's condition. Every economic and political index demonstrated the black woman's virtual powerlessness in American society. A consequence of the double jeopardy and powerlessness is the black woman's invisibility. . . .

The history of slavery has come a long way. We have learned that race relations were never so clear-cut as to be solely a matter of white over black, but that in the assimilation of culture, in the interaction of blacks and whites, there were gray areas and relationships more aptly described in terms of black over white. We have also begun to understand that despite the brutality and inhumanity, or perhaps because of it, a distinct African American culture based on close-knit kinship relationships grew and thrived, and that it was this culture that sustained black people through many trials before and after emancipation.

SOURCE: White, Deborah Gray (1985). *Ar'n't I a Woman? Female Slaves in the Plantation South*, pp. 17–18. New York: Norton.

1. Why is the origin of African American culture an important issue? What difference does it make today? If you believe Elkins is correct, what are the implications for dealing with racial inequality in the present? Could a culture that was created under a pathological system and a sick society be an adequate basis for the pursuit of equality and justice today? Is Elkins's thesis a form of blaming the victim? Is it a way of blaming the present inequality of the black community on an "inadequate" culture, thus absolving the rest of society from blame?

2. If you agree with Piersen's or White's viewpoints, what are the implications for how African Americans think about their history and about themselves? What difference does it make if your roots are in Africa or in colonial Virginia or, as White and Piersen argue, in both?

3. What does White add to the debate? What are some of the challenges in researching the experiences of female slaves? How did the experiences of female slaves differ from those of male slaves?

Main Points

- Dominant-minority relations are shaped by the characteristics of society as a whole, particularly by subsistence technology. The contact situation is the single most important factor in the development of dominant-minority relations.

- The Noel hypothesis states that when a contact situation is characterized by ethnocentrism, competition, and a differential in power, ethnic or racial stratification will result. In colonial America, Africans were enslaved instead of white indentured servants or American Indians because only they fit all three conditions. American slavery was a paternalistic system.

- Prejudice and racism are more the results of systems of racial and ethnic inequality than they are the causes. They serve to rationalize, "explain," and stabilize these systems.

- The competition with American Indians centered on control of the land. American Indian tribes were conquered and pressed into a paternalistic relationship with white society. American Indians became a colonized minority group and were subjected to forced acculturation.

- Mexican Americans were the third minority group created during the preindustrial era. Mexican Americans competed with white settlers over both land and labor. Like Africans and American Indians, Mexican Americans were a colonized minority group subjected to forced acculturation.

- Conquest and colonization affected men and women differently. Women's roles changed, and they sometimes were less constrained by patriarchal traditions. These changes were always in the context of increasing powerlessness and poverty for the group as a whole, however, and minority women have been doubly oppressed by their gender roles as well as their minority group status.

- How long do patterns of ethnic and racial stratification persist? The two public sociology assignments presented in the introduction to Part 2 give you an opportunity to research this question on your own campus in terms of the diversity and equality of the workforce and in terms of "self-segregation" in the student body.

Study Site on the Web

Don't forget the interactive quizzes and other resources and learning aids at www.pineforge .com/healeystudy5.

For Further Reading

Genovese, Eugene D. (1974). *Roll, Jordan, Roll.* New York: Pantheon.

Gutman, Herbert G. (1976). *The Black Family in Slavery and Freedom.* New York: Vintage.

Levine, Lawrence. (1977). *Black Culture and Black Consciousness.* New York: Oxford University Press.

Rawick, George P. (1972). *From Sundown to Sunup: The Making of the Black Community.* Westport, CT: Greenwood Press.

Stuckey, Sterling. (1987). *Slave Culture: Nationalist Theory and the Foundations of Black America.* New York: Harper & Row.

A short list of five vital sources on the origins and psychological and cultural impact of slavery in America.

Brown, Dee. (1970). *Bury My Heart at Wounded Knee.* New York: Holt, Rinehart & Winston.

An eloquent and moving account of the conquest of American Indians.

Nabakov, Peter. (Ed.). 1999. *Native American Testimony* (Rev. ed.). New York: Penguin.

A collection of valuable and insightful American Indian accounts of the last 500 years.

Wax, Murray. (1971). *Indian Americans: Unity and Diversity.* Englewood Cliffs, NJ: Prentice Hall.

A compact and informative analysis of the history and present situation of American Indians.

McWilliams, Carey. (1961). *North From Mexico: The Spanish-Speaking People of the United States.* New York: Monthly Review Press.

A classic overview of the historical development of Mexican Americans.

Acuna, Rodolfo. (1999). *Occupied America* (4th ed.). New York: Harper & Row.

   Acuna examines a broad sweep of Mexican American experiences and argues that their status is comparable to that of other colonized groups.

Mirandé, Alfredo. (1985). *The Chicano Experience: An Alternative Perspective.* Notre Dame, IN: University of Notre Dame Press.

   A passionate argument for a new sociological approach to the study of Mexican Americans. Many useful insights into Mexican American family structures, the problem of crime, and other areas.

Questions for Review and Study

1. State and explain the two themes presented at the beginning of the chapter. Apply each to the contact situations between white European colonists, African Americans, American Indians, and Mexican Americans. Identify and explain the key differences and similarities between the three situations.

2. Explain what a plantation system is and why this system of production is important for understanding the origins of slavery in colonial America. Why are plantation systems usually characterized by (a) paternalism, (b) huge inequalities between groups, (c) repressive systems of control, (d) rigid codes of behavior, and (e) low rates of overt conflict?

3. Explain the Noel and Blauner hypotheses and explain how they apply to the contact situations covered in this chapter. Explain each of the following key terms: ethnocentrism, competition, power, colonized minority group, immigrant minority group. How did group conflict vary when competition was over land rather than over labor?

4. Explain the role of prejudice and racism in the creation of minority group status. Do prejudice and racism help cause minority group status, or are they caused by minority group status? Explain.

5. Compare and contrast gender relations in regard to each of the contact situations discussed in this chapter. Why do the relationships vary?

6. What does it mean to say that under slavery, acculturation for African Americans was coerced? What are the implications for assimilation, inequality, and African American culture?

7. Compare and contrast the contact situations of Native Hawaiians with American Indians. What were the key differences in the contact situation, and how are these differences reflected in the current situations of the groups?

8. Compare and contrast the contact situations in colonial America, Canada, and Mexico. What groups were involved in each situation? What was the nature of the competition, and what were the consequences?

Internet Research Project

The "slave narratives" are one interesting source of information about the nature of everyday life under slavery. The narratives were compiled during the 1930s in interviews with ex-slaves, and although they are limited in many ways, the interviews do provide a close-up, personal view of the system of slavery from the perspective of its victims. To use this resource, go to http://newdeal.feri.org/asn/index.htm and read the home page carefully, especially the cautions. Select several of the narratives and analyze them in terms of the concepts introduced in this chapter (e.g., paternalism, labor-intensive systems of work, the Noel and Blauner hypotheses).

Note

1. This section is largely based on Russell (1994).

Industrialization and Dominant-Minority Relations

From Slavery to Segregation and the Coming of Postindustrial Society

One theme stated at the beginning of Chapter 4 was that a society's subsistence technology shapes dominant-minority group relations. A corollary of this theme, explored in this chapter, is that *dominant-minority group relations change as the subsistence technology changes.* As we saw in Chapter 4, dominant-minority relations in the formative years of the United States were profoundly shaped by agrarian technology and the desire to control land and labor. The agrarian era ended in the 1800s, and since that time, the United States has experienced two major transformations in subsistence technology, each of which has, in turn, transformed dominant-minority relations.

The first transformation began in the early 1800s as American society began to experience the effects of the Industrial Revolution, or the shift from agrarian

technology to machine-based, manufacturing technology. In the agrarian era, as we saw in Chapter 4, work was labor-intensive, done by hand or with the aid of draft animals. As industrialization proceeded, work became capital-intensive as machines replaced people and animals.

The new industrial technology rapidly increased the productivity and efficiency of the U.S. economy and quickly began to change all other aspects of society, including the nature of work, politics, communication, transportation, family life, birthrates and death rates, the system of education, and, of course, dominant-minority relations. The groups that had become minorities during the agrarian era (African Americans, American Indians, and Mexican Americans) faced new possibilities and new dangers, but industrialization also created new minority groups, new forms of exploitation and oppression, and for some, new opportunities to rise in the social structure and succeed in America. In this chapter, we will explore this transformation and illustrate its effects on the status of African Americans. The impact of industrialization on other minority groups will be considered in the case studies presented in Part 3.

The second transformation in subsistence technology brings us to more recent times. Industrialization is a continuous process, and beginning in the mid-20th century, the United States entered the postindustrial era, also called **deindustrialization**. This shift in subsistence technology was marked by a decline in the manufacturing sector of the economy and a decrease in the supply of secure, well-paying, blue-collar, manual-labor jobs. At the same time, there was an expansion in the service- and information-based sectors of the economy and an increase in the proportion of white-collar and "high-tech" jobs. Like the 19th-century industrial revolution, these 20th-century changes have profound implications not just for dominant-minority relations, but for every aspect of modern society. Work, family, politics, popular culture, and thousands of other characteristics of American society are being transformed as the subsistence technology continues to develop and modernize. In the latter part of this chapter, we examine this latest transformation in general terms and point out some of its implications for minority groups. We also present some new concepts and establish some important groundwork for the case studies in Part 3, in which the effects of late industrialization on America's minority groups will be considered in detail.

Industrialization and the Shift From Paternalistic to Rigid Competitive Group Relations

The Industrial Revolution began in England in the mid-1700s and spread from there to the rest of Europe, to the United States, and eventually to the rest of the world. The key innovations associated with this change in subsistence technology were the application of machine power to production and the harnessing of inanimate sources of energy, such as steam and coal, to fuel the machines. As machines replaced humans and animals, work became many times more productive, the economy grew, and the volume and variety of goods produced increased dramatically.

In an industrial economy, the close, paternalistic control of minority groups found in agrarian societies becomes irrelevant. Paternalistic relationships such as slavery are found in societies with labor-intensive technologies and are designed to organize and control a large, involuntary, geographically immobile labor force. An industrial economy, in contrast, requires a workforce that is geographically and socially mobile, skilled, and literate. Furthermore, with industrialization comes urbanization, and close, paternalistic controls are difficult to maintain in a city.

Thus, as industrialization progresses, agrarian paternalism tends to give way to **rigid competitive** group relations. Under this system, minority group members are freer to compete for jobs and other valued commodities with dominant group members, especially the lower-class segments of the dominant group. As competition increases, the threatened members of the dominant group become more hostile, and attacks on the minority groups tend to increase. Whereas paternalistic systems seek to directly dominate and control the minority group (and its labor), rigid competitive systems are more defensive in nature. The threatened segments of the dominant group seek to minimize or eliminate minority group encroachment on jobs, housing, or other valuable goods or services (van den Berghe, 1967; Wilson, 1973).

Paternalistic systems such as slavery required members of the minority group to be active, if involuntary, participants. In contrast, in rigid competitive systems, the dominant group seeks to handicap the minority group's ability to compete effectively or, in some cases, eliminate competition from the minority group altogether. We have already considered an example of a dominant group attempt to protect itself from a threat. As you recall, the National Origins Act was passed in the 1920s to stop the flow of cheaper labor from Europe and protect jobs and wages (see Chapter 2). In this chapter, we consider dominant group attempts to keep African Americans powerless and impoverished as the society shifted from an agricultural to an industrial base.

The Impact of Industrialization on African Americans: From Slavery to Segregation

Industrial technology began to transform American society in the early 1800s, but its effects were not felt equally in all regions. The northern states industrialized first, while the South remained primarily agrarian. This economic diversity was one of the underlying causes of the regional conflict that led to the Civil War. Because of its more productive technology, the North had more resources and defeated the Confederacy in a bloody war of attrition. Slavery was abolished, and black-white relations in the South entered a new era when the Civil War ended in April 1865.

The southern system of race relations that ultimately emerged after the Civil War was designed in part to continue the control of African American labor institutionalized under slavery. It was also intended to eliminate any political or economic threat from the African American community. This rigid competitive system grew to be highly elaborate and inflexible, partly because of the high racial visibility and long history of inferior status and powerlessness of African Americans in the South and partly because of the particular needs of southern agriculture. In this section, we look at black-white relations from the end of the Civil War through the ascendance of segregation in the South and the mass migration of African Americans to the cities of the industrializing North.

Reconstruction

The period of **Reconstruction**, from 1865 to the 1880s, was a brief respite in the long history of oppression and exploitation of African Americans. The Union army and other agencies of the federal government, such as the Freedman's Bureau, were used to enforce racial freedom in the defeated Confederacy. Black southerners took advantage of the Fifteenth Amendment to the Constitution, passed in 1870, which states that the right to vote cannot be denied on the grounds of "race, color, or previous condition of servitude." They registered to vote in large numbers and turned out on election day, and some were elected to high political office. Schools for the former slaves were opened, and African Americans purchased land and houses and founded businesses.

The era of freedom was short, however, and Reconstruction began to end when the federal government demobilized its armies of occupation and turned its attention to other matters. By the 1880s, the federal government had withdrawn from the South, Reconstruction was over, and black southerners began to fall rapidly into a new system of exploitation and inequality.

Reconstruction was too brief to change two of the most important legacies of slavery. First, the centuries of bondage left black southerners impoverished, largely illiterate and uneducated, and with few power resources. When new threats of racial oppression appeared, African Americans found it difficult to defend their group interests. These developments are consistent with the Blauner hypothesis: Colonized minority groups face greater difficulties in improving their disadvantaged status because they confront greater inequalities and have fewer resources at their disposal.

Second, slavery left a strong tradition of racism in the white community. Anti-black prejudice and racism originated as rationalizations for slavery but had taken on lives of their own over the generations. After two centuries of slavery, the heritage of prejudice and racism was thoroughly ingrained in southern culture. White southerners were predisposed by this cultural legacy to see racial inequality and exploitation of African Americans as normal and desirable. They were able to construct a social system based on the assumption of racial inferiority after Reconstruction ended and the federal government withdrew.

De Jure Segregation

The system of race relations that replaced slavery in the South was **de jure segregation**, sometimes referred to as the **Jim Crow** system. Under segregation, the minority group is physically and socially separated from the dominant group and consigned to an inferior position in virtually every area of social life. The phrase *de jure* ("by law") means that the system is sanctioned and reinforced by the legal code; the inferior status of African Americans was actually mandated or required by state and local laws. For example, southern cities during this era had laws requiring African Americans to ride at the back of the bus. If an African American refused to comply with this seating arrangement, he or she could be arrested.

De jure segregation came to encompass all aspects of southern social life. Neighborhoods, jobs, stores, restaurants, and parks were segregated. When new social forms, such as movie theaters, sports stadiums, and interstate buses appeared in the South, they, too, were quickly segregated.

The logic of segregation created a vicious cycle. The more African Americans were excluded from the mainstream of society, the greater their objective poverty and powerlessness became. The more inferior their status and the greater their powerlessness, the easier it was to mandate more inequality. High levels of inequality reinforced racial prejudice and made it easy to use racism to justify further separation. The system kept turning on itself, finding new social niches to segregate and reinforcing the inequality that was its starting point. For example, at the height of the Jim

Photo 5.2

One of the most serious forms of official, state-sponsored racial segregation was in the schools.

© Bettmann/Corbis.

Segregation affected virtually every aspect of Southern life including rest rooms and water fountains.

© Bettmann/Corbis.

Crow era, the system had evolved to the point that some courtrooms maintained separate Bibles for African American witnesses to swear on. Also, in Birmingham, Alabama, it was against the law for blacks and whites to play checkers and dominoes together (Woodward, 1974, p. 118).

What were the causes of this massive separation of the races? Once again, the concepts of the Noel hypothesis prove useful. Because strong anti-black prejudice was already in existence when segregation began, we do not need to account for ethnocentrism. The post-Reconstruction competition between the racial groups was reminiscent of the origins of slavery in that black southerners had something that white southerners wanted: labor. In addition, a free black electorate threatened the political and economic dominance of the elite segments of the white community. Finally, after the withdrawal of federal troops and the end of Reconstruction, white southerners had sufficient power resources to end the competition on their own terms and construct repressive systems of control for black southerners.

The Origins of De Jure Segregation.
Although the South lost the Civil War, its basic class structure and agrarian economy remained intact. The plantation elite, with their huge tracts of land, remained the dominant class, and cotton remained the primary cash crop. As was the case before the Civil War, the landowners needed a workforce to farm the land. Because of the depredations and economic disruptions of the war, the old plantation elite was short on cash and liquid capital. Hiring workers on a wage system was not feasible for them. In fact, almost as soon as the war ended, southern legislatures attempted to force African

Americans back into involuntary servitude by passing a series of laws known as the "Black Codes." Only the beginning of Reconstruction and the active intervention of the federal government halted the implementation of this legislation (Geschwender, 1978, p. 158; Wilson, 1973, p. 99).

The plantation elite solved their manpower problem this time by developing a system of **sharecropping**, or tenant farming. The sharecroppers worked the land, which was actually owned by the planters, in return for payment in shares of the profit when the crop was taken to market. The landowner would supply a place to live and food and clothing on credit. After the harvest, tenant and landowner would split the profits (sometimes very unequally), and the tenant's debts would be deducted from his share. The accounts were kept by the landowner. Black sharecroppers lacked political and civil rights and found it difficult to keep unscrupulous white landowners honest. The landowner could inflate the indebtedness of the sharecropper and claim that he was still owed money even after profits had been split. Under this system, sharecroppers had few opportunities to improve their situations and could be bound to the land until their "debts" were paid off (Geschwender, 1978, p. 163).

By 1910, more than half of all employed African Americans worked in agriculture, and more than half of the remainder (25% of the total) worked in domestic occupations, such as maid or janitor (Geschwender, 1978, p. 169). The manpower shortage in southern agriculture was solved, and the African American community once again found itself in a subservient status. At the same time, the white southern working class was protected from direct job competition with African Americans. As the South began to industrialize, white workers were able to monopolize the better-paying jobs. With a combination of direct discrimination by whites-only labor unions and strong anti-black laws and customs, white workers erected barriers that excluded black workers and reserved the better industrial jobs in cities and mill towns for themselves. White workers took advantage of the new jobs brought by industrialization, while black southerners remained a rural peasantry, excluded from participation in this process of modernization.

In some sectors of the changing southern economy, the status of African Americans actually fell lower than it had been during slavery. For example, in 1865, 83% of the artisans in the South were African Americans; by 1900, this percentage had fallen to 5% (Geschwender, 1978, p. 170). The Jim Crow system confined African Americans to the agrarian and domestic sectors of the labor force, denied them the opportunity for a decent education, and excluded them from politics. The system was reinforced by still more laws and customs that drastically limited the options and life opportunities available to black southerners.

A final force behind the creation of de jure segregation was more political than economic. As the 19th century drew to a close, a wave of agrarian radicalism known as *populism* spread across the country. This anti-elitist movement was a reaction to changes in agriculture caused by industrialization. The movement attempted to unite poor whites and blacks in the rural South against the traditional elite classes. The economic elite was frightened by the possibility of a loss of power and split the incipient coalition between whites and blacks by fanning the flames of racial hatred. The strategy of "divide and conquer" proved to be effective (as it often has both before and since this time), and the white elite classes in states throughout the South eliminated the possibility of future threats by depriving African Americans of the right to vote (Woodward, 1974).

The disenfranchisement of the black community was accomplished by measures such as literacy tests, poll taxes, and property requirements. The literacy tests were officially justified as promoting a better-informed electorate but were shamelessly rigged to favor white voters. The requirement that voters pay a tax or prove ownership of a certain amount of property could also disenfranchise poor whites, but again, the implementation of these policies was racially biased.

The policies were extremely effective, and by the early 20th century, the political power of the southern black community was virtually nonexistent. For example, as late as 1896 in Louisiana, there had been more than 100,000 registered African American voters, and African American voters were a majority in 26 parishes (counties). In 1898, the state adopted a new constitution containing stiff educational and property requirements for voting unless the voter's father or grandfather had been eligible to vote as of January 1, 1867. At that time, the Fourteenth and Fifteenth Amendments, which guaranteed suffrage for black males, had not yet been passed. Such "grandfather clauses" made it easy for white males to register while disenfranchising blacks. By 1900, only about 5,000 African Americans were registered to vote in Louisiana, and African American voters were not a majority in any parish. A similar decline occurred in Alabama, where an electorate of more than 180,000 African American males was reduced to 3,000 by provision of a new state constitution. This story repeated itself throughout the South, and African American political powerlessness had become a reality by 1905 (Franklin & Moss, 1994, p. 261).

This system of legally mandated racial privilege was approved by the U.S. Supreme Court, which ruled in the case of *Plessy v. Ferguson* (1896) that it was constitutional for states to require separate facilities (schools, parks, etc.) for African Americans as long as the separate facilities were fully equal. The southern states paid close attention to "separate" but "ignored equal."

Reinforcing the System.

Under de jure segregation, as under slavery, the subordination of the African American community was reinforced and supplemented by an elaborate system of racial etiquette. Everyday interactions between blacks and whites proceeded according to highly stylized and rigidly followed codes of conduct intended to underscore the inferior status of the African American community. Whites were addressed as "Mister" or "Ma'am," whereas African Americans were called by their first names or perhaps by an honorific title such as "Aunt," "Uncle," or "Professor." Blacks were expected to assume a humble and deferential manner, remove their hats, cast their eyes downward, and enact the role of the subordinate in all interactions with whites. If an African American had reason to call on anyone in the white community, he or she was expected to go to the back door.

These expectations and "good manners" for black southerners were systematically enforced. Anyone who ignored them ran the risk of reprisal, physical attacks, and even death by lynching. During the decades in which the Jim Crow system was being imposed, there were thousands of lynchings in the South. From 1884 until the end of the century, lynchings averaged almost one every other day (Franklin & Moss, 1994, p. 312). The bulk of this violent terrorism was racial and intended to reinforce the system of racial advantage or punish real or imagined transgressors. Also, various secret organizations, such as the Ku Klux Klan, engaged in terrorist attacks against the African American community and anyone else who failed to conform to the dictates of the system.

Increases in Prejudice and Racism. As the system of racial advantage formed and solidified, levels of prejudice and racism increased (Wilson, 1973, p. 101). The new system needed justification and rationalization, just as slavery did, and anti-black sentiment, stereotypes, and ideologies of racial inferiority grew stronger. At the start of the 20th century, the United States in general—not just the South—was a very racist and intolerant society. This spirit of rejection and scorn for all out-groups coalesced with the need for justification of the Jim Crow system and created an especially negative brand of racism in the South.

The "Great Migration"

Although African Americans lacked the power resources to withstand the resurrection of southern racism and oppression, they did have one option that had not been available under slavery: freedom of movement. African Americans were no longer legally tied to a specific master or to a certain plot of land. In the early 20th century, a massive population movement out of the South began. Slowly at first, African Americans began to move to other regions of the nation and from the countryside to the city. The movement increased when hard times hit southern agriculture and slowed down during better times. It has been said that African Americans voted against southern segregation with their feet.

As Exhibits 5.1 and 5.2 show, an urban black population living outside the South is a 20th-century phenomenon. A majority of African Americans continue to live in the South, but the group is more evenly distributed across the nation and much more urbanized than a century ago.

Exhibit 5.1 Regional Distribution of African American Population, 1890–2004

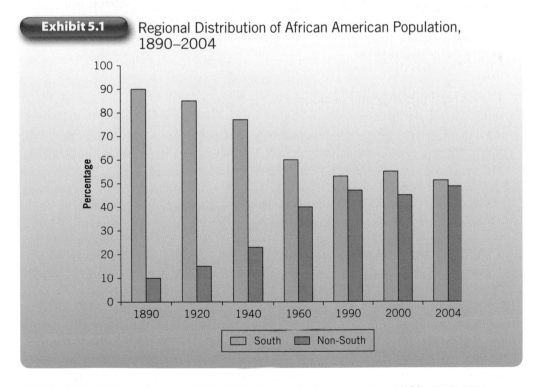

SOURCE: 1890–1960: Geschwender (1978); 1990: Heaton, Chadwick, & Jacobson (2000); 2000, 2004: U.S. Bureau of the Census (2006).

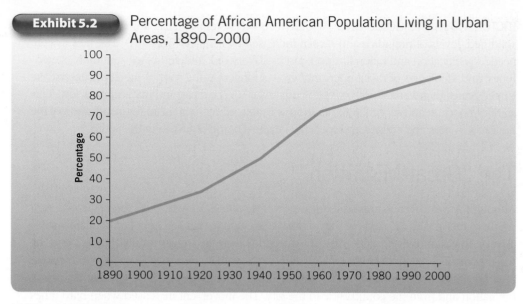

Exhibit 5.2 Percentage of African American Population Living in Urban Areas, 1890–2000

SOURCE: 1890–1960: Geschwender (1978); 1970, 1980, 1990: Pollard & O'Hare (1999, p. 27); 2000: U.S. Bureau of the Census (2000f).

The significance of this population redistribution is manifold. Most important, perhaps, was the fact that by moving out of the South and from rural to urban areas, African Americans moved from areas of great resistance to racial change to areas of lower resistance. In the northern cities, for example, it was far easier to register and to vote. Black political power began to grow and eventually provided many of the crucial resources that fueled the civil rights movement of the 1950s and 1960s.

Life in the North

What did African American migrants find when they got to the industrializing cities of the North? There is no doubt that life in the North was better for the vast majority of African American migrants. The growing Northern African American communities relished the absence of Jim Crow laws and oppressive racial etiquette, the relative freedom to pursue jobs, and the greater opportunities to educate their children. Inevitably, however, life in the North fell short of utopia. Many aspects of African American culture—literature, poetry, music—flourished in the heady new atmosphere of freedom, but on other fronts, Northern African American communities faced discrimination in housing, schools, and the job market. Along with freedom and such cultural flowerings as the Harlem Renaissance came black ghettos and new forms of oppression and exploitation.

Competition With White Ethnic Groups

It is useful to see the movement of African Americans out of the South in terms of their resultant relationships with other groups. Southern blacks began to move to the North at about the same time as the "New Immigration" from Europe (see Chapter 2) began to end. By the time

substantial numbers of black southerners began arriving in the North, European immigrants and their descendants had had years, decades, and even generations to establish themselves in the job markets, political systems, labor unions, and neighborhoods of the North. Many of the European ethnic groups had also been the victims of discrimination and rejection, and, as we discussed in Chapter 2, their hold on economic security and status was tenuous for much of the 20th century. They saw the newly arriving black migrants as a threat to their status, a perception that was reinforced by the fact that industrialists and factory owners often used African Americans as strikebreakers and scabs during strikes. The white ethnic groups responded by developing defensive strategies to limit the dangers presented by these migrants from the South. They tried to exclude African Americans from their labor unions and other associations and limit their impact on the political system. They also attempted, often successfully, to maintain segregated neighborhoods and schools (although the legal system outside the South did not sanction overt de jure segregation).

This competition led to hostile relations between black southern migrants and white ethnic groups, especially the lower- and working-class segments of those groups. Ironically, however, in another chapter of the ethnic succession discussed in Chapter 2, the newly arriving African Americans actually helped white ethnic groups become upwardly mobile. Dominant group whites became less contemptuous of white ethnic groups as their alarm over the presence of African Americans increased. The greater antipathy of the white community toward African Americans made the immigrants less undesirable and thus hastened their admittance to the institutions of the larger society. For many white ethnic groups, the increased tolerance of the larger society coincided happily with the coming of age of the more educated and skilled descendants of the original immigrants, further abetting the rise of these groups in the U.S. social class structure (Lieberson, 1980).

For more than a century, each new European immigrant group had helped to push previous groups up the ladder of socioeconomic success and out of the old, ghettoized neighborhoods. Black southerners got to the cities after immigration from Europe had been curtailed, and no newly arrived immigrants appeared to continue the pattern of succession for northern African Americans. Instead, American cities developed concentrations of low-income blacks

The Kitchenette

*R*ichard Wright (1908–1960), one of the most powerful writers of the 20th century, lived through and wrote about many of the social changes discussed in this chapter. He grew up in the South during the height of the Jim Crow system, and his passionate hatred for segregation and bigotry is expressed in his major works, Native Son (1940) and the autobiographical Black Boy (1945). In 1941, Wright helped to produce 12 Million Black Voices, a folk history of African Americans. A combination of photos and brief essays, the work is a powerful commentary on three centuries of oppression.

The following selection is adapted from "Death on the City Pavement," which expresses Wright's view of the African American [black] migration out of the South, a journey he himself experienced. This bittersweet migration often traded the harsh, rural repression of the South for the overcrowded, anonymous ghettos of the North. Housing discrimination, both overt and covert, confined African American migrants to the least desirable, most overcrowded areas of the city—in many cases, the neighborhoods that had first housed immigrants from Europe. Unscrupulous landlords subdivided buildings into the tiniest possible apartments ("kitchenettes"), and as impoverished newcomers who could afford no better, African American migrants were forced to cope with overpriced, substandard housing as best they could. Much of this passage, incidentally, could have been written about any 20th-century minority group.

Death on the City Pavement

Richard Wright

A war sets up in our emotions: one part of our feelings tells us it is good to be in the city, that we have a chance at life here, that we need but turn a corner to become a stranger, that we need no longer bow and dodge at the sight of the Lords of the Land. Another part of our feelings tells us that, in terms of worry and strain, the cost of living in the kitchenettes is too high, that the city heaps too much responsibility on us and gives too little security in return. . . .

The kitchenette, with its filth and foul air, with its one toilet for thirty or more tenants, kills our black babies so fast that in many cities twice as many of them die as white babies. . . .

The kitchenette scatters death so widely among us that our death rate exceeds our birth rate, and if it were not for the trains and autos bringing us daily into the city from the plantations, we black folk who dwell in northern cities would die out entirely over the course of a few years. . . .

The kitchenette throws desperate and unhappy people into an unbearable closeness of association, thereby increasing latent friction, giving birth to never-ending quarrels of recrimination, accusation, and vindictiveness, producing warped personalities.

The kitchenette injects pressure and tension into our individual personalities, making many of us give up the struggle, walk off and leave wives, husbands, and even children behind to shift for themselves. . . .

The kitchenette reaches out with fingers of golden bribes to the officials of the city, persuading them to allow old firetraps to remain standing and occupied long after they should have been torn down.

The kitchenette is the funnel through which our pulverized lives flow to ruin and death on the city pavement, at a profit.

SOURCE: Wright, Richard (1988). *12 Million Black Voices,* pp. 105–111. New York: Thunder's Mouth Press.

who were economically vulnerable and politically weak and whose position was further solidified by anti-black prejudice and discrimination (Wilson, 1987, p. 34).

The Origins of Black Protest

As I pointed out in Chapter 4, African Americans have always resisted their oppression and protested their situation. Under slavery, however, the inequalities they faced were so great and their resources so meager that the protest was ineffective. With the increased freedom that followed slavery, a national African American leadership developed and spoke out against oppression and founded organizations that eventually helped to lead the fight for freedom and equality. Even at its birth, the black protest movement was diverse and incorporated a variety of viewpoints and leaders.

Booker T. Washington was the most prominent African American leader prior to World War I. Washington had been born in slavery and was the founder and president of Tuskegee Institute, a college in Alabama dedicated to educating African Americans. His public advice to African Americans in the South was to be patient, to accommodate to the Jim Crow system for the time being, to raise their levels of education and job skills, and to take full advantage of whatever opportunities became available. This nonconfrontational stance earned Washington praise and support from the white community and widespread popularity in the nation. Privately, he worked behind the scenes to end discrimination and implement full racial integration and equality (Franklin & Moss, 1994, pp. 272–274; Hawkins, 1962; Washington, 1965).

Photo 5.6

Booker T. Washington, the most renowned African American of his time, dines with President Theodore Roosevelt.

© David J. & Janice L. Frent Collection/Corbis.

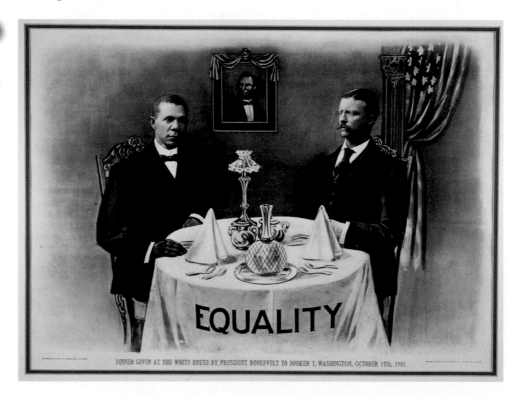

EQUALITY

DINNER GIVEN AT THE WHITE HOUSE BY PRESIDENT ROOSEVELT TO BOOKER T. WASHINGTON, OCTOBER 17TH, 1901

Washington's most vocal opponent was W. E. B. Du Bois, an intellectual and activist who was born in the North and educated at some of the leading universities of the day. Among his many other accomplishments, Du Bois was part of a coalition of blacks and white liberals who founded the National Association for the Advancement of Colored People (NAACP) in 1909. Du Bois rejected Washington's accommodationist stance and advocated immediate pursuit of racial equality and a direct assault on de jure segregation. Almost from the beginning of its existence, the NAACP filed lawsuits that challenged the legal foundations of Jim Crow segregation (Du Bois, 1961). As we shall see in Chapter 6, this legal strategy was eventually successful and led to the demise of the Jim Crow system.

Washington and Du Bois may have differed on matters of strategy and tactics, but they agreed that the only acceptable goal for African Americans was an integrated, racially equal United States. A third leader who emerged early in the 20th century called for a very different approach to the problems of U.S. race relations. Marcus Garvey was born in Jamaica and immigrated to the United States during World War I. He argued that the white-dominated U.S. society was hopelessly racist and would never truly support integration and racial equality. He advocated separatist goals, including a return to Africa. Garvey founded the Universal Negro Improvement Association in 1914 in his native Jamaica and founded the first U.S. branch in 1916. Garvey's organization was very popular for a time in African American communities outside the South, and he helped to establish some of the themes and ideas of black nationalism and pride in African heritage that would become prominent again in the pluralistic 1960s (Essien-Udom, 1962; Garvey, 1969, 1977; Vincent, 1976).

These early leaders and organizations established some of the foundations for later protest movements, but prior to the mid-20th century, they made few actual improvements in the situation of African Americans in the North or South. Jim Crow was a formidable opponent, and the African American community lacked the resources to successfully challenge the status quo until the century was well along and some basic structural features of American society had changed.

Applying Concepts

Acculturation and Integration

During this era of southern segregation and migration to the North, assimilation was not a major factor in the African American experience. Rather, the black-white relations of the time are better described as a system of structural pluralism combined with great inequality. Excluded from the mainstream but freed from the limitations of slavery, African Americans constructed a separate subsociety and subculture. In all regions of the nation, African Americans developed their own institutions and organizations, including separate neighborhoods, churches, businesses, and schools. Like immigrants from Europe in the same era, they organized their communities to cater to their own needs and problems and pursue their agenda as a group.

During the era of segregation, a small African American middle class emerged based on leadership roles in the church, education, and business. A network of black colleges and universities was constructed to educate the children of the growing middle class, as well as other classes. Through this infrastructure, African Americans began to develop the resources and leadership that in the decades ahead would attack, head-on, the structures of racial inequality.

Gender and Race

For African American men and women, the changes wrought by industrialization and the population movement to the North created new possibilities and new roles. However, as African Americans continued to be the victims of exploitation and exclusion in both the North and the South, African American women continued to be among the most vulnerable groups in society.

Following Emancipation, there was a flurry of marriages and weddings among African Americans, as they were finally able to legitimate their family relationships (Staples, 1988, p. 306). African American women continued to have primary responsibility for home and children. Historian Herbert Gutman (1976) reports that it was common for married women to drop out of the labor force and attend solely to household and family duties, because a working wife was too reminiscent of a slave role. This pattern became so widespread that it created serious labor shortages in many areas (Gutman, 1976; see also Staples, 1988, p. 307).

The former slaves were hardly affluent, however, and as sharecropping and segregation began to shape race relations in the South, women often had to return to the fields or to domestic work for the family to survive. One former slave woman noted that women "do double duty, a man's share in the field and a woman's part at home" (Evans, 1989, p. 121). During the bleak decades following the end of Reconstruction, southern black families and black women in particular lived "close to the bone" (Evans, 1989, p. 121).

In the cities and in the growing African American neighborhoods in the North, African American women played a role that in some ways paralleled the role of immigrant women from Europe. The men often moved north first and sent for the women after they had attained some level of financial stability or after the pain of separation became too great (Almquist, 1979, p. 434). In other cases, African American women by the thousands left the South to work as domestic servants; they often replaced European immigrant women, who had moved up in the job structure (Amott & Matthaei, 1991, p. 168).

In the North, discrimination and racism created constant problems of unemployment for the men, and families often relied on the income supplied by the women to make ends meet. It was comparatively easy for women to find employment, but only in the low-paying, less desirable areas, such as domestic work. In both the South and the North, African American women worked outside the home in larger proportions than did white women. For example, in 1900, 41% of African American women were employed, compared with only 16% of white women (Staples, 1988, p. 307).

In 1890, more than a generation after the end of slavery, 85% of all African American men and 96% of African American women were employed in just two occupational categories: agriculture and domestic or personal service. By 1930, 90% of employed African American women were still in these same two categories, whereas the corresponding percentage for employed African American males had dropped to 54% (although nearly all of the remaining 46% were unskilled workers) (Steinberg, 1981, pp. 206–207). Since the inception of segregation, African American women have had consistently higher unemployment rates and lower incomes than African American men and white women (Almquist, 1979, p. 437). These gaps, as we shall see in Chapter 6, persist to the present day.

During the years following Emancipation, some issues did split men and women, within both the African American community and the larger society. Prominent among these was suffrage, or the right to vote, which was still limited to men only. The abolitionist movement, which had been so instrumental in ending slavery, also supported universal suffrage.

Efforts to enfranchise women, though, were abandoned by the Republican Party and large parts of the abolitionist movement to concentrate on efforts to secure the vote for African American males in the South. Ratification of the Fifteenth Amendment in 1870 extended the vote, in principle, to African American men, but the Nineteenth Amendment enfranchising women would not be passed for another 50 years (Almquist, 1979, pp. 433–434; Evans, 1989, pp. 121–124).

Industrialization, the Shift to Postindustrial Society, and Dominant-Minority Group Relations: General Trends

The process of industrialization that began in the 19th century continued to shape the larger society and dominant-minority relations throughout the 20th century. At the start of the 21st century, the United States bears little resemblance to the society it was a century ago. The population has more than tripled in size and has urbanized even more rapidly than it has grown. New organizational forms (bureaucracies, corporations, multinational businesses) and new technologies (nuclear power, computers) dominate everyday life. Levels of education have risen, and the public schools have produced one of the most literate populations and best-trained workforces in the history of the world.

Minority groups also grew in size during this period, and most became even more urbanized than the general population. Minority group members have come to participate in an increasing array of occupations, and their average levels of education have also risen. Despite these real improvements, however, virtually all U.S. minority groups continue to face racism, poverty, discrimination, and exclusion. In this section, we outline the ways in which industrialization has changed American society and examine some of the implications for minority groups in general. We also note some of the ways in which industrialization has aided minority groups and address some of the barriers to full participation in the larger society that continue to operate in the present era. The impact of industrialization and the coming of postindustrial society will be considered in detail in the case studies that make up Part 3 of this text.

Urbanization

We have already noted that urbanization made close, paternalistic controls of minority groups irrelevant. For example, the racial etiquette required by southern de jure segregation, such as African Americans deferring to whites on crowded sidewalks, tended to disappear in the chaos of an urban rush hour.

Besides weakening dominant group controls, urbanization also created the potential for minority groups to mobilize and organize large numbers of people. As stated in Chapter 1, the sheer size of a group is a source of power. Without the freedom to organize, however, size means little, and urbanization increased both the concentration of populations and the freedom to organize.

Text continued on p. 219

South African Apartheid

Photo 5.7

Apartheid meant poverty and powerlessness for black South Africans.

© Peter Turnley/Corbis.

Photo 5.8

Nelson Mandela served nearly three decades in prison for his anti-apartheid activities. He was released in 1990 and was elected president of South Africa in 1994.

© Gideon Mendel/Corbis.

Systems of legally sanctioned racial segregation can be found in many nations and historical eras, but perhaps the most infamous system—called **apartheid**—was constructed in South Africa (see Exhibit 5.3). As in the United States, South African segregation was intended to control the labor of the black population and eliminate all political and economic threats from the group. A small minority of whites (about 30%) dominated the black African population and enjoyed a level of race-based privilege rarely equaled in the history of the world. Today, although enormous problems of inequality and racism remain, South Africa has officially dismantled the machinery of racial oppression, has enfranchised nonwhites, and has elected two black presidents.

Some background will illuminate the dynamics of the system. Europeans first came into contact with Southern Africa in the 1600s, at about the time the British were establishing colonies in North America. First to arrive were the Dutch, who established ports on the coast to resupply merchant ships for the journey between Asia and Europe. Some of the Dutch began moving into the interior to establish farms and sheep and cattle ranches. The "trekkers," as they were called, regularly fought with indigenous black Africans and with tribes moving into the area from the North. These interracial conflicts were extremely bloody and resulted in enslavement for some black Africans, genocide for others, and a gradual push of the remaining black Africans into the interior. In some ways, this contact period resembled that between European Americans and Native Americans, and in other ways, it resembled the early days of the establishment of black slavery in North America.

In the 1800s, South Africa became a British colony, and the new governing group attempted to grant more privileges to blacks. These efforts stopped far short of equality, however, and South Africa continued to evolve as a racially divided, white-dominated society into the 20th century. The white community continued to be split between people of Dutch (Boers)

Exhibit 5.3   Map of Africa Showing South Africa

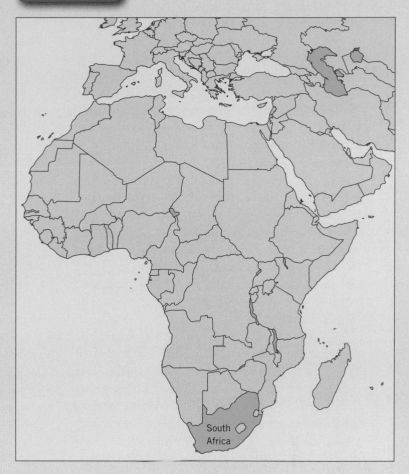

and English descent, and hostilities erupted into violence on a number of occasions. In 1899, British and Dutch factions fought each other in the Boer War, a bitter and intense struggle that widened and solidified the divisions between the two white communities. Generally, the descendants of the Dutch have been more opposed to racial change than have the descendants of the British.

In 1948, the National Party, the primary political vehicle of the Afrikaans, or Dutch, segment of the white community, came into control of the state. As the society modernized and industrialized, there was growing concern about controlling the majority black population. Under the leadership of the National Party, the system of apartheid was constructed to firmly establish white superiority. In Afrikaans, **apartheid** means "separate" or "apart"; the basic logic of the system was to separate whites and blacks in every area of life: schools, neighborhoods, jobs, buses, churches, and so forth. Apartheid resembled the Jim Crow system of segregation in the United States, but it led to results that were even more repressive, elaborate, and unequal.

Although the official government propaganda claimed that apartheid would permit blacks and whites to develop separately and equally, the system was clearly intended to solidify white privilege and black powerlessness. By keeping blacks poor and powerless, white South Africans created a pool of workers who were both cheap and docile. Whites of even modest means could afford the luxuries of personal servants, and employers could minimize their payrolls and their overhead. Of the dominant-minority situations considered in this text, perhaps only American slavery rivals apartheid for its naked, unabashed subjugation of one group for the benefit of another.

Note that the coming of apartheid reverses the relationship between modernization and control of minority groups in the United States. As the United States industrialized and modernized, group relations evolved from paternalistic (slavery) to rigid competitive forms (de jure segregation) with the latter representing a looser form of control over the minority group. In South Africa after 1948, group relations became more rigid, and the structures of control became stronger and more oppressive. Why the difference?

Just as U.S. southerners attempted to defend their privileged status and resist the end of de jure segregation in the 1950s and 1960s, white South Africans were committed to retaining their status and the benefits it created. Although South Africans of British descent tended to be more liberal in matters of race than those of Dutch descent, both groups were firmly committed to white supremacy. Thus, unlike in the United States, where there was almost constant opposition to racial oppression in any form—slavery or segregation—in South Africa, there was little opposition among whites to the creation of apartheid.

Furthermore, South African blacks in the late 1940s were comparatively more powerless than blacks were in the United States at the same time. Although South African black protest organizations existed, they were illegal and had to operate underground or from exile and under conditions of extreme repression. In the United States, in contrast, blacks living outside the South were able to organize and pool their resources to assist in the campaign against Jim Crow, and these activities were protected (more or less) by the national commitment to civil liberties and political freedom.

A final difference between the two situations has to do with numbers. Whereas in the United States, blacks are a numerical minority, they were the great majority of the population in South Africa. Part of the impetus for establishing the rigid system of apartheid was the fear among whites that they would be "swamped" by the numerical majority unless black powerlessness was perpetuated. The difference in group size helped to contribute to what has been described as a "fortress" mentality among some white South Africans: the feeling that they were defending a small (but luxurious) outpost surrounded and besieged by savage hordes who threatened their immediate and total destruction. This strong sense of threat among whites and the need to be vigilant and constantly resist the least hint of racial change made the system seem impregnable and perpetual to many observers.

Apartheid lasted about 40 years. Through the 1970s and 1980s, changes within South Africa and in the world in general built up pressure against the system. Internally, protests against apartheid by blacks began in the 1960s and continued to build in intensity. The South African government responded to these protests with violent repression, and thousands died in the confrontations with police and the army. Nonetheless, antiapartheid activism continued to attack the system from below.

Apartheid also suffered from internal weaknesses and contradictions. For example, jobs were strictly segregated, along with all other aspects of South African society. In a modern, industrial economy, however, new types of jobs are continually being created, and old jobs are continually lost to mechanization and automation, making it difficult to maintain simple, castelike rules about who can do what kinds of work. Also, many of the newer jobs required higher levels of education and special skills, and the number of white South Africans was too small to fill the demand. Thus, some black South Africans were slowly rising to positions of greater affluence and personal freedom even as the system attempted to coerce and repress the group as a whole.

Internationally, pressure on South Africa to end apartheid was significant. Other nations established trade embargoes and organized boycotts of South African goods. South Africa was officially banned from the Olympics and other international competitions. Although many of these efforts were more symbolic than real and had only minor impact on everyday social life, they sustained an outcast status for South Africa and helped create an atmosphere of uncertainty among its economic and political elite.

In the late 1980s, these various pressures made it impossible to ignore the need for reform any longer. In 1990, F. W. de Klerk, the leader of the National Party and the prime minister of the nation, began a series of changes that eventually ended apartheid. He lifted the ban on many outlawed black African protest organizations, and perhaps most significantly, he released Nelson Mandela from prison. Mandela was the leader of the African National Congress, one of the oldest and most important black organizations, and he had served a 27-year prison term for actively protesting apartheid. Together, de Klerk and Mandela helped to ease South Africa through a period of rapid racial change that saw the franchise being extended to blacks, the first open election in South African history, and in 1994, Mandela's election to a 5-year term as president. In 1999, Mandela was replaced by Thabo M. Mbeke, another black South African, who was reelected in 2004.

The future of South Africa remains unclear. Although the majority black population now has considerable political power, much of the wealth of the nation remains in white hands. Furthermore, the school system did little to prepare blacks for positions of leadership and for jobs demanding specialized skills or technical expertise. Thus, most of the crucial jobs in business and government continue to be held by whites. Tribal affiliations, language differences, and political loyalties split black South Africans, and unified action is often problematical for the minority group. This experiment in racial reform might still fail, and South Africa could still become the site of a devastating race war, but this dramatic transition away from massive racism and institutionalized discrimination could also provide a model of change for other racially divided societies.

Occupational Specialization

One of the first and most important results of industrialization, even in its earliest days, was an increase in occupational specialization and the variety of jobs available in the workforce. The growing needs of an urbanizing population increased the number of jobs available in the production, transport, and sale of goods and services. Occupational specialization was also stimulated by the very nature of industrial production. Complex manufacturing processes could be performed more efficiently if they were broken down into the narrower component tasks. It was easier and more efficient to train the workforce in the simpler, specialized jobs. Assembly lines were invented, the work was subdivided, the division of labor became increasingly complex, and the number of different occupations continued to grow.

The sheer complexity of the industrial job structure made it difficult to maintain rigid, castelike divisions of labor between dominant and minority groups. Rigid competitive forms of group relations, such as Jim Crow segregation, became less viable as the job market became more diversified and changeable. Simple, clear rules about which groups could do which jobs disappeared. As the more repressive systems of control weakened, job opportunities for minority group members sometimes increased. However, as the relationships between group memberships and positions in the job market became more blurred, conflict between groups also increased. For example, as we have noted, African Americans moving from the South often found themselves in competition for jobs with members of white ethnic groups, labor unions, and other elements of the dominant group.

Bureaucracy and Rationality

As industrialization continued, privately owned corporations and businesses came to have workforces numbering in the hundreds of thousands. Gigantic factories employing thousands of workers became common. To coordinate the efforts of these huge workforces, bureaucracy became the dominant form of organization in the economy and, indeed, throughout the society.

Bureaucracies are large-scale, impersonal, formal organizations that run "by the book." They are governed by rules and regulations (i.e., "red tape") and are "rational" in that they attempt to find the most efficient ways to accomplish their tasks. Although they typically fail to attain the ideal of fully rational efficiency, bureaucracies tend to recruit, reward, and promote employees on the basis of competence and performance (Gerth & Mills, 1946).

The stress on rationality and objectivity can counteract the more blatant forms of racism and increase the array of opportunities available to members of minority groups. Although they are often nullified by other forces (see Blumer, 1965), these antiprejudicial tendencies do not exist at all or are much weaker in preindustrial economies.

The history of the concept of race illustrates the effect of rationality and scientific ways of thinking. Today, virtually the entire scientific community regards race as a biological triviality, a conclusion based on decades of research. This scientific finding undermined and contributed to the destruction of the formal systems of privilege based solely on race (e.g., segregated school systems) and individual perceptual systems (e.g., traditional prejudice) based on the assumption that race is a crucial personal characteristic.

Growth of White-Collar Jobs and the Service Sector

Industrialization changed the composition of the labor force. As work became more complex and specialized, the need to coordinate and regulate the production process increased, and as a result, bureaucracies and other organizations grew larger still. Within these organizations, white-collar occupations, those that coordinate, manage, and deal with the flow of paperwork, continued to expand. As industrialization progressed, mechanization and automation reduced the number of manual or blue-collar workers, and white-collar occupations became the dominant sector of the job market in the United States.

Photo 5.9

Some new service jobs, such as staffing help centers, have been outsourced to nations with cheaper labor, including India.

© Sherwin Crasto/Reuters/ Corbis.

The changing nature of the workforce can be illustrated by looking at the proportional representation of three different types of jobs:

1.   **Extractive (or primary) occupations** are those that produce raw materials, such as food and agricultural products, minerals, and lumber. The jobs in this sector often involve unskilled manual labor, require little formal education, and are generally low paying.

2.   **Manufacturing (or secondary) occupations** transform raw materials into finished products ready for sale in the marketplace. Like jobs in the extractive sector, these blue-collar jobs involve manual labor, but they tend to require higher levels of skill and are more highly rewarded. Examples of occupations in this sector include the assembly line jobs that transform steel, rubber, plastic, and other materials into finished automobiles.

3.   **Service (or tertiary) occupations** are those in which the people in them do not produce "things"; rather, they provide services. As urbanization increased and self-sufficiency decreased, opportunities for work in this sector grew. Examples of tertiary occupations include police officer, clerk, waiter, teacher, nurse, doctor, and cabdriver.

The course of industrialization is traced in the changing structure of the labor market depicted in Exhibit 5.4. In 1840, when industrialization was just beginning in the United States, most of the workforce (70%) was in the extractive sector, with agriculture being the dominant occupation. As industrialization progressed, the manufacturing, or secondary, sector grew, reaching a peak after World War II. Today, the large majority of U.S. jobs (80%) are in the service, or tertiary, sector.

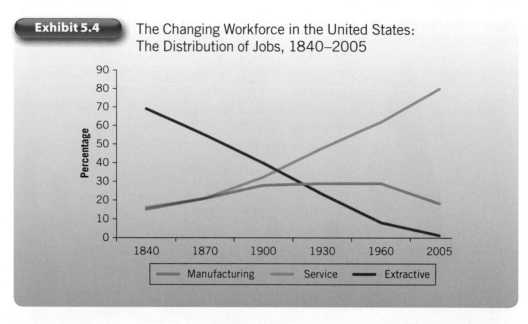

Exhibit 5.4 The Changing Workforce in the United States: The Distribution of Jobs, 1840–2005

SOURCE: 1840–1990: Adapted from Lenski, Nolan, & Lenski (1995); 2002: Calculated from U.S. Bureau of the Census (2005, pp. 385–388); 2005: Calculated from U.S. Bureau of the Census (2007b, pp. 388–391).

This shift away from blue-collar jobs and manufacturing since the 1960s is sometimes referred to as *deindustrialization* or discussed in terms of the emergence of postindustrial society. The U.S. economy has lost millions of unionized, high-paying factory jobs over the past several decades, and the downward trend will continue. The industrial jobs that sustained so many generations of American workers have moved to other nations where wages are considerably lower than in the United States or have been eliminated by robots or other automated manufacturing processes (see Rifkin, 1996).

The changing structure of the job market helps to clarify the nature of intergroup competition and the sources of wealth and power in society. Job growth in the United States today is largely in the service sector, and these occupations are highly variable. At one end are low-paying jobs with few, if any, benefits or chances for advancement (e.g., washing dishes in a restaurant). At the upper end are high-prestige, lucrative positions, such as Supreme Court justice, scientist, and financial analyst. The new service sector jobs are either highly desirable technical, professional, or administrative jobs with demanding entry requirements (e.g., physician or nurse) or low-paying, low-skilled jobs with few benefits and little security (e.g., receptionist, nurse's aide). For the last half century, job growth in the United States has been either in areas in which educationally deprived minority group members find it difficult to compete or in areas that offer little compensation, upward mobility, or security. As we will see in Part 3, the economic situation of contemporary minority groups reflects these fundamental trends.

The Growing Importance of Education

Education has been an increasingly important prerequisite for employability in the United States and in other advanced industrial societies. A high school or, increasingly, a college degree has become the minimum entry-level requirement for employment. However, opportunities for high-quality education are not distributed equally across the population. Some minority groups, especially those created by colonization, have been systematically excluded from the schools of the dominant society, and today, they are less likely to have the educational backgrounds needed to compete for better jobs.

Access to education is a key issue for all U.S. minority groups, and the average educational levels of these groups have been rising since World War II. Still, minority children continue to be much more likely to attend segregated, underfunded, deteriorated schools and to receive inferior educations (see Orfield, 2001).

A Dual Labor Market

The changing composition of the labor force and increasing importance of educational credentials has split the U.S. labor market into two segments or types of jobs. The **primary labor market** includes jobs usually located in large, bureaucratic organizations. These positions offer higher pay, more security, better opportunities for advancement, health and retirement benefits, and other amenities. Entry requirements include college degrees, even when people with fewer years of schooling could competently perform the work.

Photo 5.10

The U.S. job market is segmented with more desirable, higher-prestige jobs, such as surgeon in the primary sector, and low-paid, less prestigious jobs, such as fast-food worker in the secondary sector.

© Mark Peterson/Corbis.

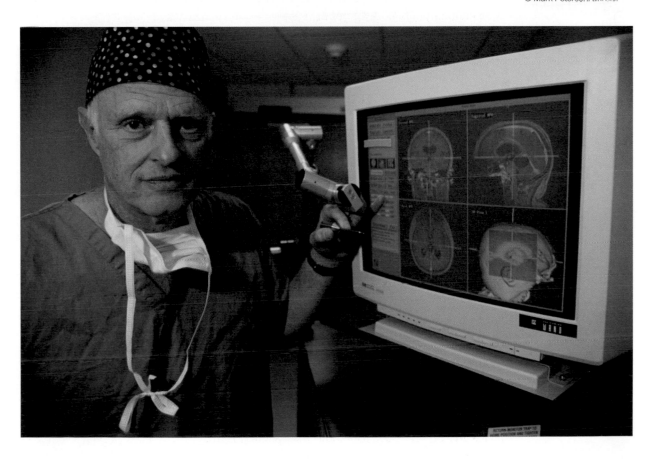

The **secondary labor market**, sometimes called the competitive market, includes low-paying, low-skilled, insecure jobs. Many of these jobs are in the service sector. They do not represent a career and offer little opportunity for promotion or upward mobility. Very often, they do not offer health or retirement benefits, have high rates of turnover, and are part-time, seasonal, or temporary.

Many American minority groups are concentrated in the secondary job market. Their exclusion from better jobs is perpetuated not so much by direct or overt discrimination as by their lack of educational and other credentials required to enter the primary sector. The differential distribution of educational opportunities, in

Photo 5.11

© Najlah Feanny/Corbis.

the past as well as in the present, effectively protects workers in the primary sector from competition from minority groups.

Globalization

Over the past century, the United States became an economic, political, and military world power with interests around the globe. These worldwide ties have created new minority groups through population movement and have changed the status of others. Immigration to this country has been considerable for the past three decades. The American economy is one of the most productive in the world, and jobs, even those in the low-paying secondary sector, are the primary goals for millions of newcomers. For other immigrants, this country continues to play its historic role as a refuge from political and religious persecution.

Many of the wars, conflicts, and other disputes in which the United States has been involved have had consequences for American minority groups. For example, both Puerto Ricans and Cuban Americans became U.S. minority groups as the result of processes set in motion during the Spanish-American War of 1898. Both World War I and World War II created new job opportunities for many minority groups, including African Americans and Mexican Americans. After the Korean War, international ties were forged between the United States and South Korea, and this led to an increase in immigration from that nation. In the 1960s and 1970s, the military involvement of the United States in Southeast Asia led to the arrival of Vietnamese, Cambodians, and other immigrant groups from Southeast Asia.

Dominant-minority relations in the United States have been increasingly played out on an international stage as the world has effectively "shrunk" in size and become more interconnected by international organizations, such as the United Nations; by ties of trade and commerce; and by modern means of transportation and communication. In a world in which two thirds of the population is nonwhite and many important nations (such as China, India, and Nigeria) are composed primarily of peoples of color, the treatment of racial minorities by the U.S. dominant group has come under increased scrutiny. It is difficult to preach principles of fairness, equality, and justice—which the United States claims as its own—when domestic realities suggest an embarrassing failure to fully implement these standards. Part of the pressure for the United States to end blatant systems of discrimination such as de jure segregation came from the desire to maintain a leading position in the world.

The Shift From Rigid to Fluid Competitive Relationships

The recent changes in the structure of American society are so fundamental and profound that they are often described in terms of a revolution in subsistence technology: from an industrial society, based on manufacturing, to a postindustrial society, based on information processing and computer-related or other new technologies.

As the subsistence technology has evolved and changed, so have American dominant-minority relations. The rigid competitive systems (such as Jim Crow) associated with earlier phases of industrialization have given way to **fluid competitive systems** of group relations. In fluid competitive relations, the formal or legal barriers to competition such as Jim Crow laws or apartheid no longer exist. Both geographic and social mobility are greater, and the limitations imposed by minority group status are less restrictive and burdensome. Rigid caste systems of stratification, in which group membership determines opportunities, adult statuses, and jobs, are replaced by more open class systems, in which there are weaker relationships between group membership and wealth, prestige, and power. Because fluid competitive systems are more open and the position of the minority group is less fixed, the fear of competition from minority groups becomes more widespread for the dominant group, and intergroup conflict increases. Exhibit 5.5 compares the characteristics of the three systems of group relations.

Compared with previous systems, the fluid competitive system is closer to the American ideal of an open, fair system of stratification in which effort and competence are rewarded and race, ethnicity, gender, religion, and other "birthmarks" are irrelevant. However, as we will see in chapters to come, race and ethnicity continue to affect life chances and limit opportunities for minority group members even in fluid competitive systems. As suggested by the Noel hypothesis, people continue to identify themselves with particular groups (ethnocentrism), and competition for resources continues to play out along group lines. Consistent with the Blauner hypothesis, the minority groups that were formed by colonization remain at a disadvantage in the pursuit of opportunities, education, prestige, and other resources.

Exhibit 5.5   Characteristics of Three Systems of Group Relationships

	Systems of Group Relations		
		Competitive	
	Paternalistic	**Rigid**	**Fluid**
Subsistence Technology:	*Agrarian*	*Early Industrial*	*Advanced Industrial*
Stratification	**Caste.** Group determines status.	**Mixed.** Elements of caste and class. Status largely determined by group.	**Variable.** Status strongly affected by group. Inequality varies within groups.
Division of labor	**Simple.** Determined by group.	**More complex.** Job largely determined by group, but some sharing of jobs by different groups.	**Most complex.** Group and job less related. Complex specialization and great variation within groups.
Contact between groups	**Common,** but statuses unequal.	**Less common,** and mostly unequal.	**More common.** Highest rates of equal status contact.
Overt intergroup conflict	**Rare**	**More common**	**Common**
Power differential	**Maximum.** Minority groups have little ability to pursue self-interests.	**Less.** Minority groups have some ability to pursue self-interests.	**Least.** Minority groups have more ability to pursue self-interests.

SOURCE: Based on Farley (2000, p. 109).

Gender Inequality in a Globalizing, Postindustrial World

Deindustrialization and globalization are transforming gender relations along with dominant-minority relations. Everywhere, even in the most traditional and sexist societies, women are moving away from their traditional wife and mother roles, taking on new responsibilities, and facing new challenges. Some women are also encountering new dangers and new forms of exploitation that perpetuate their lower status and extend it into new areas.

In the United States, the transition to a postindustrial society has changed gender relations and the status of women on a number of levels. Women and men are now equal in terms of levels of education (U.S. Bureau of the Census, 2007b, p. 143), and the shift to fluid competitive group relations has weakened the barriers to gender equality along with the barriers to racial equality. The changing role of women is also shaped by other characteristics of a modern society: smaller families, high divorce rates, and rising numbers of single mothers who must work to support their children as well as themselves.

Many of these trends have coalesced to motivate women to enter the paid labor force in unprecedented numbers over the past half century. Women are now employed at almost the same levels as men. In the year 2005, for example, 66% of single women (vs. about 70% of single men) and about 61% of married women (vs. about 77% of married men) had jobs outside the home (U.S. Bureau of the Census, 2007b, p. 379). Furthermore, between 1970 and 2005, the participation of married women with children in the workforce increased from a little less than 40% to almost 70% (U.S. Bureau of the Census, 2007b, p. 380).

Many women workers enter the paid labor force to compensate for the declining earning power of men. Before deindustrialization began to transform U.S. society, men monopolized the more desirable, higher-paid, unionized jobs in the manufacturing sector. For much of the 20th century, these blue-collar jobs paid well enough to subsidize a comfortable lifestyle, a house in the suburbs, and vacations, with enough money left over to save for a rainy day or for college for the kids. However, when deindustrialization began, many of these desirable jobs were lost to automation and to cheaper labor forces outside the United States and were replaced, if at all, by low-paying jobs in the service sector. Thus, deindustrialization tended to drive men's wages down, and many women were forced to take jobs to supplement the family income. This trend was reflected in Exhibit 3.10 in Chapter 3, which shows that average wages for men have been stagnant or actually declining since the early 1970s.

A large number of the "new" women workers have taken jobs in a limited number of female-dominated occupations, most of which are in the less-well-paid service sector, and this pattern of occupational segregation is one important reason for the continuing gender gap in income. For example, Exhibit 5.6 lists some of the occupations that were dominated by females in 1983 and 2005, along with the percentages of females in comparable but higher-status occupations. In 2005, 92% of nurses and nearly 100% of dental hygienists were female. The comparable figures for physicians and dentists were 32% and 22%, respectively.

Photo 5.12

Women are increasingly entering traditionally male professions.

© Jim Craigmyle/Corbis.

Exhibit 5.6   Percentage Female in Selected Occupations, 1983 and 2005

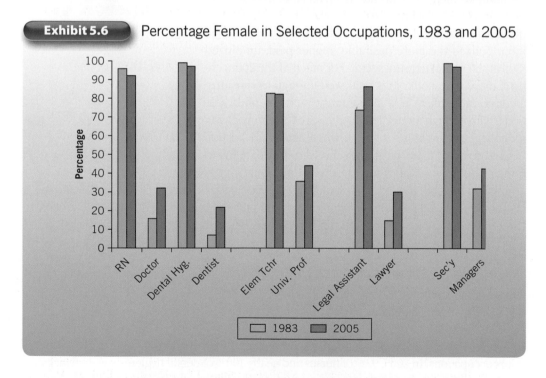

SOURCE: 1983: Calculated from U.S. Bureau of the Census (2005, pp. 383–385); 2005: Calculated from U.S Bureau of the Census (2007b, pp. 388–391).

In part, this occupational segregation is a result of the choices women make to balance the demands of their jobs with their family obligations. Whereas men are expected to make a total commitment to their jobs and careers, women have been expected to find ways to continue to fulfill their domestic roles even while working full-time, and many "female jobs" offer some flexibility in this area (Shelton & John, 1996). For example, many women become elementary educators despite the lower salaries because the job offers predictable hours and long summer breaks, both of which can help women meet their child care and other family responsibilities. This pattern of gender occupational segregation testifies to the lingering effects of minority status for women and the choices they make to reconcile the demands of career and family.

Exhibit 5.6 also shows that gender segregation in the world of work is declining, at least in some areas. Women are moving into traditionally male (and higher-paid) occupations, as reflected by the rising percentages of female physicians, dentists, college professors, and lawyers. Also, some of the occupational areas that have traditionally had high concentrations of women—for example, finance, insurance, and real estate—actually benefited from deindustrialization and the shift to a service economy. Job opportunities in the finance, insurance, and real estate sector have expanded rapidly since the 1960s and have provided opportunities for women to rise in the social structure, and this has, in turn, tended to elevate average salaries for women in general (Farley, 1996, pp. 95–101). The movement of females into these more lucrative occupations is another reason why the gender gap in income is decreasing, as reflected in Exhibit 3.10 in Chapter 3.

How have deindustrialization and globalization affected women internationally? In part, the trends worldwide parallel those in the United States. According to the United Nations (United Nations, 2006), indicators such as rising education levels for women and lower rates of early marriage and childbirth show that women around the world are moving out of their traditional (and often highly controlled and repressed) status. They are entering the labor force in unprecedented numbers virtually everywhere, and women now make up at least a third of the paid global workforce.

Although the status of women is generally rising, the movement away from traditional gender roles also brings exposure to new forms of exploitation. Around the globe, women have become a source of cheap labor, often in jobs that have recently been exported from the U.S. economy. For example, many manufacturing jobs formerly held by men in the United States have migrated just south of the border to Mexico, where they are held by women. *Maquiladoras* are assembly plants built by corporations (often headquartered in the United States) to take advantage of the plentiful supply of working-class females who will work for low wages and in conditions that would not be tolerated in the United States.

The weakening of traditional gender roles has increased women's vulnerability in other areas as well. A global sex trade in prostitution and pornography is flourishing and accounts for a significant portion of the economy of Thailand, the Philippines, and other nations. This international industry depends on impoverished women (and children) pushed out of the subsistence rural economy by industrialization and globalization and made vulnerable for exploitation by their lack of resources and power (Poulan, 2003).

Across all these changes and around the globe, women commonly face the challenge of reconciling their new work demands with their traditional family responsibilities. Also, women face challenges and issues, such as sexual harassment and domestic violence, which clearly differentiate their status from that of men. In this context, minority group women face a double disadvantage because the issues they face as women are complicated by the barriers created by racial and ethnic prejudice and discrimination. As we shall see in Part 3, minority group and immigrant women often form the poorest, most vulnerable, and exploited groups in U.S. society and around the globe.

Modern Institutional Discrimination

Virtually all American minority groups continue to lag behind national averages in income, employment, and other measures of equality (see the Appendix for examples), despite the greater fluidity of group relations, the greater openness in the U.S. stratification system, the dramatic declines in overt prejudice (see Chapter 3), and the introduction of numerous laws designed to ensure that all people are treated without regard to race, gender, or ethnicity. After all this change, shouldn't there be less minority group inequality?

As we saw in Chapter 3, many Americans attribute the persisting patterns of inequality to the minority groups' lack of willpower or motivation to get ahead. In the remaining chapters of this text, however, I argue that the major barrier facing minority groups in late-industrial, post–Jim Crow America is a more subtle but still powerful form of discrimination: **modern institutional discrimination**.

As you recall from Chapter 1, institutional discrimination is built into the everyday operation of the social structure of society. The routine procedures and policies of institutions and organizations are arranged so that minority group members are automatically put at a disadvantage. In the Jim Crow era in the South, for example, African Americans were deprived of the right to vote by overt institutional discrimination and could acquire little in the way of political power.

The forms of institutional discrimination that persist in the present are more subtle and less overt than those that defined the Jim Crow system. In fact, they are often unintentional or unconscious and are manifested more in the results for minority groups than in the intentions or prejudices of dominant group members. Modern institutional discrimination is not necessarily linked to prejudice, and the decision makers who implement it may sincerely think of themselves as behaving rationally and in the best interests of their organizations.

When employers make hiring decisions based solely on educational criteria, they may be putting minority group members at a disadvantage. When banks use strictly economic criteria to deny money for home mortgages or home improvement loans in certain run-down neighborhoods, they may be handicapping the efforts of minority groups to cope with the results of the blatant, legal housing segregation of the past. When businesspeople decide to lower their overhead by moving their operations away from center cities, they may be reducing the ability of America's highly urbanized minority groups to earn a living and educate their children. When educators rely solely on standardized tests of ability that have been developed from white, middle-class experiences to decide who will be placed in college preparatory courses, they may be limiting the ability of minority group children to compete for jobs in the primary sector.

Any and all of these decisions can and do have devastating consequences for minority individuals, even though decision makers may be entirely unaware of the discriminatory effects. Employers, bankers, and educators do not have to be personally prejudiced for their actions to have negative consequences for minority groups. Modern institutional discrimination helps to perpetuate systems of inequality that can be just as pervasive and stifling as those of the past.

To illustrate, consider the effects of **past-in-present institutional discrimination**, which involves practices in the present that have discriminatory consequences because of some pattern of discrimination or exclusion in the past (Feagin & Feagin, 1986, p. 32). One form of this discrimination is found in workforces organized around the principle of seniority. In these systems, which are quite common, workers who have been on the job longer have higher incomes; more privileges; and other benefits, such as longer vacations. The "old-timers" often have more job security and are designated in official, written policy as the last to be fired or laid off in the event of hard times. Workers and employers alike may think of the privileges of seniority as just rewards for long years of service, familiarity with the job, and so forth.

Personnel policies based on seniority may seem perfectly reasonable, neutral, and fair. However, they can have discriminatory results in the present because in the past, members of minority groups and women were excluded from specific occupations by racist or sexist labor unions, discriminatory employers, or both. As a result, minority group workers and women may have fewer years of experience than dominant group workers and may be the first to go when layoffs are necessary. The adage "last hired, first fired" describes the situation of minority group and female employees who are more vulnerable not because of some overtly racist or sexist policy, but because of the routine operation of the seemingly neutral principle of seniority.

It is much more difficult to identify, measure, and eliminate this more subtle form of institutional discrimination, and some of the most heated disputes in recent group relations have concerned public policy and law in this area. Among the most controversial issues are **affirmative action** programs that attempt to ameliorate the legacy of past discrimination or increase diversity in the workplace or in schools. In many cases, the Supreme Court has found that programs designed to favor minority employees as a strategy for overcoming overt discrimination in the past are constitutional (e.g., *Firefighters Local Union No. 1784 v. Stotts*, 1984; *Sheet Metal Workers v. EEOC*, 1986; *United Steelworkers of America, AFL-CIO-CLC v. Weber*, 1979). Virtually all these decisions, however, were based on narrow margins (votes of 5 to 4) and featured acrimonious and bitter debates. More recently, the Supreme Court narrowed the grounds on which such past grievances could be redressed and, in the eyes of many observers, dealt serious blows to affirmative action programs (e.g., *Adarand Constructors, Inc. v. Pena*, 1995).

One of the more prominent battlegrounds for affirmative action programs has been in higher education. Since the 1960s, many colleges and universities have implemented programs to increase the number of minority students on campus at both the undergraduate and graduate levels, sometimes admitting minority students who had lower GPAs (grade point averages) or test scores than dominant group students who were turned away. In general, advocates of these programs have justified them in terms of redressing the discriminatory practices of the past or increasing diversity on campus and making the student body a more accurate representation of the surrounding society. To say the least, these programs have been highly controversial and the targets of frequent lawsuits, some of which have found their way to the highest courts in the land.

Affirmative action programs in general and those in education in particular appear to be in serious jeopardy. There is very little social support for these programs. According to a public opinion survey conducted in 2006, affirmative action was supported by only 12% of white respondents. More surprising, perhaps, it was supported by less than a majority of black respondents (43%) and only 19% of female respondents (National Opinion Research Council, 1972–2007). Furthermore, the administration of President George W. Bush is generally opposed to affirmative action and has registered its opposition in documents submitted to the Supreme Court in various cases.

Most important, perhaps, recent lawsuits show that the Supreme Court is not supportive of affirmative action in education. For example, in two lawsuits involving the University of Michigan in 2003 (*Grutter v. Bollinger* and *Gratz v. Bollinger*), the Supreme Court held that the university's law school *could* use race as one criterion in deciding admissions but that undergraduate admissions *could not* award an automatic advantage to minority applicants. In other words, universities could take account of an applicant's race but only in a very limited way, as one factor among many.

In the spring of 2007, the court further limited the scope of affirmative action in a ruling that involved two public school systems (*Community Schools, Inc. v. Seattle School District* and *Meredith v. Jefferson County, Kentucky, Board of Education*). At issue were the plans in Seattle and Louisville to further racial integration and diversity in their schools despite the extensive residential segregation in their areas. Students were assigned to schools partly on the basis of race, and the Court ruled that these plans violated the equal protection clause of the Constitution (Bames, 2007).

In the face of these decisions and the low level of public support, it would not be surprising to see all affirmative action programs end in the next 5 to 10 years. If they do, one of the few tools available to combat modern institutional discrimination will be eliminated. These issues are pursued further in the Current Debate section at the end of Chapter 6.

Social Change and Minority Group Activism

This chapter has focused on the continuing Industrial Revolution and its impact on minority groups in general and black-white relations in particular. For the most part, changes in group relations have been presented as the results of the fundamental transformation of the U.S. economy from agrarian to industrial to late industrial (or postindustrial). However, the changes in the situation of African Americans and other minority groups did not "just happen" as society modernized. Although the opportunity to pursue favorable change was the result of broad structural changes in American society, the realization of these opportunities came from the efforts of the many who gave their time, their voices, their resources, and sometimes their lives in pursuit of racial justice in America. Since World War II, African Americans have often been in the vanguard of protest activity, and we focus on the contemporary situation of this group in the next chapter.

Reparations

Should African Americans be compensated for the losses they suffered as a result of their kidnapping from Africa, their centuries of slavery, and their continuing oppression under de jure segregation? What, if anything, does American society owe for the centuries of uncompensated labor performed by African Americans and the oppression and coerced inequality of the Jim Crow era? Should present-day Americans be held accountable for the actions of their ancestors? What about the families and businesses that grew rich from the labor of African Americans (and other minorities) in the past? To what extent are they responsible for the continuing racial gaps in income and wealth documented in this chapter?

The idea of reparations remains on the national agenda in a variety of forms, including bills proposed to the U.S. Congress and apologies for slavery issued by the Virginia House of Delegates in 2007. A reparations lawsuit, first filed in 2002 against a number of large corporations that allegedly benefited directly from slavery, remains active, and a number of university campuses across the nation have held demonstrations and teach-ins on the issue.

In the excerpts below, Joe Feagin and Eileen O'Brien (Brooks, 1999), while arguing for reparations, place the issue in a historical context. Manning Marable (2001), a prominent African American sociologist, and John McWhorter (2001), also an African American academic, present some of the central arguments for and against reparations.

Reparations for African Americans in Historical Context

JOE FEAGIN AND EILEEN O'BRIEN

Many discussions of reparation for African Americans seem to suggest that such compensation is a wild idea well beyond conventional U.S. practice or policy. This is not, however, the case. The principle of individual and group compensation for damages done by others is accepted by the federal government and the larger society in regard to some claims, but only grudgingly and incompletely for others, such as those by African Americans who have been harmed by racial oppression. For example, recent anti-crime legislation, in the form of the Victims of Crime Act, codifies the principle of compensation for victims of crime. In addition, as a nation, we now expect corporations to compensate the deformed children of mothers who took drugs without knowing their consequences.... The fact that those who ran the corporation in the initial period of damage are deceased does not relieve the corporation from having to pay compensation to those damaged later on from the earlier actions. Injured children can sue for redress many years later. Clearly, in some cases monetary compensation for past injustices is accepted and expected.

Long after the Nazi party had been out of power and most of its leaders had grown old or died, the U.S. government continued to press the German government to make tens of billions of dollars in reparations to the families of those killed in the Holocaust and to the state of Israel.

In recent years, the federal government has grudgingly agreed to (modest) reparations for those Japanese Americans who were interned during World War II. Federal courts have also awarded nearly a billion dollars in compensatory damages to Native American groups whose lands were stolen in violation of treaties. Significantly, however, these slow moves to compensate some victims of racial oppression have not extended, even modestly, to African Americans....

In his 1946 book, *The World and Africa,* W. E. B. DuBois argued that the poverty in Europe's African colonies was "a main cause of wealth and luxury in Europe" (1965, p. 37). DuBois argued that the history of African colonization is omitted from mainstream histories of European development and wealth. A serious understanding of European wealth must *center* on the history of exploitation and oppression in Africa, for the resources of Africans were taken to help create Europe's wealth. To a substantial degree, Europeans were rich because Africans were poor. Africa's economic development—its resources, land, and labor—had been and was being sacrificed to spur European economic progress.

In our view, a similar argument is applicable to the development of the wealth and affluence of the white population in the United States. From its first decades, white-settler colonialism in North America involved the extreme exploitation of enslaved African Americans.

European colonists built up much wealth by stealing the labor of African Americans and the land of Native Americans.

Racial oppression carried out by white Americans has lasted for nearly four centuries and has done great damage to the lives, opportunities, communities, and futures of African Americans. The actions of white Americans over many generations sharply reduced the income of African Americans, and thus their economic and cultural capital. Legal segregation in the South, where most African Americans resided until recent decades, forced black men and women into lower-paying jobs or into unemployment, where they could not earn incomes sufficient to support their families adequately, much less to save. In the 1930s, two-thirds of African Americans still lived in the South, and most were descendants of recently enslaved Americans. They were still firmly entrenched in the semi-slavery of legal segregation, which did not allow the accumulation of wealth. Significant property holding was not even available as a possibility to a majority of African Americans until the late 1960s....

Most whites do not understand the extent to which the racial oppression of the past continues to fuel inequalities in the present. Although affirmative action programs (where they still exist) attempt to redress discrimination by increasing job or educational opportunities for African Americans in a few organizations, such programs do little to address the large-scale wealth inequality between black and white Americans. All the "equal opportunity" programs and policies one could envisage would not touch the assets of whites who long ago reaped the benefits of not being subjected to legal segregation during the United States' most prosperous economic times in the 19th and 20th centuries....

Wealth transmission is a critical factor in the reproduction of racial oppression. Given the nature of whites' disproportionate share of America's wealth and the historical conditions under which it was acquired—often at the expense of African Americans—it is of little significance that legal discrimination and segregation do not exist today. The argument that "Jim Crow is a thing of the past" misses the point, because the huge racial disparities in wealth today are a direct outgrowth of the economic and social privileges one group secured unfairly, if not brutally, at the expense of another group.

SOURCE: From *When Sorry Isn't Enough: The Controversy Over Apologies and Reparations for Human Injustice,* edited by Roy L. Brooks. Copyright © 1999 by New York University. Reprinted by permission of New York University Press.

Reparations Are an Idea Whose Time Has Come

MANNING MARABLE

In 1854 my great-grandfather, Morris Marable, was sold on an auction block in Georgia for $500. For his white slave master, the sale was just "business as usual." But to Morris Marable and his heirs, slavery was a crime against our humanity. This pattern of human-rights violations against enslaved African Americans continued under Jim Crow segregation for nearly another century.

The fundamental problem of American democracy in the 21st century is the problem of "structural racism": the deep patterns of socioeconomic inequality and accumulated disadvantage that are coded by race, and constantly justified in public discourse by both racist stereotypes and white indifference. Do Americans have the capacity and vision to dismantle these structural barriers that deny democratic rights and opportunities to millions of their fellow citizens?

This country has previously witnessed two great struggles to achieve a truly multicultural democracy. The First Reconstruction (1865–1877) ... briefly gave black men voting rights, but gave no meaningful compensation for two centuries of unpaid labor. The promise of "40 acres and a mule" was for most blacks a dream deferred.

The Second Reconstruction (1954–1968), or the modern civil-rights movement, outlawed legal segregation in public accommodations and gave blacks voting rights. But these successes paradoxically obscure the tremendous human costs of historically accumulated disadvantage that remain central to black Americans' lives.

The disproportionate wealth that most whites enjoy today was first constructed from centuries of unpaid black labor. Many white institutions, including Ivy League universities, insurance companies and banks, profited from slavery. This pattern of white privilege and black inequality continues today.

Demanding reparations is not just about compensation for slavery and segregation. It is, more important, an educational campaign to highlight the contemporary reality of "racial deficits" of all kinds, the unequal conditions that impact blacks regardless of class. Structural racism's barriers include "equity inequity," the absence of black capital formation that is a direct consequence of America's history. One third of all black households actually have negative net wealth. In 1998 the typical black family's net wealth was $16,400, less than one fifth that of white families. Black families are denied home loans at twice the rate of whites.

Blacks remain the last hired and first fired during recessions. During the 1990–91 recession, African Americans suffered disproportionately. At Coca-Cola, 42 percent of employees who lost their jobs were black. At Sears, 54 percent were black. Blacks have significantly shorter life expectancies, in part due to racism in the health establishment. Blacks are statistically less likely than whites to be referred for kidney transplants or early-stage cancer surgery.

In criminal justice, African Americans constitute only one seventh of all drug users. Yet we account for 35 percent of all drug arrests, 55 percent of drug convictions and 75 percent of prison admissions for drug offenses....

White Americans today aren't guilty of carrying out slavery and segregation. But whites have a moral and political responsibility to acknowledge the continuing burden of history's structural racism.

A reparations trust fund could be established, with the goal of closing the socioeconomic gaps between blacks and whites. Funds would be targeted specifically toward poor, disadvantaged communities with the greatest need, not to individuals.

Let's eliminate the racial unfairness in capital markets that perpetuates black poverty. A national commitment to expand black homeownership, full employment and quality health care would benefit all Americans, regardless of race.

Reparations could begin America's Third Reconstruction, the final chapter in the 400-year struggle to abolish slavery and its destructive consequences. As Malcolm X said in 1961, hundreds of years of racism and labor exploitation are "worth more than a cup of coffee at a white cafe. We are here to collect back wages."

SOURCE: Marable, Manning (2001). "An Idea Whose Time Has Come.... Whites Have an Obligation to Recognize Slavery's Legacy." *Newsweek,* August 27, p. 22.

Why I Don't Want Reparations for Slavery

JOHN MCWHORTER

My childhood was a typical one for a black American in his mid-thirties. I grew up middle class in a quiet, safe neighborhood in Philadelphia. [My] mother taught social work at Temple University and my father was a student activities administrator there. My parents were far from wealthy,... but I had everything I needed plus some extras....

Contrary to popular belief, I was by no means extraordinarily "lucky" or "unusual" among black Americans of the post–Civil Rights era.... [T]oday, there are legions of black adults in the United States who grew up as I did. As a child, I never had trouble finding black peers, and as an adult, meeting black people with life histories like mine requires no searching. In short, in our moment, black success is a norm. Less than one in four black families now live below the poverty line, and the black underclass is at most one out of five blacks. This is what the Civil Rights revolution helped make possible, and I grew up exhilarated at belonging to a race that had made such progress in the face of many obstacles.

Yet today, numerous black officials tell the public that lives like mine are statistical noise, that the overriding situation for blacks is one of penury, dismissal, and spiritual desperation. Under this analysis, the blood of slavery remains on the hands of mainstream America until it allocates a large sum of money to "repair" the...damage done to our race over four centuries....

The shorthand version of the reparations idea is that living blacks are "owed" the money that our slave ancestors were denied for their unpaid servitude. But few black Americans even know the names or life stories of their slave ancestors; almost none of us have pictures or keepsakes from that far back.... Yes, my slave ancestors were "blood" to me; yes, what was done to them was unthinkable. But the 150 years between me and them has rendered our tie little more than biological. Paying anyone for the suffering of long-dead strangers ... would be more a matter of blood money than "reparation." . . .

Perhaps recognizing this, the reparations movement is now drifting away from the "back salary" argument to justifications emphasizing the effects of slavery since Emancipation. It is said blacks deserve payment for residual echoes of their earlier disenfranchisement and segregation. This justification, however, is predicated upon the misconception that in 2001, most blacks are "struggling."

This view denies the stunning success that the race has achieved over the past 40 years. It persists because many Americans, black and white, have accepted the leftist notion which arose in the mid 1960s that blacks are primarily victims in this country, that racism and structural injustice hobble all but a few individual blacks. Based on emotion, victimologist thought ignores the facts of contemporary black success and progress, because they do not square with the "blame game."

Reparations cannot logically rely on a depiction of black Americans as a race still reeling from the brutal experience of slavery and its after effects. The reality is that, by any estimation, in the year 2001 there are more middle-class blacks than poor ones. The large majority of black Americans, while surely not immune to the slings and arrows of the eternal injustices of life on earth, are now leading dignified lives as new variations on what it means to be American. . . .

Any effort to repair problems in black America must focus on helping people to help themselves. Funds must be devoted to ushering welfare mothers into working for a living, so that their children do not grow up learning that employment is something "other people" do. Inner-city communities should be helped to rebuild themselves, in part through making it easier for residents to buy their homes. Police forces ought to be trained to avoid brutality, which turns young blacks against the mainstream today, and to work with, rather than against, the communities they serve.

Finally, this country must support all possible efforts to liberate black children from the soul-extinguishing influence of ossified urban public schools, and to move them into experimental or all-minority schools where a culture of competition is fostered. This will help undo the sense that intellectual excellence is a "white" endeavor. Surely we must improve the public schools as well, including increasing the exposure of young black children to standardized tests. But we also must make sure another generation of black children are not lost during the years it will take for these schools to get their acts together....

Ultimately, a race shows its worth not by how much charity it can extract from others, but in how well it can do in the absence of charity. Black America has elicited more charity from its former oppressors than any race in human history—justifiably in my view. However, this can only serve as a spark—the real work is now ours.

SOURCE: McWhorter, John (2001). "Blood Money, An Analysis of Slavery Reparations." *American Enterprise,* 12:18.

1. Feagin and O'Brien justify reparations for African Americans, in part, by making comparisons to other situations in which victimized groups have been compensated. Are the situations they cite truly comparable to slavery and segregation? If so, what characteristics make the situations comparable? If not, explain the key differences that make the comparison invalid?

2. Feagin and O'Brien agree with Marable that whites share responsibility for "the continuing burden of history's structural racism." Explain this argument, especially in terms of the continuing racial gaps in education and income (see Chapter 6 for specific data). Does McWhorter's assessment of black success make sense? Is the difference between McWhorter and Marable merely one of emphasis? Is one seeing the glass "half empty" and the other seeing it "half full?" Or, is the division deeper than this?

3. People often think of reparations for slavery in terms of cash payments to individuals. McWhorter opposes "reparations" but approves of programs of improvement (workfare, schools, etc.). How are these programs different from "reparations?"

4. Consider Marable's point that the reparations issue can be used as an educational tool. Could the campaign for reparations be used to counteract modern racism or white indifference to racial issues? How?

5. Have reparations been considered to compensate women for centuries of exclusion from the workplace and politics? Why or why not?

- Group relations change as the subsistence technology and the level of development of the larger society change. As nations industrialize and urbanize, dominant-minority relations change from paternalistic to rigid competitive forms.

- In the South, slavery was replaced by de jure segregation, a system that combined racial separation with great inequality. The Jim Crow system was motivated by a need to control labor and was reinforced by coercion and intense racism and prejudice.

- Black southerners responded to segregation in part by moving to northern urban areas. The northern African American population enjoyed greater freedom and developed some political and economic resources, but a large concentration of low-income, relatively powerless African Americans developed in the ghetto neighborhoods.

- In response to segregation, the African American community developed a separate institutional life centered on family, church, and community. An African American middle class emerged, as well as a protest movement.

- African American women remain one of the most exploited groups. Combining work with family roles, African American females were employed mostly in agriculture and domestic service during the era of segregation.

- Industrialization continued throughout the 20th century and has profoundly affected dominant-minority relations. Urbanization, specialization, bureaucratization, and other trends have changed the shape of race relations, as have the changing structure of the occupational sector and the growing importance of education. Group relations have shifted from rigid to fluid competitive. Modern institutional discrimination is one of the major challenges facing minority groups.

Study Site on the Web

Don't forget the interactive quizzes and other resources and learning aids at www.pineforge.com/healeystudy5.

For Further Reading

Bluestone, Barry, & Harrison, Bennet. (1982). *The Deindustrialization of America*. New York: Basic Books.

The classic analysis of the shift from a manufacturing to a service-based, information society.

Feagin, Joe R., & Feagin, Clairece Booher. (1986). *Discrimination American Style: Institutional Racism and Sexism*. Malabar, FL: Robert E. Krieger.

A comprehensive and provocative look at modern institutional discrimination.

Geschwender, James A. (1978). *Racial Stratification in America*. Dubuque, IA: William C. Brown.

Wilson, William J. (1973). *Power, Racism, and Privilege: Race Relations in Theoretical and Sociohistorical Perspectives*. New York: Free Press.

Woodward, C. Vann. (1974). *The Strange Career of Jim Crow* (3rd ed., rev.). New York: Oxford University Press.

Three outstanding analyses of black-white relations in the United States, with a major focus on the historical periods covered in this chapter.

Pincus, Fred. (2003). *Reverse Discrimination: Dismantling the Myth*. Boulder, CO: Lynne Reiner.

A compact, masterful review of the myths and realities surrounding affirmative action.

Questions for Review and Study

1. A corollary to two themes from Chapter 5 is presented at the beginning of Chapter 6. How exactly does the material in the chapter illustrate the usefulness of this corollary?

2. Explain paternalistic and rigid competitive relations and link them to industrialization. How does the shift from slavery to de jure segregation illustrate the dynamics of these two systems?

3. What was the "Great Migration" to the North? How did it change American race relations?

4. Explain the transition from rigid competitive to fluid competitive relations and explain how this transition is related to the coming of postindustrial society. Explain the roles of urbanization, bureaucracy, the service sector of the job market, and education in this transition.

5. What is modern institutional discrimination? How does it differ from "traditional" institutional discrimination? Explain the role of affirmative action in combating each.

6. Explain the impact of industrialization and globalization on gender relations. Compare and contrast these changes with the changes that occurred for racial and ethnic minority groups.

7. What efforts have been made on your campus to combat modern institutional discrimination? How effective have these programs been? The public sociology assignment on affirmative action gives you a chance to research these questions.

Internet Research Project

A. Everyday Life Under Jim Crow

The daily workings of the Jim Crow system of segregation are analyzed and described in a collection of interviews, photos, and memories archived at http://www.americanradioworks .org/features/remembering/. Explore the site, look at the photos, listen to the clips, and analyze them in terms of the concepts introduced in this chapter.

B. The Debate Over Affirmative Action

Update and supplement the debate on affirmative action presented at the end of the chapter. Start with the newspaper home pages listed in the Appendix and search for recent news items or opinion pieces on the issue. Search the Internet for other viewpoints and perspectives from other groups and positions on the political spectrum. One place you might start is http://aad .english.ucsb.edu/, a Web site that presents diverse opinions on the topic and brings many different voices to the debates. Analyze events and opinions in terms of the concepts introduced in this chapter, especially modern institutional discrimination.

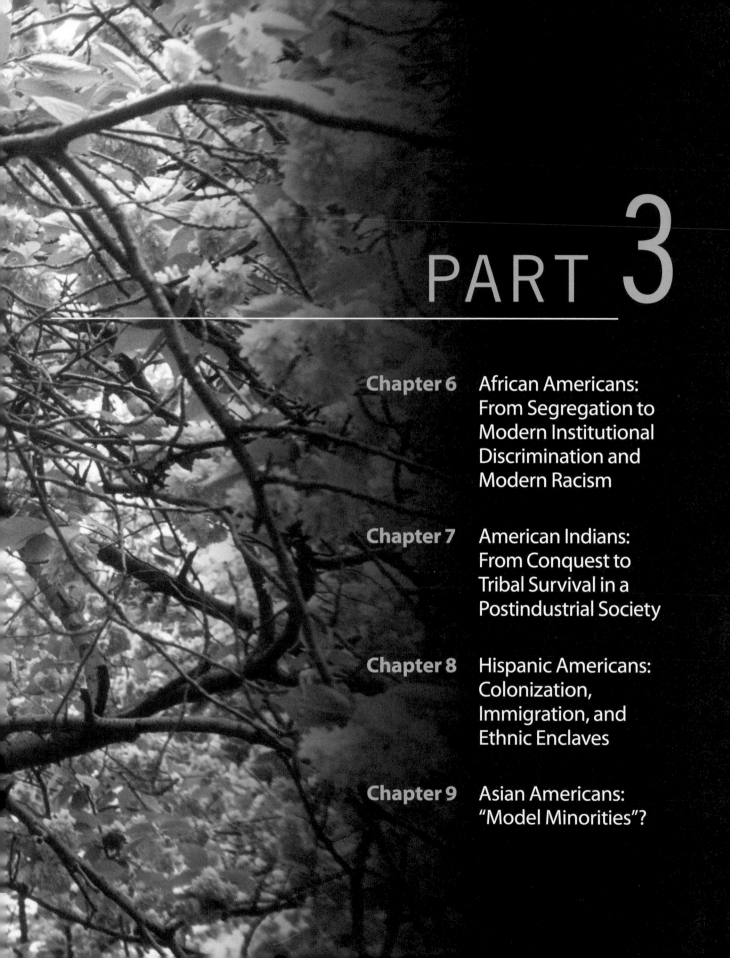

PART 3

Understanding Dominant-Minority Relations in the United States Today

In Part 3, we turn to contemporary intergroup relations. The emphasis is on the present situation of American minority groups, but the recent past is also investigated to see how present situations developed. We explore the ways minority and dominant groups respond to a changing American society and to each other and how minority groups define and pursue their own self-interests in interaction with other groups, American culture and values, and the institutions of the larger society.

The themes and ideas developed in the first two parts of this text will continue to be central to the analysis. For example, the case studies are presented in an order that roughly follows the Blauner hypothesis: Colonized groups are presented first, and we end with groups created by immigration. Also, we will continue to rely on the concepts of the Noel hypothesis to analyze and explain contemporary dominant-minority patterns.

The history and present conditions of each minority group are unique, and no two groups have had the same experiences. To help identify and understand these differences, the concepts developed in the first two parts of this text and a common comparative frame of reference are used throughout Part 3. We stress assimilation and pluralism; inequality and power; and prejudice, racism, and discrimination. For ease of comparison, the final sections of Chapters 6 through 9 use the same headings and subheadings, in the same order. Much of the conceptual frame of reference employed in these case studies can be summarized in seven themes. The first six themes are based on material from previous chapters; the last is covered in the forthcoming chapters.

1. Consistent with the Noel hypothesis, the present conditions of America's minority groups reflect their contact situations, especially the nature of their competition with the dominant group (e.g., competition over land vs. competition over labor) and the size of the power differential between groups at the time of contact.

2. Consistent with the Blauner hypothesis, minority groups created by colonization experience economic and political inequalities that have lasted longer and been more severe than those experienced by minority groups created by immigration.

3. Power and economic differentials and barriers to upward mobility are especially pronounced for groups identified by racial or physical characteristics, as opposed to cultural or linguistic traits.

4. Consistent with the themes stated in Chapters 4 and 5, dominant-minority relations reflect the economic and political characteristics of the larger

society and change as those characteristics change. Changes in the subsistence technology of the larger society are particularly consequential for dominant-minority relations. The shift from a manufacturing to a service economy (deindustrialization) is one of the key factors shaping dominant-minority relations in the United States today.

5. As we saw in Chapter 3, the "mood" of the dominant group over the past four decades combines a rejection of blatant racism with the belief that the modern United States is nondiscriminatory and that success is attainable for all who are willing to work hard enough. It is also common for dominant group Americans to believe that further reforms of the larger society or special programs or treatment for minorities are unnecessary and unjustified. Efforts to address contemporary minority group problems must deal with the pervasive "modern racism" of the dominant group.

6. The development of group relations, both in the past and for the future, can be analyzed in terms of assimilation (more unity) and pluralism (more diversity). Group relations in the past (e.g., the degree of assimilation permitted or required of the minority group) reflected mainly dominant group needs and wishes. Although the pressure for Americanization remains considerable, there is more flexibility and variety in group relations today.

7. Since World War II, minority groups have gained significantly more control over the direction of group relationships. This trend reflects the decline of traditional prejudice in the larger society and the successful efforts of minority groups to protest, resist, and change patterns of exclusion and domination. These successes have been possible in large part because American minority groups have increased their share of political and economic resources.

About the Public Sociology Assignments

The first assignment in this installment of public sociology connects you to the American Indian tribes that may once have lived in your area. As we discussed in Chapter 4, and as we will discuss further in Chapter 7, one of the most devastating consequences of the colonization of this group was the loss of their traditional homelands. In this exercise, you will explore one of the present-day aspects of that loss.

The second exercise can be done with any (or all) of the groups covered in Chapters 6 through 9. The focus is on health and health care, one of the many aspects of inequality not covered in the text. It is likely that you will find patterns reminiscent of those documented in the chapter sections titled "Secondary Structural Assimilation."

Public Sociology Assignments

Marcus Griffin

Assignment 1
American Indian Cultural Affiliation

American Indians have very little control over or ownership of land and resources that were once entirely theirs. Many tribes were forced by the federal and state governments to resettle far from their ancestral domains so that immigrant Europeans could benefit from tribal loss. Today, there are a variety of federal and state laws that protect archaeological deposits and require the repatriation of certain kinds of materials to their rightful owners: American Indians. One particular law, the Native American Graves Protection and Repatriation Act of 1990 (NAGPRA), requires that Native American human remains, funerary objects, objects of cultural patrimony, and sacred objects be returned to the tribal descendants with which they are associated.

Like many laws, there are complications to NAGPRA that present difficulties for both American Indians and federal and state agencies. The first complication is that given forced resettlement and migration of American Indian groups, which uncovered materials belong to which tribe (in a cultural sense) is not always clear—usually it is not. The second complication is that agencies are required to consult with federally recognized tribes first and foremost—namely, those that acquired recognized tribal status from the Bureau of Indian Affairs. State-recognized tribes without federal recognition, as well as other self-identified American Indian groups, do not have much legal standing insofar as repatriation is concerned.

Your assignment is to work on an American Indian cultural affiliation overview of your home region. This document can be provided to federally recognized tribes and Native American communities that once lived in the area. It may also be provided to federal and state agencies in an effort to reduce uncertainty regarding who must be consulted and who should be secondarily consulted and thereby speed up the process of repatriation when human remains or sacred items are inadvertently discovered.

Step 1

You must first familiarize yourself with legislation and policy involving American Indian archaeological deposits. Perhaps the best place to start is the National Park Service Web site devoted to NAGPRA at http://www.cr.nps.gov/nagpra/. The next government Web site you should search for background information is that of the Advisory Council on Historic Preservation, which has pages on federal, state, and tribal historic preservation programs at http://www.achp.gov/programs.html. You may conduct an Internet search for related documentation, but be careful of what you read, because the issue is quite sensitive and prone to passionate loss of objectivity. If you are not certain of the reasoned nature of material you encounter, ask your university librarians, who are experts at information literacy and may help you discern the worth of your sources.

Step 2

Using the Web-based databases of the National Park Service and Advisory Council on Historic Preservation, determine who are the federal, state, and tribal historic preservation contacts for your region. Contact them

and explain the cultural affiliation overview project you would like to conduct on their behalf. In your conversations, explore what has already been done and what remains to be completed. Your area may well already have an affiliation overview, but even so, there are likely to be areas that you could add to. Use your agency personnel as advisers on how best to proceed.

Step 3

Once you have sufficiently narrowed the focus of your cultural affiliation overview through your conversations (and, hopefully, face-to-face visits) with tribal, state, and federal historic preservation officers, begin your research. Your method will be primarily historical and literature based, and much of your time will be spent in the library or at agency offices reviewing archaeological reports and historical documents. To assist your systematic review, you may want to keep a dialogic notebook of your readings. To create this, use three-ring binder paper and draw a straight line vertically midway through each sheet, essentially creating a two-columned sheet of paper. On the left-side column of the page, write quotes and references from your readings. On the right side of the page, write your own observations, connections you have made to other material you encountered, and notes to yourself. This will aid you in your final analysis and write-up, because you will have a systematic overview of all the material read and reviewed.

Step 4

Return to your agency contacts once you are well into your review of the literature and historical documentation. Discuss with them what you are finding and obtain feedback. They are experts in their field and can provide guidance, alternatives, and insight should you feel stuck or confused in one area of the research.

Step 5

Using your dialogic notebook, begin drafting an outline of your cultural affiliation overview. Look for gaps in the research and decide whether they can be fixed or whether they should be highlighted in the executive summary and conclusion for future research efforts. Using your outline, begin crafting the narrative of your report, keeping in mind that you want to make the prose readable yet not unduly passionate or lacking in objectivity. This is where your creativity as a writer may shine, but in the end, simply try to write to the best of your ability.

Step 6

Share the draft report with your agency contacts and seek their comments and suggestions for improvement. All writing requires outside review to make it better than it is. Keep in mind that editorial comments are never about you as a writer; they are simply about communicating effectively.

Step 7

Revise your report based on the comments and suggestions you received and submit your final draft to the agency contacts you worked with from the beginning. Ask them to keep you informed of any repatriations or newly discovered materials and how repatriation consultations have used and benefited from your research.

Congratulate yourself for hard work well-done and be sure to stay in touch with your agency contacts! You may be surprised at an offer of summer employment or an internship to continue your scholarship for a good cause.

Assignment 2
Race and Class—Epidemiology and Surveillance

Social inequality often results in inadequate health care and unhealthy lifestyle choices. To understand the impact today of racism, sexism, and class-based discrimination, you can study the health and vital statistics of your county's population. This data,

presented by you in an easily understood format, may assist local social service and welfare agencies in targeting their services efficiently and communicating the magnitude of health problems effectively. Included at the end of the assignment is an Internet link to a presentation on epidemiology in Ventura, California, that will help you envision your own end product.

Step 1

Locate your local county's department of health online and search for their health and vital statistics page. This is where you will get some of your data. There may also be data already tabulated or charted in your state's annual databook. This may be found by using an Internet search engine such as Google, using keywords such as "[your state] annual databook." A third source of data is the U.S. Census Bureau at http://www.census.gov/, especially their FactFinder feature, as well as their dynamic maps (which you may capture for inclusion in your report using the Shift+PrtSc keys). Be sure to keep track of all your data sources and cite them properly. If you come across material already compiled by someone else that is just what you were looking for, an e-mail for permission to use the data is the proper professional courtesy.

Step 2

Take your time wading through the data and various sources. You want to get a good understanding of current and historical patterns in the data. Variables you may want to include in your initial survey are as follows:

- Population and ethnic makeup characteristics, by zip code
- Poverty level by zip code
- Percentage of low and very low birth weight babies, by ethnicity
- First trimester prenatal care, by ethnicity
- Childhood obesity, by ethnicity
- Asthma, by ethnicity
- Homicide, by ethnicity

Step 3

Contact a local community development organization or nongovernmental social service agency. This could be the YMCA; the Women, Infants, and Children (WIC) center; or some other entity. Make an appointment to meet with one of their personnel to discuss your research project. When you meet with him or her, share what patterns and numbers you came up with and seek to discover how this data might help the organization or agency. Listen carefully to their response to your data and their needs so that in the end you are providing them with material they can actually use rather than data that is simply interesting in and of itself.

Step 4

Make an appointment with your county department of health, perhaps asking to speak with the coroner. He or she will probably encourage you to further discuss your research with other personnel, perhaps even a statistician. Share with them your research project, which agency you are working with, what data you have obtained, and the patterns you have discerned thus far. Seek their input and guidance. They are likely to have additional data that will greatly help you in creating a fuller picture, such as data going back several years that will enable you to create a time series comparing past with present.

Step 5

Revise your compiled data and include new data provided by department of health personnel. Write a paragraph or two for each chart of data you create that explains what is implied by the chart. Do the same for any table of data you include in your report. When you have completed these, write an executive summary of the project data.

Step 6

Meet with the social service organization you are working with and share with its personnel your completed draft materials. Discuss any gaps in data that they are concerned about and revise your draft into a final form they can use.

Step 7

Submit your final draft to the social service agency. You may also want to provide a copy to the personnel who assisted you at the department of health, for their use. Do not be surprised if they ask for permission to upload the project to their Web site!

Step 8

Congratulate yourself for rewarding work well-done!

Resources

This assignment was inspired by epidemiological work of the County of Ventura (California) Public Health Department, whose Health Data/Statistics page can be seen online at http://www.vchca.org/ph/stats/index.htm.

The presentation of epidemiology and surveillance at http://www.vchca.org/ph/stats/ CDR_Apri12003_1 .ppt may also assist you in creating your report.

African Americans   CHAPTER 6

From Segregation to Modern Institutional Discrimination and Modern Racism

At the dawn of the 20th century, African Americans were primarily a southern rural peasantry, victimized by de jure segregation, exploited by the share-cropping system of agriculture, and blocked from the better-paying industrial and manufacturing jobs in urban areas. Segregation had disenfranchised them and stripped them of the legal and civil rights they had briefly enjoyed during Reconstruction. As we saw in Chapter 5, the huge majority of African Americans had very limited access to quality education; few political rights; few occupational choices; and very few means of expressing their views, grievances, and concerns to the larger society or to the world.

Today, a century later, African Americans are highly urbanized, dispersed throughout the United States, and represented in virtually every occupational grouping. Members of the group are visible at the highest levels of American society: from the Supreme Court to corporate boardrooms to the most prestigious universities. Some of the best-known, most successful, and

most respected (and wealthiest) people in the world have been African Americans: Martin Luther King Jr., Malcolm X, Michael Jordan, Shirley Chisholm, Jesse Jackson, Bill Cosby, Toni Morrison, Maya Angelou, Muhammad Ali, Oprah Winfrey, Barbara Jordan, Colin Powell, Condoleezza Rice, and Barack Obama, to name just a few. Furthermore, some of the most important and prestigious American corporations (including Merrill Lynch, American Express, and Time Warner) have been led by African Americans.

How did these changes come about, and what do they signify? What problems are obscured by these glittering success stories? Do racism, prejudice, and discrimination continue to be significant problems? Is it true that barriers to racial equality have been eliminated? How do the Noel and Blauner hypotheses and the other concepts developed earlier in this text help us understand contemporary black-white relations?

To understand the trajectories of change that have led to the present, we must deal with the watershed events in black-white relations: the end of de jure segregation, the triumph (and the limitations) of the **civil rights movement** of the 1950s and 1960s, the urban riots and **Black Power movement** of the 1960s, and the continuing racial divisions within U.S. society since the 1970s. Behind these events lie the powerful pressures of industrialization and modernization, the shift from rigid to fluid competitive group relations, changing distributions of power and forms of intergroup competition, declining levels of traditional prejudice, and new ideas about assimilation and pluralism. In less abstract terms, black-white relations changed as a direct result of protest, resistance, and the concerted actions of thousands of individuals, both blacks and whites.

The End of De Jure Segregation

As a colonized minority group, African Americans entered the 20th century facing extreme inequality, relative powerlessness, and sharp limitations on their freedom. Their most visible enemy was the system of **de jure segregation** in the South, the rigid competitive system of group relations that controlled the lives of most African Americans.

Why and how did de jure segregation come to an end? Recall from Chapter 5 that dominant-minority relationships change as the larger society and its subsistence technology change. As the United States industrialized and urbanized during the 20th century, a series of social, political, economic, and legal processes were set in motion that ultimately destroyed Jim Crow segregation.

The mechanization and modernization of agriculture in the South had a powerful effect on race relations. As farmwork became less labor-intensive and machines replaced people, the need to maintain a large, powerless workforce declined (Geschwender, 1978, pp. 175–177). Thus, one of the primary motivations for maintaining Jim Crow segregation and the sharecropping system of farming lost force.

In addition, the modernization of southern agriculture helped to spur the migration northward and to urban areas, as we discussed in Chapter 5. Outside the rural South, African Americans found it easier to register to vote and pursue other avenues for improving their situations. The weight of the growing African American vote was first felt in the 1930s and was large enough to make a difference in local, state, and even national elections by the 1940s. In 1948, for example, President Harry Truman recognized that he could not be reelected without the support of African American voters. As a result, the Democratic Party adopted a civil rights plank in the party platform, the first time since Reconstruction that a national political party had taken a stand on race relations (Wilson, 1973, p. 123).

The weight of these changes accumulated slowly, and no single date or specific event marks the end of de jure segregation. The system ended as it had begun: gradually and in a series of discrete episodes and incidents. By the mid-20th century, resistance to racial change was weakening, and the power resources of African Americans were increasing. This enhanced freedom and strength fueled a variety of efforts that sped the demise of Jim Crow segregation. Although a complete historical autopsy is not necessary here, a general understanding of the reasons for the death of Jim Crow segregation is essential for an understanding of modern black-white relations.

Wartime Developments

One of the first successful applications of the growing stock of black power resources occurred in 1941, as the United States was mobilizing for war against Germany and Japan. Despite the crisis atmosphere, racial discrimination was common, even in the defense industry. A group of African Americans, led by labor leader A. Philip Randolph, head of the Brotherhood of Sleeping Car Porters, threatened to march on Washington to protest the discriminatory treatment.

To forestall the march, President Franklin D. Roosevelt signed Executive Order No. 8802, banning discrimination in defense-related industries, and created a watchdog federal agency, the Fair Employment Practices Commission, to oversee compliance with the new antidis-criminatory policy (Franklin & Moss, 1994, pp. 436–437; Geschwender, 1978, pp. 199–200). President Roosevelt's actions were significant in two ways. First, a group of African Americans not only had their grievances heard at the highest level of society but also succeeded in getting what they wanted. Underlying the effectiveness of the planned march was the rising political and economic power of the northern African American community and the need to mobilize all segments of the population for a world war. Second, the federal government made an unprecedented commitment to fair employment rights for African Americans. This alliance between the federal government and African Americans was tentative, but it foreshadowed some of the dynamics of racial change in the 1950s and 1960s.

The Civil Rights Movement

The civil rights movement was a multifaceted campaign to end legalized segregation and ameliorate the massive inequalities faced by African Americans. The campaign lasted for decades and included lawsuits and courtroom battles as well as protest marches and demonstrations. We begin our examination with a look at the movement's successful challenge to the laws of racial segregation.

Brown v. Board of Education of Topeka.
Undoubtedly, the single most powerful blow to de jure segregation was delivered by the U.S. Supreme Court in *Brown v. Board of Education of Topeka* in 1954. The Supreme Court reversed the *Plessy v. Ferguson* decision of 1896 and ruled that racially separate facilities are inherently unequal and therefore unconstitutional. Segregated school systems—and all other forms of legalized racial

segregation—would have to end. The landmark Brown decision was the culmination of decades of planning and effort by the National Association for the Advancement of Colored People (NAACP) and individuals such as Thurgood Marshall, the NAACP's chief counsel (who was appointed to the Supreme Court in 1967).

The strategy of the NAACP was to attack Jim Crow by finding instances in which the civil rights of an African American had been violated and then bringing suit against the relevant governmental agency. These lawsuits were intended to extend far beyond the specific case being argued. The goal was to persuade the courts to declare segregation unconstitutional not only in the specific instance being tried but in all similar cases. The *Brown* (1954) decision was the ultimate triumph of this strategy. The significance of the Supreme Court's decision was not that Linda Brown—the child in whose name the case was argued—would attend a different school or even that the school system of Topeka, Kansas, would be integrated. Instead, the significance lay in the rejection of the principle of de jure segregation in the South and, by implication, throughout the nation. The *Brown* decision changed the law and dealt a crippling blow to Jim Crow segregation.

The blow was not fatal, however. Southern states responded to the *Brown* (1954) decision by stalling and mounting campaigns of massive resistance. Jim Crow laws remained on the books for years. White southerners actively defended the system of racial privilege and attempted to forestall change through a variety of means, including violence and intimidation. The Ku Klux Klan (KKK), largely dormant since the 1920s, reappeared along with other racist and terrorist groups, such as the White Citizens' Councils. White politicians and other leaders competed with each other to express the most adamant statements of racist resistance (Wilson, 1973, p. 128). One locality, Prince Edward County in central Virginia, chose to close its public schools rather than integrate. The schools remained closed for 5 years. During that time, the white children attended private, segregated academies, and the county provided no education at all for African American children (Franklin, 1967, p. 644).

Nonviolent Direct Action Protest. The principle established by *Brown* (1954) was assimilationist: It ordered the educational institutions of the dominant group to be opened up freely and equally to all. Southern states and communities overwhelmingly rejected the principle of equal access and shared facilities. Centuries of racist tradition and privilege were at stake, and considerable effort would be required to overcome southern defiance and

Photo 6.2

Freedom riders staging a sit-in at a bus terminal.

© Bettmann/Corbis.

resistance. The central force in this struggle was a protest movement, the beginning of which is often traced to Montgomery, Alabama, where on December 1, 1955, Rosa Parks, a seamstress and NAACP member, rode the city bus home from work, as she usually did. As the bus filled, she was ordered to surrender her seat to a white male passenger. When she refused, the police were called and Rosa Parks was jailed for violating a local segregation ordinance.

Although Mrs. Parks was hardly the first African American to be subjected to such indignities, her case stimulated a protest movement in the African American community, and a boycott of the city buses was organized. Participants in the boycott set up car pools, shared taxis, and walked (in some cases, for miles) to and from work. They stayed off the buses for more than a year, until victory was achieved and the city was ordered to desegregate its buses. The Montgomery boycott was led by the Reverend Martin Luther King Jr., the new minister of a local Baptist church.

From these beginnings sprang the protest movement that eventually defeated de jure segregation. The central strategy of the movement involved **nonviolent direct action**, a method by which the system of de jure segregation was confronted head-on, not in the courtroom or in the state legislature, but in the streets. The movement's principles of nonviolence were adopted from the tenets of Christianity and from the teachings of Mohandas K. Gandhi, Henry David Thoreau, and others. Dr. King expressed the philosophy in a number of books and speeches (King, 1958, 1963, 1968). Nonviolent protest was intended to confront the forces of evil rather than the people who happened to be doing evil, and it attempted to win the friendship and support of its enemies rather than to defeat or humiliate them. Above all, nonviolent protest required courage and discipline; it was not a method for cowards (King, 1958, pp. 83–84).

The movement used different tactics for different situations, including sit-ins at segregated restaurants, protest marches and demonstrations, prayer meetings, and voter registration drives. The police and terrorist groups such as the KKK often responded to these protests with brutal repression and violence, and protesters were routinely imprisoned, beaten, and attacked by police dogs. The violent resistance sometimes escalated to acts of murder, including the 1963 bombing of a black church in Birmingham, Alabama, which took the lives of four little girls, and the 1968 assassination of Dr. King. Resistance to racial change in the South was intense. It would take more than protests and marches to finally extirpate de jure segregation, and the U.S. Congress finally provided the necessary tools (see D'Angelo, 2001; Killian, 1975; King, 1958, 1963, 1968; Morris, 1984).

Landmark Legislation.

The successes of the protest movement, combined with changing public opinion and the legal principles established by the Supreme Court, coalesced in the mid-1960s to stimulate the passage of two laws that, together, ended Jim Crow segregation. In 1964, at the urging of President Lyndon B. Johnson, the U.S. Congress passed the Civil Rights Act of 1964, banning discrimination on the grounds of race, color, religion, national origin, or gender. The law applied to publicly owned facilities such as parks and municipal swimming pools, businesses and other facilities open to the public, and any programs that received federal aid. Congress followed this up with the Voting Rights Act in 1965, also initiated by President Johnson, which required that the same standards be used to register all citizens in federal, state, and local elections. The act banned literacy tests, whites-only primaries, and other practices that had been used to prevent African Americans from registering to vote. This law gave the franchise back to black southerners and laid the groundwork for increasing black political power. This landmark federal legislation, in combination with court decisions and the protest movement, finally succeeded in crushing Jim Crow.

The Success and Limitations of the Civil Rights Movement.

Why did the civil rights movement succeed? A comprehensive list of reasons would be legion, but we can cite some of the most important causes of its success, especially those consistent with the general points about dominant-minority relations that have been made in previous chapters.

The continuing industrialization and urbanization of the society as a whole—and the South in particular—weakened the Jim Crow, rigid competitive system of minority group control and segregation.

Following World War II, the United States enjoyed a period of prosperity that lasted into the 1960s. Consistent with the Noel hypothesis, this was important, because it reduced the intensity of intergroup competition, at least outside the South. During prosperous times, resistance to change tends to weaken. If the economic "pie" is expanding, the "slices" claimed by minority groups can increase without threatening the size of anyone else's portions, and the prejudice generated during intergroup competition (à la Robber's Cave, Chapter 3) is held in check. Thus, these "good times" muted the sense of threat experienced in the dominant group by the demands for equality made by the civil rights movement.

Also, some of the economic prosperity found its way into African American communities and increased their pool of economic and political resources. Networks of independent,

African-American-controlled organizations and institutions, such as churches and colleges, were created or grew in size and power. The increasingly elaborate infrastructure of the black community included protest organizations, such as the NAACP (see Chapter 5), and provided material resources, leadership, and "people power" to lead the fight against segregation and discrimination.

The goals of the civil rights movement were assimilationist; the movement embraced the traditional American values of liberty, equality, freedom, and fair treatment. It demanded civil, legal, and political rights for African Americans, rights available to whites automatically. Thus, many whites did not feel threatened by the movement because they saw it as consistent with mainstream American values, especially in contrast with the intense, often violent resistance of southern whites.

The perceived legitimacy of the goals of the movement also opened up the possibility of alliances with other groups (white liberals, Jews, college students). The support of others was crucial because black southerners had few resources of their own other than their numbers and their courage. By mobilizing the resources of other, more powerful groups, black southerners forged alliances and created sympathetic support that was brought to bear on their opposition.

Finally, widespread and sympathetic coverage from the mass media, particularly television, was crucial to the success of the movement. The oft-repeated scenario of African Americans being brutally attacked while demonstrating for their rights outraged many Americans and reinforced the moral consensus that eventually rejected "old-fashioned" racial prejudice along with Jim Crow segregation (see Chapter 3).

The southern civil rights movement ended de jure segregation but found it difficult to survive the demise of its primary enemy. The confrontational tactics that had been so effective against the Jim Crow system proved less useful when attention turned to the actual distribution of jobs, wealth, political power, and other valued goods and services. Outside the South, the allocation of opportunity and resources had always been the central concern of the African American community. Let's take a look at these concerns.

Developments Outside the South

De Facto Segregation

Chapter 5 discussed some of the difficulties encountered by African Americans as they left the rural South. Discrimination by labor unions, employers, industrialists, and white ethnic groups was common. Racial discrimination outside the South was less blatant but was still pervasive, especially in housing, education, and employment.

The pattern of racial separation and inequality outside the South is often called **de facto segregation**: segregation resulting from the apparently voluntary choices of dominant and minority groups alike. Theoretically, no person, law, or specific group is responsible for de facto segregation; it "just happens" as people and groups make decisions about where to live and work.

The distinction between de facto and de jure segregation can be misleading, however, and the de facto variety is often the de jure variety in thin disguise. Although cities and states outside the South may not have had actual Jim Crow laws, de facto segregation was often the direct result of intentionally racist decisions made by governmental and quasi-governmental agencies, such as real estate boards, school boards, and zoning boards (see Massey & Denton, 1993, pp. 74–114). For example, shortly after World War I, the real estate board in the city of Chicago adopted a policy that required its members, on penalty of "immediate expulsion," to follow a policy of racial residential segregation (Cohen & Taylor, 2000, p. 33).

Regardless of who or what was responsible for these patterns, African Americans living outside the South faced more poverty, higher unemployment, and lower-quality housing and schools than did whites, but there was no clear equivalent of Jim Crow to attack or to blame for these patterns of inequality. In the 1960s, the African American community outside the South expressed its frustration over the slow pace of change in two ways: Urban unrest and a movement for change that rose to prominence as the civil rights movement faded.

Urban Unrest

In the mid-1960s, the frustration and anger of urban African American communities erupted into a series of violent uprisings. The riots began in the summer of 1965 in Watts, a neighborhood in Los Angeles, California, and over the next 4 years, virtually every large black urban community experienced similar outbursts. Racial violence was hardly a new phenomenon in America. Race riots had existed as early as the Civil War, and various time periods had seen racial violence of considerable magnitude. The riots of the 1960s were different, however. Most race riots in the past had involved attacks by whites against blacks, often including the invasion and destruction of African American neighborhoods (see, e.g., D'Orso, 1996; Ellsworth, 1982). The urban unrest of the 1960s, in contrast, consisted largely of attacks by blacks against the symbols of their oppression and frustration. The most obvious targets were white-owned businesses operating in black neighborhoods and the police, who were seen as an army of occupation and whose excessive use of force was often the immediate precipitator of riots (Conot, 1967; National Advisory Commission, 1968).

The Black Power Movement

The urban riots of the 1960s were an unmistakable sign that the problems of race relations had not been resolved with the end of Jim Crow segregation. Outside the South, the problems were different and called for different solutions. Even as the civil rights movement was celebrating its victory in the South, a new protest movement rose to prominence. The Black Power movement was a loose coalition of organizations and spokespersons that encompassed a variety of ideas and views, many of which differed sharply from those of the civil rights movement. Some of the central ideas included racial pride ("Black is beautiful" was a key slogan of the day), interest in African heritage, and Black Nationalism. In contrast to the assimilationist goals of the civil rights movement, Black Power groups worked to increase African American control over schools, police, welfare programs, and other public services operating in black neighborhoods.

Most adherents of the Black Power movement felt that white racism and institutional discrimination, forces buried deep in the core of American culture and society, were the primary causes of racial inequality in America. Thus, if African Americans were ever to be truly empowered, they would have to liberate themselves and do it on their own terms. Some

Black Power advocates specifically rejected the goal of assimilation into white society, arguing that integration would require blacks to become part of the very system that had for centuries oppressed, denigrated, and devalued them and other peoples of color.

The Nation of Islam.
The themes of Black Power voiced so loudly in the 1960s were decades, even centuries, old. Marcus Garvey had popularized many of these ideas in the 1920s, and they were espoused and further developed by the Nation of Islam, popularly known as the Black Muslims, in the 1960s.

The Black Muslims, who formed one of the best-known organizations within the Black Power movement, were angry, impatient, and outspoken. They denounced the hypocrisy, greed, and racism of American society and advocated staunch resistance and racial separation. The Black Muslims did more than talk, however. Pursuing the goals of autonomy and self-determination, they worked hard to create a separate, independent African American economy within the United States. They opened businesses and stores in African American neighborhoods and tried to deal only with other Muslim-owned firms. Their goal was to develop the African American community economically and supply jobs and capital for expansion solely by using their own resources (Essien-Udom, 1962; Lincoln, 1961; Malcolm X, 1964; Wolfenstein, 1993).

The Nation of Islam and other black power groups distinguished between *racial separation* and *racial segregation*. The former is a process of empowerment whereby a group becomes stronger as it becomes more autonomous and self-controlled. The latter is a system of inequality in which the African American community is powerless and is controlled by the dominant group. Thus, the Black Power groups were working to find ways in which African Americans could develop their own resources and deal with the dominant group from a more powerful position, a strategy similar to that followed by minority groups that form ethnic enclaves (see Chapter 2).

The best-known spokesman for the Nation of Islam was Malcolm X, one of the most charismatic figures of the 1960s. Malcolm X forcefully articulated the themes of the Black Power movement. Born Malcolm Little, he converted to Islam and joined the Nation of Islam while serving a prison term. He became the chief spokesperson for the Black Muslims and a well-known but threatening figure to the white community. After a dispute with Elijah Muhammad, the leader of the Nation of Islam, Malcolm X founded his own organization, in which he continued to express and develop the ideas of Black Nationalism. Like so many other protest leaders of the era, Malcolm X was assassinated, in 1965.

Black power leaders such as Malcolm X advocated autonomy, independence, and a pluralistic direction for the African American protest movement. They saw the African American community as a colonized, exploited population in need of liberation from the unyielding racial oppression of white America, not integration into the system that was the source of its oppression.

Protest, Power, and Pluralism

The Black Power Movement in Perspective

By the end of the 1960s, the riots had ended, and the most militant and dramatic manifestations of the Black Power movement had faded. In many cases, the passion of Black Power activists had been countered by the violence of the police and other agencies, and many of the most powerful spokespersons of the movement were dead; others were in jail or in exile. The nation's commitment to racial change wavered and weakened as other concerns, such as the Vietnam War, competed for attention. Richard M. Nixon was elected president in 1968 and made it clear that his administration would not ally itself with the black protest movement. Pressure from the federal government for racial equality was reduced. The boiling turmoil of the mid-1960s faded, but the idea of Black Power had become thoroughly entrenched in the African American community.

In some part, the pluralistic themes of Black Power were a reaction to the failure of assimilation and integration in the 1950s and 1960s. Laws had been passed; court decisions had been widely publicized; and promises and pledges had been made by presidents, members of Congress, ministers, and other leaders. For many African Americans, though, little had changed. The problems of their parents and grandparents continued to constrain and limit their lives and, as far into the future as they could see, the lives of their children. The pluralistic Black Power ideology was a response to the failure to go beyond the repeal of Jim Crow laws and fully implement the promises of integration and equality.

Black Nationalism, however, was, and remains, more than simply a reaction to a failed dream. It was also a different way of defining what it means to be black in America. In the context of black-white relations in the 1960s, the Black Power movement served a variety of purposes. First, along with the civil rights movement, it helped carve out a new identity for African Americans. The cultural stereotypes of black Americans (see Chapter 3) stressed laziness, irresponsibility, and inferiority. This image needed to be refuted, rejected, and buried. The **black protest movements** supplied a view of African Americans that emphasized power, assertiveness, seriousness of purpose, intelligence, and courage.

Second, Black Power served as a new rallying cry for solidarity and unified action. Following the success of the civil rights movement, these new themes and ideas helped to focus attention on "unfinished business": the black-white inequalities that remained in U.S. society.

Finally, the ideology provided an analysis of the problems of American race relations in the 1960s. The civil rights movement had, of course, analyzed race relations in terms of integration, equality of opportunity, and an end to exclusion. After the demise of Jim Crow, that analysis became less relevant. A new language was needed to describe and analyze the continuation of racial inequality. Black Power argued that the continuing problems of U.S. race relations were structural and institutional, not individual or legal. To take the next steps toward actualizing racial equality and justice would require a fundamental and far-reaching restructuring of the society. Ultimately, white Americans, as the beneficiaries of the system, would not support such restructuring. The necessary energy and commitment had to come from African Americans pursuing their own self-interests.

The nationalistic and pluralistic demands of the Black Power movement evoked defensiveness and a sense of threat in white society. By questioning the value of assimilation and celebrating a separate African heritage equal in legitimacy with white European heritage, the Black Power movement questioned the legitimacy and worth of Anglo-American values. In fact, many Black Power spokespersons condemned Anglo-American values fiercely and openly and implicated them in the creation and maintenance of a centuries-long system of racial repression. Today, 40 years after the success of the civil rights movement, assertive and critical demands by the African American community continue to be perceived as threatening.

Gender and Black Protest

Both the civil rights movement and the Black Power movement tended to be male dominated. African American women were often viewed as supporters of men rather than as equal partners in liberation. Although African American women were heavily involved in the struggle, they were often denied leadership roles or decision-making positions in favor of men. In fact, the women in one organization, the Student Nonviolent Coordinating Committee, wrote position papers to protest their relegation to lowly clerical positions and the frequent references to them as "girls" (Andersen, 1993, p. 284). The Nation of Islam emphasized female subservience, imposing a strict code of behavior and dress for women and separating the sexes in many temple and community activities. Thus, the battle against racism and the battle against sexism were separate struggles with separate and often contradictory agendas, as the black protest movement continued to subordinate women (Amott & Matthaei, 1991, p. 177).

When the protest movements began, however, African American women were already heavily involved in community and church work, and they often used their organizational skills and energy to further the cause of black liberation. In the view of many, African American women were the backbone of the movement, even if they were often relegated to less glamorous but vital organizational work (Evans, 1979).

Fannie Lou Hamer of Mississippi, an African American who became a prominent leader in the black liberation movement, illustrates the importance of the role played by women. Born in 1917 to sharecropper parents, Hamer's life was so circumscribed that until she attended her first rally at the beginning of the civil rights movement, she was unaware that blacks could—even theoretically—register to vote. The day after the rally, she quickly volunteered to register:

> I guess I'd had any sense I'd a-been a little scared, but what was the point of being scared? The only thing they could do to me was kill me and it seemed like they'd been trying to do that a little bit at a time ever since I could remember. (Evans, 1989, p. 271)

As a result of her activism, Hamer lost her job, was evicted from her house, and was jailed and beaten on a number of occasions. She devoted herself entirely to the civil rights movement and founded the Freedom Party, which successfully challenged the racially segregated Democratic Party and the all-white political structure of the State of Mississippi (Evans, 1979; Hamer, 1967).

Much of the energy that motivated black protest was forged in the depths of segregation and exclusion, a system of oppression that affected all African Americans. Not all segments of the community had the same experience; the realities faced by the black community were, as always, differentiated by class as well as gender. A flavor of life in the Jim Crow South is presented in Narrative Portrait 1 in this chapter.

Photo 6.3

Fannie Lou Hamer speaks out at the Democratic Party convention in 1964.

© Bettmann/Corbis.

Growing Up Black and Female in the Jim Crow South

Feminist intellectual bell hooks was born in Kentucky in the 1950s, at the height of the Jim Crow system. Her family was rural and poor, but she rose from these humble beginnings to earn her doctorate in English. She has written over 20 books and has devoted her life to a passionate critique of white supremacy, capitalism, and patriarchy. The name under which she writes is a pseudonym, and she does not capitalize it, to stress that her ideas are more important than her name or any other aspect of her identity. She teaches at City College of New York. What class, gender, and other differentiating factors can you identify in the passage? What is the young bell hooks learning about herself and her world?

Bone Black

bell hooks

We live in the country. We children do not understand that that means we are among the poor. We do not understand that the outhouses behind many of the houses are still there because running water came here long after they had it in the city. We do not understand that our playmates who are eating laundry starch do so not because the white powder tastes so good but because they are sometimes without necessary food. We do not understand that we wash with the heavy, unsmelling, oddly shaped pieces of homemade lye soap because real soap costs money. We never think about where lye soap comes from. We only know we want to make our skin itch less—that we do not want our mouths to be washed out with it. Because we are poor, because we live in the country, we go to the country school—the little white wood-frame building where all the country kids come. They come from miles and miles away. They come so far because they are black. As they are riding the school buses they pass school after school where children who are white can attend without being bused, without getting up in the wee hours of the morning, sometimes leaving home in the dark.

We are not bused. The school is only a mile or two away from our house. We get to walk. We get to wander aimlessly in the road—until a car comes by. We get to wave at the buses. They are not allowed to stop and give us a ride. We do not understand why. . . .

School begins with chapel. There we recite the Pledge of Allegiance to the Flag. We have no feeling for the flag but we like the words; said in unison, they sound like a chant. We then listen to a morning prayer. We say the Lord's Prayer. It is the singing that makes morning chapel the happiest moment of the day. It is there I learn to sing "Red River Valley." It is a song about missing and longing. I do not understand all the words, only the feeling—warm wet sorrow, like playing games in spring rain. After chapel we go to classrooms.

In the first grade the teacher gives tasting parties. She brings us different foods to taste so that we can know what they are like because we do not eat them in our homes. All of us eagerly await the Fridays when the tasting party will begin. . . .

Mama tells us that most of that food we taste isn't good to eat all the time, that it is a waste of money. We do not understand money. We do not know that we are all poor. We cannot visit many of the friends we make because they live miles and miles away. We have each other after school.

Here at the country school we must always work to raise money—selling candy, raffle tickets, having shows for which tickets are sold. Sold to our parents, neighbors, friends, people without money who are shamed into buying little colored paper they cannot afford, tickets that will help keep the school going. The people with lots of money can buy many tickets—can show that they are "big time." Their flesh is often the color of pigs in the storybook. Somehow they have more money because they are lighter, because their flesh turns pink and pinker, because they dye their hair blond, red, to emphasize the light, lightness of their skin. We children think of them as white. We are so confused by this thing called Race.

We learn about color with crayons. We learn to tell the difference between white and pink and a color they call Flesh. The flesh-colored crayon amuses us. Like white it never shows up on the thick Manila paper they give us to draw on, or on the brown paper sacks we draw on at home. Flesh we know has no relationship to our skin, for we are brown and brown and brown like all good things. And we know that pigs are not pink or white like these flesh people. We secretly love pigs, especially me. I like to watch them lie in the mud, covering themselves in the cool red mud that is like clay, that is flaming red hot like dirt on fire. I like to watch them eat—to feed them. For some weeks now I have been feeding them the coal that is our way of keeping warm in winters. I give them little pieces at a time to hear the crunching sound. I want to give them all the tickets to eat so no one will have to sell them, so mama will not have to complain about the way it adds to her worries that she must now sell tickets. The pigs are disgusted by the tickets.

Even when I prod them with a stick they only turn away. They would rather eat coal.

I must sell tickets for a Tom Thumb wedding, one of the school shows. It isn't any fun for children. We get to dress up in paper wedding clothes and go through a ceremony for the entertainment of the adults. The whole thing makes me sick but no one cares. Like every other girl I want to be the bride but I am not chosen. It has always to do with money. The important roles go to the children whose parents have money to give, who will work hard selling tickets. I am lucky to be a bridesmaid, to wear a red crepe paper dress made just for me. I am not thrilled with such luck. I would rather not wear a paper dress, not be in a make-believe wedding. They tell me that I am lucky to be lighter skinned, not black black, not dark brown, lucky to have hair that is almost straight, otherwise I might not be in the wedding at all, otherwise I might not be so lucky.

This luck angers me and when I am angry things always go wrong. We are practicing in our paper dresses, walking down the aisle while the piano music plays a wedding march. We are practicing to be brides, to be girls who will grow up to be given away. My legs would rather be running, itch to go outdoors. My legs are dreaming, adventurous legs. They cannot walk down the aisle without protest. They go too fast. They go too slow. They make everything slow down. The girl walking behind me steps on the red dress; it tears. It moves from my flesh like wind moving against the running legs. I am truly lucky now to have this tear. I hope they will make me sit, but they say No we would not think of taking you out of the show. They know how much every girl wants to be in a wedding. The tear must be mended. The red dress like a woman's heart must break silently and in secret.

SOURCE: hooks, bell (1996). *Bone Black*, pp. 4–9. New York: Henry Holt and Company.

Race in Another America

Traditional anti-black prejudice in the United States includes an array of stereotypes alleging biological inferiority and laziness along with feelings of contempt and dislike. These ideas and emotions reflect the particular history of black-white relations in the United States, especially the centuries of slavery and decades of legally sanctioned racial inferiority. Other nations, even close neighbors to the United States, have different experiences, different histories, different cultures, and different sets of stereotypes and emotions.

One of the key characteristics of traditional U.S. anti-black prejudice is a simple "two-race" view: Everyone belongs to one and only one race, and a person is either black or white. This perception is a legacy of the assumption of black inferiority that was at the heart of both U.S. slavery and Jim Crow segregation in the South. The southern states formalized the racial dichotomy in law as well as custom with the "one-drop rule": Any trace of black ancestry, even "one drop" of African blood, meant that a person was legally black and subject to all the limitations of extreme racial inequality.

This two-race model continues in the present, and many Americans continue to insist on a single racial category for everyone, regardless of actual racial inheritance. This rigid perception may be challenged by the increases in racial intermarriage and the number of mixed-race individuals, but, in fact, "racial mixing" has always been a part of the U.S. experience, and there have always been people of mixed-race heritage. In the past, especially under slavery, interracial unions were generally coercive, and following the one-drop rule, the offspring were classified, socially and legally, as black. This nation has a very long history of ignoring the reality that people can be *both* black and white.

The U.S. perception of race contrasts sharply with the racial sensibilities in many other nations. Throughout Central and South America, for example, race is perceived as a continuum of possibilities and combinations, not as a simple split between white and black. This does not mean that these societies arc egalitarian, racially open utopias. To the contrary, they incorporate a strong sense of status and position and clear notions of who is higher and who is lower. However, other factors such as social class are considered more important than race as criteria for judging and ranking other people. In fact, social class can affect perceptions of skin color to the extent that people of higher status can be seen as "whiter" than those of lower status, regardless of actual skin color.

One interesting comparison is between the United States and Brazil, the largest nation in South America. The racial histories of Brazil and the United States run parallel in many ways, and prejudice, discrimination, and racial inequality are very much a part of Brazilian society, past and present. Like other Central and South Americans, however, Brazilians recognize many gradations of skin color and the different blends that are possible in people of mixed-race heritage. Commonly used terms in Brazil include *branco* (white), *moreno* (brown), *moreno claro* (light brown), *claro* (light), *pardo* (mixed race), and *negro* and *preto* (black). Some reports count scores of Brazilian racial categories, but Telles (2004, p. 82) reports that fewer than 10 are in common use. Still, this system is vastly more complex than the traditional U.S. perception of race.

Why the differences in racial perception? Why does Brazil have a more open-ended, less rigid system than the United States? This issue cannot be fully explored in these few paragraphs, but we can make the point that the foundation for this perception was laid in the distant past. The Portuguese, the colonial conquerors of Brazil, were mostly single males, and they took brides from other racial groups. These intermarriages produced a large class of mixed-race people. Also, slavery was not so thoroughly equated with race in Brazil as it was in North America. Although slave status was certainly regarded as undesirable and unfortunate, it did not carry the same presumption of racial inferiority as in North America, where slavery, blackness, and inferiority were tightly linked in the dominant ideology, an equation with powerful echoes in the present. Also, after slavery ended, Brazil did not go through a period of legalized racial segregation like the Jim Crow system in the U.S. South or apartheid in South Africa. Thus, there was less need politically, socially, or economically to divide people into rigid groups in Brazil.

I should stress that Brazil is not a racial utopia, as is sometimes claimed. Prejudice is an everyday reality, the legacy of slavery is strong, and there is a very high correlation between skin color and social status. Black Brazilians have much higher illiteracy, unemployment, and poverty rates and are much less likely to have access to a university education. Whites dominate the more prestigious and lucrative occupations and the leadership positions in the economy and in politics, whereas blacks are concentrated at the bottom of the class system, with mixed-race people in between (Kuperman, 2001, p. 25). It would be difficult to argue that race prejudice in Brazil is less intense than in the United States. On the other hand, given the vastly different perceptions of race in the two societies, we can conclude that Brazilian prejudice has a different content and emotional texture and reflects a different contact situation and national history.

Black-White Relations Since the 1960s

By the 1970s, the outlines of present-day black-white relations had been established. Since that time, progress has been made in integrating the society and eliminating racial inequality in some areas. In other areas, however, the progress of the African American community has stagnated, and the problems that remain are enormous, deep-rooted, and inextricably mixed with the structure and functioning of modern American society. As was the case in earlier eras, racism and racial inequality today cannot be addressed apart from the trends of change in the larger society, especially changes in subsistence technology. This section examines the racial separation that continues to characterize so many areas of U.S. society and applies many of the concepts from previous chapters to present-day black-white relations.

Continuing Separation, Continuing Violence

Almost 40 years ago, a presidential commission charged with investigating black urban unrest warned that the United States was "moving towards two societies, one black, one white, separate and unequal" (National Advisory Commission, 1968). We could object to the commission's use of the phrase "moving towards," with its suggestion that U.S. society was at one time racially unified, but the warning still seems prophetic. Without denying the progress toward integration that has been made, African Americans and white Americans continue to live in worlds that are indeed separate and unequal.

Each group has committed violence and hate crimes against the other, but the power differentials and the patterns of inequality that are the legacy of our racist past guarantee that African Americans will more often be seen as "invaders" pushing into areas where they do not belong and are not wanted. Sometimes the reactions to these perceived intrusions are immediate and bloody, but other, subtler attempts to maintain the exclusion of African Americans continue to be part of everyday life, even at the highest levels of society. For example, in a lawsuit reminiscent of Jim Crow days, a national restaurant chain was accused of

discriminating against African American customers by systematically providing poor service. In 2004, the company agreed to pay $8.7 million to settle the lawsuit (McDowell, 2004). In another example, Texaco, in 1996, was sued for discrimination by several of its minority employees. The case was settled out of court after a tape recording of company executives plotting to destroy incriminating documents and making racist remarks was made public (Eichenwald, 1996).

Many African Americans mirror the hostility of whites, and as the goals of full racial equality and justice continue to seem remote, frustration and anger continue to run high. The unrest and discontent has been manifested in violence and riots; the most widely publicized example was the racial violence that began with the 1991 arrest and beating of Rodney King by police officers in Los Angeles. The attack on King was videotaped and shown repeatedly on national and international news, and contrary to the expectations of most who saw the videotape, the police officers were acquitted of almost all charges in April 1992. On hearing word of the acquittals, African American communities in several cities erupted in violence. The worst disturbance occurred in the Watts section of Los Angeles, where 58 people lost their lives and millions of dollars of property damage was done (Wilkens, 1992).

In some ways, the riot following the 1992 King verdict was different from the riots of the 1960s. The more recent event was multiracial and involved Hispanics as well as African Americans. In fact, most of the 58 fatalities were from these two groups. Also, many of the businesses looted and burned were owned by Korean Americans, and many of the attacks were against whites directly, as in the beating of truck driver Reginald Denny (also, ironically, captured on videotape).

In other ways, the events were similar. Both were spontaneous and expressed diffuse but bitter discontent with the racial status quo. Both signaled the continuing racial inequality, urban poverty and despair, and the reality of separate nations, unequal and hostile (for more on these urban uprisings, see Gooding-Williams, 1993).

The Criminal Justice System and African Americans

No area of race relations is more volatile and controversial than the relationship between the black community and the criminal justice system. There is considerable mistrust and resentment of the police among African Americans, and the perception that the entire criminal justice system is stacked against them is widespread. These perceptions are not without justification, as black people continue to be victimized by the police in a variety of ways—some petty, some involving deadly violence. The scenario of the police viciously attacking Rodney King, mentioned earlier, is echoed in the more recent deaths of Sean Bell in 2006 and Amadou Diallo in 1999, both in New York City. Both men were black and both were shot down in a hail of bullets fired by police. In both cases, the police claimed that they were acting in the belief that their lives were in danger. Bell and Diallo, however, were unarmed. The police stood trial in both cases but were acquitted, an outcome that was widely seen as a miscarriage of justice and that reinforced negative perceptions of the police.

Photo 6.5

The "get tough" drug policy begun in the 1980s resulted in an extraordinarily high level of imprisonment for young black males.

© Ed Kashi/Corbis.

The racial bias in the criminal justice system is documented in a recent report (National Council on Crime and Delinquency, 2007), which concludes that African American youth (and youth from other minority groups) are treated more harshly at every step of the process, from arrest to imprisonment. For example, African Americans are 16% of all young people but 28% of juvenile arrests, 34% of those formally processed by the courts, and 58% of those sent to adult prison (National Council on Crime and Delinquency, 2007, p. 37). Civil rights advocates and other spokespersons for the black community charge that there is a dual justice system in the United States and that blacks, adults as well as youth, are far more likely to receive harsher treatment than whites charged with similar crimes.

Some of these tensions are exemplified by a recent series of incidents in Jena, a small town in Louisiana. At the start of the school year in 2006, a black student at the local high school asked a school official whether black students could sit under the "white tree," a shade tree in the school yard under which only white students sat. When black students approached the tree the next day, they found three nooses hanging from the branches. Three white students were expelled by the principal for their part in hanging the nooses, but this punishment was reduced to a 3-day suspension by the school superintendent.

The black community saw the action of the superintendent as evidence of racist bias, and a series of scuffles between black and white students followed, culminating in a brawl in the school yard after which six black male students were charged with attempted murder for attacking a white student. The charges were regarded as overzealous by many—not just African Americans—especially in contrast with the treatment of the white students who hung the nooses. The victim of the attack suffered no life-threatening injuries and was released from the hospital after only 2 hours of treatment. The sheriff of Jena supported the steep charges and argued that the case was not about race. Members of the black community felt otherwise. One said, "It's always about race in Jena" (Fears, 2007b).

On another level, more pervasive if less dramatic, is the issue of racial profiling: the police use of race as an indicator when calculating whether a person is suspicious or dangerous (Kennedy, 2001, p. 3). The tendency to focus more on blacks and to disproportionately stop, question, and follow them is a form of discrimination that generates resentment and increases the distrust (and fear) many African Americans feel toward their local police forces. According to some, humiliating encounters with police (for example, being stopped and questioned for "driving while black") are virtually a rite of passage for black men (Kennedy, 2001, p. 7). According to one national survey, more than half of all black men and 25% of black females feel that they have been unfairly stopped by police (Morin & Cottman, 2001; see also Weitzer & Tuch, 2005).

Black males are much more likely than white males to be involved in the criminal justice system, and in many communities, a third or more of young African American men are under the supervision of the system: in jail or prison or on probation or parole (Mauer & Huling, 2000, p. 417). This phenomenal level of imprisonment is largely the result of a national "get tough" policy on drugs and especially on crack cocaine that began in the 1980s. Crack cocaine is a cheap form of the drug that has devastated certain largely minority neighborhoods, and the street-level dealers who have felt the brunt of the national anti-drug campaign have been disproportionately young African American males. Some see this crackdown as a not-so-subtle form of racial discrimination. For example, a 1986 federal law required a minimal prison sentence of 10 years for anyone convicted of possession with intent to distribute 50 grams or more of crack, a drug much more likely to be dealt by poor blacks. In contrast, comparable levels of sentencing for dealing powder cocaine—the more expensive form of the drug—were not reached until the accused possessed a minimum of 5,000 grams (Kennedy, 2001, p. 15). The result was a double victimization of the African American community: first from the drug itself and then from the attempt to police the drug.

The scope of the relationship between the African American community and the criminal justice system is documented in two recent studies. The first (Pettit & Western, 2004) focused on men born between 1965 and 1969 and found that 3% of whites, compared with 20% of blacks, had been imprisoned by the time they were 30 years old. Also, the study found that education was a key variable affecting the probability of imprisonment: Nearly 60% of African American men in this cohort who had not completed high school went to prison. The second (Pew Charitable Trust, 2008) found that black men are imprisoned at far higher rates than white men: While less than 1% of all white men are in prison or jail, the rate for black men is 7%. Furthermore, 11% of black men aged 20 to 34 are imprisoned.

The charges of racial profiling and discrimination in the war against drugs are controversial. Many argue that racial profiling is at some level based on the fact that blacks are statistically more likely to be involved in street crime and in the illegal drug trade (for example, see Taylor & Whitney, 2002; an excerpt is included in the Current Debates at the end of Chapter 3). At another level, these patterns sustain the ancient perceptions of African Americans as dangerous outsiders, and they feed the tradition of resentment and anger toward the police in the African American community.

Increasing Class Inequality

As black Americans moved out of the rural South and as the repressive force of de jure segregation receded, social class inequality within the African American population increased. Since the 1960s, the black middle class has grown, but black poverty continues to be a serious problem.

The Black Middle Class.

A small African American middle class, based largely on occupations and businesses serving only the African American community, had been in existence since before the Civil War (Frazier, 1957). Has this more affluent segment benefited from increasing tolerance in the larger society, civil rights legislation, and affirmative action programs? Is the African American middle class growing in size and affluence?

The answers to these questions are not entirely clear, but research strongly suggests that the size and affluence of the African American middle class is less than is often assumed. For example, one study (Kochhar, 2004) found that between 1996 and 2002, the percentage of blacks that could be considered middle and upper class never exceeded 25% of the black population. The comparable figure for whites was almost 60%. Thus, by this definition, the black middle and upper class was less than half the size of the white middle and upper class.

Another recent study (Oliver & Shapiro, 2006) indicates that the African American middle class is not only smaller but also much less affluent. The researchers studied racial differences in wealth, which includes not only income but all other financial assets: the value of houses, cars, savings, other property, and so forth. Exhibit 6.1 compares the wealth of blacks and whites, using two different definitions of "middle class" and two different measures of "wealth." Middle-class status is defined, first, in terms of level of education, with a college education indicating middle-class status and, second, in terms of occupation, with a white-collar occupation indicating middle-class status. Wealth is defined first in terms of *net worth,* which includes all assets (houses, cars, and so forth) minus debt. The second measure, *net financial assets,* is the same as net worth but excludes the value of a person's investments in home and cars. This second measure is a better indicator of the resources that are available to invest in educating the next generation or financing new businesses (Oliver & Shapiro, 2006, pp. 60–62).

By either definition, the black middle class is at a distinct disadvantage. There are huge differentials in net worth between blacks and whites and even greater differences in net financial assets. Note, in fact, that the figure for net financial assets of blacks in white-collar occupations is exactly zero. Once their equity in houses and cars is subtracted out, they are left with no wealth at all, a statistic that strongly underscores the greater precariousness of middle-class standing for blacks. (For other studies the document the lower size and affluence of the black middle class, see Avery & Rendall, 2002; Pollard & O'Hare, 1999; Shapiro, 2004).

These economic differences are due partly to discrimination in the present and partly to the racial gaps in income, wealth, and economic opportunity inherited from past generations.

Exhibit 6.1 Wealth by Definition of "Middle Class" by Race

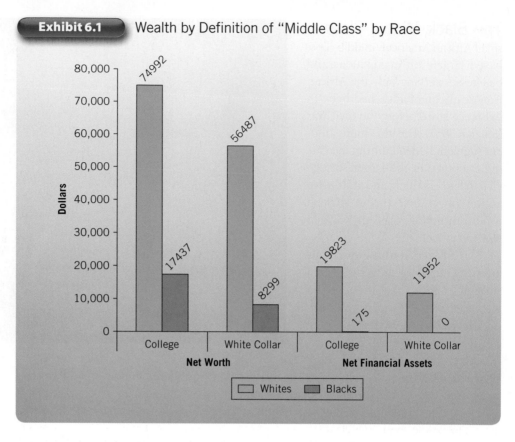

SOURCE: Oliver & Shapiro (2006, p. 96).

As suggested by the concept of net financial assets in Exhibit 6.1, economically more-advantaged white families have passed along a larger store of resources, wealth, and property to the present generation. Thus, the greater economic marginality of the African American middle class today is a form of "past-in-present" institutional discrimination (see Chapter 5). It reflects the greater ability of white parents (and grandparents) to finance higher education and to subsidize business ventures and home mortgages (Oliver & Shapiro, 2006).

Not only is their economic position more marginal; middle-class African Americans commonly report that they are unable to escape the narrow straitjacket of race. No matter what their level of success, occupation, or professional accomplishments, race continues to be seen as their primary defining characteristic in the eyes of the larger society (Benjamin, 2005; Cose, 1993; Hughes & Thomas, 1998). Without denying the advances of some, many analysts argue that the stigma of race continues to set sharp limits on the life chances of African Americans.

There is also a concern that greater class differentiation may decrease solidarity and cohesion within the African American community. There is greater income inequality among African Americans than ever before, with the urban poor at one extreme and some of the wealthiest, most recognized figures in the world at the other: millionaires, celebrities, business moguls, politicians, and sports and movie stars. Will the more affluent segment of the African American community disassociate itself from the plight of the less fortunate and move away from the urban neighborhoods, taking with it its affluence, articulateness, and leadership skills? If this happens, it would reinforce the class division and further seal the fate of impoverished African Americans, who are largely concentrated in urban areas.

Urban Poverty.
African Americans have become an urban minority group, and the fate of the group is inextricably bound to the fate of America's cities. The issues of black-white relations cannot be successfully addressed without dealing with urban issues, and vice versa.

As we saw in Chapter 5, automation and mechanization in the workplace have eliminated many of the manual labor jobs that sustained city dwellers in earlier decades (Kasarda, 1989). The manufacturing, or secondary, segment of the labor force has declined in size, and the service sector has continued to expand (see Exhibit 5.4). The more desirable jobs in the service sector have more and more demanding educational prerequisites. The service sector jobs available to people with lower educational credentials pay low wages, often less than the minimum necessary for the basics, including food and shelter, and offer little in the way of benefits, security, and links to more rewarding occupations. This form of past-in-present institutional discrimination constitutes a powerful handicap for colonized groups such as African Americans, who have been excluded from educational opportunities for centuries.

Furthermore, many of the blue-collar jobs that have escaped automation have migrated away from the cities. Industrialists have been moving their businesses to areas where labor is cheaper, unions have less power, and taxes are lower. This movement to the suburbs, to the Sunbelt, and offshore has been devastating for the inner city. Poor transportation systems, the absence of affordable housing outside the center city, and outright housing discrimination have combined to keep urban poor people of color confined to center-city neighborhoods, distant from opportunities for jobs and economic improvement (Feagin, 2001, pp. 159–160; Kasarda, 1989; Massey & Denton, 1993).

Sociologist Rogelio Saenz (2005) recently analyzed the situation of blacks in the 15 largest metropolitan areas in the nation and found that they are much more likely than whites to be living in highly impoverished neighborhoods, cut off from the "economic opportunities, services, and institutions that families need to succeed" (p. 1). We referred to this pattern in Chapter 1 when we discussed the vulnerability of African Americans to natural (and man-made) disasters, such as Hurricane Katrina. Saenz found that the greater vulnerability and social and geographical isolation of blacks is pervasive, however, and includes not only higher rates of poverty and unemployment but also large differences in access to cars and even phones, amenities taken for granted in the rest of society. In the areas studied by Saenz, blacks were as much as 3 times as likely not to have a car (and thus a means to get to jobs outside center-city areas) and as much as 8 times as likely not to have a telephone.

Some of these industrial and economic forces affect all poor urbanites, not just minority groups or African Americans in particular. The dilemma facing many African Americans is in some part not only racism or discrimination; the impersonal forces of evolving industrialization and social class structures contribute as well. However, when immutable racial stigmas and centuries of prejudice (even disguised as modern racism) are added to these economic and urban developments, the forces limiting and constraining many African Americans become extremely formidable.

For the past 60 years, the African American poor have been increasingly concentrated in narrowly delimited urban areas ("the ghetto") in which the scourge of poverty has been compounded and reinforced by a host of other problems, including joblessness, high rates of school dropout, crime, drug use, teenage pregnancy, and welfare dependency. These increasingly isolated neighborhoods are fertile grounds for the development of oppositional cultures, which reject or invert the values of the larger society. The black urban counterculture may be most visible in music, fashion, speech, and other forms of popular culture, but it is also manifest in widespread lack of trust in the larger society and whites in particular. **An urban underclass**, barred from the mainstream economy and the primary labor force and consisting largely of poor African Americans and other minority groups of color, is quickly becoming a permanent feature of the American landscape (Kasarda, 1989; Massey & Denton, 1993; Wilson, 1987, 1996).

Consider the parallels and contrasts between the plight of the present urban underclass and black southerners under de jure segregation:

- In both eras, a large segment of the African American population was cut off from opportunities for success and growth.
- In the earlier era, African Americans were isolated in rural areas; now they are isolated in urban areas, especially center cities.
- In the past, escape from segregation was limited primarily by political and legal restrictions and blatant racial prejudice; escape from poverty in the present is limited by economic and educational deficits and a more subtle and amorphous prejudice.

The result is the same: Many African Americans remain as a colonized minority group, isolated, marginalized, and burdened with a legacy of powerlessness and poverty.

Race Versus Class.

One of the livelier debates in contemporary race relations concerns the relative importance of race and class in shaping the lives of African Americans and other minority groups. One position argues that race is no longer the primary controlling influence in the lives of African Americans and that blacks and whites at the same social class level or with the same credentials have the same opportunities. The playing field is level, it is argued, and what matters is competence and willingness to work hard, not skin color.

This position is often associated with *The Declining Significance of Race,* a book written in the late 1970s by William J. Wilson, an African American and prominent sociologist. Wilson concluded that there is a segmented job market for African Americans. The black urban underclass is restricted to the low-wage sector and faces high rates of unemployment and crushing poverty. Talented and educated African Americans, in contrast, have job prospects that are "at least comparable to those of whites with equivalent qualifications" (Wilson, 1980, p. 151). Wilson attributed the improved situation of the African American middle class partly to the expansion of white-collar occupations and partly to affirmative action programs and pressure from the federal government to include African Americans and other minorities in colleges, universities, professional schools, and the job market.

Wilson's assessment may have been accurate for the 1970s. It follows, however, that these improvements would be sustained only to the extent that white-collar jobs continued to grow and affirmative action programs continued to be enforced. In the decade following the publication of Wilson's book, neither of these conditions was fulfilled. Economic growth slowed in the 1980s and 1990s, the racial gap in wages actually widened (especially among younger workers), and, under the administrations of Presidents Reagan and George H. W. Bush, federal affirmative action programs were de-emphasized (Cancio, Evans, & Maume, 1996, pp. 551–554). There is some evidence that the race/gender gap closed during the economic boom of the 1990s, but these gains were lost as racial wage inequality has increased since the beginning of the 21st century (see Exhibits 6.3 and 6.10, later in this chapter). At any rate, Wilson's conclusion that race is declining in significance seems, at best, premature (Hughes & Thomas, 1998; Thomas, 1993; Wilson, 1997).

Other critics of Wilson's thesis argue that the forces of institutional discrimination and racism remain strong in modern America, even though they may be less blatant than in the past. Race remains the single most important feature of a person's identity and the most important determinant of life chances. Contrary to the beliefs of many white Americans, especially modern racists, reports of the death of racism and the coming of a color-blind society have been greatly exaggerated (Feagin, 2001; Margolis, 1989, p. 99; Willie, 1989).

Closed Networks and Racial Exclusion.
The continuing importance of race as a primary factor in the perpetuation of class inequality is dramatically illustrated in a recent research project. Royster (2003) interviewed black and white graduates of a trade school in Baltimore. Her respondents had completed the same curricula and earned similar grades. In other words, they were nearly identical in terms of the credentials they brought to the world of work. Nonetheless, the black graduates were employed less often in the trades for which they had been educated, had lower wages, got fewer promotions, and experienced longer periods of unemployment. Virtually every white graduate found secure and reasonably lucrative employment. The black graduates, in stark contrast, usually were unable to stay in the trades and became, instead, low-skilled, low-paid workers in the service sector.

What accounts for these differences? Based on extensive interviews with the subjects, Royster concluded that the differences could not be explained by training or by personality characteristics. Instead, she found that what really mattered was not "what you know" but "who you know." The white graduates had access to networks of referrals and recruitment that linked them to the job market in ways that simply were not available to black graduates. In their search for jobs, whites were assisted more fully by their instructors and were able to use intraracial networks of family and friends, connections so powerful that they "assured even the worst [white] troublemaker a solid place in the blue collar fold" (Royster, 2003, p. 78).

Needless to say, these results run contrary to some deeply held American values, most notably the widespread, strong support for the idea that success in life is due to individual effort, self-discipline, and the other attributes enshrined in the Protestant ethic. The strength of this faith is documented in a recent survey that was administered to a representative sample of adult Americans. The respondents were asked whether they thought that people got ahead by hard work, luck, or a combination of the two. Fully 69% of the sample chose "hard work," and another 20% chose "hard work and luck equally" (National Opinion Research Council, 1972–2007). This overwhelming support for the importance of individual effort is echoed in human capital theory and many "traditional" sociological perspectives on assimilation (see Chapter 2).

Royster's results demonstrate that the American faith in the power of hard work alone is simply wrong. To the contrary, access to jobs is controlled by nepotism, cronyism, personal relationships, and networks of social relations that are decidedly not open to everyone. These subtle patterns of exclusion and closed intraracial networks are more difficult to document than the blatant discrimination that was at the core of Jim Crow segregation, but they can be just as devastating in their effects and just as powerful as mechanisms for perpetuating racial gaps in income and employment.

The Family Institution and the Culture of Poverty

The nature of the African American family institution has been a continuing source of concern and controversy. On one hand, some analysts see the African American family as structurally weak, a cause of continuing poverty and a variety of other problems. No doubt the most famous study in this tradition was the Moynihan (1965) report, which focused on the higher rates of divorce, separation, desertion, and illegitimacy among African American families and the fact that black families were far more likely to be female headed than were white families. Moynihan concluded that the fundamental barrier facing African Americans was a family structure that he saw as crumbling, a condition that would perpetuate the cycle of poverty entrapping African Americans (p. iii). Today, most of the differences between black and white family institutions identified by Moynihan are even more pronounced. Exhibit 6.2, for example, compares the percentage of households headed by females (black and white) with the percentage of households headed by married couples. (Note that the trends seem to have stabilized since the mid-1990s.)

The line of analysis implicit in the Moynihan (1965) report locates the problem of urban poverty in the characteristics of the African American community, particularly in the African American family. These structures are "broken" in important ways and need to be "fixed." This argument is consistent with the **culture of poverty theory**, which argues that poverty is perpetuated by the particular characteristics of the poor. Specifically, poverty is said to encourage **fatalism** (the sense that one's destiny is beyond one's control) and an orientation to the present rather than the future. The desire for instant gratification is a central trait of the culture of poverty, as opposed to the ability to defer gratification, which is thought to be essential for middle-class success. Other characteristics include violence, authoritarianism, and high rates of alcoholism and family desertion by males (Lewis, 1959, 1965, 1966).

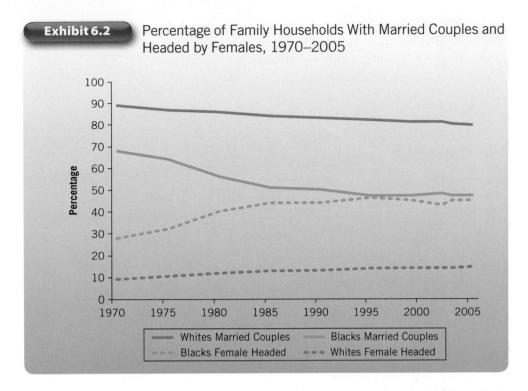

Exhibit 6.2 Percentage of Family Households With Married Couples and Headed by Females, 1970–2005

Legend:
— Whites Married Couples   — Blacks Married Couples
- - - Blacks Female Headed   ▪ ▪ ▪ Whites Female Headed

SOURCE: 1977: U.S. Bureau of the Census (1978, p. 13); 2007: U.S. Bureau of the Census (2007b, p. 56).

The culture of poverty theory leads to the conclusion that the problem of urban poverty would be resolved if female-headed family structures and other cultural characteristics correlated with poverty could be changed. Note that this approach is consistent with the traditional assimilationist perspective and human capital theory: The poor have "bad" or inappropriate values. If they could be equipped with "good" (i.e., white, middle-class) values, the problem would be resolved.

An opposed perspective, more consistent with the concepts and theories that underlie this text, sees the matriarchal structure of the African American family as the result of urban poverty—rather than a cause—and a reflection of racial discrimination and the scarcity of jobs for urban African American males. In impoverished African American urban neighborhoods, the supply of men able to support a family is reduced by high rates of unemployment, incarceration, and violence, and these conditions are in turn created by the concentration of urban poverty and the growth of the "underclass" (Massey & Denton, 1993; Wilson, 1996). Thus, the burden of child rearing tends to fall on females, and female-headed households are more common than in more-advantaged neighborhoods.

Female-headed African American families tend to be poor, not because they are weak in some sense, but because of the lower wages accorded to women in general and to African American women in particular, as documented in Exhibit 6.3. Note that black female workers have the lowest wages throughout the time period. Also note that the gap between black women and white men has narrowed over the years. In 1955, black women earned about a third of what white men earned. In 2005, the gap had shrunk to about 70%, largely because

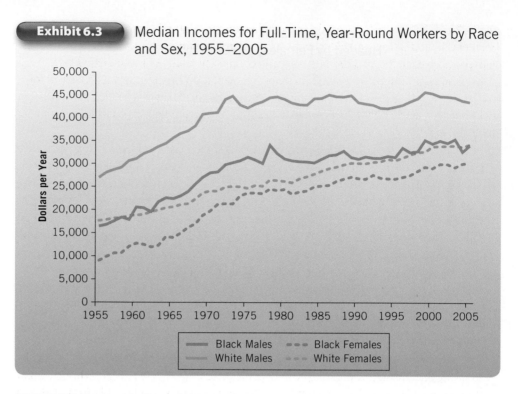

Exhibit 6.3 Median Incomes for Full-Time, Year-Round Workers by Race and Sex, 1955–2005

SOURCE: U.S. Bureau of the Census (2007c).

male wages (for blacks as well as whites) have been relatively flat since the 1970s, while women's wages (again for whites and blacks) have risen. This pattern reflects the impact of deindustrialization: the shift away from manufacturing, which has eliminated many good blue-collar jobs, and the rise of employment sectors in which women tend to be more concentrated. A similar pattern was documented in Exhibit 3.10, which compared the wages of all full-time, year-round workers by sex.

The poverty associated with black female-headed households reflects the interactive effects of sexism and racism on black women, not some weakness in the black family. African American urban poverty is the result of the complex forces of past and present institutional discrimination, American racism and prejudice, the precarious position of African American women in the labor force, and continuing urbanization and industrialization. The African American family is not in need of "fixing," and the attitudes and values of the urban underclass are more the results of impoverishment than they are the causes. The solution to African American urban poverty lies in fundamental changes in the urban industrial economy and sweeping alterations in the distribution of resources and opportunities.

Prejudice and Discrimination

Modern racism, the more subtle form of prejudice that seems to dominate contemporary race relations, was discussed in Chapter 3 . Although the traditional, more overt forms of prejudice have certainly not disappeared, contemporary expressions of prejudice are often amorphous and indirect. For example, the widespread belief among whites that racial discrimination has been eliminated in the United States may be a way of blaming African Americans—rather than themselves or the larger society—for the continuing reality of racial inequality.

A parallel process of evolution from blunt and overt forms to more subtle and covert forms has occurred in patterns of discrimination. The clarity of Jim Crow has yielded to the ambiguity of modern institutional discrimination and the continuing legacy of past discrimination in the present.

The dilemmas of the African American urban underclass provide a clear, if massive, example of modern institutional discrimination. As long as American businesses and financial and political institutions continue to operate as they do, jobs will continue to migrate, cities will continue to lack the resources to meet the needs of their poorer citizens, and urban poverty will continue to sustain itself, decade after decade. The individual politicians, bankers, industrialists, and others who perpetuate and benefit from this system are not necessarily prejudiced and may not even be aware of these minority group issues. Yet their decisions can and do have profound effects on the perpetuation of racial inequality in America.

The effects of past discrimination on the present can be illustrated by the relatively low level of African American business ownership. From the beginning of slavery through the end of Jim Crow segregation less than 40 years ago, the opportunities for African Americans to start their own businesses were severely restricted (or even forbidden) by law. The black-owned businesses that did exist were confined to the relatively less affluent market provided by the African American community, a market they had to share with firms owned by dominant group members. At the same time, customs and laws prevented the black-owned businesses from competing for more affluent white customers. The lack of opportunity to develop and maintain a strong business base in the past—and the consequent inability to accumulate wealth, experience, and other resources—limits the ability of African Americans to compete successfully for economic opportunities in the present (Oliver & Shapiro, 2001, p. 239).

How can the pervasive problems of racial inequality be addressed in the present atmosphere of modern racism, low levels of sympathy for the urban poor, and subtle but powerful institutional discrimination? Many people advocate a "color-blind" approach to the problems of racial inequality: The legal and political systems should simply ignore skin color and treat everyone the same. This approach seems sensible to many people because, after all, the legal and overt barriers of Jim Crow discrimination are long gone, and at least at first glance, there are no obvious limits to the life chances of blacks.

In the eyes of others, a color-blind approach is doomed to failure: In order to end racial inequality and deal with the legacy of racism, the society must follow race-conscious programs that explicitly address the problems of race and racism. Color-blind strategies amount to inaction: All we need to do to perpetuate (or widen) the present racial gap is to do nothing. This issue is taken up in the Current Debates section at the end of this chapter.

Assimilation and Pluralism

Acculturation. The Blauner hypothesis states that the culture of groups created by colonization will be attacked, denigrated, and, if possible, eliminated, and this assertion seems well validated by the experiences of African Americans. African cultures and languages were largely eradicated under slavery. As a powerless, colonized minority group, slaves had few opportunities to preserve their heritage even though traces of African homelands have been found in black language patterns, kinship systems, music, folk tales, and family legends (see Levine, 1977; Stuckey, 1987).

Cultural domination continued under the Jim Crow system, albeit through a different structural arrangement. Under slavery, slaves and their owners worked together, and interracial contact was common. Under de jure segregation, intergroup contact diminished, and blacks and whites generally became more separate. After slavery ended, the African American community had somewhat more autonomy (although still few resources) to define itself and develop a distinct culture.

The centuries of cultural domination and separate development have created a unique black experience in America. African Americans share language, religion, values, beliefs, and norms with the dominant society but have developed distinct variations on the general themes.

The acculturation process may have been slowed (or even reversed) by the Black Power movement. Beginning in the 1960s, on one hand, there has been an increased interest in African culture, language, clothing, and history and a more visible celebration of unique African American experiences (e.g., Kwanzaa) and the innumerable contributions of African Americans to the larger society. On the other hand, many of those traditions and contributions have been in existence all along. Perhaps all that really changed was the degree of public recognition.

Secondary Structural Assimilation.
Structural assimilation, or integration, involves two different phases. Secondary structural assimilation refers to integration in more public areas, such as the job market, schools, and political institutions. We can assess integration in this area by comparing residential patterns, income distributions, job profiles, political power, and levels of education of the different groups. Each of these areas is addressed in the next section. (See the Appendix for additional information on how African Americans compare to other U.S. groups.) We then discuss the second phase of primary structural assimilation (integration in intimate associations, such as friendship and intermarriage).

Residential Patterns. After a century of movement out of the rural South, African Americans today are highly urbanized and much more spread out across the nation. As displayed in Exhibit 6.4, about 90% of African Americans are urban, and over 80% reside in the larger cities of the nation. A slim majority of African Americans continue to reside in the South, and about 37% of African Americans now live in the Northeast and Midwest (overwhelmingly in urban areas). Exhibit 6.5 clearly shows the concentration of African Americans in the states of the old Confederacy; the urbanized East Coast corridor from Washington, D.C., to Boston; the industrial centers of the Midwest; and, to a lesser extent, California.

In the decades since Jim Crow segregation ended in the 1960s, residential integration has advanced slowly, if at all. Black and white Americans continue to live in separate areas, and racial residential segregation has been the norm. This pattern is reinforced by the fact that African Americans are more urbanized than whites and especially concentrated in densely populated center-city areas. Today, the extent of residential segregation varies around the nation, but African Americans continue to be residentially isolated, especially in the older industrial cities of the Northeast and Midwest and in the South.

Is racial residential segregation increasing or decreasing? Looking at the nation as a whole, the answer to this question is somewhat unclear, because the studies that have been done use

Exhibit 6.4 Urban-Rural Residence for Whites and Blacks, 2000

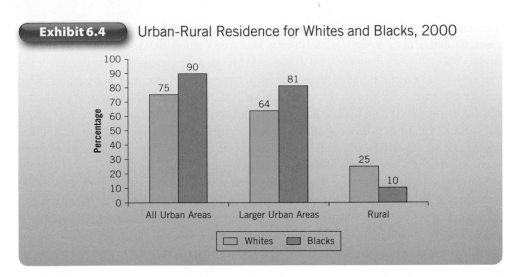

SOURCE: U.S Bureau of the Census (2000f).

Exhibit 6.5 Geographical Distribution of the African American Population, 2000

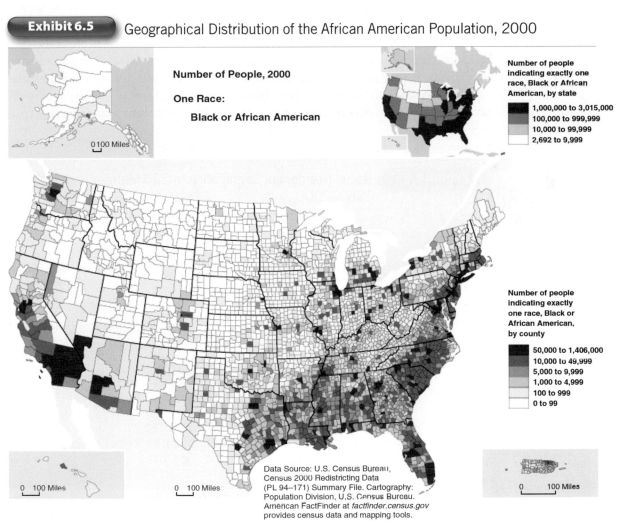

Number of People, 2000

One Race:

Black or African American

0 100 Miles

Number of people indicating exactly one race, Black or African American, by state

- 1,000,000 to 3,015,000
- 100,000 to 999,999
- 10,000 to 99,999
- 2,692 to 9,999

Number of people indicating exactly one race, Black or African American, by county

- 50,000 to 1,406,000
- 10,000 to 49,999
- 5,000 to 9,999
- 1,000 to 4,999
- 100 to 999
- 0 to 99

0 100 Miles

0 100 Miles

Data Source: U.S. Census Bureau, Census 2000 Redistricting Data (PL 94–171) Summary File. Cartography: Population Division, U.S. Census Bureau. American FactFinder at *factfinder.census.gov* provides census data and mapping tools.

0 100 Miles

SOURCE: U.S. Bureau of the Census (2000b).

different methodologies, definitions, and databases and come to different conclusions (for example, see Glaeser & Vigdor, 2001; Lewis Mumford Center, 2001). One illustrative study (Iceland, Weinberg, & Steinmetz, 2002) examined residential segregation within each of the four major regions of the United States. Exhibit 6.6 presents a measure of segregation called the *dissimilarity index* for African Americans for 1980, 1990, and 2000. This index indicates the degree to which a group is *not* evenly spread across neighborhoods or census tracts. Specifically, the index is the proportion of each group that would have to move to a different tract or area to achieve integration, and scores over .6 are considered to indicate extreme segregation.

In 1980, all regions scored at or above the .6 mark, with the highest levels of segregation found in the Midwest. By 2000, there were declines in all regions, and two (the South and West) had fallen slightly below the .6 mark. Thus, according to this study, racial residential segregation is declining but remains quite high across the nation.

The continuing patterns of residential segregation are reinforced by a variety of practices, including racial steering (guiding clients to same-race housing areas) by realtors and barely disguised discrimination. For example, in an investigation of housing discrimination in the rental apartment market conducted over the telephone, Massey (2000, p. 4) demonstrated that compared with speakers of "white English," speakers of "black English" were less likely to be told that an advertised unit was available, more likely to be required to pay an application fee, and more likely to have credit mentioned as an issue. Also, banks and other financial institutions are more likely to refuse home mortgages to black applicants than to white applicants and are more likely to "redline," or deny, home improvement loans for houses in minority group neighborhoods (Feagin, 2001, pp. 155–159). "White flight" away from integrated areas

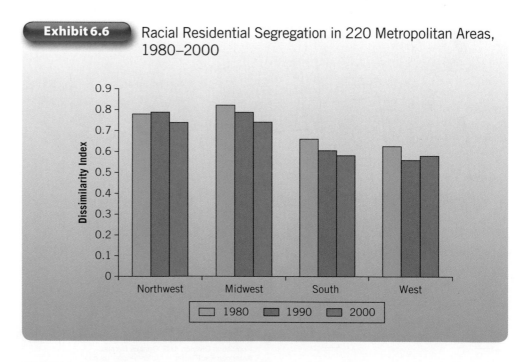

Exhibit 6.6   Racial Residential Segregation in 220 Metropolitan Areas, 1980–2000

SOURCE: Iceland, Weinberg, & Steinmetz (2002, p. 64).

also contributes to the pattern of racial separation, as whites flee from even minimal neighborhood integration. These practices are sometimes supplemented with harassment and even violence against African Americans who move into white-majority neighborhoods.

Contrary to a popular belief among whites, an African American preference for living in same-race neighborhoods plays a small role in perpetuating these patterns. For example, one study of representative samples of African Americans from four major American cities (Atlanta, Boston, Detroit, and Los Angeles) found that African Americans overwhelmingly preferred to live in areas split 50/50 between blacks and whites (Krysan & Farley, 2002, p. 949). Finally, the social class and income differences between blacks and whites are also relatively minor factors in perpetuating residential segregation, as the African American middle class is just as likely to be segregated as the African American poor (Stoll, 2004, p. 26).

School Integration. In 1954, the year of the landmark Brown desegregation decision, the great majority of African Americans lived in states operating segregated school systems. Compared with white schools, Jim Crow schools were severely underfunded and had fewer qualified teachers, shorter school years, and inadequate physical facilities. School integration was one of the most important goals of the civil rights movement in the 1950s and 1960s, and aided by pressure from the courts and the federal government, considerable strides were made toward this goal for several decades. More recently, the pressure from the federal government has eased, and one recent report found that schools are being resegregated today at the fastest rate since the 1950s. For example, as displayed in Exhibit 6.7, schools in the southern states actually reached their highest levels of racial integration in the late 1980s—20 years ago—when 44% of black students attended white-majority schools. Since that time, this percentage has drifted downward and reached a low of less than 30% in 2003 (Orfield & Lee, 2006).

Exhibit 6.7 Percentage of Black Students Attending Majority-White Schools in the South, 1954–2003

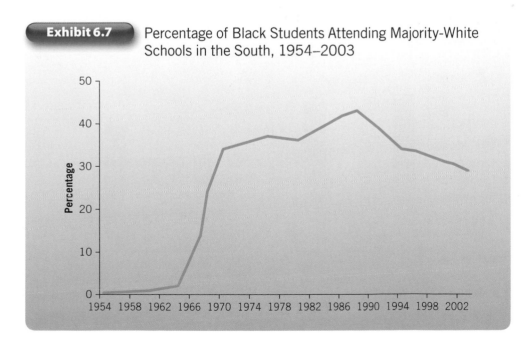

SOURCE: Orfield & Lee (2006, p. 14).

Exhibit 6.8 shows the extent of school segregation for the nation as a whole in the 1993–1994 and 2005–2006 school years. Three indicators of school segregation are used. The first is the percentage of white and black students in majority-white schools, and the second is the percentage of each in "majority-minority" schools, or schools in which at least 51% of the student body is nonwhite. The third indicator is the percentage attending schools that are extremely segregated: Minorities make up 90% to 100% of the student body.

Exhibit 6.8 clearly shows that the goal of racial integration in the public schools has not been achieved. In both school years, the overwhelming majority of white students attended predominantly white schools, while the great majority of black students attended schools that were predominantly minority. Both the percentage of black students in "majority-minority" schools and the percentage in extremely segregated schools was higher in the 2005–2006 school year than in the 1993–1994 year. The degree of racial isolation declined slightly between the two time periods as the percentage of white students in majority-white schools dropped from 91% to 87%. According to analyst Richard Fry, this was due to a massive increase (55%) in Hispanic students in the schools, not an increase in black-white contacts (Fry, 2007, p. 1).

Underlying and complicating the difficulty of school integration is the widespread residential segregation mentioned previously. The challenges for school integration are especially evident in those metropolitan areas, such as Washington, D.C., that consist of a largely black-populated inner city surrounded by largely white-populated rings of suburbs. Even with busing, political boundaries would have to be crossed before the school systems could be substantially integrated. Without a renewed commitment to integration, American schools will continue to resegregate. This is a particularly ominous trend, because it directly affects the quality of education. For example, years of research demonstrate that the integration of schools—by social class as well as by race—is related to improved test scores (Orfield & Lee, 2006).

Exhibit 6.8   School Integration, 1993–1994 and 2005–2006

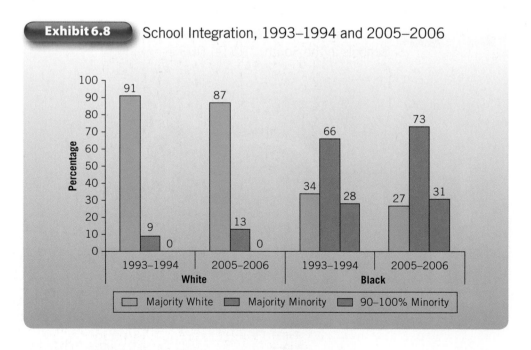

SOURCE: Fry (2007).

In terms of the quantity of education, the gap between whites and blacks has generally decreased over the past several decades. Exhibit 6.9 displays the percentage of the population over 25 years old, by race and sex, who have high school diplomas. The racial gap has shrunk dramatically at the high school level, even though it remains noticeable. Part of the remaining difference in educational attainment is due to social class factors. For example, African American students are more likely to drop out of high school. Research has shown that "students are more likely to drop out . . . when they get poor grades, are older than their classmates, come from a single-parent family, have parents who dropped out . . . or live in a central city" (O'Hare, Pollard, Mann, & Kent, 1991, p. 21). On the average, African American students are more exposed to these risk factors than are white students. When the effects of social class background are taken into account, differences in dropout rates nearly disappear (O'Hare et al., 1991, p. 21).

At the college level, the trends somewhat parallel the narrowing gap in levels of high school education, as shown in Exhibit 6.10. In 1960, white males held a distinct advantage over all other race/gender groups. For example, white males were about 3½ times more likely than African American males to have a college degree. By 2005, the advantage of white males had shrunk, but they were still about twice as likely as black males to have a college degree. These racial differences are larger with more-advanced degrees, however, and differences such as these will be increasingly serious in an economy in which jobs increasingly require an education beyond high school.

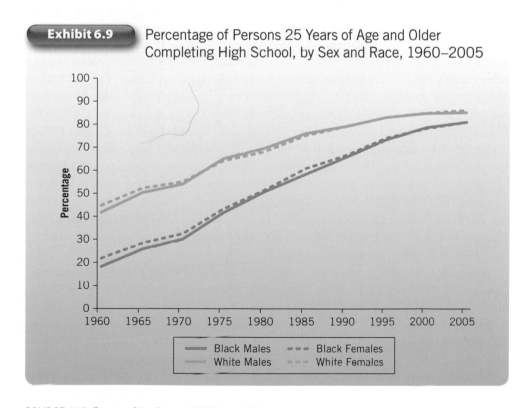

Exhibit 6.9   Percentage of Persons 25 Years of Age and Older Completing High School, by Sex and Race, 1960–2005

Legend:
—— Black Males   ● ● ● Black Females
—— White Males   - - - White Females

SOURCE: U.S. Bureau of the Census (2007b, p. 143).

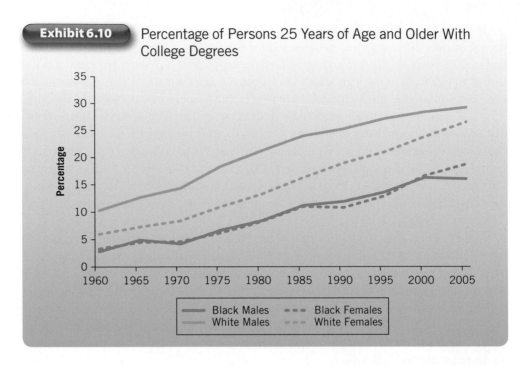

Exhibit 6.10 Percentage of Persons 25 Years of Age and Older With College Degrees

Black Males ▬ Black Females ▪▪▪
White Males ▬ White Females ▪▪▪

SOURCE: U.S. Bureau of the Census (2007b, p. 143).

Political Power. Two trends have increased the political power of African Americans since World War II. One is the movement out of the rural South, a process that concentrated African Americans in areas in which it was easier to get people registered to vote. The first African American representative to the U.S. Congress (other than those elected during Reconstruction) was elected in 1928. By 1954, there were still only three African American members in the House of Representatives (Franklin, 1967, p. 614), and currently there are 42, about 9% of the total (U.S. Bureau of the Census, 2007b, p. 251). In 2004, Barack Obama was elected to the U.S. Senate from the state of Illinois, the third African American senator since Reconstruction (the other two were Edward Brooke, R-Mass., who served two terms beginning in 1967, and Carol Mosely-Braun, D-Ill., who served one term beginning in 1993). In 2007, Senator Obama became a candidate for the nomination of the Democratic Party for president. By spring 2008, Senator Obama was the leader in the race, with more pledged delegates than his remaining rival, Senator Hillary Clinton.

The number of African American elected officials at all levels of government increased from virtually zero at the turn of the 20th century to more than 9,000 in 2001 (U.S. Bureau of the Census, 2005, p. 255). In Virginia in 1989, Douglas Wilder became the first African American to be elected to a state governorship, and both Colin Powell and Condoleezza Rice have served as secretary of state, the highest governmental office—along with Supreme Court justice—ever held by African Americans. African American communities are virtually guaranteed some political representation by their high degree of geographical concentration at the local level. Today, most large American cities, including Los Angeles, Chicago, Atlanta, New York, and Washington, D.C., have elected African American mayors.

Representative John Conyers (D-Mich.) is one of the most powerful members of Congress.

© Stefan Zaklin/epa/Corbis.

The other trend is the dismantling of the institutions and practices that disenfranchised southern blacks during Jim Crow segregation (see Chapter 5). In particular, the Voting Rights Act of 1965 specifically prohibited many of the practices (poll taxes, literacy tests, and whites-only primaries) traditionally used to keep African Americans politically powerless. The effect of these repressive policies can be seen in the fact that as late as 1962, only 5% of the African American population of Mississippi and 13% of the African American population of Alabama were registered to vote (O'Hare et al., 1991, p. 33).

Since the 1960s, the number of African Americans in the nation's voting age population has increased from slightly less than 10% to about 13%. This increasing potential for political power was not fully mobilized in the past, however, and actual turnout has generally been much lower for blacks than for whites. In the hotly contested presidential races of 2000 and 2004, however, a variety of organizations (such as the NAACP) made a concerted and largely successful effort to increase turnout for African Americans. In both years, black turnout was comparable to that of whites. In 2000, for example, black turnout nationally was only 3% lower than white turnout and, in the view of many, might have made the difference in the razor-close race in Florida had the votes been counted differently. Black voters have been a very important constituency for the Democratic Party and, even with low turnout, figured prominently in the elections of John F. Kennedy in 1960, Jimmy Carter in 1976, and Bill Clinton in 1992 and 1996. In 2004, President George W. Bush made a slight gain in the support of black voters for the Republican Party, and African Americans may perhaps amplify their political power if the rivalry between the parties for this small but potentially crucial vote increases.

Jobs and Income. Integration in the job market and racial equality in income follow the trends established in many other areas of social life: The situation of African Americans has improved since the end of de jure segregation but has stopped well short of equality. Among males, whites are much more likely to be employed in the highest-rated and most lucrative occupational areas, whereas blacks are overrepresented in the service sector and in unskilled labor. Although huge gaps remain, we should also note that the present occupational distribution represents a rapid and significant upgrading, given the fact that as recently as the 1930s, the majority of African American males were unskilled agricultural laborers (Steinberg, 1981, pp. 206–207).

A similar improvement has occurred for African American females. In the 1930s, about 90% of employed African American women worked in agriculture or in domestic service (Steinberg, 1981, pp. 206–207). The percentage of African American women in these categories has dropped dramatically, and the majority of African American females are employed in the two highest occupational categories, although typically at the lower levels of these categories. For example, in the top-rated "managerial and professional" category, women are more likely to be concentrated in less-well-paid occupations, such as nurse or elementary school teacher (see Exhibit 5.6), whereas men are more likely to be physicians and lawyers.

Unemployment rates vary by sex and by age, and African American males frequently have higher unemployment rates than do African American females. Among white Americans, females have always had a higher unemployment rate. The reasons for greater unemployment among African Americans are various and complex. As we have seen, lower levels of education and concentration in the job-poor center cities play a part. So, too, does lower seniority (because integration is so recent, African American workers have less seniority and are more often the victims of the "last hired, first fired" pattern) and the concentration of African Americans in positions more likely to become obsolete in a developing economy. At the core of these patterns of unemployment and disadvantage, however, are discrimination, both individual and institutional, and the continuing presence of prejudice and racism (Feagin, 2001, pp. 159–166).

The racial differences in education and jobs are reflected in a persistent racial income gap, as shown in Exhibit 6.11. In the early 1970s, black household income was about 58% of white household income. The gap remained relatively steady through the 1980s, closed during the boom years of the 1990s and, since the turn of the century, has widened again.

Exhibit 6.11 depicts the racial income gap in terms of the median, an average that shows the difference between "typical" white and black families. Exhibit 6.12 supplements this information by comparing the distribution of income within each racial group for 2006 and highlights the differences in the percentage of each group in low-, middle-, and upper-income categories. To read this graph, note that income categories are arrayed from top to bottom and that the horizontal axis has a zero point in the middle of the graph. The percentage of white households in each income category is represented by the bars to the left of the zero

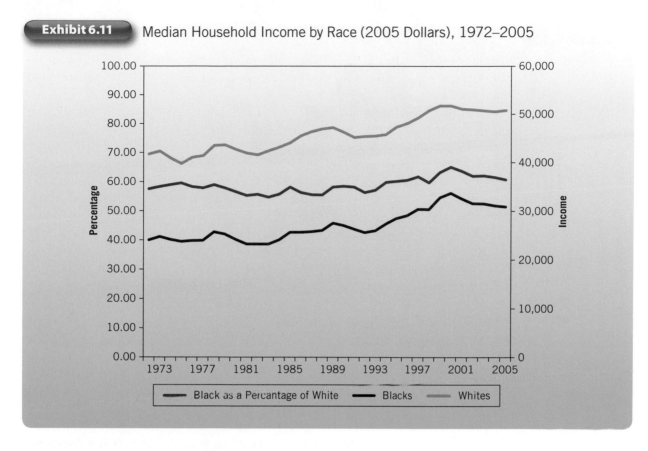

Exhibit 6.11 Median Household Income by Race (2005 Dollars), 1972–2005

Legend: Black as a Percentage of White — Blacks — Whites

SOURCE: DeNavas-Walt, Proctor, & Lee (2006, pp. 32–35).

point, and the same information is presented for black households by the bars to the right of the center point.

Starting at the bottom, note that the bars representing black households are considerably wider than those for white households: This reflects the fact that black Americans are more concentrated in the lower income brackets. For example, 16% of black households had incomes of $10,000 or less, almost triple the percentage of white households (6%) in this range.

Moving up the figure, we can see that black households continue to be overrepresented in the income categories at the bottom and middle of the figure. As we continue upward, note that there is a noticeable clustering for both black and white households in the $50,000 to $124,000 categories, income ranges that would be associated with an upper-middle-class lifestyle. In this income range, however, it is the white households that are overrepresented: 40% of white households versus only 28% of black households had incomes in this range. The racial differences are even more dramatic in the two highest income ranges: Over 8% of white households had incomes greater than $150,000 versus only 2% of black households. Graphs such as this convincingly refute the notion, common among "modern racists" and many other Americans, that there are no important racial inequalities in the United States today.

Exhibit 6.12 Distribution of Household Income for Non-Hispanic Whites and Blacks, 2006

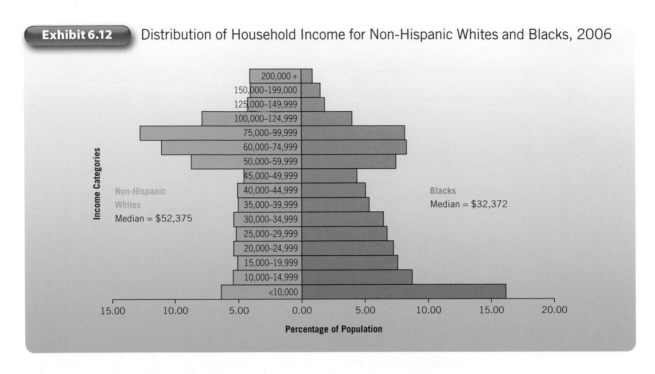

SOURCE: U.S. Census Bureau (2007a).

Finally, poverty affects African Americans at much higher rates than it does white Americans. Exhibit 6.13 shows the percentage of white and black Americans living below the federally established, "official" poverty level from 1966 through 2006. The poverty rate for African American families runs about 3 times greater than the rate for whites, even though the rate for both groups trends down. For example, in 1970, African American poverty was more than 3.3 times the rate of white poverty (33% vs. 10%). By 2006, fewer families of both races were living in poverty (about 22% for blacks and 8% for whites), but the racial differential was still almost 3 times greater for African American families. Tragically, the highest rates of poverty continue to be found among children, especially African American children. Note the increase in poverty rates for black families and black and white children in the early years of the 21st century, after falling for nearly a decade. Again, graphs like this convincingly refute the notion that serious racial inequality is a thing of the past for U.S. society.

Primary Structural Assimilation. Interracial contact in the more public areas of society, such as schools or the workplace, is certainly more common today, and as Gordon's model of assimilation predicts, this has led to increases in more intimate contacts across racial lines. For example, the percentage of African Americans who say they have "good friends" who are white increased from 21% in 1975 to 78% in 1994. Comparable increases have occurred for whites: In 1975, only 9% said they had "good friends" who were black, and that percentage rose to 73% in 1995 (Thernstrom & Thernstrom, 1997, p. 521). One

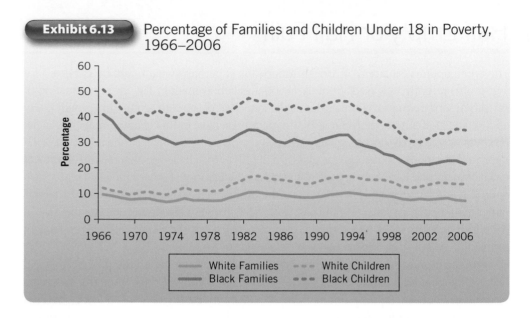

Exhibit 6.13 Percentage of Families and Children Under 18 in Poverty, 1966–2006

Legend:
- White Families
- White Children
- Black Families
- Black Children

SOURCE: 1966–2005: DeNavas-Walt, Proctor, & Lee (2006, pp. 47–49); 2006: U.S. Bureau of the Census (2007a).

study looked at changing intimate relationships among Americans by asking a nationally representative sample about the people with whom they discuss "important matters." Although the study did not focus on black-white relations per se, the researchers did find that the percentage of whites who included African Americans as intimate contacts increased from 9% to over 15% between 1984 and 2004 (McPherson, Smith-Lovin, & Brashears, 2006). While this increase would be heartening to those committed to a more integrated, racially unified society, these low percentages could also be seen as discouraging, as they suggest that about 85% of white Americans maintain racially exclusive interpersonal networks of friends and acquaintances.

Consistent with the decline in traditional, overt prejudice, Americans are much less opposed to interracial dating and marriage today. A Gallup Poll, for example, reports that 75% of white Americans express approval of black-white marriage, up from just 20% approval in 1968. The comparable percentage of black Americans was 85%, up from 56% in 1968 (Gallup Organization, 2007). Approval of interracial dating and marriage appears to be especially high among younger people: In a 2007 poll, 86% of Americans in the 18-to-29 age range approved of interracial marriage, as opposed to 30% of those aged 65 and older (Wellner, 2007).

Behavior appears to be following attitudes as the rates of interracial dating and marriage are increasing. A number of studies find that interracial dating is increasingly common (see Wellner, 2007) and marriages between blacks and whites are also increasing in number, although still a tiny percentage of all marriages. According to the U.S. Bureau of the Census, there were 65,000 black-white married couples in 1970 (including persons of Hispanic origin), about 0.10% of all married couples. By 2005, the number of black-white married couples had increased more than sixfold, to 422,000, but this is still only about 0.70% of all married couples (U.S. Bureau of the Census, 2007b, p. 52).

Is the Glass Half Empty or Half Full?

The contemporary situation of African Americans is perhaps what might be expected for a group so recently "released" from exclusion and subordination. The average situation of African Americans improved vastly during the latter half of the 20th century in virtually every area of social life. As demonstrated by the data presented in this chapter, however, racial progress stopped well short of equality. In assessing the present situation, one might stress the improved situation of the group (the glass is half full) or the challenges that remain before full racial equality and justice are achieved (the glass is half empty). Perhaps the most reasonable approach is to recognize that in many ways, the overall picture of racial progress is "different" rather than "better" and that over the past century of change, a large percentage of the African American population has traded rural peasantry for urban poverty and now faces an array of formidable and deep-rooted problems.

The situation of African Americans is intimately intermixed with the plight of our cities and the changing nature of the labor force. It is the consequence of nearly 400 years of prejudice, racism, and discrimination, but it also reflects broader social forces, such as urbanization and industrialization. Consistent with their origin as a colonized minority group, the relative poverty and powerlessness of African Americans has persisted long after other groups (e.g., the descendants of the European immigrants who arrived between the 1820s and the 1920s) have achieved equality and acceptance. African Americans were enslaved to meet the labor demands of an agrarian economy, became a rural peasantry under Jim Crow segregation, were excluded from the opportunities created by early industrialization, and remain largely excluded from the better jobs in the emerging postindustrial economy.

Progress toward racial equality has slowed considerably since the heady days of the 1960s, and in many areas, earlier advances seem hopelessly stagnated. Public opinion polls indicate that there is little support or sympathy for the cause of African Americans (see Chapter 3). Traditional prejudice has declined, only to be replaced by modern racism. In the court of public opinion, African Americans are often held responsible for their own plight. Biological racism has been replaced by indifference to racial issues or by blaming the victims.

Of course, in acknowledging the challenges that remain, we should not downplay the real improvements that have been made in the lives of African Americans. Compared with their forebears in the days of Jim Crow, African Americans today are on the average more prosperous and more politically powerful, and some are among the most revered of current popular heroes (the glass is half full). However, the increases in average income and education and the glittering success of the few obscures a tangle of problems for the many, problems that may well grow worse as America moves further into the postindustrial era. Poverty, unemployment, a failing educational system, residential segregation, subtle racism, and continuing discrimination continue to be inescapable realities for millions of African Americans. In many African American neighborhoods, crime, drugs, violence, poor health care, malnutrition, and a host of other factors compound these problems (the glass is half empty).

Given this gloomy situation, it should not be surprising to find significant strength in pluralistic, nationalistic thinking, as well as resentment and anger in the African American community. Black Nationalism and Black Power remain powerful ideas, but their goals of development and autonomy for the African American community remain largely rhetorical sloganeering without the resources to bring them to actualization.

The situation of the African American community in the early days of the 21st century might be characterized as structural pluralism combined with inequality. The former characterization testifies to the failure of assimilation and the latter to the continuing effects, in the present, of a colonized origin. The problems that remain are less visible (or perhaps just better hidden from the average white middle-class American) than those of previous eras. Responsibility is more diffused, the moral certainties of opposition to slavery or to Jim Crow laws are long gone, and contemporary racial issues must be articulated and debated in an environment of subtle prejudice and low levels of sympathy for the grievances of African Americans. Urban poverty, modern institutional discrimination, and modern racism are less dramatic and more difficult to measure than an overseer's whip, a lynch mob, or a sign that says "Whites Only," but they can be just as real and just as deadly in their consequences.

CURRENT DEBATES

Should the United States Be Colorblind?

Many people believe that U.S. society should officially ignore race and that the way to finally get past the injustices of the past is to treat everyone exactly the same in schools, jobs, politics, and every other American institution. This argument resonates strongly with fundamental American values and appeals to many as simple common sense: If we want to have a society in which only character matters—not race or skin color—we need to start treating people as individuals, not as representatives of groups. From this viewpoint, programs such as affirmative action perpetuate rather than solve the problems of racial inequality in America.

Others, a distinct minority of public opinion, feel that to ignore race is to perpetuate the inequalities of the past. Colorblindness leads not to a more equal and open society but, rather, simply perpetuates white privilege and dominance. The only way to end racial inequality is to build programs and policies that take explicit notice of race and confer an affirmative advantage on blacks and on other colonized, marginalized groups. Without a strong program to force employers to balance their workforces and to require college admission programs to seek out qualified minority candidates, the racial status quo will be perpetuated indefinitely.

The view that America needs to be colorblind is presented below in an interview with Ward Connerly, an African American and a very prominent leader of anti–affirmative action programs in California and across the nation. The interview was published in The American Enterprise (TAE) in 2003. The opposing view is presented by Ian F. Haney Lopez, a professor of law at the University of California at Berkeley and author of White by Law: The Legal Construction of Race (2006).

Creating Equal: The Importance of Being Colorblind

WARD CONNERLY INTERVIEW

The American Enterprise (TAE): What are the biggest problems facing young black Americans today?

Connerly: The problems that face black Americans are really no different from the threats that face all young Americans. I would sum them up this way: How do we preserve a culture in which every American citizen is treated as an equal without regard to his race or color?

TAE: Is it easier to be a white person in America than a black person?

Connerly: Maybe, but that really should not be important. It certainly is a lot easier for a black person growing up today than it was 40 years ago. But that didn't stop blacks 40 years ago from overcoming their problems. And they didn't do it alone; the nation grew with them.

There is no obstacle in the way of any black kid or Latino kid today that is insurmountable. A lot of things that we present as barriers for black people are barriers that are created by expecting the worst. When you expect the worst you get it. So I don't think that the challenges facing black people once they step outside the prism of blackness are any greater than they are for anybody else.

TAE: There now exists a sizable, reasonably well-off generation of African Americans who have never faced legal discrimination. Is this group eventually going to conclude that affirmative action is no longer needed, and how soon do you think that might happen?

Connerly: There is indeed a sizable black middle class, and also a sizable group of very wealthy blacks.... But there's still an element of political correctness that stops black Americans from...saying, "We don't need affirmative action." That won't happen until the cultural and political waters are warmer for them to say that.

Today's successful blacks have taken advantage of opportunities that were there. They were prepared, worked hard, and made it. But it's not yet fashionable among blacks to say that. If you do, the wrath of the "professional" blacks—people for whom being black is their profession—will come down on you. If you're the CEO of a big company, you don't want Jesse Jackson and the Congressional Black Caucus ragging on you every day. So you just roll over—and let the Connerlys of the world do the dirty work.

TAE: So what do you think a modern civil rights movement should focus on?

Connerly: A modern civil rights movement should focus on making sure that every American understands that civil rights are not just for black people. They're for everybody. I think it's time for the conservative movement to conduct a friendly, or perhaps a hostile, takeover of the civil rights movement.... The next step, I think, is to articulate the absolute importance of deregulating race. Getting it out of the equation. Getting to the point where you no longer have to ask me about black people.

TAE: Tell us about the Racial Privacy Initiative.

Connerly: The Racial Privacy Initiative is aimed at breathing life into what I think is at the core of America—taking people from all around the globe who come here, and saying to them: Once you are fully here, you're just an American citizen, no more, no less. You have the same expectations, same privileges, same benefits as any other American citizen. You're not a black American citizen. You're not Irish. You're just an American. In the privacy of your own life you can celebrate anything you want to celebrate. But the government will not be a party to that. The government doesn't give a damn about whether you are black or white or whatever.

TAE: How hopeful are you that that is going to happen? It seems like racial identity politics has become very entrenched.

Connerly: Let's step back for a moment. Just a short nine years ago . . . to even think of challenging affirmative action was unthinkable. Now affirmative action is on the ropes. . . .

TAE: Are public schools leaving black youths ill-prepared for competitive colleges? Isn't this one of the main factors creating the pressure for admission quotas by race?

Connerly: Yeah, I think that public schools are a large part of the problem. But you cannot dismiss the role of the family. Public schools provide lesson plans and homework assignments, and babysit the kids during the day. When kids get home it's the parents who make sure that they're learning. Before children have their first day in school they need to know their ABCs, and they need to be disciplined. In all too many black families, they have not been taught how to speak proper English. And therein lies the basic problem. A kid who comes to school speaking little proper English is severely handicapped.

[M]any black kids . . . are taught that learning is a white man's game. Many of the black kids we are worried about are low-income kids; kids without parents who understand the importance of getting them prepared. These are not problems of their skin color, and the minute we say they're black that just translates into a whole different approach to how we deal with the problem. We think they're being discriminated against yadda, yadda, yadda, and we never get to the real core of the problem, which is that the kid is in a dysfunctional family setting where race isn't the real problem. . . .

TAE: Do you consider yourself black?

Connerly: It is a testimony to my endurance that I've sat through this interview, with nearly every question being about color, and I'm still civil at the end of it. My origin is of African descent, Choctaw Indian, French, and Irish. Two of my grandkids are all of that plus their grandmother, who is Irish, and their father, who is of German descent. And two other grandkids are all of those ingredients plus their mother, who is half Vietnamese.

So you see, for me, checking these racial-identification boxes is rather personal. I don't like it. I don't buy into it. I say I'm black for the sake of not spending the whole interview quarreling about classification. But I don't like it. I'm brown in color. What is black? It's a term we use because we're lazy. It's easier to put somebody into a box and use that as a shortcut for something. But it's not useful.

SOURCE: *The American Enterprise* (2003, April/May). "Ward Connerly: Interview." *The American Enterprise,* 14:18–22.

Colorblindness Will Perpetuate Racial Inequality

IAN F. HANEY LOPEZ

How will race as a social practice evolve in the United States over the next few decades? The American public, and indeed many scholars, increasingly believe that the country is leaving race and racism behind. . . . My sense of our racial future differs. Not only do I fear that race will continue to fundamentally skew American society over the coming decades, but I worry that the belief in the diminished salience of race makes that more likely rather than less. . . . We find ourselves now in the midst of a racial era marked by what I term "colorblind white dominance," in which a public consensus committed to formal anti-racism deters effective remediation of racial inequality, protecting the racial status quo while insulating new forms of racism and xenophobia.

We remain a racially stratified country, though for some that constitutes an argument for rather than against colorblindness. . . . For the first half of the 20th century, colorblindness represented the radical . . . aspiration of dismantling de jure racial subordination. . . . In the wake of the civil rights movement's limited but significant triumphs, the relationship between colorblindness and racial reform changed markedly. The greatest potency of colorblindness came to lie in preserving, rather than challenging, the racial status quo. When the end of explicit race-based subordination did not eradicate stubborn racial inequalities, progressives increasingly recognized the need for state and private actors to intervene along racial lines. Rather than call for colorblindness, they began to insist on the need for affirmative race-conscious remedies. In that new context, colorblindness appealed to those opposing racial integration. . . . Colorblindness provided cover for opposition to racial reform. . . .

Wielding the ideal of colorblindness as a sword, in the past three decades racial conservatives on the Supreme Court have increasingly . . . [cut] back on protections against racial discrimination as well as severely limiting race-conscious remedies. In several cases in the 1970s . . . the court ruled that the need to redress the legacy of segregation made strict colorblindness impossible. But as the 1980s went on . . . the court presented race as a phenomenon called into existence just when someone employed a racial term. Discrimination existed only [when] . . . someone used racial language. . . .

That approach ignores the continuing power of race as a society-altering category. The civil rights movement changed the racial zeitgeist of the nation by rendering illegitimate all explicit invocations of white supremacy, a shift that surely marked an important step toward a more egalitarian society. But it did not bring into actual existence that ideal, as white people remain dominant across virtually every social, political, and economic domain. . . . Those many in our society who are darker, poorer, more identifiably foreign will continue to suffer the poverty, marginalization, immiseration, incarceration, and exclusion historically accorded to those whose skin and other features socially mark them as nonwhite. . . . Racial hierarchy will continue as the links are strengthened between nonwhite identity and social disadvantage on the one hand, and whiteness and privilege on the other. . . .

Contemporary colorblindness . . . define[s] how people comprehend, rationalize, and act on race. [It] continues to retard racial progress. It does so for a simple reason: It focuses on the surface, on the bare fact of racial classification, rather than looking down into the nature of social practices. It gets racism and racial remediation exactly backward, and insulates new forms of race baiting.

White dominance continues with few open appeals to race. Consider the harms wrought by segregated schools today. Schools in predominantly white suburbs are far more likely to have adequate buildings, teachers, and books, while the schools serving mainly minority children are more commonly underfinanced, unsafe, and in a state of disrepair. Such harms accumulate, encouraging white flight to avoid the expected deterioration in schools and the violence that is supposedly second nature to "them," only to precipitate the collapse in the tax base that in fact ensures a decline not only in schools but also in a range of social services. Such material differences in turn buttress seemingly commonsense ideas about disparate groups, so that we tend to see pristine schools and suburbs as a testament to white accomplishment and values. When violence does erupt, it is laid at the feet of alienated and troubled teenagers, not a dysfunctional culture. Yet we see the metal detectors guarding entrances to minority schoolhouses (harbingers of the prison bars to come) as evidence not of the social dynamics of exclusion and privilege, but of innate pathologies. No one need talk about the dynamics of privilege and exclusion. No one need cite white-supremacist arguments nor openly refer to race—race exists in the concrete of our gated communities and barrios, in government policies and programs, in cultural norms and beliefs, and in the way Americans lead their lives. . . .

To break the interlocking patterns of racial hierarchy, there is no other way but to focus on, talk about, and put into effect constructive policies explicitly engaged with race. To be sure, inequality in wealth is a major and increasing challenge for our society, but class is not a substitute for a racial analysis—though, likewise, racial oppression cannot be lessened without sustained attention to poverty. It's no accident that the poorest schools in the country warehouse minorities, while the richest serve whites; the national education crisis reflects deeply intertwined racial and class politics. One does not deny the imbrication of race and class by insisting on the importance of race-conscious remedies: The best strategies for social repair will give explicit attention to race as well as to other sources of inequality, and to their complex interrelationship. . . .

Contemporary colorblindness loudly proclaims its antiracist pretensions. To actually move toward a racially egalitarian society, however, requires that we forthrightly respond to racial inequality today. The alternative is the continuation of colorblind white dominance. As Justice Harry Blackmun enjoined in defending affirmative action in *Bakke:* "In order to get beyond racism, we must first take account of race. There is no other way."

SOURCE: Lopez, Ian F. Haney (2006). "Colorblind to the Reality of Race in America." *Chronicle of Higher Education,* 53(11), November 3, p. B6.

Debate Questions to Consider

1. What assumptions does Connerly make about the overall fairness of American society? Are there any similarities between his position and human capital theory (see Chapter 2)? Judging from the evidence presented in this chapter, how credible is his statement that young black Americans face essentially the same problems as all young Americans? Is he thinking about all African Americans? Middle-class African Americans? Male as well as female African Americans? How close is the United States to Connerly's "Racial Privacy Initiative"?

2. What, according to Lopez, would be the consequences of official color blindness? Would the progress toward racial equality that has been made be reversed? How is color blindness a disguised form of white domination?

3. Which author(s) directly addresses "past-in-present" discrimination? How?

4. Which of these two positions is most appealing to you? If you agree with Connerly, how would you combat modern institutional discrimination? If you agree with Lopez, how would you respond to the charge that programs like affirmative action are a form of "reverse discrimination"?

Main Points

- At the beginning of the 20th century, the racial oppression of African Americans took the form of a rigid competitive system of group relations, de jure segregation. This system ended because of changing economic and political conditions, changing legal precedents, and a mass movement of protest initiated by African Americans.

- The U.S. Supreme Court decision in *Brown v. Board of Education of Topeka* (1954) was the single most powerful blow struck against legalized segregation. A nonviolent direct action campaign was launched in the South to challenge and defeat segregation. The U.S. Congress delivered the final blows to de jure segregation in the 1964 Civil Rights Act and the 1965 Voting Rights Act.

- Outside the South, the concerns of the African American community had centered on access to schooling, jobs, housing, health care, and other opportunities. African Americans' frustration and anger were expressed in the urban riots of the 1960s. The Black Power movement addressed the massive problems of racial inequality remaining after the victories of the civil rights movement.

- Black-white relations since the 1960s have been characterized by continuing inequality, separation, and hostility, along with substantial improvements in status for some African Americans. Class differentiation within the African American community is greater than ever before.

- The African American family has been perceived as weak, unstable, and a cause of continuing poverty. Culture of poverty theory attributes poverty to certain characteristics of the poor. An alternative view sees problems such as high rates of family desertion by men as the result of poverty, rather than the cause.

- Anti-black prejudice and discrimination are manifested in more subtle, covert forms (modern racism and institutional discrimination) in contemporary society.

- African Americans are largely acculturated, but centuries of separate development have created a unique black experience in American society.

- Despite real improvements in their status, the overall secondary structural assimilation of African Americans remains low. Evidence of racial inequalities in residence, schooling, politics, jobs, income, unemployment, and poverty is massive and underlines the realities of the urban underclass.

- In the area of primary structural assimilation, interracial interaction and friendships appear to be rising. Interracial marriages are increasing, although they remain a tiny percentage of all marriages.

- Compared with their situation at the start of the 20th century, African Americans have made considerable improvements in quality of life. The distance to true racial equality remains enormous.

- As suggested by the Blauner hypothesis, the legacy of racial inequality extends far beyond the matters of income, occupation, and poverty documented in this chapter. Public sociology Assignment 2 in the introduction to Part 3 will permit you to document racial inequalities in health in your area. Are these comparable in magnitude to the racial inequalities documented in this chapter?

Study Site on the Web

Don't forget the interactive quizzes and other resources and learning aids at www.pineforge .com/healeystudy5.

For Further Reading

Feagin, Joe. (2001). *Racist America: Roots, Current Realities, and Future Reparations*. New York: Routledge.

Hacker, Andrew. (1992). *Two Nations: Black and White, Separate, Hostile, Unequal*. New York: Scribner's.

Two very readable overviews of contemporary black-white relations.

Massey, Douglas, & Denton, Nancy. (1993). *American Apartheid: Segregation and the Making of the Underclass*. Cambridge, MA: Harvard University Press.

The authors argue powerfully that residential segregation is the key to understanding urban black poverty.

Morris, Aldon D. (1984). *The Origins of the Civil Rights Movement*. New York: Free Press.

An indispensable source.

Thernstrom, Stephan, & Thernstrom, Abigail. (1997). *America in Black and White*. New York: Simon & Schuster.

A comprehensive review of American race relations.

Smelser, N., Wilson, W., & Mitchell, F. (Eds.). (2001). *America Becoming: Racial Trends and Their Consequences*. Washington, DC: National Academy Press.

A two-volume collection of articles by leading scholars that presents a comprehensive analysis of black-white relations in America.

Williams, Juan. (1987). *Eyes on the Prize: America's Civil Rights Years, 1954–1965*. New York: Penguin.

Commentaries and accounts. See also the acclaimed television documentary of the same name.

Questions for Review and Study

1. What forces led to the end of de jure segregation? To what extent was this change a result of broad social forces (e.g., industrialization), and to what extent was it the result of the actions of African Americans acting against the system (e.g., the southern civil rights movement)? By the 1960s and 1970s, how had the movement for racial change succeeded, and what issues were left unresolved? What issues remain unresolved today?

2. What are the differences between de jure segregation and de facto segregation? What are the implications of these differences for movements to change these systems? That is, how must movements against de facto segregation differ from movements against de jure segregation in terms of tactics and strategies?

3. Describe the differences between the southern civil rights movement and the Black Power movement. Why did these differences exist? Do these movements remain relevant today? How?

4. How does gender affect contemporary black-white relations and the African American protest movement? Is it true that African American women are a "minority group within a minority group"? How?

5. What are the implications of increasing class differentials among African Americans? Does the greater affluence of middle-class blacks mean that they are no longer a part of a minority group? Will future protests by African Americans be confined only to working-class and lower-class blacks?

6. Regarding contemporary black-white relations, is the glass half empty or half full? Considering the totality of evidence presented in this chapter, which of the following statements would you agree with? Why? (1) American race relations are the best they've ever been; racial equality has been essentially achieved (even though some problems remain) or (2) American race relations have a long way to go before society achieves true racial equality.

Internet Research Project

In the year 2000, a team of reporters from the *New York Times* conducted a yearlong investigation of how black-white relations are being lived out by ordinary people in churches, schools, neighborhoods, and other venues. A series of 15 articles detailing and analyzing these experiences were published, and all are available online at http://www.nytimes.com/library/national/race/. Read at least three or four of these stories and analyze them in terms of the concepts and conclusions presented in this chapter. What do these stories imply about black-white inequality, prejudice, discrimination, assimilation, pluralism, and racial separation? Is the glass half empty or half full?

American Indians   CHAPTER 7

From Conquest to Tribal Survival in a Postindustrial Society

We discussed the contact period for American Indians in Chapter 4. As you recall, the contact period began in the earliest colonial days and lasted nearly 300 years, ending only with the final battles of the Indian Wars in the late 1800s. The Indian nations fought for their land and to preserve their cultures and ways of life. The tribes had enough power to win many battles, but they eventually lost all the wars. The superior resources of the burgeoning white society made the eventual defeat of American Indians inevitable, and by 1890, the last of the tribes had been conquered, their leaders had been killed or were in custody, and their people were living on government-controlled reservations.

Early in the 20th century, American Indians were, in Blauner's (1972) terms, a conquered and colonized minority group. Like the slave plantations, the reservations were paternalistic systems that controlled American Indians with federally mandated regulations and government-appointed Indian agents. For most of the 20th century, as Jim Crow segregation, Supreme Court decisions, industrialization, and urbanization shaped the

status of other minority groups, American Indians subsisted on the fringes of development and change, marginalized, relatively powerless, and isolated. Their links to the larger society were weaker and, compared with other minority groups, they were less affected by the forces of social and political evolution.

The very last years of the 20th century witnessed some improvement in the status of American Indians in general and some tribes, especially those with casinos and other gaming establishments, made notable progress toward parity with national standards. Also, the tribes are now more in control of their own affairs, and many have used their increased autonomy and independence to effectively address problems in education, health, joblessness, and other areas. Despite this progress, however, large gaps remain between American Indians and the dominant group in virtually every area of social and economic life.

In this chapter, we will bring the history of American Indians up to the present and explore both recent progress and persisting problems. Some of the questions we address include the following: What accounts for the lowly position of this group for much of the last 100 years? How can we explain the improvements in the most recent decades? Now, early in the 21st century, what problems remain, and how does the situation of American Indians compare with that of other colonized and conquered minority groups? What are the most promising strategies for closing the remaining gaps between American Indians and the larger society?

Please note that this chapter presents information about American Indians in a variety of formats. The main focus is on American Indians residing in the "lower" 48 states (i.e., excluding Hawaii and Alaska). As I did with African Americans, I will rely primarily on information from the U.S. Census to characterize the situation of this group. Unfortunately, much of the most important information about American Indians and the different tribes dates from the 2000 census. More recent data (from 2006) includes Alaska Natives along with American Indians (this broader category is often labeled "AIAN"), but, since American Indians outnumber Alaska Natives by about 20 to 1, information about the AIAN category is fairly representative of the situation of the former group. Finally, a few figures and graphs presented in this chapter refer only to American Indians living on reservations or other Indian lands, not to all American Indians.

Size of the Group

How many Indians are there? There are several different answers to this question, partly because of the way census information is collected and partly because of the social and subjective nature of race and group membership. The most current answers come from the American Community Survey (ACS), conducted every year by the U.S. Bureau of the Census since the last full census in 2000. This survey provides estimates for the number of American Indians and Alaska Natives (AIAN) and figures for each group separately and for some of the larger American Indian tribes.

The task of determining the size of the group is also complicated by the way the census collects information on race. As you recall, beginning with the 2000 census, people were allowed to claim membership in more than one racial category. If we define "American Indians" as consisting of people who identify themselves *only* as American Indian, we will get one estimate of the size of the group. If we use a broader definition and include people who claim mixed racial ancestry, our estimate of group size will be much larger.

At any rate, Exhibit 7.1 shows that there were almost 4.5 million people who claimed at least some American Indian or Alaska Native ancestry but only about 2.3 million if we confine the group to people who select one race only. By either count, the group is a tiny minority (about 1%) of the total population of the United States. Exhibit 7.1 also presents information for American Indians and Alaska Native separately and for the 10 largest tribal groupings.

American Indians have been growing rapidly over the past several decades, but this fact needs to be seen in the full context of American Indian history. As I mentioned in Chapter 4, in 1492, there were at least 1 million American Indians living in what is now the continental ("lower 48") United States (Snipp, 1992, p. 354). Losses suffered during the contact period

Exhibit 7.1 American Indians and Alaska Natives (AIAN), 2006

	Alone (One Race)	Alone or in Combination (Two or More Races)
Total AIAN	2,369,431	4,329,799
American Indian	1,969,896	3,424,177
Ten Largest Tribal Groupings		
Cherokee	301,750	974,328
Navaho	296,076	335,905
Choctaw	79,236	185,874
Sioux	116,737	175,799
Chippewa	109,149	169,301
Apache	71,737	133,026
Iroquois	N/A	93,419
Pueblo	75,679	90,508
Creek	N/A	77,908
Lumbee	N/A	70,287
Alaska Native	103,741	145,720
Tribal Groupings (Based on 2000 Census Only)		
Eskimo	47,239	56,824
Tlingit-Haida	15,212	22,786
Alaska Athabascan	14,700	18,874
Aleut	12,069	7,551

SOURCE: U.S. Bureau of the Census (2007a).

reduced the population to less than 250,000 by 1900, a loss of at least 75%. Recent population growth has restored the group to its pre-Columbian size.

As displayed in Exhibit 7.2, growth was slow in the early decades of the 20th century but much more rapid in recent decades. The more recent growth is due, in part, to higher birthrates. Mainly, however, the growth is a result of changing definitions of race in the larger society and a much greater willingness of people to claim Indian ancestry, a pattern that again underscores the basically social nature of race (Thornton, 2001, p. 137).

American Indian Cultures

The dynamics of American Indian and Anglo-American relationships have been shaped by the vast differences in culture, values, and norms between the two groups. These differences have hampered communication in the past and continue to do so in the present. A comprehensive analysis of American Indian cultures is well beyond the scope of this text, but the past experiences and present goals of the group can be appreciated only with some understanding of their views of the world.

We must note here, as we did in Chapter 4, that there were (and are) hundreds of different tribes in what is now the United States, each with its own language and heritage, and that a complete analysis of American Indian culture would have to take this diversity into account. However, some patterns and cultural characteristics are widely shared across the tribes, and we will concentrate on these similarities.

Before exploring the content of their culture, we should note that most Native American tribes that existed in what is now the United States relied on hunting and gathering, although some cultivated gardens as well, to satisfy their basic needs. This is important because, as noted by Lenski (see Chapter 1), societies are profoundly shaped by their subsistence technology. Hunting-and-gathering societies typically live on the thin edge of hunger and

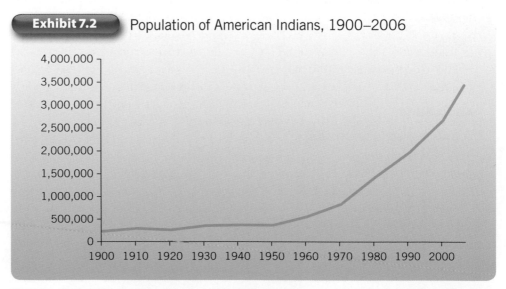

Exhibit 7.2   Population of American Indians, 1900–2006

SOURCE: 1900–1990, Thornton (2001, p. 142); 2000: U.S. Bureau of the Census (2007b, p. 14); 2006: U.S. Bureau of the Census (2007a).

want. They survive by stressing cultural values such as sharing and cooperation and by maintaining strong bonds of cohesion and solidarity. As you will see, American Indian societies are no exception to this fundamental survival strategy.

The relatively lower level of development of Native Americans is reflected in what is perhaps their most obvious difference with people in Western cultures: their ideas about the relationship between human beings and the natural world. In the traditional view of many American Indian cultures, the universe is a unity. Humans are simply a part of a larger reality, no different from or more important than other animals, plants, trees, and the earth itself. The goal of many American Indian tribes was to live in harmony with the natural world, not "improve" it or use it for their own selfish purposes, views that differ sharply from Western concepts of development, commercial farming, and bending the natural world to the service of humans. The gap between the two worldviews is evident in the reaction of one American Indian to the idea that his people should become farmers: "You ask me to plow the ground. . . . Shall I take a knife and tear my mother's bosom? You ask me to cut grass and make hay . . . but how dare I cut my mother's hair?" (Brown, 1970, p. 273).

The concept of private property, or the ownership of things, was not prominent in American Indian cultures and was, from the Anglo-American perspective, most notably absent in conceptions of land ownership. The land simply existed, and the notion of owning, selling, or buying it was foreign to American Indians. In the words of Tecumseh, a chief of the Shawnee, a man could no more sell the land than the "sea or the air he breathed" (Josephy, 1968, p. 283).

As is typical at the hunting-and-gathering level of development, American Indian cultures and societies also tended to be more oriented toward groups (e.g., the extended family, clan, or tribe) than toward individuals. The interests of the self were subordinated to those of the group, and child-rearing practices strongly encouraged group loyalty (Parke & Buriel, 2002). Cooperative, group activities were stressed over those of a competitive, individualistic nature. The bond to the group was (and is) so strong that "students go hungry rather than ask their parents for lunch money, for in asking they would be putting their needs in front of the group's needs" (Locust, 1990, p. 231).

Many American Indian tribes were organized around egalitarian values that stressed the dignity and worth of every man, woman, and child. Virtually all tribes had a division of labor based on gender, but women's work was valued, and women often occupied far more important positions in tribal society than was typical for women in Anglo-American society. In many of the American Indian societies that practiced gardening, women controlled the land. In other tribes, women wielded considerable power and held the most important political and religious offices. Among the Iroquois, for example, a council of older women appointed the chief of the tribe and made decisions about when to wage war (Amott & Matthaei, 1991, pp. 34–35).

These differences in values, compounded by the power differentials that emerged, often placed American Indians at a disadvantage when dealing with the dominant group. The American Indians' conception of land ownership and their lack of experience with deeds, titles, contracts, and other Western legal concepts often made it difficult for them to defend their resources from Anglo-Americans. At other times, cultural differences led to disruptions of traditional practices, further weakening American Indian societies. For example, Christian missionaries and government representatives tried to reverse the traditional American Indian division of labor, in which women were responsible for the gardening. In the Western view, only males did farmwork. Also, the military and political representatives of the dominant society usually ignored female tribal leaders and imposed Western notions of patriarchy and male leadership on the tribes (Amott & Matthaei, 1991, p. 39).

Relations With the Federal Government After the 1890s

By the end of the Indian Wars in 1890, Americans Indians had few resources with which to defend their self-interests. In addition to being confined to the reservations, the group was scattered throughout the western two thirds of the United States and split by cultural and linguistic differences. Politically, the power of the group was further limited by the facts that the huge majority of American Indians were not U.S. citizens and that most tribes lacked a cultural basis for understanding representative democracy as practiced in the larger society.

Economically, American Indians were among the most impoverished groups in the society. Reservation lands were generally of poor quality, traditional food sources such as buffalo and other game had been destroyed, and traditional hunting grounds and gardening plots had been lost to white farmers and ranchers. The tribes had few means of satisfying even their most basic needs. Many became totally dependent on the federal government for food, shelter, clothing, and other necessities.

Prospects for improvement seemed slim. Most reservations were in remote areas, far from sites of industrialization and modernization, and American Indians had few of the skills (knowledge of English, familiarity with Western work habits and routines) that would have enabled them to compete for a place in the increasingly urban and industrial American society of the early 20th century. Off the reservations, racial prejudice and strong intolerance limited them. On the reservations, they were subjected to policies designed either to maintain their powerlessness and poverty or to force them to Americanize. Either way, the future of American Indians was in serious jeopardy, and their destructive relations with white society continued in peace as they had in war.

Reservation Life

As would be expected for a conquered and still hostile group, the reservations were intended to closely supervise American Indians and maintain their powerlessness. Relationships with the federal government were paternalistic and featured a variety of policies designed to coercively acculturate the tribes.

Paternalism and the Bureau of Indian Affairs

The reservations were run not by the tribes but by an agency of the federal government: the U.S. **Bureau of Indian Affairs** (BIA) of the U.S. Department of the Interior. The BIA and its local superintendent controlled virtually all aspects of everyday life, including the reservation budget, the criminal justice system, and the schools. The BIA (again, not the tribes) even determined tribal membership.

The traditional leadership structures and political institutions of the tribes were ignored as the BIA executed its duties with little regard for, and virtually no input from, the people it supervised. The BIA superintendent of the reservations "ordinarily became the most powerful influence on local Indian affairs, even though he was a government employee, not responsible to the Indians but to his superiors in Washington" (Spicer, 1980, p. 117). The superintendent controlled the food supply and communications to the world outside the reservation. This control was used to reward tribal members who cooperated and to punish those who did not.

Coercive Acculturation: The Dawes Act and Boarding Schools

Consistent with the Blauner hypothesis, American Indians on the reservations were subjected to coercive acculturation or forced Americanization. Their culture was attacked, their languages and religions were forbidden, and their institutions were circumvented and undermined. The centerpiece of U.S. Indian policy was the Dawes Allotment Act of 1887, a deeply flawed attempt to impose white definitions of land ownership and to transform American Indians into independent farmers by dividing their land among the families of each tribe. The intention of the act was to give each Indian family the means to survive like their white neighbors.

Although the law might seem benevolent in intent (certainly thousands of immigrant families would have been thrilled to own land), it was flawed by a gross lack of understanding of American Indian cultures and needs, and in many ways, it was a direct attack on those cultures. Most American Indian tribes did not have a strong agrarian tradition, and little or nothing was done to prepare the tribes for their transition to peasant yeomanry. More important, American Indians had little or no concept of land as private property, and it was relatively easy for settlers, land speculators, and others to separate Indian families from the land allocated to them by this legislation. By allotting land to families and individuals, the legislation sought to destroy the broader kinship, clan, and tribal social structures and replace them with Western systems that featured individualism and the profit motive (Cornell, 1988, p. 80).

About 140 million acres were allocated to the tribes in 1887. By the 1930s, nearly 90 million of those acres—almost 65%—had been lost. Most of the remaining land was desert or otherwise nonproductive (Wax, 1971, p. 55). From the standpoint of the Indian Nations, the Dawes Allotment Act was a disaster and a further erosion of their already paltry store of resources (for more details, see Josephy, 1968; Lurie, 1982; McNickle, 1973; Wax, 1971).

Coercive acculturation also operated through a variety of other avenues. Whenever possible, the BIA sent American Indian children to boarding schools, sometimes hundreds of miles away from parents and kin, where they were required to speak English, convert to Christianity, and become educated in the ways of Western civilization. Consistent with the Blauner (1972) hypothesis, tribal languages, dress, and religion were forbidden, and to the extent that native cultures were mentioned at all, they were attacked and ridiculed. Children of different tribes were mixed together as roommates to speed the acquisition of English. When school was not in session, children were often boarded with local white families, usually as unpaid domestic helpers or farmhands, and prevented from visiting their families and revitalizing their tribal ties (Hoxie, 1984; Spicer, 1980; Wax, 1971).

American Indians were virtually powerless to change the reservation system or avoid the campaign of acculturation. Nonetheless, they resented and resisted coerced Americanization, and many languages and cultural elements survived the early reservation period, although often in altered form. For example, the traditional tribal religions remained vital through the period despite the fact that by the 1930s, the great majority of Indians had affiliated with one Christian faith or another. Furthermore, many new religions were founded, some combining Christian and traditional elements (Spicer, 1980, p. 118). Narrative Portrait 1 in this chapter gives an intimate account of the dynamics of coercive acculturation.

Civilize Them With a Stick

I n recent decades, boarding schools for American Indian children have been much improved. Facilities have been modernized and faculties upgraded. The curriculum has been updated and often includes elements of American Indian culture and language. Still, it was not that long ago that coercive acculturation at its worst was the daily routine.

In the following passage, Mary Crow Dog, a member of the Sioux tribe who became deeply involved in the Red Power movement that began in the 1960s, recalls some of the horrors of her experiences at a reservation boarding school. As you read her words, keep in mind that she was born in 1955 and started school in the early 1960s, just a generation or two ago.

Lakota Woman

Mary Crow Dog

It is almost impossible to explain to a sympathetic white person what a typical old Indian boarding school was like; how it affected the Indian child suddenly dumped into it like a small creature from another world, helpless, defenseless, bewildered, trying desperately to survive and sometimes not surviving at all. Even now, when these schools are so much improved, when . . . the teachers [are] well-intentioned, even trained in child psychology—unfortunately the psychology of white children, which is different from ours—the shock to the child upon arrival is still tremendous. . . .

In the traditional Sioux family, the child is never left alone. It is always surrounded by relatives, carried around, enveloped in warmth. It is treated with the respect due to any human being, even a small one. It is seldom forced to do anything against its will, seldom screamed at, and never beaten. . . . And then suddenly a bus or car arrives full of strangers, who yank the child out of the arms of those who love it, taking it screaming to the boarding school. The only word I can think of for what is done to these children is kidnapping. . . .

The mission school at St. Francis was a curse for our family for generations. My grandmother went there, then my mother, then my sisters and I. At one time or another, every one of us tried to run away. Grandma told me about the bad times she experienced at St. Francis. In those days they let students go home only for one week every year. Two days were used up for transportation, which meant spending just five days out of every 365 with her family. . . . My mother had much the same experiences but never wanted to talk about them, and then there was I, in the same place. . . . Nothing had changed since my grandmother's days. I have been told that even in the '70s they were still beating children at that school. All I got out of school was being taught how to pray. I learned quickly that I would be beaten if I failed in my devotions or, God forbid, prayed the wrong way, especially prayed in Indian to Wakan Tanka, the Indian creator. . . .

My classroom was right next to the principal's office and almost every day I could hear him swatting the boys. Beating was the common punishment for not doing one's homework, or for being late to school. It had such a bad effect upon me that I hated and mistrusted every white person on sight, because I met only one kind. It was not until much later that I met sincere white people I could relate to and be friends with. Racism breeds racism in reverse.

SOURCE: Crow Dog, Mary (1990). *Lakota Woman*, pp. 28–34. New York: HarperCollins. Copyright © 1990 by Mary Crow Dog and Richard Erdoes. Used by permission of Grove/Atlantic, Inc.

The Indian Reorganization Act

By the 1930s, the failure of the reservation system and the policy of forced assimilation had become obvious to all who cared to observe. The quality of life for American Indians had not improved, and there was little economic development and fewer job opportunities on the reservations. Health care was woefully inadequate, and education levels lagged far behind national standards.

The plight of American Indians eventually found a sympathetic ear in the administration of Franklin D. Roosevelt, who was elected president in 1932, and John Collier, the man he appointed to run the BIA. Collier was knowledgeable about American Indian issues and concerns and was instrumental in securing the passage of the **Indian Reorganization Act** (IRA) in 1934.

This landmark legislation contained a number of significant provisions for American Indians and broke sharply with the federal policies of the past. In particular, the IRA rescinded the Dawes Act of 1887 and the policy of individualizing tribal lands. It also provided means by which the tribes could expand their landholdings. Many of the mechanisms of coercive Americanization in the school system and elsewhere were dismantled. Financial aid in various forms and expertise were made available for the economic development of the reservations. In perhaps the most significant departure from earlier policy, the IRA proposed an increase in American Indian self-governance and a reduction of the paternalistic role of the BIA and other federal agencies.

Although sympathetic to American Indians, the IRA had its limits and shortcomings. Many of its intentions were never realized, and the empowerment of the tribes was not unqualified. The move to self-governance generally took place on the dominant group's terms and in conformity with the values and practices of white society. For example, the proposed increase in the decision-making power of the tribes was contingent on their adoption of Anglo-American political forms, including secret ballots, majority rule, and written constitutions. These were alien concepts to those tribes that selected leaders by procedures other than popular election (e.g., leaders might be chosen by councils of elders) or that made decisions by open discussion and consensus building (i.e., decisions required the agreement of everyone with a voice in the process, not a simple majority). The incorporation of these Western forms illustrates the basically assimilationist intent of the IRA.

The IRA had variable effects on American Indian women. In tribes that were male dominated, the IRA gave women new rights to participate in elections, run for office, and hold leadership roles. In other cases, new political structures replaced traditional forms, some of which, as in the Iroquois culture, had accorded women considerable power. Although the political effects were variable, the programs funded by the IRA provided opportunities for women on many reservations to receive education and training for the first time. Many of these opportunities were oriented toward domestic tasks and other traditionally Western female roles, but some prepared American Indian women for jobs outside the family and off the reservation, such as clerical work and nursing (Evans, 1989, pp. 208–209).

In summary, the Indian Reorganization Act of 1934 was a significant improvement over prior federal Indian policy but was bolder and more sympathetic to American Indians in intent than in execution. On one hand, not all tribes were capable of taking advantage of the opportunities provided by the legislation, and some ended up being further victimized. For example, in the Hopi tribe, located in the Southwest, the act allowed a Westernized group of

American Indians to be elected to leadership roles, with the result that dominant group firms were allowed to have access to the mineral resources, farmland, and water rights controlled by the tribe. The resultant development generated wealth for the white firms and their Hopi allies, but most of the tribe continued to languish in poverty (Churchill, 1985, pp. 112–113). On the other hand, some tribes prospered (at least comparatively speaking) under the IRA. One impoverished, landless group of Cherokee in Oklahoma acquired land, equipment, and expert advice through the IRA, and between 1937 and 1949, they developed a prosperous, largely debt-free farming community (Debo, 1970, pp. 294–300). Many tribes remained suspicious of the IRA, and by 1948, fewer than 100 tribes had voted to accept its provisions.

Termination and Relocation

The IRA's stress on the legitimacy of tribal identity seemed "un-American" to many. There was constant pressure on the federal government to return to an individualistic policy that encouraged (or required) Americanization. Some viewed the tribal structures and communal-property-holding patterns as relics of an earlier era and as impediments to modernization and development. Not so incidentally, some elements of dominant society still coveted the remaining Indian lands and resources, which could be more easily exploited if property ownership were individualized.

Photo 7.1

Indians often live in more deteriorated, less desirable urban areas. Here, an Indian boy rides his bike near a man passed out in a doorway.

© Rubin Steven/Corbis Sygma.

In 1953, the assimilationist forces won a victory when Congress passed a resolution calling for an end to the reservation system and to the special relationships between the tribes and the federal government. The proposed policy, called **termination**, was intended to get the federal government "out of the Indian business." It rejected the IRA and proposed a return to the system of private land ownership imposed on the tribes by the Dawes Act. Horrified at the notion of termination, the tribes opposed the policy strongly and vociferously. Under this policy, all special relationships—including treaty obligations—between the federal government and the tribes would end. Tribes would no longer exist as legally recognized entities, and tribal lands and other resources would be placed in private hands (Josephy, 1968, pp. 353–355).

About 100 tribes, most of them small, were terminated. In virtually all cases, the termination process was administered hastily, and fraud, misuse of funds, and other injustices were common. The Menominee of Wisconsin and the Klamath on the West Coast were the two largest tribes to be terminated. Both suffered devastating economic losses and precipitous declines in quality of life. Neither tribe had the business or tax base needed to finance the services (e.g., health care and schooling) formerly provided by the federal government, and both were forced to sell land, timber, and other scarce resources to maintain minimal standards of living. Many poor American Indian families were forced to turn to local and state agencies, which placed severe strain on welfare budgets. The experience of the Menominee was so disastrous that at the concerted request of the tribe, reservation status was restored in 1973 (Deloria, 1969, pp. 60–82; McNickle, 1973, pp. 103–110; Raymer, 1974). The Klamath reservation was restored in 1986 (Snipp, 1996, p. 394).

At about the same time the termination policy came into being, various programs were established to encourage American Indians to move to urban areas. The movement to the city had already begun in the 1940s, spurred by the availability of factory jobs during World War II. In the 1950s, the movement was further encouraged with programs of assistance and by the declining government support for economic development on the reservation, the most dramatic example of which was the policy of termination (Green, 1999, p. 265). Centers for American Indians were established in many cities, and various services (e.g., job training, housing assistance, English instruction) were offered to assist in the adjustment to urban life. The urbanization of the American Indian population is displayed in Exhibit 7.3. Note the rapid increase in the movement to the city that began in the 1950s. Almost 60% of all American Indians are now urbanized, and since 1950, Indians have urbanized faster than the general population. Nevertheless, American Indians are still the least urbanized minority group. The population as a whole is about 80% urbanized; in contrast, African Americans (see Exhibit 6.4) are about 90% urbanized.

As with African Americans, American Indians arrived in the cities after the mainstream economy had begun to de-emphasize blue-collar or manufacturing jobs. Because of their relatively low average levels of educational attainment and their racial and cultural differences, American Indians in the city tended to encounter the same problems experienced by African Americans and other minority groups of color: high rates of unemployment, inadequate housing, and all of the other travails of the urban underclass.

American Indian women also migrated to the city in considerable numbers. The discrimination, unemployment, and poverty of the urban environment often made it difficult for the men of the group to fulfill the role of breadwinner; thus, the burden of supporting the family tended to fall on the women. The difficulties inherent in combining child rearing and

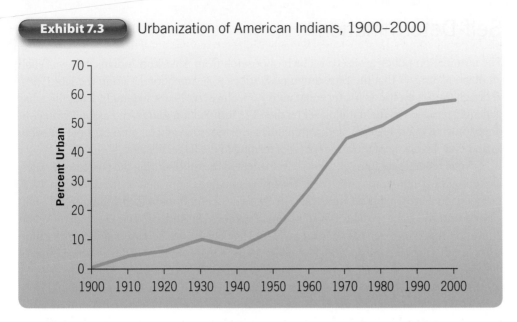

Exhibit 7.3 Urbanization of American Indians, 1900–2000

SOURCE: 1900–1990: Thornton (2001, p. 142); 2000: U.S. Bureau of the Census (2000a).

a job outside the home are compounded by isolation from the support networks provided by extended family and clan back on the reservations. Nevertheless, one study found that American Indian women in the city continue to practice their traditional cultures and maintain the tribal identity of their children (Joe & Miller, 1994, p. 186).

American Indians living in the city are, on the average, better off than those living on reservations, where unemployment can reach 80% or even 90%. The improvement is relative, however. Although many individual Indians prosper in the urban environment, income figures for urban Indians as a whole are comparable to those for African Americans and well below those for whites. American Indian unemployment rates run about twice the national average (Cornell, 1988, p. 132). Thus, a move to the city often means trading rural poverty for the urban variety, with little net improvement in life chances.

American Indians will probably remain more rural than other minority groups for years to come. Despite the poverty and lack of opportunities for schooling and jobs, the reservation offers some advantages in services and lifestyle. On the reservation, there may be opportunities for political participation and leadership roles that are not available in the cities, where American Indians are a tiny minority. Reservations also offer kinfolk, friends, religious services, and tribal celebrations (Snipp, 1989, p. 84). Lower levels of education, work experience, and financial resources combine with the prejudice, discrimination, and racism of the larger society to lower the chances of success in the city and will probably sustain a continuing return to the reservations.

Although the economic benefits of urbanization have been slim for the group as a whole, other advantages have accrued from life in the city. It was much easier to establish networks of friendship and affiliation across tribal lines in the cities, and urban Indians have been one of the sources of strength and personnel for a movement of protest that began early in the 20th century. Virtually all of the organizational vehicles of American Indian protest have had urban roots.

Self-Determination

The termination policy aroused so much opposition from American Indians and was such an obvious disaster that the pressure to push tribes to termination faded in the late 1950s, although the act itself was not repealed until 1975. Since the 1960s, federal Indian policy has generally returned to the tradition set by the IRA. Termination and forced assimilation continue to be officially rejected, and within limits, the tribes have been granted more freedom to find their own way, at their own pace, of relating to the larger society.

Several federal programs and laws have benefited the tribes during the past few decades, including the antipoverty and "Great Society" campaigns launched in the 1960s. In 1970, President Richard Nixon affirmed the government's commitment to fulfilling treaty obligations and the right of the tribes to self-governance. The Indian Self-Determination and Education Assistance Act was passed in 1975. This legislation increased aid to reservation schools and American Indian students and increased tribal control over the administration of the reservations, from police forces to schools to road maintenance.

The Self-Determination Act primarily benefited the larger tribes and those that had well-established administrative and governing structures. Smaller and less-well-organized tribes have continued to rely heavily on the federal government (Snipp, 1996, p. 394). Nonetheless, in many cases, this new phase of federal policy has allowed American Indian tribes to plot their own courses free of paternalistic regulation, and just as important, it gave them the tools and resources to address their problems and improve their situations. Decision making was returned to local authorities, who were "held more accountable to local needs, conditions, and cultures than outsiders" (Taylor & Kalt, 2005, p. xi).

In the view of many, self-determination is a key reason for the recent improvements in the status of American Indians, and we will look at some of these developments after examining the American Indian protest movement.

Protest and Resistance

Early Efforts

As BIA-administered reservations and coercive Americanization came to dominate tribal life in the 20th century, new forms of Indian activism appeared. The modern protest movement was tiny at first and, with few exceptions, achieved a measure of success only in recent decades. In fact, the American Indian protest movement in the past was not so much unsuccessful as simply ignored. The movement has focused on several complementary goals: protecting American Indian resources and treaty rights, striking a balance between assimilation and pluralism, and finding a relationship with the dominant group that would permit a broader array of life chances without sacrificing tribal identity and heritage.

Formally organized American Indian protest organizations have existed since the 1910s, but the modern phase of the protest movement began during World War II. Many American Indians served in the military or moved to the city to take jobs in aid of the war effort and were thereby exposed to the world beyond the reservation. Also, political activism on the reservation, which had been stimulated by the IRA, continued through the war years, and the recognition that many problems were shared across tribal lines grew.

These trends helped to stimulate the founding of the National Congress of American Indians (NCAI) in 1944. This organization was pantribal (i.e., included members from many different tribes); its first convention was attended by representatives of 50 different tribes and reservations (Cornell, 1988, p. 119). The leadership consisted largely of American Indians educated and experienced in the white world. However, the NCAI's program stressed the importance of preserving the old ways and tribal institutions as well as protecting Indian welfare. An early victory for the NCAI and its allies came in 1946 when an Indian Claims Commission was created by the federal government. This body was authorized to hear claims brought by the tribes with regard to treaty violations. The commission has settled hundreds of claims, resulting in awards of millions of dollars to the tribes, and it continues its work today (Weeks, 1988, pp. 261–262).

In the 1950s and 1960s, the protest movement was further stimulated by the threat of termination and by the increasing number of American Indians living in the cities who developed friendships across tribal lines. Awareness of common problems, rising levels of education, and the examples set by the successful protests of other minority groups also increased readiness for collective action.

Red Power

By the 1960s and 1970s, American Indian protest groups were finding ways to express their grievances and problems to the nation. The Red Power movement, like the Black Power movement (see Chapter 6), encompassed a coalition of groups, many considerably more assertive than the NCAI, and a varied collection of ideas, most of which stressed self-determination and pride in race and cultural heritage. Red Power protests included a "fish-in" in Washington State in 1965, an episode that also illustrates the nature of American Indian demands. The state of Washington had tried to limit the fishing rights of several different tribes on the grounds that the supply of fish was diminishing and needed to be protected. The tribes depended on fishing for subsistence and survival and argued that their right to fish had been guaranteed by treaties signed in the 1850s and that it was the pollution and commercial fishing of the dominant society that had depleted the supply of fish. They organized a "fish-in" in violation of the state's policy and were met by a contingent of police officers and other law officials. Violent confrontations and mass arrests ensued. Three years later, after a lengthy and expensive court battle, the tribes were vindicated, and the U.S. Supreme Court confirmed their treaty rights to fish the rivers of Washington State (Nabakov, 1999, pp. 362–363).

Another widely publicized episode took place in 1969, when American Indians from various tribes occupied Alcatraz Island in San Francisco Bay, the site of a closed federal prison. The protesters were acting on an old law that granted American Indians the right to reclaim abandoned federal land. The occupation of Alcatraz was organized in part by the American Indian Movement (AIM), founded in 1968. More militant and radical than the previously established protest groups, AIM aggressively confronted the BIA, the police, and other forces that were seen as repressive. With the backing of AIM and other groups, Alcatraz was occupied for nearly 4 years and generated a great deal of publicity for the Red Power movement and the plight of American Indians.

Photo 7.2

Indian activists occupy an abandoned missile base.

In 1972, AIM helped to organize a march on Washington, D.C., called the "Trail of Broken Treaties." Marchers came from many tribes and represented both urban and reservation Indians. The intent of the marchers was to dramatize the problems of the tribes. The leaders demanded the abolition of the BIA, the return of illegally taken land, and increased self-governance for the tribes, among other things. When they reached Washington, some of the marchers forcibly occupied the BIA offices. Property was damaged (by which side is disputed), and records and papers were destroyed. The marchers eventually surrendered, but none of their demands were met. The following year, AIM occupied the village of Wounded Knee in South Dakota to protest the violation of treaty rights. Wounded Knee was the site of the last armed confrontation between Indians and whites in 1890 and was selected by AIM for its deep symbolic significance. The occupation lasted more than 2 months and involved several armed confrontations with federal authorities. Again, the protest ended without achieving any of the demands made by the Indian leadership (Olson & Wilson, 1984, pp. 172–175). Since the early 1970s, the level of protest activity has declined, just as it has for the African American protest movement. Lawsuits and court cases have predominated over dramatic, direct confrontations.

Ironically, the struggle for Red Power encouraged assimilation as well as pluralism. The movement linked members of different tribes and forced Indians of diverse heritages to find common ground, often in the form of a "generic" American Indian culture. Inevitably, the protests were conducted in English, and the grievances were expressed in ways that were understandable to white society, thus increasing the pressure to acculturate even while arguing for the survival of the tribes. Furthermore, successful protest required that American Indians be fluent in English, trained in the law and other professions, skilled in dealing with bureaucracies, and knowledgeable about the formulation and execution of public policy. American Indians who became proficient in these areas thereby took on the characteristics of their adversaries (Hraba, 1979, p. 235).

As the pantribal protest movement forged ties between members of diverse tribes, the successes of the movement and changing federal policy and public opinion encouraged a rebirth of commitment to tribalism and "Indian-ness." American Indians were simultaneously stimulated to assimilate (by stressing their common characteristics and creating organizational forms that united the tribes) and to retain a pluralistic relationship with the larger society (by working for self-determination and enhanced tribal power and authority). Thus, part of the significance of the Red Power movement was that it encouraged both pantribal unity and a continuation of tribal diversity (Olson & Wilson, 1984, p. 206). Today, American Indians continue to seek a way of existing in the larger society that merges assimilation with pluralism.

Exhibit 7.4 summarizes this discussion of federal policy and Indian protest. The four major policy phases since the end of overt hostilities in 1890 are listed on the left. The thrust of the government's economic and political policies are listed in the next two columns, followed by a brief characterization of tribal response. The last column shows the changing bases for federal policy, sometimes aimed at weakening tribal tribes and individualizing American Indians and sometimes (including most recently) aimed at working with and preserving tribal structures.

The Continuing Struggle for Development in Contemporary American Indian-White Relations

Conflicts between American Indians and the larger society are far from over. Although the days of deadly battle are (with occasional exceptions) long gone, the issues that remain are serious, difficult to resolve, and, in their way, just as much matters of life and death. American Indians face enormous challenges in their struggle to improve their status, but largely as a result of their greater freedom from stifling federal control since the 1970s, they also have some resources, some opportunities, and a leadership that is both talented and resourceful (Bordewich, 1996, p. 11).

Natural Resources

Ironically, land allotted to American Indian tribes in the 19th century sometimes turned out to be rich in resources that became valuable in the 20th century. These resources include

Exhibit 7.4   Federal Indian Policy and Indian Response

Period	Economic Impact	Political Impact	Indian Response	Government Approach
Reservation. Late 1800s–1930s	Land loss (Dawes Act) and welfare dependency	Government control of reservation and coerced acculturation	Some resistance, growth of religious movements	Individualistic, creation of self-sufficient farmers
Reorganization (IRA). 1930s and 1940s	Stabilize land base and support some development of reservations	Establish federally sponsored tribal governments	Increased political participation in many tribes, some pantribal activity	Incorporate tribes as groups, creation of self-sufficient "Americanized" communities
Termination and Relocation. Late 1940s–early 1960s	Withdrawal of government support for reservations, promotion of urbanization	New assault on tribes, new forms of coercive acculturation	Increased pantribalism, widespread and intense opposition to termination	Individualistic; dissolve tribal ties and promote incorporation into the modern, urban labor market
Self-Determination. 1960s–present	Develop reservation economies, increased integration of Indian labor force	Support for tribal governments	Greatly increased political activity	Incorporate tribes as self-sufficient communities with access to federal programs of support and welfare

SOURCE: Based on Cornell, Kalt, Krepps, & Taylor (1998, p. 5).

oil, natural gas, coal, and uranium, basic sources of energy in the larger society. In addition (and despite the devastation wreaked by the Dawes Act of 1887), some tribes hold title to water rights, fishing rights, woodlands that could sustain a lumbering industry, and wilderness areas that could be developed for camping, hunting, and other forms of recreation. These resources are likely to become more valuable as the earth's natural resources and undeveloped areas are further depleted in the future.

The challenge faced by American Indians is to retain control of these resources and to develop them for their own benefit. Threats to the remaining tribal lands and assets are common. Mining and energy companies continue to cast envious eyes on American Indian land, and other tribal assets are coveted by real estate developers, fishermen (recreational as well as commercial), backpackers and campers, and cities facing water shortages (Harjo, 1996).

Some tribes have succeeded in developing their resources for their own benefit, in part because of their increased autonomy and independence since the passage of the 1975 Indian Self-Determination Act. For example, the White Mountain Apaches of Arizona operate nine tribally owned enterprises, including a major ski resort, a logging operation and sawmill, and a small casino. These businesses are the primary economic engines of the local area, and unemployment on the White Mountain reservation is only a quarter of the national reservation average (Cornell & Kalt, 1998, pp. 3–4). On many other reservations, however, even rich stores of resources lie dormant, awaiting the right combination of tribal leadership, expertise, and development capital. The Crow tribe of Montana, for example, controls a huge supply of coal and has extensive timber, water, mineral, and other resources. Yet unemployment on the reservation runs 60%, and the tribe gets very little return on their wealth. "All those resources have not produced wealth. Nor have they produced a viable, working economy" (Cornell & Kalt, 1998, p. 5).

On a broader level, tribes are banding together to share expertise and negotiate more effectively with the larger society. For example, 25 tribes founded the Council of Energy Resource Tribes in 1975 to coordinate and control the development of the mineral resources on reservation lands. Since its founding, the council has successfully negotiated a number of agreements with dominant group firms, increasing the flow of income to the tribes and raising their quality of life (Cornell, 1988; Snipp, 1989).

Attracting Industry to the Reservation

Many efforts to develop the reservations have focused on creating jobs by attracting industry through such incentives as low taxes, low rents, and a low-wage pool of labor—not unlike the package of benefits offered to employers by less developed nations in Asia, South America, and Africa. With some notable exceptions, these efforts have not been particularly successful (for a review, see Vinje, 1996; Cornell, 2006). Reservations are often so geographically isolated that transportation costs become prohibitive. The jobs that have materialized are typically low wage and have few benefits; usually, non-Indians fill the more lucrative managerial positions. Thus, the opportunities for building economic power or improving the standard of living from these jobs are sharply limited. These new jobs may transform "the welfare poor into the working poor" (Snipp, 1996, p. 398), but their potential for raising economic vitality is low.

To illustrate the problems of developing reservations by attracting industry, consider the Navajo, the second-largest American Indian tribe. The Navajo reservation spreads across Arizona, New Mexico, and Utah and encompasses about 20 million acres, an area a little smaller than either Indiana or Maine. Although the reservation seems huge on a map, much of the land is desert not suitable for farming or other uses. As they have for the past several centuries, the Navajo today rely heavily on the cultivation of corn and sheepherding for sustenance.

Most wage-earning jobs on the reservation are with the agencies of the federal government (e.g., the BIA) or with the tribal government. Tourism is large and growing, but the jobs available in that sector are typically low wage and seasonal. There are reserves of coal, uranium, and oil on the reservation, but these resources have not generated many jobs. In some cases, the Navajo have resisted the damage to the environment that would be caused by mines and oil wells because of their traditional values and respect for the land. When exploitation of these resources has been permitted, the companies involved often use highly automated technologies that generate few jobs (Oswalt & Neely, 1996, pp. 317–351).

Exhibits 7.5 and 7.6 contrast Navaho income, poverty, and education with that of non-Hispanic whites. Median income for the Navaho men is a third lower than the income for non-Hispanic whites, and Navajo women earn, on the average, almost $4,000 less than the men of their tribe and $8,000 less than non-Hispanic white women. Thus, there is a sizable gender gap alongside the racial gap in incomes. The poverty rate for the Navajo is about three times greater than the rate for non-Hispanic whites, and the tribe is far below national standards in terms of education.

On the other hand, some tribes have managed to achieve relative prosperity by bringing jobs to their people. The Choctaw Nation of Mississippi, for example, has become one of the largest employers in the state. Tribal leaders have been able to attract companies such as Xerox and Harley-Davidson by promising (and delivering) high-quality labor for relatively low wages. Incomes have risen, unemployment is relatively low, and the tribe has built schools, hospitals, and a television station and administers numerous other services for its members (Bordewich, 1996, pp. 300–305). The median income for Choctaw men, although still only about 80% of the figure for non-Hispanic whites, is $7,000 greater than that of Navajo men, and Choctaw women also earn more, on the average, than Navajo women. The Choctaw

Exhibit 7.5   Poverty and Education for Non-Hispanic Whites, American Indians, Navajo, and Choctaw, 2006

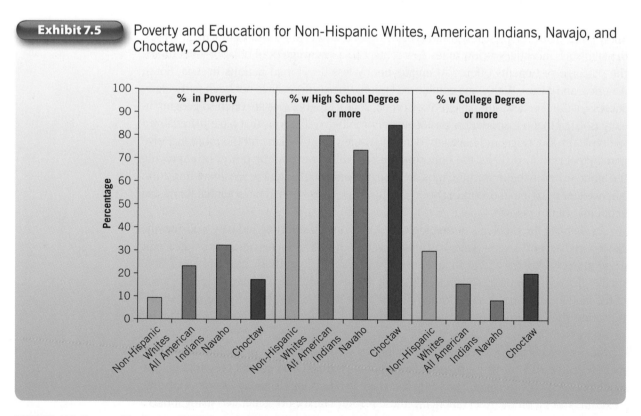

SOURCE: U.S. Bureau of the Census (2007a).

UNDERSTANDING DOMINANT-MINORITY RELATIONS

Exhibit 7.6 Median Incomes for Full-Time Year-Round Workers, Males and Females, 2006

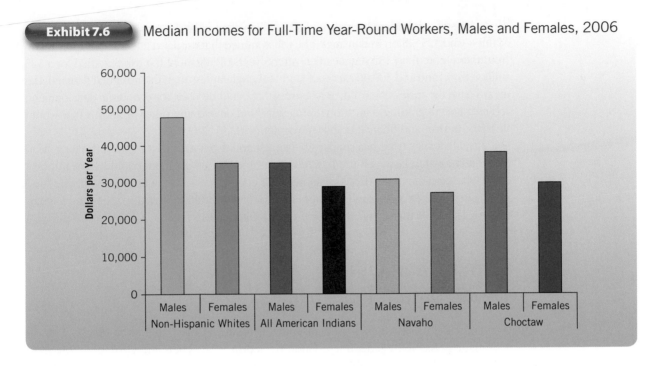

SOURCE: U.S. Bureau of the Census (2007a).

poverty rate is about half that of the Navajo, and Choctaws almost match non-Hispanic whites in high school education. Twenty percent of the Choctaw are college educated, more than twice the comparable figure for the Navajo.

The Choctaw are not the most affluent tribe, and the Navajo are far from being the most destitute. They illustrate the mixture of partial successes and failures that typify efforts to bring prosperity to the reservations; together, these two cases suggest that attracting industry and jobs to the reservations is a possible—but difficult and uncertain—strategy for economic development.

It is worth repeating that self-determination, the ability of tribes to control development on the reservation, seems to be one of the important keys to success. Tribes like the Choctaw are, in a sense, developing ethnic enclaves (see Chapter 2) in which they can capitalize on local networks of interpersonal relationships. As with other groups that have followed this strategy, success in the enclave depends on solidarity and group cohesion, not Americanization and integration (see Cornell, 2006).

Broken Treaties

For many tribes, the treaties signed with the federal government in the 19th century offer another potential resource. These treaties were often violated by white settlers, the military, state and local governments, the BIA, and other elements and agencies of the dominant group, and many tribes are pursuing this trail of broken treaties and seeking compensation for the wrongs of the past. For example, in 1972, the Passamaquoddy and Penobscot tribes filed a lawsuit demanding the return of 12.5 million acres of land—more than half the state of Maine—and $25 billion in damages. The tribes argued that this land had been illegally taken from them more than 150 years earlier. After 8 years of litigation, the tribes settled for a $25 million trust fund and 300,000 acres of land. Although far less than their original demand, the award gave the tribes control over resources that could be used for economic development, job creation, upgrading educational programs, and developing other programs that would enhance human and financial capital (Worsnop, 1992, p. 391).

Virtually every tribe has similar grievances, and if pursued successfully, the long-dead treaty relationship between the Indian nations and the government could be a significant fount of economic and political resources. Of course, lawsuits require considerable (and expensive) legal expertise and years of effort to bring to fruition. Because there are no guarantees of success, this avenue has some sharp limitations and risks.

Gaming and Other Development Possibilities

Another resource for American Indians is the gambling industry, the development of which was made possible by federal legislation passed in 1988. There are currently more than 200 tribes with gaming establishments (National Indian Gaming Commission, 2004), and the industry has grown more than 100 times over, from $212 million in revenues in 1988 (Spilde, 2001) to about $25 billion in 2006 (National Indian Gaming Commission, n.d.). Exhibit 7.7 charts the growth of revenues from gaming on American Indian reservations from 1995 to 2006.

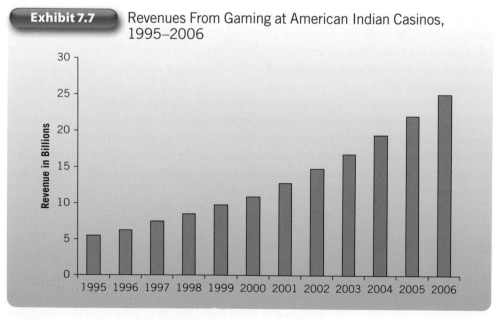

Exhibit 7.7 Revenues From Gaming at American Indian Casinos, 1995–2006

SOURCE: National Indian Gaming Commission (2007).

The single most profitable Indian gambling operation is the Foxwoods Casino in Connecticut, operated by the Pequot tribe. The casino is said to be the largest in the world and to generate more revenue than the casinos of Atlantic City. The profits from the casino are used to benefit tribal members in a variety of ways, including the repurchase of tribal lands, housing assistance, medical benefits, educational scholarships, and public services, such as a tribal police force (Bordewich, 1996, p. 110). Other tribes have used gambling profits to purchase restaurants and marinas and to finance the development of outlet malls, aquacultural programs, manufacturing plants, and a wide variety of other businesses and enterprises (Spilde, 2001).

The power of gaming to benefit the tribes is suggested by the information displayed in Exhibit 7.8. The table shows that on a number of indicators, both gaming and nongaming reservations enjoyed significant improvements in their quality of life in the last decade of the 20th century but that gaming reservations improved more rapidly. For example, all reservations increased their per capita income faster than the nation as a whole (+11%), but gaming reservations improved faster (+36%) than nongaming reservations (+21%).

Various tribes have sought other ways to capitalize on their freedom from state regulation and taxes. Some have established small but profitable businesses selling cigarettes tax-free. Also, because they are not subject to state and federal environmental regulations, some reservations are exploring the possibility of housing nuclear waste and other refuse of industrialization—a somewhat ironic and not altogether attractive use of the remaining Indian lands.

Clearly, the combination of increased autonomy, treaty rights, natural resources, and gambling means that American Indians today have an opportunity to dramatically raise their standards of living and creatively take control of their own destinies. Some tribes have enjoyed enormous benefits, but for others, these assets remain a potential waiting to be actualized. Without denying the success stories or the improvements in recent years, the lives of many American Indians continue to be limited by poverty and powerlessness, prejudice, and discrimination. We document these patterns in the next section.

Photo 7.3

This Apache-owned facility combines a casino and a resort.

© Anders Ryman/Corbis.

Exhibit 7.8 Various Indicators of Improvement on Gaming vs. Nongaming Reservations and Total U.S., 1990–2000

Indicator	Nongaming	Gaming	U.S.
Per capita income	+21%	+36%	+11%
Family poverty	–7%	–12%	–1%
Unemployment	–2%	–5%	–1%
High school graduates	–1%	+2%	–1%
College graduates	+2%	+3%	+4%

SOURCE: Taylor & Kalt (2005, p. xi).

Contemporary American Indian-White Relations

This section uses many of the terms and concepts we have developed over the first seven chapters to analyze the contemporary situation of American Indians. Compared with other groups, information about American Indians is scant. Nonetheless, a relatively clear picture emerges. The portrait stresses a mixed picture for this group: improvements for some tribes combined with continued colonization, marginalization, and impoverishment for others. American Indians as a group face continuing discrimination and exclusion and continue the search for a meaningful course between assimilation and pluralism.

Prejudice and Discrimination

Anti-Indian prejudice has been a part of American society from the beginning. Historically, negative feelings such as hatred and contempt have been widespread and strong, particularly during the heat of war, and various stereotypes of Indians have been common. One stereotype, especially strong during periods of conflict, depicts Indians as bloodthirsty, ferocious, cruel savages capable of any atrocity. The other image of American Indians is that of "the noble Red Man" who lives in complete harmony with nature and symbolizes goodwill and pristine simplicity (Bordewich, 1996, p. 34). Although the first stereotype tended to fade away as hostilities drew to a close, the latter image retains a good deal of strength in modern views of Indians found in popular culture and among environmentalist and "new age" spiritual organizations.

A variety of studies have documented continued stereotyping of Native Americans in the popular press, textbooks, the media, cartoons, and various other places (for example, see Aleiss, 2005; Bird, 1999; Rouse & Hanson, 1991). In the tradition of "the noble Red Man," American Indians are often portrayed as bucks and squaws, complete with headdresses, bows, tepees, and other such "generic" Indian artifacts. These portrayals obliterate the diversity of American Indian culture and lifestyles. American Indians are often referred to in the past tense, as if their present situation were of no importance or, worse, as if they no longer existed. Many history books continue to begin the study of American history in Europe or with the "discovery" of America, omitting the millennia of civilization prior to the arrival of European explorers and colonizers. Contemporary portrayals of American Indians, such as in the movie *Dances With Wolves* (1990), are more sympathetic but still treat the tribes as part of a bucolic past forever lost, not as peoples with real problems in the present.

The persistence of stereotypes and the extent to which they have become enmeshed in modern culture is illustrated by continuing controversies surrounding nicknames for athletic teams (the Washington Redskins, the Cleveland Indians, and the Atlanta Braves) and the use of American Indian mascots, tomahawk "chops," and other practices offensive to many American Indians (see the Current Debates section at the end of this chapter for more). Protests have been staged at some athletic events to increase awareness of these derogatory depictions, but as was the case so often in the past, the protests have been attacked, ridiculed, or simply ignored. Public opinion polls indicate that the public sees the issue as trivial and regards the protesters as attention-seeking troublemakers (Giago, 1992).

There are relatively few studies of anti-Indian prejudices in the social science literature, and it is therefore difficult to characterize changes over the past several decades. We do not know whether there has been a shift to more symbolic or "modern" forms of anti-Indian racism, as there has been for anti-black prejudice, or whether the stereotypes of American Indians have declined in strength or changed in content.

One of the few records of national anti-Indian prejudice over time is that of social distance scale results (see Exhibit 3.4). When the scales were first administered in 1926, American Indians were ranked in the middle third of all groups (18th out of 28), at about the same level as Southern and Eastern Europeans and slightly above Mexicans, another colonized group. The ranking of American Indians remained stable until 1977, when there was a noticeable rise in their position relative to other groups. In the most recent polls, the social distance scores of American Indians fell (indicating less prejudice), but the relative ranking still placed them with other racial minority groups. These shifts may reflect a decline in levels of prejudice, a change from more overt forms to more subtle modern racism, or both. Remember, however, that the samples for the social distance research were college students for the most part and do not necessarily reflect trends in the general population (see also Hanson & Rouse, 1987; Smith & Dempsey, 1983).

Research is also unclear about the severity or extent of discrimination against American Indians. Certainly, the group's lower average levels of education limit their opportunities for upward mobility, choice of occupations, and range of income. This is a form of institutional discrimination in the sense that the opportunities to develop human capital are much less available to American Indians than to much of the rest of the population. In terms of individual discrimination or more overt forms of exclusion, there is simply too little evidence to sustain clear conclusions (Snipp, 1992, p. 363). The situation of American Indian women is also underresearched, but Snipp reports that like their counterparts in other minority groups and the dominant group, they "are systematically paid less than their male counterparts in similar circumstances" (p. 363).

The very limited evidence available from social distance scales suggests that overt anti-Indian prejudice has declined, perhaps in parallel with anti-black prejudice. A great deal of stereotyping remains, however, and demeaning, condescending, or negative portrayals of American Indians are common throughout the dominant culture. Institutional discrimination is a major barrier for American Indians, who have not had access to opportunities for education and employment.

Assimilation and Pluralism

Acculturation.
Despite more than a century of coercive Americanization, many tribes have been able to preserve a large portion of their traditional cultures. For example, many tribal languages continue to be spoken on a daily basis. The huge majority (72%) of American Indians in the continental United States speak only English, but a sizable minority (28%) speak a tribal language as well. Exhibit 7.9 suggests the extent of language acculturation. For most of the 10 largest tribes, less than 20% of their members speak a tribal language in addition to English. In some tribes, however, the picture is dramatically different. For example, most Navajo and Pueblo Indians speak the tribal language at home, and about 25% of Navajo and 18% of Pueblo speak English "less than very well" (Ogunwole, 2006, p. 7).

Traditional culture is retained in other forms besides language. Religions and value systems, political and economic structures, cuisine, and recreational patterns have all survived the military conquest and the depredations of reservation life; each pattern has been altered, however, by contact with the dominant group. Cornell (1987), for example, argues that although American Indians have been affected by the "American dream" of material success through hard, honest work, their individual values continue to reflect their greater orientation to the group rather than to the individual.

The tendency to filter the impact of the larger society through continuing, vital American Indian culture is also illustrated by the Native American Church. The Native American Church is an important American Indian religion, with over 100 congregations across the nation.

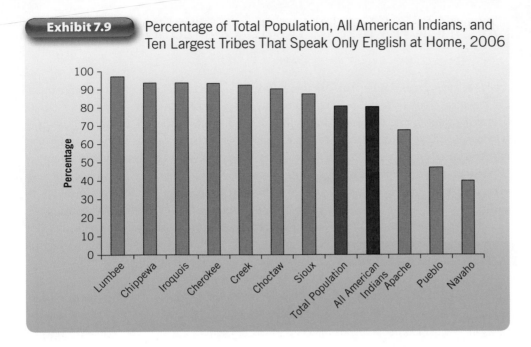

Exhibit 7.9 Percentage of Total Population, All American Indians, and Ten Largest Tribes That Speak Only English at Home, 2006

SOURCE: U.S. Bureau of the Census (2007a).

This religion combines elements from both cultures, and church services freely mix Christian imagery and the Bible with attempts to seek personal visions by using peyote, a hallucinogenic drug. The latter practice is consistent with the spiritual and religious traditions of many tribes but clashes sharply with the laws and norms of the larger society. The difference in traditions has generated many skirmishes with the courts, and as recently as 2004, the right of the Native American Church to use peyote was upheld by the Supreme Court of Utah ("Utah Supreme Court," 2004).

American Indians have been considerably more successful than African Americans in preserving their traditional cultures. The differences in the relationship between each minority group and the dominant group help explain this pattern. African Americans were exploited for labor, whereas the competition with American Indians involved land. African cultures could not easily survive, because the social structures that transmitted the cultures and gave them meaning were destroyed by slavery and sacrificed to the exigencies of the plantation economy.

In contrast, American Indians confronted the dominant group as tribal units, intact and whole. The tribes maintained integrity throughout the wars and throughout the reservation period. Tribal culture was indeed attacked and denigrated during the reservation era, but the basic social unit that sustained the culture survived, albeit in altered form. The fact that American Indians were placed on separate reservations, isolated from one another and the "contaminating" effects of everyday contact with the larger society, also abetted the preservation of traditional languages and culture (Cornell, 1990). Narrative Portrait 2 in this chapter illustrates the persistence of a distinct Indian culture and point of view.

Indian cultures seem healthy and robust in the current atmosphere of greater tolerance and support for pluralism in the larger society combined with increased autonomy and lower government regulation on the reservations. However, a number of social forces are working against pluralism and the survival of tribal cultures. Pantribalism may threaten the integrity

An Indian View of White Civilization

*W*ho's the savage? One stereotype of American Indians portrays them as "cruel, barbaric, and savage." Is it possible, however, that American Indians are more advanced than the dazzling sophisticates of urban America? In a 1972 interview, John Lame Deer, a Sioux, gives his view of the technologically advanced society that surrounds him. Through his words, we can hear the voices of the Indian cultures that have survived.

Listening to the Air

John Lame Deer

You have made it hard for us to experience nature in the good way by being part of it. Even here [a Sioux reservation in South Dakota] we are conscious that somewhere out in those hills there are missile silos and radar stations. White men always pick the few unspoiled, beautiful, awesome spots for these abominations. You have raped and violated these lands, always saying, "gimme, gimme, gimme," and never giving anything back.... You have not only despoiled the earth, the rocks, the minerals, all of which you call "dead" but which are very much alive; you have even changed the animals, ... changed them in a horrible way, so no one can recognize them. There is power in a buffalo—spiritual, magic power—but there is no power in an Angus, in a Hereford.

There is power in an antelope, but not in a goat or a sheep, which holds still while you butcher it, which will eat your newspaper if you let it. There was great power in a wolf, even in a coyote. You made him into a freak—a toy poodle, a Pekinese, a lap dog. You can't do much with a cat, which is like an Indian, unchangeable. So you fix it, alter it, declaw it, even cut its vocal cords so you can experiment on it in a laboratory without being disturbed by its cries. . . .

You have not only altered, declawed, and malformed your winged and four-legged cousins; you have done it to yourselves. You have changed men into chairmen of boards, into office workers, into time-clock punchers. You have changed women into housewives, truly fearful creatures. . . . You live in prisons which you have built for yourselves, calling them "homes," offices, factories. We have a new joke on the reservations: "What is cultural deprivation?" Answer: "Being an upper-middle-class white kid living in a split-level suburban home with a color TV." . . .

I think white people are so afraid of the world they created that they don't want to see, feel, smell, or hear it. The feeling of rain or snow on your face, being numbed by an icy wind and thawing out before a smoking fire, coming out of a hot sweat bath and plunging into a cold stream, these things make you feel alive, but you don't want them anymore. Living in boxes that shut out the heat of the summer and the chill of winter, living inside a body that no longer has a scent, hearing the noise of the hi-fi rather than listening to the sounds of nature, watching some actor on TV have a make-believe experience when you no longer experience anything for yourself, eating food without taste—that's your way. It's no good.

SOURCE: Lame Deer, John (Fire), & Erdoes, Richard (1972). "Listening to the Air." In *Lame Deer, Seeker of Visions*, pp. 119–121. New York: Simon & Schuster.

of individual tribal cultures as it represents American Indian grievances and concerns to the larger society. Opportunities for jobs, education, and higher incomes draw American Indians to more developed urban areas and will continue to do so as long as the reservations are underdeveloped. Many aspects of the tribal cultures can be fully expressed and practiced only with other tribal members on the reservations. Thus, many American Indians must make a choice between "Indian-ness" on the reservation and "success" in the city. The younger, more educated American Indians will be most likely to confront this choice, and the future vitality of traditional American Indian cultures and languages will hinge on which option is chosen.

Secondary Structural Assimilation.
This section assesses the degree of integration of American Indians into the various institutions of public life, following the general outlines of the parallel section in Chapter 6.

Residential Patterns. Since the Indian Removal Act of 1830 (see Chapter 4), American Indians have been concentrated in the western two thirds of the nation, as illustrated in Exhibit 7.10, although some pockets of population still can be found in the East. The states with the largest concentrations of American Indians—California, New Mexico, and Arizona—together include about one third of all American Indians, and another 10% live in Oklahoma. American Indians belong to hundreds of different tribes, the 10 largest of which were listed in Exhibit 7.1

Exhibit 7.10 Percentage of County Populations Choosing AIAN, Alone and in Combination, 2000

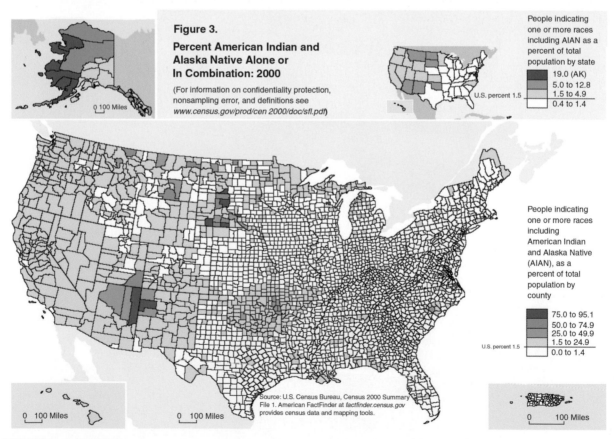

SOURCE: Ogunwole (2002).

Exhibit 7.11 provides some information about the levels of residential segregation of American Indians. The data in the exhibit are limited to metropolitan areas only. Since American Indians are such a small, rural group, Exhibit 7.11 is limited to only 13 metropolitan areas, most in the West. The Northeast is not included because of the small numbers of American Indians living in the metropolitan areas of that region. Residential segregation is measured using the dissimilarity index, the same statistic used in Exhibit 6.6 for African Americans.

Although based on small numbers, the exhibit shows that residential segregation is much lower for American Indians than for African Americans (see Exhibit 6.6) and approaches the "high" range (.6) only in the western region. Also, the level of residential segregation declined slightly between 1980 and 2000, but remember that more than a third of American Indians live on rural reservations where the levels of residential segregation are quite high.

School Integration and Educational Attainment. As a result of the combined efforts of missionaries and federal agencies, American Indians have had a long but not necessarily productive acquaintance with Western education. Until the last few decades, schools for American Indians were primarily focused on Americanizing children, not on educating them. For many tribes, the percentage of high school graduates has increased in the recent past, but American Indians as a whole are still somewhat below national levels. On the other hand, several tribes now exceed the national standard. The gap in college education is closing as well but remains large. None of the 10 largest tribes approaches the national norm on this variable. The differences in schooling are especially important because the lower levels of educational attainment limit mobility and job opportunities in the postindustrial job market. The educational levels of American Indians are displayed in Exhibit 7.12.

Exhibit 7.11 Residential Segregation of American Indians, 1980–2000

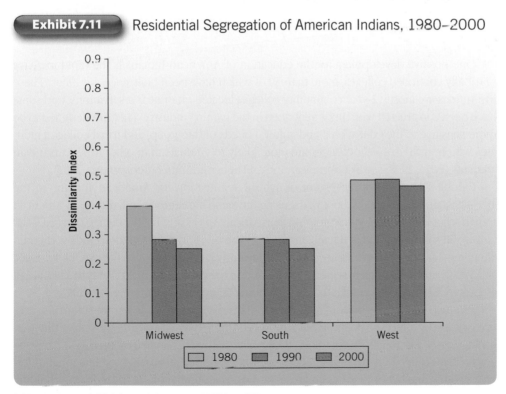

SOURCE: Iceland, Weinberg, & Steinmetz (2002, p. 23).

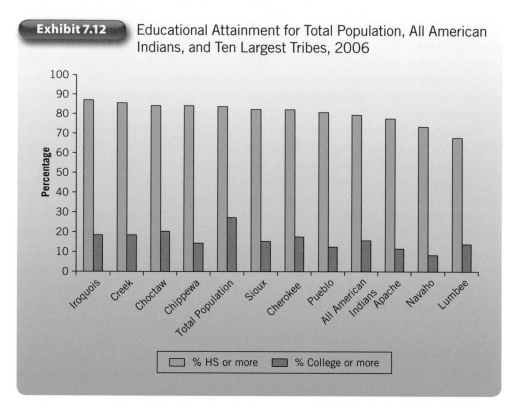

Exhibit 7.12 Educational Attainment for Total Population, All American Indians, and Ten Largest Tribes, 2006

SOURCE: U.S. Bureau of the Census (2007a).

One positive development for the education of American Indians is the rapid increase in tribally controlled colleges, more than 30 of which have been built since the 1960s. These institutions are mostly 2-year community colleges located on or near reservations, and some have been constructed with funds generated in the gaming industry. They are designed to be more sensitive to the educational and cultural needs of the group, and tribal college graduates who transfer to 4-year colleges are more likely to graduate than other American Indian students (Pego, 1998; see also American Indian Higher Education Consortium, 2001).

Exhibit 7.13 displays the extent of school segregation for American Indians in the 1993–1994 and 2005–2006 school years, using the same measures as in Exhibit 6.8. American Indian schoolchildren are less segregated than African Americans, but the degree of racial isolation is still substantial and is actually increasing. The percentage of American Indian children attending "majority-minority" schools increased from 44% to 49% between the two school years. The percentage in extremely segregated schools, on the other hand, held steady at 21%, about 10 percentage points lower than the corresponding figure for African American children.

Political Power. The ability of American Indians to exert power as a voting bloc or to otherwise directly affect the political structure is very limited by group size; they are a tiny percentage of the electorate. Furthermore, their political power is limited by their lower average levels of education, language differences, lack of economic resources, and fractional differences within and between tribes and reservations. The number of American Indians holding

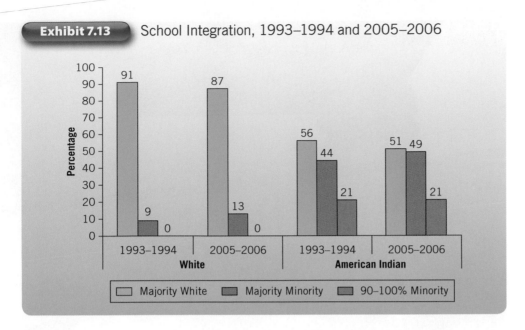

Exhibit 7.13   School Integration, 1993–1994 and 2005–2006

Majority White   Majority Minority   90–100% Minority

SOURCE: Fry (2007).

elected office is minuscule, far less than 1% (Pollard & O'Hare, 1999). In 1992, however, Ben Nighthorse Campbell, of Colorado, a member of the Northern Cheyenne tribe, was elected to the U.S. Senate and served until 2005.

Jobs and Income. Some of the most severe challenges facing American Indians relate to work and income. The problems are especially evident on the reservations, where jobs have traditionally been scarce and affluence rare. As in the case of African Americans, the overall unemployment rate for all American Indians is about double the rate for whites. For Indians living on or near reservations, however, the rate is much higher, sometimes rising to 70% to 80% on the smaller, more isolated reservations (U.S. Bureau of Indian Affairs, 1997). According to one report, the unemployment rate on reservations declined between 1990 and 2000 but still exceeded national levels by a substantial margin (Taylor & Kalt, 2005, p. 28).

Nationally, American Indians are underrepresented in the higher-status, more lucrative professions and overrepresented in unskilled labor and service jobs (Ogunwole, 2006, p. 10). As is the case for African Americans, American Indians who hold white-collar jobs are more likely than whites to work in relatively low-level occupations, such as typist or retail salesperson (Pollard & O'Hare, 1999).

The income data in Exhibit 7.14 show median household income in 2006 for the total U.S. population, all American Indians, and the 10 largest tribes. Overall, American Indian per capita income is about 75% of national levels. There is a good deal of variability among the 10 largest tribes, but again, none approaches national norms. These incomes reflect lower levels of education as well as the interlocking forces of past discrimination and lack of development on many reservations. The rural isolation of much of the population and their distance from the more urbanized centers of economic growth limit possibilities for improvement and raise the likelihood that many reservations will remain the rural counterparts to urban underclass ghettos.

Photo 7.5

Ben Cheyenne looks out over a reservation in South Dakota. Poverty, unemployment, and alcoholism continue to be major problems on many reservations.

© NewSport/Corbis.

Exhibit 7.14 Median Household Income for Total Population, All American Indians, and Ten Largest Tribes, 2006

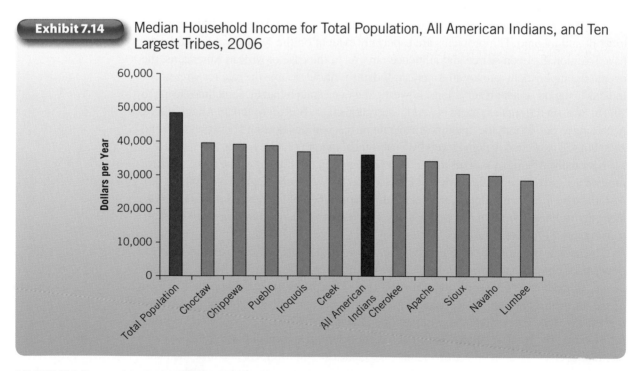

SOURCE: U.S. Bureau of the Census (2007a).

Exhibit 7.15 supplements the information in Exhibit 7.14 by displaying the distribution of income for American Indians and Alaska Natives (AIAN) compared with non-Hispanic Whites. This type of graph was introduced in the chapter on African Americans and follows the same format as Exhibit 6.12. In both graphs, the pattern of income inequality is immediately obvious. Starting at the bottom, we see that like African Americans, AIAN are overrepresented in the lowest income groups. For example, almost 15% of AIAN have incomes less than $10,000, more than double the percentage for non-Hispanic whites (7%) in this range.

Moving up the figure through the lower- and middle-income brackets, we see that AIAN households continue to be overrepresented. As was the case with Exhibit 6.12, there is a notable clustering of both groups in the $50,000 to $100,000 categories, but it is whites who are overrepresented at these higher-income levels: Almost a third of white households compared with only 25% of AIAN households are in these categories. The income differences between the groups are especially obvious at the top of the figure. About 13% of white households versus 5% of AIAN households are in the top three income categories. Exhibit 7.15 also shows the median household income for both groups in 2006, and the difference of almost $20,000 further illustrates the lower socioeconomic level of American Indians.

Finally, Exhibit 7.16 shows the poverty levels for the total population, all American Indians, and the 10 largest tribes. The poverty rate for American Indian families is almost double the national rate, and 6 of the 10 largest tribes have an even higher percentage of families living in poverty. The poverty rates for children show a similar pattern, with very high rates for the Navajo and Sioux.

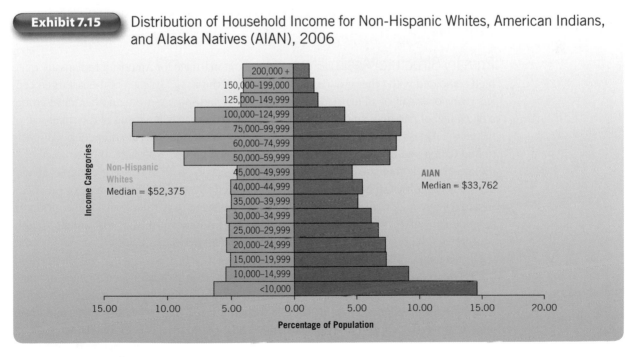

Exhibit 7.15 Distribution of Household Income for Non-Hispanic Whites, American Indians, and Alaska Natives (AIAN), 2006

SOURCE: U.S. Bureau of the Census (2007a).

Exhibit 7.16 Poverty Levels for Families and for Children for Total Population, All American Indians, and Ten Largest Tribes, 2006

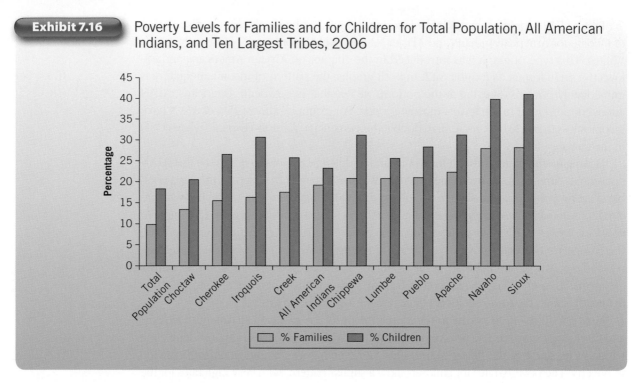

SOURCE: U.S. Bureau of the Census (2007a).

Taken together, this information on income and poverty shows that despite the progress that American Indians have made over the past several decades, a very sizable socioeconomic gap persists.

Primary Structural Assimilation.
Rates of out-marriage for American Indians are quite high compared with other groups, as displayed in Exhibit 7.17. In each of the last three census years, over half of all married American Indians had spouses from another racial group, a much higher rate than any other group. This pattern is partly the result of the small size of the group. As less than 1% of the total population, American Indians are numerically unlikely to find dating and marriage partners within their own group, especially in those regions of the country and urban areas where the group is especially small in size. For example, an earlier study found that in New England, which has the lowest relative percentage of American Indians of any region, over 90% of Indian marriages were to partners outside the group. In the mountain states, which have a greater number of American Indians who are also highly concentrated on reservations, only about 40% of Indian marriages involved partners outside the group (Snipp, 1989, pp. 156–159).

The high rate of out-marriage is also an indication of the extent of acculturation and integration for some American Indians. Marriages with non-Indians are associated with higher levels of education, greater participation in the labor force, higher income levels, and lower rates of poverty (Snipp, 1989, pp. 160–164). Thus, out-marriage is more characteristic of American Indians who have left the reservation to pursue opportunities for education and careers in the cities.

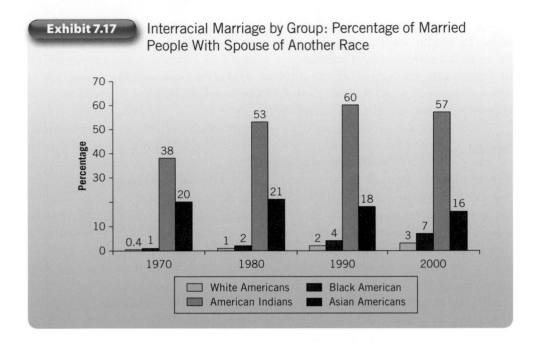

Exhibit 7.17 Interracial Marriage by Group: Percentage of Married People With Spouse of Another Race

SOURCE: Lee & Edmonston (2005).

Comparing Minority Groups

Comparing the experiences of American Indians with those of other groups will further our understanding of the complexities of dominant-minority relationships and permit us to test the explanatory power of the concepts and theories that are central to this text. No two minority groups have had the same experiences, and our concepts and theories should help us understand the differences and the similarities. We will make it a point to compare groups in each of the chapters in this part of the text. We begin by comparing American Indians with African Americans.

First, note the differences in the stereotypes attached to the two groups during the early years of European colonization. While Indians were seen as cruel savages, African Americans under slavery were seen as lazy, irresponsible, and in constant need of supervision. The two stereotypes are consistent with the outcomes of the contact period. The supposed irresponsibility of blacks under slavery helped justify their subordinate, highly controlled status, and the alleged savagery of American Indians helped to justify their near extermination by white society.

Second, both American Indians and African Americans were colonized minority groups, but their contact situations were governed by very different dynamics (competition for labor vs. land) and a very different dominant group agenda (the capture and control of a large, powerless workforce vs. the elimination of a military threat). These differing contact situations shaped subsequent relationships with the dominant group and the place of the groups in the larger society.

For example, consider the situations of the two groups a century ago. The most visible enemy for African Americans was de jure segregation, the elaborate system of repression in the South that controlled them politically, economically, and socially (see Chapters 5 and 6). In particular, the southern system of agriculture needed the black population—but only as a powerless, cheap workforce. The goals of African Americans centered on dismantling this oppressive system, assimilation, and equality.

American Indians, in contrast, were not viewed as a source of labor and, after their military defeat, were far too few in number and dispersed geographically to constitute a political threat. Thus, there was little need to control them in the same way African Americans were controlled. The primary enemies of the tribes were the reservation system, various agencies of the federal government (especially the BIA), rural isolation, and the continuing attacks on their traditional cultures and lifestyles, which are typical for a colonized minority group. American Indians had a different set of problems, different resources at their disposal, and different goals in mind. They have always been more oriented toward a pluralistic relationship with the larger society and preserving what they could of their autonomy, their institutions, and their heritage. African Americans spent much of the 20th century struggling for inclusion and equality; American Indians were fighting to maintain or recover their traditional cultures and social structures. This difference in goals reflects the different histories of the two groups and the different circumstances surrounding their colonization.

Progress and Challenges

What does the future hold for American Indians? Their situation has certainly changed over the past 100 years, but is it "better" or just "different," as is the case for large segments of the African American community? The answer seems to be a little of both, as the group grows in size and improves its status. To reach some conclusions, we will look at several aspects of the situation of American Indians and assess the usefulness of our theoretical models and concepts.

Since the 1960s, the decline of intolerance in the society at large, the growth of pride in ancestry in many groups (e.g., Black Power), and the shift in federal government policy to encourage self-determination have all helped to spark a reaffirmation of commitment to tribal cultures and traditions. As was the case with African Americans and the Black Power movement, the Red Power movement asserted a distinct and positive Indian identity, a claim for the equal validity of American Indian cultures within the broad framework of the larger society. During the same time period, the favorable settlements of treaty claims, the growth in job opportunities, and the gambling industry have enhanced the flow of resources and benefits to the reservations. In popular culture, American Indians have enjoyed a strong upsurge of popularity and sympathetic depictions. This enhanced popularity accounts for much of the growth in population size as people of mixed ancestry resurrect and reconstruct their Indian ancestors and their own ethnic identities.

Linear or simplistic views of assimilation do not fit the current situation or the past experiences of American Indians very well. Some American Indians are intermarrying with whites and integrating into the larger society; others strive to retain a tribal culture in the midst of an urbanized, industrialized society; and still others labor to use the profits from gaming and other enterprises for the benefit of the tribe as a whole. Members of the group can be found at every degree of acculturation and integration, and the group seems to be moving toward assimilation in some ways and away from it in others.

From the standpoint of the Noel and Blauner hypotheses, we can see that American Indians have struggled with conquest and colonization, experiences made more difficult by the loss of so much of their land and other resources and by the concerted, unrelenting attacks on their culture and language. The legacy of conquest and colonization was poor health and housing, an inadequate and misdirected education system, and slow (or nonexistent) economic development. For most of the 20th century, American Indians were left to survive as best they could on the margins of the larger society, too powerless to establish meaningful pluralism and too colonized to pursue equality.

Today, the key to further progress for many, if not all, members of this group is economic development on reservation lands and the further strengthening of the tribes as functioning social units. Some tribes do have assets—natural resources, treaty rights, and the gambling industry—that could fuel development. However, they often do not have the expertise or the capital to finance the exploitation of these resources. They must rely, in whole or in part, on non-Indian expertise and white-owned companies and businesses. Thus, non-Indians, rather than the tribes, may be the primary beneficiaries of some forms of development (this would, of course, be quite consistent with American history). For those reservations for which gambling is not an option and for those without natural resources, investments in human capital (education) may offer the most compelling direction for future development.

Urban Indians confront the same patterns of discrimination and racism that confront other minority groups of color. Members of the group with lower levels of education and job skills face the prospects of becoming a part of a permanent urban underclass. More-educated and skilled American Indians share with African Americans the prospect of a middle-class lifestyle that is more partial and tenuous than that of comparable segments of the dominant group.

The situation of American Indians today is vastly superior to the status of the group a century ago, and this chapter has documented the notable improvements that have occurred since 1990. Given the depressed and desperate conditions of the reservations in the early 20th century, however, it would not take much to show an improvement. American Indians are growing rapidly in numbers and are increasingly diversified by residence, education, and degree of assimilation. Some tribes have made dramatic progress over the past several decades, but enormous problems remain, both on and off the reservations. The challenge for the future, as it was in the past, is to find a course between pluralism and assimilation, pantribalism and traditional lifestyles that will balance the issues of quality of life against the importance of retaining an Indian identity.

Australian Aborigines and American Indians

The history of American Indians—their conquest and domination by a larger, more powerful society—has a number of parallels from around the globe, a reflection of the rise of European societies to power and their frequent conquest of indigenous societies in Africa, North and South America, and Asia. A comparative analysis of these episodes suggests that similar dynamics have come into play, even though each has its own unique history. To illustrate, we will use some of the concepts developed in this text to compare the impact of European domination on Australian Aborigines and the indigenous peoples of North America.

Australia came under European domination in the late 1700s, nearly two centuries after the establishment of Jamestown and the beginning of Anglo-American Indian relations. In other ways, however, the two contact situations shared many features. In both cases, the colonial power was Great Britain, and first contacts occurred in the preindustrial era (although Britain had begun to industrialize by the late 1700s). Also, the indigenous peoples of both North America and Australia were thinly spread across vast areas and were greatly inferior to the British in their technological development.

The Aboriginal peoples had lived in Australia for 50,000 years by the time the British arrived. Estimates of their population size vary, but there may have been as many as a million Aborigines at the time of contact with the British ("A Sorry Tale," 2000). They were organized into small, nomadic hunting-and-gathering bands and were generally much less developed than the tribes of North America, lacking the population base, social organization, and resources that would have permitted sustained resistance to the invasion of their land. There was plenty of violence in the contact situation, but unlike the situation in North America, there were no sustained military campaigns pitting large armies against each other.

The initial thrust of colonization was motivated by Great Britain's need for a place to send its convicts after losing the Revolutionary War to the fledgling United States. The European population in Australia grew slowly at first and consisted mostly of prisoners. The early economic enterprises centered on subsistence farming and sheepherding, not large-scale enterprises that required forced labor (at least not on the same scale as in North America).

Early relations between the English and the Aborigines were hostile and centered on competition for land. In their ethnocentrism, the invaders denied that the Aborigines had any claims to the land and simply pushed them aside or killed them if they resisted. As in the Americas, European diseases took their toll, and the indigenous population declined rapidly. Because they were not desired as laborers (although many became semi-unfree servants), they were pushed away from the areas of white settlement into the fringes of development, where they and their grievances could be ignored. As in North America, they were seen as "savages": a culture that would (and in the view of the emerging dominant group, should) wither away and disappear.

To the extent that there was contact with the larger society, it was often in the form of coercive acculturation. For example, throughout much of the 20th century, the Australian government, aided by various church organizations, actually removed children of mixed parentage from their Aboriginal mothers and placed them in orphanages. The idea behind this program was to give these children a chance to leave their Aboriginal culture behind, marry whites, and enter the larger society. This policy, abandoned only in the 1960s, resulted in the state-sponsored orphaning of thousands of Aboriginal children. Some of the angriest and most militant members of the current generation of Aborigines belong to this "stolen generation" (for a report on this program, see Australian Human Rights and Equal Opportunity Commission, 1997).

The contemporary situation of Australian Aborigines has many parallels with American Indians, as does their past. The group is largely rural and continues to live on land that is less desirable. After the initial—and dramatic—declines, their numbers have been increasing of late, partly because of higher birthrates and partly because of changing perceptions, growing sympathy for their plight, and increased willingness of people to claim their aboriginal heritage. The population fell to a low of less than 100,000 at the start of the 20th century but is now put at 427,000, or about 2% of the total population (Australian Bureau of Statistics, 2002).

Just as in North America, there is a huge gap between the indigenous population and the rest of society on every statistic that measures quality of life, equality, and access to resources. Life expectancy for Aborigines is as much as 20 years lower than that of the general population, and their infant mortality rate is 2 to 3 times higher. They have much less access to health care, and Aboriginal communities are much more afflicted with alcoholism, suicide, and malnutrition than the general population. Unemployment rates are double the rate in the general population, average income is about 65% of the national average, and only about a third as many Aboriginal people (13.6%) as compared with the national population (34.4%) are in school at age 19 ("Asia: Original Sin," 2007; Brace, 2001; see also Australian Bureau of Statistics, 2002). The issues animating Aboriginal affairs

have a familiar ring for anyone familiar with American Indians. They include concerns for the preservation of Aboriginal culture, language, and identity; self-determination and autonomy; the return of lands illegally taken by the Anglo invaders; and an end to discrimination and unequal treatment.

As are relations with American Indians in North America, Aboriginal relations are in flux, and the overall picture is mixed. For example, in 1998, the federal government of Australia was condemned by the United Nations Committee on the Elimination of Racial Discrimination for its handling of Aboriginal land claims. Australia is the only developed nation to have ever received this censure (Pilger, 2000). On the other hand, the opening ceremonies of the 2000 Olympic Games in Sydney featured a celebration of Aboriginal culture, dance, music, and art, and Aboriginal athlete Cathy Freeman lit the Olympic flame.

The Aboriginal peoples of Australia, like American Indians, face many—often overwhelming—challenges to secure a better future for themselves and for their children. Their history and their present situation clearly validate both the Blauner and Noel hypotheses: They are a colonized minority group, victims of European domination, with all that that status implies.

CURRENT DEBATES

Are Indian Sports Team Mascots Offensive?

American Indians face many challenges as they address persistent problems such as unemployment and poverty. Some of the issues they face are not about money and jobs, but are, rather, symbolic and perceptual. How are American Indians seen by the larger society? What stereotypes linger in American popular culture? How might these stereotypes affect the ability of American Indians to argue their causes?

The controversies over using Indian mascots for athletic teams illustrate these symbolic battles. Is

there any real harm in using team names such as "Indians," "Seminoles," or "Braves"? Are people who object to these names carrying political correctness and sensitivity too far?

The excerpts below present both sides of this argument. Journalists Price and Woo, in the March 4, 2002, issue of Sports Illustrated (SI), argue that the team names are not offensive to sports fans and, in fact, to most American Indians. The opposing point of view is presented by a group of five academics and Indian activists. They raise a number of issues about

Indian Symbols and Mascots Are Not Offensive

S. L. PRICE AND ANDREA WOO

[The thorniest word problem in sports today is] the use of Native American names and mascots by high school, college and professional teams. For more than 30 years the debate has been raging over whether names such as Redskins, Braves, Chiefs and Indians honor or defile Native Americans, whether clownish figures like the Cleveland Indians' Chief Wahoo have any place in today's racially sensitive climate and whether the sight of thousands of non-Native Americans doing the tomahawk chop at Atlanta's Turner Field is mindless fun or mass bigotry. It's an argument that, because it mixes mere sports with the sensitivities of a people who were nearly exterminated, seems both trivial and profound. . . .

[The case of Betty Ann Gross, a member of the Sisseton-Wahpeton Sioux tribe] illustrates how slippery the issue can be. She grew up on a reservation in South Dakota and went to Sisseton High, a public school on the reservation whose teams are called the Redmen. Gross, 49, can't recall a time when people on the reservation weren't arguing about the team name, evenly divided between those who were proud of it and those who were ashamed. Gross recently completed a study that led the South Dakota state government to change the names of 38 places and landmarks around the state, yet she has mixed feelings on the sports issue. She wants Indian mascots and the tomahawk chop discarded, but she has no problem with team names like the Fighting Sioux (University of North Dakota) or even the Redskins. "There's a lot of division," Gross says. . . .

Although most Native American activists and tribal leaders consider Indian team names and mascots offensive, neither Native Americans in general nor a cross-section of U.S. sports fans agree. That is one of the findings of a poll conducted for *SI.* . . . The pollsters interviewed 351 Native Americans (217 living on reservations and 134 living off) and 743 fans. Their responses were weighted according to U.S. census figures for age, race and gender and for distribution of Native Americans on and off reservations. With a margin of error of ±4%, 83% of the Indians said that professional teams should not stop using Indian nicknames, mascots or symbols, and 79% of the fans agreed with them. . . . When pollsters asked about the Washington Redskins, they found no great resentment toward the name. Instead, they again found agreement between Native Americans and fans (69% of the former and 74% of the latter do not object to the name). . . .

Regardless, the campaign to erase Indian team names and symbols nationwide has been a success. Though Native American activists have made little progress at the highest level of pro sports . . . their single-minded pursuit of the issue has literally changed the face of sports in the U.S. Since 1969 more than 600 school teams and minor league professional clubs have dropped nicknames deemed offensive by Native American groups. . . .

While those who support names such as Seminoles (Florida State) and [Atlanta] Braves can argue that the words celebrate Native American traditions, applying that claim to the Redskins is absurd. Nevertheless, Redskins vice president Karl Swanson says the name "symbolizes courage, dignity and leadership and has always been employed in that manner"—conveniently ignoring the fact that in popular usage dating back four centuries, the word has been a slur based on skin color. . . . Many experts on Native American history point out that . . . the word redskin was first used by whites who paid and received bounties for dead Indians. . . .

However, what's most important, Swanson counters, is intent: Because the Redskins and their fans mean nothing racist by using the nickname, it isn't racist or offensive. Not so, says Suzan Harjo (a Native American activist): "There's no more derogatory word that's used against us . . . in the English language. . . . Everyone knows that it has never been an honorific. It's a terrible insult." . . .

That the name is offensive to Native Americans is easy for non-Natives to presume. It resonates when an Olympic hero and former Marine Corps captain such as Billy Mills (a Native American and a Gold Medal winner in the 1964 Olympics), who speaks out against Indian names and mascots at schools around the country, insists that a team named Redskins in the capital of the nation that committed genocide against Native Americans is the equivalent of a soccer team in Germany being called the Berlin Kikes.

Somehow that message is lost on most of Mills's fellow Native Americans. Asked if they were offended by the name Redskins, 75% of Native American respondents in *SI*'s poll said they were not, and even on reservations, where Native American culture and influence are perhaps felt most intensely, 62% said they weren't offended. . . . Only 29% of Native Americans . . . thought [the owner of the Redskins] should change his team's name. Such indifference implies a near total disconnect between Native American activists and the general Native American population on this issue. . . .

The Utes's experience with the University of Utah might serve as a model for successful resolution of conflicts over Indian nicknames. Four years ago the council met with university officials, who made it clear that they would change their teams' name, the Running Utes, if the tribe found it objectionable. . . . The council was perfectly happy to have the Ute name continue to circulate in the nation's sports pages. . . . Florida State, likewise, uses the name Seminoles for its teams with the express approval of the Seminole nation. . . . Like the Ute tribe, most Native Americans have no problem with teams using [Indian] names. . . .

SOURCE: Price, S. L., & Woo, Andrea (2002). "The Indian Wars: The Campaign Against Indian Nicknames and Mascots Presumes That They Offend Native Americans—But Do They? We Took a Poll, and You Won't Believe the Results" (Special report). *Sports Illustrated*, March 4, pp. 66–73.

Mascots Are Offensive

C. RICHARD KING, ELLEN J. STAUROWSKY, LAWRENCE BACA, R. DAVIS, AND CORNEL PEWEWARDY

To fully understand both the *SI* article and ongoing controversy about mascots, one must grasp the history of Indian symbols in sports. . . . Native American mascots emerged (mainly) in the early 1900s, after [the end of military hostilities]. . . . These mascots were part of a larger phenomenon of increased prevalence of Native American images in U.S. popular culture, including Western movies, symbols for beer and butter, and art in homes. One of the reasons why most Americans find the mascots unremarkable . . . is because of the prevalence of similar images throughout U.S. popular culture. . . .

Historically, the most popular sport mascots have been animals associated with aggression (e.g., Tigers) and Native Americans (e.g., Indians, Chiefs, Braves, and so forth). Although other ethnic groups have been occasionally used as mascots, these mascots differ from Native American mascots in several ways: [these mascots] are often (a) a people that do not exist today (e.g., Spartans); (b) less associated with aggression (e.g., Scots); (c) selected by people from the same ethnicity (e.g., Irish Americans at Notre Dame); and (d) not mimicked to nearly the same degree.

Native American mascots emerged in a context in which many non-Native Americans were "playing Indian." Still today, children don "Indian" costumes at Halloween, "act like Indians" during "Cowboy and Indian" games, "become Indian Princesses" at the YMCA, and perform "Indian rituals" at summer camps. Adults belong to organizations that involve learning "Indian ways" and performing "Indian rituals." Non-Native Americans have created an imaginary version of Indianness that they sometimes enact, and they expect real Native Americans to either ignore, affirm, or validate such myths and practices. Similar practices applied to other races/ethnicities, such as "playing Black" or "playing Jewish," would not be accepted in our society today.

Activism against Native American mascots has been evident for more than 30 years. Since the early 1990s, this activism has become more widespread [and] emerged from Native American individuals, groups, and communities that work on a variety of other issues, such as treaty, economic, cultural, environmental, health, and educational issues. Although many U.S. citizens see the mascot issue as emerging "out of the blue," many Native American organizations see the elimination of such mascots as part of a larger agenda of reducing societal stereotyping about Native Americans (in the media, school curriculums, and so forth) and informing the public about the realities of Native American lives. An increase in accurate information about Native Americans is viewed as necessary for the achievement of other goals such as poverty reduction, educational advancements, and securing treaty rights.

Anti-mascot activists articulate many different arguments against the mascots. First, they assert that the mascots stereotype Native Americans as only existing in the past, having a single culture, and being aggressive fighters. Second, they hold that these stereotypes influence the way people perceive and treat Native Americans. Such imagery is seen as affecting Native American images of themselves, creating a hostile climate for many Native Americans, and preventing people from understanding current Native American realities, which affects public policy relative to Native Americans. Third, the activists state that no racial/cultural group should be mimicked (especially in regard to sacred items/practices), even if such mimicking is "culturally accurate." And fourth, they argue that Native Americans should have control over how they are represented. . . .

Native American mascots are rooted in the bloodthirsty savage stereotype, as it is this stercotype that is linked to desirable athletic qualities such as having a fighting spirit and being aggressive, brave, stoic, proud, and persevering. . . .

Of course, even [this] so-called positive stereotype [is] ultimately negative. [All] stereotypes fail to recognize diversity among the people who are being stereotyped. . . . Most people deny that they believe any racial stereotypes. . . . When we do notice our own stereotyping, it is often because our beliefs are very negative (e.g., believing that African Americans are criminal or Puerto Ricans are lazy). When our stereotypes are "positive" (e.g., Jews as good at business or Asians as smart), we tend to think that these beliefs are not stereotypical and thus not racist.

Sport mascots are based on what is today perceived as "positive" ideas about Native Americans: that they are brave, principled, persevering, good fighters. This "positive cast" to the mascot stereotype leads most to conclude that the mascots are not racist. In fact, it is this "positive cast" to the mascot stereotype that leads many mascot supporters to think that the mascots actually counter racism by "honoring" Native Americans. . . .

It is not surprising that some Native Americans embrace "positive" stereotypes of Native Americans, and thus that some are not critical of Native American mascots. There are several factors that encourage Native Americans to accept, internalize, celebrate, and even capitalize on, "positive" stereotypes of Native Americans. First, many people do not define so-called positive stereotypes as stereotypes or racist. In fact, a group that experiences a great deal of inequality may be especially attracted to any imagery that is positive, as such imagery might be a relief from the negative. Second, throughout much of U.S. history, Native people have faced intense pressures to acculturate and have been exposed to many of the same stereotypical images of Native Americans as non-Natives have. These pressures have certainly resulted in some Natives adopting "dominant/White/outsider views" of Native Americans. Third, given the destruction of Native economies and the resulting economic destitution, some Native people have turned to the marketing of their ethnicity, or an acceptable Hollywood version of their ethnicity, to survive, including teaching "Native spirituality" to non-Native Americans; selling Native jewelry and art; and managing Native tourist establishments.

In conclusion, to understand the Native American mascot issue, and the *SI* article, one needs to understand the social context surrounding the mascots. Most important, one must understand the historically rooted, but contemporarily alive, stereotypes of Native Americans. Native American mascots emerged from these stereotypes, and these mascots continue to reinforce these stereotypes. The continued prevalence of these stereotypes inhibits social changes that would better contemporary Native American lives.

SOURCE: King, C. Richard, Staurowsky, Ellen J., Baca, Lawrence, Davis, R., & Pewewardy, Cornel (2002). "Of Polls and Race Prejudice: Sports Illustrated's Errant 'Indian Wars.' *Journal of Sport and Social Issues,* 26:381–403.

Debate Questions to Consider

1. Price and Woo argue that the majority of American Indians polled did not object to the use of Indian team mascots. How relevant is this point to the debate? Should questions such as these be decided by "popular vote," or are there deeper principles that should guide public policy? If so, what are those principles, and how should they be applied?

2. Price and Woo quote an official of the Washington Redskins franchise as arguing that the team uses the term to honor American Indians for their courage and dignity. Should "intent" matter in deciding whether a term is insulting or offensive? Who should decide these matters? The team? The tribes? Someone else?

3. What arguments do King et al. make about why these matters are important? What real harm comes from using Indian team mascots? Are their arguments convincing? Why or why not? What are "positive stereotypes," and how do they differ (if at all) from negative stereotypes? Are positive stereotypes less harmful than negative stereotypes?

4. Is there a gender dimension to these arguments? Price and Woo mention the controversy about a South Dakota High School using "Redmen" as a team name. What do you suppose the women's teams at this school were called? Lady Redmen? Redwomen? How is this handled on your campus? Are the women's athletic teams distinguished by adding the modifier "Lady" or "Women"? What issues arise from this (very common) pattern? How do these issues matter?

5. Ultimately, is all of this just a matter of political correctness? What is at stake here (if anything)?

Main Points

*   American Indian and Anglo-American cultures are vastly different, and these differences have hampered communication and understanding, usually in ways that harmed American Indians or weakened the integrity of their tribal structures.

*   At the beginning of the 20th century, American Indians faced the paternalistic reservation system, poverty and powerlessness, rural isolation and marginalization, and the BIA. American Indians continued to lose land and other resources.

- The Indian Reorganization Act (IRA) of 1934 attempted to increase tribal autonomy and to provide mechanisms for improving the quality of life on the reservations. The policy of termination was proposed in the 1950s. The policy was a disaster, and the tribes that were terminated suffered devastating economic losses and drastic declines in quality of life.

- American Indians began to urbanize rapidly in the 1950s but are still less urbanized than the population as a whole. They are the least urbanized American minority group.

- The Red Power movement rose to prominence in the 1960s and had some successes but was often simply ignored. The Red Power movement was partly assimilationist even though it pursued pluralistic goals and greater autonomy for the tribes.

- Current conflicts between American Indians and the dominant group center on control of natural resources, preservation of treaty rights, and treaties that have been broken in the past. Another possible source of development and conflict is in the potentially lucrative gambling industry.

- There is some indication that anti-Indian prejudice has shifted to more "modern" forms. Institutional discrimination and access to education and employment remain major problems confronting American Indians.

- American Indians have preserved much of their traditional culture, although in altered form. The secondary structural assimilation of American Indians remains relatively low, despite recent improvements in quality of life for many tribes. Primary structural assimilation is comparatively high.

- Over the course of the last 100 years, American Indians have struggled from a position of powerlessness and isolation. Today, the group faces an array of problems similar to those faced by all American colonized minority groups of color as they try to find ways to raise their quality of life and continue their commitment to their tribes and to an Indian identity.

- The public sociology assignment in the introduction to Part 3 will acquaint you with the history of Indian loss of land in your area and with the continuing unique relationship between American Indian tribes and the federal government. How did the loss of land you will document contribute to the present status of the tribe?

Study Site on the Web

Don't forget the interactive quizzes and other resources and learning aids at www.pineforge.com/healeystudy5.

For Further Reading

Amott, Teresa, & Matthaei, Julie. (1991). "I Am the Fire of Time: American Indian Women." In T. Amott & J. Matthaei (Eds.), *Race, Gender, and Work: A Multicultural History of Women in the United States* (pp. 31–62). Boston: South End Press.

Good overview of the history and present situation of American Indian women.

Bordewich, Fergus. (1996). *Killing the White Man's Indian*. New York: Doubleday.

   A comprehensive, dispassionate analysis of current problems and future possibilities.

Brown, Dee. (1970). *Bury My Heart at Wounded Knee*. New York: Holt, Rinehart & Winston.

   A passionately written, highly readable account of the military defeat and the establishment of dominance over American Indians.

Deloria, Vine. (1969). *Custer Died for Your Sins*. New York: Macmillan.

Deloria, Vine. (1970). *We Talk, You Listen*. New York: Macmillan.

Deloria, Vine. (1995). *Red Earth, White Lies*. New York: Scribner's.

   The three major works of the well-known American Indian activist, writer, and professor of Indian studies.

The Harvard Project on American Indian Economic Development. (2008). *The State of the Native Nations*. New York: Oxford University Press.

   A comprehensive look at economic development and other issues on reservations across the nation.

Nabakov, Peter. (Ed.). 1999. *Native American Testimony*. New York: Penguin.

   A collection of personal accounts by American Indians from pre-Columbian times to the present day.

Snipp, C. Matthew. (1989). *American Indians: The First of This Land*. New York: Russell Sage Foundation.

   A valuable scholarly study covering a variety of aspects of the American Indian condition.

Questions for Review and Study

   1.   What were the most important cultural differences between American Indian tribes and the dominant society? How did these affect relations between the two groups?

   2.   Compare and contrast the effects of paternalism and coercive acculturation on American Indians after the end of the contact period with those of African Americans under slavery. What similarities and differences existed in the two situations? Which system was more oppressive and controlling? How? How did these different situations shape the futures of the groups?

   3.   How did federal Indian policy change over the course of the 20th century? What effects did these changes have on the tribes? Which were more beneficial? Why? What was the role of the Indian protest movement in shaping these policies?

   4.   What options do American Indians have for improving their position in the larger society and developing their reservations? Which strategies seem to have the most promise? Which seem less effective? Why?

   5.   Compare and contrast the contact situations of American Indians, African Americans, and Australian Aborigines. What are the most crucial differences in the situations? What implications did these differences have for the development of each group's situation after the initial contact situation?

   6.   Characterize the present situation of American Indians in terms of acculturation and integration. How do they compare with African Americans? What factors in the experiences of the two groups might help explain contemporary differences?

7. What gender differences can you identify in the experiences of American Indians? How do these compare with the gender differences in the experiences of African Americans?

8. Given the information and ideas presented in this chapter, speculate about the future of American Indians. How likely are American Indian cultures and languages to survive? What are the prospects for achieving equality?

Internet Research Project

Use the Internet to develop a profile of American Indians by answering the questions asked here. Some addresses are provided as starting points, but you will have to use your own initiative to cruise the Internet and answer all questions fully.

A. Numbers (U.S. Bureau of the Census: http://www.census.gov; Bureau of Indian Affairs: http://www.doi.gov/bureau-indian-affairs.html)

1. Counting people who select only one racial category, how many American Indians are there?

2. How does the number change when people who selected more than one category are counted as members of the group?

3. Which of these two totals (if either) should be regarded as the "true" number of American Indians? Why?

4. How many separate tribes are recognized by the federal government?

5. How many federal reservations are there? In what regions of the nation are they concentrated? Which is the largest? Which is the smallest?

B. Gambling (National Indian Gaming Association: http://www.indiangaming.org/)

1. How many reservations are involved in gaming or gambling?

2. What is the approximate annual revenue from these enterprises?

3. How is that revenue used?

C. Health (Indian Health Services: http://www.ihs.gov)

1. What are the birthrates and death rates for Native Americans?

2. Are these higher or lower than national norms or the rates for white Americans?

3. What are the mortality rates for various age-groups compared with national norms?

	Death Rates	National Norms
Infants (age 0–1)	_____	_____
Young adults (18–25)	_____	_____
Senior Citizens (65+)	_____	_____

4. Select two age-groups and find the five most common causes of death for the group:

Age-Group 1	Age-Group 2
1. _____	1. _____
2. _____	2. _____
3. _____	3. _____
4. _____	4. _____
5. _____	5. _____

5. Describe how these patterns vary from national norms.

D. Issues (National Congress of American Indians: http://www.ncai.org. Also, search for American Indian newspapers or periodicals that are online. For example, Indian Country Today, "America's Leading Indian News Source," is available at http://www.indiancountry.com)

1. Cite and briefly explain three current issues in *Indian Country Today* or whatever newspaper or periodical you've found.

2. Analyze each issue in terms of the concepts used in the text (especially assimilation, pluralism, self-determination or development of the reservation, institutional discrimination, protest and resistance, and inequality).

3. How would members of other groups (e.g., white or black Americans) view each issue?

Hispanic Americans CHAPTER 8

Colonization, Immigration, and Ethnic Enclaves

The United States is home to many different Spanish-origin groups. Before the Declaration of Independence was signed, before slavery began, even before Jamestown was founded, the ancestors of some of these groups were already in North America. Other Hispanic groups are recent immigrants and new members of U.S. society. The label *Hispanic American* includes a number of groups that are diverse and distinct from each other. These groups connect themselves to a variety of traditions; like the larger society, they are dynamic and change-able, unfinished and evolving. Hispanic Americans share a language and some cultural traits but do not generally think of themselves as a single social entity. Many identify with their national-origin groups (e.g., Mexican American) rather than broader, more encompassing labels.

In this chapter, we look at the development of Hispanic American groups over the past century, exam-ine their contemporary relations with the larger society, and assess their current status. We focus on the three largest Hispanic groups, Mexican Americans, Puerto Ricans, and Cuban Americans, but include several smaller groups as well: Exhibit 8.1 shows the size of the largest Hispanic groups and some information

Exhibit 8.1 — Size and Growth of Hispanic Groups by Nation or Territory of Origin, 1990–2006

Country of Origin	1990	2000	2006	Growth (Number of Times Larger), 1990–2006	Percentage of Total Population, 2006
Mexico	13,496,000	20,641,000	28,339,354	2.1	9.5
Puerto Rico[a]	2,728,000	3,406,000	3,987,947	1.5	1.3
Cuba	1,044,000	1,242,000	1,520,276	1.5	0.5
Dominican Republic	520,521	799,768	1,217,225	2.3	0.4
El Salvador	565,081	708,741	1,371,666	2.4	0.5
Colombia	378,726	496,748	801,363	2.1	0.3
Other Hispanics[b]	3,621,672	4,794,763	7,014,447	1.9	2.3
Total Hispanic	22,355,990	32,091,000	44,252,278	2.0	14.8
Percentage of U.S. Population	9.0%	11.4%	14.8%		
Total U.S. Population	248,710,000	281,422,000	299,398,485	1.2	

SOURCE: 1990: U.S. Bureau of the Census (1990); 2000: U.S. Bureau of the Census (2000f); 2006: U.S. Bureau of the Census (2007a).

a. Living on U.S. mainland only.

b. Includes people from Colombia, Peru, Ecuador, Argentina, and many other nations.

on growth since 1990. Mexican Americans, the largest single group, are 9.5% of the total U.S. population (and about two thirds of all Hispanic Americans), but the other groups are small in size. Considered as a single group, however, Hispanic Americans are more than 14% of the total population, and they became the largest U.S. minority group, surpassing African Americans, in the spring of 2004. The relative sizes of the major subgroups of Latino Americans are displayed in Exhibit 8.2, and Exhibit 8.3 shows the countries of origin of the three largest Hispanic American groups.

Latinos are growing rapidly, partly because of their relatively high birthrates, but mainly because of immigration. The number of Mexican Americans more than doubled between 1990 and 2005, and Hispanic groups in general are growing at rates above the national

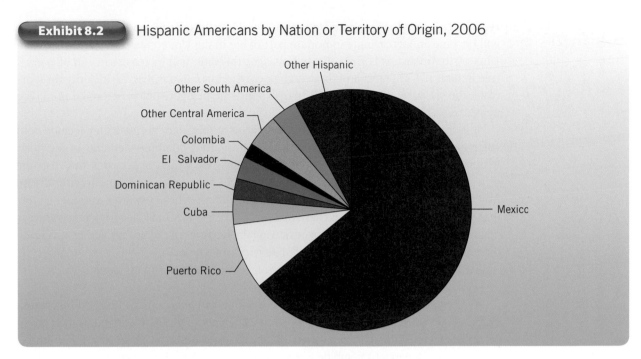

Exhibit 8.2 Hispanic Americans by Nation or Territory of Origin, 2006

Other Hispanic

Other South America

Other Central America

Colombia

El Salvador

Dominican Republic

Cuba

Puerto Rico

Mexico

SOURCE: U.S. Bureau of the Census (2007a).

Exhibit 8.3 Points of Origin for Mexicans, Cuban Americans, and Puerto Ricans

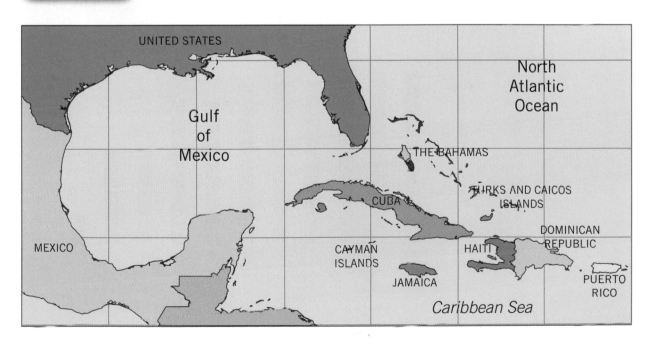

average. This growth is projected to continue well into the century, and Hispanic Americans will become an increasingly important part of life in the United States. Today, more than 1 out of 10 Americans is Hispanic, but by 2050, this ratio will increase to 1 out of every 4 (see Exhibit 1.1). One result of these high rates of immigration is that the majority (in some cases, the great majority) of many Hispanic groups are first generation or foreign-born. The percentages are displayed in Exhibit 8.4.

It is appropriate to discuss Hispanic Americans at this point because they include both colonized and immigrant groups, and in that sense, they combine elements of the polar extremes of Blauner's typology of minority groups. We would expect that the Hispanic groups that were more colonized in the past would have much in common with African Americans and Native Americans today. Hispanic groups whose experiences more closely model those of immigrants would have different characteristics and follow different pathways of adaptation. We test these ideas by reviewing the histories of the groups and by analyzing their current status and degree of acculturation and integration.

Two additional introductory comments can be made about Hispanic Americans:

• Hispanic Americans are partly an ethnic minority group (i.e., identified by cultural characteristics such as language) and partly a racial minority group (identified by their physical appearance). Latinos bring a variety of racial backgrounds to U.S. society. For example, most Mexican Americans combine European and Native American ancestries and are identifiable by their physical traits as well as by their culture and language. Puerto Ricans, in

Exhibit 8.4 Percentage Foreign-Born by Country of Origin, 2006

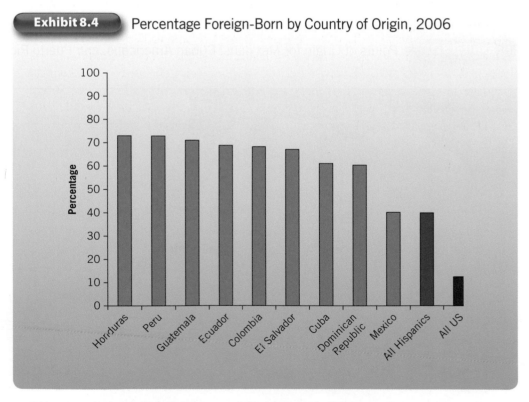

SOURCE: U.S. Bureau of the Census (2007a).

contrast, are a mixture of white and black ancestry. The original inhabitants of the island, the Arawak and Caribe tribes, were decimated by the Spanish conquest, and the proportion of Native American ancestry is much smaller in Puerto Rico than it is in Mexico. Africans were originally brought to the island as slaves, and there has been considerable intermarriage between whites and blacks. The Puerto Rican population today varies greatly in its racial characteristics, combining every conceivable combination of white and African ancestry. Hispanic Americans are often the victims of racial discrimination in the United States. Racial differences often (but not always) overlap with cultural distinctions and reinforce the separation of Hispanic Americans from Anglo-American society. Even members of the group who are completely acculturated may still experience discrimination based on their physical appearance.

- As is the case with all American minority groups, labels and group names are important. The term *Hispanic American* is widely applied to this group and might seem neutral and inoffensive to non-Hispanics. In fact, a recent survey shows that the preferred designation varies widely by the primary language and generation of the respondent. About two thirds of Spanish speakers and first-generation (foreign-born) individuals prefer to identify themselves in terms of their countries of origin, while a slight majority of English speakers and third-generation Hispanics prefer to be called simply "American" (Pew Hispanic Center, 2005). An earlier study showed that a sizable majority (67%) of the group prefer the *Hispanic* label to *Latino* (Jones, 2001). At any rate, both the Hispanic and Latino labels are similar to *American Indian,* in that they were invented and applied by the dominant group and may reinforce the mistaken perception that all Spanish-speaking peoples are the same. Also, the term *Hispanic* highlights Spanish heritage and language but does not acknowledge the roots of these groups in African American and Native American civilizations. Further, the label is sometimes mistakenly applied to immigrant groups that bring French, Portuguese, or English traditions (e.g., Haitians, Brazilians, and Jamaicans, respectively). On the other hand, the *Latino* label stresses the common origins of these groups in Latin America and the fact that each culture is a unique blend of diverse traditions. In this chapter, the terms *Latino* and *Hispanic* are used interchangeably.[1]

Mexican Americans

We applied the Noel and Blauner hypotheses to this group in Chapter 4. Mexicans were conquered and colonized in the 19th century and used as a cheap labor force in agriculture, ranching, mining, railroad construction, and other areas of the dominant group economy in the Southwest. In the competition for control of land and labor, they became a minority group, and the contact situation left them with few power resources with which to pursue their self-interests.

By the dawn of the 20th century, the situation of Mexican Americans resembled that of American Indians in some ways. Both groups were small, numbering about 0.5% of the total population (Cortes, 1980, p. 702). Both differed from the dominant group in culture and language, and both were impoverished, relatively powerless, and isolated in rural areas distant from the centers of industrialization and modernization. In other ways, Mexican Americans resembled African Americans in the South in that they also supplied much of the labor power for the agricultural economy of their region and both were limited to low-paying occupations and subordinate status in the social structure. All three groups were colonized and, at least in the early decades of the 20th century, lacked the resources to end their exploitation and protect their cultural heritages from continual attack by the dominant society (Mirandé, 1985, p. 32).

There were also some important differences in the situation of Mexican Americans and the other two colonized minority groups. Perhaps the most crucial difference was the proximity of the sovereign nation of Mexico. Population movement across the border was constant, and Mexican culture and the Spanish language were continually rejuvenated, even as they were attacked and disparaged by Anglo-American society.

Photo 8.1

Dancers celebrate Cinco de Mayo, Mexican Independence Day.

© Morton Beebe/Corbis.

Cultural Patterns

Besides language differences, Mexican American and Anglo-American cultures differ in many ways. Whereas the dominant society is largely Protestant, the overwhelming majority of Mexican Americans are Catholic, and the church remains one of the most important institutions in any Mexican American community. Religious practices also vary; Mexican Americans (especially men) are relatively inactive in church attendance, preferring to express their spiritual concerns in more spontaneous, less routinized ways.

In the past, everyday life among Mexican Americans was often described in terms of the "culture of poverty" (see Chapter 6), an idea originally based on research in several different Hispanic communities (see Lewis, 1959, 1965, 1966). This perspective asserts that Mexican Americans suffer from an unhealthy value system that includes a weak work ethic, fatalism, and other negative attitudes. Today, this characterization is widely regarded as exaggerated or simply mistaken. More recent research shows that the traits associated with the culture of poverty tend to characterize people who are poor and uneducated, rather than any particular racial or ethnic group. In fact, a number of studies show that there is little difference between the value systems of Mexican Americans and other Americans of similar length of residence in the United States, social class, and educational background (e.g., see Buriel, 1993; Moore & Pinderhughes, 1993; Pew Hispanic Center, 2005, p. 20; Valentine & Mosley, 2000).

Another area of cultural difference involves **machismo**, a value system that stresses male dominance, honor, virility, and violence. The stereotypes of the dominant group exaggerate the negative aspects of machismo and often fail to recognize that machismo can also be expressed through being a good provider and a respected father, as well as in other nondestructive ways. In fact, the concern for male dignity is not unique to Hispanics and can be found in many cultures in varying strengths and expressions, including Anglo-American. Thus, this difference is one of degree rather than kind (Moore & Pachon, 1985).

Compared with Anglo-Americans, Mexican Americans tend to place more value on family relations and obligations. Strong family ties can be the basis for support networks and cooperative efforts but can also conflict with the emphasis on individualism and individual success in the dominant culture. For example, strong family ties may inhibit geographical mobility and people's willingness to pursue educational and occupational opportunities distant from their home communities (Moore, 1970, p. 127).

These cultural and language differences have inhibited communication with the dominant group and have served as the basis for excluding Mexican Americans from the larger society. However, they also have provided a basis for group cohesion and unity that has sustained common action and protest activity.

Immigration

Although Mexican Americans originated as a colonized minority group, their situation since the early 1900s (and especially since the 1960s) has been largely shaped by immigration. The numbers of legal Mexican immigrants to the United States are shown in Exhibit 8.5. The fluctuations in the rate of immigration can be explained by conditions in Mexico; the varying demand for labor in the low-paying, unskilled sector of the U.S. economy; broad changes in North America and the world; and changing federal immigration policy. As you will see, competition, one of the key variables in Noel's hypothesis, has shaped the relationships between Mexican immigrants and the larger American society.

Exhibit 8.5 Legal Immigrants From Mexico, 1900s–2005

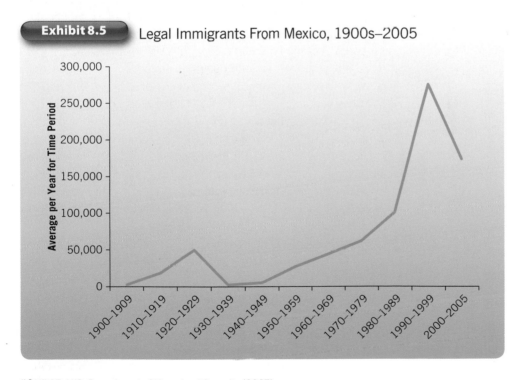

SOURCE: U.S. Department of Homeland Security (2007).

The Meaning of *Macho*

Words as well as people can immigrate, and in both cases, the process can be transforming. In the following passage, Rose Guilbault (1993), a newspaper editor and columnist, reflects on the meaning of one term that has become central to the dominant group's view of Hispanic males. The image evoked by the term *macho* changed from positive to negative as it found its way into American English, a process that reflects dominant-minority relations and partly defines them.

Americanization Is Tough on "Macho"

Rose Del Castillo Guilbault

What is macho? That depends on which side of the border you come from. . . . The negative connotations of macho in this country are troublesome to Hispanics.

The Hispanic macho is manly, responsible, hardworking, a man in charge, a patriarch. A man who expresses strength through silence. . . .

The American macho is a chauvinist, a brute, uncouth, loud, abrasive, capable of inflicting pain, and sexually promiscuous.

Quintessential macho models in this country are Sylvester Stallone, Arnold Schwarzenegger, and Charles Bronson. . . . They exude toughness, independence, masculinity. But a closer look reveals their machismo is really violence masquerading as courage, sullenness disguised as silence and irresponsibility camouflaged as independence. . . .

In Spanish, macho ennobles Latin males. In English it devalues them. This pattern seems consistent with the conflicts ethnic minority males experience in this country. Typically the cultural traits other societies value don't translate as desirable characteristics in America.

I watched my own father struggle with these cultural ambiguities. He worked on a farm for 20 years. He laid down miles of irrigation pipe, carefully plowed long, neat rows in fields, . . . stoically worked 20-hour days during the harvest season, accepting the long hours as part of agricultural work. When the boss complained or upbraided him for minor mistakes, he kept quiet, even when it was obvious that the boss had erred.

He handled the most menial tasks with pride. At home he was a good provider. . . . Americans regarded my father as decidedly un-macho. His character was interpreted as non-assertive, his loyalty non-ambition, and his quietness, ignorance. I once overheard the boss's son blame him for plowing crooked rows. . . . My father merely smiled at the lie, knowing the boy had done it, . . . confident his good work was well-known . . . . Seeing my embarrassment, my father dismissed the incident, saying "They're the dumb ones. Imagine me fighting with a kid."

I tried not to look at him with American eyes because sometimes the reflection hurt. . . .

In the United States, I believe it was the feminist movement of the early '70s that changed macho's meaning. Perhaps my generation of Latin women was in part responsible. I recall Chicanas complaining about the chauvinistic nature of Latin men and the notion they wanted their women barefoot, pregnant, and in the kitchen. The generalization that Latin men embodied chauvinistic traits led to this . . . twist of semantics. Suddenly a word that represented something positive in one culture became a negative stereotype in another. . . .

The impact of language in our society is undeniable. And the misuse of macho hints at a deeper cultural misunderstanding that extends beyond mere word definitions.

SOURCE: Guilbault, Rose Del Castillo (1993). "Americanization Is Tough on 'Macho.'" In D. La Guardia & H. Guth (Eds.), *American Voices*, pp. 163–165. Mountain View, CA: Mayfield Press. First published in "This World," *San Francisco Chronicle*, August 20, 1989.

Push and Pull. Like the massive wave of immigrants from Europe that arrived between the 1820s and the 1920s (see Chapter 2), Mexicans have been pushed from their homeland and toward the United States by a variety of sweeping changes in their society and in the global system of societies. European immigration was propelled by the fundamental changes in European society wrought by industrialization, urbanization, and rapid population growth. Mexican immigrants have been motivated by similarly broad forces, including continuing industrialization and globalization.

At the heart of the immigration lies a simple fact: The almost 2,000-mile-long border between Mexico and the United States is the longest continuous point of contact between a less developed and a more developed nation in the world. For the past century, the United States has developed faster than Mexico, moving from an industrial to a postindustrial society and sustaining a substantially higher standard of living. The continuing wage gap between the two nations has made even menial work in the North attractive to millions of Mexicans (and other Central and South Americans). The less-developed Mexican economy has been unable to supply full employment for its population, creating a symbiotic gap between the two nations: Mexico has generally produced a large number of people who need work, and the United States has offered jobs that pay more—often much more—than the wages available south of the border. Just as the air flows from high to low pressure, people move from areas of lower to higher economic opportunities. The flow is not continuous, however, and has been affected by conditions in both the sending and receiving nations.

Conditions in Mexico, Fluctuating Demand for Labor, and Federal Immigration Policy

Generally, for the past 100 years, Mexico has served as a reserve pool of cheap labor for the benefit of U.S. businesses, agricultural interests, and other groups, and the volume of immigration largely reflects changing economic conditions in the United States. Immigration increased with good times in the United States and decreased when times were bad, a pattern reinforced by the policies and actions of the federal government. The most important events in the complex history of Mexican immigration to the United States are presented in Exhibit 8.6, along with some comments regarding the nature of the event and its effects.

Prior to the early 1900s, the volume of immigration was generally low and largely unregulated. People crossed the border—in both directions—as the need arose, informally and without restriction. The volume of immigration and concern about controlling the border began to rise with the increase of political and economic turmoil in Mexico in the early decades of the 20th century but still remained a comparative trickle.

Immigration increased in the 1920s when federal legislation curtailed the flow of cheap labor from Europe and then decreased in the 1930s when hard times came to the United States (and the world) during the Great Depression. Many Mexicans in the United States returned home during that decade, sometimes voluntarily, often by force. As competition for jobs increased, efforts began to expel Mexican laborers, just as the Noel hypothesis would predict. The federal government instituted a **repatriation** campaign aimed specifically at deporting

Exhibit 8.6 Significant Dates in Mexican Immigration

Dates	Event	Result	Effect on Immigration
1910	Mexican Revolution	Political turmoil and unrest in Mexico	Increased
Early 20th century	Mexican industrialization	Many groups (especially rural peasants) displaced	Increased
1920s	U.S. passes the National Origins Act of 1924	Decreased immigration from Europe	Increased
1930s	Great Depression	Decreased demand for labor and increased competition for jobs leads to repatriation campaign	Decreased, many return to Mexico
1940s	World War II	Increased demand for labor leads to Bracero Guest Worker Program	Increased
1950s	Concern over illegal immigrants	Operation Wetback	Decreased, many return to Mexico
1965	Repeal of National Origins Act	New immigration policy gives high priority to close family of citizens	Increased (see Exhibit 8.5)
1986	IRCA	Illegal immigrants given opportunity to legalize status	Many illegal immigrants gain legal status
1994	NAFTA	Borders more open, many groups in Mexico (especially rural peasants) displaced	Increased

IRCA: Immigration Reform and Control Act.
NAFTA: North American Free Trade Agreement.

illegal Mexican immigrants. In many localities, repatriation was pursued with great zeal, and the campaign intimidated many legal immigrants and native-born Mexican Americans into moving to Mexico. The result was that the Mexican American population of the United States declined by an estimated 40% during the 1930s (Cortes, 1980, p. 711).

When the depression ended and U.S. society began to mobilize for World War II, federal policy toward immigrants from Mexico changed once more as employers again turned to Mexico for workers. In 1942, the *Bracero program* was initiated to permit contract laborers, usually employed in agriculture and other areas requiring unskilled labor, to work in the United States for a limited amount of time. When their contracts expired, the workers were required to return to Mexico.

The Bracero program continued for several decades after the end of the war and was a crucial source of labor for the American economy. In 1960 alone, braceros supplied 26% of the nation's seasonal farm labor (Cortes, 1980, p. 703). The program generated millions of dollars of profit for growers and other employers, because they were paying braceros much less than American workers would have received (Amott & Matthaei, 1991, pp. 79–80).

At the same time that the Bracero program permitted immigration from Mexico, other programs and agencies worked to deport undocumented (or illegal) immigrants, large numbers of whom entered the United States with the braceros. Government efforts reached a peak in the early 1950s with "**Operation Wetback**," a program under which federal authorities deported almost 4 million Mexicans (Grebler, Moore, & Guzman, 1970, p. 521).

During Operation Wetback, raids on the homes and places of business of Mexican Americans were common, and authorities often ignored their civil and legal rights. In an untold number of cases, U.S. citizens of Mexican descent were deported along with illegal immigrants. These violations of civil and legal rights have been a continuing grievance of Mexican Americans (and other Latinos) for decades (Mirandé, 1985, pp. 70–90).

In 1965, the overtly racist national immigration policy incorporated in the 1924 National Origins Act (see Chapter 2) was replaced by a new policy that gave a high priority to immigrants who were family and kin of U.S. citizens. The immediate family (parents, spouses, and children) of U.S. citizens could enter without numerical restriction. Some numerical restrictions were placed on the number of immigrants from each sending country, but about 80% of these restricted visas were reserved for other close relatives of citizens. The remaining 20% of the visas went to people who had skills needed in the labor force (Bouvier & Gardner, 1986, pp. 13–15, 41; Rumbaut, 1991, p. 215).

Immigrants have always tended to move along chains of kinship and other social relationships, and the new policy reinforced those tendencies. The social networks connecting Latin America with the United States expanded, and the rate of immigration from Mexico increased sharply after 1965 (see Exhibit 8.5) as immigrants became citizens and sent for other family members.

Most of the Mexican immigrants, legal as well as undocumented, who have arrived since 1965 continue the pattern of seeking work in the low-wage, unskilled sectors of the labor market in the cities and fields of the Southwest. For many, work is seasonal or temporary. When the work ends, they often return to Mexico, commuting across the border as has been done for decades.

In 1986, Congress attempted to deal with illegal immigrants, most of whom were thought to be Mexican, by passing the Immigration Reform and Control Act (IRCA). This legislation allowed illegal immigrants who had been in the country continuously since 1982 to legalize their status. According to the U.S. Immigration and Naturalization Service (1993, p. 17), about 3 million people, 75% of them Mexican, have taken advantage of this provision, but this program has not slowed the volume of illegal immigration. In 1988, at the end of the amnesty application period, there were still almost 3 million undocumented immigrants in the United States. In 2006, the number of undocumented immigrants was estimated at 11.6 million (Hoefer, Rytina, & Campbell, 2007).

Immigration From Mexico Today. Mexican immigration to the U.S. continues to reflect the difference in level of development and standard of living between the two societies. Mexico remains a much more agricultural nation and continues to have a much lower standard of living, as measured by average wages, housing quality, health care, or any number of other criteria. About 40% of Mexicans live in poverty, and the population is growing rapidly, faster than good jobs can be provided. Thus, many Mexicans are unable to find a secure place in their home economy and are drawn to the opportunities for work provided by their affluent northern neighbor. Mexicans have lower levels of education, averaging just over 7 years of schooling ("Average Years of Schooling," n.d.), and consequently, they bring much lower levels of job skills and continue to compete for work in the lower levels of the U.S. job structure.

The impetus to immigrate has been reinforced by the recent globalization of the Mexican economy. In the past, the Mexican government insulated its economy from foreign competition with a variety of tariffs and barriers. These protections have been abandoned over the past several decades, and Mexico, like many less developed nations, has opened its doors to the world economy. The result has been a flood of foreign goods and capital, which, while helpful in some parts of the economy, has disrupted social life and forced many Mexicans, especially the poor and rural dwellers, out of their traditional way of life.

Probably the most significant changes to Mexican society have come from the North American Free Trade Agreement (NAFTA). Starting in 1994, this policy united the three nations of North America in a single trading zone. U.S. companies began to move their manufacturing operations to Mexico, attracted by lower wages, less stringent environmental regulations, and weak labor unions. They built factories, called *maquiladoras,* along the border and brought many new jobs to the Mexican economy. However, other jobs—no longer protected from global competition—were lost, more than offsetting these gains, and Mexican wages have actually declined since NAFTA, increasing the already large number of Mexicans living in poverty. One analyst estimates that over 2½ million families have been driven out of the rural economy because they cannot compete with U.S. and Canadian agribusinesses (Faux, 2004).

Thus, globalization in general and NAFTA in particular seem to have reinforced the long-term relationship between the two nations. Mexico, like other nations of the less developed "South," continues to produce a supply of unskilled, less-educated workers, while the United States, like other nations of the more developed and industrialized "North," provides a seemingly insatiable demand for cheap labor. Compared with what is available at home, the wages in *el Norte* are quite attractive, even when the jobs are at the margins of the mainstream economy or in the irregular, underground economy (e.g., day laborers paid off the books, illegal sweatshop jobs in the garment industry, and sex work) and even when the journey

requires Mexican immigrants to break American laws, pay large sums of money to "coyotes" to guide them across borders, and live in constant fear of raids by *La Migra*.

The Continuing Debate Over Immigration Policy

Immigration has once again become a hotly debated issue in the United States. How many immigrants should be admitted? From which nations? With what skills? Should the relatives of U.S. citizens continue to receive a high priority? And, perhaps the issue that generates the most passion, what should be done about illegal immigrants?

Virtually all of these questions, even those that are phrased in general, abstract terms, are mainly about the large volume of immigration from Mexico and the porous U.S. southern border.

The federal government is attempting to reduce the flow by building a wall on the border with Mexico and beefing up the Border Patrol, with both increased personnel and more high-tech surveillance technology. Still, communities across the nation—not just in border states—are feeling the impact of Mexican immigration and wondering how to respond. Many citizens support extreme measures to close the borders—bigger, thicker walls and even the use of deadly force—while others ponder ways to absorb the newcomers without disrupting or bankrupting local school systems, medical facilities, or housing markets. The nation is divided on many of the issues related to immigration. For example, a May 2006 poll indicated that the public is nearly evenly split on whether immigration should be kept at present levels (39%) or decreased (34%). In the same poll, a healthy minority of respondents chose a third alternative: 22% felt that immigration should be increased (Pew Hispanic Center, 2006).

A variety of reforms for immigration policy have been proposed and continue to be debated. One key issue is the treatment of illegal immigrants: Should the undocumented be summarily deported, or should some provision be made for them to legalize their status, as was done in the IRCA legislation of 1986? If the latter, should the opportunity to attain legal status be extended to all or only to immigrants who meet certain criteria (e.g., those with steady jobs and clean criminal records)? Many feel that amnesty is unjust because immigrants who entered illegally have, after all, broken the law and should be punished. Others point to the economic contributions and the damage to the economy that would result from summary, mass expulsions. Still others worry about the negative impact illegal immigrants might be having on the job prospects for the less skilled members of the larger population, including the urban underclass that is disproportionately minority. We address some of these issues later in this chapter and in Chapters 9 and 10.

Immigration, Colonization, and Intergroup Competition.

Three points can be made about Mexican immigration to the United States. First, the flow of population from Mexico was and is stimulated and sustained by powerful political and economic interests in the United States. Systems of recruitment and networks of communication and transportation have been established to routinize the flow of people and make it a predictable source of labor for the benefit of U.S. agriculture and other employers. The movement of people back and forth across the border was well established long before current efforts to regulate and control it. Depending on U.S. policy, this immigration is sometimes legal and encouraged and sometimes illegal and discouraged. Regardless of the label, the river of people has been steadily flowing for decades in response to opportunities for work in the North (Portes, 1990, pp. 160–163).

Second, Mexican immigrants enter a social system in which a colonized status for the group has already been established. The paternalistic traditions and racist systems that were established in the 19th century shaped the positions that were open to Mexican immigrants in the 20th century. Mexican Americans continued to be treated as a colonized group despite the streams of new arrivals, and the history of the group in the 20th century has many parallels with African Americans and American Indians. Thus, Mexican Americans might be thought of as a colonized minority group that happens to have a large number of immigrants or, alternatively, as an immigrant group that incorporates a strong tradition of colonization.

Third, this brief review of the twisting history of U.S. policy on Mexican immigration should serve as a reminder that levels of prejudice, racism, and discrimination increase as competition and the sense of threat between groups increases. The very qualities that make Mexican labor attractive to employers have caused bitter resentment among those segments of the Anglo population who feel that their own jobs and financial security are threatened. Often caught in the middle, Mexican immigrants and Mexican Americans have not had the resources to avoid exploitation by employers or rejection and discrimination by others. The ebb and flow of the efforts to regulate immigration (and sometimes even deport U.S. citizens of Mexican descent) can be understood in terms of competition, differentials in power, and prejudice.

Developments in the United States

As the flow of immigration from Mexico fluctuated with the need for labor, Mexican Americans struggled to improve their status. In the early decades of the 20th century, like other colonized minority groups, they faced a system of repression and control in which they were accorded few rights and had little political power.

Continuing Colonization. Throughout much of the 20th century, Mexican Americans have been limited to less desirable, low-wage jobs. Split labor markets, in which Mexican Americans are paid less than Anglos for the same jobs, have been common. The workforce has often been further split by gender, with Mexican American women assigned to the worst jobs and receiving the lowest wages in both urban and rural areas (Takaki, 1993, pp. 318–319).

Men's jobs often took them away from their families to work in the mines and fields. In 1930, 45% of all Mexican American men worked in agriculture, with another 28% in unskilled nonagricultural jobs (Cortes, 1980, p. 708). The women were often forced by economic necessity to enter the job market; in 1930, they were concentrated in farmwork (21%), unskilled manufacturing jobs (25%), and domestic and other service work (37%) (Amott & Matthaei, 1991, pp. 76–77). They were typically paid less than both Mexican American men and Anglo women. In addition to their job responsibilities, Mexican American women had to maintain their households and raise their children, often facing these tasks without a spouse (Zinn & Eitzen, 1990, p. 84).

As the United States industrialized and urbanized during the century, employment patterns became more diversified. Mexican Americans found work in manufacturing, construction, transportation, and other sectors of the economy. Some Mexican Americans, especially those of the third generation or later, moved into middle- and upper-level occupations, and some began to move out of the Southwest. Still, Mexican Americans in all regions (especially recent immigrants) tended to be concentrated at the bottom of the occupational ladder. Women increasingly worked outside the home, but their employment was largely limited to agriculture, domestic service, and the garment industry (Amott & Matthaei, 1991, pp. 76–79; Cortes, 1980, p. 708).

Like African Americans in the segregated South, Mexican Americans were excluded from the institutions of the larger society by law and by custom for much of the 20th century. There were separate (and unequal) school systems for Mexican American children, and in many communities, Mexican Americans were disenfranchised and accorded few legal or civil rights. There were "whites-only" primary elections modeled after the Jim Crow system, and residential segregation was widespread. The police and the court system generally abetted or ignored the rampant discrimination against the Mexican American community. Discrimination in the criminal justice system and civil rights violations have been continual grievances of Mexican Americans throughout the century.

Protest and Resistance. Like all minority groups, Mexican Americans have attempted to improve their collective position whenever possible. The beginnings of organized resistance and protest stretch back to the original contact period in the 19th century, when protest was usually organized on a local level. Regional and national organizations made their appearance in the 20th century (Cortes, 1980, p. 709).

As with African Americans, Mexican Americans' early protest organizations were integrationist and reflected the assimilationist values of the larger society. For example, one of the earlier and more significant groups was the League of United Latin American Citizens (LULAC), founded in Texas in 1929. LULAC promoted Americanization and greater educational opportunities for Mexican Americans. The group also worked to expand civil and political rights and to increase equality for Mexican Americans. LULAC fought numerous court battles against discrimination and racial segregation (Moore, 1970, pp. 143–145).

The workplace has been a particularly conflictual arena for Mexican Americans. Split labor market situations increased anti–Mexican American prejudice; some labor unions tried to exclude Mexican immigrants from the United States, along with immigrants from Asia and Southern and Eastern Europe (Grebler et al., 1970, pp. 90–93).

At the same time, Mexican Americans played important leadership roles in the labor movement. Since early in the century, Mexican Americans have been involved in union organizing, particularly in agriculture and mining. When excluded by Anglo labor unions, they often formed their own unions to work for the improvement of working conditions. As the 20th century progressed, the number and variety of groups pursuing the Mexican American cause increased. During World War II, Mexican Americans served in the armed forces, and, as with other minority groups, this experience increased their impatience with the constraints on their freedoms and opportunities. After the war ended, a number of new Mexican American organizations were founded, including the Community Service Organization in Los Angeles and the American GI Forum in Texas. Compared with older organizations such as LULAC, the new groups were less concerned with assimilation per se, addressed a broad range of community problems, and attempted to increase Mexican American political power (Grebler et al., 1970, pp. 543–545).

Chicanismo.

The 1960s were a time of intense activism and militancy for Mexican Americans. A protest movement guided by an ideology called **Chicanismo** began at about the same time as the Black Power and Red Power movements. Chicanismo encompassed a variety of organizations and ideas, united by a heightened militancy and impatience with the racism of the larger society and strongly stated demands for justice, fairness, and equal rights. The movement questioned the value of assimilation and sought to increase awareness of the continuing exploitation of Mexican Americans; it adapted many of the tactics and strategies (marches, rallies, voter registration drives, etc.) of the civil rights movement of the 1960s.

Chicanismo is similar in some ways to the Black Power ideology (see Chapter 7). It is partly a reaction to the failure of U.S. society to implement the promises of integration and equality. It rejected traditional stereotypes of Mexican Americans, proclaimed a powerful and positive group image and heritage, and analyzed the group's past and present situation in American society in terms of victimization, continuing exploitation, and institutional discrimination. The inequalities that separated Mexican Americans from the larger society were seen as the result of deep-rooted, continuing racism and the cumulative effects of decades of exclusion. According to Chicanismo, the solution to these problems lay in group empowerment, increased militancy, and group pride, not in assimilation to a culture that had rationalized and abetted the exploitation of Mexican Americans (Acuna, 1988, pp. 307–358; Grebler et al., 1970, p. 544; Moore, 1970, pp. 149–154).

Some of the central thrusts of the 1960s protest movement are captured in the widespread adoption of **Chicanos**, which had been a derogatory term, as a group name for Mexican Americans. Other minority groups underwent similar name changes at about the same time. For example, African Americans shifted from *Negro* to *black* as a group designation. These name changes were not merely cosmetic; they marked fundamental shifts in group goals and desired relationships with the larger society. The new names came from the minority groups themselves, not from the dominant group, and they expressed the pluralistic themes of group pride, self-determination, militancy, and increased resistance to exploitation and discrimination.

Organizations and Leaders.

The Chicano movement saw the rise of many new groups and leaders, one of the most important of whom was Reies Lopez Tijerina, who formed the Alianza de Mercedes (Alliance of Land Grants) in 1963. The goal of this group was to correct what Tijerina saw as the unjust and illegal seizure of land from Mexicans during the 19th century. The Alianza was militant and confrontational, and to bring attention to their cause, members of the group seized and occupied federal lands. Tijerina spent several years in jail as a result of his activities, and the movement eventually lost its strength and faded from view in the 1970s.

Another prominent Chicano leader was Rodolfo Gonzalez, who founded the Crusade for Justice in 1965. The crusade focused on abuses of Mexican American civil and legal rights and worked against discrimination by police and the criminal courts. In a 1969 presentation at a symposium on Chicano liberation, Gonzalez expressed some of the nationalistic themes of Chicanismo and the importance of creating a power base within the group (as opposed to assimilating or integrating):

> Where [whites] have incorporated themselves to keep us from moving into their neighborhoods, we can also incorporate ourselves to keep them from controlling our neighborhoods. We...have to understand economic revolution.... We have to understand that liberation comes from self-determination, and to start to use the tools of nationalism to win over our barrio brothers.... We have to understand that we can take over the institutions within our community. We have to create the community of the Mexicano here in order to have any type of power. (Moquin & Van Doren, 1971, pp. 381–382)

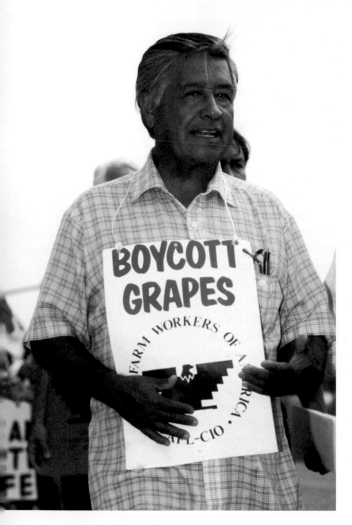

A third important leader was José Angel Gutierrez, organizer of the party La Raza Unida (People United). La Raza Unida offered alternative candidates and ideas to Democrats and Republicans. Its most notable success was in Crystal City, Texas, where, in 1973, it succeeded in electing its entire slate of candidates to local office (Acuna, 1988, pp. 332–451).

Without a doubt, the best-known Chicano leader of the 1960s and 1970s was the late César Chávez, who organized the United Farm Workers, the first union to successfully represent migrant workers. Chávez was as much a labor leader as a leader of the Mexican American community, and he also organized African Americans, Filipinos, and Anglo-Americans. Migrant farmworkers have few economic or political resources, and the migratory nature of their work isolates them in rural areas and makes them difficult to contact. In the 1960s (and still today), many were undocumented immigrants who spoke little or no English and returned to the cities or to their countries of origin at the end of the season. As a group, farmworkers were nearly invisible in the social landscape of the United States in the 1960s, and organizing this group was a demanding task. Chávez's success in this endeavor is one of the more remarkable studies in group protest.

Like Dr. Martin Luther King Jr., Chávez was a disciple of Gandhi and a student of nonviolent direct protest (see Chapter 7). His best-known tactic was the boycott; in 1965, he organized a grape-pickers' strike and a national boycott of grapes. The boycott lasted 5 years and ended when the growers recognized the United Farm Workers as the legitimate representative of farmworkers. Chávez and his organization achieved a major victory, and the agreement provided for significant improvements in the situation of the workers (for a biography of Chávez, see Levy, 1975).

Gender and the Chicano Protest Movement.
Mexican American women were heavily involved in the Chicano protest movement. Jessie Lopez and Dolores Huerta were central figures in the movement to organize farmworkers and worked closely with César Chávez. However, as was the case for African American women, Chicano women encountered sexism and gender discrimination within the movement even as they worked for the benefit of the group as a whole. Their dilemmas are described by activist Sylvia Gonzales:

> Along with her male counterpart, she attended meetings, organized boycotts, did everything asked of her.... But, if she [tried to assume leadership roles], she was met with the same questioning of her femininity which the culture dictates when a woman is not self-sacrificing and seeks to fulfill her own needs.... The Chicano movement seemed to demand self-actualization for only the male members of the group. (Amott & Matthaei, 1991, p. 83)

Despite these difficulties, Chicano women contributed to the movement in a variety of areas. They helped to organize poor communities and worked for welfare reform. Continuing issues include domestic violence, child care, the criminal victimization of women, and the racial and gender oppression that limits women of all minority groups (Amott & Matthaei, 1991, pp. 82–86; see also Mirandé & Enriquez, 1979, pp. 202–243).

Mexican Americans and Other Minority Groups

Like the Black Power and Red Power movements, Chicanismo began to fade from public view in the 1970s and 1980s. The movement could claim some successes, but perhaps the clearest victory was in raising the awareness of the larger society about the grievances and problems of Mexican Americans. Today, many Chicanos continue to face poverty and powerlessness and continuing exploitation as a cheap agricultural labor force. The less-educated, urbanized segments of the group share the prospect of becoming a permanent urban underclass with other minority groups of color.

Over the course of the 20th century, the ability of Chicanos to pursue their self-interests has been limited by both internal and external forces. Like African Americans, the group has been systematically excluded from the institutions of the larger society. Continuing immigration from Mexico has increased the size of the group, but these immigrants bring few resources with them that could be directly or immediately translated into economic or political power in the United States.

Unlike immigrants from Europe, who settled in the urban centers of the industrializing East Coast, Mexican Americans tended to work and live in rural areas distant from and marginal to urban centers of industrialization and opportunities for education, skill development, and upward mobility. They were a vitally important source of labor in agriculture and other segments of the economy but only to the extent that they were exploitable and powerless. As Chicanos moved to the cities, they continued to serve as a colonized, exploited labor force concentrated at the lower end of the stratification system. Thus, the handicaps created by discrimination in the past were reinforced by continuing discrimination and exploitation in the present, perpetuating the cycles of poverty and powerlessness.

At the same time, however, the flow of immigration and the constant movement of people back and forth across the border kept Mexican culture and the Spanish language alive. Unlike African Americans under slavery, Chicanos were not cut off from their homeland and native culture. Mexican American culture was attacked and disparaged, but, unlike African culture, it was not destroyed.

Clearly, the traditional model of assimilation does not describe the experiences of Mexican Americans very well. They have experienced less social mobility than European immigrant groups and have maintained their traditional culture and language more completely. Like African Americans, the group is split along lines of social class. Although many Mexican Americans (particularly of the third generation and later) have acculturated and integrated, a large segment of the group continues to fill the same economic role as their ancestors: an unskilled labor force for the development of the Southwest, augmented with new immigrants at the convenience of U.S. employers. In 2004, over 41% of employed Mexican Americans—nearly double the percentage for non-Hispanic whites—were in the construction, unskilled labor, and farm sectors of the labor force (U.S. Bureau of the Census, 2007a). For the less educated and for recent immigrants, cultural and racial differences combine to increase their social visibility, mark them for exploitation, and rationalize their continuing exclusion from the larger society.

Puerto Ricans

Puerto Rico became a territory of the United States after the defeat of Spain in the Spanish-American War of 1898. The island was small and impoverished, and it was difficult for Puerto Ricans to avoid domination by the United States. Thus, the initial contact between Puerto Ricans and U.S. society was made in an atmosphere of war and conquest. By the time Puerto Ricans began to migrate to the mainland in large numbers, their relationship to U.S. society was largely that of a colonized minority group, and they generally retained that status on the mainland.

Migration (Push and Pull) and Employment

At the time of initial contact, the population of Puerto Rico was overwhelmingly rural and supported itself by subsistence farming and by exporting coffee and sugar. As the century wore on, U.S. firms began to invest in and develop the island economy, especially the sugarcane industry. These agricultural endeavors took more and more of the land. Opportunities for economic survival in the rural areas declined, and many peasants were forced to move into the cities (Portes, 1990, p. 163).

Movement to the mainland began gradually and increased slowly until the 1940s. In 1900, there were about 2,000 Puerto Ricans living on the mainland. By the eve of World War II, this number had grown to only 70,000, a tiny fraction of the total population. Then, during the 1940s, the number of Puerto Ricans on the mainland increased more than fourfold, to 300,000, and during the 1950s, it nearly tripled, to 887,000 (U.S. Commission on Civil Rights, 1976, p. 19).

This massive and sudden population growth was the result of a combination of circumstances. First, Puerto Ricans became citizens of the United States in 1917, so their movements were not impeded by international boundaries or immigration restrictions. Second, unemployment was a major problem on the island. The sugarcane industry continued to displace the rural population, urban unemployment was high, and the population continued to grow. By the 1940s, a considerable number of Puerto Ricans were available to seek work off the island and, like Chicanos, could serve as a cheap labor supply for U.S. employers.

Third, Puerto Ricans were "pulled" to the mainland by the same labor shortages that attracted Mexican immigrants during and after World War II. Whereas the latter responded to job opportunities in the West and Southwest, Puerto Ricans moved to the Northeast. The job profiles of these two groups were similar; both were concentrated in the low-wage, unskilled sector of the job market. However, the Puerto Rican migration began many decades after the Mexican migration, at a time when the United States was much more industrialized and urbanized. As a result, Puerto Ricans have been more concentrated than Mexican immigrants in urban labor markets (Portes, 1990, p. 164).

Movement between the island and the mainland was facilitated by the commencement of affordable air travel between San Juan and New York City in the late 1940s. New York had been the major center of settlement for Puerto Ricans on the mainland even before annexation. A small Puerto Rican community had been established in the city, and as with many groups, organizations and networks were established to ease the transition and help newcomers with housing, jobs, and other issues. Although they eventually dispersed to other regions and cities, Puerto Ricans on the mainland remain centered in New York City. More than two thirds currently reside in the cities of the Northeast (U.S. Bureau of the Census, 2004b).

Economics and jobs were at the heart of the move to the mainland. The rate of Puerto Rican migration has followed the cycle of boom and bust, just as it has for Mexican immigrants. The 1950s, the peak decade for Puerto Rican migration, was a period of rapid U.S. economic growth. Migration was encouraged, and job recruiters traveled to the island to attract workers. By the 1960s, however, the supply of jobs on the island had expanded appreciably, and the average number of migrants declined from the peak of 41,000 per year in the 1950s to about 20,000 per year. In the 1970s, the U.S. economy faltered, unemployment grew, and the flow of Puerto Rican migration actually reversed itself, with the number of returnces exceeding the number of migrants in various years (U.S. Commission on Civil Rights, 1976, p. 25). The migrations continued: A little more than 3.4 million Puerto Ricans, or about 47% of all Puerto Ricans, were living on the mainland in 1999.

As the U.S. economy expanded and migration accelerated after World War II, Puerto Ricans moved into a broad range of jobs and locations in the society, and the group grew more economically diversified and more regionally dispersed. Still, the bulk of the group remains concentrated in lower-status jobs in the larger cities of the Northeast. Puerto Rican men have often found work as unskilled laborers or in service occupations, particularly in areas where English language facility is not necessary (e.g., janitorial work). The women have often been employed as domestics or seamstresses for the garment industry in New York City (Portes, 1990, p. 164).

Transitions

Although Puerto Ricans are not "immigrants," the move to the mainland does involve a change in culture and language (Fitzpatrick, 1980, p. 858). Despite nearly a century of political affiliation, Puerto Rican and Anglo cultures differ along many dimensions. Puerto Ricans are overwhelmingly Catholic, but the religious practices and rituals on the mainland are quite different from those on the island. Mainland Catholic parishes often reflect the traditions and practices of other cultures and groups. On the island, "Religious observance reflects the spontaneous and expressive practices of the Spanish and the Italian and not the restrained and well-organized worship of the Irish and Germans" (Fitzpatrick, 1980, p. 865). Also, there are few Puerto Rican priests or even Spanish-speaking clergy on the mainland; thus, members of the group often feel estranged from and poorly served by the church (Fitzpatrick, 1987, pp. 117–138).

A particularly unsettling cultural difference between the island and the mainland involves skin color and perceptions of race. Puerto Rico has a long history of racial intermarriage. Slavery was less monolithic and total, and the island had no periods of systematic, race-based segregation like the Jim Crow system. Thus, although skin color prejudice still exists in Puerto Rico, it has never been as categorical as on the mainland. On the island, race is perceived as a continuum of possibilities and combinations, not as a simple dichotomous split between white and black.

Furthermore, in Puerto Rico, other factors, such as social class, are considered to be more important than race as criteria for judging and classifying others. In fact, as we discussed in Chapter 6, social class can affect perceptions of skin color, and people of higher status might be seen as lighter skinned. Coming from this background, Puerto Ricans find the rigid racial thinking of U.S. culture disconcerting and even threatening.

The confusion and discomfort that can result was documented and illustrated by a study of Puerto Rican college students in New York City. Dramatic differences were found between the personal racial identification of the students and their perceptions of how Anglos viewed them. When asked for their racial identification, most of the students classified themselves as "tan," with one third labeling themselves "white" and only 7% considering themselves "black." When asked how they thought they were racially classified by Anglos, however, none of the students used the "tan" classification: 58% felt that they were seen as "white," and 41% felt that they were seen as "black" (Rodriguez, 1989, pp. 60–61; see also Rodriguez & Cordero-Guzman, 1992).

Another study documented dramatic differences in the terms used to express racial identity between women on the mainland and those in Puerto Rico. The latter identified their racial identities primarily in skin color terms: black, white, or *trigueña* (a "mixed-race" category with multiple skin tones), while mainland women identified themselves in nonracial terms, such as

Hispanic, Latina, Hispanic American, or American. In the view of the researchers, these labels serve to deflect the stigma associated with black racial status in the United States (Landale & Oropesa, 2002). In the racially dichotomized U.S. culture, many Puerto Ricans feel they have no clear place. They are genuinely puzzled when they first encounter prejudice and discrimination based on skin color and are uncertain about their own identities and self-image. The racial perceptions of the dominant culture can be threatening to Puerto Ricans to the extent that they are victimized by the same web of discrimination and disadvantage that affects African Americans. There are still clear disadvantages to being classified as black in U.S. society. Institutionalized racial barriers can be extremely formidable, and in the case of Puerto Ricans, they may combine with cultural and linguistic differences to sharply limit opportunities and mobility.

Puerto Ricans and Other Minority Groups

Puerto Ricans arrived in the cities of the Northeast long after the great wave of European immigrants and several decades after African Americans began migrating from the South. They have often competed with other minority groups for housing, jobs, and other resources. A pattern of ethnic succession can be seen in some neighborhoods and occupational areas in which Puerto Ricans have replaced other groups that have moved out (and sometimes up).

Because of their more recent arrival, Puerto Ricans on the mainland were not subjected to the more repressive paternalistic or rigid competitive systems of race relations like slavery or Jim Crow. Instead, the subordinate status of the group is manifested in their occupational, residential, and educational profiles and by the institutionalized barriers to upward mobility that they face. Puerto Ricans share many problems with other urban minority groups of color: poverty, failing educational systems, and crime. Like African Americans, Puerto Ricans find their fate to be dependent on the future of the American city, and a large segment of the group is in danger of becoming part of a permanent urban underclass.

Like Mexican Americans, Puerto Ricans on the mainland combine elements of both an immigrant and a colonized minority experience. The movement to the mainland is voluntary in some ways, but in others, it is strongly motivated by the transformations in the island economy that resulted from modernization and U.S. domination. Like Chicanos, Puerto Ricans tend to enter the labor force at the bottom of the occupational structure and face similar problems of inequality and marginalization. Also, Puerto Rican culture retains a strong vitality and is continually reinvigorated by the considerable movement back and forth between the island and the mainland.

Cuban Americans

The contact period for Cuban Americans, as for Puerto Ricans, dates back to the Spanish-American War. At that time, Cuba was a Spanish colony but became an independent nation as a result of the war. Despite Cuba's nominal independence, the United States remained heavily involved in Cuban politics and economics for decades, and U.S. troops actually occupied the island on two different occasions.

Gender Images of Latinas

O ne part of the minority group experience is learning to deal with the stereotypes, images, and expectations of the larger society. Of course, everyone (even white males) has to respond to the assumptions of others, but given the realities of power and status, minority group members have fewer choices and a narrower range in which to maneuver: The images imposed by the society are harder to escape and more difficult to deny.

In her analysis, Judith Ortiz Cofer (1995), a writer, poet, professor of English, and Puerto Rican, describes some of the images and stereotypes of Latinas with which she has had to struggle and some of the dynamics that have created and sustained those images. She writes from her own experiences, but the points she makes illustrate many of the sociological theories and concepts that guide this text.

The Island Travels With You

Judith Ortiz Cofer

On a bus trip from London to Oxford University . . . a young man, obviously fresh from a pub, spotted me and as if struck by inspiration went down on his knees in the aisle. With both hands over his heart he broke into an Irish tenor's rendition of "Maria" from West Side Story. My politely amused fellow passengers gave his lovely voice the round of gentle applause that it deserved. Though I was not quite as amused, I managed my version of an English smile: no show of teeth, no extreme contortions of the facial muscles—I was at this time in my life practicing reserve and cool. . . . But Maria had followed me to London, reminding me of a prime fact of my life: You can leave the island, master the English language, and travel as far as you can, but if you are a Latina, . . . the Island travels with you.

This is sometimes a very good thing—it may win you the extra minute of somebody's attention. But with some people, the same things can make you an island—not so much a tropical paradise as an Alcatraz, a place nobody wants to visit. As a Puerto Rican girl growing up in the United States and wanting like most children to "belong," I resented the stereotypes that my Hispanic appearance called forth from many people I met.

Our family lived in a large urban center in New Jersey during the sixties, where life was designed as a microcosm of my parents' casas on the island. We spoke Spanish, we ate Puerto Rican food bought at the bodega, and we practiced strict Catholicism. . . .

As a girl, I was kept under strict surveillance, since virtue and modesty were, by cultural equation, the same as family honor. As a teenager, I was instructed on how to behave as a proper senorita. But it was a conflicting message girls got, since the Puerto Rican mothers also encouraged their daughters to look and act like women and to dress in clothes our Anglo friends found too "mature" for our age. . . . At a Puerto

Rican festival, neither the music nor the colors we wore could be too loud. I still experience a vague sense of letdown when I'm invited to a "party" and it turns out to be a marathon conversation in hushed tones rather than a fiesta with salsa, laughter, and dancing—the kind of celebration I remember from my childhood. . . .

Mixed cultural signals have perpetuated certain stereotypes—for example, that of the "Hot Tamale" or sexual firebrand. It is a . . . view that the media have found easy to promote. In their special vocabulary, advertisers have designated "sizzling" and "smoldering" as the adjectives of choice for describing not only the foods but the women of Latin America. . . .

It is custom, however, not chromosomes, that leads us to choose scarlet over pale pink. As young girls, we were influenced in our decisions about clothes and colors by the women . . . who had grown up on a tropical island where the natural environment was a riot of primary colors, where showing your skin was one way to keep cool as well as to look sexy. Most important of all, on the island, women perhaps felt freer to dress and move more provocatively, since . . . they were protected by the traditions, mores, and laws of a Spanish/ Catholic system of morality and machismo whose main rule was: You may look at my sister, but if you touch her I will kill you. The extended family and church structure could provide a young woman with a circle of safety in her small pueblo on the Island; if a man "wronged" a girl, everyone would close in to save her family honor. . . .

Because of my education and proficiency with the English language, I have acquired many mechanisms for dealing with the anger I experience. This was not true for my parents, nor is it true for the many Latin women working at menial jobs who must put up with stereotypes about our ethnic group such as: "They make good domestics." This is another facet of the myth of the Latin women in the United States. . . . The myth of the Hispanic menial has been maintained by the same media phenomenon that made "Mammy" from *Gone With the Wind* America's idea of a black woman for generations: Maria, the housemaid or counter girl, is now indelibly etched into the national psyche. The big and little screens have presented us with the picture of the funny Hispanic maid, mispronouncing words and cooking up a spicy storm in the kitchen. . . .

I am one of the lucky ones. My parents made it possible for me to acquire a stronger footing in the mainstream culture by giving me the chance at an education. . . . There are thousands of Latinas without the privilege of an education or the entrée into society that I have. For them, life is a struggle against the misconceptions perpetuated by the myth of the Latina as whore, domestic, or criminal. My personal goal in my public life is to try to replace the old pervasive stereotypes and myths about Latinas with a much more interesting set of realities. Every time I give a reading [of my poetry], I hope the stories I tell, the dreams and fears I examine in my work, can achieve some universal truth which will get my audience past the particulars of my skin color, my accent, or my clothes.

SOURCE: From Cofer, Judith Ortiz (1995). "The Myth of the Latin Woman: I Just Met a Girl Named Maria." In her *The Latin Deli: Prose and Poetry*, pp. 148–154. Athens, GA: University of Georgia Press.

The development of a Cuban American minority group bears little resemblance to the experience of either Chicanos or Puerto Ricans. As recently as the 1950s, there had not been much immigration from Cuba to the United States, even during times of labor shortages, and Cuban Americans were a very small group, numbering no more than 50,000 (Perez, 1980, p. 256).

Immigration (Push and Pull)

The conditions for a mass immigration were created in the late 1950s, when a Marxist revolution brought Fidel Castro to power in Cuba. Castro's government was decidedly anti-American and began to restructure Cuban society along socialist lines. The middle and upper classes lost political and economic power, and the revolution made it difficult, even impossible, for Cuban capitalists to remain in business. Thus, the first Cuban immigrants to the United States tended to come from the more elite classes and included affluent and powerful people who controlled many resources.

The United States was a logical destination for those displaced by the revolution. Cuba is only 90 miles from southern Florida, the climates are similar, and the U.S. government, which was as anti-Castro as Castro was anti-American, welcomed the new arrivals as political refugees fleeing from Communist tyranny. Prior social, cultural, and business ties also pulled the immigrants in the direction of the United States. Since gaining its independence in 1898, Cuba has been heavily influenced by its neighbor to the north, and U.S. companies helped to develop the Cuban economy. At the time of Castro's revolution, the Cuban political leadership and the more affluent classes were profoundly Americanized in their attitudes and lifestyles (Portes, 1990, p. 165). Furthermore, many Cuban exiles viewed southern Florida as an ideal spot from which to launch a counterrevolution to oust Castro.

Immigration was considerable for several years. More than 215,000 Cubans arrived between the end of the revolution and 1962, when an escalation of hostile relations resulted in the cutoff of all direct contact between Cuba and the United States. In 1965, an air link was reestablished, and an additional 340,000 Cubans made the journey. When the air connection was terminated in 1973, immigration slowed to a trickle once more. In 1980, however, the Cuban government permitted another period of open immigration. Using boats of every shape, size, and degree of seaworthiness, about 124,000 Cubans crossed to Florida. These immigrants are often referred to as the **Marielitos**, after the port of Mariel from which many of them departed. This wave of immigrants generated a great deal of controversy in the United States, because the Cuban government used the opportunity to rid itself of a variety of convicted criminals and outcasts. However, the Marielitos also included people from every segment of Cuban society, a fact that was lost in the clamor of concern about the "undesirables" (Portes & Manning, 1986, p. 58).

Regional Concentrations

The overwhelming majority of Cuban immigrants settled in southern Florida, especially in Miami and the surrounding Dade County. Today, Cuban Americans remain one of the most spatially concentrated minority groups in the United States, with 67% of all Cuban Americans residing in Florida, 52% in the Miami area alone (U.S. Bureau of the Census, 2001). This dense concentration has led to a number of disputes and conflicts between the Hispanic, Anglo-, and African American communities in the area. Issues have centered on language (see the Current Debates section in Chapter 2), jobs, and discrimination by the police and other governmental agencies. The conflicts have often been intense, and on more than one occasion, they have erupted into violence and civil disorder.

Socioeconomic Characteristics

Compared with other streams of immigrants from Latin America, Cubans are, on the average, unusually affluent and well educated. Among the immigrants in the early 1960s were large numbers of professionals, landowners, and businesspeople. In later years, as Cuban society was transformed by the Castro regime, the stream included fewer elites, largely because there were fewer left in Cuba, and more political dissidents and working-class people. Today (as will be displayed in the exhibits presented later in this chapter), Cuban Americans rank higher than other Latino groups on a number of dimensions, a reflection of the educational and economic resources they brought with them from Cuba and the favorable reception they enjoyed from the United States (Portes, 1990, p. 169).

These assets gave Cubans an advantage over Chicanos and Puerto Ricans, but the differences between the three Latino groups run deeper and are more complex than a simple accounting of initial resources would suggest. Cubans adapted to U.S. society in a way that is fundamentally different from the experiences of the other two Latino groups.

The Ethnic Enclave

Most of the minority groups we have discussed to this point have been concentrated in the unskilled, low-wage segments of the economy in which jobs are not secure and not linked to opportunities for upward mobility. Many Cuban Americans have bypassed this sector of the economy and much of the discrimination and limitations associated with it. Like several other groups, such as Jewish Americans, Cuban Americans are an enclave minority (see Chapter 2). An ethnic enclave is a social, economic, and cultural subsociety controlled by the group itself. Located in a specific geographical area or neighborhood inhabited solely or largely by members of the group, the enclave encompasses sufficient economic enterprises and social institutions to permit the group to function as a self-contained entity, largely independent of the surrounding community.

The first wave of Cuban immigrants brought with them considerable resources and business expertise. Although much of their energy was focused on ousting Castro and returning to Cuba, they generated enough economic activity to sustain restaurants, shops, and other small businesses that catered to the exile community.

As the years passed and the hope of a return to Cuba dimmed, the enclave economy grew. Between 1967 and 1976, the number of Cuban-owned firms in Dade County

increased ninefold, from 919 to about 8,000. Six years later, the number had reached 12,000. Most of these enterprises are small, but some factories employ hundreds of workers (Portes & Rumbaut, 1996, pp. 20–21). In addition to businesses serving their own community, Cuban-owned firms are involved in construction, manufacturing, finance, insurance, real estate, and an array of other activities. Over the decades, Cuban-owned firms have become increasingly integrated into the local economy and increasingly competitive with firms in the larger society. The growth of economic enterprises has been paralleled by a growth in the number of other types of groups and organizations and in the number and quality of services available (schools, law firms, medical care, funeral parlors, etc.). The enclave has become a largely autonomous community capable of providing for its members from cradle to grave (Logan, Alba, & McNulty, 1994; Peterson, 1995; Portes & Bach, 1985, p. 59).

The fact that the enclave economy is controlled by the group itself is crucial; it separates the ethnic enclave from "the ghetto," or neighborhoods that are impoverished and segregated. In ghettos, members of other groups typically control the local economy; the profits, rents, and other resources flow out of the neighborhood. In the enclave, profits are reinvested and kept in the neighborhood. Group members can avoid the discrimination and limitations imposed by the larger society and can apply their skills, education, and talents in an atmosphere free from language barriers and prejudice. Those who might wish to venture into business for themselves can use the networks of cooperation and mutual aid for advice, credit, and other forms of assistance. Thus, the ethnic enclave provides a platform from which Cuban Americans can pursue economic success independent of their degree of acculturation or English language ability.

The effectiveness of the ethnic enclave as a pathway for adaptation is illustrated by a study of Cuban and Mexican immigrants, all of whom entered the United States in 1973. At the time of entry, the groups were comparable in levels of skills, education, and English language ability. The groups were interviewed on several different occasions, and although they remained comparable on many variables, there were dramatic differences between the groups that reflected their different positions in the labor market. The majority of the Mexican immigrants were employed in the low-wage job sector. Less than 20% were self-employed or employed by another person of Mexican descent. Conversely, 57% of the Cuban immigrants were self-employed or employed by another Cuban (i.e., they were involved in the enclave economy). Among the subjects in the study, self-employed Cubans reported the highest monthly incomes ($1,495), and Cubans otherwise employed in the enclave earned the second-highest incomes ($1,111). The lowest incomes ($880) were earned by Mexican immigrants employed in small, nonenclave firms; many of these people worked as unskilled laborers in seasonal, temporary, or otherwise insecure jobs (Portes, 1990, p. 173; see also Portes & Bach, 1985).

The ability of the Mexican immigrants to rise in the class system and compete for place and position was severely constrained by the weight of past discrimination, the preferences of employers in the present, and their own lack of economic and political power. Cuban immigrants who found jobs in the enclave did not need to expose themselves to American prejudices or rely on the job market of the larger society. They entered an immigrant context that had networks of mutual assistance and support and linked them to opportunities more consistent with their ambitions and their qualifications.

The fact that success came faster to the group that was less acculturated reverses the prediction of many theories of assimilation. The pattern has long been recognized by some leaders of other groups, however, and is voiced in many of the themes of Black Power, Red Power, and Chicanismo that emphasize self-help, self-determination, nationalism, and separation. However, ethnic enclaves cannot be a panacea for all immigrant or other minority groups. They develop only under certain limited conditions, namely, when business and financial expertise and reliable sources of capital are combined with a disciplined labor force willing to work for low wages in exchange for on-the-job training, future assistance and loans, or other delayed benefits. Enclave enterprises usually start on a small scale and cater only to other ethnics. Thus, the early economic returns are small, and prosperity follows only after years of hard work, if at all. Most important, eventual success and expansion beyond the boundaries of the enclave depend on the persistence of strong ties of loyalty, kinship, and solidarity. The pressure to assimilate might easily weaken these networks and the strength of group cohesion (Portes & Manning, 1986, pp. 61–66).

Cuban Americans and Other Minority Groups

The adaptation of Cuban Americans contrasts sharply with the experiences of colonized minority groups and with the common understanding of how immigrants are "supposed" to acculturate and integrate. Cuban Americans are neither the first nor the only group to develop an ethnic enclave, and their success has generated prejudice and resentment from the dominant group and from other minority groups. Whereas Puerto Ricans and Chicanos have been the victims of stereotypes labeling them "inferior," higher-status Cuban Americans have been stereotyped as "too successful," "too clannish," and "too ambitious." The former stereotype commonly emerges to rationalize exploitative relationships; the latter expresses disparagement and rejection of groups that are more successful in the struggle to acquire resources (see Chapter 3). Nonetheless, the stereotype of Cubans is an exaggeration and a misperception that obscures the fact that poverty and unemployment are major problems for many members of this group (see the exhibits at the end of this chapter).

New Hispanic Groups: Immigrants From the Dominican Republic, El Salvador, and Colombia

Immigration from Latin America, the Caribbean, and South America has been considerable, even excluding Mexico. As with other sending nations, the volume of immigration from these regions increased after 1965 and has averaged about 200,000 per year since the 1980s. Generally, Latino immigrants—not counting those from Mexico—have been 20% to 25% of all immigrants since the 1960s.

The sending nations for these immigrants are economically less developed, and most have long-standing relations with the United States. We have already discussed the roles that Mexico and Puerto Rico have historically played as sources of cheap labor and the ties that led Cubans to immigrate to the United States. Each of the other sending nations has been similarly linked to the United States, the dominant economic and political power in the region.

Although the majority of these immigrants bring educational and occupational qualifications that are modest by U.S. standards, they tend to be more educated, more urbanized, and more skilled than the average citizens of the nations from which they come. Contrary to widely held beliefs, these immigrants do not represent the poorest of the poor, the "wretched refuse" of their homelands. They tend to be rather ambitious, as evidenced by their willingness to attempt to succeed in a society that has not been notably hospitable to Latinos or people of color in the past. Most of these immigrants are not so much fleeing poverty or joblessness as they are attempting to pursue their ambitions and seek opportunities for advancement that are simply not available in their countries of origin (Portes & Rumbaut, 1996, pp. 10–11).

This characterization applies to legal and unauthorized immigrants alike. In fact, the latter may illustrate the point more dramatically, because the cost of illegally entering the United States can be considerable, much higher than the cost of a legal entry. The venture may require years of saving money or the combined resources of a large kinship group. Forged papers and other costs of being smuggled into the country can easily amount to thousands of dollars, a considerable sum in nations in which the usual wage is a tiny fraction of the U.S. average (Orreniou, 2001, p. 7). Also, the passage can be extremely dangerous and can require a level of courage (or desperation) not often associated with the undocumented and illegal. Many Mexican would-be immigrants have died along the border, and many other immigrants have been lost at sea (for example, see "Dominicans Saved From Sea," 2004).

Rather than attempting to cover all South and Central American groups, we will select the three largest to serve as "case studies" and consider immigrants from the Dominican Republic, El Salvador, and Colombia (see Exhibit 8.7). Together, these three groups have made up 7% to 8% of all immigrants in recent years and about 20% of the immigrants from Central and South America and the Caribbean. These groups had few members in the United States before the 1960s, and all have had high rates of immigration over the past four decades. However, the motivation of the immigrants and the immigration experience has varied from group to group, as we shall see later.

Three Case Studies

Each of the groups selected for case studies has a high percentage of foreign-born members (see Exhibit 8.4), and, predictably with so many members in the first generation, proficiency

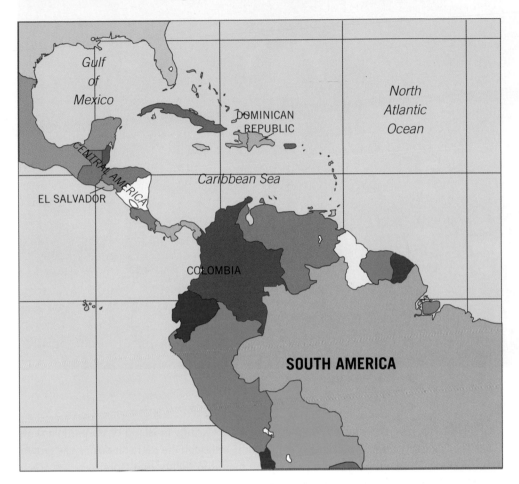

in English is an important issue. Although Colombians approach national norms in education, the other two groups have relatively low levels of human capital (education), and all are well above national norms in terms of poverty.

Although these groups share some common characteristics, there are also important differences between them. They differ in their "racial" characteristics, with Dominicans being more African in appearance, Colombians more European, and Salvadorans more Indian. The groups tend to settle in different places. Dominicans and Colombians are clustered along the East Coast, particularly in New York, New Jersey, and Florida, but Salvadorans are more concentrated on the West Coast (U.S. Department of Homeland Security, 2003). Finally, the groups differ in the conditions of their entry or their contact situation, a difference that, as we have seen, is quite consequential. Salvadorans are more likely to be political refugees fleeing a brutal civil war and political repression, while Dominicans and Colombians are more likely to be motivated by economics and the employment possibilities offered in the United States. We will consider each of these groups briefly and explore some of these differences further.

Dominicans. The Dominican Republic shares the Caribbean island of Hispaniola with Haiti. The island economy is still largely agricultural, although the tourist industry has grown in recent years. Unemployment and poverty are major problems, and Dominicans average less than 5 years of education ("Average Years of Schooling," n.d.). Dominican immigrants, like those from Mexico, are motivated largely by economics, and they compete for jobs with Puerto Ricans, other immigrant groups, and native-born workers with lower levels of education and jobs skills. Although Dominicans are limited in their job options by the language barrier, they are somewhat advantaged by their willingness to work for lower wages, and they are especially concentrated in the service sector, as day laborers (men) or domestics (women). Dominicans maintain strong ties with home and are a major source of income and support for the families left behind.

In terms of acculturation and integration, Dominicans are roughly similar to Mexican Americans and Puerto Ricans, although some studies suggest that they are possibly the most impoverished immigrant group (see, for example, Camarota, 2002). A high percentage of Dominicans are undocumented, and many spend considerable money and take considerable risks to get to the United States. If these less visible members of the community were included in the official, government-generated statistics used in exhibits presented later in this chapter, it is very likely that the portrait of poverty and low levels of education and jobs skills would be even more dramatic.

Salvadorans. El Salvador, like the Dominican Republic, is a relatively poor nation, with a high percentage of the population relying on subsistence agriculture for survival. It is estimated that about 50% of the population lives below the poverty level, and there are major problems with unemployment and underemployment. About 80% of the population is literate, and the average number of years of school completed is a little more than 5 ("Literacy, Total Population," n.d.).

El Salvador, like many sending nations, has a difficult time providing sufficient employment opportunities for its population, and much of the pressure to immigrate is economic. However, El Salvador also suffered through a brutal civil war in the 1980s, and many of the Salvadorans in the United States today are actually political refugees. The United States, under the administration of President Reagan, refused to grant political refugee status to Salvadorans, and many were returned to El Salvador. This federal policy resulted in high numbers of undocumented immigrants and also stimulated a sanctuary movement, led by American clergy, which helped Salvadoran immigrants, both undocumented and legal, to stay in the United States. As was the case with Dominicans, if the undocumented immigrants from El Salvador were included in official government statistics, the picture of poverty would become even more extreme.

Colombians. Colombia is somewhat more developed than most other Central and South American nations but has suffered from more than 40 years of internal turmoil, civil war, and government corruption. The nation is a major center for the production and distribution of drugs to the world in general and the United States in particular, and the drug industry and profits are complexly intertwined with domestic strife. Colombian Americans are closer to U.S. norms of education and income than other Latino groups, and recent immigrants are a mixture of less-skilled laborers and well-educated professionals seeking to further their careers. Colombians are residentially concentrated in urban areas, especially in Florida and the Northeast, and often settle in areas close to other Latino neighborhoods. Of course, the huge majority of Colombian Americans are law-abiding and not connected with the drug trade, but still they must deal with the pervasive stereotype that pictures Colombians as gangsters and drug smugglers (not unlike the Mafia stereotype encountered by Italian Americans).

Contemporary Hispanic-White Relations

As in previous chapters, we will use the central concepts of this text to review the status of Latinos in the United States. Where relevant, comparisons are made between the major Latino groups and the minority groups discussed in previous chapters.

Prejudice and Discrimination

The American tradition of prejudice against Latinos was born in the 19th-century conflicts that created minority group status for Mexican Americans. The themes of the original anti-Mexican stereotypes and attitudes were consistent with the nature of the contact situation: As

Immigration in Europe Versus Immigration to the United States

The volume of immigration in the world today is at record levels. Almost 200 million people, about 3% of the world's population, live outside their countries of birth, and there is hardly a nation or region that has not been affected (Population Reference Bureau, 2007b). The United States has by far the highest number of foreign-born citizens, and the flow of immigrants (illegal as well as legal) from Mexico to the United States is the single largest population movement. However, the United States is only one of many destination nations, and the issues of immigration and assimilation that are being debated so fervently here are echoed in many other nations.

In particular, the nations of Western Europe—highly developed, advanced industrial economies—are prime destinations for immigrants. Like the United States, these nations have very high standards of living, and they offer myriad opportunities for economic survival, even though the price may be to live at the margins of the larger society or to take jobs scorned by the native-born. In addition, a powerful factor that "pulls" people to this region is that Western European nations have very low birthrates, and in some cases (e.g., Germany and Italy), their populations are projected to actually decline in coming decades (Population Reference Bureau, 2007a). The labor force shortages thus created will continue to attract immigrants to Western Europe for decades to come.

The immigration to Western Europe is varied and includes people from all walks of life, from highly educated professionals to peasant laborers. The most prominent flows include movements from Turkey to Germany, from Africa to Spain and Italy, and from many former British colonies (Jamaica, India, Nigeria, etc.) to the United Kingdom. This immigration is primarily an economic phenomenon motivated by the search for jobs and survival, but the stream also includes refugees and asylum seekers spurred by civil war, genocide, and political unrest.

In terms of numbers, the volume of immigration to Western Europe is much smaller than the flow to the United States, but its proportional impact is comparable. About 13% of the U.S. population is foreign-born, and many Western European nations (including Belgium, Germany, and Sweden) have a similar profile (Organization for Economic Cooperation and Development [OECD], 2008). Thus, it is not surprising that in both cases, immigration has become a major concern and a significant political issue. A major difference, as we saw when discussing Ireland in Chapter 2, is that Western European nations have less experience in dealing with a large influx of newcomers or managing a pluralistic society. Furthermore, many Western European nations make it difficult or impossible for immigrants to achieve citizenship or full membership in their societies.

To focus on one example, Germany has by far the largest immigrant community of any Western European nation and has been dealing with a large foreign-born population for decades. Germany began to allow large numbers of immigrants to enter as temporary workers or "guest workers" (*Gastarbeiter*) to help staff its expanding economy beginning in the 1960s. Most of these immigrants came from Turkey, and they were seen by Germans as temporary workers only, people who would return to their homeland when they were no longer needed. Thus, the host society saw no particular need to encourage immigrants to acculturate and integrate.

Contrary to this perception, many immigrants stayed and settled permanently, and their millions of descendants today speak only German and have no knowledge of or experience with their "homeland." Although acculturated, they are not integrated, and, in fact— and in stark contrast with the United States—they were denied the opportunity to become citizens until recently. A German law passed nearly a century ago reserved citizenship for ethnic Germans, regardless of place of birth. Under this policy, a recent immigrant from, say, Ukraine was eligible for citizenship if they could prove that they had German ancestors—even if they spoke no German and had no familiarity with German culture or traditions. In contrast, a Turk living in Germany was not eligible for citizenship regardless of how long they or their family had been residents. This law was changed in 1999 to permit greater flexibility in qualifying for citizenship, but still more recently, Germany has passed new laws that make it harder for foreigners to enter the country. To gain admission, immigrants may have to pass a language test and have a guaranteed job or a place in school. The immigrant community sees these new laws as a form of rejection, and there have been bitter (and sometimes violent) demonstrations in response ("Europe: The Integration Dilemma," 2007).

Clashes of this sort have been common across Western Europe in recent years, especially with the growing Muslim communities. Many Europeans see Islamic immigrants as unassimilable, too foreign or exotic to ever fit into the mainstream of their society. These conflicts have been punctuated by violence and riots in France, Germany, the Netherlands, and other places.

Across Europe, just as in the United States (and Canada), nations are wrestling with issues of inclusion and diversity: What should it mean to be German, or French, or British, or Dutch? How much diversity can be tolerated before national cohesion is threatened? What are the limits of tolerance? What is the best balance between assimilation and pluralism? Struggles over the essential meaning of national identity are increasingly common throughout the developed world.

Mexicans were conquered and subordinated, they were characterized as inferior, lazy, irresponsible, low in intelligence, and dangerously criminal (McWilliams, 1961, pp. 212–214). The prejudice and racism, supplemented with the echoes of the racist ideas and beliefs brought to the Southwest by many Anglos, helped to justify and rationalize the colonized, exploited status of the Chicanos.

These prejudices were incorporated into the dominant culture and transferred to Puerto Ricans when they began to arrive on the mainland. As we have already mentioned, this stereotype does not fit Cuban Americans. Instead, their affluence has been exaggerated and perceived as undeserved or achieved by unfair or "un-American" means, a characterization similar to the traditional stereotype of Jews but just as prejudiced as the perception of Latino inferiority.

There is some evidence that the level of Latino prejudice has been affected by the decline of explicit American racism (discussed in Chapter 3). For example, social distance scale results show a decrease in the scores of Mexicans, although their group ranking tends to remain stable. On the other hand, prejudice and racism against Latinos tend to increase during times of high immigration.

Although discrimination of all kinds, institutional as well as individual, has been common against Latino groups, it has not been as rigid or as total as the systems that controlled African American labor under slavery and segregation. However, discrimination against Latinos has not dissipated to the same extent as it has against European immigrant groups and their descendants. Because of their longer tenure in the United States and their original status as a rural labor force, Mexican Americans have probably been more victimized by the institutionalized forms of discrimination than have other Latino groups.

Assimilation and Pluralism

Acculturation. Latinos are highly variable in their extent of acculturation but are often seen as "slow" to change, learn English, and adopt Anglo customs. Contrary to this perception, research shows that Hispanics are following many of the same patterns of assimilation as European groups. Their rates of acculturation increase with length of residence and are higher for the native-born (Espinosa & Massey, 1997; Goldstein & Suro, 2000; Valentine & Mosley, 2000).

One study found a generational pattern in the pattern of language acculturation for the children and grandchildren of three Hispanic groups. The subjects were age 5 through 16 at the time of the study and classified as second generation if at least one of their parents was foreign-born and third generation if both parents were born in the United States. The "mother-tongue" third generation children were those who had at least one parent who spoke a language other than English at home, even though both parents were born in the United States. If the traditional patterns of language acculturation applied to contemporary immigrant groups, we would expect the percentage that speaks only English at home would increase sharply from the second to the third generation with the mother-tongue third generation intermediate, exactly the pattern displayed in Exhibit 8.8.

A different study showed that the values of Hispanics come to approximate the values of the society as a whole as the generations pass. Exhibit 8.9 shows some results of a 2002 survey of Latinos and compares cultural values by English language proficiency, which increases with length of residence and by generation. For example, most Latinos (72%) who speak predominantly Spanish are first generation, while most (78%) who speak predominantly English are third generation. The second generation is most likely to be bilingual.

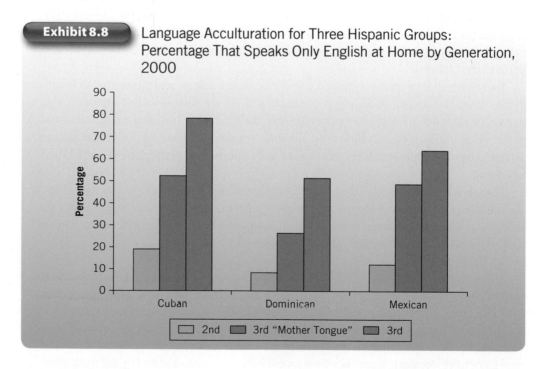

Exhibit 8.8 Language Acculturation for Three Hispanic Groups: Percentage That Speaks Only English at Home by Generation, 2000

SOURCE: Alba, Logan, Lutz, & Stults (2002, p. 472).

Exhibit 8.9 shows the results for four different survey items that measure values and opinions. The values of predominantly Spanish speakers are distinctly different from non-Latinos, especially on the item that measures support for the statement that "children should live with their parents until they are married." Virtually all of the predominantly Spanish speakers supported the statement, but English-speaking Latinos approximate the more individualistic values of Anglos. For each of the other three items, a similar acculturation to American values occurs.

Even while acculturation continues, however, Hispanic culture and the Spanish language are revitalized by immigration. By its nature, assimilation is a slow process that can require decades or generations to complete. In contrast, immigration can be fast, often accomplished in less than a day. Thus, even as Hispanic Americans acculturate and integrate, Hispanic culture and language are sustained and strengthened. What is perceived to be slow acculturation for these groups is mostly the result of fast and continuous immigration.

Furthermore, colonized minority groups such as Chicanos and Puerto Ricans were not encouraged to assimilate in the past. Valued primarily for the cheap labor they supplied, they were seen as otherwise inferior or undesirable and unfit for integration. For much of the 20th

Exhibit 8.9 Percentage of Latinos Agreeing by Primary Language

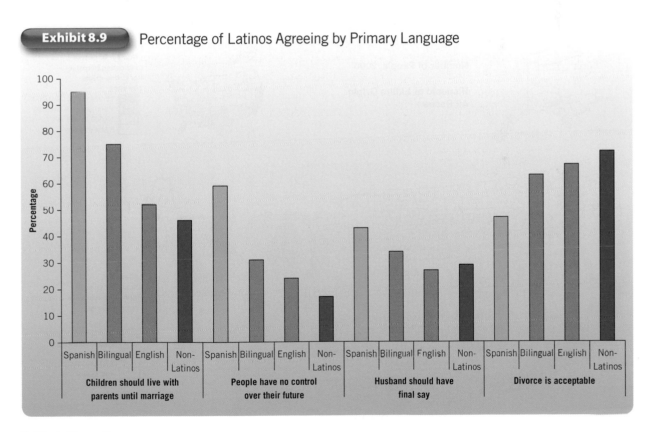

Full Text of Survey Items:
"It is better for children to live in their parents' home until they are married."
"It doesn't do any good to plan for the future because you don't have any control over it."
"In general, the husband should have the final say in family matters."
"Divorce is acceptable."

SOURCE: Pew Hispanic Center (2004).

century, Latinos were excluded from the institutions and experiences (e.g., school) that could have led to greater equality and higher rates of acculturation. Prejudice, racism, and discrimination combined to keep most Latino groups away from the centers of modernization and change and away from opportunities to improve their situation.

Finally, for Cubans, Dominicans, and other groups, cultural differences reflect the fact that they are largely recent immigrants. Their first generations are alive and well, and as is typical for immigrant groups, they keep the language and traditions alive.

Secondary Structural Assimilation.
In this section, we survey the situation of Latinos in the public areas and institutions of American society, beginning with where people live. Additional information on the relative standing of Hispanic American groups can be found in the Appendix.

Residence. Exhibit 8.10 shows the regional concentrations of Latinos in 2000. The legacies of the varied patterns of entry and settlement for the largest groups are evident. The higher concentrations in the Southwest reflect the presence of Mexican Americans; those in Florida

Exhibit 8.10 Geographical Distribution of People of Hispanic or Latino Origin (All Races), 2000

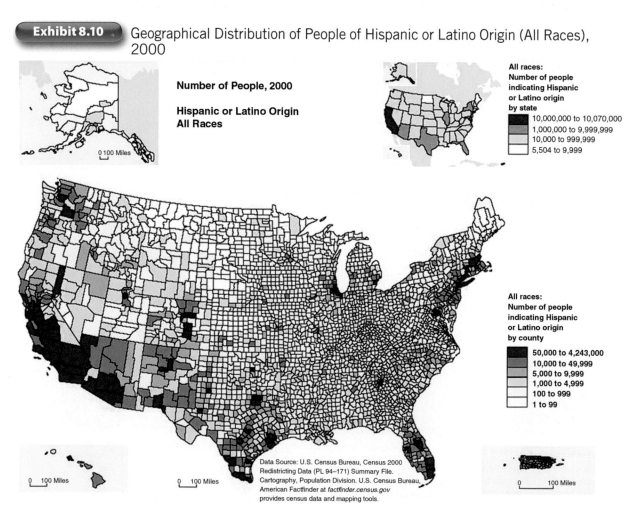

SOURCE: U.S. Bureau of the Census (2000d).

are the result of the Cuban immigration, and those in the Northeast display the settlement patterns of Puerto Ricans.

Within each of these regions, Latino groups are highly urbanized, as shown in Exhibit 8.11. More than 90% of all groups live in cities, and this percentage rises to nearly 100% for some. Mexican Americans are more rural than the other groups, but in sharp contrast to their historical role as an agrarian workforce, the percentage of the group living outside urban areas is tiny today.

The extent of residential segregation for Hispanic Americans is displayed in Exhibit 8.12, which shows the average dissimilarity index for 220 metropolitan areas grouped into four regions. Hispanic Americans are less residentially segregated than African Americans (see Exhibit 6.6), but in contrast to African Americans, their segregation has generally held steady or slightly increased over the 20-year period. Among other factors, this is a reflection of high rates of immigration and "chain" patterns of settlement, which concentrate newcomers in ethnic neighborhoods.

Education. Exhibit 8.13, like Exhibit 6.8 for the black population, shows the extent of school segregation for Hispanic Americans for the 1993–1994 and the 2005–2006 school years. In both years, Hispanic American children were more segregated than either American Indian or African American children. Furthermore, the percentages of Hispanic children in both majority-minority and extremely segregated schools increased over the time period. These patterns reflect recent high rates of immigration and the tendency for newcomers to reside in the same neighborhoods as their coethnics (see patterns of residential segregation in Exhibit 8.12).

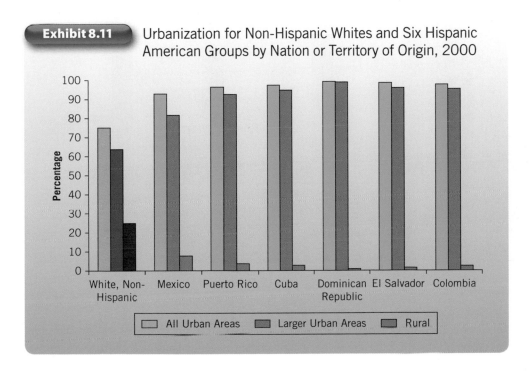

Exhibit 8.11 Urbanization for Non-Hispanic Whites and Six Hispanic American Groups by Nation or Territory of Origin, 2000

SOURCE: U.S. Bureau of the Census (2000f).

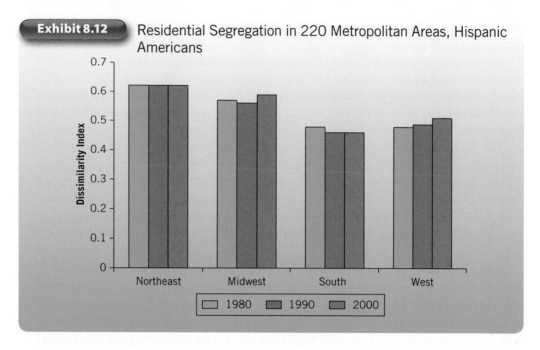

Exhibit 8.12 Residential Segregation in 220 Metropolitan Areas, Hispanic Americans

SOURCE: Iceland, Weinberg, & Steinmetz (2002, p. 84).

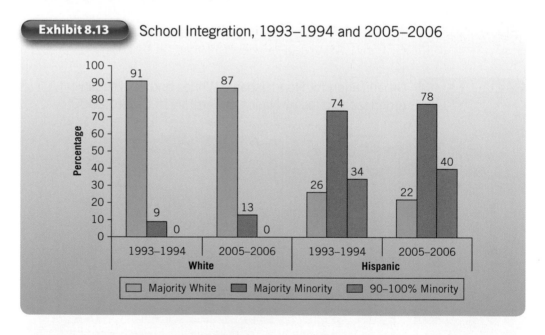

Exhibit 8.13 School Integration, 1993–1994 and 2005–2006

SOURCE: Fry (2007).

Levels of education for Hispanic Americans have risen in recent years but still are far below national standards (see Exhibit 8.14). Hispanic Americans in general and all six subgroups, except Colombian Americans, fall well below non-Hispanic whites for high school education. In particular, a little more than half of Mexican Americans and only 45% of Salvadorans have high school degrees. At the college level, Colombian and Cuban Americans match national norms, but the other groups and Hispanic Americans as a whole are far below non-Hispanic whites. For all Hispanic groups, there is very little difference by gender: Males and females have about the same record of educational attainment.

The lower levels of education are the cumulative results of decades of systematic discrimination and exclusion for Mexican Americans and Puerto Ricans. These levels have been further reduced by the high percentage of recent immigrants from Mexico, the Dominican Republic, and El Salvador who have very modest educational backgrounds.

Given the role that educational credentials have come to play in the job market, these figures are consistent with the idea that assimilation may be segmented for some Hispanic groups (see Chapters 2 and 10), who may contribute in large numbers, along with African Americans and Native Americans, to the growth of an urban underclass.

Political Power. The political resources available to Hispanic Americans have increased over the years, but the group is still proportionally underrepresented. The number of Hispanics of voting age has doubled in the past two decades, and Hispanics today constitute more than 10% of the voting-age population. Yet because registration rates and actual turnout have been low, the Hispanic community has not had an impact on the political structure proportionate to its size. For example, in the presidential elections between 1992 and 2004, actual voter turnout for Hispanic Americans was less than 30%, less than half the comparable

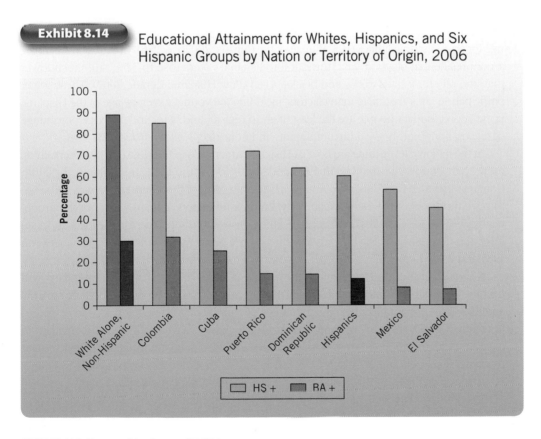

Exhibit 8.14 Educational Attainment for Whites, Hispanics, and Six Hispanic Groups by Nation or Territory of Origin, 2006

SOURCE: U.S. Bureau of the Census (2007a).

Photo 8.7

A polling station in New
Mexico uses English
and Spanish signs.

© Steven Clevenger/Corbis.

rate for non-Hispanic whites (U.S. Bureau of the Census, 2007b, p. 256). In the 2006 elections, a nonpresidential election year, turnout for Hispanic voters rose to 32%, still much lower than the rate for whites (52%) and blacks (41%) (Pew Hispanic Center, 2007). These lower participation rates are due to many factors, including the younger average age of the Hispanic population (younger people are the least likely to register and vote) and the large percentage of recent, non-English-speaking immigrants and noncitizens in the group.

At the national level, there are now 24 Hispanic Americans in the House of Representatives, more than double the number in 1990 and about 6% of the total. In addition, the 110th Congress included three Hispanic American senators. Most of these representatives and senators are members of the Democratic Party, but in a reflection of the diversity of the group, nearly 20% are Republicans (U.S. Bureau of the Census, 2007b, p. 251). On the local and state level, the number of public officials identified as Hispanic increased by over 50% between 1985 and 2005, from 3,147 to 4,853 (U.S. Bureau of the Census, 2007b, p. 255).

Although still underrepresented, these figures suggest that Hispanic Americans will become increasingly important in American political life as their numbers continue to grow and their rates of naturalization rise. A preview of their increasing power has been displayed in recent years as Hispanic communities across the nation have mobilized and engaged in massive demonstrations to express their opposition to restrictive immigration policies (for example, see Alzenman, 2006).

Jobs and Income. The economic situation of Hispanic Americans is mixed. Many members of these groups, especially those who have been in the United States for several generations, are doing "just fine. They have, in ever increasing numbers, accessed opportunities in education and employment and have carved out a niche of American prosperity for themselves and their children" (Camarillo & Bonilla, 2001, pp. 130–131). For many others, however, the picture is not so promising. They face the possibility of becoming members of an impoverished, powerless, and economically marginalized urban underclass, like African Americans and other minority groups of color.

Occupationally, Hispanic American groups are concentrated in the less-desirable, lower-paid service and unskilled segments of the job market, although the groups with higher levels of human capital (e.g., education) compare more favorably with the dominant group. This is generally what would be expected for a group with such a high percentage of first-generation members who bring such modest levels of education and job skills.

Unemployment, low income, and poverty continue to be issues for all Hispanic groups. The official unemployment rates for Hispanic Americans run about twice the rate for non-Hispanic whites, and Exhibit 8.15 shows that Hispanics in general and all subgroups have dramatically lower median household incomes than non-Hispanic whites.

Exhibit 8.16 supplements the information on median income by displaying the overall distribution of income for Hispanic Americans and non-Hispanic whites for 2006. The figure shows a greater concentration (wider bars) of Hispanics in the lower-income categories and a lower concentration (narrower bars) in the income groups at the very top of the figure. There is a noticeable concentration of both groups in the $60,000 to $100,000 categories, but whites outnumber Hispanics by about 32% to 23% in these income ranges. Recent detailed income information is not available for the separate subgroups, but we can assume that although all groups have members in all income categories, Mexican Americans, Dominican Americans, and Puerto Ricans would be disproportionately represented in the lowest-income categories and Cuban and Colombian Americans in the higher groups.

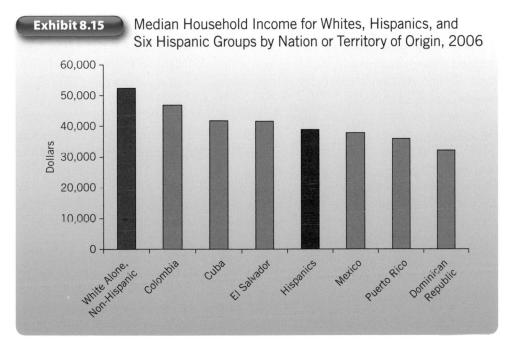

Exhibit 8.15 Median Household Income for Whites, Hispanics, and Six Hispanic Groups by Nation or Territory of Origin, 2006

SOURCE: U.S. Bureau of the Census (2007a).

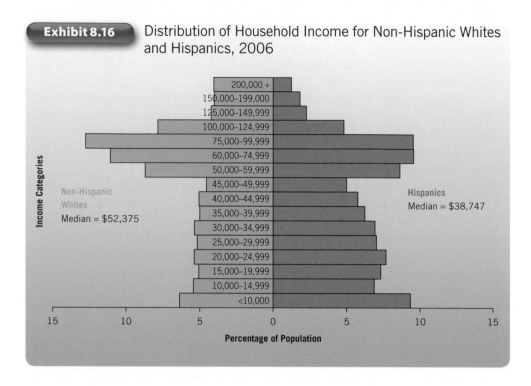

Exhibit 8.16 Distribution of Household Income for Non-Hispanic Whites and Hispanics, 2006

Income Categories:
200,000 +
150,000–199,000
125,000–149,999
100,000–124,999
75,000–99,999
60,000–74,999
50,000–59,999
45,000–49,999
40,000–44,999
35,000–39,999
30,000–34,999
25,000–29,999
20,000–24,999
15,000–19,999
10,000–14,999
<10,000

Non-Hispanic Whites
Median = $52,375

Hispanics
Median = $38,747

Percentage of Population

SOURCE: U.S. Bureau of the Census (2007a).

Exhibit 8.17 finishes the socioeconomic profile by displaying the varying levels of poverty for Hispanic Americans, a pattern that is consistent with previous information on income and education. The poverty rate for all Hispanic families is more than double the national norm and at about the same level as that of African Americans (see Exhibit 6.13). However, there is considerable diversity across the subgroups, with Colombians and Cubans very close to national norms and Dominicans the most impoverished. For all groups, children have higher poverty rates than families.

These socioeconomic profiles reflect the concentration of many Hispanic groups in the low-wage sector of the economy, a long tradition of discrimination and exclusion for Mexican Americans and Puerto Ricans, high rates of recent immigration, and the lower amounts of human capital (education, job training) controlled by these groups. The higher rates of unemployment for these two groups reflect not only discrimination but also the lack of security and the seasonal nature of many of the jobs they hold. Cuban Americans, buoyed by a more privileged social class background and their enclave economy, rank higher on virtually all measures of wealth and prosperity.

There is a split labor market differentiated by gender, within the dual market differentiated by race and ethnicity. Hispanic women—like minority group women in general—are among the lowest-paid, most-exploitable, and least-protected segments of the U.S. labor force. The impact of poverty is especially severe for Latino women, who often find themselves with the responsibility of caring for their children alone. In 2004, about 19% of all Hispanic American households were headed by females, and for the six subgroups covered in this chapter, this percentage ranged from a low of 15% for Cuban Americans to a high of 32% for Dominican

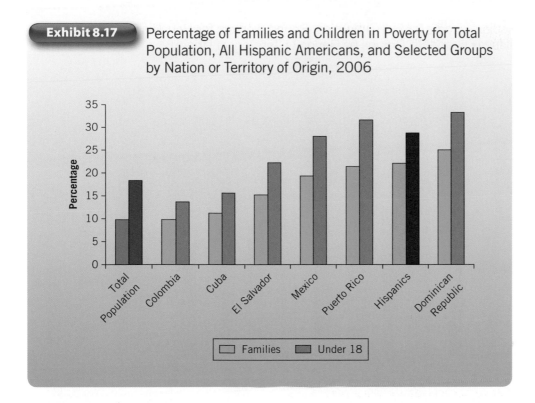

Exhibit 8.17 Percentage of Families and Children in Poverty for Total Population, All Hispanic Americans, and Selected Groups by Nation or Territory of Origin, 2006

SOURCE: U.S. Bureau of the Census (2007a).

Americans. In the same year, about 13% of all households were headed by females (U.S. Bureau of the Census, 2007a, p. 10). This pattern is the result of many factors, among them the status of Latino men in the labor force. The jobs available to Latino men often do not pay enough to support a family, and many jobs are seasonal, temporary, or otherwise insecure.

Female-headed Latino families are affected by a triple economic handicap: They have only one wage earner, whose potential income is limited by discrimination against both women and Latinos. The result of these multiple disadvantages is an especially high rate of poverty. Whereas 22% of non-Hispanic, white, female-headed households fall below the poverty line, the percentage is nearly 40% for Hispanic households headed by females (U.S. Bureau of the Census, 2007a; see Exhibit 8.18).

Summary. The socioeconomic situation of Latinos is complex and diversified. Although members of all groups have successfully entered the mainstream economy, poverty and exclusion continue to be major issues. Highly concentrated in deteriorated urban areas (barrios), segments of these groups, like other minority groups of color, face the possibility of permanent poverty and economic marginality.

Primary Structural Assimilation. Overall, the extent of intimate contact between Hispanic Americans and the dominant group probably has been higher than for either African Americans or American Indians (see, e.g., Quillian & Campbell, 2003; Rosenfield, 2002). This pattern may reflect the fact that Latinos form partly ethnic minority groups and partly racial minority groups. Some studies report that contact is greater for the more affluent social

Median Income for Full-Time, Year-Round Workers for Non-Hispanic Whites, Hispanics, and Six Groups by Nation or Territory of Origin

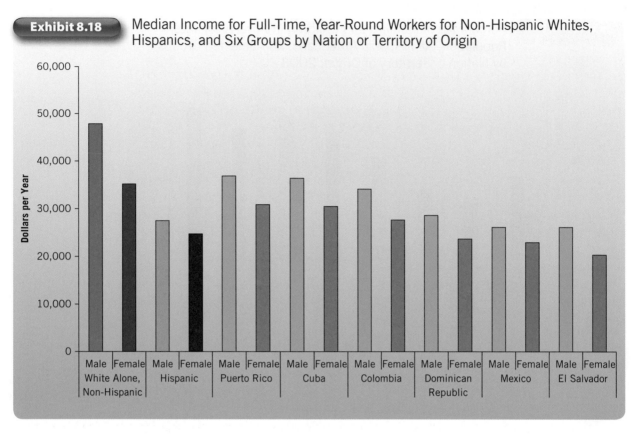

SOURCE: U.S. Bureau of the Census (2007a).

classes, in the cities, and for the younger generations (who are presumably more American-ized) (Fitzpatrick, 1976; Grebler et al., 1970, p. 397; Rodriguez, 1989, pp. 70–72). On the other hand, the rate of contact has probably been decreased by the rapid increase in immigration and the tendency of the first generation to socialize more with their coethnics.

Rates of intermarriage are higher for Latinos than for African Americans, but neither are a very high percentage of all marriages. Black and white interracial couples make up less than 1% of all marriages, and the comparable figure for Latinos is 3.7% of all marriages (U.S. Bureau of the Census, 2007b, p. 52).

Assimilation and Hispanic Americans

As test cases for what we have called the traditional view of American assimilation, Latinos fare poorly. Mexican Americans continue to be concentrated in the low-wage sector of the labor market, a source of cheap labor for the dominant group's economy. Puerto Ricans, who are more recent arrivals, occupy a similar profile and position.

The fundamental reality faced by both groups, in their histories and in their present situations, is their colonized status in U.S. society. Both Mexican Americans and Puerto Ricans have struggled to rise from their subordinate positions in the United States, and some members have been successful. Yet both groups continue to resemble other colonized minority groups and share many problems with other urban minority groups of color.

The traditional views of the nature of assimilation likewise fail to describe the experiences of Cuban Americans. They are more prosperous, on the average, than either Mexican Americans or Puerto Ricans, but they became successful by remaining separate. Since their immigration is so recent, it may be too early to tell how Dominicans, Salvadorans, and Colombians will fare in the assimilation process. We can be sure, however, that their experiences will be as varied and volatile as those of the three larger Hispanic groups.

There is no single Hispanic American experience or pattern of adjustment to the larger society. We have focused mainly on three of the many Latino groups in the United States, and the diversity of their experiences suggests the variety and complexity of what it means to be a minority group in U.S. society. Their experiences also illustrate some of the fundamental forces that shape the experiences of minority groups: the split labor market and the U.S. appetite for cheap labor, the impact of industrialization, the dangers of a permanent urban underclass, the relationships between competition and levels of prejudice and rejection, and the persistence of race as a primary dividing line between people and groups.

CURRENT DEBATES

Is the United States Threatened by "Hispanization"?

As we have seen in this chapter, immigration from Latin America—and especially from Mexico—is voluminous and shows no sign of slowing. How will these new immigrants shape American culture? Will traditional American values such as individualism, the Protestant Ethic, democracy, and loyalty and patriotism be compromised? Are we developing into two nations, one Anglo and the other Hispanic?

Many people are deeply concerned that American culture cannot survive in its present form. For example, political scientist Samuel Huntington, in his influential book Who Are We? (2004), argues that large-scale immigration (particularly from Mexico) is leading the United States away from its historical roots and its central values. Others have taken up his argument, and in the article below, John Fonte

(2004) presents a case for patriotic assimilation as an antidote to the threats presented by our growing cultural diversity.

In opposition to the alarms raised by Huntington and Fonte, Professor Francis Fukuyama (2004), a leading American academic, argues that the immigrants are the true carriers of the "Protestant Ethic" and that the United States is corrupting their stronger family and traditional values, not the other way around.

How to Make an American

JOHN FONTE

Browsing through my grandmother's citizenship textbook from the 1930s one day, I found Lesson

61 on the Americanization policies of Theodore Roosevelt:

> [Roosevelt] loved America above all else and his last public message was a plea for the "complete Americanization" of our people in which he said: "...[if] the immigrant who comes here in good faith becomes an American and assimilates himself to us, he shall be treated on an exact equality with everyone else, for it is an outrage to discriminate against any such man because of creed, or birthplace, or origin. But this is predicated upon the man's becoming an American, and nothing but an American. There can be no divided allegiance here. We have room for but one soul [sic] loyalty and that is loyalty to the American people."

The textbook captured the spirit of Americanization—that immigrants are expected to assimilate patriotically and become loyal Americans. More than one hundred years earlier George Washington had written to John Adams that he envisioned immigrants "assimilated to our customs, measures, and laws," and because of this, Washington declared, native-born citizens and immigrants would "soon become one people."

This sentiment is roughly the view of the majority of Americans today, but clearly not the opinion of many American elites. As Samuel Huntington argues...elites in government, business, education, academia, and the media have for decades been actively involved in efforts to "deconstruct"[2] the American nation and its traditional concepts of assimilation and citizenship.

Huntington explains in his new book *Who Are We?* that arguments over multiculturalism, bilingualism, ethnic and gender group preferences, dual citizenship, history standards, transnationalism—and immigration and assimilation—are all part of the same conflict over the nature of the American liberal democratic regime. He is right to maintain that a "deconstructionist coalition" challenges the core principles of the American nation on all fronts. At the end of the day, the deconstructionists would transform an American nation based on the principles of individual citizenship, equality of opportunity, and self-government within Constitutional limits, into a new form of regime built on ethnic, racial, and gender group rights with decision-making increasingly in the hands of unelected elites....What is ultimately at stake is whether the traditional American regime will be transmitted to future generations intact or wholly transformed.

Clearly, all of this means that the issue of immigration/assimilation (and these two issues should always be considered as one) must be examined within the broader context of the leftist assault on traditional American political principles. To help clarify the problem, let us explore a series of assimilation-related issues that will soon confront both elite and popular opinion. These include initiatives to revise the oath of allegiance [and] design a new citizenship test....

Implicit in Huntington's thesis is that just below the surface of the policy debate there exists unapologetic public support for vigorous Americanization policies that would explicitly promote the patriotic integration of immigrants into what was once called "the American way of life." Besides public support, there appears to be a bloc in Congress...strongly interested in patriotic, as well as economic and linguistic, integration. Last year when the United States Citizenship and Immigration Services (USCIS) wanted to simplify the citizenship oath, some members of Congress immediately protested, and the USCIS pulled back. Worried that the traditional oath (in which new citizens promise to "renounce" their old allegiances and "bear arms" on behalf of the United States) will be weakened, Senator Lamar Alexander (R-TN) and Congressman Jim Ryun (R-KS) have introduced legislation to codify it into law.

In addition, it appears that the forces of patriotic renewal are being heard in discussions over the development of a new citizenship test.... Advocates of patriotic integration in veterans groups, think tanks, and Congress...declare that we must start with first principles by asking: What is the purpose of the history/government citizenship test?

The law states that applicants for citizenship must have: 1) "a knowledge and understanding of the history, and of the principles and form of government of the United States" and 2) possess "good moral character, attachment to the principles of the Constitution, and be well disposed to the good order and happiness of the United States." This leads naturally to the conclusion that the purpose of the test as a whole is not merely to get new citizens to know certain facts, but also to be "attached" to the principles of the Constitution—evidence of the explicit normative purpose of naturalization.

The citizenship naturalization process should be a life-altering experience, a rite of passage, such as a wedding, graduation, first communion, or bar mitzvah, which fosters emotional attachment to our nation and strengthens patriotism. . . . The oath is especially crucial to American democracy, because citizenship in America is not based on race, religion, or ethnicity, but on political loyalty. In taking the oath, the new citizen transfers allegiance from the land of his birth to the United States.

Oath-takers have a moral obligation to give up all political loyalty to their birth nations . . . . The oath of allegiance, like wedding vows, represents not only a moral obligation for individuals, but a norm for our democracy. . . .

If it becomes routine for large numbers of new citizens to keep old political loyalties, the nature of American citizenship will be transformed, just as, say, legal polygamy would transform the nature of marriage. The principle that we are a people united by political allegiance rather than the ascriptive characteristics of race, ethnicity, and birth would be effectively repudiated.

"Patriotic Renewalists" on Capitol Hill could very well demand that . . . we should get serious about patriotic assimilation . . . . Like Theodore Roosevelt, . . . we should insist that immigration policy be combined with serious Americanization initiatives and that immigration levels remain dependent on how well we integrate newcomers patriotically. After all, we are a nation, not just a market.

SOURCE: Fonte, John (2004). "How to Make an American." *American Enterprise*, 15(6):4–5.

Why We Shouldn't Worry About the "Hispanization" of the United States

FRANCIS FUKUYAMA

It is not politically correct today to say that America is fundamentally a Protestant country, or that a specific form of religion is critical to its success as a democracy. Yet as historical facts, these statements are undoubtedly true, and they are the premise of *Who Are We?*, Samuel Huntington's new book. The United States, he argues, is a liberal democracy based on certain universal political principles regarding liberty and equality, summed up traditionally as the American Creed. But the country's success as a free and prosperous democratic society was not due simply to the goodness of these principles or the strength of America's formal institutions. There was a crucial supplement: cultural values that Huntington describes as "Anglo-Protestant." . . .

Huntington is following in the path of innumerable observers of the United States [who] have noted that the dissident, sectarian nature of the Protestantism transplanted to North America was critical to shaping American values like individualism, antistatism, tolerance, moralism, the work ethic, the propensity for voluntary association, and a host of other informal habits and customs that augment our Constitution and legal system. *Who Are We?* is also perfectly consistent with Huntington's [work] in arguing that liberal democracy is less a universalistic system for organizing political life than an outgrowth of a certain northern European Christian culture, the appeal and feasibility of which will be limited in other cultural settings.

Huntington goes on to argue that . . . immigration [is a] threat to that traditional American identity. In his view, the American elite, from corporate executives to professors to journalists, sees itself as cosmopolitan, secular, and attached to the principle of diversity as an end in itself. That elite no longer feels emotionally attached to America and is increasingly out of touch with the vast majority of non-elite Americans who remain patriotic, morally conservative, and Christian....

On no issue are elites and ordinary Americans further apart than on immigration, and Huntington takes the latter's concerns about the threat posed by Mexican immigration very seriously. This is because of the numbers involved, ... the concentration of Mexican immigrants in a few Southwestern states and cities, and the proximity of their country of origin. The wave has occurred, moreover, at a time when American elites have lost confidence in their own cultural values and are no longer willing to use the public school system to assimilate these new immigrants to Anglo-Protestant culture. Huntington worries that unchecked immigration will sow the seeds of a later backlash, and may even lead one day to something new in the American experience, an ethnolinguistic minority with strong ties to a neighboring country that could potentially make territorial claims on much of the Southwest.

I am glad that a scholar like Huntington has raised these issues, since they deserve serious discussion.... Huntington poses some real questions about whether the large Mexican immigrant population will assimilate as other immigrant groups have done before them.... He is right that "culture matters" and he is right that the thoughtless promotion of multiculturalism and identity politics threatens important American values. But his book, ironically, offers grist for a rather different perspective on the problem: *Who Are We?* suggests that the more serious threat to American culture comes perhaps from its own internal contradictions than from foreigners.

Let's begin with the question of who the true bearers of "Anglo-Protestant" values are.... His chapter describing "core" Anglo-Protestant values ends up focusing almost entirely on the work ethic: "from the beginning," he writes, "America's religion has been the religion of work." But who in today's world works hard? Certainly not contemporary Europeans with their six-week vacations. The real Protestants are those Korean grocery-store owners, or Indian entrepreneurs, or Taiwanese engineers, or Russian cab drivers working two or three jobs in America's free and relatively unregulated labor market. I lived in Los Angeles for nearly a decade, and remember passing groups of Chicanos gathered at certain intersections at 7 a.m. waiting for work as day laborers. No lack of a work ethic here: That's why Hispanics have pushed native-born African-Americans out of low-skill jobs in virtually every city where they compete head-to-head....

There are a number of grounds for thinking that the United States will assimilate Hispanic immigrants just as it has earlier ethnic groups. Most important is the fact that they are Christian—either Catholic or, to an increasing degree, Evangelical Protestant. When controlling for socioeconomic status, they have stronger traditional family values than their native-born counterparts. This means that culturally, today's Mexican immigrants are much less distant from mainstream "Anglos" than were, say, the southern Italian immigrants or Eastern European Jews from mainstream WASPs at the beginning of the 20th century. Their rates of second- and third-generation intermarriage are much closer to those of other European groups than for African-Americans. And, from Gen. Ricardo Sanchez on down, they are serving honorably today in the U.S. armed forces in numbers disproportionate to their place in the overall population.

The problem ... is not that Mexican and other Latino immigrants come with the wrong values, but rather that they are corrupted by American practices. Many young Hispanics are absorbed into the underclass culture of American inner cities, which has then re-exported gang violence back to Mexico and Central America; or else their middle-class leaders have absorbed the American post-civil rights era sense of victimization and entitlement. There is a sharp divide between elites—organizations like the National Council of La Raza, or the Mexican-American Legal Defense Fund—and the general population of Hispanic immigrants. The latter, overall, tend to be socially conservative, want to learn English and assimilate into the American mainstream, and were even supportive initially of California's Proposition 187 (denying benefits to illegal immigrants) and 227 (ending bilingualism in public education)....

If it is the case that high levels of immigration are inevitable for developed societies, then what we need to do is to shift the focus from immigration per se to the issue of assimilation....

This will be a huge challenge for the United States, but I am more confident than Huntington that we can meet it. Indeed, Hispanic immigrants will help to reinforce certain cultural values like the emphasis on family and work, and the Christian character of American society.

SOURCE: Fukuyama, Francis (2004). *Identity Crisis: Why We Shouldn't Worry About Mexican Immigration*. Retrieved April 2, 2005, from http://slate.msn.com/id/2101756/#continuearticle.

Debate Questions to Consider

1. Analyze these arguments in terms of assimilation and pluralism. Are these authors using Gordon's model of assimilation? Can these issues and concerns be expressed in terms of pluralism? How?

2. Is "patriotic assimilation" a reasonable policy to deal with the concerns over "Hispanization"? What would this policy look like if implemented in schools and other institutions?

3. What points does Fukuyama make in response to the arguments presented by Fonte and Huntington? What evidence does he present to back up his points? How convincing is the evidence?

4. Is it fair to say that Fonte is a pessimist and Fukuyama is an optimist about the future of American culture? Does immigration really threaten traditional American values?

Main Points

• Hispanic Americans are a diverse and growing part of U.S. society. There are many distinct groups, but the three largest are Mexican Americans, Puerto Ricans, and Cuban Americans. The various Hispanic groups do not think of themselves as a single entity.

• Hispanic Americans have some characteristics of colonized groups and some of immigrant groups. Similarly, these groups are racial minorities in some ways and ethnic minorities in others.

• Since the beginning of the 20th century, Mexico has served as a reserve labor force for the development of the U.S. economy. Immigrants from Mexico entered a social system in which the colonized status of the group was already established. Mexican Americans remained a colonized minority group despite the large numbers of immigrants in the group and have been systematically excluded from opportunities for upward mobility by institutional discrimination and segregation.

- A Mexican American protest movement has been continuously seeking to improve the status of the group. In the 1960s, a more intense and militant movement emerged, guided by the ideology of Chicanismo.

- Puerto Ricans began to move to the mainland in large numbers only in recent decades. The group is concentrated in the urban Northeast, in the low-wage sector of the job market.

- Cubans began immigrating after Castro's revolution in the late 1950s. They settled primarily in southern Florida, where they created an ethnic enclave.

- Dominicans, Salvadorans, and Colombians are three of the many Hispanic groups that began immigrating to the United States in large numbers after the 1965 change in federal immigration policy.

- The overall levels of anti-Hispanic prejudice and discrimination seem to have declined, along with the general decline in explicit, overt racism in American society. Recent high levels of immigration seem to have increased anti-Hispanic prejudice and discrimination, however, especially in areas with large numbers of immigrants.

- Levels of acculturation are highly variable from group to group and generation to generation. Acculturation increases with length of residence. The vitality of Latino cultures has been sustained by recent immigration.

- Secondary structural assimilation also varies from group to group. Poverty, unemployment, lower levels of educational attainment, and other forms of inequality continue to be major problems for Hispanic groups, even the relatively successful Cuban Americans.

- Primary structural assimilation with the dominant group is greater than for African Americans.

- Public sociology Assignment 2 in the introduction to Part 3 will permit you to document racial and ethnic inequalities in health in your area. What differences in health can you document between Hispanic groups and non-Hispanic whites? Are there differences between specific Hispanic groups? Do these differences parallel the patterns of inequality documented in this chapter?

Study Site on the Web

Don't forget the interactive quizzes and other resources and learning aids at www.pineforge.com/healeystudy5.

For Further Reading

Acuna, Rodolfo. (1999). *Occupied America* (4th ed.). New York: Harper & Row.

The author reviews Mexican American history and argues that the experiences of this group resemble those of colonized groups.

Garcia, Maria Cristina. (1996). *Havana USA: Cuban Exiles and Cuban Americans in South Florida, 1959–1994.* Berkeley: University of California Press.

A comprehensive history of the Cuban community in southern Florida.

Fitzpatrick, Joseph P. (1987). *Puerto Rican Americans: The Meaning of Migration to the Mainland* (2nd ed.). Englewood Cliffs, NJ: Prentice Hall.

Good overview of the history and present situation of Puerto Ricans.

Mirandé, Alfredo. (1985). *The Chicano Experience: An Alternative Perspective.* Notre Dame, IN: University of Notre Dame Press.

A passionate analysis of the Mexican American experience. Separate chapters on work, crime, education, the church, and family.

Portes, Alejandro, & Bach, Robert L. (1985). *Latin Journey: Cuban and Mexican Immigrants in the United States.* Berkeley: University of California Press.

A landmark analysis of Latino immigration, ethnic enclaves, and the United States and assimilation.

Questions for Review and Study

1. At the beginning of this chapter, it is stated that Hispanic Americans "combine elements of the polar extremes [immigrant and colonized] of Blauner's typology of minority groups" and that they are "partly an ethnic minority group and partly a racial minority group." Explain these statements in terms of the rest of the material presented in the chapter.

2. What important cultural differences between Mexican Americans and the dominant society shaped the relationships between the two groups?

3. How does the history of Mexican immigration demonstrate the usefulness of Noel's concepts of differentials in power and competition?

4. Compare and contrast the protest movements of Mexican Americans, American Indians, and African Americans. What similarities and differences existed in Chicanismo, Red Power, and Black Power? How do the differences reflect the unique experiences of each group?

5. In what ways are the experiences of Puerto Ricans and Cuban Americans unique compared with those of other minority groups? How do these differences reflect other differences, such as differences in contact situation?

6. The Cuban American enclave has resulted in a variety of benefits for the group. Why don't other minority groups follow this strategy?

7. What images of Latinas are common in U.S. society? How do these images reflect the experiences of these groups?

8. Describe the situation of the major Hispanic American groups in terms of acculturation and integration. Which groups are closest to equality? What factors or experiences might account for the differences between groups? In what ways might the statement "Hispanic Americans are remaining pluralistic even while they assimilate" be true?

Internet Research Project

The Mexican Migration Project was created to learn more about the complex process of Mexican migration to the United States. The project is binational and has been gathering data since 1982. A number of individual stories of Mexican migrants are available online at http://mmp.opr.princeton.edu/expressions/stories-en,aspx. Read the introduction and then select several of the stories to read. Analyze each using the concepts developed in this chapter, especially the idea that Mexico serves as a reserve pool of cheap labor for the benefit of U.S. businesses.

Notes

1. *Latino* refers to the group in general or to males. The correct form for females is *Latina*.
2. In this context, to "deconstruct" means to critically analyze values and traditions in order to expose contradictions and inconsistencies.

Asian Americans

CHAPTER 9

"Model Minorities"?

A variety of groups from Asia are becoming increasingly prominent in the United States. Although they are often seen as the same and classified into a single category in government reports, these groups vary in their languages, in their cultural and physical characteristics, and in their experiences in the United States. Some of these groups are truly newcomers to America, but others have roots in this country stretching back for more than 150 years.

In this chapter, we will begin with an overview of the largest Asian American groups and then briefly examine the traditions and customs that they bring with them to America. We will then focus on the two oldest Asian American groups, Chinese Americans and Japanese Americans, and cover some of the newer Asian groups more briefly. Throughout the chapter, we will be especially concerned with the perception that Asian Americans in general and Chinese and Japanese Americans in particular are *model minorities*: successful, affluent, highly educated people who do not suffer from the problems usually associated with minority group status. How accurate is this view? Have Asian Americans forged a pathway to upward mobility that could be followed by other groups? Do the concepts and theories that have guided this text (particularly the Blauner and Noel hypotheses) apply? Does the success of these groups mean that the United States is truly an open, fair, and just society? We explore these questions throughout the chapter.

Exhibit 9.1 lists the largest Asian American groups and illustrates their diversity. As was the case with American Indians and Hispanic Americans, *Asian American* is a convenient label imposed by the larger society (and by government agencies like the Census Bureau) that de-emphasizes the differences between the groups. The six largest groups are distinct from each other in culture and physical appearance, and each has had its own unique experience in America. A variety of smaller Asian American groups (Hmongs, Pakistanis, Cambodians, and Laotians, for example), not covered in this chapter, further add to this diversity.

Several features of Exhibit 9.1 are worth noting. First, Asian Americans are a small fraction of the total U.S. population. Even when aggregated, they account for less than 5% of all Americans. In contrast, African Americans and Hispanic Americans are each more than 12% of the total population (see Exhibit 1.1). Second, most Asian American groups have grown dramatically in recent decades, largely because of high rates of immigration since the 1965 changes in U.S. immigration policy. All of the groups listed in Exhibit 9.1 grew faster than the total population between 1990 and 2006. The Japanese American population grew at the

Exhibit 9.1 Size and Growth of Asian American Groups by Nation or Territory of Origin, 1990–2006 (Alone and in Combination)

Group	1990	2000	2006	Growth (Number of Times Larger), (1990–2006)	Percentage of Total Population, 2006
Chinese	1,645,472	2,633,849	3,565,458	2.2	1.2
Filipino	1,406,770	2,089,701	2,915,745	2.1	1.0
Asian Indians	815,447	1,785,336	2,662,112	3.3	0.9
Vietnamese	614,547	1,171,776	1,599,394	2.6	0.5
Koreans	798,849	1,148,951	1,520,703	1.9	0.5
Japanese	847,562	958,945	1,221,773	1.4	0.4
All Asian American Groups	6,908,638	11,070,913	14,656,608	2.1	4.5
Percentage of U.S. Population	2.8%	3.9%	4.5%	2.2	
Total U.S. Population	248,710,000	281,422,000	299,398,485	1.2	

SOURCE: 1990: U.S. Bureau of the Census (1990); 2000: U.S. Bureau of the Census (2000f); 2006: U.S. Bureau of the Census (2007a).

slowest rate (largely because immigration from Japan has been low in recent decades), but the number of Asian Indians more than tripled, and several other groups more than doubled. This rapid growth is projected to continue for decades to come, and the impact of Asian Americans on everyday life and American culture will increase accordingly. Today, fewer than 5 out of every 100 Americans are in this group, but this ratio will grow to nearly 10 out of every 100 by the year 2050 (see Exhibit 1.1). The relative sizes of the largest Asian American groups are presented in Exhibit 9.2, and their nations of origin are displayed in Exhibit 9.3.

Like Hispanic Americans, most Asian American groups have a high percentage of foreign-born members. The great majority of four of the six groups listed in Exhibit 9.4 are first generation, and even Japanese Americans, the lowest-ranked group, more than double the national norm for foreign-born members.

Origins and Cultures

Asian Americans have brought a wealth of traditions to the United States. They speak many different languages and practice religions as diverse as Buddhism, Confucianism, Islam, Hinduism, and Christianity. Asian cultures predate the founding of the United States by centuries or even millennia. Although no two of these cultures are the same, some

Exhibit 9.2 Largest Asian American Groups by Nation of Origin, 2006

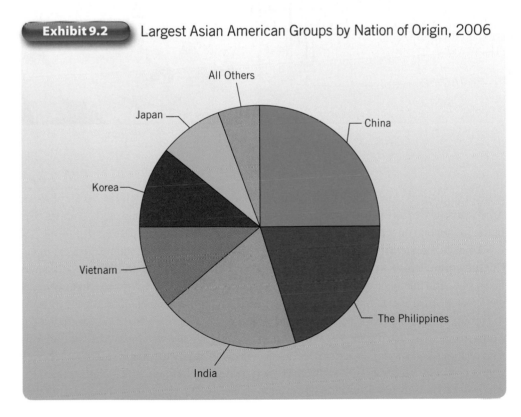

SOURCE: U.S. Bureau of the Census (2007a).

Exhibit 9.3 Map Showing China, the Philippines, India, Vietnam, Korea, and Japan

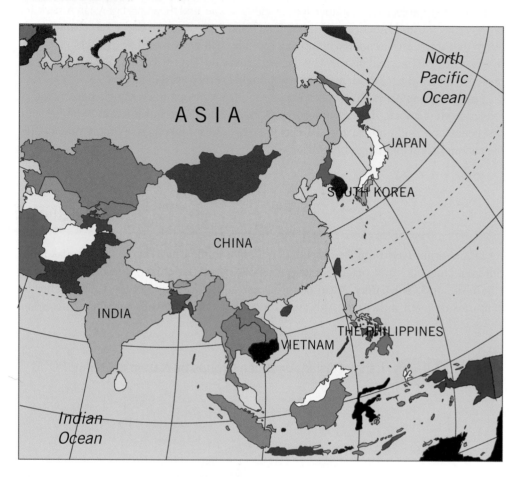

general similarities can be identified. These cultural traits have shaped the behavior of Asian Americans, as well as the perceptions of members of the dominant group, and compose part of the foundation on which Asian American experiences have been built.

Asian cultures tend to stress group membership over individual self-interest. For example, Confucianism, which was the dominant ethical and moral system in traditional China and had a powerful influence on many other Asian cultures, counsels people to see themselves as elements in larger social systems and status hierarchies. Confucianism emphasizes loyalty to the group, conformity to societal expectations, and respect for one's superiors. In traditional China, as in other Asian societies, the business of everyday life was organized around kinship relations, and most interpersonal relations were with family members and other relatives (Lyman, 1974, p. 9). The family or the clan often owned the land on which all depended for survival, and kinship ties determined inheritance patterns. The clan also performed a number of crucial social functions, including arranging marriages, settling disputes between individuals, and organizing festivals and holidays.

Exhibit 9.4 Percentage Foreign-Born by Country of Origin, 2006

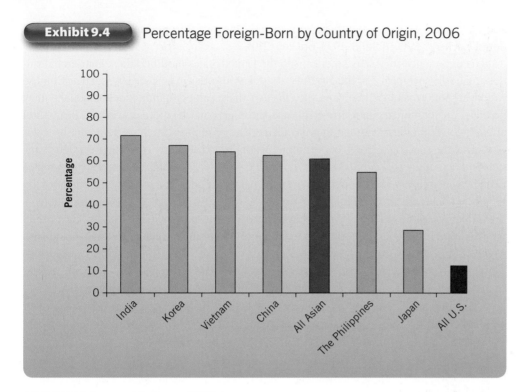

SOURCE: U.S. Bureau of the Census (2007a).

Asian cultures stress sensitivity to the opinions and judgments of others and the importance of avoiding public embarrassment and not giving offense. Especially when discussing Japanese culture, these cultural tendencies are often contrasted with Western practices in terms of "guilt versus shame" and the nature of personal morality (Benedict, 1946). In Western cultures, individuals are encouraged to develop and abide by a conscience, or an inner moral voice, and behavior is guided by one's personal sense of guilt. In contrast, Asian cultures stress the importance of maintaining the respect and good opinion of others and avoiding shame and public humiliation. Group harmony, or *wa* in Japanese, is a central concern, and displays of individualism are discouraged. These characteristics are reflected in the Japanese proverb "The nail that sticks up must be hammered down" (Whiting, 1990, p. 70). Asian cultures emphasize proper behavior, conformity to convention and the judgments of others, and avoiding embarrassment and personal confrontations ("saving face").

Traditional Asian cultures were male dominated, and women were consigned to subordinate roles. A Chinese woman was expected to serve first her father, then her husband, and, if widowed, her eldest son. Confucianism also decreed that women should observe the Four Virtues: chastity and obedience, shyness, a pleasing demeanor, and skill in the performance of domestic duties (Amott & Matthaei, 1991, p. 200). Women of high status in traditional China symbolized their subordination by binding their feet. This painful, crippling practice began early in life and required women to wrap their feet tightly to keep them artificially small. The bones in the arch were broken so that the toes could be bent under the foot, further decreasing the size of the foot. Bound feet were considered beautiful, but they also immobilized women and were intended to prevent them from "wandering away" from domestic and household duties (Jackson, 2000; Takaki, 1993, pp. 209–210).

The experiences of Asian Americans in the United States modified these patriarchal values and traditional traits. For the groups with longer histories in U.S. society, such as Chinese Americans and Japanese Americans, the effects of these values on individual personality may be slight, but for more recently arrived groups, the effects may be more powerful. The cultural and religious differences among the Asian American groups also reflect the recent histories of each of the sending nations. For example, Vietnam was a colony of China for 1,000 years, but for much of the past century, it was a colony of France. Although Vietnamese culture has been heavily influenced by China, many Vietnamese are Catholic, a result of the efforts of the French to convert them. The Philippines and India were also colonized by Western nations— the former by Spain and then by the United States and the latter by Great Britain. As a result, many Filipinos are Catholic, and many Indian immigrants are familiar with English and with Anglo culture.

These examples are, of course, the merest suggestion of the diversity of these groups. In fact, Asian Americans, who share little more than a slight physical resemblance and some broad cultural similarities, are much more diverse than Hispanic Americans, who are overwhelmingly Catholic and share a common language and a historical connection with Spain (Min, 1995, p. 25).

Contact Situations and the Development of the Chinese American and Japanese American Communities

The earliest Asian groups to arrive in substantial numbers were from China and Japan. Their contact situations not only shaped their own histories but also affected the present situation of all Asian Americans in many ways. As we will see, the contact situations for both Chinese Americans and Japanese Americans featured massive rejection and discrimination. Both groups adapted to the racism of the larger society by forming enclaves, a strategy that eventually produced some major benefits for their descendants.

Chinese Americans

Early Immigration and the Anti-Chinese Campaign.
Immigrants from China to the United States began to arrive in the early 1800s and were generally motivated by the same kinds of social and economic forces that have inspired immigration everywhere for the past two centuries. Chinese immigrants were "pushed" to leave their homeland by the disruption of traditional social relations, caused by the colonization of much of China by more industrialized European nations, and by rapid population growth (Chan, 1990; Lyman, 1974; Tsai, 1986). At the same time, these immigrants were "pulled" to the West Coast of the United States by the Gold Rush of 1849 and by other opportunities created by the development of the West.

The Noel hypothesis (see Chapter 4) provides a useful way to analyze the contact situation that developed between Chinese and Anglo-Americans in the mid-19th century. As you recall, Noel argues that racial or ethnic stratification will result when a contact situation is characterized by three conditions: ethnocentrism, competition, and a differential in power. Once all three conditions were met on the West Coast, a vigorous campaign against the Chinese began, and the group was pushed into a subordinate, disadvantaged position.

Ethnocentrism based on racial, cultural, and language differences was present from the beginning, but at first, competition for jobs between Chinese immigrants and native-born workers was muted by a robust, rapidly growing economy and an abundance of jobs. At first, politicians, newspaper editorial writers, and business leaders praised the Chinese for their industriousness and tirelessness (Tsai, 1986, p. 17). Before long, however, the economic boom slowed, and the supply of jobs began to dry up. The Gold Rush petered out, and the transcontinental railroad, which thousands of Chinese workers had helped to build, was completed in 1869. The migration of Anglo-Americans from the East continued, and competition for jobs and other resources increased. An anti-Chinese campaign of harassment, discrimination, and violent attacks began. In 1871, in Los Angeles, a mob of "several hundred whites shot, hanged, and stabbed 19 Chinese to death" (Tsai, 1986, p. 67). Other attacks against the Chinese occurred in Denver; Seattle; Tacoma; and Rock Springs, Wyoming (Lyman, 1974, p. 77).

As the West Coast economy changed, the Chinese came to be seen as a threat, and elements of the dominant group tried to limit competition. The Chinese were a small group—there were only about 100,000 in the entire country in 1870—and by law, they were not permitted to become citizens. Hence, they controlled few power resources with which to withstand these attacks. During the 1870s, Chinese workers were forced out of most sectors of the mainstream economy, and in 1882, the anti-Chinese campaign experienced its ultimate triumph when the U.S. Congress passed the Chinese Exclusion Act, banning virtually all immigration from China. The act was one of the first restrictive immigration laws and was aimed solely at the Chinese. It established a "rigid competitive" relationship between the groups (see Chapter 5) and eliminated the threat presented by Chinese labor by excluding Chinese from American society.

Consistent with the predictions of split labor market theory (see Chapter 3), the primary antagonists of Chinese immigrants were native-born workers and organized labor. White owners of small businesses, feeling threatened by Chinese-owned businesses, also supported passage of the Chinese Exclusion Act (Boswell, 1986). Other social classes, such as the capitalists who owned larger factories, might actually have benefited from the continued supply of cheaper labor created by immigration from China. Conflicts such as the anti-Chinese campaign can be especially intense because they can confound racial and ethnic antagonisms with disputes between different social classes.

The ban on immigration from China remained in effect until World War II, when China was awarded a yearly quota of 105 immigrants in recognition of its wartime alliance with the United States. However, large-scale immigration from China did not resume until federal policy was revised in the 1960s.

Population Trends and the "Delayed" Second Generation. Following the Chinese Exclusion Act, the number of Chinese in the United States actually declined (see Exhibit 9.5),

as some immigrants passed away or returned to China and were not replaced by newcomers. The huge majority of Chinese immigrants in the 19th century had been young adult male sojourners who intended to work hard, save money, and return to their homes in China (Chan, 1990, p. 66). After 1882, it was difficult for anyone from China, male or female, to enter the United States, and the Chinese community in the United States remained overwhelmingly male for many decades. At the end of the 19th century, for example, males outnumbered females by more than 25 to 1, and the sex ratio did not approach parity for decades (Wong, 1995, p. 64; see also Ling, 2000). The scarcity of Chinese women in the United States delayed the second generation (the first born in the United States), and it wasn't until the 1920s, 80 years after immigration began, that as many as one third of all Chinese in the United States were native-born (Wong, 1995, p. 64).

The delayed second generation may have reinforced the exclusion of the Chinese American community, which began as a reaction to the overt discrimination of the dominant group (Chan, 1990, p. 66). The children of immigrants are usually much more acculturated, and their language facility and greater familiarity with the larger society often permits them to represent the group and speak for it more effectively. In the case of Chinese Americans (and other Asian groups), members of the second generation were citizens of the United States by birth, a status from which the immigrants were barred, and they had legal and political rights not available to their parents. Thus, the decades-long absence of a more Americanized, English-speaking generation increased the isolation of Chinese Americans.

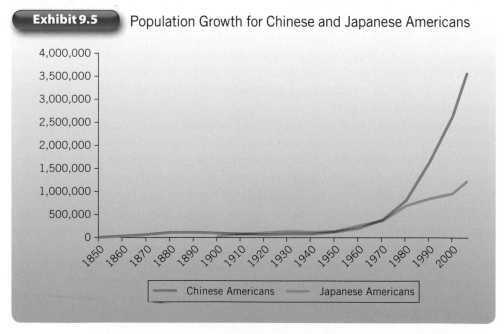

Exhibit 9.5 Population Growth for Chinese and Japanese Americans

SOURCE: Kitano (1980, p. 562); Lee (1998, p. 15); U.S. Bureau of the Census (2007a); Xie & Goyette (2004).

UNDERSTANDING DOMINANT MINORITY RELATIONS

The Ethnic Enclave.

The Chinese became increasingly urbanized as the anti-Chinese campaign and rising racism took their toll. Forced out of towns and smaller cities, they settled in larger urban areas, such as San Francisco, which offered the safety of urban anonymity and ethnic neighborhoods where the old ways could be practiced and contact with the hostile larger society minimized. Chinatowns had existed since the start of the immigration, and they now took on added significance as safe havens from the storm of anti-Chinese venom. The Chinese withdrew to these neighborhoods and became an "invisible minority" (Tsai, 1986, p. 67).

These early Chinatowns were ethnic enclaves like those founded by Jews on the East Coast and the more recently founded Cuban community in Miami, and a similar process formed them. The earliest urban Chinese included merchants and skilled artisans who, like the early wave of Cuban immigrants, were experienced in commerce (Chan, 1990, p. 44). They established businesses and retail stores that were typically small in scope and modest in profits. As the number of urban Chinese increased, the market for these enterprises became larger and more spatially concentrated. New services were required, the size of the cheap labor pool available to Chinese merchants and entrepreneurs increased, and the Chinatowns became the economic, cultural, and social centers of the community.

Within the Chinatowns, elaborate social structures developed that mirrored traditional China in many ways. The enforced segregation of the Chinese in America helped preserve much of the traditional food, dress, language, values, and religions of their homeland from the pressures of Americanization. The social structure was based on a variety of types of organizations, including family and clan groups and **huiguan**, or associations based on the region or district in China from which the immigrant had come. These organizations performed various, often overlapping, social and welfare services, including settling disputes, aiding new arrivals from their regions, and facilitating the development of mutual aid networks (Lai, 1980, p. 221; Lyman, 1974, pp. 32–37, 116–118). Life was not always peaceful in Chinatown, and there were numerous disputes over control of resources and the organizational infrastructure. In particular, secret societies called **tongs** contested the control and leadership of the merchant-led huiguan and the clan associations. These sometimes bloody conflicts were sensationalized in the American press as "Tong Wars," and they contributed to the popular stereotypes of Asians as exotic, mysterious, and dangerous (Lai, 1980, p. 222; Lyman, 1974, pp. 37–50).

Photo 9.1

Japanese American farmer hauling cauliflower, 1942. Within weeks, he will be in an internment camp.

© Corbis.

Despite these internal conflicts, American Chinatowns evolved into highly organized, largely self-contained communities, complete with their own leadership and decision-making structures. The internal "city government" of Chinatown was the Chinese Consolidated Benevolent Association (CCBA). Dominated by the larger huiguan and clans, the CCBA coordinated and supplemented the activities of the various organizations and represented the interests of the community to the larger society.

The local CCBAs, along with other organizations, also attempted to combat the anti-Chinese campaign, speaking out against racial discrimination and filing numerous lawsuits to contest racist legislation (Lai, 1980, p. 223). The effectiveness of the protest efforts was handicapped by the lack of resources in the Chinese community and by the fact that Chinese immigrants could not become citizens. Attempts were made to mobilize international pressure to protest the treatment of the Chinese in the United States. At the time, however, China was itself colonized and dominated by other nations (including the United States). China was further weakened by internal turmoil and could mount no effective assistance for its citizens in the United States (Chan, 1990, p. 62).

Survival and Development.
The Chinese American community survived despite the widespread poverty, discrimination, and pressures created by the unbalanced sex ratio. Members of the group began to seek opportunities in other regions, and Chinatowns appeared and grew in New York, Boston, Chicago, Philadelphia, and many other cities.

The patterns of exclusion and discrimination that began during the 19th-century anti-Chinese campaign were common throughout the nation and continued well into the 20th century. Chinese Americans responded by finding economic opportunity in areas where dominant group competition for jobs was weak, continuing their tendency to be an "invisible" minority group. Very often, they started small businesses that either served other members of their own group (restaurants, for example) or relied on the patronage of the general public (laundries, for example). The jobs provided by these small businesses were the economic lifeblood of the community but were limited in the amount of income and wealth they could generate. Until recent decades, for example, most restaurants served primarily other Chinese, especially single males. Since their primary clientele was poor, the profit potential of these businesses was sharply limited. Laundries served the more affluent dominant group, but the returns from this enterprise declined as washers and dryers became increasingly widespread in homes throughout the nation. The population of Chinatown was generally too small to sustain more than these two primary commercial enterprises (Zhou, 1992, pp. 92–94).

As the decades passed, the enclave economy and the complex subsociety of Chinatown evolved. However, discrimination, combined with defensive self-segregation, ensured the continuation of poverty, limited job opportunities, and substandard housing. Relatively hidden from general view, Chinatown became the world in which the second generation grew to adulthood.

The Second Generation.
Whereas the immigrant generation generally retained its native language and customs, the second generation was much more influenced by the larger culture. The institutional and organizational structures of Chinatown were created to serve the older, mostly male immigrant generation, but younger Chinese Americans tended to look beyond the enclave to fill their needs. They came in contact with the larger society through schools, churches, and voluntary organizations such as the YMCA and YWCA.

They abandoned many traditional customs and were less loyal to and interested in the clan and regional associations that the immigrant generation had constructed. They founded organizations of their own that were more compatible with their Americanized lifestyles (Lai, 1980, p. 225).

As with other minority groups, World War II was an important watershed for Chinese Americans. During the war, job opportunities outside the enclave increased, and after the war, many of the 8,000 Chinese Americans who served in the armed forces were able to take advantage of the GI Bill to further their education (Lai, 1980, p. 226). In the 1940s and 1950s, many second-generation Chinese Americans moved out of the enclave, away from the traditional neighborhoods, and pursued careers in the larger society. This group was mobile and Americanized, and with educational credentials comparable to the general population, they were prepared to seek success outside Chinatown.

In another departure from tradition, the women of the second generation also pursued education, and as early as 1960, median years of schooling for Chinese American women were slightly higher than for Chinese American men (Kitano & Daniels, 1995, p. 48). Chinese American women also became more diverse in their occupational profile as the century progressed. In 1900, three quarters of all employed Chinese American women worked in manufacturing (usually in garment industry sweatshops or in canning factories) or in domestic work. By 1960, less than 2% were in domestic work, 32% were in clerical occupations, and 18% held professional jobs, often as teachers (Amott & Matthaei, 1991, pp. 209–211).

An American Success Story? The men and women of the second generation achieved considerable educational and occupational success and helped to establish the idea that Chinese Americans are a "model minority." A closer examination reveals, however, that the old traditions of anti-Chinese discrimination and prejudice continued to limit the life chances of even the best-educated members of this generation. Second-generation Chinese Americans earned less, on the average, and had less-favorable occupational profiles than comparably educated white Americans, a gap between qualifications and rewards that reflects persistent discrimination. Kitano and Daniels (1995, p. 50) conclude, for example, that although well-educated Chinese Americans could find good jobs in the mainstream economy, the highest, most lucrative positions—and those that required direct supervision of whites—were still closed to them (see also Hirschman & Wong, 1984).

Furthermore, many Chinese Americans, including many of those who stayed in the Chinatowns to operate the enclave economy, and the immigrants who began arriving after 1965, do not fit the image of success at all. A large percentage of these Chinese Americans face the same problems as do members of other colonized, excluded, exploited minority groups of color. They rely for survival on low-wage jobs in the garment industry, the service sector, and the small businesses of the enclave economy and are beset by poverty and powerlessness, much like the urban underclass segments of other groups.

Thus, Chinese Americans can be found at both ends of the spectrum of success and affluence, and the group is often said to be "bipolar" in its occupational structure (see Barringer, Takeuchi, & Levin, 1995; Takaki, 1993, pp. 415–416; Wong, 1995, pp. 77–78; Zhou & Logan, 1989). Although a high percentage of Chinese Americans are found in more desirable occupations—sustaining the idea of Asian success—others, less visible, are concentrated at the lowest levels of the society. Later in this chapter, we will again consider the socioeconomic status of Chinese Americans and the accuracy of the image of success and affluence.

Japanese Americans

Immigration from Japan began to increase shortly after the Chinese Exclusion Act of 1882 took effect, in part to fill the gap in the labor supply created by the restrictive legislation (Kitano, 1980). The 1880 census counted only a few hundred Japanese in the United States, but the group increased rapidly over the next few decades. By 1910, the Japanese in the United States outnumbered the Chinese and remained the larger of the two groups until large-scale immigration resumed in the 1960s (see Exhibit 9.5).

The Anti-Japanese Campaign.
The contact situation for Japanese immigrants resembled that of the Chinese. They immigrated to the same West Coast regions as the Chinese, entered the labor force in a similar position, and were a small group with few power resources. Predictably, the feelings and emotions generated by the anti-Chinese campaign transferred to them. By the early 1900s, an anti-Japanese campaign to limit competition was in full swing. Efforts were being made to establish a rigid competitive system of group relations and to exclude Japanese immigrants in the same way the Chinese had been barred (Kitano, 1980, p. 563; Kitano & Daniels, 1995, pp. 59–60; Petersen, 1971, pp. 30–55).

Japanese immigration was partly curtailed in 1907 when a "gentlemen's agreement" was signed between Japan and the United States limiting the number of laborers Japan would allow to emigrate (Kitano & Daniels, 1995, p. 59). This policy remained in effect until the United States changed its immigration policy in the 1920s and barred immigration from Japan completely. The end of Japanese immigration is largely responsible for the slow growth of the Japanese American population displayed in Exhibit 9.5.

Most Japanese immigrants, like the Chinese, were young male laborers who planned to eventually return to their homeland or bring their wives after they were established in their new country (Duleep, 1988, p. 24). The agreement of 1907 curtailed the immigration of men, but because of a loophole, females were able to continue to immigrate until the 1920s. Japanese Americans were thus able to maintain a relatively balanced sex ratio, marry, and begin families, and a second generation of Japanese Americans began to appear without much delay. Native-born Japanese numbered about half of the group by 1930 and were a majority of 63% on the eve of World War II (Kitano & Daniels, 1995, p. 59).

The anti-Japanese movement also attempted to dislodge the group from agriculture. Many Japanese immigrants were skilled agriculturists, and farming proved to be their most promising avenue for advancement (Kitano, 1980, p. 563). In 1910, between 30% and 40% of all Japanese in California were engaged in agriculture; from 1900 to 1909, the number of independent Japanese farmers increased from fewer than 50 to about 6,000 (Jibou, 1988, p. 358).

Most of these immigrant farmers owned small plots of land, and they made up only a minuscule percentage of West Coast farmers (Jibou, 1988, pp. 357–358). Nonetheless, their presence and relative success did not go unnoticed and eventually stimulated discriminatory legislation, most notably the **Alien Land Act**, passed by the California legislature in 1913 (Kitano, 1980, p. 563). This bill made aliens who were ineligible for citizenship (effectively meaning only immigrants from Asia) to be also ineligible to own land. The act did not achieve its goal of dislodging the Japanese from the rural economy. They were able to dodge the discriminatory legislation by various devices, mostly by putting titles of land in the names of their American-born children, who were citizens by law (Jibou, 1988, p. 359).

The Alien Land Act was one part of a sustained campaign against the Japanese in the United States. In the early decades of this century, the Japanese were politically disenfranchised and segregated from dominant group institutions in schools and residential areas. They were discriminated against in movie houses, swimming pools, and other public facilities (Kitano & Daniels, 1988, p. 56). The Japanese were excluded from the mainstream economy and confined to a limited range of poorly paid occupations (see Yamato, 1994). Thus, there were strong elements of systematic discrimination, exclusion, and colonization in their overall relationship with the larger society.

The Ethnic Enclave.

Spurned and disparaged by the larger society, the Japanese, like the Chinese, constructed a separate subsociety. The immigrant generation, called **Issei** (from the Japanese word *ichi,* meaning "one"), established an enclave in agriculture and related enterprises, a rural counterpart of the urban enclaves constructed by other groups we have examined.

By World War II, the Issei had come to dominate a narrow but important segment of agriculture on the West Coast, especially in California. Although the Issei were never more than 2% of the total population of California, Japanese-American-owned farms produced as much as 30% to 40% of various fruits and vegetables grown in that state. As late as 1940, more than 40% of the Japanese American population was involved directly in farming, and many more were dependent on the economic activity stimulated by agriculture, including the marketing of their produce (Jibou, 1988, pp. 359–360). Other Issei lived in urban areas, where they were concentrated in a narrow range of businesses and services, such as domestic service and gardening, some of which catered to other Issei and some of which served the dominant group (Jibou, 1988, p. 362).

Japanese Americans in both the rural and urban sectors maximized their economic clout by doing business with other Japanese-owned firms as often as possible. Gardeners and farmers purchased supplies at Japanese-owned firms, farmers used other members of the group to haul their products to market, and businesspeople relied on one another and mutual credit associations, rather than dominant group banks, for financial services. These networks helped the enclave economy to grow and also permitted the Japanese to avoid the hostility and racism of the larger society. However, these very same patterns helped sustain the stereotypes that depicted the Japanese as clannish and unassimilable. In the years before World War II, the Japanese American community was largely dependent for survival on their networks of cooperation and mutual assistance, not on Americanization and integration.

The Second Generation (Nisei).

In the 1920s and 1930s, anti-Asian feelings continued to run high, and Japanese Americans continued to be excluded and discriminated against despite (or perhaps because of) their relative success. Unable to find acceptance in Anglo society, the second generation, called **Nisei**, established clubs, athletic leagues, churches, and a multitude of other social and recreational organizations within their own communities (Kitano & Daniels, 1995, p. 63). These organizations reflected the high levels of Americanization of the Nisei and expressed values and interests quite compatible with those of the dominant culture. For example, the most influential Nisei organization was the Japanese American Citizens League, whose creed expressed an ardent patriotism that was to be sorely tested: "I am proud that I am an American citizen. . . . I believe in [American] institutions, ideas and traditions; I glory in her heritage; I boast of her history, I trust in her future" (Kitano & Daniels, 1995, p. 64).

Although the Nisei enjoyed high levels of success in school, the intense discrimination and racism of the 1930s prevented most of them from translating their educational achievements into better jobs and higher salaries. Many occupations in the mainstream economy were closed to even the best-educated Japanese Americans, and anti-Asian prejudice and discrimination did not diminish during the hard times and high unemployment of the Great Depression in the 1930s. Many Nisei were forced to remain within the enclave, and in many cases, jobs in the produce stands and retail shops of their parents were all they could find. Their demoralization and anger over their exclusion were eventually swamped by the larger events of World War II.

The Relocation Camps.
On December 7, 1941, Japan attacked Pearl Harbor, killing almost 2,500 Americans. President Franklin D. Roosevelt asked Congress for a declaration of war the next day. The preparations for war stirred up a wide range of fears and anxieties among the American public, including concerns about the loyalty of Japanese Americans. Decades of exclusion and anti-Japanese prejudice had conditioned the dominant society to see Japanese Americans as sinister, clannish, cruel, unalterably foreign, and racially inferior. Fueled by the ferocity of the war itself and fears about a Japanese invasion of the mainland, the tradition of anti-Japanese racism laid the groundwork for a massive violation of civil rights.

Two months after the attack on Pearl Harbor, President Roosevelt signed Executive Order 9066, which led to the relocation of Japanese Americans living on the West Coast. By the late summer of 1942, more than 110,000 Japanese Americans, young and old, male and female—virtually the entire West Coast population—had been transported to **relocation camps**, where they were imprisoned behind barbed-wire fences patrolled by armed guards. Many of these people were American citizens, yet no attempt was made to distinguish between citizen and alien. No trials were held, and no one was given the opportunity to refute the implicit charge of disloyalty.

The government gave families little notice to prepare for evacuation and secure their homes, businesses, and belongings. They were allowed to bring only what they could carry, and many possessions were simply abandoned. Businesspeople sold their establishments and farmers sold their land at panic sale prices. Others locked up their stores and houses and walked away, hoping that the evacuation would be short-lived and their possessions undisturbed.

The internment lasted for nearly the entire war. At first, Japanese Americans were not permitted to serve in the armed forces, but eventually more than 25,000 escaped the camps by volunteering for military service. Nearly all of them served in segregated units or in intelligence work with combat units in the Pacific Ocean. Two all-Japanese combat units served in Europe and became the most decorated units in American military history (Kitano, 1980, p. 567). Other Japanese Americans were able to get out of the camps by means other than the military. Some, for example, agreed to move to militarily nonsensitive areas far away from the West Coast (and their former homes). Still, when the camps closed at the end of the war, about half of the original internees remained (Kitano & Daniels, 1988, p. 64).

The strain of living in the camps affected Japanese Americans in a variety of ways. Lack of activities and privacy, overcrowding, boredom, and monotony were all common complaints. Narrative Portrait 1 in this chapter summarizes the experiences of one Japanese American.

Prejudice and Discrimination Against Japanese Americans

On December 7, 1941, Japan bombed Pearl Harbor. Fear of a Japanese invasion and of subversive acts by Japanese Americans prompted President Franklin D. Roosevelt to sign Executive Order 9066 on February 19, 1942. The order designated the West Coast as a military zone from which "any or all persons may be excluded." Although not specified in the order, Japanese Americans were singled out for evacuation. More than 110,000 people of Japanese ancestry were removed from California, southern Arizona, and western Washington and Oregon and sent to 10 relocation camps. Those forcibly removed from their homes, businesses, and possessions included Japanese immigrants who were legally forbidden to become U.S. citizens (Issei), the American born (Nisei), and children of the American born (Sansei).

After the internment of Japanese Americans from the Seattle region, barber G. S. Hante points proudly to his bigoted sign that reads, "We Don't Want Any Japs Back Here . . . EVER!"

© Bettmann/Corbis.

Dust storm blows at this War Relocation Authority center (Manzanar) where evacuees of Japanese ancestry spent the duration of World War II. (California; July 3, 1942)

© Corbis/Dorothea Lange.

Persons of Japanese ancestry arrive at the Santa Anita Assembly Center from San Pedro. Evacuees lived at this center at the former Santa Anita race track before being moved inland to relocation centers. (Arcadia, CA; April 5, 1942)

© Corbis/Clem Albers.

The Relocation

Joseph Kurihara was born in Hawaii in 1895. He moved to California at age 20 and served with the U.S. Army in World War I, completed a college education, and was a businessman working within the Japanese American enclave until World War II. He worked actively to promote acculturation and better relations with the larger society during the interwar years. He was sent to the relocation camp at Manzanar, California, in the spring of 1942 and continued to play an active role in the dislocated Japanese American community. Although he had never visited Japan and had no interest or connection with the country of his parents' birth, his experiences in the camp were so bitter that he renounced his American citizenship and expatriated to Japan following the war.

We Were Just Japs

Joseph Kurihara

[The evacuation] . . . was really cruel and harsh. To pack and evacuate in forty-eight hours was an impossibility. Seeing mothers completely bewildered with children crying from want and peddlers taking advantage and offering prices next to robbery made me feel like murdering those responsible without the slightest compunction in my heart.

The parents may be aliens but the children are all American citizens. Did the government of the United States intend to ignore their rights regardless of their citizenship? Those beautiful furnitures [sic] which the parents bought to please their sons and daughters, costing hundreds of dollars were robbed of them at the single command, "Evacuate!" Here my first doubt of American Democracy crept into the far corners of my heart with the sting that I could not forget. Having had absolute confidence in Democracy, I could not believe my very eyes what I had seen that day. America, the standard bearer of Democracy had committed the most heinous crime in its history. . . .

[The camp was in an area that is largely desert.] The desert was bad enough. The . . . barracks made it worse. The constant cyclonic storms loaded with sand and dust made it worst. After living in well furnished homes with every modern convenience and suddenly forced to live the life of a dog is something which one can not so readily forget. Down in our hearts we cried and cursed this government every time when we were showered with sand.

We slept in the dust; we breathed the dust; and we ate the dust. Such abominable existence one could not forget, no matter how much we tried to be patient, understand the situation, and take it bravely. Why did not the government permit us to remain where we were? Was it because the government was unable to give us the protection? I have my doubt. The government could have easily declared Martial Law to protect us.

It was not the question of protection. It was because we were Japs! Yes, Japs!

After corralling us like a bunch of sheep in a hellish country, did the government treat us like citizens? No! We were treated like aliens regardless of our rights. Did the government think we were so without pride to work for $16.00 a month when people outside were paid $40.00 to $50.00 a week in the defense plants? Responsible government officials further told us to be loyal and that to enjoy our rights as American citizens we must be ready to die for the country. We must show our loyalty. If such is the case, why are the veterans corralled like the rest of us in the camps? Have they not proven their loyalty already? This matter of proving one's loyalty to enjoy the rights of an American citizen was nothing but a hocus-pocus.

My American friends . . . no doubt must have wondered why I renounced my citizenship. This decision was not that of today or yesterday. It dates back to the day when General DeWitt [the officer in charge of the evacuation] ordered evacuation. It was confirmed when he flatly refused to listen even to the voices of the former World War Veterans and it was doubly confirmed when I entered Manzanar. We who already had proven our loyalty by serving in the last World War should have been spared. The veterans asked for special consideration but their requests were denied. They too had to evacuate like the rest of the Japanese people, as if they were aliens.

I did not expect this of the Army. . . . I expected that at least the Nisei would be allowed to remain. But to General DeWitt, we were all alike. "A Jap's a Jap. Once a Jap, always a Jap." . . . I swore to become a Jap 100 percent and never to do another day's work to help this country fight this war. My decision to renounce my citizenship there and then was absolute.

[Just before he left for Japan (in 1946), Kurihara wrote:]

It is my sincere desire to get over there as soon as possible to help rebuild Japan politically and economically. The American Democracy with which I was infused in my childhood is still unshaken. My life is dedicated to Japan with Democracy my goal.

SOURCE: Swaine, Thomas, & Nishimoto, Richard S. (1946). *The Spoilage*, pp. 363–369. Berkeley: University of California Press. Retrieved February 11, 2005, from http://www.geocities.com/Athens/8420/kurihara.html.

The camps disrupted the traditional forms of family life, as people had to adapt to barracks living and mess hall dining. Conflicts flared between those who counseled caution and temperate reactions to the incarceration and those who wanted to protest in more vigorous ways. Many of those who advised moderation were Nisei intent on proving their loyalty and cooperating with the camp administration.

Despite the injustice and dislocations of the incarceration, the camps did reduce the extent to which women were relegated to a subordinate role. Like Chinese women, Japanese women were expected to devote themselves to the care of the males of their family. In Japan, for example, education for females was not intended to challenge their intellect so much as to make them better wives and mothers. In the camps, however, pay for the few jobs available was the same for both men and women, and the mess halls and small living quarters freed women from some of the burden of housework. Many took advantage of the free time to take classes to learn more English and other skills. The younger women were able to meet young men on their own, weakening the tradition of family controlled, arranged marriages (Amott & Matthaei, 1991, pp. 225–229).

Some Japanese Americans protested the incarceration from the start and brought lawsuits to end the relocation program. Finally, in 1944, the Supreme Court ruled that detention was unconstitutional. As the camps closed, some Japanese American individuals and organizations began to seek compensation and redress for the economic losses the group had suffered. In 1948, Congress passed legislation to authorize compensation to Japanese Americans. About 26,500 people filed claims under this act. These claims were eventually settled for a total of about $38 million—less than one tenth of the actual economic losses. Demand for meaningful redress and compensation continued, and in 1988, Congress passed a bill granting reparations of about $20,000 in cash to each of the 60,000 remaining survivors of the camps. The law also acknowledged that the relocation program had been a grave injustice to Japanese Americans (Biskupic, 1989, p. 2879).

The World War II relocation devastated the Japanese American community and left it with few material resources. The emotional and psychological damage inflicted by this experience is incalculable. The fact that today, only six decades later, Japanese Americans are equal or superior to national averages on measures of educational achievement, occupational prestige, and income is one of the more dramatic transformations in minority group history.

Japanese Americans After World War II.
In 1945, Japanese Americans faced a world very different from the one they had left in 1942. To escape the camps, nearly half of the group had scattered throughout the country and lived everywhere but on the West Coast. As Japanese Americans attempted to move back to their former homes, they found their fields untended, their stores vandalized, their possessions lost or stolen, and their lives shattered. In some cases, there was simply no Japanese neighborhood to return to; the Little Tokyo area of San Francisco, for example, was now occupied by African Americans who had moved to the West Coast to take jobs in the defense industry (Amott & Matthaei, 1991, p. 231).

Japanese Americans themselves had changed as well. In the camps, the Issei had lost power to the Nisei. The English-speaking second generation had dealt with the camp administrators and held the leadership positions. Many Nisei had left the camps to serve in the armed forces or to find work in other areas of the country. For virtually every American minority group, the war brought new experiences and a broader sense of themselves, the nation, and the world. A similar transformation occurred for the Nisei. When the war ended, they were unwilling to rebuild the Japanese community as it had been before.

Like second-generation Chinese Americans, the Nisei had a strong record of success in school, and they also took advantage of the GI Bill to further their education. When anti-Asian prejudice began to decline in the 1950s and the job market began to open, the Nisei were educationally prepared to take advantage of the resultant opportunities (Kitano, 1980, p. 567).

The Issei-dominated enclave economy did not reappear after the war. One indicator of the shift away from an enclave economy was the fact that the percentage of Japanese American women in California who worked as unpaid family laborers (i.e., worked in family-run businesses for no salary) declined from 21% in 1940 to 7% in 1950 (Amott & Matthaei, 1991, p. 231). Also, between 1940 and 1990, the percentage of the group employed in agriculture declined from about 50% to 3%, and the percentage employed in personal services fell from 25% to 5% (Nishi, 1995, p. 116).

By 1960, Japanese Americans had an occupational profile very similar to that of whites except that they were actually overrepresented among professionals. Many were employed in the primary economy, not in the ethnic enclave, but there was a tendency to choose "safe" careers (e.g., in engineering, optometry, pharmacy, accounting) that did not require extensive contact with the public or supervision of whites (Kitano & Daniels, 1988, p. 70).

Within these limitations, the Nisei, their children (**Sansei**), and their grandchildren (**Yonsei**) have enjoyed relatively high status, and their upward mobility and prosperity have contributed to the perception that Asian Americans are a "model minority." An additional factor contributing to the high status of Japanese Americans (and to the disappearance of Little Tokyos) is that unlike Chinese Americans, immigrants from Japan have been few in number, and the community has not had to devote many resources to newcomers. Furthermore, recent immigrants from Japan tend to be highly educated professional people whose socioeconomic characteristics add to the perception of success and affluence.

The Sansei and Yonsei are highly integrated into the occupational structure of the larger society. Compared with their parents, their connections with their ethnic past are more tenuous, and in their values, beliefs, and personal goals, they resemble dominant group members of similar age and social class (Kitano & Daniels, 1995, pp. 79–81; also see Spickard, 1996).

Comparing Minority Groups

What factors account for the differences in the development of Chinese Americans and Japanese Americans and other racial minority groups? First, unlike the situation of African Americans in the 1600s and Mexican Americans in the 1800s, the dominant group had no desire to control the labor of these groups. The contact situation featured economic competition (e.g., for jobs) during an era of rigid competition between groups (see Exhibit 5.5), and Chinese Americans and Japanese Americans were seen as a threat to security that needed to be eliminated, not as a labor pool that needed to be controlled. Second, unlike American Indians, Chinese Americans and Japanese Americans in the early 20th century presented no military danger to the larger society, so there was little concern with their activities once the economic threat had been eliminated. Third, Chinese Americans and Japanese Americans had the ingredients and experiences necessary to form enclaves. The groups were allowed to "disappear," but unlike other racial minority groups, the urban location of their enclaves left them with opportunities for schooling for later generations. As many scholars argue, the particular mode of incorporation developed by Chinese Americans and Japanese Americans is the key to understanding the present status of these groups.

Contemporary Immigration From Asia

Immigration from Asia has been considerable since the 1960s, averaging close to 300,000 per year and running about 30% to 35% of all immigrants. As was the case with Hispanic immigrants, the sending nations are considerably less developed than the United States, and the primary motivation for most of these immigrants is economic. However, the Asian immigrant stream also includes a large contingent of highly educated professionals seeking opportunities to practice their careers and expand their skills. While these more elite immigrants contribute to the image of "Asian success," other Asian immigrants are low skilled, less educated, and undocumented. Thus, this stream of immigrants, like Chinese Americans, is "bipolar" and includes a healthy representation of people from both the top and the bottom of the occupational and educational hierarchies.

Of course, other factors besides mere economics attract these immigrants to the United States. The United States has maintained military bases throughout the region (including South Korea and the Philippines) since the end of World War II, and many Asian immigrants are the spouses of American military personnel. Also, U.S. involvement in the war in Southeast Asia in the 1960s and 1970s created interpersonal ties and governmental programs that drew refugees from Vietnam, Cambodia, and Laos.

As before, rather than attempting to cover all the separate groups in this category, we will concentrate on four case studies and consider immigrant groups from India, Vietnam, Korea, and the Philippines. Together, these four groups make up about half of all immigrants from Asia.

Four Case Studies

These groups are small, and they all include a high percentage of foreign-born members (see Exhibits 9.2 and 9.4). The groups are quite variable in their backgrounds, their occupational profiles, their levels of education, and their incomes. In contrast with Hispanic immigrants, however, they tend to have higher percentages of members who are fluent in English, higher levels of education, and relatively more members prepared to compete for good jobs in the American job market.

As we have done so often, we must note the diversity across these four groups. First, we can repeat the point that the category "Asian American" is an arbitrary designation imposed on peoples who actually have little in common and who come from nations that vary in language, culture, religion, "racial" characteristics, and scores of other ways. More specifically, these four groups are quite different from each other. Perhaps the most striking contrast is between immigrants from India, many of whom are highly educated and skilled, and Vietnamese Americans, who have a socioeconomic profile that in some ways resembles non-Asian racial minorities in the United States. Part of the difference between these two groups relates to their contact situations and can be illuminated by applying the Blauner hypothesis. Immigrants from India are at the "immigrant" end of Blauner's continuum. They bring strong educational credentials and are well equipped to compete for favorable positions in the occupational hierarchy. The Vietnamese, in contrast, began their American experience as a refugee group fleeing the turmoil of war. Although they do not fit Blauner's "conquered or colonized" category, most Vietnamese Americans had to adapt to American society with few resources and few contacts with an established immigrant community. The consequences of these vastly different contact situations are suggested by the data presented in the exhibits at the end of this chapter.

These groups also vary in their settlement patterns. Most are concentrated along the West Coast, but Indians are roughly equally distributed on both the East and West Coasts, and Vietnamese have a sizable presence in Texas, in part related to the fishing industry along the Gulf Coast.

Asian Indians.
India is the second most populous nation in the world, and its huge population of more than a billion people incorporates a wide variety of different languages (India has 19 official languages, including English), religions, and ethnic groups. Overall, the level of education is fairly low: The population averages about 5 years of formal schooling and is about 61% literate ("Average Years of Schooling," n.d.). However, about 10% of the population does reach the postsecondary level of education, which means that there are roughly 100 million (10% of a billion) well-educated Indians looking for careers commensurate with their credentials. Because of the relative lack of development in the Indian economy, many members of this educated elite must search for career opportunities abroad, and not just in the United States. It is also important to note that as a legacy of India's long colonization by the British, English is the language of the educated. Thus, Indian immigrants tend to be not only well educated but also English speaking.

Immigration from India was low until the mid-1960s, and the group was quite small at that time. The group more than quadrupled in size between 1980 and 2000, and Indians are now the third-largest Asian American group (behind Chinese and Filipinos).

Immigrants from India tend to be a select, highly educated, and skilled group. According to the 2000 census, Indians are very overrepresented in some of the most prestigious occupations, including computer engineering, medicine, and college teaching (U.S. Bureau of the Census, 2000f). Immigrants from India are part of a worldwide movement of educated peoples from less developed countries to more developed countries. One need not ponder the differences in career opportunities, technology, and compensation for long to get some insight into the reasons for this movement. Other immigrants from India are more oriented to commerce and small business, and there is a sizable Indian ethnic enclave in many cities (Kitano & Daniels, 1995, pp. 96–111; Sheth, 1995).

Koreans.
Immigration from Korea to the United States began early in the 20th century, when laborers were recruited to help fill the void in the job market left by the 1882 Chinese Exclusion Act. This group was extremely small until the 1950s, when the rate of immigration rose because of refugees and "war brides" after the Korean War. Immigration did not become substantial, however, until the 1960s. The size of the group increased fivefold in the 1970s and tripled between 1980 and 2000 but is still only 0.5% of the total population.

Recent immigrants from Korea consist mostly of families and include many highly educated people. Although differences in culture, language, and race make Koreans visible targets of discrimination, the high percentage of Christians among them (about 30% of South Koreans are Christian; see "Religion Statistics," n.d.) may help them appear more "acceptable" to the dominant group. Certainly, Christian church parishes play a number of important roles for the Korean American community, offering assistance to newcomers and the less fortunate, serving as a focal point for networks of mutual assistance, and generally assisting in the completion of the myriad chores to which immigrant communities must attend (e.g., government paperwork, registering to vote, etc.) (Kitano & Daniels, 2001, p. 123).

Korean American immigrants have formed an enclave, and the group is heavily involved in small businesses and retail stores, particularly fruit and vegetable retail stores, or greengroceries. According to one study, Koreans had the second-highest percentage of self-employment among immigrant groups (Greeks were the highest), with about 24% of the group in this occupational category (Kritz & Girak, 2004, p. 36). Another data source, also based on the 2000 census, shows that Koreans have the highest rate of business ownership among 11 different minority groups (U.S. Bureau of the Census, 2002), including other enclave minorities. Japanese Americans had the second-highest rate (108 businesses per 1,000 population), Chinese Americans were third (104 per 1,000 population), and Cuban Americans were fourth (101 per 1,000 population). In contrast, racial minority groups with strong histories of colonization and exclusion were at the bottom of the rankings: African Americans (24 businesses per 1,000) and Puerto Ricans (21 per 1,000) (see also Pollard & O'Hare, 1999; Kim, Hurh, & Fernandez, 1989; Logan, Alba, & McNulty, 1994; Min, 1995, pp. 208–212).

As is the case for other groups that have pursued this course, the enclave allows Korean Americans to avoid the discrimination and racism of the larger society yet survive in an economic niche in which lack of English fluency is not a particular problem. However, the enclave has its perils and its costs. For one thing, the success of Korean enterprises depends heavily on the mutual assistance and financial support of other Koreans and the willingness of family members to work long hours for little or no pay (recall the story of Kim Park from

Chapter 1). These resources would be weakened or destroyed by acculturation, integration, and the resultant decline in ethnic solidarity. Only by maintaining a distance from the dominant culture and its pervasive appeal can the infrastructure survive.

Furthermore, the economic niches in which Mom-and-Pop greengroceries and other small businesses can survive are often in deteriorated neighborhoods populated largely by other minority groups. There has been a good deal of hostility and resentment expressed against Korean shop owners by African Americans, Puerto Ricans, and other urbanized minority groups. For example, anti-Korean sentiments were widely expressed in the 1992 Los Angeles riots that followed the acquittal of the policemen who had been charged in the beating of Rodney King. Korean-owned businesses were some of the first to be looted and burned, and when asked why, one participant in the looting said simply, "Because we hate 'em. Everybody hates them" (Cho, 1993, p. 199). Thus, part of the price of survival for many Korean merchants is to place themselves in positions in which antagonism and conflict with other minority groups is common (Kitano & Daniels, 1995, pp. 112–129; Light & Bonacich, 1988; Min, 1995, pp. 199–231; see also Hurh, 1998).

Filipino Americans.

Ties between the United States and the Philippines were established in 1898 when Spain ceded the territory after its defeat in the Spanish-American war. The Philippines achieved independence following World War II, but the United States has maintained a strong military presence there for much of the past 60 years. The nation has been heavily influenced by American culture, and English remains one of two official languages. Thus, Filipino immigrants are often capable of conversation in English, at least as a second language (see Exhibit 9.6, page 430, on language acculturation).

Today, Filipinos are the second-largest Asian American group, but their numbers became sizable only in the last few decades. There were fewer than 1,000 Filipinos in the United States in 1910, and by 1960, the group still numbered fewer than 200,000. Most of the recent growth has come from increased post-1965 immigration. The group more than doubled in size between 1980 and 2000.

Many of the earliest immigrants were agricultural workers recruited for the sugar plantations of Hawaii and the fields of the West Coast. Because the Philippines was a U.S. territory, Filipinos could enter without regard to immigration quotas until 1935, when the nation became a self-governing commonwealth.

The most recent wave of immigrants is diversified, and like Chinese Americans, Filipino Americans are "bipolar" in their educational and occupational profiles. Many recent immigrants have entered under the family preference provisions of the U.S. immigration policy. These immigrants are often poor and compete for jobs in the low-wage secondary labor market (Kitano & Daniels, 1995, p. 94). More than half of all Filipino immigrants since 1965, however, have been professionals, many of them in the health and medical fields. Many female immigrants from the Philippines were nurses actively recruited by U.S. hospitals to fill gaps in the labor force (Amott & Matthaei, 1991, p. 245). Thus, the Filipino American community includes some members in the higher-wage primary labor market and others who are competing for work in the low-wage secondary sector (Agbayani-Siewart & Revilla, 1995; Espiritu, 1996; Kitano & Daniels, 1995, pp. 83–94; Mangiafico, 1988; Posadas, 1999).

Vietnamese.

A flow of refugees from Vietnam began in the 1960s as a direct result of the war in Southeast Asia. The war began in Vietnam but expanded when the United States attacked Communist forces in Cambodia and Laos. Social life was disrupted, and people were displaced throughout the region. In 1975, when Saigon (the South Vietnamese capital) fell and the U.S. military withdrew, many Vietnamese and other Southeast Asians who had collaborated with the United States and its allies fled in fear for their lives. This group included high-ranking officials and members of the region's educational and occupational elite. Later groups of refugees tended to be less well educated and more impoverished. Many Vietnamese waited in refugee camps for months or years before being admitted to the United States, and they often arrived with few resources or social networks to ease their transition to the new society (Kitano & Daniels, 1995, pp. 151–152). The Vietnamese are the largest of the Asian refugee groups, and contrary to Asian American success stories and notions of model minorities, they have incomes and educational levels that are sometimes comparable to colonized minority groups (see Exhibits 9.11 to 9.16 and the Appendix).

Contemporary Relations

In this section, we once more use our guiding concepts to assess the situation of Chinese Americans and Japanese Americans and the other Asian groups discussed in the next chapter. This section is organized around the same concepts used in previous case study chapters.

Prejudice and Discrimination

American prejudice against Asians first became prominent during the anti-Chinese movement of the 19th century. The Chinese were believed to be racially inferior, docile, and subservient, but also cruel and crafty, despotic, and threatening (Lai, 1980, p. 220; Lyman, 1974, pp. 55–58). The Chinese Exclusion Act of 1882 was justified by the idea that the Chinese were unassimilable and could never be part of U.S. society. The Chinese were seen as a threat to the working class, to American democracy, and to other American institutions. Many of these stereotypes and fears transferred to the Japanese later in the 19th century and then to other groups as they, in turn, arrived in the United States. The social distance scales presented in Exhibit 3.4 provide the only long-term record of anti-Asian prejudice in the society as a whole. In 1926, the five Asian groups included in the study were grouped in the bottom third of the scale, along with other racial and colonized minority groups. Twenty years later, in 1946, the Japanese had fallen to the bottom of the rankings, and the Chinese had risen seven positions, changes that reflect America's World War II conflict with Japan and alliance with China. This suggests that anti-Chinese prejudice may have softened during the war as distinctions were made between "good" and "bad" Asians. For example, an item published in a 1941 issue of *Time* magazine, "How to Tell Your Friends From the Japs," provided some tips for identifying "good" Asians: "The Chinese expression is likely to be more placid, kindly, open; the Japanese more positive, dogmatic, arrogant. . . . Japanese are nervous in conversation, laugh loudly at the wrong time" (p. 33).

In more recent decades, the average social distance scores of Asian groups have fallen even though the ranking of the groups has remained relatively stable. The falling scores probably reflect the society-wide increase in tolerance and the shift from blatant prejudice to modern racism that we discussed in Chapter 3. However, the relative position of Asians in the American hierarchy of group preferences has remained remarkably consistent since the 1920s. This stability may reflect the cultural or traditional nature of much of American anti-Asian prejudice.

Although prejudice against Asian and Pacific Island groups may have weakened overall, there is considerable evidence that it remains a potent force in American life. The continuing force of anti-Asian prejudice is marked most dramatically, perhaps, by hate crimes against members of the group. Asian Americans of all types—citizens, immigrants, and tourists—have been attacked, beaten, and even murdered in recent years. According to official statistics on hate crimes, there were 231 attacks on Asian Americans and Pacific Islanders[1] in 2005 (FBI, 2006), a little less than 5% of all racially motivated racially based incidents. This percentage is roughly consistent with the relative size of the group in U.S. society (see Exhibit 9.1), but some of the most notorious hate crimes in recent history have been directed at Asian Americans, including the murder of Vincent Chin in 1982 by autoworkers in Detroit. More recently, in 1996, an unemployed meat cutter named Robert Page murdered a randomly selected Chinese American male. Page said that he hated the Chinese because they "got all the good jobs" (Fong, 2002, p. 162). Other attacks include the murder of Filipino postman Joseph Ileto in 1999 and the murder of an Indian gas station owner in Mesa, Arizona, in the aftermath of the September 11, 2001, attacks on the World Trade Center and the Pentagon. Incidents such as these suggest that the tradition of anti-Asian prejudice is close to the surface and could be activated under the right combination of competition and threat.

Asian Americans have also been the victims of "positive" stereotypes. The perception of Asian Americans as a "model minority" is exaggerated and, for some Asian American groups, simply false. This label has been applied to these groups by the media, politicians, and others. It is not an image that the Asian American groups themselves developed or particularly advocate. As you might suspect, people who apply these labels to Asian Americans have a variety of hidden moral and political agendas, and we explore these dynamics later in this chapter.

Assimilation and Pluralism

Acculturation. The extent of acculturation of Asian Americans is highly variable from group to group. Japanese Americans represent one extreme. They have been a part of American society for more than a century, and the current generations are highly acculturated. Immigration from Japan has been low throughout the century and has not revitalized the traditional culture or language. As a result, Japanese Americans are the most acculturated of the Asian American groups, as illustrated in Exhibit 9.6. Japanese Americans have the highest percentage of members who speak only English at home and the lowest percentage, along with Filipinos, who speak English "less than very well."

Chinese Americans, in contrast, are highly variable in their extent of acculturation. Many are members of families who have been American for generations and are highly acculturated. Others, including many here illegally, are new immigrants who have little knowledge of English or of Anglo culture. In this dimension, as in occupations, Chinese Americans are "bipolar." This great variability within the group makes it difficult to characterize their overall degree of acculturation.

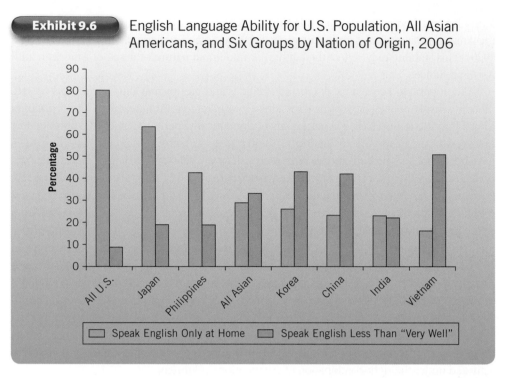

Exhibit 9.6 English Language Ability for U.S. Population, All Asian Americans, and Six Groups by Nation of Origin, 2006

SOURCE: U.S. Bureau of the Census (2007a).

Secondary Structural Assimilation. We will cover this complex area in roughly the order followed in previous chapters. The Appendix presents additional information on the relative standing of Asian American groups.

Residence. Exhibit 9.7 shows the regional concentrations of all Asian Americans. The tendency to reside on either coast and around Los Angeles, San Francisco, and New York stands out clearly. Note also the sizable concentrations in a variety of metropolitan areas, including Chicago, Atlanta, Miami, Denver, and Houston.

Asian Americans in general are highly urbanized, a reflection of the entry conditions of recent immigrants as well as the appeal of ethnic neighborhoods, such as Chinatowns, with long histories and continuing vitality. As displayed in Exhibit 9.8, all six Asian American groups discussed in this chapter are more than 90% urbanized, and several approach the 100% mark.

Asian Americans are much less residentially segregated than either African Americans or Hispanic Americans in all four regions. Exhibit 9.9 shows the average dissimilarity index for 220 metropolitan areas using the same format as in the previous three chapters. Asian Americans are not "extremely" (dissimilarity scores greater than .60) segregated in any region, but the level of residential segregation is holding steady or slightly rising, a reflection of high rates of immigration and the tendency for newcomers to settle close to other members of their group.

Exhibit 9.7   Regional Distribution of Asian Americans, 2000

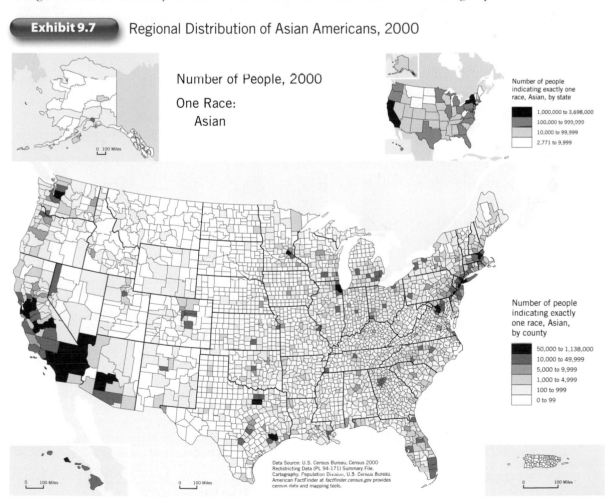

SOURCE: U.S. Bureau of the Census (2000e).

Exhibit 9.8   Urbanization of Six Asian American Groups, 2000

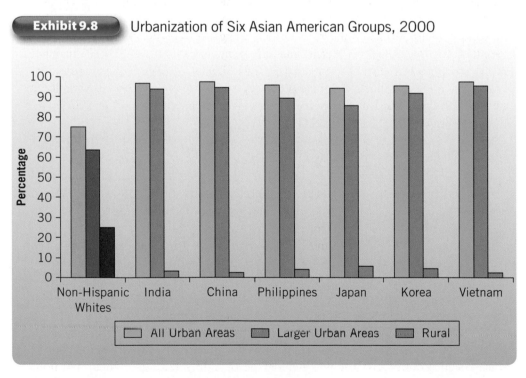

SOURCE: U.S. Bureau of the Census (2000f).

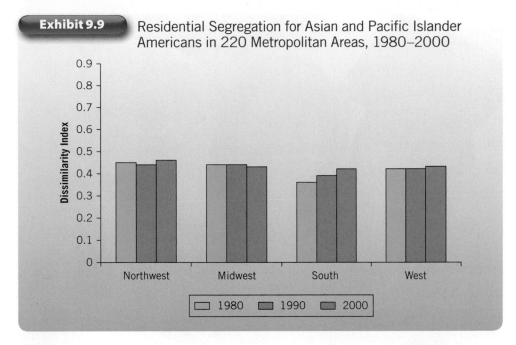

Exhibit 9.9 Residential Segregation for Asian and Pacific Islander Americans in 220 Metropolitan Areas, 1980–2000

SOURCE: Iceland, Weinberg, & Steinmetz (2002, p. 43).

Asian Americans are also moving away from their traditional neighborhoods and enclaves into the suburbs of metropolitan areas, most notably in the areas surrounding Los Angeles, San Francisco, New York, and other cities where the groups are highly concentrated. For example, Asian Americans have been moving in large numbers to the San Gabriel Valley, just east of downtown Los Angeles. Once a bastion of white, middle-class suburbanites, these areas have taken on a distinctly Asian flavor in recent years. Monterey Park, once virtually all white, is now 62% Chinese and is often referred to as "America's first suburban Chinatown" or the "Chinese Beverly Hills" (Fong, 2002, p. 49).

Education. The extent of school segregation for Asian Americans for the 1993–1994 and the 2005–2006 school years is displayed in Exhibit 9.10, as was done in previous chapters. In the 2005–2006 school year, Asian American children were much less likely to attend "majority-minority" or extremely segregated schools than either Hispanic American or African American children. However, the extent of school segregation has increased over the time period, a reflection of the pattern of residential segregation in Exhibit 9.9.

The extent of schooling for Asian Americans and for Chinese and Japanese Americans is very different from that for other U.S. racial minority groups. Considered as a whole, Asian Americans compare favorably with society-wide standards for educational achievement, and they are above those standards on many measures. Exhibit 9.11 shows that most Asian American groups are equal to or higher than non-Hispanic whites in high school education and far higher in college education, a pattern that has been very much reinforced by the high levels of education of many recent Asian immigrants. Four of the six Asian groups have a higher percentage of high school graduates than non-Hispanic whites, and all groups except the Vietnamese have a higher percentage of college graduates.

Photo 9.5

An Asian American family celebrates a graduation.

© moodboard/Corbis.

Exhibit 9.10 School Integration, 1993–1994 and 2005–2006

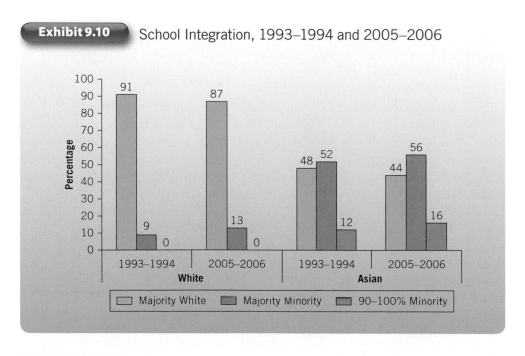

SOURCE: Fry (2007).

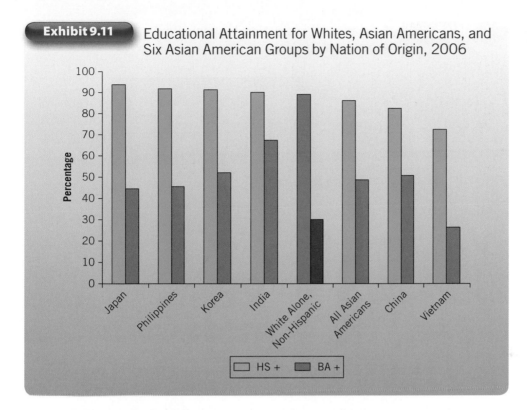

Exhibit 9.11 Educational Attainment for Whites, Asian Americans, and Six Asian American Groups by Nation of Origin, 2006

SOURCE: U.S. Bureau of the Census (2007a).

Exhibit 9.11 reinforces the "model minority" image, but recall that Chinese Americans (and several other Asian American groups) are "bipolar" and have a sizable underclass group. This reality is captured in Exhibit 9.12, which compares the distribution of levels of education for non-Hispanic whites and Chinese Americans. Over 50% of Chinese Americans hold college and graduate degrees, far outnumbering whites (30%) at this level. Many of these highly educated Chinese Americans are recent immigrants seeking to pursue their professions in one of the world's most advanced economies.

Note, however, that Chinese Americans are also disproportionately concentrated at the lowest level of educational achievement. Some 18% of the group has less than a high school diploma, as opposed to 11% of non-Hispanic whites. Many of these less educated Chinese Americans are also recent immigrants (many of them undocumented), and they supply the unskilled labor force, in retail shops, restaurants, and garment industry "sweatshops," that staffs the lowest levels of the Chinatown economy. Thus, the image of achievement and success needs to be balanced by the recognition that there is a full range of success and failure among Asian Americans and by the fact that average levels of achievement are "inflated" for some groups by recent immigrants who are highly educated, skilled professionals.

Political Power. The ability of Asian Americans to pursue their group interests has been sharply limited by a number of factors, including their relatively small size, institutionalized discrimination, and the same kinds of racist practices that have limited the power resources of other minority groups of color. However, and contrary to the perception that Asian Americans

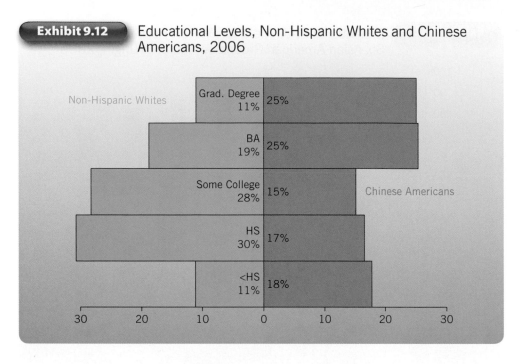

Exhibit 9.12 Educational Levels, Non-Hispanic Whites and Chinese Americans, 2006

Non-Hispanic Whites		Chinese Americans
Grad. Degree 11%	25%	
BA 19%	25%	
Some College 28%	15%	
HS 30%	17%	
<HS 11%	18%	

SOURCE: U.S. Bureau of the Census (2007a).

are a "quiet" minority, the group has a long history of political action, including a civil rights movement in the 1960s and 1970s (Fong, 2002, pp. 273–281).

The political power of Asian Americans and Pacific Islanders today is also limited by their high percentages of foreign-born members. Rates of political participation for the group (e.g., voting in presidential elections) are somewhat lower than national norms but may rise as more members Americanize, learn English, and become citizens (Lee, 1998, p. 30). Even today, there are signs of the growing power of the group, especially in areas where they are most residentially concentrated. Of course, Asian Americans have been prominent in Hawaiian politics for decades, but they are increasingly involved in West Coast political life as well. For example, in 1996, the state of Washington elected Gary Locke as governor, the first Chinese American to hold this high office. Governor Locke was reelected in 2000.

Jobs and Income. The image of success is again sustained by the occupational profiles of Asian American groups. Both males and females are overrepresented in the highest occupational categories, a reflection of the high levels of educational attainment for the group. Asian American males are underrepresented among manual laborers, but otherwise, the occupational profiles of the groups are in rough proportion to the society as a whole.

Exhibit 9.13 shows median household incomes for Asian Americans as a whole and for six Asian American subgroups. Four of the six groups and the group as a whole are well above the incomes of non-Hispanic whites, yet again sustaining the notion of success and affluence. This image is somewhat qualified, however, when we observe the distribution of income for the group as a whole, as presented in Exhibit 9.14. Asian Americans are overrepresented in the most affluent groups but also in the lower income category, a reflection of the "bipolar" distribution of Chinese Americans and some other groups.

Exhibit 9.13 Median Household Income for Whites, All Asian Americans, and Six Asian American Groups by Nation of Origin, 2006

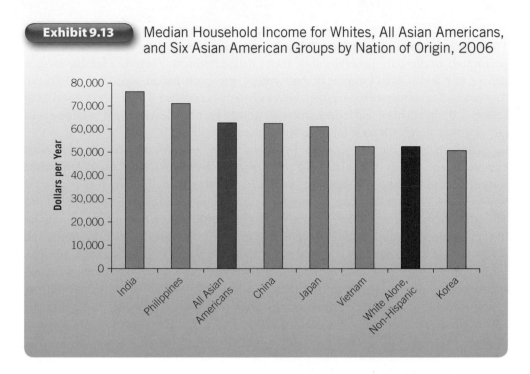

SOURCE: U.S. Bureau of the Census (2007a).

Exhibit 9.14 Distribution of Household Income for Non-Hispanic Whites and Asian Americans, 2006

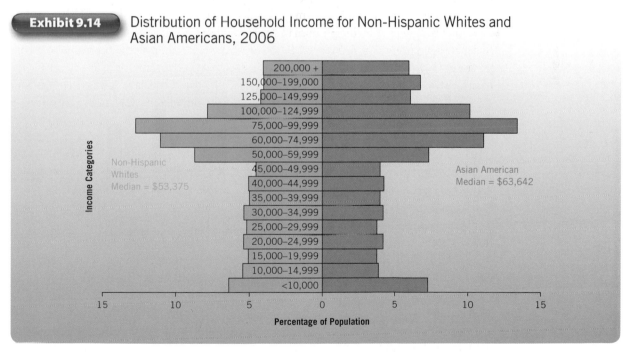

SOURCE: U.S. Bureau of the Census (2007a).

Exhibits 9.15 and 9.16 return us to the picture of relative affluence for Asian Americans. Their poverty rates are generally well below national norms, and the incomes of full-time, year-round workers are generally at or above national norms. There is a sizable income gap for men and women for some of these groups, especially Indian, Japanese, and Korean Americans. The women of these groups are much more concentrated in the service and retail sectors of the job market, and Indian American women are much less involved in professional and managerial jobs, the most lucrative occupations.

Although these data generally support the image of economic success, we must examine some qualifications before coming to any conclusions. First, Asian Americans in general and Chinese and Japanese Americans in particular generally reside in areas with higher-than-average costs of living (e.g., San Francisco, Los Angeles, New York); thus, their higher incomes have relatively less purchasing power. Second, they are more likely than the general population to have multiple wage earners in each household, and differences in per capita income are smaller than differences in median family income. For example, Exhibit 9.13 shows that Asian Americans as a group had median household incomes almost $10,000 greater than non-Hispanic whites. The difference in per capita income reverses the comparison: In 2006, Asian Americans earned $26,515 per capita, while non-Hispanic whites earned $29,406 per capita (U.S. Bureau of the Census, 2007a).

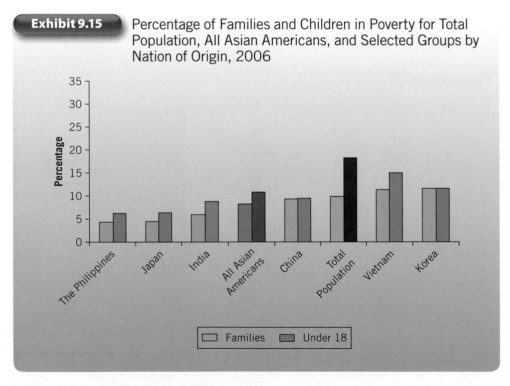

Exhibit 9.15 Percentage of Families and Children in Poverty for Total Population, All Asian Americans, and Selected Groups by Nation of Origin, 2006

SOURCE: U.S. Bureau of the Census (2007a).

Exhibit 9.16 Median Incomes for Full-Time, Year-Round Workers, 2006

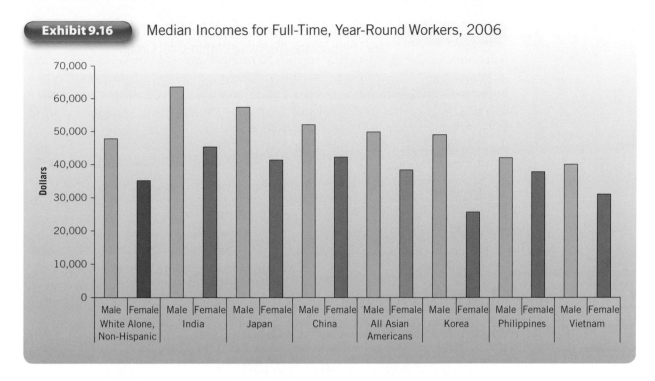

SOURCE: U.S. Bureau of the Census (2007a).

Primary Structural Assimilation.

Studies of integration at the primary level for Asian Americans generally find high rates of interracial friendship and intermarriage. For example, using 1980 census data, Lee and Yamanaka (1990) report higher rates of intermarriage for Asian Americans than for other minority groups. They report out-marriage rates at 2% for African Americans, 13% for Hispanic Americans, and from 15% to 34% for Asian Americans. They also found that native-born Asian Americans were much more likely to marry outside their groups than the foreign-born (see also Kitano & Daniels, 1995; Min, 1995; Sung, 1990). Some studies have found that the rate of intermarriage has been decreasing in recent years in the nation as a whole and specifically in California, a pattern that perhaps reflects the high rates of immigration, the tendency for the first generation to marry within the group, and the growing number of potential partners within Asian American groups (Lee & Fernandez, 1998; Shinagawa & Pang, 1996; see also Xie & Goyette, 2004).

Dr. C. N. Le, a sociologist who maintains the Asian Nation Web site (http://www.asian-nation .org) has analyzed the intermarriage patterns from the 2006 U.S. census. His data can be found at http://www.asian-nation.org/interracial.shtml and is summarized in Exhibit 9.17. Japanese Americans, the most acculturated of the groups, are the most likely to marry outside of their group. Also, many Japanese Americans are "war brides" who married American GIs stationed in Japan. The groups with the highest percentage of foreign-born, Asian Indians, Koreans, and Vietnamese (see Exhibit 9.4), are also the most likely to marry within their groups.

Exhibit 9.17	Intermarriage Rates for Asian Americans by Group and Sex, Percentage Marrying Within Own Group

Group	Men	Women
Asian Indians	92	94
Chinese	90	82
Filipino	82	61
Japanese	64	47
Korean	91	69
Vietnamese	92	83

Comparing Minority Groups: Explaining Asian American Success

To conclude this chapter, let's return to a question raised in the opening pages: How can we explain the apparent success of Asian Americans? Relative affluence and high status are not characteristic of the other racial minority groups we have examined, and at least at first glance, there seems to be little in our theories and concepts to help us understand the situation of Asian Americans. Even after we recognize that the "success" label is simplistic and even misleading, the relatively high status of many Asian Americans begs a closer look.

The Current Debates section at the end of this chapter presents several different views on the nature and causes of Asian American success. In this section, we compare Asian Americans with European immigrant groups and with colonized minority groups. What crucial factors differentiate the experiences of these groups? Can we understand these differences in terms of the framework provided by the Blauner and Noel hypotheses and the other concepts developed in this text?

The debate over the causes of Asian American success often breaks down into two different viewpoints. One view offers a cultural explanation, which accepts the evidence of Asian American success at face value and attributes it to the "good values" of traditional Asian cultures that we briefly explored at the beginning of this chapter. These values—including respect for elders and for authority figures, hard work and thriftiness, and conformity and politeness—are highly compatible with U.S. middle-class Protestant value systems and presumably helped Asian Americans gain acceptance and opportunities. The cultural explanation is consistent with traditional assimilation theory and human capital theory, and an example of it can be found in the selection by Professor Harry Kitano in the Current Debates section.

The second point of view stresses the ways in which these groups entered American society and the reactions of Asian Americans to the barriers of racism and exclusion they faced. This approach could be called a "structural explanation," and it emphasizes contact situations, modes of incorporation, enclave economies, group cohesion, position in the labor market, and institutionalized discrimination rather than cultural values. Also, this approach questions the notion that Asian Americans are successful and stresses the realities of Asian American poverty and the continuing patterns of racism and exclusion. The structural approach is more compatible with the theories and concepts used throughout this text, and it identifies several of the important pieces needed to solve the puzzle of Asian "success" and put it in perspective. This is not to suggest that the cultural approach is wrong or irrelevant, however. The issues we raise are complex and will probably require many approaches and perspectives before they are fully resolved.

Asian Americans and White Ethnics

Chinese and Japanese immigrants arrived in America at about the same time as immigrants from Southern and Eastern Europe (see Chapter 2). Both groups consisted mainly of sojourning young men who were largely unskilled, from rural backgrounds, and not highly educated. European immigrants, like Asian immigrants, encountered massive discrimination and rejection and were also victims of restrictive legislation. Yet the barriers to upward mobility for European immigrants (or at least for their descendants) fell away more rapidly than the barriers for immigrants from Asia. Why?

Some important differences between the two immigrant experiences are clear, the most obvious being the greater racial visibility of Asian Americans. Whereas the cultural and linguistic markers that identified Eastern and Southern Europeans faded with each passing generation, the racial characteristics of the Asian groups continued to separate them from the larger society. Thus, Asian Americans are not "pure immigrant" groups (see Blauner, 1972, p. 55). For most of the 20th century, Chinese Americans and Japanese Americans remained in a less favorable position than European immigrants and their descendants, excluded by their physical appearance from the mainstream economy until the decades following World War II.

Another important difference relates to position in the labor market. Immigrants from Southern and Eastern Europe entered the industrializing East Coast economy, where they took industrial and manufacturing jobs. Although such jobs were poorly paid and insecure, this location in the labor force gave European immigrants and their descendants the potential for upward mobility in the mainstream economy. At the very least, these urban industrial and manufacturing jobs put the children and grandchildren of European immigrants in positions from which skilled, well-paid, unionized jobs were reachable, as were managerial and professional careers.

In contrast, Chinese and Japanese immigrants on the West Coast were forced into ethnic enclaves and came to rely on jobs in the small business and service sector and, in the case of the Japanese, in the rural economy. By their nature, these jobs did not link Chinese and Japanese immigrants or their descendants to the industrial sector or to better-paid, more secure, unionized jobs. Furthermore, their exclusion from the mainstream economy was reinforced by overt discrimination based on race from both employers and labor unions (see Fong & Markham, 1991).

Asian Americans and Colonized Racial Minority Groups

Comparisons between Asian Americans and African Americans, American Indians, and Hispanic Americans have generated a level of controversy and a degree of heat and passion that may be surprising at first. An examination of the issues and their implications, however, reveals that the debate involves some thinly disguised political and moral agendas and evokes sharply clashing views on the nature of U.S. society. What might appear on the surface to be merely an academic comparison of different minority groups turns out to be an argument about the quality of American justice and fairness and the very essence of the value system of U.S. society.

What is *not* in dispute in this debate is that some Asian groups (e.g., Japanese Americans) rank far above other racial minority groups on all the commonly used measures of secondary structural integration and equality. What *is* disputed is how to interpret these comparisons and assess their meanings. First, we need to recognize that gross comparisons between entire groups can be misleading. If we confine our attention to averages (mean levels of education or median income), the picture of Asian American success is sustained. However, if we also observe the full range of differences within each group (e.g., the "bipolar" nature of occupations among Chinese Americans), we see that the images of success have been exaggerated and need to be placed in a proper context (see the selection by Takaki in the Current Debates section). Even with these qualifications, however, discussion often slides on to more ideological ground, and political and moral issues begin to cloud the debate. Asian American success is often taken as proof that American society is truly the land of opportunity and that people who work hard and obey the rules will get ahead: In America, anyone can be anything they want as long as they work hard enough.

When we discussed modern racism in Chapter 3, I pointed out that a belief in the openness and fairness of the United States can be a way of blaming the victim and placing the responsibility for change on the minority groups rather than on the structure of society or on past-in-present or institutionalized discrimination. Asian success has become a "proof" of the validity of this ideology. The none-too-subtle implication is that other groups (African Americans, Hispanic Americans, American Indians) could achieve the same success Asian Americans have achieved but, for various reasons, choose not to. Thus, the relative success of Chinese Americans and Japanese Americans has become a device for scolding other minority groups.

A more structural approach to investigating Asian success begins with a comparison of the history of the various racial minority groups and their modes of incorporation into the larger society. When Chinese Americans and Japanese Americans were building their enclave economies in the early part of the 20th century, African Americans and Mexican Americans were concentrated in unskilled agricultural occupations. American Indians were isolated from the larger society on their reservations, and Puerto Ricans had not yet begun to arrive on the mainland. The social class differences between these groups today flow from their respective situations in the past.

Many of the occupational and financial advances made by Chinese Americans and Japanese Americans have been due to the high levels of education achieved by the second generations. Although education is traditionally valued in Asian cultures, the decision to invest limited resources in schooling is also quite consistent with the economic niche occupied by these immigrants. Education is one obvious, relatively low-cost strategy to upgrade the productivity and profit of a small-business economy and improve the economic status of the group as a whole. An educated, English-speaking second generation could bring expertise and business acumen to the family enterprises and lead them to higher levels of performance. Education might also be the means by which the second generation could enter professional careers. This strategy may have been especially attractive to an immigrant generation that was itself relatively uneducated and barred from citizenship (Hirschman & Wong, 1986, p. 23; see also Bonacich & Modell, 1980, p. 152; Sanchirico, 1991).

The efforts to educate the next generation were largely successful. Chinese Americans and Japanese Americans achieved educational parity with the larger society as early as the 1920s. One study found that for men and women born after 1915, the median years of schooling completed were actually higher for Chinese Americans and Japanese Americans than for whites (Hirschman & Wong, 1986, p. 11). Before World War II, both Asian groups were barred from the mainstream economy and from better jobs. When anti-Asian prejudice and discrimination declined in the 1950s, however, the Chinese and Japanese second generations had the educational background necessary to take advantage of the increased opportunities.

Thus, there was a crucial divergence in the development of Chinese Americans and Japanese Americans and the colonized minority groups. At the time that native-born Chinese Americans and Japanese Americans reached educational parity with whites, the vast majority of African Americans, American Indians, and Mexican Americans were still victimized by Jim Crow laws and legalized segregation and excluded from opportunities for anything but rudimentary education. The Supreme Court decision in *Brown v. Board of Education of Topeka* (1954) was decades in the future, and American Indian schoolchildren were still being subjected to intense Americanization in the guise of a curriculum. Today, these other racial minority groups have not completely escaped from the disadvantages imposed by centuries of institutionalized discrimination. African Americans have approached educational parity with white Americans only in recent years (see Chapter 6), and American Indians and Mexican Americans remain far below national averages (see Chapters 7 and 8).

The structural explanation argues that the recent upward mobility of Chinese Americans and Japanese Americans is the result of the methods by which they incorporated themselves into American society, not so much their values and traditions. The logic of their enclave economy led the immigrant generation to invest in the education of their children, who would be better prepared to develop their businesses and seek opportunity in the larger society.

As a final point, note that the structural explanation is not consistent with traditional views of the assimilation process. The immigrant generation of Chinese Americans and Japanese Americans responded to the massive discrimination they faced by withdrawing, developing ethnic enclaves, and becoming "invisible" to the larger society. Like Jewish and Cuban Americans, Chinese Americans and Japanese Americans used their traditional cultures and patterns of social life to create and build their own subcommunities, from which they launched the next generation. Contrary to traditional ideas about how assimilation is "supposed" to happen, we see again that integration can precede acculturation and that the smoothest route to integration may be the creation of a separate subsociety independent of the surrounding community.

CURRENT DEBATES

Asian American "Success": What Are the Dimensions, Causes, and Implications for Other Minority Groups?

The following selections continue the discussion of the causes of Asian American success. The first selection, from the writings of sociologist Harry Kitano (1980), is consistent with cultural explanations for *the upward mobility of Asian groups. It argues that the success of the Japanese in America is due in part to their culture and in part to their strength of character, resilience, and flexibility.*

In opposition to Kitano's views are two other selections. The first counterargument, by sociologists Alejandro Portes and Min Zhou (1992), presents a structural analysis that links the success of Chinese Americans to their enclave economy. Portes and Zhou also draw some provocative comparisons between Chinese Americans and African Americans, suggesting that the "thorough acculturation" of the African American community has weakened its economic vitality.

The second counterargument, by sociologist Ronald Takaki, sharply questions the whole notion of the "model minority" and points out the limits and qualifications that need to be observed when comparing Asian Americans with other groups. Takaki (1993) also points to a hidden agenda of those who single out Asian Americans as a "model minority": the chastisement of other minority groups, particularly African Americans.

The Success of Japanese Americans Is Cultural

HARRY KITANO

Social interaction among Japanese Americans is governed by behavioral norms such as *enryo* and *amae*. These derive from Confucian ideas about human relationships and define the dimensions of interaction and exchange between superior and inferior members of a social group. Although these forms of behavior were brought over by Issei immigrants, they still survive in attenuated form among the Nisei and even the Sansei.

Enryo prescribes the way in which a social inferior must show deference and self-abnegation before a superior. Hesitancy to speak out at meetings, the automatic refusal of a second helping, and selecting a less desired object are all manifestations of enryo....

Amae behavior softens a power relationship through the acting out of dependency and weakness, and expresses the need for attention, recognition, acceptance, and nurture. A child displays amae to gain the sympathy and indulgence of a parent. A young, anxious-to-please employee in a business firm will act with exaggerated meekness and confusion to give his superior an opportunity to provide paternal advice and treat him as a protégé. Through the ritual display of weakness and dependency, reciprocal bonds of loyalty, devotion, and trust are formed. In this way, amae creates strong emotional ties that strengthen cohesion within the family, business organization, and community.

Japanese Americans inherit an almost reverential attitude toward work. Their ancestors struggled for survival in a crowded island country with limited natural resources, and they placed great value on industry and self-discipline. Certain traditional attitudes encourage resilient behavior in the face of setbacks and complement the moral imperative to work hard. Many Japanese Americans are familiar with the common expressions *gaman* and *gambotte* which mean "don't let it bother you," "don't give up." These dicta, derived from Buddhist teachings, encourage Japanese people to conceal frustration or disappointment and to carry on. A tradition that places great value on work and persistence has helped many Japanese Americans to acquire good jobs and to get ahead.

The submerging of the individual to the interest of the group is another basic Japanese tradition, and one that produces strong social cohesion and an oblique style of behavior, one manifestation of which is the indirection or allusiveness of much communication between Japanese; another is the polite, consensual behavior expected in all social contacts. Both are common in Japan and visible among Japanese Americans. Today, even third- and fourth-generation Japanese Americans are apt to be seen by others as agreeable, unaggressive, willing to accept subordinate roles, and reluctant to put themselves forward....

The history of the Japanese Americans in the United States is one of both resilience and adaptation. Suffering from discriminatory laws and racial hostility in the first half of the 20th century, Japanese Americans were nonetheless able to create stable ethnic communities and separate, but vital, social organizations. Since the end of World War II, with the disappearance of legal discrimination and the weakening of social restrictions, they have assimilated more readily into American society and shown rapid economic progress. Scholars have searched for the key to their remarkable record of adaptation. Some have pointed to the Japanese family, others to a strong group orientation, and still others to Japanese moral training; all of these theories often tend to overemphasize the degree to which Japanese traditions have been maintained. Japanese Americans have displayed a pragmatic attitude toward American life. [Rather] than rigidly maintaining their traditions, Japanese Americans have woven American values and behavior into the fabric of their culture and have seized new social, cultural, and economic avenues as they have become available, extending the limits of ethnicity by striking a workable balance between ethnic cohesion and accommodation.

SOURCE: Kitano, Harry (1980). "Japanese." In S. Thernstrom, A. Orlov, & O. Handlin (Eds.), *Harvard Encyclopedia of American Ethnic Groups,* pp. 570–571. Cambridge, MA: Harvard University Press.

Reprinted by permission of the publisher from HARVARD ENCYCLOPEDIA OF AMERICAN ETHNIC GROUPS, edited by Stephan Thernstrom, Ann Orlov, & Oscar Handlin, pp. 570–571, Cambridge, MA: The Belknap Press of Harvard University Press, Copyright © 1980 by the President and Fellows of Harvard College.

The "Success" of Chinese Americans Is Structural

ALEJANDRO PORTES AND MIN ZHOU

[What lessons for ethnic poverty can we find in the experiences of Chinese Americans and other groups that have constructed ethnic enclaves?] A tempting option—and one to which many experts have not been averse—is to resort to culturalistic explanations. According to these interpretations, certain groups do better because they possess the "right" kind of values. This view is, of course, not too different from assimilation theory except that, instead of learning the proper values after arrival, immigrants bring them ready made. A moment's reflection suffices to demonstrate the untenability of this explanation. . . .

The very diversity of [the] groups [that have constructed enclave economies] conspires against explanations that find the roots of economic mobility in the unique values associated with a particular culture. If we had to invoke a particular "ethic" to account for the business achievements of Chinese and Jews, Koreans and Cubans, Lebanese and Dominicans, we would wind up with a very messy theory. In terms of professed religions alone, we would have to identify those unique values leading Confucianists and Buddhists, Greek Orthodox and Roman Catholics into successful business ventures. In addition, culturalistic explanations have little predictive power since they are invoked only after a particular group has demonstrated its economic prowess. . . .

There is no alternative but to search for the relevant causal process in the social structure of the ethnic community. [Several] common aspects in the economic experience of the immigrant communities [are] relevant. . . .

[First is] the "bounded solidarity" created among immigrants by virtue of their foreignness and being treated as [different]. As consumers, immigrants manifest a consistent preference for items associated with the country of origin, both for their intrinsic utility and as symbolic representations of a distinct identity. As workers, they often prefer to work among "their own," interacting in their native language even if this means sacrificing some material benefits. As investors, they commonly opt for firms in the country of origin or in the ethnic community rather than trusting their money to impersonal outside organizations.

Bounded solidarity [is accompanied by] "enforceable trust" against malfeasance among prospective ethnic entrepreneurs. Confidence that business associates will not resort to double-dealing is cemented in something more tangible than generalized cultural loyalty since it also relies on the ostracism of violators, cutting them off from sources of credit and opportunity. [Enforceable trust] is the key mechanism underlying the smooth operation of rotating credit associations among Asian immigrant communities.

Bounded solidarity and enforceable trust as sources of social capital do not inhere in the moral convictions of individuals or in the value orientations in which they were socialized. [These benefits] accrue by virtue of [the group's] minority [status] in the host country and as a result of being subjected to mainstream pressure to accept their low place in the ethnic hierarchy. Such pressures prompt the revalorization of the symbols of a common nationality and the privileging of the ethnic community as the place where the status of underprivileged menial labor can be avoided. . . .

Black Americans, Mexican Americans, and mainland Puerto Ricans today lag significantly behind the immigrant groups in their entrepreneurial orientation. [This] lack of entrepreneurial presence is even more remarkable because of the large size of these minorities and the significant consumer market that they represent. . . .

We believe that the dearth of entrepreneurship among these groups is related to the dissolution of the structural underpinnings of the social capital resources noted above: bounded solidarity and enforceable trust. A thorough process of acculturation among U.S.-born members of each of these groups has led to a gradual weakening of their sense of community and to a reorientation towards the values, expectations, and preferences of the cultural mainstream. [Complete] assimilation among domestic minorities leads to identification with the mainstream views, including a disparaging evaluation of their own group. . . .

[Even] groups with a modest level of human capital have managed to create an entrepreneurial presence when the necessary social capital, created by specific historical conditions, was present. This was certainly the case among turn-of-the-century Chinese. [It] was also true of segregated black communities during the same time period. The current desperate conditions in many inner-city neighborhoods have led some black leaders to recall wistfully the period of segregation. [As one black leader said]:

[T]he same kind of business enclave that exists in the Cuban community or in the Jewish community existed in the black community when the consumer base was contained [i.e., segregated from the larger society] and needed goods and services that had to be provided by someone in the neighborhood. Today, blacks will not buy within their neighborhood if they can help it; they want to go to the malls and blend with mainstream consumers."

Hence, thorough acculturation and the formal end of segregation led to the dissipation of the social capital formerly present in restricted black enclaves and the consequent weakening of minority entrepreneurship. As blacks attempted to join the mainstream, they found that lingering discrimination barred or slowed down their progress in the labor market, while consumption of outside goods and services undermined their own community business base.

SOURCE: Portes, Alejandro, & Zhou, Min (1992). "Gaining the Upper Hand: Economic Mobility Among Immigrant and Domestic Minorities." *Ethnic and Racial Studies*, 15:513–518.

The Success of Asian Americans Has Been Exaggerated, in Part, to Criticize Other Minority Groups

RONALD TAKAKI

African American "failure" has been contrasted with Asian American "success." In 1984, William Raspberry of the *Washington Post* noted that Asian Americans on the West Coast had "in fact" "outstripped" whites in income. Blacks should stop blaming racism for their plight, he argued, and follow the example of the self-reliant Asian Americans. In 1986, *NBC Nightly News* and *McNeil/Lehrer Report* aired special segments on Asian Americans and their achievements. *U.S. News and World Report* featured Asian American advances in a cover story, and *Newsweek* focused a lead article on "Asian Americans: A 'Model Minority'" while *Fortune* applauded them as "America's super minority."

But in their celebration of this "model minority," these media pundits have exaggerated Asian American "success." Their comparisons of income between Asians and whites fail to recognize the regional location of the Asian American population. Concentrated in California, Hawaii, and New York, most Asian Americans reside in states with higher incomes but also higher costs of living than the national average. . . .

Asian American families have more persons working per family than white families. Thus, the family incomes of Asian Americans indicate the presence of more workers in each family rather than higher individual incomes. Actually, in terms of personal incomes, Asian Americans have not reached equality.

While many Asian Americans are doing well, others find themselves mired in poverty: They include Southeast-Asian refugees such as the Hmong, as well as immigrant workers trapped in Chinatowns. Eighty percent of the people in New York Chinatown, 74% of San Francisco Chinatown, and 88% of Los Angeles Chinatown are foreign-born. Like the nineteenth century Chinese immigrants in search of Gold Mountain, they came here to seek a better life. But what they found instead was work in Chinatown's low wage service and garment industries. . . .

The myth of the Asian American "model minority" has been challenged, yet it continues to be widely believed. One reason for this is its instructional value. For whom are Asian Americans supposed to be a "model"? . . .

Asian Americans are being used to discipline blacks. If the failure of blacks on welfare warns Americans in general how they should not behave,

the triumph of Asian Americans affirms the deeply rooted values of the Protestant ethic and self-reliance. Our society needs an Asian American "model minority" in an era anxious about a growing black underclass. If Asian Americans can make it on their own, why can't other groups? . . .

Betraying a certain nervousness over the seeming end of the American dream's boundlessness, praise for this "super minority" has become society's most recent jeremiad—a call for a renewed commitment to the traditional values of hard work, thrift, and industry. After all, it has been argued, the war on poverty and affirmative action were not really necessary. Look at the Asian Americans! They did it by pulling themselves up by their bootstraps. For blacks shut out of the labor market, the Asian American model provides the standards for acceptable behavior: Blacks should not depend on welfare or affirmative action. While congratulating Asian Americans for their family values, hard work, and high incomes, President Ronald Reagan chastised blacks for their dependency on the "spider's web of welfare" and their failure to recognize that the "only barrier" to success was "within" them.

SOURCE: Takaki, Ronald (1993). *A Different Mirror: A History of Multicultural America*, pp. 414–417. Boston: Little, Brown. Copyright © 1993 by Ronald Takaki. By permission of LITTLE, BROWN & COMPANY.

Debate Questions to Consider

1. If Kitano's analysis is correct, what could other minority groups learn from the Japanese experience? If Portes and Zhou are correct, what could other minority groups learn from the Chinese experience? Do Portes and Zhou use cultural factors as part of their explanation? How? Are Portes and Zhou advocating segregation? Pluralism? Assimilation?

2. Why would the United States "need" a "model minority"? How would you answer Takaki's question: "For whom are Asian Americans supposed to be a model?" Whose interests are being served by these comparisons? Do Asian Americans gain anything from these labels and comparisons? Do they lose anything?

3. Which of these views are consistent with traditional assimilation theory? How? Which are consistent with human capital theory? How? Which views are consistent with the thinking of Noel and Blauner? How?

Japan's "Invisible" Minority

One of the first things I did in this text was to list the five characteristics that, together, define a minority group. The first and most important of these characteristics was the disadvantage and inequality that minority groups face, and the second was visibility: Minority group members must be easily identifiable, either culturally (language, accent, dress) or physically (skin color, stature). These two traits work in tandem. Members of the dominant group must be able to determine a person's group membership quickly and easily, preferably at a glance, so that the systematic discrimination that is the hallmark of minority group status can be practiced.

Cultural and racial visibility is such an obvious precondition for discrimination that it almost seems unnecessary to state it. However, every generalization about human beings seems to have an exception, and there is at least one minority group, the Buraku of Japan, that has been victimized by discrimination and prejudice for hundreds of years but is virtually indistinguishable from the general population. That is, the Buraku are a minority and fit all parts of the definition stated in Chapter 1—except that there is no physical, cultural, religious, or linguistic difference between them and other Japanese. How could such an "invisible" minority come into being? How could the disadvantaged status be maintained through time?

The Buraku were created centuries ago, during feudal times in Japan. At that time, the society was organized into a caste system (see Chapter 4) based on occupation, and the ancestors of today's Buraku people did work that brought them into contact with death (gravediggers, executioners) or required them to handle meat or meat products (leather workers, butchers). These occupations were regarded as very low in status, and their practitioners were seen as being "unclean" or polluted. In fact, an alternative name for the group, *eta,* means "extreme filth." The Buraku people were required to live in separate, segregated villages and to wear leather patches for purposes of identification (thus raising their social visibility). They were forbidden to marry outside their caste, and any member of the general population who touched a Buraku had to be ritually purified or cleansed of pollution (Lamont-Brown, 1993, p. 137).

The caste system was officially abolished in the 19th century, at about the time Japan began to industrialize. The Buraku today, however, continue to suffer from discrimination and rejection, even though most observers agree that the levels of discrimination today are lower than in the past and that the overall situation of the Buraku people is improving. The Buraku still have much lower levels of education than the general population. For example, the enrollment rate of the Buraku in higher education is about 60% of the national average (Buraku Liberation League, 2001). Lower levels of education in Japan, as in the United States, limit occupational mobility and lead to higher unemployment rates. The educational deficits also help to maintain gaps between the Buraku and the general population in income and poverty rates.

The Buraku are a small group, about 2% or 3% of Japan's population. About 1 million still live in the thousands of traditional Buraku areas that remain, and another 2 million or so live in non-Buraku areas, mostly in larger cities. They continue to be seen as "filthy," "not very bright," and "untrustworthy"—stereotypical traits that are often associated with minority groups mired in subordinate and unequal positions (see Chapter 3). Also, as is the case for many American minority groups, the Buraku have a vocal and passionate protest organization—the Buraku Liberation League (http://www.blhrri.org/index_e.htm)—that is dedicated to improving the conditions of the group.

The situation of the Buraku might seem puzzling. If it is disadvantageous to be a member of the group and if the group is indistinguishable from the general population, why don't the Buraku simply blend into the larger society and avoid the discrimination and prejudice? What keeps them attached to their group? In fact, it is relatively easy for those who choose to do so to disappear into the mainstream and to "pass," as attested by the fact that two thirds of the group no longer live in the traditional Buraku areas. Why doesn't the group integrate into the larger society?

One answer to this question, at least for some Buraku, is that they are committed to their group identity and are proud of their heritage. They refuse to surrender to the dominant culture, insist on being accepted for who they are, and have no intention of trading their identity for acceptance or opportunity. For others, even those attempting to pass, the tie to the group and a subtle form of social visibility are maintained by the ancient system of residential segregation. The identity of the traditional Buraku villages and areas of residence are matters of public record, and it is this information—not race or culture—that establishes the boundaries of the group and forms the ultimate barrier to Buraku assimilation.

Japanese firms keep lists of local Buraku addresses and use the lists to screen out potential employees, even though this practice is now illegal. Also, the telltale information may be revealed when applying to rent an apartment (some landlords refuse to rent rooms to Buraku because of their alleged "filthiness")

or purchase a home (banks may be reluctant to make loans to members of a group that is widely regarded as "untrustworthy"). A particularly strong line of resistance to the complete integration of the Buraku arises if they attempt to marry outside of the group. It is common practice for Japanese parents to research the family history of a child's fiancé, and any secret Buraku connections are very likely to be unearthed by this process. Thus, members of the Buraku who pass undetected at work and in their neighborhood are likely to be "outed" if they attempt to marry into the dominant group.

This link to the traditional Buraku residential areas means that this group is not really invisible. Although their social visibility is much lower than the visibility of racial and ethnic minority groups, there is a way to determine group membership, a mark or sign of who belongs and who doesn't. Consistent with the definition presented in Chapter 1, this "birthmark" is the basis for a socially constructed boundary that differentiates "us" from "them" and for systematic discrimination, prejudice, inequality, and all the other disabilities and disadvantages associated with minority group status.

Main Points

- Asian Americans and Pacific Islanders are diverse and have brought many different cultural and linguistic traditions to the United States. These groups are growing rapidly but are still only a tiny fraction of the total population.

- Chinese immigrants were the victims of a massive campaign of discrimination and exclusion and responded by constructing enclaves. Chinatowns became highly organized communities, largely run by the local CCBAs and other associations. The second generation faced many barriers to employment in the dominant society, although opportunities increased after World War II.

- Japanese immigration began in the 1890s and stimulated a campaign that attempted to oust the group from agriculture and curtail immigration from Japan. The Issei formed an enclave, but during World War II, Japanese Americans were forced into relocation camps, and this experience devastated the group economically and psychologically.

- Recent immigration from Asia is diverse in terms of national origins, contact situation, levels of human capital, and mode of incorporation into U.S. society.

- Overall levels of anti-Asian prejudice and discrimination have probably declined in recent years but remain widespread. Levels of acculturation and secondary structural assimilation are variable. Members of these groups whose families have been in the United States longer tend to be highly acculturated and integrated. Recent immigrants from China, however, are "bipolar." Many are highly educated and skilled, but a sizable number are "immigrant laborers" who bring modest educational credentials and are likely to be living in poverty.

- The notion that Asian Americans are a "model minority" is exaggerated, but comparisons with European immigrants and colonized minority groups suggest some of the reasons for the relative "success" of these groups.

- Public sociology Assignment 2 in the introduction to Part 3 focuses on racial and ethnic inequalities in health in your area. Can you document any differences in health between Asian groups and whites?

- Are there differences between specific Asian groups? Do these differences parallel the patterns of inequality documented in this chapter?

Study Site on the Web

Don't forget the interactive quizzes and other resources and learning aids at www.pineforge.com/healeystudy5.

For Further Reading

Espiritu, Yen. (1997). *Asian American Women and Men*. Thousand Oaks, CA: Sage.

Analyzes the intersections of race, class, and gender among Asian Americans.

Kitano, Harry H. (1976). *Japanese Americans*. Englewood Cliffs, NJ: Prentice Hall.

Lyman, Stanford. (1974). *Chinese Americans*. New York: Random House.

Two comprehensive case studies of the Asian American groups with the longest histories in the United States.

Kitano, Harry H. L., & Daniels, Roger. (1995). *Asian Americans: Emerging Minorities* (2nd ed.). Englewood Cliffs, NJ: Prentice Hall.

Min, Pyong Gap. (Ed.). (1995). *Asian Americans: Contemporary Trends and Issues*. Thousand Oaks, CA: Sage.

Two good overviews of all the Asian American groups covered in this chapter.

Kwong, Peter. (1987). *The New Chinatown*. New York: Hill & Wang.

Zhou, Min. (1992). *Chinatown*. Philadelphia: Temple University Press.

Two excellent analyses of Chinatowns, with a behind-the-scenes look at the realities often hidden from outsiders.

Questions for Review and Study

1. Describe the cultural characteristics of Asian American groups. How did these characteristics shape relationships with the larger society? Did they contribute to the perception of Asian Americans as "successful"? How?

2. Compare and contrast the contact situation for Chinese Americans, Japanese Americans, and Cuban Americans. What common characteristics led to the construction of ethnic enclaves for all three groups? How and why did these enclaves vary from each other?

3. In what sense was the second generation of Chinese Americans "delayed"? How did this affect the relationship of the group with the larger society?

4. Compare and contrast the campaigns that arose in opposition to the immigration of Chinese and Japanese. Do the concepts of the Noel hypothesis help to explain the differences? Do you see any similarities with the changing federal policy toward Mexican immigrants across the 20th century? Explain.

5. Compare and contrast the Japanese relocation camps with Indian reservations in terms of paternalism and coerced acculturation. What impact did this experience have on the Japanese Americans economically? How were Japanese Americans compensated for their losses? Does the compensation paid to Japanese Americans provide a precedent for similar payments (reparations) to African Americans for their losses under slavery? Why or why not?

6. How do the Buraku in Japan illustrate "visibility" as a defining characteristic of minority group status? How is the minority status of this group maintained?

7. What gender differences characterize Asian American groups? What are some of the important ways in which the experiences of women and men vary?

8. Describe the situation of the Chinese and Japanese Americans in terms of prejudice and discrimination, acculturation, and integration. Are these groups truly "success stories"? How? What factors or experiences might account for this "success"? Are all Asian American groups equally successful? Describe the important variations from group to group. Compare the integration and level of equality of these groups with other American racial minorities. How would you explain the differences? Are the concepts of the Noel and Blauner hypotheses helpful? Why or why not?

Internet Research Project

A. Updating the Chapter

The Asian-Nation Web site at http://www.asian-nation.org/index.html provides comprehensive coverage on a number of issues raised in this chapter. Update and expand the chapter by selecting one or two topics (e.g., the "model minority" image) and searching the Web site. Be sure to follow some of the links provided to see what additional information and perspectives you can uncover.

B. Learning More About Asian Americans

Select one of the Asian groups discussed in this chapter other than Japanese Americans and Chinese Americans and conduct an Internet search using the name of the group. Follow the links and see what information you can add to the profile provided in the chapter. You might focus your search by seeking answers to basic questions such as these: How large is the group? Where do the members live in the United States (region of the country, rural vs. urban)? How acculturated is the group in terms of language? How does the group compare with national norms in terms of education, occupational profile, and income? What are the major issues from the perspective of the group?

Note

1. The FBI does not provide separate estimates for the two groups.

PART 4

Challenges for the Present and the Future

In this section, we analyze the new immigration, continuing issues of assimilation, and equality, inclusion, and racism. Many of these issues—as they relate to what it means to be an American—have been discussed throughout this text, as they have been discussed and debated throughout the history of this society. In the final chapter, we summarize the major themes of this text, bring the analysis to a close, and speculate about the future of American race and ethnic relations.

About the Public Sociology Assignments

The two assignments in this part are global in scope. The first focuses on natural and man-made disasters, public policy, emergency relief efforts, and the most vulnerable and exploitable segments of society. As we have seen throughout this text, minority groups (especially colonized groups) and women frequently have the fewest resources and the least ability to protect their self-interests. When disaster strikes, they are often the most exposed and victimized segment of the society. What policies, if any, do your community and state have to protect these most vulnerable populations? How can these policies be improved?

The second assignment connects to one of the most distressing and horrifying acts of which people are capable: genocide. The most well-known episode of genocide was the Nazi extermination of millions of people, especially Jews, during World War II, but more recent examples can be found in the former Yugoslavia, Rwanda, and the Darfur region of Sudan What is known about the causes of these horrors? What can be done to prevent them? This exercise allows you to develop and present information about a particular genocide. Unfortunately, there are many from which to choose.

Public Sociology Assignments

Marcus Griffin

Assignment 1

Social Justice and Disaster Preparedness Planning

Each year, the world experiences a plethora of natural and man-made disasters. Hurricanes, typhoons, earthquakes, tsunamis, flooding, drought, and heavy snowfall are a few of the natural disasters. Oil tanker spills and terrorist and war-based attacks are prominent man-made disasters. These events have devastating effects on local populations. For example, the December 29, 2004, tsunami that impacted eastern Africa, South Asia, and parts of Southeast Asia killed in excess of 120,000 people. Many died due to water contamination, vulnerability to dengue fever and malaria, and other communicable diseases promoted by numerous unburied corpses. The

September 11, 2001, terrorist attack on the World Trade Center killed 2,752 people and caused billions of dollars in damages. The human suffering caused by incidents such as these is inestimable and is on a scale difficult to comprehend.

We learned in this text that societies experience a range of social inequalities. Many times, especially vulnerable segments of the population are, for all practical purposes, invisible. During natural and man-made disasters, women, children, the aged, the underprivileged, and ethnic minorities may experience more severe trauma due to their "invisibility" or to lack of awareness on the part of disaster relief agencies and the policies they follow. For example, women and children in the December 29 tsunami experienced not simply loss of life, injuries, separation from loved ones, and basic needs but also rape and sexual exploitation. Disaster plans do not always include explicit gender perspectives in all responses to humanitarian and recovery needs. This assignment is designed for you to explore local, state, and federal disaster preparedness and response policy, to discern whether particular populations are invisible and likely to inadvertently experience unequal treatment and unmitigated trauma. Responding rapidly and effectively to a disaster is extremely complex, and officials and personnel involved often put their lives at risk to help others get out of harm's way and recover. Your state department of emergency management may be able to use your research to examine its policy and response in an effort to serve the citizenry best.

Step 1

You will first need to gain a basic understanding of disaster preparedness and how agencies cooperate with each other to serve the populace during times of crisis. Start with the Federal Emergency Management Agency (FEMA) Web site at http://www.fema.gov and conduct a literature review of their resources (which are quite good). If you want to focus on man-made disasters or terrorist attacks, you may want to explore the federal Department of Homeland Security (to

which FEMA reports) at http://www.dhs.gov/. Next, go to your state department of emergency management's Web site and conduct a similar literature review.

Three resources are listed at the end of this assignment to help you get started. The first is a United Nations report on environmental management and mitigation of natural disasters from a gender perspective. Other variables, such as age, ethnicity, and socioeconomic status, may be used instead of gender, as you prefer: The issues of inequality are similar from a policy point of view. The second resource is the Commonwealth of Virginia's Disaster Preparedness Plan, which will give you exposure to how one state approaches the problem. Your particular state will have its own plan and should be searched. The final resource is the U.S. National Response Plan, from the Department of Homeland Security. This gives you a global perspective useful to looking at how local county, state, and federal agencies in the United States must coordinate activities and prioritize relief efforts.

Step 2

Choose a particular variable (e.g., gender, age, or race) on which to focus your policy and procedure review. Return to your literature review and reexamine the material to glean information on your variable from global, federal, state, and local points of view.

Step 3

Using the information you obtained from your literature and resource reviews, draft a set of questions to refer to when speaking with agency and government officials. Your goal is to come up with information and material that the agency will find useful and helpful in carrying out its duties.

Step 4

Contact your state director of emergency management. Discuss with her or him your interest in exploring the disaster preparedness plan and contributing information that may be used to ensure that especially vulnerable populations are not inadvertently overlooked in relief efforts. You will probably be directed to speak with a number of other agency contacts and should keep a log of conversations. Be open to suggestions they provide to you to customize your efforts in light of the needs they agree exist. In short, if an agency does not agree there is a need for such information, what you give them in the end will not be used, and so you must adjust realistically to their interest.

Step 5

Using the resources you uncovered in Steps 1 and 2 plus the resources you obtained from the agencies, begin a policy analysis on the relative invisibility of the group or groups on which you are focused. If the group you have chosen is indeed invisible or is only tangentially addressed, you must explore other disaster preparedness plans from other states, countries, and transnational agencies (i.e., International Federation of Red Cross and Red Crescent Societies, http://www.ifrc.org/; United Nations, http://www.un.org/; Doctors Without Borders, http://www.doctorswithoutborders.org). You need to find relief protocols that already exist that your agency can consider adopting, along with the reasoning behind the protocols.

Step 6

Examine the structure of your state's disaster preparedness plan and decide how to insert the content you obtained from your research. Your wording and language use must be consistent and conform to the existing document. Once you have worked this out, submit your finished content to your agency contacts and ask them to keep you informed of any adoption of the material you put together and revision of the disaster plan. Thank them for their assistance and commitment and for providing you with the opportunity to contribute!

Step 7

Congratulate yourself for hard work well-done! Do not be surprised if you have worked yourself into an agency internship!

Resources

Commonwealth of Virginia's Disaster Preparedness Plan: http://www.vdem.state.va.us/library/eopv012/eopvolume2.pdf

U.N. Division for the Advancement of Women. 2001. Environmental Management and the Mitigation of Natural Disasters: A Global Perspective: http://www.un.org/womenwatch/daw/csw/env_manage/documents/EGM-Turkey-final-report.pdf

U.S. National Response Plan: http://www.dhs.gov/dhspublic/display?theme=15& content=4269. If your computer can handle all 426 pages (4 MB) of the full text version, go straight to http://www.dhs.gov/interweb/assetlibrary/NRP_FullText.pdf.

Assignment 2
Global Genocide Awareness and Education

Most students are familiar with the genocide during World War II perpetrated by Adolf Hitler and the German Nazi soldiers under his command against Jews, Romany, and other ethnic groups. There have been many other genocides since World War II. In fact, they seem to occur with alarming frequency. As inequalities increase among people not just in the United States but worldwide, the incidence of genocide seems to increase as well. Therefore, understanding genocide as an international war crime as well as a crime against humanity is paramount. In this assignment, you will create educational and informational materials for a local school, your college or university community, or a broader audience on a genocide of your choosing.

Step 1

Review the different genocides. You will do this by reviewing the published literature on past and present genocides in your school library as well as online databases and Web sites. When using online resources, you must be careful to exercise good information literacy skills, because there is little editorial control over the content of sites, and there exist people who argue that certain genocides, such as the Jewish Holocaust during World War II, never happened. When in doubt, consult your university or college librarians for assistance, as they are experts in information literacy. A few online resources are suggested at the end of this assignment to get you started.

Step 2

Choose a genocide to study in detail. These may be genocides in Cambodia in the late 1970s, the former Yugoslavia in the 1990s, the Darfur region of Sudan in 2004, or another genocide. As a general rule, however, you might consider focusing on an event that has not already been covered in depth in history textbooks so that that your audience will be informed of the scope of the problem and its continuing prevalence.

Step 3

Once your background research is completed, assess what audience and presentation format you feel best targets and promotes the knowledge you have synthesized. You may wish to compile learning aids for your alma mater high school or a grade school with which you are connected. You may wish to share your knowledge with your fellow university or college classmates and faculty through a poster or presentation kiosk exhibition in the local student center or union. If you are computer savvy and graphically inclined, you may wish to construct a Web site hosted on your college or university account or by a third-party account such as Geocities.

Step 4

After deciding the final product format and audience, compile your resources and construct your learning materials. Be careful to cite your sources correctly and appropriately. If you are using Internet site links or relying on a Web site's resources, e-mail the site managers for each link to inform them of your link and purpose.

Step 5

With a draft of your materials completed, share it with an impartial reviewer, such as a professor, teacher (especially if providing learning resources to a school), or community advocate or authority.

Step 6

Consider the revisions your reviewer suggests and make appropriate changes to your materials. Polish your presentation, Web site, poster series, or learning resources into a final draft that makes an impact on the viewer.

Step 7

Exhibit your materials and make yourself available to answer questions from your audience.

Step 8

Send a thank-you message to those advocates who helped you with your materials and provide them with a copy, if appropriate, of your final product for them to make available to others. Do not forget to congratulate yourself for emotionally difficult yet rewarding work well-done!

Suggested Resources

Australian Institute for Holocaust and Genocide Studies: http://www.aihgs.com/

Prevent Genocide International: http://www.preventgenocide.org/

United Nations Human Rights Web site: http://www.un.org/rights/

New Americans, Assimilation, and Old Challenges

CHAPTER 10

In this chapter, we focus on the current wave of immigration to the United States and the myriad issues stimulated by this influx of newcomers. We have already addressed some new groups in American society in Chapters 8 and 9. Here, we will look at recent immigrants in general terms and then address some additional groups of new Americans: non-Hispanic groups from the Caribbean, Arab Americans and Middle Easterners, and immigrants from sub-Saharan Africa. A consideration of these groups will broaden your understanding of the wide cultural variations, motivations, and human capital of the current immigration stream to the United States. To conserve space, I consider only groups that number at least 100,000 members.

We will then address the most important immigration issues facing U.S. society and conclude with a brief return to the "traditional" minority groups: African, Hispanic, and Native American, peoples of color that continue to face issues of equality and full integration and must now pursue their long-standing grievances in an atmosphere where public attention and political energy are focused on other groups and newer issues.

Current Immigration

As you are aware, the United States has experienced two different waves of mass immigration. In Chapter 2, we discussed the first wave, which lasted from the 1820s to the 1920s. During this century, over 37 million people immigrated to the United States, an average rate of a little less than 400,000 per year. This wave of newcomers, overwhelmingly from Europe, transformed American society on every level: its neighborhoods and parishes and cities, its popular culture, its accent and dialect, its religion, and its cuisine.

The second wave of mass immigration may well prove to be equally transformative. This wave began in the 1960s and includes people from every corner of the globe. Over the past four decades, over 30 million newcomers have arrived (not counting undocumented immigrants), a rate that far exceeds the pace of the first mass immigration. Since the 1960s, the United States has averaged about 650,000 newcomers each year, a number that generally has increased year by year (see Exhibit 10.1). The record for most immigrants in a year was set in 1907, when almost 1.3 million people arrived on these shores. That number was almost equaled in 2006, and if undocumented immigrants were included in the count, the 1907 record would certainly have been eclipsed several times since the 1960s.

The more recent wave of immigration is much more global than the first. In 2006 alone, immigrants arrived from over 200 separate nations, from Albania to Zimbabwe. Only about 13% of the newcomers were from Europe. A third were from North America (most from Mexico), and another third were from the nations of Asia, while South America supplied another 11%. The top 20 sending nations for 2006 are listed in Exhibit 10.2. Note that Mexico accounted for more than double the number of immigrants from the next-highest sending nation.

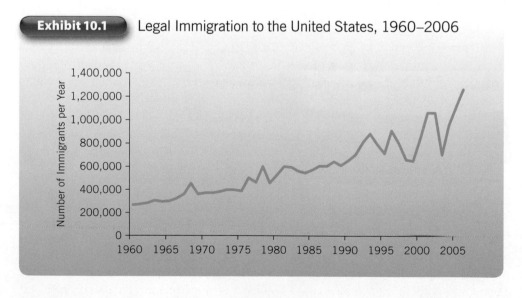

Exhibit 10.1 Legal Immigration to the United States, 1960–2006

SOURCE: U.S. Department of Homeland Security (2007, p. 5).

Exhibit 10.2   Top 20 Sending Nations, 2006

Rank	Nation	No. of Immigrants	Rank	Nation	No. of Immigrants
1	Mexico	173,753	11	Korea	24,386
2	China	87,345	12	Guatemala	24,146
3	Philippines	74,607	13	Haiti	22,228
4	India	61,369	14	Peru	21,718
5	Cuba	45,614	15	Canada	18,207
6	Colombia	43,151	16	Brazil	17,910
7	Dominican Republic	38,069	17	Ecuador	17,490
8	El Salvador	31,783	18	Pakistan	17,418
9	Vietnam	30,695	19	United Kingdom	17,207
10	Jamaica	24,976	20	Ukraine	17,142

SOURCE: U.S. Department of Homeland Security (2007, p. 16).

Key:

Blue = Western Hemisphere

Red = Asia

Black = Europe

How will this new wave of immigration transform the United States? How will these new immigrants be transformed by the United States? What do they contribute? What do they cost? Will they assimilate and adopt the ways of the dominant society? What are the implications if assimilation fails?

We have been asking questions like this throughout this text, and in this chapter, we will apply them to the recent wave of immigrants. First, however, we will review several more case studies of new Americans, focusing on information and statistics comparable to those used in Chapters 6 through 9. Also, additional data in the relative standing of these groups is presented in the Appendix.

Each of the groups covered in this chapter has had some members in the United States for decades, some for more than a century. However, in all cases, the groups were quite small until the latter third of the 20th century. Although they are growing rapidly now, all remain relatively small, and none are larger than 1% of the population. Nonetheless, some will have a greater impact on American culture and society in the future, and some groups—Arab Americans, Muslims, and Middle Easterners—have already become a focus of concern and controversy because of the events of 9/11 and the ensuing war on terrorism.

Recent Non-Hispanic Immigration From the Caribbean

We discussed immigration from Latin America and the Caribbean in Chapter 8. The groups we discussed in that chapter were Hispanic, but there are several other traditions represented in the region, and in this chapter, we discuss two prominent non-Latino Caribbean groups: Haitians and Jamaicans. Haiti and Jamaica are economically much less developed than the United States, and this is reflected in the educational and occupational characteristics of their immigrants. A statistical profile of both groups is presented in Exhibit 10.3, along with non-Hispanic whites for purposes of comparison.

Haitians.
Haiti is the poorest country in the Western Hemisphere, and most of the population relies on small-scale subsistence agriculture for survival. Estimates are that 80% of the population lives below the poverty line, and fewer than one third of adults hold formal jobs. Only about half the population is literate, and Haitians average less than 3 years of formal education ("Literacy, Total Population," n.d.).

Haitian immigration was virtually nonexistent until the 1970s and 1980s, when thousands began to flee the brutal political repression of the Duvalier dictatorship, which—counting both father ("Papa Doc") and son ("Baby Doc")—lasted until the mid-1980s. In stark contrast to the treatment of Cuban immigrants (see Chapter 8), however, the United States government defined Haitians as economic refugees ineligible for asylum, and an intense campaign has been conducted to keep Haitians out of the United States. Thousands have been returned to Haiti, some to face political persecution, prison, and even death. Others have been incarcerated in the United States, and in the view of some, "During the 1970s and 1980s, no other immigrant group suffered more U.S. government prejudice and discrimination than Haitians" (Stepick, Stepick, Eugene, Teed, & Labissiere, 2001, p. 236).

Exhibit 10.3 Characteristics of Two Caribbean-Origin Groups

Group	Number	% Foreign-Born	% That Speak English "Less Than Very Well"	% High School Degree or More	% College Degree or More	% of Families in Poverty	% in Managerial or Professional Occupations	Median Household Income (U.S. Dollars)
Non-Hispanic Whites	—	3.9	1.8	88.9	29.9	6.1	37.6	52,375
Jamaica	910,979	62.3	1.5	82.1	22.8	11.5	30.7	47,106
Haiti	762,925	61.2	37.6	75.7	18.5	15.4	21.7	41,666

SOURCE: U.S. Bureau of the Census (2007a).

Exhibit 10.4   Map of Caribbean Showing Haiti and Jamaica

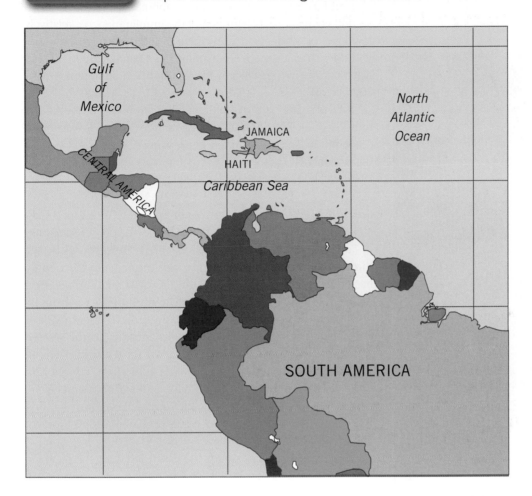

What accounts for this cold, negative reception? Some reasons are not hard to identify. The first Haitian immigrants to come brought low levels of human capital and education. This created concerns about their ability to support themselves in the United States and also meant that they had relatively few resources with which to defend their self-interests. In addition, Haitians speak Creole, a language spoken by almost no one else, and a high percentage of Haitian immigrants spoke English poorly or not at all. Perhaps the most important reason for the rejection, however, is that Haitians are black and must cope with the centuries-old traditions of rejection, racism, and prejudice that are such an integral part of American culture (Stepick et al., 2001).

Haitian Americans today are still mostly first generation, and roughly a third of the group arrived after 1990. Overall, they are comparable to Hispanic Americans in terms of such measures of equality as level of education, income, and poverty. Still, research shows that some Haitians continue to face the exclusion and discrimination long associated with nonwhite ancestry. One important study of Haitians in South Florida found that a combination of factors—their hostile reception, their poverty and lack of education, and their racial background—combined to lead the Haitian second generation (the children of the immigrants) to a relatively low level of academic achievement and a tendency to identify with the African American community. "Haitians are becoming American but in a specifically black ethnic fashion" (Stepick et al., 2001, p. 261).

The ultimate path of Haitian assimilation will unfold in the future, but these tendencies—particularly Haitians' low levels of academic achievement—suggest that some of the second generation are unlikely to move into the middle class and that their assimilation will be segmented (Stepick et al., 2001, p. 261).

Jamaicans. The Jamaican economy is more developed than Haiti's, and this is reflected in the higher levels of education of Jamaican immigrants (see Exhibit 10.3). However, as is true throughout the less developed world, the Jamaican economy has faltered in recent decades, and the island nation has been unable to provide full employment opportunities to its population. Jamaica is a former British colony, and immigrants have journeyed to the United Kingdom in addition to the United States. In both cases, the immigrant stream tends to be more skilled and educated and represents something of a "brain drain," a pattern we have seen with other groups, including Asian Indians. Needless to say, the loss of the more-educated Jamaicans to immigration exacerbates problems of development and growth on the island.

Jamaicans typically settle on the East Coast, particularly in the New York City area. Because they come from a former British colony, they have the advantage of speaking English as their native tongue. On the other hand, they are black, and like Haitians, they must face the barriers of discrimination and racism faced by all nonwhite groups in the United States. On the average, they are significantly higher than Haitians (and native-born African Americans) in socioeconomic standing, but poverty and institutionalized discrimination limit the mobility of a segment of the group. Like all other groups of color in the United States, they face a danger of segmented assimilation and permanent exclusion from the economic mainstream that is very real.

Middle Eastern and Arab Americans

Immigration from the Middle East and the Arab world began in the 19th century but has never been particularly large. The earliest immigrants tended to be merchants and traders, and the Middle Eastern community in the United States has been constructed around an ethnic, small-business enclave. The number of Arab Americans and Middle Easterners has grown rapidly over the past several decades but still remains a tiny percentage of the total

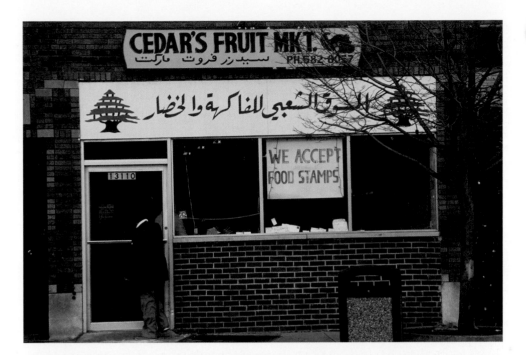

Arab-owned stores in Dearborn, Michigan.

population. Exhibit 10.5 displays some statistical information on the group, broken down by ancestry group with which individuals identify. Middle Easterners and Arab Americans rank relatively high in income and occupation. Most groups are at or above national norms in terms of percentage of high school graduates, and all groups have a higher percentage of college graduates than non-Hispanic whites, with some (Egyptians and Iranians) far more educated. Although poverty is a problem for all groups (especially Lebanese), many of the groups compare quite favorably in terms of occupation and income. Additional information on the relative standing of these groups is presented in the Appendix.

Many recent Middle Eastern immigrants are, like Asian immigrants, highly educated people who take jobs in the highest levels of the American job structure. Also, consistent with the heritage of being an enclave minority, the groups are overrepresented in sales and underrepresented in occupations involving manual labor. One study, using 1990 census data and a survey mailed to a national sample of Arab American women in 2000, found that immigrant Arab American women have a very low rate of employment, the lowest of any immigrant group. The author's analysis of this data strongly suggests that this pattern is due to traditional gender roles and family norms regarding the proper role of women (Read, 2004).

Arab Americans and Middle Easterners are diverse and vary along a number of dimensions. They bring different national traditions and cultures and also vary in religion. Although Islam is the dominant religion and most are Muslim, many members of these groups are Christian. Also, not all Middle Easterners are Arabic; Iranians, for example, are

Exhibit 10.5 Characteristics of Middle Eastern Americans by Arab Self-Identification and by Nation of Origin (Groups Larger Than 100,000 Only)

Group	Number	% Foreign-Born	% That Speak English "Less Than Very Well"	% High School Degree or More	% College Degree or More	% of Families in Poverty	% in Managerial or Professional Occupations	Median Household Income (U.S. Dollars)
Non-Hispanic Whites	—	3.9	1.8	88.9	29.9	6.1	37.6	52,375
Arab	257,864	47.8	25.4	83.3	34.6	15.8	34.1	45,666
Egypt	177,534	63.7	22.9	94.9	64.5	9.3	50.4	64,118
Iran	414,016	65.0	28.3	91.5	57.8	9.7	51.2	63,069
Lebanon	481,675	23.1	9.3	90.6	43.5	7.8	46.6	62,053
Syria	155,718	24.8	11.2	87.7	36.8	8.6	42.4	53,906

SOURCE: U.S. Bureau of the Census (2007a).

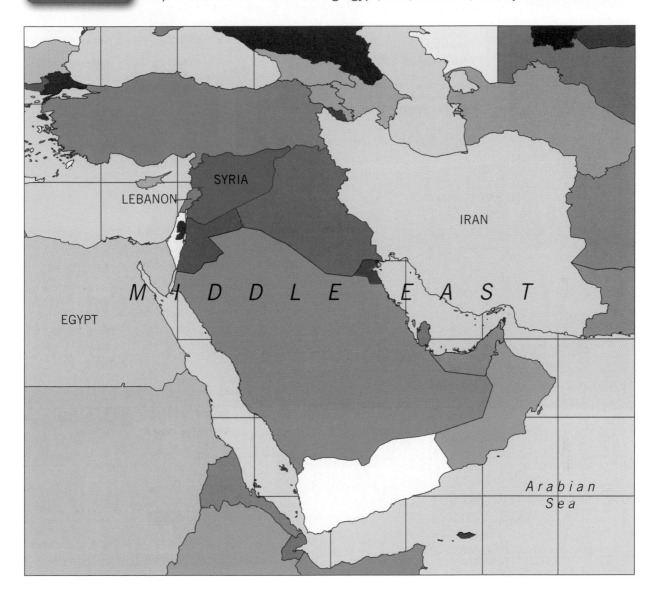

Persian. (Also, about a third of all Muslims in the United States are native-born, and about 20% are African American.)

Residentially, Arab Americans and Middle Easterners are highly urbanized, and almost 50% live in just five states (California, New Jersey, New York, Florida, and Michigan). This settlement pattern is not too different from that of other recent immigrant groups except for the heavy concentration in Michigan, especially in the Detroit area. Arab Americans account for 1.2% of the total population of Michigan, a far higher representation than in any other

Exhibit 10.7   Regional Distribution of Arab Americans, 2000

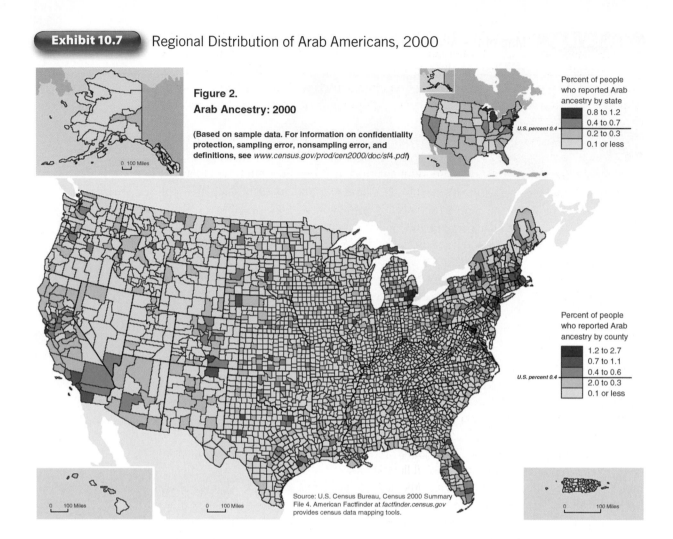

Figure 2.
Arab Ancestry: 2000

(Based on sample data. For information on confidentiality protection, sampling error, nonsampling error, and definitions, see *www.census.gov/prod/cen2000/doc/sf4.pdf*)

Percent of people who reported Arab ancestry by state

	0.8 to 1.2
	0.4 to 0.7
	0.2 to 0.3
	0.1 or less

U.S. percent 0.4

Percent of people who reported Arab ancestry by county

	1.2 to 2.7
	0.7 to 1.1
	0.4 to 0.6
	2.0 to 0.3
	0.1 or less

U.S. percent 0.4

Source: U.S. Census Bureau, Census 2000 Summary File 4. American Factfinder at *factfinder.census.gov* provides census data mapping tools.

SOURCE: de la Cruz & Brittingham (2003, p. 6).

state. Arab Americans make up 30% of the population of Dearborn, Michigan, the highest percentage of any city in the nation. (On the other hand, the greatest single concentration is in New York City, which has a population of about 70,000 Arab Americans.) These settlement patterns reflect chains of migration, some set up decades ago. Exhibit 10.7 shows the regional distribution of the group and clearly displays the clusters in Michigan, Florida, and Southern California.

9/11 and Arab Americans.
There has always been at least a faint strain of prejudice directed at Middle Easterners in American culture (e.g., see the low position of Turks in the 1926 social distance scales presented in Chapter 3; most Americans probably are not aware that Turks and Arabs are different groups). These vague feelings have intensified in recent decades as relations with various Middle Eastern nations and groups

worsened. For example, in 1979, the U.S. Embassy in Tehran, Iran, was attacked and occupied, and more than 50 Americans were held hostage for more than a year. The attack stimulated a massive reaction in the United States, in which anti-Arab and anti-Muslim feelings figured prominently. Continuing anti-American activities across the Middle East in the 1980s and 1990s stimulated a backlash of resentment and growing intolerance in the United States.

These earlier events pale in comparison, of course, to the events of September 11, 2001. Americans responded to the attacks on the World Trade Center and the Pentagon by Arab terrorists with an array of emotions that included bewilderment, shock, anger, patriotism, deep sorrow for the victims and their families, and—perhaps predictably in the intensity of the moment—increased prejudicial rejection of Middle Easterners, Arabs, Muslims, and any group that seemed even vaguely associated with the perpetrators of the attacks. In the 9 weeks following September 11, more than 700 violent attacks were reported to the Arab-American Anti-discrimination Committee, followed by another 165 violent incidents in the first 9 months of 2002. In this same time period, there were more than 80 incidents in which Arab Americans were removed from aircraft after boarding because of their ethnicity, more than 800 cases of employment discrimination, and "numerous instances of denial of service, discriminatory service, and housing discrimination" (Ibish, 2003, p. 7).

Anti-Arab passions may have cooled somewhat since the multiple traumas of 9/11, but the Arab American community faces a number of issues and problems, including profiling at airport security checks and greater restrictions on entering the country. Also, the USA Patriot Act, passed in 2001 to enhance the tools available to law enforcement to combat terrorism, allows for long-term detention of suspects, a wider scope for searches and surveillance, and other policies that many (not just Arab Americans) are concerned will encourage violations of due process and suspension of basic civil liberties.

Thus, although the Arab American and Middle Eastern communities are small in size, they have assumed a prominent place in the attention of the nation. The huge majority of these groups denounce and reject terrorism and violence, but, like Colombians and Italians, they are victimized by a strong stereotype that is often applied uncritically and without qualification. A recent survey of Muslim Americans, a category that includes the huge majority of Arab Americans and Middle Easterners, finds them to be "middle class and mostly mainstream." They have a positive view of U.S. society and espouse distinctly American values. At the same time, they are very concerned about becoming scapegoats in the war on terror, and a majority (53%) say that it became more difficult to be a Muslim in the United States after 9/11 (Pew Research Center, 2007).

Relations between Arab Americans and the larger society are certainly among the most tense and problematic of any minority group, and given the continuing U.S. occupation of Iraq and Afghanistan and the threat of further, even more damaging terrorist attacks by Al-Qaeda or other groups, they will not ease anytime soon. Some of the consequences of these relationships are discussed in Narrative Portrait 1 in this chapter.

The Arab American Community in Detroit, Michigan by *Steve Gold*

The events of September 11, 2001, focused attention on Arab American communities. The Detroit area is home to more than 300,000 Arab Americans, one of the largest ethnic enclaves in the United States. Nineteenth-century immigrants from Syria and Lebanon were the first to arrive. With the increased demand for automobiles and the steel to make them at the beginning of the 20th century, more immigrants from the Middle East came to work in Detroit's many factories. By 1916, the Ford motor company counted 555 Arab men among its workforce. The first Islamic mosque in America was established in Highland Park in 1919. The relationship between Arab immigrants and auto manufacturing endures. Next to Ford's famous River Rouge plant is Dearborn's "Arab village."

Immigrants continue to arrive in Detroit, reuniting families that have been divided across borders and continents. Whether from Iraq, Yemen, or Palestine, they seek economic advancement and escape from the Middle East's chronic violence. In 1990, more than one-third of Michigan's residents of Arab origin had been born outside of the United States; about 40 percent had immigrated after 1980. Although all are Arab, their religious affiliations are diverse: Lebanese Christians; Sunni and Shiite Muslims; Palestinians and Jordanians who are Catholic, Protestant, Greek Orthodox, and Sunni Muslims; Eastern rite Catholic Chaldeans; and Yemenis of different Muslim sects.

The Arab community is also socioeconomically diverse, but the 1990 Census showed them to be generally well-off as a group. College graduation rates are high, and comparatively few are unemployed or struggling on below-poverty incomes. Besides careers in the auto industry, Arab Americans also become professionals, and many are self-employed.

With their new visibility since September 2001, Arab Americans have experienced renewed negative attention. But this, too, has deep roots. Metropolitan Detroit has a long history of racial and ethnic violence, and Arab American residents have become well acquainted with discrimination and stereotyping—from ethnic slurs like being called "camel jockeys" to the more pernicious dominance of European traditions and standards in schools. Neither is this the first conflict in the Middle East for which Arabs were demonized. With a rich community life, Arab Americans have developed a range of organizational supports that provide succor in the face of the episodic but persistent hostilities they face in America.

Recommended Resources

Abraham, Sameer Y. 1983. "Detroit's Arab-American Community," pp. 84–108 in *Arabs in the New World,* ed. Sameer Y. Abraham and Nabeel Abraham. Detroit: Wayne State University Center for Urban Studies.

Abraham, Nabeel, and Andrew Shryock, eds. 2000. *Arab Detroit: From Margins to Mainstream.* Detroit: Wayne State University Press.

Johnson, Nan E. 1995. *Health Profiles of Michigan Populations of Color.* Lansing: Michigan Department of Public Health.

SOURCE: From Gold, S., *The Arab American Community in Detroit, Michigan.* Reprinted with permission of the University of California Press.

9/11 and Middle Eastern Americans

*A*mir Marvasti and Karyn McKinney are sociologists who, between 2002 and 2004, conducted in-depth interviews with 20 Middle Eastern Americans. The interviews covered a variety of topics, but most centered on the reactions of the respondents to the attacks of 9/11, the ensuing public reaction, and their own rethinking of what it means to be an American. What follows are the personal reactions of the respondents, knit together by the narrative written by Marvasti and McKinney.

Middle Eastern Americans and the American Dream

Amir Marvasti and Karyn McKinney

Difficulty with cultural assimilation is a common experience for most ethnic groups, but being designated public enemy number one is not. In the hours following the tragic attacks of September 11, 2001, being or just looking Middle Eastern became an instant offense. For members of this group, this was a turning point in terms of both the way they were viewed by others and the way they defined themselves. While the feeling of shock is similar to what everyone must have felt that day, in the case of Middle Eastern Americans, there was also a feeling of impending doom, the knowledge that their lives would never be exactly the same. Many of our respondents stated that after their sense of initial shock and sadness, the next thought they remember was that they hoped that the incident was perpetrated by domestic terrorists, as was the case with the Oklahoma City bombing. One Pakistani American stated,

> I was on my way to the gym listening to radio when it happened. And I thought it was a hoax. And then I got to the gym and it was on TV and I was like "Oh my God, please don't let it be Muslims." That was the first thing came to my mind, "God please don't let this be one of us."

As the day went by, a chasm began to form between Middle Eastern Americans and their fellow citizens. The perception that Middle Easterners were the aggressors and Americans the victims began to take hold, and out of this perception grew anger:

> I went to class that day and came back and from then on for two days, I was glued to CNN. . . . Wherever you went you always—that day even among my friends there was talk about anger and they looked really angry. . . . There was talk about "We should bomb Palestine." And "Who cares about these people now." In a way, I understood their anger because of what had just happened. I guess it was kind of lonely that day.

In the days following the attacks, Middle Eastern Americans had to accept the fact that they were seen by many as legitimate targets of anger. The news media were full of messages about hate being an acceptable emotion under the circumstances. In that atmosphere, it was indeed very "lonely" to be Middle Eastern American. What was most striking was the ordinary tone with which retaliatory violence was talked about. For example, in an introductory race and ethnicity course taught by [Marvasti], a young man passionately exclaimed, "I say we go bomb the Taj Mahal!" Although others in the class corrected his error in terms of his misplaced target, his general idea of bombing buildings where civilians would be the primary casualties was not disputed.

Some Middle Eastern Americans also felt a strong sense of impending doom related to this tragedy. . . . Perhaps the most significant realization for many Middle Eastern Americans was the awareness that their right to be part of the American Dream could be taken away for actions that they were not in any way responsible for. With this realization came the sense of not belonging and the real possibility of being physically separated from the rest of society and placed in an internment camp. One young Middle Eastern American remembered,

> I really thought I was going to be sent to like a camp. . . . It didn't—for those couple of days—it didn't feel like we were going to be back to normal again. Like I really didn't feel like—along with going to internment camp—I thought my life was never going to be the same. I no longer had a home here.

As this respondent puts it, realizing that one no longer has a home here, was tantamount to realizing that the American Dream applied to some more than others. . . .

September 11 was an important turning point in the psyche of Middle Eastern Americans to the extent that it caused them to reevaluate their place in American society and its promises of freedom and equality. Consider, for example, how this Pakistani American woman (who was born in Pennsylvania) rethinks her status as an American in light of how she and her family have been treated since September 11:

> My brother was assaulted three days after September 11th. It was part of the backlash. . . . I feel I'm even considered an outsider a lot of the times. I sound just as American as anyone else, and I was born and raised here. . . . [After September 11] I think a lot of people thought that if you're not going to consider me American, why am I going to consider myself an American. If you're not going to protect me like other Americans, if you are going to create laws that are going to undermine me, then I shouldn't be trying so hard to fit into a culture that consistently and perpetually rejects me.

According to this respondent, . . . it became particularly apparent that the ideals of equality in the American Dream did not apply to her and her family. Her ethnicity transcends her identity as an American and places her in the position of a second-class citizen. . . .

One of the most profound effects of September 11 on the lives of Middle Eastern Americans was the realization that their daily routines (i.e., the mundane tasks of going on a trip or even to a grocery store) would be subjected to scrutiny and potentially make them vulnerable to acts of violence. An Iranian American man describes how September 11 affected his life:

> I actually canceled a trip. We usually take a trip on Thanksgiving with about 30–40 Iranian Americans. And that's when I realized there's a difference in this war [War on Terrorism]. There is a new order. . . . We can't go somewhere and not play our own music. We like our own music, we like our own dance, we like our own food and tradition so we couldn't do that therefore I canceled that trip. That's when it occurred to me there's a difference.
>
> *Interviewer:* Did you put any other limitations on your life because of it? Did you restrict your life in any other way?
>
> *Respondent:* I'm more alert these days about how I answer people. . . . In the past I wouldn't mind if they asked right off the bat where I'm from. . . . But now most of the time I say "God, please don't let them ask the question.". . . I don't volunteer information. . . . I'm more guarded about what I say. . . .

Collectively, these post–9/11 experiences have caused some Middle Eastern Americans to question the meaning of the American Dream and the extent to which its lofty promises apply to them. They have recognized that full assimilation into American culture will not provide protection against acts of ignorance and that their future in this country is uncertain. . . .

The very value of civility is that it should offer protection when things are the most tense. If it fails to do so, then it is in fact, just a "veneer." Similarly, laws . . . are of no value unless they defend those who are least able to protect themselves (e.g., the newest immigrants) at times when they are most vulnerable. . . . The fact that . . . constitutional rights (i.e., due process protections) are undermined with the passage of new laws, such as the Patriot Act, further reveals how thin this "veneer of civility" really is.

SOURCE: Marvasti, Amir, & McKinney, Karyn (2004). *Middle Eastern Lives in America*, pp. 121–126. Lanham, MD: Rowman & Littlefield.

Immigrants From Africa

Our final group of new Americans consists of immigrants from Africa. Immigration from Africa has been quite low over the past 50 years. However, there was the usual increase after the 1960s, and Africans have made up about 5% of all immigrants in the past few years.

Exhibit 10.8 shows the total number of sub-Saharan Africans in the United States in 2006, along with the two largest national groups. The number of native Africans in the United States has more than doubled since 1990, and this rapid growth suggests that these groups may have a greater impact on U.S. society in the future. The category *sub-Saharan African* is extremely broad and encompasses destitute black refugees from African civil wars and relatively affluent white South Africans. In the remainder of this section, we will focus on Nigerians and Ethiopians rather than this very broad category (see Exhibit 10.9). See the Appendix for additional information on the relative standing of these groups.

Clearly, although they may be growing, Nigerians and Ethiopians are tiny minorities: Neither group is as much as 0.1% of the total population. They are recent immigrants and have a high representation of first-generation members. They both compare favorably to national norms in education, an indication that this is another example of a "brain drain" from the countries of origin. Nigerian and Ethiopian immigrants tend to be highly skilled and educated, and they bring valuable abilities and advanced educational credentials to the United States. Like some other groups, many of the immigrants from Nigeria and Ethiopia are motivated by a search for work, and they compete for positions in the higher reaches of the job structure.

Exhibit 10.8 Characteristics of Africans by Area and by Nation of Origin (Groups Larger Than 100,000 Only)

Group	Number	% Foreign-Born	% That Speak English "Less Than Very Well"	% High School Degree or More	% College Degree or More	% of Families in Poverty	% in Managerial or Professional Occupations	Median Household Income (U.S. Dollars)
Non-Hispanic Whites	—	3.9	1.8	88.9	29.9	6.1	37.6	52,375
Sub-Saharan Africa	1,588,718	24.3	7.0	83.3	22.7	18.5	29.6	36,335
Ethiopia	151,491	74.2	36.6	87.4	25.5	16.5	26.2	35,199
Nigeria	237,527	65.6	11.2	96.2	62.8	11.9	49.7	51,082

SOURCE: U.S. Bureau of the Census (2007a).

Exhibit 10.9   Map of Africa Showing Ethiopia and Nigeria

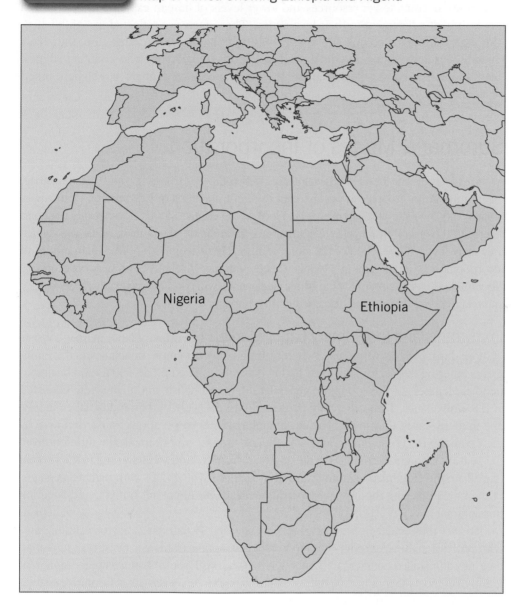

Nigeria is a former British colony, so the relatively high level of English fluency of the immigrants is not surprising. Exhibit 10.8 shows that, on the average, members of the group have been able to translate their relatively high levels of human capital and English fluency into a favorable position in the U.S. economy. They compare quite favorably with national norms in their occupational profiles and their income levels.

Compared with Nigerians, Ethiopians rank lower in their English fluency and are more mixed in their backgrounds. They include refugees from domestic unrest along with the educated elite. For example, almost 50% of Ethiopian immigrants in 2006 were admitted as "refugees and asylees" versus only 5% of Nigerian immigrants. Refugees, virtually by definition, bring fewer resources and lower levels of human capital and thus have a more difficult adjustment to their host nation. These facts are reflected in Exhibit 10.8. Although Ethiopians compare favorably with national norms in education, they have much higher rates of poverty and much lower levels of income. These contrasts suggest that Ethiopians are less able to translate their educational credentials into higher-ranked occupations.

Summary: Modes of Incorporation

As the case studies included in this chapter (as well as those in Chapters 8 and 9) demonstrate, recent immigrant groups can occupy very different positions in U.S. society. One way to address this diversity of relationships is to look at the contact situation, especially the characteristics the groups bring with them (their race and religion, the human capital with which they arrive) and the reaction of the larger society. There seem to be three main modes of incorporation for immigrants in the United States: entrance through the primary or secondary labor markets (see Chapter 5) or the ethnic enclave. We will consider each pathway separately and relate them to the groups discussed in this chapter.

Immigrants and the Primary Labor Market. The primary labor market consists of more desirable jobs with greater security, higher pay, and more benefits, and the immigrants entering this sector tend to be highly educated, skilled professionals and business-people. Members of this group are generally fluent in English, and many were educated at U.S. universities. They are highly integrated into the global urban-industrial economy, and in many cases, they are employees of multinational corporations transferred here by their companies. These immigrants are affluent, urbane, and dramatically different from the peasant laborers so common in the past (e.g., from Ireland and Italy) and in the present (e.g., from the Dominican Republic and from Mexico). The groups with high percentages of members entering the primary labor market include Egyptian, Iranian, and Nigerian immigrants.

Because they tend to be affluent and enter a growing sector of the labor force, immigrants with professional backgrounds tend to attract less notice and fewer racist reactions than their more unskilled counterparts. Although they come closer to Blauner's pure immigrant group than most other minority groups we have considered, racism can still complicate their assimilation. In addition, Arab Americans must confront discrimination and prejudice based on their religious affiliation.

Immigrants and the Secondary Labor Market. This mode of incorporation is more typical for immigrants with lower levels of education and fewer job skills. Jobs in this sector are less desirable and command lower pay, little security, and few benefits and are often seasonal or in the underground or informal economy. This labor market includes jobs in construction or the garment industry, in which workers are paid "off the books" and working conditions are unregulated by government authorities or labor unions; domestic work; and some forms of criminal or deviant activity, such as drug sales and prostitution. The employers

who control these jobs often prefer to hire undocumented immigrants because they are easier to control and less likely to complain to the authorities about abuse and mistreatment. The groups with high percentages of members in the secondary labor market include Haitians and the less skilled and less educated kinfolk of the higher-status immigrants.

Immigrants and Ethnic Enclaves. As we have seen, some immigrant groups—especially those that can bring financial capital and business experience—have established ethnic enclaves. Some members of these groups enter U.S. society as entrepreneurs and become owners of small retail shops and other businesses; their less-skilled and -educated coethnics serve as a source of cheap labor to staff the ethnic enterprises. The enclave provides contacts, financial and other services, and social support for the new immigrants of all social classes. Some Arab Americans, along with Cuban Americans and Jewish Americans in the past, have been particularly likely to follow this path.

This classification suggests some of the variety of relationships between the new Americans and the larger society. The contemporary stream of immigrants entering the United States is extremely diverse and includes people ranging from the most sophisticated and urbane to the most desperate and despairing. The variety is suggested by considering a list of occupations in which recent immigrants are overrepresented. For men, the list includes biologists and other natural scientists, taxi drivers, farm laborers, and waiters. For women, the list includes chemists, statisticians, produce packers, laundry workers, and domestics (Kritz & Girak, 2004).

Immigration: Issues and Controversies

How Welcoming Are Americans?

One factor that affects the fate of immigrant groups is the attitude of the larger society, particularly, the groups in the larger society that have the most influence with governmental policymakers. Overall, we can say that native-born Americans (even those with immigrant parents) have never been particularly open to newcomers. The history of this nation is replete with movements to drastically reduce immigration or even eliminate it completely. We have already mentioned some of the anti-immigration movements directed against the first mass wave of immigrants from Europe (Chapter 2), Mexico (Chapter 8), and China and Japan (Chapter 9). Here we will look at attitudes and reactions to contemporary immigrants.

First, although Americans have a lot of reservations about immigration, it seems that attitudes are somewhat more open now than in the past. Exhibit 10.10 shows some results of a survey administered to nationally representative samples for 3 different years between 1993 and 2006 (National Opinion Research Council, 1972–2007). In all years, the majority of respondents felt that the volume of immigration should be decreased, and only a small minority advocated an increase. However, and contrary to what many would expect, the percentage of Americans who favor decreasing the number of immigrants is actually lowest in the latest year of the survey.

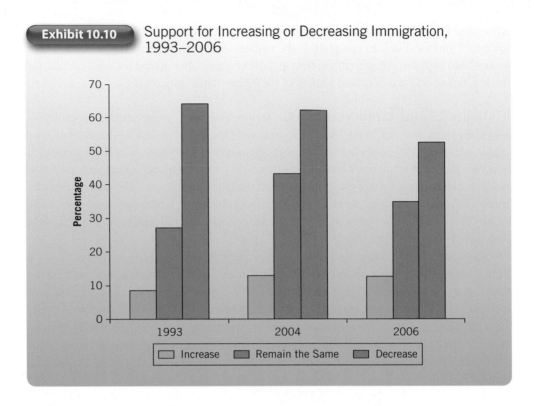

Exhibit 10.10 Support for Increasing or Decreasing Immigration, 1993–2006

Increase   Remain the Same   Decrease

SOURCE: National Opinion Research Council (1972–2007).

One survey found that people's opinions about the volume of immigration were related to their perceptions of their personal financial situations. Predictably, white Americans who felt that their financial situations had worsened over the past few years were more likely to support a reduction in immigration. This relationship is displayed in Exhibit 10.11. The table shows that there is a great deal of support for decreasing immigration regardless of people's perceptions of their financial situations. However, support for decreasing immigration is strongest among people who feel that their own personal financial situations have gotten worse. This relationship is consistent with the Noel hypothesis and the Robber's Cave experiment and should come as no surprise at this point in the text.

We should also note that support for decreasing immigration is affected by contact across group lines. In Chapter 3, we investigated a report that showed a relationship between contact and attitudes about immigrants in Europe. Exhibit 10.12 shows a parallel relationship in the United States. Whites who had more contact with Hispanic Americans, the largest single group of contemporary immigrants, show the lowest support for decreasing immigration.

Of course, these are simple tests that do not take all factors into consideration—for example, we do not know whether the intergroup contact measured in Exhibit 10.12 was with newly arrived immigrants or with Hispanic Americans from old, long-established families. Still, the relationships are suggestive and a reminder of the power of some of the central ideas and theories presented in this text.

Exhibit 10.11 Position on Immigration by Perception of Financial Situation, 2006 (Whites Only)

Do you think that the number of immigrants to America should be:	Over the past few years, do you feel that your financial situation has been getting better, worse, or has it stayed the same?		
	Better	Stayed the Same	Worse
Increased	11%	9%	9%
Remain the same	35%	34%	23%
Decreased	54%	57%	68%
	100%	100%	100%

SOURCE: National Opinion Research Council (1972–2007).

Exhibit 10.12 Position on Immigration by Number of Hispanic Acquaintances, 2006 (Whites Only)

Do you think that the number of immigrants to America should be:	Number of Hispanic Acquaintances		
	None	Some (1 to 5)	Many (6 or More)
Increased	10%	10%	13%
Remain the same	23%	37%	48%
Decreased	67%	53%	39%
	100%	100%	100%

SOURCE: National Opinion Research Council (1972–2007).

Views of the Immigrants

One recent survey of immigration issues (National Public Radio, 2004) included a representative sample of immigrant respondents. Not surprisingly, the researchers found that their attitudes and views differed sharply from those of native-born respondents on a number of dimensions. For example, immigrant respondents were more likely to see immigration as a positive force for the larger society and more likely to say that immigrants work hard and pay their fair share of taxes.

More relevant for the ultimate impact of the contemporary wave of immigration, the survey found that only about 30% were sojourners (i.e., planning ultimately to return to their homelands), a finding that suggests that issues of assimilation and immigration will remain at the forefront of U.S. concerns for many decades.

The survey also showed that immigrants are very grateful for the economic opportunities available in the United States, with 84% agreeing that there are more opportunities to get ahead here than in their countries of origin. On the other hand, the immigrant respondents were ambivalent about U.S. culture and values. For example, nearly half (47%) said that the family was stronger in their homelands than in the United States, and only 28% saw U.S. society as having stronger moral values than in their homelands.

Costs and Benefits

What concerns do Americans have about immigration? One common set of concerns revolves around economics. Americans are concerned that immigrant take jobs from native-born workers, place too much strain on institutions such as schools and medical facilities, and do not pay their fair share of taxes. These issues are complex and hotly debated at all levels of U.S. society, so much so that passion and intensity of feeling on all sides often compromises the objective analysis of data. The debate is further complicated because conclusions about these economic issues can change depending on the type of immigrants being discussed and the level of analysis being used.

While most people are concerned about the local impact of less-skilled (and illegal) immigrants, the assessment of costs and benefits can lead to very different conclusions when attention is directed to highly educated professionals entering the primary job market or to the national level rather than to local communities.

Contrary to the tenor of public opinion, many studies, especially those done at the national level, find that immigrants are not a burden. For example, a study conducted by the National Academy of Sciences (1997) found that immigrants are a positive addition to the economy. They add to the labor supply in areas as disparate as the garment industry, agriculture, domestic work, and college faculty (National Academy of Sciences, 1997). Other researchers have found that low-skilled immigrants tend to find jobs in areas of the economy in which few U.S. citizens work or in the enclave economies of their own groups, taking jobs that would not have existed without the economic activity of their coethnics (Heer, 1996, pp. 190–194; Smith & Edmonston, 1997). One important recent study of the economic impact of recent immigrants concluded that there is a relatively small effect on the wages and employment of native workers, although there do seem to be negative consequences for earlier immigrants and for African Americans (Bean & Stevens, 2003, pp. 221–223).

Another concern is the strain that immigrants place on taxes and services such as schools and welfare programs. Again, these issues are complex and far from settled, but some research projects suggest that immigrants cost less than they contribute. Taxes are automatically deducted from their paychecks (unless, of course, they are being paid "under the table"), and their use of such services as unemployment compensation, Medicare, food stamps, and Social Security is actually lower than their proportional contributions. This is particularly true for undocumented immigrants, whose use of services is sharply limited by their vulnerable legal status (Marcelli & Heer, 1998; Simon, 1989). Bean and Stevens (2003, pp. 66–93), in their recent study, find that immigrants are not overrepresented on the welfare rolls. Rather, the key determinant of welfare use is refugee status. Groups such as Haitians, Salvadorans, and

Photo 10.4

Becoming a U.S. citizen is an important step in the process of assimilation.

© Carlos Barria/Reuters/ Corbis.

Vietnamese—who arrive without resources and, by definition, are in need of assistance on all levels—are the most likely to be on the welfare rolls.

Final conclusions about the impact and costs of immigration must await further research, and many local communities are experiencing real distress as they try to deal with the influx of newcomers in their housing markets, schools, and health care facilities. The fears and concerns about the economic impact of immigrants are not unfounded, but they may be confounded with and exaggerated by prejudice and racism directed at newcomers and strangers. The current opposition to immigration may be a reaction to "who" as much as to "how many" or "how expensive." The Current Debates section at the end of this chapter presents some of the common arguments for and against continued immigration.

Finally, we can repeat the finding of many studies (e.g., Bean & Stevens, 2003) that immigration is generally a positive force in the economy and that, as has been true for decades, immigrants, legal and illegal, continue to find work with Anglo employers and niches in American society in which they can survive. The networks that have delivered cheap immigrant labor for the low-wage secondary job market continue to operate, and frequently, the primary beneficiaries of this long-established system are not the immigrants (although they are often grateful for the opportunities), but employers, who benefit from a cheaper, more easily exploited workforce, and American consumers, who benefit from lower prices in the marketplace.

Illegal Immigration

Americans are particularly concerned with undocumented immigrants, and many are frustrated with what they see as ineffective government efforts to curtail this flow of illegal aliens. For example, in a 2006 survey, 59% of the respondents said the problem of illegal immigration was "very serious," and another 30% said that they felt that the problem was "somewhat serious" (Pew Research Center, 2006b). There is no question that the volume of illegal immigration is huge. In 2000, it was estimated that there were 8.5 million people living in United States illegally, more than double the number in 1992 (Martin & Widgren, 2002, p. 13). In 2006, the number of illegal immigrants was estimated at 11.6 million (Hoefer, Rytina, & Campbell, 2007). Some undocumented immigrants enter the country on tourist, temporary worker, or student visas and simply remain in the nation when their visas expire. In 2000 alone, more than 33 million tourists and more than a million temporary workers and foreign students entered the United States, and these numbers suggest how difficult it would be to keep tabs on this source of illegal immigrants. Others cross the border illegally in hopes of escaping the border police and finding their way into some niche in the American economy. The very fact that people keep coming suggests that most succeed.

A variety of efforts continue to be made to curtail and control the flow of illegal immigrants. Various states have attempted to lower the appeal of the United States by limiting benefits and opportunities. One of the best known of these attempts occurred in 1994, when California voters passed Proposition 187, which would have denied educational, health, and other services to illegal immigrants. The policy was declared unconstitutional, however, and was never implemented. Other efforts to decrease the flow of illegal immigration have included proposals to limit welfare benefits for immigrants, to deny in-state college tuition to

The United States is attempting to stem the flow of illegal immigration by reinforcing the border and building taller and bigger walls. These crosses commemorate those who lost their lives crossing the border.

© Christopher Morris/
Corbis.

the children of illegal immigrants, to increase in the size of the Border Patrol, and to construct taller and wider walls along the border with Mexico. President Bush has proposed a "guest worker" program that would allow immigrants (including those illegally in the country now) to apply for temporary work permits. The program has been hotly debated at the highest levels of government but does not appear to be close to passage.

Although Americans will continue to be concerned about this problem, it seems unlikely that much can be done (within the framework of a democratic, humane society) to curtail the flow of people. The social networks that deliver immigrants—legal as well as illegal—are too well established, and the demand for cheap labor in the United States is simply insatiable. In fact, denying services, as envisioned in Proposition 187, may make illegal immigrants more attractive as a source of labor by reducing their ability to resist exploitation. For example, if the children of illegal immigrants were not permitted to attend school, they would become more likely to join the army of cheap labor on which some employers depend. Who would benefit from closing public schools to the children of illegal immigrants?

New Americans, Assimilation, and Old Challenge **485**

Is Contemporary Assimilation Segmented?

In Chapter 2, we reviewed some of the patterns of acculturation and integration that typified the adjustment of Europeans who immigrated to the United States before the 1930s. Although the process of adjustment was anything but smooth or simple, these groups eventually Americanized and achieved levels of education and affluence comparable to national norms. Will contemporary immigrants from Latin America and the Caribbean experience similar success? Will their sons and daughters and grandsons and granddaughters rise in the occupational structure to a position of parity with the dominant group? Will the cultures and languages of these groups gradually fade and disappear?

Final answers to these questions must await future developments. In the meantime, there is considerable debate on these issues. Some analysts argue that assimilation will be segmented and that the success story of the white ethnic groups will not be repeated. Others find that the traditional perspective on assimilation—particularly the model of assimilation developed by Milton Gordon—continues to be a useful and accurate framework for understanding the experience of contemporary immigrants. We will review some of the most important and influential arguments from each side of this debate and, finally, attempt to come to some conclusions about the future of assimilation.

The Case for Segmented Assimilation

Sociologist Douglas Massey (1995) presents a compelling argument in favor of the segmented-assimilation perspective. He argues that there are three crucial differences between the European assimilation experience of the past and the contemporary period that call the traditional perspective into question. First, the flow of immigrants from Europe to the United States slowed to a mere trickle after the 1920s because of restrictive legislation, the worldwide depression of the 1930s, and World War II. Immigration in the 1930s, for example, was less than 10% of the flow of the early 1920s. Thus, as the children and grandchildren of the immigrants from Europe Americanized and grew to adulthood in the 1930s and 1940s, few new immigrants fresh from the old country replaced them in the ethnic neighborhoods. European cultural traditions and languages weakened rapidly with the passing of the first generation and the Americanization of their descendants.

For contemporary immigration, in contrast, the networks and the demand for cheap labor are so strong that it is unlikely that there will be a similar hiatus in the flow of people. Immigration has become continuous, argues Massey, and as some contemporary immigrants (or their descendants) Americanize and rise to affluence and success, new arrivals will replace them and continuously revitalize the ethnic cultures and languages.

Second, the speed and ease of modern transportation and communication will help to maintain cultural and linguistic diversity. A century ago, immigrants from Europe could maintain contact with the old country only by mail, and most had no realistic expectation of ever returning. Most modern immigrants, in contrast, can return to their homes in a day or less and can use telephones, television, e-mail, and the Internet to stay in intimate contact with the families and friends they left behind. According to one recent survey (National Public Radio, 2004), a little more than 40% of immigrants return to their homelands at least every year or two, and some (6%) return every few months. Thus, the cultures of modern immigrants can be kept vital and whole in ways that were not available (and not even imagined) 100 years ago.

Third, and perhaps most important, contemporary immigrants face an economy and a labor market that are vastly different from those faced by European immigrants of the 19th and early 20th centuries. The latter group generally rose in the class system as the economy shifted from manufacturing to service (see Exhibit 5.4). Today, rates of upward mobility have decreased, and just when the importance of education has increased, schools available to the children of immigrants have fallen into neglect (Massey, 1995, pp. 645–646).

For the immigrants from Europe a century ago, assimilation meant a gradual rise to middle-class respectability and suburban comfort, even if it took four or five generations to accomplish. Assimilation today, according to Massey, is segmented, and a large percentage of the descendants of contemporary immigrants—especially many of the Hispanic groups and Haitians—face permanent membership in a growing underclass population and continuing marginalization and powerlessness.

A recent study reinforces some of Massey's points. Sociologists Telles and Ortiz (2008) studied a sample of Mexican Americans in 1965 and again in 2000. They found evidence of strong movements toward acculturation and integration on some dimensions (e.g., language) but not on others. Even fourth-generation members of their sample continued to live in "the Barrio," marry within the group; and contrary to evidence presented in Exhibit 10.13 (which is from a different study), do not reach economic equality with Anglos. The authors single out institutional discrimination (e.g., underfunding of schools) as a primary cause for the continuing separation, a point that is consistent with Massey's conclusion regarding the decreasing rates of upward mobility in American society.

The Case Against Segmented Assimilation

Several recent studies have resurrected the somewhat tattered body of traditional assimilation theories. These studies argue that contemporary assimilation will ultimately follow the same course as did European immigrant groups 100 years ago and as described in Gordon's theory (see Chapter 2). For example, two recent studies (Bean & Stevens, 2003, and Alba & Nee, 2003) find that most contemporary immigrant groups are acculturating and integrating at the "normal" three-generation pace. Those groups (notably Mexicans) that appear to be lagging behind this pace may take as many as four to five generations, but their descendants will eventually find their way into the primary job market and the cultural mainstream.

Studies of acculturation show that values Americanize and that English language proficiency grows with time of residence and generation (Bean & Stevens, 2003, p. 168). We discussed some of these patterns in Chapter 8 (see Exhibits 8.8 and 8.9).

In terms of structural integration, contemporary immigrant groups may be narrowing the income gap over time, although many groups (e.g., Dominicans, Mexicans, Haitians, and Vietnamese) are handicapped by very low levels of human capital at the start (Bean & Stevens, 2003, p. 142). Exhibits 10.13a and 10.13b illustrate this process with respect to wage differentials between Mexican and white males and females of various generations and levels of education. In these two exhibits, complete income equality with non-Hispanic whites would be indicated if the bar touched the 100% line at the top of the graphs. Looking first at

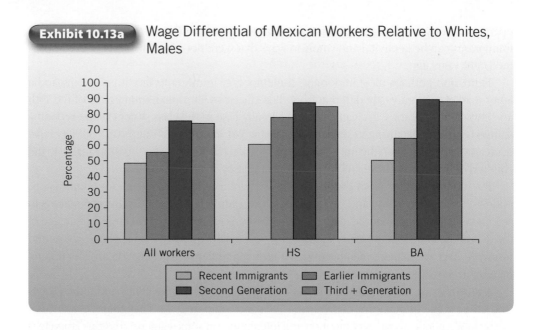

Exhibit 10.13a Wage Differential of Mexican Workers Relative to Whites, Males

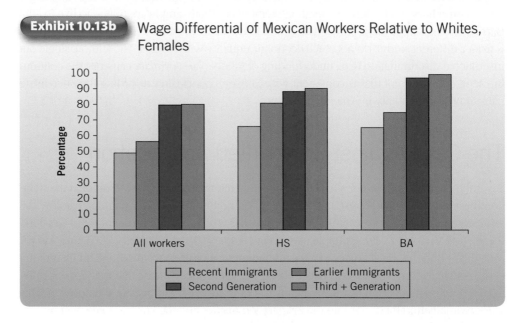

Exhibit 10.13b Wage Differential of Mexican Workers Relative to Whites, Females

SOURCE: Bean, Frank D., & Gillian Stevens (2003). Table 6.8, "Hourly Wage Differentials by Ethnicity and Generation, Ages Twenty-Five to Sixty-Four." In *America's Newcomers and the Dynamics of Diversity.* © 2003 Russell Sage Foundation, 112 East 64th Street, New York, NY 10021. Reprinted with permission.

males, recent Mexican immigrants earn a little less than half of what white males earn. The differential is lower for earlier immigrants, lower still for Mexican males of the second and third generation, and lowest for the most-educated ("BA") members of those generations. (On the other hand, males of the third generation do not rise compared with the second generation, as would be predicted by traditional assimilation theory.) For females, the wage differential also shrinks as the generations pass and level of education increases. Note that for third-generation, college-educated females, the wage differential shrinks virtually to zero, indicating complete integration on this variable.

Note how these patterns generally support the traditional perspective on assimilation. The wage gap shrinks by generation and level of education, and integration is substantial by the third generation (although complete only for one group). This pattern suggests that the movement of Mexican immigrants is toward the economic mainstream, even though they do not close the gap completely. Bean and Stevens (2003) conclude that this pattern is substantially consistent with the "three-generation model": The assimilation trajectory of Mexican Americans and other recent immigrant groups is not into the urban poor, the underclass, or the disenfranchised, disconnected, and marginalized. Assimilation is not segmented, but is substantially repeating the experiences of the European groups on which Gordon based his theory.

How can we reconcile these opposed points of view? In large part, this debate concerns the nature of the evidence and judgments about how much weight to give to various facts and trends. On one hand, Massey's points about the importance of the postindustrial economy, declining opportunities for less-educated workers, and the neglect that seems typical of inner-city schools are very well taken, as is the evidence supplied by Telles and Ortiz. On the other hand, it seems that even the least educated immigrant groups have been able to find economic niches in which they and their families can survive and eke out an existence long enough for their children and grandchildren to rise in the structure, a pattern that has been at the core of the American immigrant experience for almost two centuries.

Of course, this debate will continue, and new evidence and interpretations appear. Ultimately, however, the debate may continue until immigration stops (which, as Massey points out, is extremely unlikely) and the fate of the descendants of the last immigrant groups is measured.

Recent Immigration in Historical Context

The current wave of immigration to the United States is part of a centuries-old process that spans the globe. Underlying this immense and complex population movement is the powerful force of the continuing industrial revolution. The United States and other industrialized nations are the centers of growth in the global economy, and immigrants flow to the areas of greater opportunity. In the 19th century, population moved largely from Europe to the Western Hemisphere. Over the past 50 years, the movement has been from south to north. This pattern reflects the simple geography of industrialization and opportunity and the fact that the more developed nations are in the Northern Hemisphere.

The United States has been the world's dominant economic, political, and cultural power for much of the century and the preferred destination of most immigrants. Newcomers from around the globe continue the collective, social nature of past population movements (see Chapter 2). The direction of their travels reflects contemporary global inequalities: Labor continues to flow from the less developed nations to the more developed nations. The direction of this flow is not accidental or coincidental. It is determined by the differential rates of industrialization and modernization across the globe. Immigration contributes to the wealth and affluence of the more developed societies and particularly to the dominant groups and elite classes of those societies.

New Immigrants and Old Issues

In this chapter, we focused on some of the issues raised by high levels of immigration since the 1960s. As we discuss, debate, and consider these issues, we need to remember a fundamental fact about modern American society: The issues of the "traditional" minority groups—African Americans and American Indians, for example—have not been resolved. As we saw in earlier chapters, these groups have been a part of American society from the beginning, but they remain, in many ways, distant from achieving complete equality and integration.

Many of the current issues facing these groups relate to class as well as race. The urban underclass is disproportionately made up of peoples of color and remains marginal to the mainstream society in terms of access to education and job opportunities, decent housing, and good health care. While it is probably true that American society is more open and tolerant than ever before, we must not mistake a decline in blatant racism or a reduction in overt discrimination for its demise. In fact, as we have seen, there is abundant evidence that shows that racism and discrimination have not declined, but have merely changed form, and that the patterns of exclusion and deprivation they have sustained in the past continue in the present.

Similarly, gender issues and sexism remain on the national agenda. As we have seen at various points throughout the text, blatant sexism and overt discrimination against women are probably at a historic low, but, again, we cannot mistake change for disappearance. Most important, minority women remain the victims of a double jeopardy and are among the most vulnerable and exploited segments of the society. Many female members of the new immigrant groups find themselves in similarly vulnerable positions.

These problems of exclusion and continuing prejudice and sexism are exacerbated by a number of trends in the larger society. For example, the continuing shift in subsistence technology away from manufacturing to the service sector privileges groups that, in the past as well as today, have had access to education. The urban underclass consists disproportionately of groups that have been excluded from education in the past and have less access in the present.

The new immigrant groups have abundant problems of their own, of course, and need to find ways to pursue their self-interests in their new society. Some segments of these groups—the well-educated professionals seeking to advance their careers in the world's most advanced economy—will be much more likely to find ways to avoid the harshest forms of American rejection and exclusion. Similarly, the members of the "traditional" minority groups that have gained access to education and middle-class status will enjoy more opportunities than previous generations could have imagined (although, as we have seen, their middle-class position will be more precarious than it is for their dominant group counterparts).

Will we become a society in which ethnic and racial groups are permanently segmented by class, with the more favored members enjoying a higher, if partial, level of acceptance while other members of their groups languish in permanent exclusion and segmentation? What does it mean to be an American? What should it mean?

Is Immigration Harmful or Helpful to the United States?

The continuing debate over U.S. immigration has generated plenty of controversy but little consensus. Following are two positions in the debate. The first argues against immigration on the grounds that it is harmful to native-born workers, especially those in the low-wage sector. Steven Camarota is director of research at the Center for Immigration Studies, a well-known "think tank" for immigration studies. The rejoinder is from columnist and novelist Anna Quindlen, who argues that immigrants are essential for the continuing health of the nation's economy.

Immigration Is Hurting the U.S. Worker

STEVEN A. CAMAROTA

The United States needs fewer immigrants, not more. . . . The growing number of undereducated people crossing our borders has hurt less-educated native-born workers. The U.S. needs to focus on reducing overall immigration levels. . . .

The number of immigrants—legal and illegal—living in the U.S. is growing at an unprecedented rate. U.S. Census Bureau data indicate that 1.6 million legal and illegal immigrants settle in the country each year. In 2006, the immigrant, or foreign-born population, reached about 38 million in the United States. . . . The U.S. has never confronted an immigrant population that has grown this much, this fast.

Low-paid American workers have borne the heaviest impact of immigration. This is largely because of the educational profile of the bulk of today's immigrants. Nine percent of adult native-born Americans (age 18 to 64) were high school dropouts in 2006, while 34 percent of recent adult immigrants had not completed high school. (The rate was 60 percent for illegal immigrants.)

Common sense, economic theory, and a fair reading of the research on this question indicate that allowing in so many immigrants (legal and illegal) with relatively little education reduces the wages and job prospects for Americans with little education. These are the Americans who are already the poorest workers. Between 2000 and 2005, the number of jobless natives (age 18 to 64) with no education beyond a high school degree increased by over two million, to 23 million, according to the Current Population Survey. During the same period, the number of less-educated immigrants (legal and illegal) holding a job grew 1.5 million.

Of greater concern, the percentage of employed native-born without a high school degree fell from 53 to 48 percent in the last five years. African Americans have particularly been affected. A September 2006 National Bureau of Economic Research paper found that immigration accounted for about a third of the decline in the employment rate of the least-educated African American men over the last few decades.

The disproportionate flow of undereducated immigrants to the U.S. has also depressed wages for native-born workers on the lower rungs of the economic ladder. In the last two-and-a-half decades, average hourly wages for male workers with less than a high school education declined more than 20 percent relative to inflation. For those with only a high school degree they are down almost 10 percent.

Typically, pro-immigration voices argue that immigration is essential because there are not enough Americans to fill all the low wage jobs. But if this were so, then the wages and employment rates of such workers should be rising as employers try desperately to retain and attract workers. Yet quantitative evidence for such a phenomenon doesn't exist. The only evidence of a labor shortage comes from the employers.

In addition to harming the poorest and least educated American workers, our immigration system has created a large burden for taxpayers. The best predictor of poverty and welfare dependence in modern America is education level. Given the low educational levels of most recent immigrants, we would expect them to be a greater drain on public coffers than the immigrants who came before them. Indeed this is the case. In 1997, the National Academy of Sciences (NAS) estimated that immigrant households consumed $20 billion more in public services than they paid in taxes each year. Adjusted for inflation, with the current size of the immigrant population today, this figure would be over $40 billion.

Immigrants from Latin America place an especially heavy burden on American taxpayers. For example, 57 percent of households headed by Dominican immigrants in 2004 used at least one major welfare program; 43 percent of Mexicans took advantage of at least one welfare program; and about a third of the households headed by immigrants from Central America, Cuba and Colombia use the welfare system. In contrast only 18 percent of native households receive welfare assistance.

The biggest problem for taxpayers is not illegal aliens—though they are a drain. The biggest problem is less-educated legal immigrants, who represent the majority of the immigrants from Mexico and Central America. My own research indicates that the net costs (taxes paid minus services used) to the federal government alone would roughly triple if illegal aliens were legalized and began to use services and pay taxes like legal immigrants with the same level of education. . . .

SOURCE: Camarota, Steven (2007). *Immigration Is Hurting the U.S. Worker.* Center for Immigration Studies. Retrieved March 15, 2008, from http://www.cis.org/articles/2007/sacoped071107.html.

Immigration Is Essential

ANNA QUINDLEN

Some people talk about immigration in terms of politics, some in terms of history. But the crux of the matter is numbers. The Labor Department says that immigrants make up about 15 percent of the work force. It's estimated that a third of those are undocumented workers, or what those who want to send them back to where they came from call "illegals."

The Pew Hispanic Center estimates that one in four farmhands in the United States is an undocumented immigrant, and that they make up a significant portion of the people who build our houses, clean our office buildings and prepare our food.

All the thundering about policing the border and rounding up those who have slipped over it ignores an inconvenient fact: America has become a nation dependent on the presence of newcomers, both those with green cards and those without. Mayor Michael Bloomberg of New York testified before a Senate committee that they are a linchpin of his city's economy. The current and former chairmen of the Federal Reserve have favored legal accommodations for undocumented workers because of their salutary effect on economic growth—and the downturn that could follow their departure. Business leaders say agriculture, construction, meatpacking and other industries would collapse without them.

Last year the town of Hazleton, Pa., became known for the most draconian immigration laws in the country, laws making English the official city language, levying harsh fines against landlords who rent to undocumented immigrants and revoking the business permit of anyone who employs them. There was a lot of public talk about crime and gangs and very little about hard work in local factories and new businesses along the formerly moribund Wyoming Street. In that atmosphere, those with apartments to let and jobs to fill could be excused if they avoided any supplicant with an accent. Oh, the mayor and his supporters insisted that the laws were meant only to deal with those here illegally, but the net effect was to make all Latinos feel unwelcome.

When the law was struck down by a federal judge, there was rejoicing among Hazleton's immigrants, but some said an exodus had already begun.

Longtime residents seemed to think that was just fine.

This is a shortsighted approach. Economists say immigrants buying starter homes will keep the bottom from falling out of the housing market in the years ahead. Latinos are opening new businesses at a rate three times faster than the national. If undocumented immigrants were driven out of the work force, there would be a domino effect: prices of things ranging from peaches to plastering would rise. Nursing homes would be understaffed. Hotel rooms wouldn't get cleaned.

Sure, it would be great if everyone were here legally, if the immigration service weren't such a disaster that getting a green card is a life's work. It would be great if other nations had economies robust enough to support their citizens so leaving home wasn't the only answer. But at a certain point public policy means dealing not only with how things ought to be but with how they are. Here's how they are: these people work the jobs we don't want, sometimes two and three jobs at a time. They do it on the cheap, which is tough, so that their children won't have to, which is good. They use services like hospitals and schools, which is a drain on public coffers, and they pay taxes, which contribute to them.

In towns like Hazleton, whose aging populations were on the wane before the immigrants arrived, those who remain will find themselves surrounded by empty storefronts, deserted restaurants and houses that will not sell. It's the civic equivalent of starving to death because you don't care for the food. But at least everyone involved can tell themselves their town wasted away while they were speaking English.

SOURCE: Quindlen, Anna (2007). "Newcomers by Numbers." *Newsweek:* August 20, p. 90.

Debate Questions to Consider

1.   Consider the nature of the arguments presented by Camarota and Quindlen. To what extent do they appeal to emotion? To what extent do they base their arguments in evidence and logic? What specific disagreements over "facts" can you identify? What information would you need to resolve these disagreements?

2.   Use the evidence presented in this chapter and in Chapters 8 and 9 to further evaluate these arguments. How persuasive is Camarota's argument that immigrants have a negative impact on low-wage American workers? How about Quindlen's point that immigrants make essential contributions?

3.   The arguments in this Current Debate are mostly economic. What new dimensions should be added (cultural, linguistic, and so forth) to the debate? What arguments were raised in previous chapters that should be considered here?

4.   What are the implications of this debate for the "traditional" minority groups? What gender and class dimensions can you identify in this debate?

Main Points

- Since the mid-1960s, immigrants have been coming to the United States at nearly record rates. Most of these immigrant groups have coethnics who have been in the United States for years, but others are "new Americans." How will this new wave of immigration transform America? Will they assimilate? How?

- Non-Hispanic immigrants from the Caribbean include Haitians and Jamaicans. Some are driven by economic needs; others are political refugees. All face the issues of racism and institutionalized discrimination.

- Arab Americans, like other new Americans, have been growing rapidly in number, and their local communities tend to be centered in economic enclaves. The events of 9/11 make this group a special target for hate crimes and for security concerns.

- Immigrants from Africa remain a relatively small group, and many bring high levels of education and occupational skills, although others are concentrated in the lower levels of the occupational structure.

- Contemporary immigrants are generally experiencing three different modes of incorporation into U.S. society: the primary labor market, the secondary labor market, and the enclave. The pathway of each group is strongly influenced by the amount of human capital they bring, their race, the attitude of the larger society, and many other factors.

- Relations between immigrants and the larger society are animated by a number of issues, including the relative costs and benefits of immigration, concerns about undocumented immigrants, and the speed of assimilation. One important issue currently being debated by social scientists is whether assimilation for new Americans will be segmented or will ultimately follow the pathway established by immigrant groups from Europe in the 19th and 20th centuries.

- The public sociology assignments presented in the introduction to Part 4 are very likely to bring you face-to-face with new Americans and the increasing diversity of the United States. It is also likely that you will encounter a variety of issues and problems that have been discussed in this and previous chapters, including illegal immigration, costs and benefits of immigration, and bilingual education.

Study Site on the Web

Don't forget the interactive quizzes and other resources and learning aids at www.pineforge.com/healeystudy5.

For Further Reading

Portes, Alejandro, & Rumbaut, Rubén. (2001). *Ethnicities: Children of Immigrants in America*. New York: Russell Sage Foundation.

Portes, Alejandro, & Rumbaut, Rubén. (2001). *Legacies: The Story of the Immigrant Second Generation*. New York: Russell Sage Foundation.

Two landmark studies of new American groups whose findings are generally consistent with the segmented assimilation hypothesis.

Alba, Richard, & Nee, Victor. (2003). *Remaking the American Mainstream: Assimilation and Contemporary Immigration*. Cambridge, MA: Harvard University Press.

Bean, Frank, & Stevens, Gillian. (2003). *America's Newcomers and the Dynamics of Diversity*. New York: Russell Sage Foundation.

Two landmark studies of contemporary immigrants that find that assimilation is generally following a course consistent with the "traditional" model of assimilation.

Questions for Review and Study

1. What differences exist between these new Americans in terms of their motivations for coming to the United States? What are the implications of these various "push" factors for their reception and adjustment to the United States?

2. Compare Arab and Middle Eastern immigrant groups with those from the Caribbean. Which group is more diverse? What differences exist in their patterns of adjustment and assimilation? Why do these patterns exist?

3. Compare and contrast African immigrants with the other groups. How do they differ? What are the implications of these differences for their adjustment to the larger society?

4. What, in your opinion, are the most important issues facing the United States in terms of immigration and assimilation? How are these issues playing out in your community? What are the implications of these issues for the future of the United States?

5. Will assimilation for contemporary immigrants be segmented? After examining the evidence and arguments presented by both sides and using information from this and previous chapters, which side of the debate seems more credible? Why? What are the implications of this debate? What will the United States look like in the future if assimilation is segmented? How would the future change if assimilation is not segmented? Which of these scenarios is more desirable for immigrant groups? For the society as a whole? For various segments of U.S. society (e.g., employers, labor unions, African Americans, consumers, the college educated, the urban underclass, etc.)?

Internet Research Project

A. Update and Expand This Chapter by an Internet Search

Many of the groups covered in this chapter have Web sites dedicated to them (e.g., Arab Americans are the subject of http://www.allied-media.com/ArabAmerican/default.htm). Select several of the groups covered in this chapter and conduct a search for relevant Web sites. See what you can learn about the concerns and situations of each group, and compare the information to what has been presented in this text. What information can you collect about their socioeconomic profiles? What can you learn about their points of view regarding the United States and their treatment by the larger society? What issues are most important for them (e.g., learning English, job discrimination, hate crimes, availability of welfare services, etc.)?

B. Update and Expand This Chapter With Data From the U.S. Census

The U.S. Bureau of the Census collects an array of information about most of the groups covered in this chapter, and the information is available online. Go to http://www.census .gov and click on "American Factfinder" on the left-hand panel of the home page. Next, click on "Data Sets" on the left-hand panel and select "American Community Survey," and, in the next window, select "Selected Population Profiles." On the next window, click "Add" to move the United States to the bottom window and click "Next." Choose the "Ancestry Groups" tab and find a group covered in this text or some other group in which you are interested. Click "Show Result" and a statistical profile of the group and the U.S. population will be displayed. Extend the analysis in this chapter by selecting several variables and comparing the profile of your group with the total population.

Minority Groups and U.S. Society

CHAPTER 11

Themes, Patterns, and the Future

Over the past 10 chapters, we have analyzed ideas and theories about dominant-minority relations, examined the historical and contemporary situations of minority groups in U.S. society, and surveyed a variety of dominant-minority situations around the globe. Now it is time to reexamine our major themes and concepts and determine what conclusions can be derived from our analysis.

Six Americans Revisited

Let's begin with an exercise. Turn back to Chapter 1 and reread the biographies of the six Americans at the beginning of the chapter. After reading this text, you should now see these people through different eyes.

You should recognize that Kim Park lives in an enclave economy and that Shirley Umphlett's life was profoundly affected by the migration of African Americans from the rural South to the urban North. Mary Ann O'Brien's family history exemplifies the slow rise to middle-class status characteristic of so many European American immigrants, whereas George Snyder seems trapped by the urban poverty and underclass marginality confronting so many racial minority groups today. Hector Gonzalez has a strong attachment to the culture of his Mexican ancestors even though he has been thoroughly integrated into the U.S. job market. In contrast, William Buford occupies an elite social and economic position but has no interest in his or anyone else's ethnic origin. He often argues that anyone, regardless of social class or race, could duplicate his success with sufficient diligence and hard work, conveniently forgetting that his wealth was inherited.

You might think that Buford's conclusions are not particularly insightful or informed. However, his superficial analysis is shared by millions of other Americans. Americans traditionally see success or failure as a matter of individual choice and personal effort. Blaming the victims of racism for their situations can be comforting because it absolves the more fortunate of guilt or complicity in the perpetuation of minority group poverty and powerlessness. More accurate analyses and more compelling conclusions might be found in the thinking of people (like George Snyder) who are the victims of the system. Unlike the beneficiaries of the status quo, minority group members are sensitized to the dynamics of racism and discrimination by their efforts to avoid victimization. We should remember, however, that our understandings are always limited by who we are, where we come from, and what we have experienced. Our ability to imagine the realities faced by others is never perfect, and what we can see of the world depends very much on where we stand.

If we are to understand the forces that have created racial and ethnic minority groups in the United States and around the globe, we must find ways to surpass the limitations of our personal experiences and honestly confront the often ugly realities of the past and present. I believe that the information and the ideas developed in this text can help liberate our sociological imaginations from the narrow confines of our own experiences and perspectives.

In this final chapter, I restate the general themes of this text and draw conclusions from the material we have covered. I also raise speculative questions about the future. As we look backward to the past and forward to the future, it seems appropriate to paraphrase the words of the historian Oscar Handlin (1951): "Once I thought to write a history of the minority groups in America. Then, I discovered that the minority groups were American history" (p. 3).

The Importance of Subsistence Technology

Perhaps the most important sociological idea we have developed is that dominant-minority relations are shaped by large social, political, and economic forces and change as these broad characteristics change. To understand the evolution of America's minority groups is to understand the history of the United States, from the earliest colonial settlement to the modern megalopolis. As we have seen throughout the text, these same broad forces have left their imprint on many societies around the globe.

Subsistence technology is the most basic force shaping a society and the relationships between dominant and minority groups in that society. In the colonial United States, minority relations were bent to the demands of a land-hungry, labor-intensive agrarian technology, and the early relationships between Africans, Europeans, and American Indians flowed from the colonists' desire to control both land and labor. By the mid-1800s, two centuries after Jamestown was founded, the same dynamics that had enslaved African Americans and nearly annihilated American Indians made a minority group out of Mexican Americans.

The agrarian era came to an end in the 19th century as the new technologies of the Industrial Revolution increased the productivity of the economy and eventually changed every aspect of life in the United States. The paternalistic, oppressive systems used to control the labor of minority groups in the agrarian system were abolished and replaced by competitive systems of group relations. These newer systems evolved from more rigid forms to more fluid forms as industrialization and urbanization progressed.

As the United States grew and developed, new minority groups were created, and old minority groups were transformed. Rapid industrialization combined with the opportunities available on the frontier made the United States an attractive destination for immigrants from Europe, Asia, Latin America, and other parts of the world. Immigrants helped to farm the Great Plains, mine the riches of the West, and above all, supply the armies of labor required by industrialization.

The descendants of the immigrants from Europe benefited from the continuing industrialization of the economy, rising in the social class structure as the economy grew and matured. Immigrants from Asia and Latin America were not so fortunate. Chinese Americans and Japanese Americans survived in ethnic enclaves on the fringes of the mainstream society, and Mexican Americans and Puerto Ricans supplied low-paid manual labor for both the rural and the urban economy. Both Asian Americans and Hispanic Americans were barred from access to dominant group institutions and higher-paid jobs.

The racial minority groups, particularly African Americans, Mexican Americans, and Puerto Ricans, began to enter the urban working class after European American ethnic groups had started to move up in the occupational structure, at a time when the supply of manual, unskilled jobs was starting to dwindle. Thus, the processes that allowed upward mobility for European Americans failed to work for the racial minority groups, who confronted urban poverty and bankrupt cities in addition to the continuing barriers of racial prejudice and institutional discrimination.

We can only speculate about what the future holds, but the emerging information-based, high-tech society is unlikely to offer many opportunities to people with lower levels of education and few occupational skills. It seems fairly certain that members of the racial and colonized minority groups and some recent immigrant groups will be participating in the mainstream economy of the future at lower levels than the dominant group, the descendants of the European immigrants, and the more advantaged recent immigrant groups. Upgraded urban educational systems, job training programs, and other community development programs might alter the grim scenario of continuing exclusion. As we discussed at the end of Chapter 3, current public opinion about matters of race and discrimination makes it unlikely that such programs will be created.

Photo 11.1 to 11.3

In a postindustrial society, education is a key pathway for upward mobility and an important venue in which members of different groups can encounter each other. In dormitories, classrooms, and cafeterias and across campus, the opportunities for meaningful, equal-status contact can enhance the education of all.

© Ed Kashi/Corbis.

© moodboard/Corbis.

© A. Inden/zefa/Corbis.

Inaction and perpetuation of the status quo will bar a large percentage of the population from the emerging mainstream economy. Those segments of the African American, Hispanic American, and Asian American communities currently mired in the urban underclass will continue to compete with some of the newer immigrants for jobs in the low-wage, secondary labor market or in alternative opportunity structures, including crime.

The Importance of the Contact Situation, Group Competition, and Power

We have stressed the importance of the contact situation—the conditions under which the minority group and dominant group first come into contact with each other—throughout this text. Blauner's distinction between immigrant and colonized minority groups is fundamental, a distinction so basic that it helps to clarify minority group situations centuries after the initial contact period. In Part 3, we used Blauner's distinction as an organizing principle and covered American minority groups in approximate order from "most colonized" to "most immigrant." The groups covered first (African Americans and American Indians) are clearly at a greater disadvantage in contemporary society than the groups covered last (especially immigrants from Asia with high levels of human capital) and the white ethnic groups covered in Chapter 2. For example, prejudice, racism, and discrimination against African Americans remain formidable forces in contemporary America even though they may have softened into more subtle forms. In contrast, prejudice and discrimination against European American groups such as the Irish, Italians, and Polish Americans have nearly disappeared today even though they were quite formidable just a few generations ago. In the same way, contemporary immigrant groups that are nonwhite and bring few resources and low levels of human capital (e.g., Haitians) may experience segmented assimilation and find themselves in situations resembling those of colonized minority groups. Contemporary immigrant groups that are at the opposite end of the continuum (e.g., Asian Indians) are more likely to approximate the experiences of white ethnics and find themselves in some version of middle-class suburbia. See the Appendix for further information on the relative standings of colonized and immigrant groups.

Noel's hypothesis states that if three conditions are present in the contact situation—ethnocentrism, competition, and the differential in power—ethnic or racial stratification will result. The relevance of ethnocentrism is largely limited to the actual contact situation, but the other two concepts help to clarify the changes occurring after initial contact.

We have examined numerous instances in which group competition—or even the threat of competition—increased prejudice and led to greater discrimination and more repression. Recall, for example, the opposition of the labor movement (dominated by European American ethnic groups) to Chinese immigrants. The anti-Chinese campaign led to the Chinese Exclusion Act of 1882, the first significant restriction on immigration to the United States. There are parallels between campaigns for exclusion in the past and current ideas about ending or curtailing immigration. Clearly, some part of the current opposition to immigration is motivated by a sense of threat and the fear that immigrants are a danger not only to jobs and to the economy but also to the cultural integrity of U.S. society.

Noel's third variable, the differential in power, determines the outcome of the initial contact situation and which group becomes dominant and which becomes minority. Following the initial contact, the superior power of the dominant group helps it sustain the inferior position of the minority group. Minority groups by definition have fewer power resources, but they characteristically use what they have in an attempt to improve their situations. The improvements in the situations of American minority groups since the middle of the 20th century have been due in large part to the fact that they (especially African Americans, who typically led the way in protest and demands for change) finally acquired some power resources of their own. For example, one important source of power for the civil rights movement in the South during the 1950s and 1960s was the growth of African American voting strength in the North. After World War II, the African American electorate became too sizable to ignore, and its political power helped pressure the federal government to take action and pass the legislation that ended the Jim Crow era.

Minority status being what it is, however, each of the groups we have discussed (with the exception of the white ethnic groups) still controls relatively few power resources and is limited in its ability to pursue its own self-interests. Many of these limitations are economic and related to social class; many minority groups simply lack the monetary resources to finance campaigns for reform or to exert significant pressure on political institutions. Other limitations include small group size (e.g., Asian American groups), language barriers (e.g., many Hispanic groups), and divided loyalties within the group (e.g., American Indians separated by tribal allegiances).

At any rate, the relative powerlessness of minority groups today is a legacy of the contact situations that created the groups in the first place. In general, colonized groups are at a greater power disadvantage than immigrant groups. Contact situations set agendas for group relations that have impacts centuries after the initial meeting.

Given all that we have examined in this text, it is obvious that competition and differences in power resources will continue to shape intergroup relations (including relations between minority groups themselves) well into the future. Because they are so basic and consequential, jobs will continue to be primary objects of competition, but there will be plenty of other issues to divide the nation. Included on this divisive list will be debates about crime and the criminal justice system, welfare reform, national health care policy, school busing, bilingual education, immigration policy, and multicultural curricula in schools.

These and other public issues will continue to separate us along ethnic and racial lines because those lines have become so deeply embedded in the economy, in politics, in our schools and neighborhoods, and in virtually every nook and cranny of U.S. society. These deep divisions reflect fundamental realities about who gets what in the United States, and they will continue to reflect the distribution of power and stimulate competition along group lines for generations to come.

Diversity Within Minority Groups

All too often, and this text is probably no exception, minority groups are seen as unitary and undifferentiated. Although overgeneralizations are sometimes difficult to avoid, I want to stress again the diversity within each of the groups we have examined. Minority group members vary from each other by age, sex, region of residence, levels of education, urban versus rural residence, political ideology, and many other variables. The experience of one segment of the group (college-educated, fourth-generation, native-born Chinese American females) may bear little resemblance to the experience of another (illegal Chinese male immigrants with less than a high school education), and the problems of some members may not be the problems of others.

I have tried to highlight the importance of this diversity by exploring gender differentiation within each minority group. Study of minority groups by U.S. social scientists has focused predominantly on males, and the experiences of minority women have been described in much less depth. All the cultures examined in this text have strong patriarchal traditions. Women of the dominant group as well as minority women have had much less access to leadership roles and higher-status positions and have generally occupied a subordinate status, even in their own groups. The experiences of minority group women and the extent of their differences from minority group males and dominant group women are only now being fully explored.

One clear conclusion we can make about gender is that minority group females are doubly oppressed and disempowered. Limited by both their minority and their gender roles, they are among the most vulnerable and exploited segments of the society. At one time or another, the women of every minority group have taken the least desirable, lowest-status positions available in the economy, often while trying to raise children and attend to other family needs. They have been expected to provide support for other members of their families, kinship groups, and communities, often sacrificing their own self-interests to the welfare of others. Jade Snow Wong (1993), a Chinese American daughter of immigrant parents, describes the subordinate role and circumscribed world of minority group females in a remembrance of her mother:

> My mother dutifully followed my father's leadership. She was extremely thrifty, but the thrifty need pennies to manage, and the old world had denied her those. Upon arrival in the new world of San Francisco, she accepted the elements her mate had selected to shape her new life: domestic duties, seamstress work in the factory-home, mothering each child in turn, church once a week, and occasional movies. (p. 50)

In their roles outside the family, minority women have encountered discrimination based on their minority group membership, compounded with discrimination based on their gender. The result is, predictably, an economic and social status at the bottom

Photo 11.4

Jade Snow Wong (1922–2005) was an artist and writer. She was born to a poor, very traditional immigrant family and wrote two autobiographical volumes about her experiences.

AP Photo/Ernest K. Bennett

of the social structure. For example, average incomes of African American females today are lower than those of white males, white females, and black males (see Exhibit 6.3). The same pattern holds for other groups, and the women of many minority groups are highly concentrated in the low-paid secondary labor market and employed in jobs that provide services to members of more privileged groups.

The inequality confronted by minority women extends beyond matters of economics and jobs: Women of color have higher rates of infant mortality and births out of wedlock and a host of other health-related, quality-of-life problems. In short, there is ample evidence to document a pervasive pattern of gender inequality within America's minority groups. Much of this gender inequality is complexly interconnected with rising rates of poverty and female-headed households, teenage pregnancy, and unemployment for minority males in the inner city.

Gender differentiation cuts through minority groups in a variety of ways. Specific issues might unite minority women with women of the dominant group (e.g., sexual harassment in schools and the workplace), and others might unite them with the men of their minority groups (e.g., the enforcement of civil rights legislation). The problems and issues of minority women are complexly tied to the patterns of inequality and discrimination in the larger society and within their own groups. Solving the problems faced by minority groups will not resolve the problems faced by minority women and neither will resolving the problems of gender inequality alone. Women of color are embedded in structures of inequality and discrimination that limit them in two independent but simultaneous ways. Articulating and addressing these difficulties requires recognition of the complex interactions between gender and minority group status.

Assimilation and Pluralism

It seems fair to conclude that the diversity and complexity of minority group experiences in the United States are not well characterized by some of the traditional, or "melting pot," views of assimilation. For example, the idea that assimilation is a linear, inevitable process has little support. Immigrants from Europe probably fit that model better than other groups, but as the ethnic revival of the 1960s demonstrated, assimilation and ethnic identity can take surprising turns.

Also without support is the notion that there is always a simple, ordered relationship between the various stages of assimilation: acculturation, integration into public institutions, integration into the private sector, and so forth. We have seen that some groups integrated before they acculturated, others have become *more* committed to their ethnic or racial identity over the generations, and still others have been acculturated for generations but are no closer to full integration. New expressions of ethnicity come and go, and minority groups emerge, combine, and recombine in unexpected and seemingly unpredictable ways. The 1960s saw a reassertion of ethnicity and loyalty to old identities among some groups, even as other groups developed new coalitions and invented new ethnic identities (for example, pantribalism among American Indians). No simple or linear view of assimilation can begin to make sense of the array of minority group experiences.

Indeed, the very desirability of assimilation has been subject to debate. Since the 1960s, many minority spokespersons have questioned the wisdom of becoming a part of a socio-cultural structure that was constructed by the systematic exploitation of minority groups. Pluralistic themes increased in prominence as the commitment of the larger society to racial equality faltered. Virtually every minority group proclaimed the authenticity of its own experiences, its own culture, and its own version of history, separate from but as valid as that of the dominant groups. From what might have seemed like a nation on the verge of integration in the 1950s, America evolved into what might have seemed like a Tower of Babel in the 1960s. The consensus that assimilation was the best solution and the most sensible goal for all of America's minority groups was shattered (if it ever really existed at all).

Let's review the state of acculturation and integration in the United States on a group-by-group basis, following the order of the case studies in Part 3. African Americans are highly acculturated. Despite the many unique cultural traits forged in America and those that survive from Africa, black Americans share language, values and beliefs, and most other aspects of culture with white Americans of similar class and educational background. In terms of integration, in contrast, African Americans present a mixed picture. For middle-class, more-educated members of the group, American society offers more opportunities for upward mobility and success than ever before. Without denying the prejudice, discrimination, and racism that remain, this segment of the group is in a favorable position to achieve higher levels of affluence and power for their children and grandchildren. At the same time, a large percentage of African Americans remain mired in urban poverty, and for them, affluence, security, and power are just as distant (perhaps more so) than they were a generation ago. Considering the group as a whole, African Americans are still highly segregated in their residential and school attendance patterns, and their political power, although rising, is not proportional to their size. Unemployment, lower average incomes, and poverty in general remain serious problems and may be more serious than they were a generation ago.

American Indians are less acculturated than African Americans, and there is evidence that American Indian culture and language may be increasing in strength and vitality. On measures of integration, there is some indication of improvement, but many American Indians are among the most isolated and impoverished minority groups in the United States. One possible bright spot for some reservations lies in the further development of the gambling industry and the investment of profits in the tribal infrastructure to upgrade schools, health clinics, job training centers, and so forth.

Members of the largest Hispanic American groups are also generally less acculturated than African Americans. Hispanic traditions and the Spanish language have been sustained by the exclusion and isolation of these groups within the United States and have been continually renewed and revitalized by immigration. Cubans have moved closer to equality than Mexican Americans and Puerto Ricans but did so by resisting assimilation and building an ethnic enclave economy. Mexican Americans and Puerto Ricans share many of the problems of urban poverty that confront African Americans, and they are below national norms on measures of equality and integration.

The smaller Hispanic groups consist mostly of new immigrants who are just beginning the assimilation process. Many members of these groups, along with Mexican Americans and Puerto Ricans, are less educated and have few occupational skills, and they face the dangers of blending into a permanent urban underclass. Nonetheless, there is some evidence that these groups (or, more accurately, their descendants) may eventually find their way into the American mainstream (recall the debate over segmented assimilation in Chapter 10).

As with Hispanic Americans, the extent of assimilation among Asian Americans is highly variable. Some groups (for example, third- and fourth-generation Japanese Americans and Chinese Americans) have virtually completed the assimilation process and are remarkably successful; others (the more elite immigrants from India and the Philippines) seem to be finding a place in the American mainstream. Other Asian American groups consist largely of newer immigrants with occupational and educational profiles that resemble colonized minority groups, and these groups face the same dangers of permanent marginalization and exclusion. Still other Asian American groups (e.g., Korean Americans) have used their cohesiveness and solidarity to construct ethnic enclaves in which they have achieved relative economic equality by resisting acculturation.

Only European American ethnic groups, covered in Chapter 2, seem to approximate the traditional model of assimilation. The development even of these groups, however, has taken unexpected twists and turns, and the pluralism of the 1960s and 1970s suggests that ethnic traditions and ethnic identity, in some form, may withstand the pressures of assimilation for generations to come. Culturally and racially, these groups are the closest to the dominant group. If they still retain a sense of ethnicity, even if merely symbolic, after generations of

Ronald Takaki (b. 1939) is Professor Emeritus of Ethnic Studies at the University of California, Berkeley. He is the grandson of Japanese immigrants and is an award-winning author, researcher, and educator.

© Ronald Takaki.

acculturation and integration, what is the likelihood that the sense of group membership will fade in the racially stigmatized minority groups?

Assimilation is far from accomplished. The group divisions that remain are real and consequential; they cannot be willed away by pretending we are all "just American." Group membership continues to be important because it continues to be linked to fundamental patterns of exclusion and inequality. The realities of pluralism, inequality, and ethnic and racial identity continue to persist to the extent that the American promise of a truly open opportunity structure continues to fail. The group divisions forged in the past and perpetuated over the decades by racism and discrimination will remain to the extent that racial and ethnic group membership continues to be correlated with inequality and position in the social class structure.

Along with economic and political pressures, other forces help to sustain the pluralistic group divisions. Some argue that ethnicity is rooted in biology and can never be fully eradicated (see van den Berghe, 1981). Although this may be an extreme position, there is little doubt that many people find their own ancestries to be a matter of great interest. Some (perhaps most) of the impetus behind the preservation of ethnic and racial identity may be a result of the most vicious and destructive intergroup competition. In other ways, though, ethnicity can be a positive force that helps people locate themselves in time and space and understand their position in the contemporary world. Ethnicity remains an important aspect of self-identity and pride for many Americans from every group and tradition. It seems unlikely that this sense of a personal link to particular groups and heritages within U.S. society will soon fade.

Can we survive as a pluralistic, culturally and linguistically fragmented, racially and ethnically unequal society? What will save us from balkanization and fractionalization? Given our history of colonization and racism, can U.S. society move closer to the relatively harmonious models of race relations found in societies such as Hawaii? As we deal with these questions, we need to remember that in and of itself, diversity is no more "bad" than unity is "good." Our society has grown to a position of global preeminence despite, or perhaps because of, our diversity. In fact, many have argued that our diversity is a fundamental and essential characteristic of U.S. society and a great strength to be cherished and encouraged. Sociologist Ronald Takaki (1993) ended his history of multicultural America, *A Different Mirror,* with an eloquent endorsement of our diversity and pluralism:

> As Americans, we originally came from many different shores and our diversity has been at the center of the making of America. While our stories contain the memories of different communities, together they inscribe a larger narrative. Filled with what Walt Whitman celebrated as the "varied carols" of America, our history generously gives all of us our "mystic chords of memory."
>
> Throughout our past of oppressions and struggles for equality, Americans of different races and ethnicities have been "singing with open mouths their strong melodious songs" in the textile mills of Lowell, the cotton fields of Mississippi, on the Indian reservations of South Dakota, the railroad tracks high in the Sierras of California, in the garment factories of the Lower East Side, the canefields of Hawaii, and a thousand other places across the country. Our denied history "bursts with telling." As we hear America singing, we find ourselves invited to bring our cultural diversity [into the open], to accept ourselves. (p. 428)

The question for our future might not be so much "Unity or diversity?" as "What blend of pluralistic and assimilationist policies will serve us best in the 21st century?" Are there ways in which the society can prosper without repressing our diversity? How can we increase the degree of openness, fairness, and justice without threatening group loyalties? The one-way, Anglo-conformity mode of assimilation of the past is too narrow and destructive to be a blueprint for the future, but the more extreme forms of minority group pluralism and separatism might be equally dangerous.

How much unity do we need? How much diversity can we tolerate? These are questions you must answer for yourself, and they are questions you will face in a thousand different ways over the course of your life. Let me illustrate by citing some pertinent issues:

- Is it desirable to separate college dormitories by racial or ethnic group? Is this destructive self-segregation or a positive strategy for group empowerment? Will such practices increase prejudice (remember the contact hypothesis from Chapter 3), or will they work like ethnic enclaves and strengthen minority group cohesion and solidarity and permit the groups to deal with the larger society from a stronger position? For the campus as a whole, what good could come from residential separation? In what ways would minority students benefit? Is there a "correct" balance between separation and unity in this situation? Who gets to define what the balance is?

- How much attention should be devoted to minority group experiences in elementary and high school texts and curricula? Who should write and control these curricula? What should they say? How candid and critical should they be about America's often dismal past? How should such topics as slavery, genocide, and the racist exclusion of certain immigrant groups be presented in elementary school texts? In high school texts? Will educating children about the experiences of U.S. minority groups be an effective antidote to prejudice? Is it proper to use classrooms to build respect for the traditions of other groups and an appreciation of their experiences? If the realities of the experiences of minority groups are not addressed in school, what message will children hear? In the absence of minority group voices, what's left?

• What are the limits of free speech with respect to minority relations? When does an ethnic joke become offensive? When are racial and ethnic epithets protected by the First Amendment? As long as lines of ethnicity and race divide the nation and as long as people feel passionately about these lines, the language of dominant-minority relationships will continue to have harsh, crude, and intentionally insulting components. Under what conditions, if any, should a civil society tolerate disparagement of other groups? Should the racial and ethnic epithets uttered by minority group members be treated any differently than those uttered by dominant group members?

• What should the national policy on immigration be? How many immigrants should be admitted each year? How should immigrants be screened? What qualifications should be demanded? Should immigration policy continue to favor the family and close relatives of citizens and permanent residents? What should be done about illegal immigrants? Should they be given an opportunity to legalize their status? Should illegal immigrants or their children receive health care and schooling? If so, who should pay for these services?

I do not pretend that the ideas presented in this text can fully resolve these issues or others that will arise in the future. As long as immigrants and minority groups are a part of the United States, as long as prejudice and discrimination persist, the debates will continue and new issues will arise as old ones are resolved.

As U.S. society attempts to deal with new immigrants and unresolved minority grievances, we should recognize that it is not diversity per se that threatens stability, but the realities of split labor markets, racial and ethnic stratification, urban poverty, and institutionalized discrimination. We need to focus on the issues that confront us with an honest recognition of the past and the economic, political, and social forces that have shaped us. As the United States continues to remake itself, an informed sense of where we have been will help us decide where we should go. Clearly, the simplistic, one-way, Anglo-conformity model of assimilation of the past does not provide a basis for dealing with these problems realistically and should not be the blueprint for the future of U.S. society.

Minority Group Progress and the Ideology of American Individualism

There is so much sadness, misery, and unfairness in the history of minority groups that evidence of progress sometimes goes unnoticed. Lest we be guilty of ignoring the good news in favor of the bad, let us note some ways in which the situations of American minority groups are better today than they were in the past. Evidence of progress is easy to find for some groups; we need look only to the relative economic, educational, and income equality of European American ethnic groups and some Asian American groups. The United States has become more tolerant and open, and minority group members can be found at the highest levels of success, affluence, and prestige.

One of the most obvious changes is the decline of traditional racism and prejudice. As we discussed in Chapter 3, the strong racial and ethnic sentiments and stereotypes of the past are no longer the primary vocabulary for discussing race relations among dominant group members, at least not in public. Although the prejudices unquestionably still exist, Americans have become more circumspect and discreet in their public utterances.

The demise of blatant bigotry in polite company is, without doubt, a positive change. However, it seems that negative intergroup feelings and stereotypes have not so much disappeared as changed form. The old racist feelings are now being expressed in other guises, specifically in what has been called "modern" or "symbolic" racism: the view that holds that once Jim-Crow-type segregation ended in the 1960s, the opportunity channels and routes of upward mobility of American society were opened to all. This individualistic view of social mobility is consistent with the human capital perspective and the traditional, melting-pot view of assimilation. Taken together, these ideologies present a powerful and widely shared perspective on the nature of minority group problems in modern American society. Proponents of these views tend to be unsympathetic to the plight of minorities and to programs such as school busing and affirmative action, which are intended to ameliorate these problems. The overt bigotry of the past has been replaced by blandness and an indifference more difficult to define and harder to measure than "old-fashioned" racism, yet still unsympathetic to racial change.

This text has argued that the most serious problems facing contemporary minority groups, however, are structural and institutional, not individual or personal. For example, the paucity of jobs and high rates of unemployment in the inner cities are the result of economic and political forces beyond the control not only of the minority communities but also of local and state governments. The marginalization of the minority group labor force is a reflection of the essence of modern American capitalism. The mainstream, higher-paying, blue-collar jobs available to people with modest educational credentials are controlled by national and multinational corporations, which maximize profits by automating their production processes and moving the jobs that remain to areas, often outside the United States, with abundant supplies of cheaper labor.

We have also seen that some of the more effective strategies for pursuing equality require strong in-group cohesion and networks of cooperation, not heroic individual effort. Immigration to this country is (and always has been) a group process that involves extensive, long-lasting networks of communication and chains of population movement, usually built around family ties and larger kinship groups. Group networks continue to operate in America and assist individual immigrants with early adjustments and later opportunities for jobs and upward mobility. A variation on this theme is the ethnic enclave found among so many different groups.

Survival and success in America for all minority groups has had more to do with group processes than with individual will or motivation. The concerted, coordinated actions of the minority community provided support during hard times and, when possible, provided the means to climb higher in the social structure during good times. Far from being a hymn to individualism, the story of U.S. minority groups is profoundly sociological.

A Final Word

U.S. society and its minority groups are linked in fractious unity. They are part of the same structures but are separated by lines of color and culture and by long histories (and clear memories) of exploitation and unfairness. This society owes its prosperity and position of prominence in the world no less to the labor of minority groups than to that of the dominant group. By harnessing the labor and energy of these minority groups, the nation has grown prosperous and powerful, but the benefits have flowed disproportionately to the dominant group.

Since the middle of the 20th century, minority groups have demanded greater openness, fairness, equality, respect for their traditions, and justice. Increasingly, the demands have been made on the terms of the minority groups, not on those of the dominant group. Some of these demands have been met, at least verbally, and the society as a whole has rejected the oppressive racism of the past. Minority group progress has stalled well short of equality, however, and the patterns of poverty, discrimination, marginality, hopelessness, and despair continue to limit the lives of millions.

As we begin the 21st century, the dilemmas of America's minority groups remain perhaps the primary unresolved domestic issue facing the nation. The answers of the past—the simple faith in assimilation and the belief that success in America is open to all who simply try hard enough—have proved inadequate, even destructive and dangerous, because they help to sustain the belief that the barriers to equality no longer exist and that any remaining inequalities are the problems of the minority groups, not the larger society.

These problems of equality and access will not solve themselves or simply fade away. They will continue to manifest themselves in myriad ways; through protest activities, rancorous debates, diffused rage, and pervasive violence. The solutions and policies that will carry us through these coming travails are not clear. Only by asking the proper questions, realistically and honestly, can we hope to find the answers that will help our society fulfill its promises to the millions who are currently excluded from achieving the American Dream.

The United States is one of many ethnically and racially diverse nations in the world today. As the globe continues to shrink and networks of communication, immigration, trade, and transportation continue to link all peoples into a single global entity, the problems of diversity will become more international in their scope and implications. Ties will grow between African Americans and the nations of Africa, agreements between the United States and the nations of Latin America will have direct impact on immigration patterns, Asian Americans will be affected by international developments on the Pacific Rim, and so forth. Domestic and international group relations will blend into a single reality. In many ways, the patterns of dominant-minority relations discussed in this text have already been reproduced on the global stage. The mostly Anglo industrialized nations of the Northern Hemisphere have continuously exploited the labor and resources of the mostly nonwhite, undeveloped nations of the Southern Hemisphere. Thus, the tensions and resentments we have observed in U.S. society are mirrored in the global system of societies.

The United States is neither the most nor the least diverse country in the world. Likewise, our nation is neither the most nor the least successful in confronting the problems of prejudice, discrimination, and racism. However, the multigroup nature of our society, along with the present influx of immigrants from around the globe, do present an opportunity to improve on our record and make a lasting contribution. A society that finds a way to deal fairly and humanely with the problems of diversity and difference, prejudice and inequality, and racism and discrimination can provide a sorely needed model for other nations and, indeed, for the world.

Appendix A

This appendix presents summary information on the relative standing of most of the groups covered in this text. The data come from the American Community Survey (ACS), a data-gathering program of the U.S. Bureau of the Census. The ACS has been conducted every year since the last full census in 2000 and is based on randomly selected samples of Americans, not the entire population. Thus, the values presented in the tables and graphs of this appendix are *estimates* of the characteristics of the groups. The technology used to create these estimates is well established and very trustworthy, and the probability that these estimates are close approximations of the actual group characteristics is very high. Still, you should regard the values in this appendix as accurate within a small error band rather than literally true or an exact representation of the characteristics of the entire group. Also, you should remember that these values are summaries or averages and that each group includes a full range of scores. For example, even the most affluent group includes people who are desperately poor, and the most impoverished group includes some wealthy members.

There is a great deal of information in this appendix and, to improve readability, I have used a color key for the groups:

Black = African Americans

Blue = Asian American groups (Chinese, Japanese, Filipino, Korean, Indian, and Vietnamese Americans). The striped blue bar represents all Asian Americans.

Brown = African groups (Ethiopians and Nigerians)

Gray = Non-Hispanic white Americans (German, Irish, Italian, and Polish Americans).[1] The striped gray bar represents all non-Hispanic white Americans.

Green = Middle Eastern and Arab Americans (Arab, Egyptian, Lebanese, Iranian,[2] and Syrian Americans). The striped green bar represents all Arab Americans.

Light Blue = American Indians

Purple = Non-Hispanic Caribbean groups (Haitian and Jamaican Americans)

Red = Hispanic Americans (Colombian, Cuban, Dominican, Salvadoran, Puerto Rican, and Mexican Americans). The striped red bar represents all Hispanic Americans.

APPENDIX TABLE 1: Summary Characteristics by Group

This table presents a summary of information for the groups, followed by graphs for several of the variables.

APPENDIX TABLE 1 Summary Characteristics of All Groups

Group	Size	% of U.S. Population	Median Household Income[3] (Dollars per Year)	% Families Poor	% Children Poor	% HS	% BA	% Foreign-Born	% Speaking English "Less Than Very Well"	% Managerial and Professional
All Non-Hispanic Whites	201,973,636	67.5	52,375	6.2	10.7	88.9	29.9	3.8	1.8	37.6
Germans	50,764,352	16.9	55,203	5.0	8.6	92.1	31.5	1.4	0.7	38.3
Irish	35,975,855	12.0	54,531	6.0	9.9	91.0	31.1	0.7	0.4	38.4
Italian	17,829,184	6.0	59,877	5.5	8.6	90.4	32.0	3.4	2.0	39.0
Polish	10,024,683	3.3	58,207	4.5	7.3	92.0	34.4	5.5	3.4	39.8
Non-Hispanic Blacks	**38,167,719**	**12.8**	**32,465**	**21.4**	**34.5**	**79.6**	**17.1**	**8.5**	**2.6**	**26.7**
American Indians	3,424,177	1.2	36,011	19.2	29.8	79.9	15.7	3.5	4.9	27.2
All Hispanics	44,252,278	14.7	38,747	19.3	24.1	60.2	12.3	40.0	39.1	17.2
Colombians	801,363	0.3	46,777	9.8	13.7	84.9	31.7	68.3	45.0	28.3
Cubans	1,520,276	0.5	41,823	11.1	15.6	74.7	25.5	61.1	42.3	30.9
Dominicans	1,217,225	0.4	32,013	25.0	33.2	63.8	14.3	60.4	48.5	17.0
Salvadorans	1,371,666	0.5	41,620	15.1	22.2	45.4	7.4	67.1	58.6	10.3
Puerto Ricans	3,987,947	1.3	35,899	21.4	31.5	71.8	14.6	—	20.1	25.6
Mexicans	28,339,354	9.5	37,660	21.0	29.7	53.7	8.3	40.2	41.3	14.1
All Asians	14,656,608	4.9	62,738	8.2	10.8	85.9	48.4	61.1	33.1	46.0
Chinese	3,565,458	1.2	62,333	9.3	9.5	82.2	50.5	62.7	42.0	51.9
Filipinos	2,915,745	1.0	71,163	4.3	6.2	91.7	45.4	54.6	18.8	39.5
Indians	2,662,112	0.9	76,172	5.9	8.8	90.0	67.3	71.6	22.1	61.3
Japanese	1,221,773	0.4	61,011	4.4	6.4	93.7	44.5	28.5	18.9	48.4
Koreans	1,520,203	0.5	50,510	11.6	11.6	91.3	51.9	67.1	43.0	43.2
Vietnamese	1,599,394	0.5	52,408	11.3	15.0	72.3	26.2	64.1	50.9	30.3
Haitians	762,925	0.3	41,666	15.4	24.0	75.7	18.5	61.2	37.6	21.7
Jamaicans	910,979	0.3	47,106	11.5	19.1	82.1	22.8	62.3	1.5	30.7
All Arabs	1,466,874	0.5	53,979	12.0	20.1	87.7	42.3	41.8	19.1	41.7
Arabs	**257,864**	**0.0**	**45,666**	**15.8**	**25.1**	**83.3**	**34.6**	**47.8**	**25.4**	**34.1**
Egyptians	**177,534**	**0.0**	**64,118**	**9.3**	**17.0**	**94.9**	**64.5**	**63.8**	**22.9**	**50.4**
Iranians	**414,016**	**0.0**	**63,069**	**9.7**	**11.0**	**91.5**	**57.8**	**65.0**	**28.3**	**51.2**
Lebanese	**481,675**	**0.0**	**62,053**	**7.8**	**11.0**	**90.6**	**43.5**	**23.1**	**9.3**	**46.6**
Syrians	**155,718**	**0.0**	**53,906**	**8.6**	**13.7**	**87.7**	**36.8**	**24.8**	**11.2**	**42.4**
Ethiopians	**151,491**	**0.0**	**35,199**	**16.5**	**29.7**	**87.4**	**25.5**	**74.2**	**36.6**	**26.2**
Nigerians	**237,527**	**0.0**	**51,082**	**11.9**	**14.6**	**96.2**	**62.8**	**65.6**	**11.2**	**49.7**

SOURCE: All data are from the "American Community Survey, 2006," of the U.S. Bureau of the Census (pub. 2007). This information is available at http://factfinder.census.gov/servlet/DatasetMainPageServlet?_program=ACS&_submenuId=&_lang=en&_ts=

NOTE: Racial groups are "alone and in combination." That is, they include people who claimed only one race (e.g., Asian American) and people with multiple racial ancestry (e.g., Asian and African Americans).

APPENDIX GRAPH 1: Percentage Foreign-Born

The groups are highly variable in their percentage in the first generation (or foreign-born). The groups that have immigrated more recently (after the new immigration policy that was instituted in 1965) have the largest percentage, of course, and the lowest percentages are for the groups that immigrated before the 1924 Quota Act (see Chapter 2 for a discussion of changing American immigration policy) and groups that have been a part of this society from the beginning (American Indians and African Americans).

Also, note that some groups that are often thought to be newcomers have a relatively low percentage of foreign-born. For example, only 40% of Mexican Americans and less than 30% of Japanese Americans are first generation. As discussed in Chapters 4 and 8, Mexican Americans have been a part of this society since the first half of the 19th century. As discussed in Chapter 9, Japanese Americans began immigrating to the United States more than a century ago, stopped immigrating in large numbers after the 1920s, and have not been particularly involved in the post-1965 wave of immigration. Also note the low percentage of foreign-born in two Middle Eastern groups—Syrian and Lebanese Americans—which, again, have been part of U.S. society for more than a century.

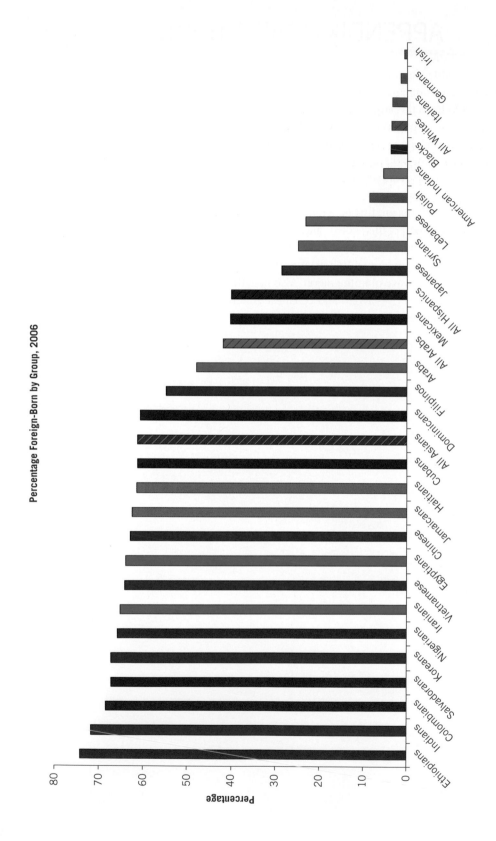

Percentage Foreign-Born by Group, 2006

RACE, ETHNICITY, GENDER, AND CLASS

Education, as we have noted throughout the text, is a key resource in a postindustrial society. Nearly 90% of non-Hispanic whites (the "dominant group") have at least a high school degree, but many groups exceed this standard. The groups with the highest levels of achievement include recent immigrant groups that bring high levels of human capital (see Chapter 2 for a discussion of human capital) as well as white ethnic groups that are well established in the social structure. The groups with lower levels of educational achievement are colonized groups (see Chapter 4 for a discussion of colonized versus immigrant groups and the importance of the contact situation) and recent immigrant groups with low levels of human capital.

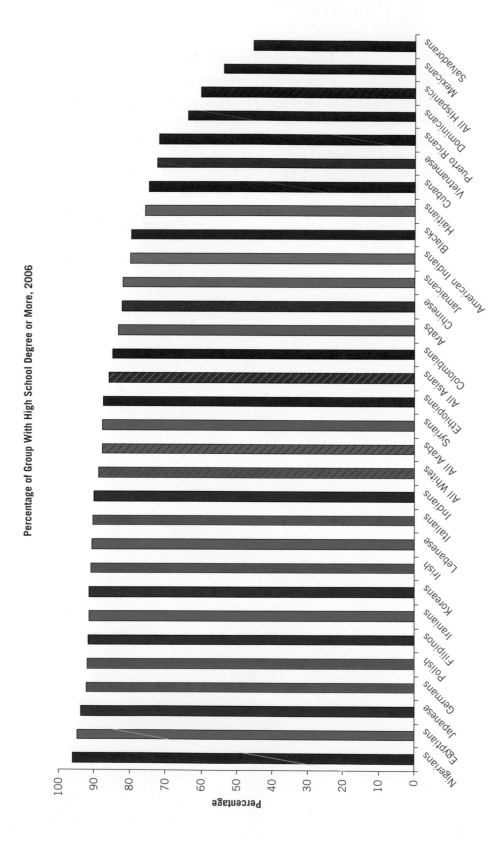

Percentage of Group With High School Degree or More, 2006

RACE, ETHNICITY, GENDER, AND CLASS

APPENDIX GRAPH 3:
Percentage With College Degree or More

Some post-1965 immigrant groups, especially groups from Asia and the Middle East, bring very high levels of human capital and in some cases, extraordinarily high levels of education. For three groups—Indians, Egyptians, and Nigerians—the percentage of the college educated is more than double the percentage for non-Hispanic whites. Many (but not all) of the Asian American groups score higher than non-Hispanic whites on this variable, as do all of the Middle Eastern groups. These groups are largely "elite" immigrants who arrive with many of the skills they will need to make a successful adjustment to the United States, although many also include less affluent members. (See Chapter 9, for example, about the "bipolar" distribution of Chinese Americans.) The groups to the right of the graph have lower levels of education and are colonized groups or non-elite immigrant groups with low levels of human capital. The latter may become the victims of segmented assimilation, as discussed in Chapters 2 and 10.

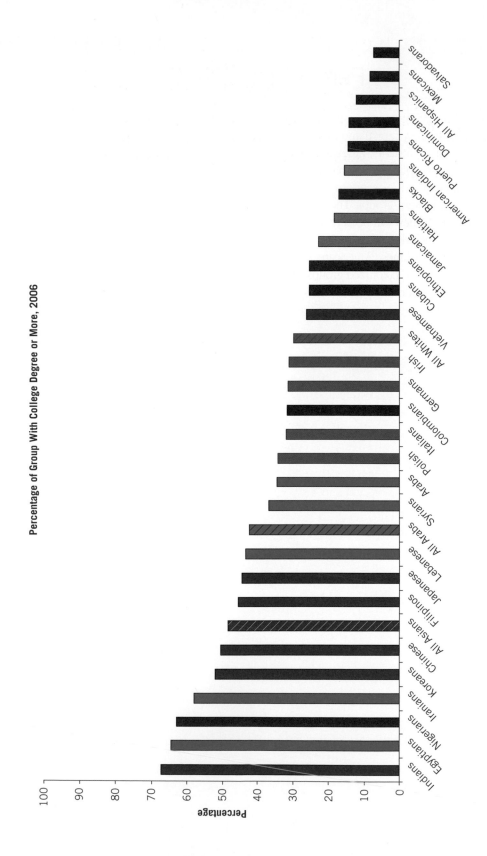

Percentage of Group With College Degree or More, 2006

RACE, ETHNICITY, GENDER, AND CLASS

APPENDIX GRAPH 4: Median Household Income

The differences in levels of education are associated with differences in levels of income and other measures of socioeconomic standing and general well-being. Once again, the groups on the left side of the graph are "elite" immigrant groups and white ethnic groups, the descendants of immigrants who arrived more than a century ago and are now well established in the society. The groups on the right side of the graph are colonized groups and immigrant groups with low levels of human capital.

Median Household Income by Group, 2006

RACE, ETHNICITY, GENDER, AND CLASS

The patterns of poverty echo the patterns of education and income. Like the other graphs in this appendix, this graph should reinforce the importance of the contact situation and the relevance of the Noel and Blauner hypotheses presented in Chapter 4 and applied throughout the remainder of the text. Groups to the right of the graph may become the victims of segmented assimilation.

Percentage of Families in Poverty by Group, 2006

RACE, ETHNICITY, GENDER, AND CLASS

As I have pointed out throughout this text, minority group status does not affect all members in the same way. Minority groups are differentiated by age, social class, geographical region, rural versus urban residence, and a host of other variables. Appendix Table 2 and the graphs that follow illustrate this variation by presenting information on gender differences within minority groups. I also present two additional variables that refer to some important gender-related characteristics: percentage of households headed by females and percentage of females in the paid labor force. The former is often an indicator of general poverty, lack of job opportunities for men, and the central importance of women in the group. The latter can be an indicator of lower prestige and power for women. As before, all information is from the 2006 American Community Survey.

	Percentage of Group With High School Degree or More			Percentage of Group With College Degree or More			Mean Income, Full-Time, Year-Round Workers			% of Households Headed by Females	% of Females in Paid Labor Force
	Men	Women	Women as a % of Men	Men	Women	Women as a % of Men	Men	Women	Women as a % of Men		
All Whites	88.6	89.1	100.56	31.3	28.4	90.73	64126	43231	67.42	34.8	71.8
Germans	91.6	92.5	100.98	32.6	30.5	93.56	62863	43024	68.44	29.3	70.0
Irish	90.6	91.3	100.77	31.1	32.5	104.50	66380	44696	67.33	26.9	68.9
Italians	90.5	90.4	99.89	32.0	33.7	105.31	70593	47247	66.93	25.5	68.2
Polish	92.2	91.8	99.57	34.4	35.8	104.07	68644	46282	67.42	23.6	67.2
Blacks	**78.6**	**80.7**	**102.67**	**15.6**	**18.3**	**117.31**	**41958**	**35445**	**84.48**	**19.2**	**65.4**
American Indians	78.9	80.9	**102.53**	15.1	16.2	**107.28**	44105	33969	**77.02**	19.0	64.6
All Hispanics	*58.7*	*61.7*	**105.11**	*11.5*	*13.1*	**113.91**	*36097*	*30528*	**84.57**	*18.4*	*63.2*
Colombians	86.0	84.0	**97.67**	32.7	31.0	**94.80**	43454	33875	**77.96**	17.9	63.0
Cubans	74.7	74.7	**100.00**	25.6	25.3	**98.83**	53406	38198	**71.52**	16.9	62.9
Puerto Ricans	70.9	72.5	**102.26**	13.0	16.0	**123.08**	44737	36010	**80.49**	14.6	62.5
Dominicans	61.4	63.5	**103.42**	13.2	15.1	**114.39**	35349	28669	**81.10**	13.9	61.7
Mexicans	52.5	55.1	**104.95**	7.7	9.0	**116.88**	33120	28378	**85.68**	13.8	61.4
Salvadorans	45.9	44.9	**97.82**	7.1	7.7	**108.45**	31294	25473	**81.40**	12.3	59.6
All Asians	*88.1*	*83.9*	**95.23**	*51.6*	*45.6*	**88.37**	*64501*	*48316*	**74.91**	*12.2*	*59.5*
Chinese	83.5	81.1	**97.13**	53.6	47.7	**88.99**	67207	53331	**79.35**	10.2	59.2
Japanese	95.0	92.7	**97.58**	48.7	41.2	**84.60**	73254	50230	**68.57**	10.0	59.1
Filipinos	93.0	90.8	**97.63**	41.6	48.1	**115.63**	52150	45793	**87.81**	9.6	58.4
Koreans	95.3	88.3	**92.65**	59.9	46.1	**76.96**	65570	46180	**70.43**	9.3	58.0
Indians	92.6	86.9	**93.84**	71.9	62.0	**86.23**	79448	57040	**71.80**	9.0	57.4
Vietnamese	76.1	68.6	**90.14**	28.9	23.5	**81.31**	50535	39174	**77.52**	9.0	57.2
Haitians	78.1	73.6	**94.24**	19.4	17.7	**91.24**	34890	32244	**92.42**	9.0	55.7
Jamaicans	80.2	83.7	**104.36**	19.8	25.2	**127.27**	47461	39892	**84.05**	8.8	55.6
All Arabs	*89.1*	*86.1*	**96.63**	*45.8*	*38.0*	**82.97**	*74043*	*48917*	**66.07**	*8.7*	*55.5*
Arabs	84.9	80.8	**95.17**	36.6	31.5	**86.07**	60996	47479	**77.84**	8.6	55.5
Egyptians	96.5	92.5	**95.85**	67.4	60.2	**89.32**	72344	49362	**68.23**	8.5	55.1
Iranians	94.8	87.8	**92.62**	65.6	49.3	**75.15**	93193	56571	**60.70**	8.4	54.6
Lebanese	91.1	90.1	**98.90**	48.0	39.2	**81.67**	86362	52775	**61.11**	8.3	53.4
Syrians	88.7	86.7	**97.75**	41.9	31.9	**76.13**	93623	44094	**47.10**	8.0	52.7
Ethiopians	91.2	83.7	**91.78**	29.7	21.3	**71.72**	46046	33417	**72.57**	4.9	51.6
Nigerians	97.6	94.2	**96.52**	67.0	56.9	**84.93**	52,428	48,237	**92.01**	4.0	41.9

APPENDIX GRAPH 6:
Gender Differences in High School Education

Women are not equally disadvantaged in all groups. In the groups on the left side of the graph and above the horizontal 100% line, women have higher levels of education than the men in their groups. Note that these groups are generally colonized or immigrant groups with low levels of human capital. Opportunities for education and occupation are often more open to women in these groups for a variety of reasons, including stereotypes and patterns of institutional discrimination that attach more to males than to females (e.g., see the study summarized in Chapter 3 by Morris that addresses the intersections of gender, class, and race).

In the groups on the right side of the graph and below the 100% line, women have lower levels of education than the men in their groups. These groups tend to be "elite" immigrants that bring high levels of human capital, but this capital seems to be more invested in the males. Also, many of these groups are Asian American and Middle Eastern, and the traditions of these groups are often very patriarchal and support traditional roles and limited opportunities for females.

**Percentage of Females With High School Degree or More as a
Percentage of Males With a High School Degree or More, 2006**

* In groups on the left side of the graph and above the 100% horizontal line, women have higher status relative to men on this variable.
* In groups close to the 100% horizontal line, men and women have approximately equal status on this variable.
* In groups on the right side of the graph and below the 100% horizontal line, women have lower status relative to men on this variable.

RACE, ETHNICITY, GENDER, AND CLASS

Once again, we see a wide variety of gender differences across the groups. The patterns here echo those in Graph 6: Colonized groups and immigrant groups with low levels of human capital tend to fall on the left side of the graph and above the 100% line (these women have higher status relative to the men in their group); and "elite" immigrant groups, Middle Eastern groups, and Asian American groups tend to fall on the right side (these women have lower status relative to the men in their groups).

Percentage of Women With College Degrees as a Percentage of Men With College Degrees, 2006

* In groups on the left side of the graph and above the 100% horizontal line, women have higher status relative to men on this variable.
* In groups close to the 100% horizontal line, men and women have approximately equal status on this variable.
* In groups on the right side of the graph and below the 100% horizontal line, women have lower status relative to men on this variable.

Females as a Percentage of Males

RACE, ETHNICITY, GENDER, AND CLASS

The most significant point about this graph is that the relatively higher educational achievements of women do not translate into higher incomes. In *no* group do women have average incomes that equal—or even approach—those of men. The extent of gender inequality tends to be less for colonized and low-human-capital immigrant groups (these groups tend to be on the left side of the graph), where incomes are lowest (see Appendix Graph 4), and greatest for Middle Eastern groups.

Females as a Percentage of Males

Mean Income of Females as a Percentage of Mean Income of Males, Full-Time, Year-Round Workers Only, 2006

* In groups to the left of this graph, women have higher (but not equal) status relative to men on this variable.
* In groups to the right of this graph, women have lower status relative to men on this variable.

Haitians
Nigerians
Filipinos
Mexicans
All Hispanics
Blacks
Jamaicans
Salvadorans
Dominicans
Puerto Ricans
Chinese
Colombians
Arabs
Vietnamese
American Indians
All Asians
Ethiopians
Indians
Cubans
Koreans
Japanese
Germans
Egyptians
Polish
All Whites
Irish
Italians
All Arabs
Lebanese
Iranians
Syrians

APPENDIX GRAPH 9: Percentage of Households That Are Female Headed

The groups that rank highest on this variable are colonized and low-human-capital immigrant groups, in which unemployment rates for men are higher and good jobs that pay enough to support a family are scarcer. See, especially, Chapter 6 for more.

Percentage of Households That Are Female Headed, 2006

Percentage

Dominicans, Blacks, Jamaicans, Puerto Ricans, Haitians, Salvadorans, American Indians, All Hispanics, Colombians, Mexicans, Ethiopians, Filipinos, Cubans, Vietnamese, Nigerians, Irish, Italians, Koreans, All Asians, All Whites, Arabs, Lebanese, Japanese, Germans, Polish, Chinese, Iranians, Syrians, All Arabs, Egyptians, Indians

RACE, ETHNICITY, GENDER, AND CLASS

1. The ACS lists almost 40 European ancestry groups. I chose these four groups because they include the two largest groups overall (German and Irish Americans), the largest Southern European group (Italians), and the largest Eastern European group (Polish).

2. Iranians are not Arabic.

3. The median is the point that splits a distribution of scores into two equal halves. Thus, half the households in the group have an income higher than the median, and half have an income lower than the median.

The Obama Presidency

Can Barack Obama Deliver the Change He Promises?

Kenneth Jost and the *CQ Researcher* Staff

They came to Washington in numbers unprecedented and with enthusiasm unbounded to bear witness and be a part of history: the inauguration of Barack Hussein Obama on Jan. 20, 2009, as the 44th president of the United States and the first African-American ever to serve as the nation's chief executive.

After taking the oath of office from Chief Justice John G. Roberts Jr., Obama looked out at the estimated 1.8 million people massed at the Capitol and National Mall and delivered an inaugural address nearly as bracing as the subfreezing temperatures.

With hardly the hint of a smile, Obama, 47, outlined the challenges confronting him as the fifth-youngest president in U.S. history. The nation is at war, he noted, the economy "badly weakened" and the public beset with "a sapping of confidence."

"Today I say to you that the challenges we face are real," Obama continued in his 18-minute speech. "They are serious and they are many. They will not be met easily or in a short span of time. But know this, America — they will be met."[1] (See economy sidebar, p. 286; foreign policy sidebar, p. 292.)

The crowd received Obama's sobering message with flag-waving exuberance and a unity of spirit unseen in Washington for decades. Despite Democrat Obama's less-than-landslide 7 percentage-point victory over John McCain on Nov. 4, hardly any sign of political dissent or partisan opposition surfaced on Inauguration Day or during the weekend of celebration that preceded it. (See maps, p. 278; poll, p. 280.)

From *CQ Researcher,*
January 30, 2009.

The largest crowd in Washington history cheers President Barack Obama after his swearing in on Jan. 20, 2009. An estimated 1.8 million high-spirited, flag-waving people gathered at the Capitol and National Mall, but thousands more were turned away by police due to overcrowding.

AP Photo/Evan Vucci

"It's life-changing for everyone," said Rhonda Gittens, a University of Florida journalism student, "because of who he is, because of how he represents everyone." Gittens traveled to Washington with some 50 other members of the school's black student union.

The inaugural crowd included tens of thousands clustered on side streets after the U.S. Park Police determined the mall had reached capacity. The crowd was bigger than for any previous inauguration — at least three times larger than when the outgoing president, George W. Bush, had first taken the oath of office eight years earlier. The total number also exceeded independent estimates cited for any of Washington's protest marches or state occasions in the past.*

The spectators came from all over the country and from many foreign lands. "He's bringing change here," said Clayton Preira, a young Brazilian accompanying three fellow students on a two-month visit to the United States. "He's bringing change all over the world." The spectators were of all ages, but overall the crowd seemed disproportionately young. "He really speaks to young people," said Christian McLaren, a white University of Florida student.

Most obviously and most significantly, the crowd was racially and ethnically diverse — just like the new first family. Obama himself is the son of a black Kenyan father and a white Kansan mother. His wife Michelle, he often remarks, carries in her the blood of slaves and of slave owners. Among those behind the first lady on the dais were Obama's half-sister, Maya Soetoro-Ng, whose father was Indonesian, and her husband, Konrad Ng, a Chinese-American. Some of Obama's relatives from Kenya came as well, wearing colorful African garb.

The vast numbers of black Americans often gave the event the air of an old-time church revival. In quieter moments, many struggled to find the words to convey the significance, both historic and personal. "It hasn't sunk in yet," Marcus Collier, a photographer from New York City, remarked several hours later.

David Moses, a health-care supervisor in New York City, carried with him a picture of his late father, who had encouraged him and his brother to join the anti-segregation sit-ins of the early 1960s in their native South Carolina. "It's the culmination of a long struggle," Moses said, "that still has a long way to go."

Shannon Simmons, who had not yet been born when Congress passed major civil rights legislation in the 1960s, brought her 12-year-old daughter from their home in New

---

* Crowd estimates for President Obama's inauguration ranged from 1.2 million to 1.8 million. Commonly cited estimates for other Washington events include: March on Washington for Jobs and Freedom, 1963, 250,000; President John F. Kennedy's funeral, 1963, 800,000; inauguration of President Lyndon B. Johnson, 1965, 1.2 million; Peace Moratorium, 1969, 250,000; Million Man March, 1995, 400,000-800,000; March for Life, 1998, 225,000; March for Women's Lives, 2004, 500,000-800,000.

Orleans. "It's historic," said Simmons, who made monthly contributions to the Obama campaign. "It's about race, but it's more than that. I believe he can bring about change." (*See sidebar, p. 282.*)

For black Americans, old and young alike, the inauguration embodied the lesson that Obama himself had often articulated — that no door need be viewed as closed to any American, regardless of race. For Obama himself, the inauguration climaxed a quest that took him from the Illinois legislature to the White House in only 12 years.

To win the presidency, Obama had to defy political oddsmakers by defeating then-Sen. Hillary Rodham Clinton, the former first lady, for the Democratic nomination and then beating McCain, the veteran Arizona senator and Vietnam War hero. Obama campaigned hard against the Bush administration's record, blaming Bush, among other things, for mismanaging the U.S. economy as well as the wars in Iraq and Afghanistan.

After a nod to Bush's record of service and help during the transition, Obama hinted at some of those criticisms in his address. "The nation cannot prosper long when it favors only the prosperous," he declared, referencing tax cuts enacted in Bush's first year in office that Obama had called for repealing.

On national defense, "we reject the false choice between our safety and our ideals," Obama continued. The Bush administration had come under fierce attack from civil liberties and human rights advocates for aggressive detention and interrogation policies adopted after the Sept. 11, 2001, terrorist attacks on the United States. (*See "At Issue," p. 302.*)

Obama Victory Changed Electoral Map

Barack Obama won nine traditionally Republican states in the November 2008 election that George W. Bush had won easily in 2004, and his electoral and popular vote totals were significantly higher than Bush's. In 2004, Bush won with 50.7 percent of the vote to John Kerry's 48.3 percent. By comparison Obama garnered 52.9 percent to Sen. John McCain's 45.7. In the nation's new political map, the Democrats dominate the landscape, with the Republicans clustered in the South, the Plains and the Mountain states.

Presidential Election, 2004

Democrat: John Kerry
Republican: George W. Bush

Total electoral vote:	
Republican	**286**
Democrat	**251**

Total popular vote:	
Republican	**62,040,610**
Democrat	**59,028,444**

* One "unfaithful" elector voted for John Edwards.

Presidential Election, 2008

Democrat: Barack Obama
Republican: John McCain

Total electoral vote:	
Democrat	**365**
Republican	**173**

Total popular vote:	
Democrat	**69,456,897**
Republican	**59,934,814**

* Due to the Nebraska's proportional allocation system, McCain received four electoral votes and Obama one.

Source: Federal Election Commission

Despite the attacks, Obama also sounded conservative notes throughout the speech, blaming economic woes in part on a "collective failure to make hard choices" and calling for "a new era of responsibility." Republicans in the audience were pleased. "He wasn't pointing fingers just toward Bush," said Rhonda Hamlin, a social worker from Alexandria, Va. "He was pointing fingers toward all of us."

With the inauguration behind him, Obama went quickly to work. Within hours, the administration moved to institute a 120-day moratorium on legal proceedings against the approximately 245 detainees still being held at the Guantánamo Bay Naval Base in Cuba. Obama had repeatedly pledged during the campaign to close the prison; two days later he signed a second decree, ordering that the camp be closed within one year.

Then on his first full day as president, Obama on Jan. 21 issued stringent ethics rules for administration officials and conferred separately with his top economic and military advisers to begin mapping plans to try to lift the U.S. economy out of its year-long recession and bring successful conclusions to the conflicts in Iraq and Afghanistan.

By then, the Inauguration Day truce in partisan conflict was beginning to break down. House Republicans pointed to a Congressional Budget Office study questioning the likely impact of the Democrats' $825-billion economic stimulus package, weighted toward spending instead of tax cuts. "The money that they're going to throw out the door, at the end of the day, is not going to work," said Rep. Devin Nunes, R-Calif., a member of the tax-writing House Ways and Means Committee. (*See "At Issue," p. 303.*)

The partisan division raised questions whether Democratic leaders could stick to the promised schedule of getting a stimulus plan to Obama's desk for his signature by the time of the Presidents' Day congressional recess in mid-February. More broadly, the Republicans' stance presaged continuing difficulties for Obama as he turned to other ambitious agenda items, including his repeated pledge to overhaul the nation's health-care system. (*See sidebar, p. 296.*)

Obama included health care in his inaugural litany of challenges, along with education, climate change and technology. For now, those initiatives lie in the future. In the immediate days after his euphoric inauguration, here are some of the major questions being debated:

Is President Obama on the right track in fixing the U.S. economy?

As president-elect, Obama spent his first full week in Washington in early January first warning of trillion-dollar federal budget deficits for years to come and then making urgent appeals for public support for a close to trillion-dollar stimulus to get the economy moving.

Members of Congress from both parties and advocates and economic experts of all persuasions agree on the need for a good-sized federal recovery program for the seriously ailing U.S. economy. And most agree on a prescription that combines spending increases and tax cuts. But there is sharp disagreement as to the particulars between tax-cutting conservatives and pump-priming liberals, with deficit hawks worried that both of the prescribed remedies could get out of hand.

With the plan's price tag then being estimated somewhere around $800 billion, Obama made his first sustained appeal for public support in a somber, half-hour address on Jan. 8 at George Mason University in Fairfax, Va., outside Washington. Any delay, he warned, could risk double-digit unemployment. He outlined plans to "rebuild America" ranging from alternative energy facilities and new school classrooms to computerized medical records, but he insisted the plan would not entail "a slew of new government programs." He reiterated his campaign promise of a "$1,000 tax cut for 95 percent of working-class families" but made no mention of business tax cuts being included as sweeteners for Republican lawmakers.

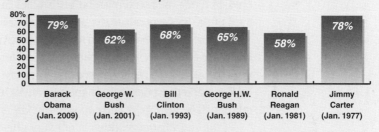

Public Gives Obama Highest Rating

Barack Obama began his presidency with 79 percent of Americans having a favorable impression of him — higher than the five preceding presidents. George W. Bush entered office with a 62 percent favorability rating; he left with a 33 percent approval rating, lowest of post-World War II presidents except Harry S. Truman and Richard M. Nixon.

Do you have a favorable impression of . . . ?

Barack Obama (Jan. 2009)	George W. Bush (Jan. 2001)	Bill Clinton (Jan. 1993)	George H.W. Bush (Jan. 1989)	Ronald Reagan (Jan. 1981)	Jimmy Carter (Jan. 1977)
79%	62%	68%	65%	58%	78%

Source: The Washington Post, Jan. 18, 2009

Within days, Obama's plan was taking flack from left and right in the blogosphere. Writing on the liberal HuffingtonPost.com, Robert Kuttner, co-editor of *American Prospect* magazine, denounced the spending plan as too small and the business tax cuts as "huge concessions" in a misguided effort at "post-partisanship." From the right, columnist Neal Boortz accused Obama on the conservative TownHall.com of using the economic crisis as "cover for increased government spending that he's been promising since the day he announced his candidacy."

Allen Schick, a professor of economics at the University of Maryland in College Park and formerly an economics specialist with the Congressional Research Service, sees weaknesses with both components of the Obama plan. "We really have no model to deal with the question of what's the right number" for the stimulus, he says. "And we're not even sure that the stimulus will do the job, especially if a lot of the spending is wasteful."

As for the tax cuts, Schick calls them "harebrained, more intended to look good and buy support than to actually get the economy moving." In particular, he criticized a proposed $3,000 jobs credit for employers. "We know from the past that employers don't hire people for just a few shekels," he says. Eventually, the jobs credit was dropped, but the package still includes business tax breaks such as a $16 billion provision to allow businesses to use 2008 and 2009 losses to offset profits for the previous five years instead of two.

Conservatives favor tax cuts, but not the middle-class tax cut that Obama is proposing. "A well-designed tax cut is the only effective short-term stimulus," says J. D. Foster, a senior fellow at the Heritage Foundation. But Foster, who worked in the Office of

Management and Budget in the Bush administration, calls either for extending or making permanent Bush's across-the-board rate cuts, which primarily benefited upper-income taxpayers.

From the opposite side, Chad Stone, chief economist with the liberal Center on Budget Policy and Priorities, endorses Obama's approach. "Tax cuts should be focused on people of low and moderate means, who are much more likely to spend the extra money they get," he says.

Academic economists, however, caution that tax cuts may not deliver a lot of bang for the buck in terms of short-term stimulus. Studies indicate that taxpayers pocketed at least one-third of the $500 tax rebate the government disbursed to counteract the 2001 recession.

Advocates and observers on both sides warn that the spending side of the package may also be less effective than hoped if political forces play too large a role in shaping it. "If it goes to pork, if it goes to green jobs that may sound good in the short term but may not have a market response or a market for them, then it's a waste," Paul Gigot, editorial page editor of *The Wall Street Journal*, said on NBC's "Meet the Press" on Jan. 11.

"If the stuff that gets added is not very effective as stimulus or the things that are good get pulled out, that would not be good," says Stone.

For its part, the budget-restraint advocacy group Concord Coalition sees political forces as driving up the total cost of the package — in spending and tax cuts alike — with no regard for the long-term impact. "Nothing is ever taken off the table," says Diane Lim Rogers, the coalition's chief economist.

Rogers complains of "political pressure to come up with tax cuts even though economists are having trouble figuring out whether they're going to do any good." At the same time, she says spending has to be designed "as thoughtfully as possible, not in a way that the federal government ends up literally just throwing money out the door."

A range of experts also call for renewed efforts to solve the mortgage and foreclosure crisis, saying that homeowners are not going to start spending again without confidence-restoring steps. Indeed, Federal Reserve Chairman Ben Bernanke pointedly told a conference in December that steps to reduce foreclosures "should be high on the agenda" in any economic recovery plan.[2]

Despite questions and concerns about the details, however, support for strong action is all but universal. "We have no choice," said Mark Zandi, chief economist of Moody's Economy.com and a former adviser to the McCain campaign, also on "Meet the Press." "If we don't do something like this — a stimulus package, a foreclosure mitigation plan — the economy is going to slide away."

Is President Obama on the right track in Iraq and Afghanistan?

At the start of his presidential campaign in February 2007, candidate Obama was unflinchingly calling for withdrawing all U.S. combat forces from Iraq within 16 months after taking office. But his tone began changing as he neared the Democratic nomination in summer 2008. And in his first extended broadcast interview after the election, President-elect Obama said on NBC's "Meet the Press" on Dec. 7 only that he would summon military advisers on his first day in office and direct them to prepare a plan for "a responsible drawdown."

Obama also did nothing to knock down host Tom Brokaw's forecast of a "residual force" of 35,000 to 50,000 U.S. troops in Iraq through the end of his term. "I'm not going to speculate on the numbers," Obama said, but he went on to promise "a large enough force in the region" to protect U.S. personnel and to "ferret out any terrorist activity." In addition, Obama voiced disappointment with developments in Afghanistan and said that "additional troops" and "more effective diplomacy" would be needed to achieve U.S. goals there.

Many foreign policy observers are viewing Obama's late campaign and post-election stances as a salutary shift from ideology to pragmatism. "It seems very clear that he will not fulfill his initial pledge to withdraw all U.S. forces from Iraq in 16 months — which is only wise," says Thomas Donnelly, a resident fellow on defense and national security issues at the American Enterprise Institute (AEI).

"I personally have been very impressed with [Obama's] thinking and his way of assembling a national security team," says Kenneth Pollack, director of the Brookings Institution's Saban Center for Middle East Policy. "This is not a man who plays by the traditional American political rules."

First Black President Made Race a Non-Issue

Obama's personal attributes swept voters' doubts aside.

Barack Obama took the oath of office the day after this year's Martin Luther King holiday, and he accepted the Democratic presidential nomination last August on the 45th anniversary of King's celebrated "I Have a Dream" speech.

For millions of Americans, Obama's election as the nation's first African-American president seemed to fulfill the promise of King's "dream" of a nation in which citizens "will not be judged by the color of their skin, but by the content of their character."

"Obviously, for an African-American to win the presidency, given the history of this country . . . is a remarkable thing," Obama said after the election. "If you think about grandparents who are alive today who grew up under Jim Crow, that's a big leap."[1]

While Obama clearly benefited from the sacrifices of the civil rights generation — to which he has paid homage — his politics are different from the veterans of that movement. Older black politicians such as the Rev. Jesse Jackson seemed to base their candidacies mainly on issues of particular concern to African-Americans. But black politicians of Obama's generation, such as Massachusetts Gov. Deval Patrick and Newark Mayor Cory Booker (both Democrats), have run on issues of broader concern — in Obama's case, first on the war in Iraq and later on the economic meltdown.

"The successful ones start from the outside by appealing to white voters first, and work back toward their base of black voters," said broadcast journalist Gwen Ifill, author of the new book The Breakthrough: Politics and Race in the Age of Obama.[2]

Black voters initially were reluctant to support Obama — polls throughout 2007 showed Sen. Hillary Rodham Clinton with a big lead among African-Americans — but he picked up their support as it became clear he was the first black candidate with a realistic hope of winning the White House. Clinton's support among blacks dropped markedly in the wake of remarks by former President Bill Clinton that many found demeaning.

(Continued)

(Continued)

But many white Democratic voters remained reluctant to support Obama, particularly in Appalachia. Exit polling during the Pennsylvania primary, for example, showed that 16 percent of whites had considered race in making their pick, with half of those saying they would not support Obama in the fall.[3]

Obama also was bedeviled by videotaped remarks of his pastor, the Rev. Jeremiah Wright, which were incendiary and deemed unpatriotic. But Obama responded with a widely hailed speech on race in March 2008 in which he acknowledged both the grievances of working-class whites and the continuing legacy of economic disadvantages among blacks. Obama said his own life story "has seared into my genetic makeup the idea that this nation is more than the sum of its parts — that out of many, we are truly one."[4]

As the general election campaign got under way, it was clear that race would continue to be a factor. One June poll showed that 30 percent of Americans admit prejudice.[5] And, despite Obama's lead, there was debate throughout the campaign about the so-called Bradley effect — the suggestion that people will lie to pollsters about their true intentions when it comes to black candidates.*

But neither Obama nor Arizona Sen. John McCain, his Republican rival, made explicit pleas based on race, with McCain refusing to air ads featuring Wright. As the campaign wore on, no one forgot that Obama is black — but most doubters put that fact aside in favor of more pressing concerns.

"For a long time, I couldn't ignore the fact that he was black. I'm not proud of that," Joe Sinitski, a 48-year-old Pennsylvania voter, told The New York Times. "I was raised to think that there aren't good black people out there."[6] But Sinitski ended up voting for Obama, along with many other whites won over by Obama's personal attributes or convinced that issues such as the economy trumped race.

Exit polls showed that Obama prevailed among those who considered race a significant factor, 53 to 46 percent.[7] "In difficult economic times, people find the price of prejudice is just a little too high," said outgoing North Carolina Gov. Mike Easley, a Democrat.[8]

"The Bradley effect really was not a significant factor, despite much concern, fear and hyperventilation about it leading up to the election," says Scott Keeter, a pollster with the Pew Research Center. "Race was a consideration to people, but what it wasn't, invariably, was a negative consideration for white voters. It was a positive consideration for many white voters who saw Obama as a candidate who could help the country toward racial reconciliation."

Obama carried more white voters than former Vice President Al Gore or Sen. John Kerry of Massachusetts, the two previous Democratic nominees. Still, he could not have prevailed without black and Hispanic voters, particularly in the three Southern states he carried. In Virginia — a state that had voted Republican since 1964 — Obama lost by 21 points among white voters, according to exit polls.

His victory clearly did not bring racial enmity to its end. In December, Chip Saltsman, a candidate for the Republican Party chairmanship, sent potential supporters a CD containing the song "Barack the Magic Negro," a parody popularized by right-wing talk show host Rush Limbaugh during the campaign. And, when Senate Democrats initially balked in January at seating Roland Burris as Obama's replacement, Rep. Bobby Rush, D-Ill, played the race card, warning them not to "hang or lynch the appointee," comparing the move to Southern governors who sought to block desegregation.[9]

But still polls suggest that most Americans believe Obama's presidency will be a boon for race relations. A USA Today/Gallup Poll taken the day after the November election showed that two-thirds predicted black-white relations "will eventually be worked out" — by far the highest total in the poll's history.[10]

_____

*The Bradley effect refers to Tom Bradley, an African-American who lost the 1982 race for governor in California despite being ahead in voter polls going into the election.

In the future, white males may no longer be the default inhabitants of America's most powerful position. The present generation and those in the future are likely to grow up thinking it's a normal state of affairs for the country to be led by a black president. "For a lot of African-Americans, it already has made them feel better and more positive about the country and American society," says David Bositis, an expert on black voting at the Joint Center for Political and Economic Studies.

"When you ask my kids what they want to be when they grow up, they always say they want to work at McDonald's or Wal-Mart," said Joslyn Reddick, principal at a predominantly black school in Selma, Ala., a city from which King led an historic march for voting rights in 1965.

"Now they will see that an African-American has achieved the highest station in the United States," Reddick said. "They can see for themselves that dreams can come true."[11]

— Alan Greenblatt, staff writer, Governing magazine

Michelle Obama holds the Bible used to swear in President Abraham Lincoln as Barack Obama takes the oath of office from Supreme Court Chief Justice John G. Roberts Jr.

AFP/Getty Images/Tim Sloan

---

[1] Bryan Monroe, "The Audacity of Victory," Ebony, January 2009, p. 16.

[2] Sam Fulwood III, "The New Face of America," Politico.com, Jan. 13, 2009.

[3] Alan Greenblatt, "Changing U.S. Electorate," CQ Researcher, May 30, 2008, p. 459.

[4] The Obama speech, "A More Perfect Union," is at www.youtube.com/watch?v=pWe7wTVbLUU. The text of the March 18, 2008, speech, "A More Perfect Union," is found in Change We Can Believe In: Barack Obama's Plan to Renew America's Promise (2008), pp. 215-232.

[5] Jon Cohen and Jennifer Agiesta, "3 in 10 Americans Admit to Race Bias," The Washington Post, June 22, 2008, p. A1.

[6] Michael Sokolove," The Transformation," The New York Times, Nov. 9, 2008, p. WK1.

[7] John B. Judis, "Did Race Really Matter?" Los Angeles Times, Nov. 9, 2008, p. 34.

[8] Rachel L. Swarns, "Vaulting the Racial Divide, Obama Persuaded Americans to Follow," The New York Times, Nov. 5, 2008, p. 7.

[9] Clarence Page, "Hiding Behind Black Voters," Chicago Tribune, Jan. 4, 2009, p. 24.

[10] Susan Page, "Hopes Are High for Race Relations," USA Today, Nov. 7, 2008, p. 1A.

[11] Dahleen Glanton and Howard Witte, "Many Marvel at a Black President," Chicago Tribune, Nov. 5, 2008, p. 6.

Obama invited speculation about a shift toward the center by selecting Clinton and Robert Gates as the two Cabinet members on his national security team along with a retired Marine general, James Jones, as national security adviser. (*See chart, at left.*) Clinton had voted for the Iraq War in late 2002, though she echoed Obama during the campaign in calling for troop withdrawals. As Bush's secretary of Defense, Gates had overseen the "surge" in U.S. forces during 2007.

"This is a group of people who are very sober, very intelligent, fully aware of the importance of Iraq to America's security interests and of the fragility of the situation there," says Pollack.

Cabinet Includes Stars, Superstars and Surprises

President Obama made his Cabinet selections in record time, and his appointees run the gamut of race, ethnic origin, gender, age and even party affiliation. Those in top posts include Sen. Hillary Rodham Clinton at State and Robert Gates continuing at Defense. Besides Gates, one other Republican was chosen: Transportation's Ray LaHood. New Mexico Gov. Bill Richardson's withdrawal left the Commerce post unfilled along with the director of Drug Control Policy. Cabinet-level appointees include four women, two Asian-Americans, two Hispanics and two African-Americans.

Name, Age Department	Date of Nomination	Date of Confirmation	Previous Positions
Hillary Rodham Clinton, 61, State	Dec. 1	Jan. 21	New York U.S. senator (2001-09); first lady (1993-2001); Arkansas first lady (1979-81, 1983-92)
Timothy Geithner, 47, Treasury	Nov. 24	Jan. 26	President, Federal Reserve Bank of New York (2003-09); under secretary, Treasury (1998-2001)
Robert Gates, 65, Defense*	Dec. 1	Dec. 6, 2006 *	Defense secretary (2006-present); director, CIA (1991-93); deputy national security adviser (1989-91)
Eric Holder, 57, Attorney General	Dec. 1		Deputy attorney general (1997-2001); U.S. attorney (1993-97); judge, D.C. Superior Court (1988-93)
Ken Salazar, 53, Interior	Dec. 17	Jan. 20	Colorado U.S. senator (2005-09); Colorado attorney general (1999-2005)
Tom Vilsack, 58, Agriculture	Dec. 17	Jan. 20	Iowa governor (1999-2007); Iowa state senator (1992-99)
Hilda Solis, 51, Labor	Dec. 19		California U.S. representative (2001-09); California state senator (1995-2001)
Tom Daschle, 61, Health & Human Services	Dec. 11		South Dakota U.S. senator (1987-2005); Senate majority leader (2001, 2001-03); South Dakota U.S. representative (1979-87)
Shaun Donovan, 42, Housing and Urban Development	Dec. 13	Jan. 22	Commissioner, New York City Dept. of Housing Preservation and Development (2004-08); deputy assistant secretary, HUD (2000-01)

Some anti-war activists were voicing concern about Obama's seeming shift within days of his election. "Obama has very successfully branded himself as anti-war, but the fact remains that he's willing to keep a residual force in Iraq indefinitely, [and] he wants to escalate in Afghanistan," said Matthis Chiroux of Iraq Veterans Against the War. "My hope is that he starts bringing home the troops from Iraq immediately, but I think those of us in the anti-war movement could find ourselves disappointed."[3]

Since then, however, criticism of Obama's emerging policies has been virtually non-existent from the anti-war and Democratic Party left. "He seems to be accelerating the withdrawal, which is terrific," says Robert Borosage, co-director of the Campaign for America's Future. Borosage is "concerned" about the residual force in Iraq because of the risk that U.S. troops will become involved in "internecine battles." But he adds, "That's what he's promised, and I think he'll fulfill his promise."

Donnelly and Pollack, however, both view a continuing U.S. role in Iraq as vital. "There's good progress, but a long way to go," says Donnelly. "A huge American role is going to be needed through the four years of the Obama administration." Pollack agrees. "Iraq is far from solved. Whether we like it or not, Iraq is a vital interest for the United States of America."

In his campaign and since, Obama has treated Afghanistan as more important to U.S. interests and harshly criticized the Bush administration for — in his view — ignoring the conflict there. Afghanistan "had had a huge rhetorical place in the Obama campaign," says Donnelly. "The idea being that Afghanistan was the good war, the more important war, and that Iraq was a dead end strategically."

P. J. Crowley, a senior fellow at the liberal think tank Center for American Progress, calls Obama's focus on Afghanistan "correct" but emphasizes the need for a multipronged effort to stabilize and reform the country's U.S.-backed government. "Returning our weight of effort [to Afghanistan] is a right approach," says Crowley, who was spokesman for the National Security Council under President Bill Clinton.

"More troops may help in a narrow sense," Crowley continues, "but I don't think anyone suggests that more troops are the long-term solution in Afghanistan. The insertion of U.S. forces is logical in the short- to mid-term, but it has to be part of a broader strategy."

But Pollack questions the value of any additional U.S. troops at all. "The problems of Afghanistan are not principally military; they are principally political and diplomatic," he says. "Unless this new national security team can create a military mission that is of value to what is ultimately a diplomatic problem, it's going to be tough to justify to the country the commitment of those additional troops."

Borosage also worries about an increased U.S. military presence in Afghanistan. "A permanent occupation of Afghanistan is a recipe for defeat," he says.

All of the experts stress that U.S. policy in Afghanistan now plays a secondary part in the fight with the al Qaeda terrorist group, which carried out the 9/11 attacks in the United States. "There is no al Qaeda in Afghanistan," says Donnelly. "Al Qaeda has now reconstituted itself in the tribal areas of northwest Pakistan."

Donnelly questions Afghanistan's importance to U.S. interests altogether but ultimately supports continued U.S. involvement. "The only thing worse than being engaged in Afghanistan," he says, "is turning our backs on it."

Name, Age, Department	Date of Nomination	Date of Confirmation	Previous Positions
Ray LaHood, 63, Transportation	Dec. 19	Jan. 22	Illinois U.S. representative (1995-2009); state representative (1982-83)
Steven Chu, 60, Energy	Dec. 15	Jan. 20	Director, Lawrence Berkeley National Laboratory, Dept. of Energy (2004-09); professor, UC-Berkeley (2004-present); Nobel Prize winner, physics (1997)
Arne Duncan, 44, Education	Dec. 16	Jan. 20	C.E.O, Chicago Public Schools (2001-09)
Eric Shinseki, 66, Veterans Affairs	Dec. 7	Jan. 20	Chief of staff, Army (1999-2003)
Janet Napolitano, 51, Homeland Security	Dec. 1	Jan. 20	Arizona governor (2003-09); attorney general (1999-2002)
Rahm Emmanuel, 49, Chief of Staff	Nov. 6	NA	Illinois U.S. representative (2003-09); senior adviser to the president (1993-98)
Lisa Jackson, 46, Environmental Protection Agency	Dec. 15	Jan. 22	Chief of staff, governor of New Jersey (2008-09); commissioner, New Jersey Dept. of Environmental Protection (2006-2008)
Peter Orszag, 40, Office of Management and Budget	Nov. 25	Jan. 20	Director, Congressional Budget Office (2007-08); adviser, National Economic Council (1997-98)
Susan Rice, 44, Ambassador to the United Nations	Dec. 1	Jan. 22	Assistant secretary, State (1997-2001); National Security Council (1993-97)
Ron Kirk, 54, Trade Representative	Dec. 19		Mayor of Dallas (1995-2002)

Department heads are listed in order of succession under Presidential Succession Act; nondepartment heads were given Cabinet-level status.

* Gates was confirmed when first nominated by President George W. Bush and did not have to be re-confirmed.

Compiled by Vyomika Jairam; all photos by Getty Images

Bleak Economy Getting Bleaker

Economists widely agree a stimulus plan is needed.

When Barack Obama took office on Jan. 20, he inherited the most battered U.S. economy since World War II — and one of the shakiest to confront a new president in American history.

And the view from the Oval Office is likely to get bleaker before the gloom begins to lift.

"There are very serious questions on the financial side and apprehension among many parties that there may be more bad news to come," says Kent Hughes, director of the Program on Science, Technology, America and the Global Economy at the Woodrow Wilson Center for Scholars.

Already, Obama has stepped into the worst unemployment picture in 16 years, with the jobless rate at 7.2 percent and 11.1 million people out of work. The economy lost 1.9 million jobs during the last four months of 2008 — 524,000 in December alone.[1]

Economists worry that rising unemployment in manufacturing, construction, retailing and other sectors foreshadows an even more dismal future, at the very least in the short term. Dean Baker, co-director for the Center for Economic and Policy Research, a liberal think tank in Washington, says he expects another million or so jobs to disappear through February, then the pace of job loss to slow if Congress acts to stimulate the economy.

Obama must figure out not only how to get people back to work but also how to restore their confidence in the economy. A punishing credit crisis and cascade of grim news from Wall Street has led consumers to stop spending on everything from restaurant meals to houses and autos.[2]

Home sales have plunged in recent months, foreclosures are hitting record levels and a study by PMI Mortgage Insurance Co. estimates that half of the nation's 50-largest Metropolitan Statistical Areas have an "elevated or high probability" of experiencing lower home prices by the end of the third quarter of 2010 compared to the same quarter of 2008.[3]

Retail sales, a key indicator of consumer confidence, fell in December 2008 for the sixth month in a row, according to the Commerce Department.[4] The International Council of Shopping Centers said chain-store sales in December posted their biggest year-to-year decline since researchers began tracking figures in 1970.[5]

Rebecca Blank, a senior fellow at the Brookings Institution and former member of President Bill Clinton's Council of Economic Advisers, says the unemployment numbers "suggest the economy is still on the way down," and the decline in holiday sales is "surely going to lead to some bankruptcies and belt tightening in the retail sector."

Indeed, such trouble is already occurring. The shopping centers group estimated that 148,000 retail stores closed last year and that more than 73,000 will be shuttered in the first half of 2009.[6] Among the latest examples: Bankrupt electronics chain Circuit City said in January that it was closing its remaining 567 stores, putting some 30,000 employees out of work.

To revive the economy, the new administration — most visibly Obama himself — is urging Congress to quickly approve a stimulus package that could approach $900 billion. Much of the money would likely go toward tax cuts and public infrastructure projects, though how, exactly, the government would allocate it remains a matter of intense political debate.

One thing seems certain, though: The cost of a stimulus package, added to the hundreds of billions of dollars already spent to shore up the nation's flagging financial system, will add to the bulging federal deficit.

"The thing you know for sure is that a stimulus is going to add to the debt, which is [now] quite frightening, and it's going to make it worse," says June O'Neill, an economics professor at the City University of New York's Baruch College and a former director of the Congressional Budget Office (CBO) during the Clinton administration.

In January the CBO projected a $1.2 trillion deficit for the fiscal year. A stimulus plan would add even more pressure on Obama to get federal spending under control. "My own economic and budget team projects that, unless we take decisive action, even after our economy pulls out of its slide, trillion-dollar deficits will be a reality for years to come," Obama said.[7]

Still, a wide spectrum of economists — including conservatives who typically look askance at government spending — agree that a stimulus plan is necessary.

Martin Feldstein, a Harvard University economist and former chair of the Council of Economic Advisers in the Reagan administration, told a House committee in January that stopping the economic slide and restoring "sustainable growth" requires fixing the housing crisis and adopting a "fiscal stimulus of reduced taxes and increased government spending."[8]

Feldstein pointed out that past recessions started after the Federal Reserve raised short-term interest rates to fight inflation. Once inflation was under control, the Fed cut rates, which spurred a recovery. But the current recession is different, Feldstein said: It wasn't caused by the Fed tightening up on fiscal policy, and thus rate cuts haven't succeeded in reviving the economy.

"Because of the dysfunctional credit markets and the collapse of housing demand, monetary policy has had no traction in its attempt to lift the economy," he said.

That poses an especially daunting challenge for Obama.

Baker of the Center for Economic and Policy Research says that the current crisis, occurring amid a broad collapse of the financial markets, more closely resembles the Great Depression than any other recession since then.

Most postwar recessions "were the result of the Fed raising rates," says Baker. "That meant we knew how to reverse it. This one, there's not an easy answer to. We're not going to see [another] Great Depression — not double-digit unemployment for a decade." But in terms of the severity of the problem, Baker adds, the Great Depression is the "closest match" to what confronts the new administration.

— Thomas J. Billitteri

The battered economy that confronts President Obama includes record foreclosure rates and plummeting home values. Above, a foreclosed home in Nevada, the state with the nation's highest foreclosure rate.

Getty Images/Ethan Miller

[1] Bureau of Labor Statistics, "Employment Situation Summary," Jan. 9, 2009, www.bls.gov/news.release/empsit.nr0.htm.

[2] For coverage of the economic crisis, see the following CQ Researcher reports: Thomas J. Billitteri, "Financial Bailout," Oct. 24, 2008, pp. 865-888; Kenneth Jost, "Financial Crisis," May 9, 2008, pp. 409-432; Marcia Clemmitt, "Regulating Credit Cards," Oct. 10, 2008, pp. 817-840; and Marcia Clemmitt, "The National Debt," Nov. 14, 2008, pp. 937-960.

[3] News release, "PMI Winter 2009 Risk Index Indicates Broader Risk Spreading Across Nation's Housing Markets," PMI Mortgage Insurance Co., Jan. 14, 2009.

[4] Bob Willis, "U.S. Economy: Retail Sales Decline for a Sixth Month," Bloomberg, Jan. 14, 2009, www.bloomberg.com.

[5] V. Dion Haynes and Howard Schneider, "A Brutal December for Retailers," The Washington Post, Jan. 9, 2009, p. 2D.

[6] Ibid.

[7] Quoted in David Stout and Edmund L. Andrews, "$1.2 Trillion Deficit Forecast as Obama Weighs Options," The New York Times, Jan. 8, 2009, www.nytimes.com/2009/01/08/business/economy/08deficit.html?scp=2&sq=deficit&st=cse.

[8] Martin Feldstein, "The Economic Stimulus and Sustained Economic Growth," statement to the House Democratic Steering and Policy Committee, Jan. 7, 2009, www.nbcr.org/feldstein/EconomicStimulusandEconomicGrowthStatement.pdf.

Is President Obama on the right track in winning support for his programs in Congress?

State Department staffers greet new Secretary of State Hillary Rodham Clinton on her first day of work, Jan. 22, 2009.

AFP/Getty Images/Mark Ralston

As president of Harvard University, Lawrence Summers clashed so often and so sharply with faculty and others that he was forced out after only five years in office. But when Summers went to Capitol Hill as President-elect Obama's designee to be top White House economic adviser, the normally self-assured economist told lawmakers that he and other administration officials plan to be all ears.

"All of us have been instructed that when it comes to Congress, to listen and not just talk," Summers told House Democrats in a Jan. 9 meeting to discuss Obama's economic recovery plan.[4]

Within days after the new Congress was sworn in on Jan. 6, however, lawmakers on both sides of the political aisle were, in fact, taking pot shots at Obama's plan. Republicans were calling for hearings after the plan was unveiled — a move seen as jeopardizing Obama's goal of signing a stimulus bill into law before Congress' mid-February recess. Meanwhile, some Democratic lawmakers were questioning the business tax cuts being considered for the package, calling them examples of what they considered the discredited philosophy of "trickle-down economics."

Despite the criticisms, Obama was upbeat about his relations with Congress in an interview broadcast on ABC's "This Weekend" on Jan. 11. "One of the things that we're trying to set a tone of is that, you know, Congress is a co-equal branch of government," Obama told host George Stephanopoulos. "We're not trying to jam anything down people's throats."

Veteran Congress-watchers in Washington are giving Obama high marks in his dealings with Capitol Hill so far, while also praising Congress for asserting its own constitutional prerogatives.

"Obama is off to a very good start with Congress, and, just as importantly, Congress is off to a good start with him," says Thomas Mann, a senior fellow at the Brookings Institution. "No more [status as a] potted plant for the first branch or an inflated sense of presidential authority by the second, but instead a serious engagement between the players at the opposite ends of Pennsylvania Avenue."

Obama is "in good shape," says Stephen Hess, a senior fellow emeritus at Brookings who began his Washington career as a White House staffer under President Dwight D. Eisenhower in the 1950s. Hess credits Obama in particular with seeking to consult with Republican as well as Democratic lawmakers.

"He was very shrewd after talking with Democrats to talk with Republicans," says Hess, who also teaches at George Washington University. "He has given the opposition the sense that he's open, he's listening. He's reached out to them when he doesn't need them — which of course is the right time to reach out to them."

Norman Ornstein, a resident scholar at the American Enterprise Institute, similarly credits Obama with having gone "further in consulting members of the opposition party than any president I can remember." Writing in the Capitol Hill newspaper *Roll Call*, Ornstein also said Obama is well aware of lawmakers' "issues and sensitivities." For example, Ornstein noted the president-elect's personal apology to Senate Intelligence Committee Chair Dianne Feinstein, D-Calif., for failing to give her advance word in early January of the planned nomination of Leon Panetta to head the Central Intelligence Agency.[5]

The lapse of protocol on the Panetta nomination — which Feinstein later promised to support — may well have been the only avoidable misstep by the Obama team in its dealings with Congress. Criticisms of the economic recovery program as it took shape could hardly have been avoided. And Republican senators natu- rally looked for ways to find fault with some of Obama's Cabinet nominees — such as their criticism of Attorney

Big-Name Policy 'Czars' Head for West Wing

Appointments may signal decline in Cabinet's influence.

President Barack Obama has tapped several high-profile Washington insiders to fill new and existing senior White House positions, indicating the new administration is shifting policy making from the Cabinet to the influential White House West Wing.

The new so-called policy "czars" include former Sen. Tom Daschle, D-S.D., at the Office of Health Reform (he is also Health and Human Services secretary); former assistant Treasury secretary Nancy Killefer, leading efforts to cut government waste as the nation's first chief performance officer; former Environmental Protection Agency Administrator Carol Browner as the new coordinator of energy and climate policy; and former New York City Council member Adolfo Carrion Jr., who is expected to head the Office of Urban Affairs.

"We're going to have so many czars," said Thomas J. Donohue, president of the U.S. Chamber of Commerce. "It's going to be a lot of fun, seeing the czars and the regulators and the czars and the Cabinet secretaries debate."[1]

In another major West Wing appointment, former Treasury secretary and Harvard President Lawrence Summers becomes director of the existing National Economic Council. In the weeks leading up to the inauguration, analysts noted that Summers, and not then-Treasury secretary-designate Timothy Geithner, was leading then-President-elect Obama's efforts to draft a new financial stimulus package.

But Paul Light, an expert on governance at New York University, questions the role the new "czars" will play. "It's a symbolic gesture of the priority assigned to an issue, and I emphasize the word symbolic," he said. "There've been so many czars over the last 50 years, and they've all been failures. Nobody takes them seriously anymore."[2]

— Vyomika Jairam

---

[1] Michael D. Shear and Ceci Connolly, "Obama Assembles Powerful West Wing; Influential Advisers May Compete With Cabinet," *The Washington Post*, Jan. 14, 2009, p. A1.

[2] Laura Meckler " 'Czars' Ascend at White House," *The Wall Street Journal*, Dec. 15, 2005, p. A6.

General-designate Eric Holder for his role in President Clinton's pardon of fugitive financier Marc Rich and Treasury Secretary-designate Timothy Geithner for his late payment of tens of thousands of dollars in federal income taxes.

A prominent, retired GOP congressman, however, says Obama is doing well so far and predicts the economic crisis may give him a longer than usual pass with lawmakers from both parties. "He has the advantage of a honeymoon, and perhaps the second advantage of the economic conditions of the country, which I think will help the Congress to gather around his program," says Bill Frenzel, a guest scholar at the Brookings Institution and a Minnesota congressman for two decades before his retirement in 1991.

"We're talking about both Republicans and Democrats," Frenzel continues. "Democrats are going to want to be independent, and Republicans are going to want to take whacks at him when they can. But I think there is a mood of wanting to help the president when they can for a while."

Ornstein and Hess caution, however, that new presidents cannot expect the honeymoon to last very long. Ornstein writes that Obama's hoped-for supermajority support in Congress "may be doable on stimulus" and "perhaps even on health care." But he says an era of "post-partisan politics" will require "some serious steps" by party leaders and rank-and-file members.

For his part, Hess says Obama may eventually begin to disappoint some within his own party — but not yet. "Democrats will for a while cut him a great deal of slack," Hess explains. "Reason No. 1, he's not George W. Bush. Reason No. 2, they're going to get some of what they want. And reason No. 3, some of those folks have become wiser about the way politics is played in this town."

Background

'A Mutt, Like Me'

Barack Obama's inauguration as president represents a 21st-century version of the American dream: the election of a native-born citizen, both black and white, with roots in Kansas and Kenya. Abandoned by his father and later living apart from his mother, Obama was nurtured in his formative years by doting white grandparents and educated in elite schools before turning to community organizing in inner-city Chicago and then to a political career that moved from the Illinois statehouse to the White House in barely 12 years.[6]

Barack Hussein Obama was born in Honolulu on Aug. 4, 1961, to parents he later described in his memoir *Dreams from My Father* as a "white as vanilla" American mother and a "black as pitch" Kenyan father. Barack Obama Sr. and Stanley Ann Dunham married, more or less secretly, after having met as students at the University of Hawaii. Stanley Ann's "moderately liberal" parents accepted the union. In Kenya — where Barack Sr. already had a wife and child — the family did not. The marriage lasted only two years;

1960s-1970s *Obama born to biracial, binational couple; begins education in Indonesia after mother's remarriage, then returns to Hawaii.*

1961 Barack Hussein Obama born on Aug. 4, 1961, in Honolulu; parents Stanley Ann Dunham and Barack Obama Sr. meet as students at University of Hawaii; father leaves family behind two years later for graduate studies at Harvard, return to native Kenya.

1967-1971 Obama's mother remarries, family moves to Indonesia; Obama attends a secular public elementary school with a predominantly Muslim student body until mother decides he should return to Hawaii for schooling.

1971-1979 "Barry" Obama lives with grandparents Stanley and Madelyn Dunham; graduates with honors from Punahou School, one of three black students at the elite private school; enrolls in Occidental College in Los Angeles but transfers later to Columbia University in New York City.

1980s-1990s *Works as community organizer in Chicago, gets law degree, enters politics.*

1983 Obama graduates with degree in political science from Columbia University; floods civil rights organizations with job applications.

1985-1988 Works on housing, employment issues as community organizer in Far South Side neighborhood in Chicago.

Summer 1988 Visits Kenya for first time.

1988-1991 Enrolls in Harvard Law School in fall 1988; graduates in 1991 after serving as president of *Harvard Law Review* — the first African-American to hold that position.

1992-1995 Returns to Chicago; marries Michelle Robinson in 1992; runs voter registration project; works as lawyer, lecturer at University of Chicago Law School.

1995 *Dreams from My Father* is published; mother dies just after publication (Nov. 7, 1995).

1996 Elected to Illinois legislature as senator representing Chicago's Hyde Park area; serves for eight years.

2000-2006 *Enters national political stage as U.S. senator, Democratic keynoter.*

2000 Loses badly in Democratic primary for U.S. House seat held by Rep. Bobby Rush.

2002 Opposes then-imminent war in Iraq.

2004 Gains Democratic nomination for U.S. Senate from Illinois. . . . Wins wide praise for keynote address to Democratic National Convention. . . . Elected U.S. senator from Illinois: third African-American to serve in Senate since Reconstruction.

2005-2006 Earns reputation as hard worker in Senate; compiles liberal voting record; manages Democrats' initiative on ethics reform. . . . *Audacity of Hope* is published (October 2006). . . . Deflects intense speculation about possible presidential bid.

Barack left his wife and child behind to go to graduate school at Harvard. Stanley Ann filed for divorce, citing standard legal grounds.

His mother's second marriage, to an Indonesian student, Lolo Soetoro, took young Barry, as he was then called, to his Muslim stepfather's native country at the age of 6. Lolo worked as a geologist in post-colonial Indonesia; his mother taught English. They had a child, Obama's half-sister, Maya. (Maya Soetoro-Ng now teaches high school history in Honolulu.) Barry attended a predominantly Muslim school that would be falsely depicted as an Islamist madrassa during the 2008 campaign. His mother, meanwhile, taught her son about the civil rights struggles in America and eventually sent him back to Hawaii for schooling. The marriage ended later, a victim of cultural and personality differences.

2007 *Obama enters presidential race as underdog to New York Sen. Hillary Rodham Clinton; nearly matches Clinton in "money primary" in advance of Iowa caucuses.*

Feb. 10, 2007 Obama announces candidacy for Democratic nomination for president at rally in Springfield, Ill., three weeks after Clinton, former first lady, joined race; Democratic field eventually includes eight candidates.

March-December 2007 Democratic candidates engage in 17 debates, with no knockout punches; Obama closes gap with Clinton in polls, fundraising.

2008 *Obama gains Democratic nomination after drawn-out contest with Clinton; beats Republican Sen. John McCain as economic issues take center stage.*

January-February Obama scores upset in Iowa caucuses (Jan. 3); Clinton wins New Hampshire primary (Jan. 9); field narrows to two candidates by end of January.

March-April Clinton wins big-state primaries, including Ohio (March 4) and Pennsylvania (April 22); Obama edges ahead in delegates.

May-June Obama gains irreversible lead after Indiana, North Carolina primaries (May 6); clinches nomination after final primaries (June 2).

July Obama goes to Iraq, reaffirms 16-month pullout timetable; speaks at big rally in Berlin, Germany.

August Obama picks Delaware Sen. Joseph R. Biden as running mate; accepts nomination with speech promising Iraq withdrawal, domestic initiatives; McCain chooses Alaska Gov. Sarah Palin as running mate.

September-October Obama holds his own in three debates with McCain (Sept. 26, Oct. 7, Oct. 15); McCain challenge to go to Washington to push financial bailout plan ends with advantage to Obama.

Nov. 4 Obama victory is signaled with victories in "red states" in East, Midwest; networks declare him winner as polls close in West (11 p.m., Eastern time).

November-December Obama completes Cabinet selections; works on economic recovery plan; vacations in Hawaii.

2009 *Obama inaugurated before largest crowd in Washington history.*

Jan. 5-19 Obama, in Washington, starts public campaign for economic recovery plan. . . . Congress reconvenes with Democrats holding 256-178 majority in House with one vacancy, 57-41 majority in Senate with two seats vacant. . . . More high-level nominations; Commerce post in limbo after Bill Richardson withdraws because of ethics investigation in New Mexico.

Jan. 20 Obama is inaugurated as 44th president; uses inaugural address to detail "serious" challenges at home, abroad; promises that challenges "will be met." . . . President moves quickly over next week to reverse some Bush administration policies; lobbies Congress on economic stimulus package, but Republicans continue to push for less spending, more tax cuts.

Barry returned to live with grandparents Stanley and Madelyn Dunham — "Gramps" and "Toot" (her nickname came from the Hawaiian word for grandmother). They provided him the stable, supportive home life that he had somewhat lacked so far. He gained admission to the prestigious Punahou School as one of only three black students. His father visited once — Barack's only time spent with him after the divorce — and spoke to one of his son's classes about life in Africa. Obama's mother came back to Hawaii for studies in anthropology, but when she returned to Indonesia for field work Barack chose to stay in Hawaii.

Myriad Global Problems Confront Obama

Two wars, the Middle East and terrorism top the list.

President Barack Obama faces immense foreign-policy challenges — two wars and a turbulent global scene that includes continuing conflict in the Middle East — all against the backdrop of a global economic crisis.

Tens of thousands of U.S. troops are at war in Iraq and Afghanistan. Israel, America's closest Mideast ally, has just suspended a devastating military offensive in the Gaza Strip that could restart at any time. And Islamist terrorism remains a constant threat, with al Qaeda leader Osama bin Laden still at large.[1]

Obama divided his early days in office between wartime matters, the latest Mideast crisis and the economic meltdown. By all indications, he will be walking a tightrope between domestic and international affairs for the foreseeable future.

"A president in these circumstances is going to want to do everything possible to ensure that the transformative and ambitious and very difficult projects of domestic policy that have been designated as the priority for this new administration are not inhibited or disrupted by early failures, in counterterrorism or foreign policy," Steve Coll, president and CEO of the New America Foundation, a nonpartisan think tank, told a pre-inauguration conference on security issues.

Obama's inaugural address restated his commitment to withdraw U.S. forces from Iraq, which is more peaceful after more than five years of war but still violent and torn by political intrigue.[2]

In Afghanistan, however, escalating warfare is tied to another source of U.S. worries: Pakistan. Concern escalated in late November following coordinated terrorist attacks on hotels and other sites in Mumbai — India's financial and cultural capital — which were traced to a jihadist group in Pakistan with deep ties to that country's intelligence agency.[3] Some 175 people were killed and 200 wounded.

The group, Lashkar-e-Taiba, also has at least some operational link to al Qaeda and bin Laden, who is believed to be hiding in Pakistan's northern tribal region, bordering Afghanistan. Another al Qaeda ally, the Taliban guerrillas who are fighting the Afghan government and U.S. and NATO troops in Afghanistan, use Pakistan as a headquarters.[4]

"Moreover," a government commission on weapons of mass destruction and terrorism said in December, "given Pakistan's tense relationship with India, its buildup of nuclear weapons is exacerbating the prospect of a dangerous nuclear arms race in South Asia that could lead to a nuclear conflict."[5]

The other daunting foreign-policy issue facing the new Obama administration — conflict between Israel and the Palestinians — offers slender prospects for peace. "Two states living side by side in peace and security — right now that stands about as much chance as Bozo the Clown becoming president of the United States," says Aaron David Miller, a former Mideast peace adviser to six secretaries of State.

The biggest obstacle, Miller says, is the "broken and dysfunctional" state of the Palestinian national movement. Fatah, the secular party that runs the West Bank, has a negotiating relationship with Israel. Hamas, the elected Islamist party and militia that initially seized power in an anti-Fatah coup in Gaza in 2007, deems Israel illegitimate. Hamas sponsored or tolerated rocket fire into Israel from Gaza but halted rocketing at the beginning of a cease-fire that began in June 2008. But Israel accused Hamas of building up its arsenal and retaliated by limiting the flow of goods into the region. In December, Hamas announced it wouldn't renew the already shaky truce, blaming the Israeli embargo and military moves. From then on, Hamas stepped up rocketing.

Israel's recent 22-day anti-Hamas offensive in Gaza cost some 1,300 Palestinian lives. The Palestinians estimated the civilian death toll at 40 percent to 70 percent of the fatalities; Israel put the toll at about 25 percent of the total. Israeli fatalities totaled 13, including three civilians.[6]

The scale of Israel's Gaza offensive is renewing calls for the U.S. government to change its relationship to Israel. "The days of America's exclusive ties to Israel may be coming to an end," Miller wrote in *Newsweek* in January. Obama, however, reaffirmed his support for Israel in his Jan. 26 interview with the Arabic-language network Al Arabiya.[7]

Those interests also would require devising a response to what the United States believes is a nuclear arms development project by Iran, which supports Hamas politically and financially — a sign, for some, of how all Middle Eastern issues are interconnected.

(Continued)

(Continued)

Palestinians in Gaza search the rubble of their homes for usable items after an Israeli air strike on Jan. 5, 2009.

Getty Images

"One of the great mistakes we have made has been to believe we can compartmentalize these different policies, that we can somehow separate what is happening between Israel and the Palestinians from what's happening in Iraq and what's happening in Iran and what's happening in Egypt and Saudi Arabia and everywhere else in the Middle East," said Kenneth M. Pollack, a senior fellow at the Brookings Institution and former CIA analyst of the region. "Linkage is a reality."[8]

Another set of connections ties past U.S. support for NATO membership by Ukraine and Georgia to chilled U.S. relations with Russia, which views the potential presence of Western military allies — and U.S. missiles — on its borders as hostile.

Despite the Cold War echoes of that dispute, some foreign-affairs experts argue that Obama actually confronts a less perilous international panorama than some of his recent predecessors. "We don't have the Cold War and World War II," says Michael Mandelbaum, director of the foreign policy program at Johns Hopkins University's School of Advanced International Studies. "Those were existential threats. What the incoming president faces are annoying and troublesome, but not existential threats."

That picture could change if jihadist radicals took over nuclear-armed Pakistan. For now, Mandelbaum argues the biggest international and domestic dangers are one and the same — the economic meltdown.

But success for the huge spending package that Obama wants will require participation by China, America's major creditor. "China has been lending us money by buying our bonds," Mandelbaum says. "That huge stimulus package is not going to work unless we get some cooperation from the Chinese."

In short, the American way of life very much depends on China, Mandelbaum says: "For what Americans care about, for what matters in the world, the issue of where and how we borrow money for the stimulus and where and how we rebalance the economy dwarfs Gaza in importance, and is more important than Iraq and Afghanistan."

— Peter Katel

[1] For coverage of the Iraq and Afghanistan wars, the Middle East and Islamic fundamentalism, see the following *CQ Researcher* reports: Peter Katel, "Cost of the Iraq War," April 25, 2008, pp. 361-384; Peter Katel, "New Strategy in Iraq," Feb. 23, 2007, pp. 169-192; and Peter Katel, "Middle East Tension," Oct. 27, 2006, pp. 889-912. Also see the following *CQ Global Researcher* reports: Roland Flamini, "Afghanistan on the Brink," June 2007, pp. 125-150; Robert Kiener, "Crisis in Pakistan," December 2008, pp. 321-348; and Sarah Glazer, "Radical Islam in Europe," November 2007, pp. 265-294.

[2] Alissa J. Rubin, "Iraq Unsettled by Political Power Plays," *The New York Times*, Dec. 25, 2008, www.nytimes.com/2008/12/26/world/middleeast/26baghdad.html; and Alissa J. Rubin, "Bombs Kill 5 in Baghdad, but Officials Avoid Harm," *The New York Times*, Jan. 20, 2009, www.nytimes.com/2009/01/21/world/middleeast/21iraq.html.

[3] Jane Perlez and Somini Sengupta, "Mumbai Attack is Test for Pakistan on Curbing Militants," *The New York Times*, Dec. 3, 2008, www.nytimes.com/2008/12/04/world/asia/04pstan.html?scp=5&sq=MumbaiLashkarISI&st=cse.

[4] For a summary and analysis, see K. Alan Kronstadt and Kenneth Katzman, "Islamist Militancy in the Pakistan-Afghanistan Border Region and U.S. Policy," Congressional Research Service, Nov. 21, 2008, http://fpc.state.gov/documents/organization/113202.pdf.

[5] See "World at Risk," Commission on the Prevention of Weapons of Mass Destruction Proliferation and Terrorism, December 2008, p. xxiii.

[6] See Steven Erlanger, "Weighing Crimes and Ethics in the Fog of Urban Warfare," *The New York Times*, Jan. 16, 2009, www.nytimes.com/2009/01/17/world/middleeast/17israel.html?scp=1&sq=Gazaciviliandeathpercent&st=cse; Amy Teibel, "Last Israeli troops leave Gaza, completing pullout," The Associated Press, Jan. 21, 2009, http://news.yahoo.com/s/ap/ml_israel_palestinians.

[7] Aaron David Miller, "If Obama Is Serious, He should get tough with Israel," *Newsweek*, Jan. 3, 2009, www.newsweek.com/id/177716.

[8] Quoted in Adam Graham-Silverman, "Conflict in Gaza Strip Presents Immediate Challenge for New President," *CQ Today*, Jan. 20, 2009.

At Punahou, Obama excelled as a student and played with the state championship basketball team his senior year. He graduated in 1979 and enrolled at Occidental College in Los Angeles. Two years later, he transferred to Columbia University in New York. By now, Obama was well aware of racial issues in the United States — and his ambiguous place in the story. "I learned to slip back and forth between my black and white worlds," he wrote in *Dreams from My Father.* More recently, as president-elect, Obama referred self-deprecatingly to his background. In describing the kind of puppy he would have preferred to get for his two young daughters, but for Malia's allergies, Obama said, "A mutt, like me."

Barack Obama's riveting, highly personal keynote address at the 2004 Democratic National Convention made him an overnight star and presidential contender.

AFP/Getty Images/Timothy A. Clary

Graduating from Columbia in 1983 with a degree in political science, Obama decided to take on the so-called Reagan revolution by becoming a community organizer — aiming, as he wrote, to bring about "change . . . from a mobilized grass roots." Obama flooded civil rights organizations to no avail until he was hired in 1985 by Gerald Kellman, a white organizer looking for an African-American to help with community development and mobilization in a Far South Side section of Chicago. Obama's three years in Chicago brought him face to face with the gritty realities of urban life and the disillusionment of the disadvantaged. He later described the time as "the best education I ever had."[7]

Obama enrolled in Harvard Law School in 1988.[8] He wrote nothing about the decision in his memoir and has said little about it elsewhere. Before going, he visited Kenya, where his father had died in an automobile accident six years earlier. Obama described enjoying the meeting with his extended family while acutely conscious of the cultural gap. At Harvard, he excelled as a student, played pick-up basketball and had only a limited social life after meeting his future wife, Michelle Robinson, a lawyer he had met while working for a Chicago law firm as a summer associate. His election in 1990 as president of the *Harvard Law Review* — as a compromise between conservative and liberal factions — marked the first time an African-American had held the prestigious position.

His barrier-breaking gained enough attention to get Obama an invitation from a literary agent, Jane Dystel, to write a book.[9] Obama planned to write about race relations, but in the three years of writing it turned into more of a personal memoir. Obama has said he was unmindful of political consequences in the writing and that he rejected a suggestion from one of his editors to delete references to drug use while in college. The book garnered respectable reviews — and the audio version won a Grammy — but no more than middling sales. Obama's mother read page proofs and lived just long enough to see it published. She died of ovarian cancer in November 1995.[10]

Red, Blue and Purple

Obama needed only 10 years to rise from the back benches of the Illinois legislature to a front seat on the national political stage. His political ambition misled him only once:

in a failed run for the U.S. House. But he succeeded in other endeavors on the strength of hard work, personal intelligence, political acumen and earnest efforts to bridge the differences of race, class and partisan affiliation.

Obama entered politics in 1995 as the chosen successor of a one-term state senator, Alice Palmer. But he turned on his mentor when she sought re-election after all, following a losing bid in a special election for a U.S. House seat. Obama successfully challenged signatures on Palmer's nominating petitions and had her disqualified (and the other candidates too) to win the Democratic nomination unopposed and eventual election.

As a Democrat in a Republican-controlled legislature and a liberal with no connection to his party's organization, Obama worked to develop personal ties — some formed in a weekly poker game. Among his accomplishments: ethics legislation, a state earned-income tax credit and a measure, backed by law enforcement, to require videotaped interrogations in all capital cases.[11]

After four years in office, Obama decided in 2000 to mount a primary challenge to the popular and much better known Democratic congressman, Bobby Rush. The race was foolhardy from the outset. But — as Obama recounts in his second book, *The Audacity of Hope* — he suffered a grave embarrassment when he failed to return from a family vacation in Hawaii in time to vote on a major gun control bill in a specially called legislative session. Rush won handily.[12] In the 2008 presidential campaign, Obama's absence on the gun control vote was cited along with many other instances when he voted "present" as evidence of risk-averse gamesmanship on his part — a depiction vigorously disputed by the campaign.

His ambition unquenched, Obama began deciding by fall 2002 to run for the U.S. Senate seat then held by Republican Peter Fitzgerald, a vulnerable incumbent who eventually decided not to seek re-election. In October, at the invitation of a peace activist group, he delivered to an anti-war rally in Chicago his now famous speech opposing the then-imminent U.S. war in Iraq. Obama formally entered the Senate race in 2003 as the underdog to multimillionaire Blair Hull and state Comptroller Dan Hynes. But Hull's candidacy collapsed after allegations of abuse against his ex-wife. Hynes ran a lackluster campaign, while Obama waged a determined, disciplined drive that netted him nearly 53 percent of the vote in a seven-way race.[13]

Obama's debut on the national stage came in July 2004 after the presumptive Democratic presidential nominee, Massachusetts Sen. John Kerry, picked him to deliver the keynote address at the party's convention. Obama drafted the speech himself, according to biographer David Mendell. The night before, he told a friend, "My speech is pretty good." It was better than that. Obama wove his personal story together with verbal images of working-class America to lead up to the passage — rebroadcast thousands of times since — envisioning a unified nation instead of the "pundits' " image of monochromatic "Red States" and "Blue States." The speech "electrified the convention hall," *The Washington Post* reported the next day, and made Obama a rising star to be watched.[14]

By the time of the speech, political fortune had already shone on Obama back in Illinois. Divorce files of his Republican opponent in the Senate race, Jack Ryan, made public in June, showed that Ryan had pressured his wife to go with him to sex clubs and have sex in front of others. Ryan, a multimillionaire businessman, resisted pressure to withdraw for more than a month. Once Ryan bowed out — three days after Obama's speech — GOP leaders had to scramble for an opponent. They eventually lured Alan

Keyes, a conservative African-American from Maryland, to be the sacrificial lamb in the race. Obama won with a record-setting 70 percent of the vote to take his seat in January 2005 as only the third African-American to serve in the U.S. Senate since Reconstruction.

Obama entered the Senate with the presidency on his mind but also the recognition that he must succeed first in a club with low tolerance for celebrity without substance. A profile in Congressional Quarterly's *Politics in America* published with his presidential campaign under way in 2007 credited Obama with "a reputation as a hard worker, a good listener and a quick study."[15]

With Democrats in the majority, Obama was designated in 2007 to spearhead the party's work on ethics reform — a role that prompted an icy exchange with his future opponent, Sen. McCain, who had expected to work with Democrats on a bipartisan approach. The eventual package included a ban on senators' discounted trips on corporate jets, but not — as Obama had pushed for — outside enforcement of ethics rules.

Obama had more success working with other Republicans, including Oklahoma's Tom Coburn (Internet access to government databases) and Indiana's Richard Lugar (international destruction of conventional weapons). Overall, however, his voting record was solidly liberal and reliably party-line. In the 2008 race, the McCain campaign repeatedly tried to debunk Obama's image of post-partisanship by challenging him to cite a significant example of departing from Democratic Party positions.

'Yes, We Can'

Obama won the Democratic nomination for president in a come-from-behind victory over frontrunner Hillary Clinton on the strength of fundraising prowess, message control and a pre-convention strategy focused on amassing delegates in caucus as well as primary states. He took an even bigger financial advantage into the general election but pulled away from McCain only after the nation's dire economic news in October drove the undecideds decisively toward the candidate promising "change we can believe in."[16]

Despite intense speculation and Obama's evident interest, he decided to run only after heart-to-heart talks with Michelle while vacationing in Hawaii in December 2006. Michelle's reluctance stemmed from the effects on the family and fear for Obama's personal safety. In the end, she agreed — with one stipulation: Obama had to give up smoking. That promise remains a work in progress. In his post-election appearance on NBC's "Meet the Press" on Dec. 7, Obama promised only that, "you will not see any violations" of the White House's no-smoking rule while he is president.

Obama entered the race with a speech to an outdoor rally on a cold Feb. 10, 2007, in Springfield, Ill. After acknowledging the "audacity" of his campaign, Obama laid out a platform of reshaping the economy, tackling the health-care crisis and ending the war in Iraq. He started well behind Clinton in the polls and in organization. In the early debates — with eight candidates in all — Obama himself rated his performance as "uneven," according to *Newsweek*'s post-election account.[17] By December, however, Obama had pulled ahead of Clinton in some New Hampshire polling and was in a virtual dead-heat in the all-important "money primary."

The Iowa caucuses on Jan. 3, 2007, gave Obama an unexpected win with about 38 percent of the vote and left only two other viable candidates standing: former North

Daschle Appointment Shows Commitment to Health-Care Reforms

But a vote on a specific plan may be delayed until next year.

"The flaws in our health system are pervasive and corrosive. They threaten our health and economic security," said former Sen. Tom Daschle, D-S.D., President Obama's nominee for secretary of Health and Human Services (HHS), at his initial confirmation hearing before the Senate Health, Education, Labor, and Pensions (HELP) Committee on Jan. 8.[1]

Throughout his campaign, Obama promised to make good-quality health care accessible to all Americans. Many observers see his choice of Daschle — who recently coauthored a book laying out a plan for universal insurance coverage — to lead both HHS and a new White House Office of Health Policy as a sign of the new president's commitment to health-care reform, which he has called the key to economic security.[2] "I talk to hardworking Americans every day who worry about paying their medical bills and getting and keeping health insurance for their families," Obama said.[3]

In the final presidential debate on Oct. 15, 2008, Obama laid out the essence of his health overhaul. "If you've got health insurance through your employer, you can keep your health insurance," he said. "If you don't have health insurance, then what we're going to do is to provide you the option of buying into the same kind of federal pool [of private insurance plans] that [Republican presidential nominee] Sen. McCain and I enjoy as federal employees, which will give you high-quality care, choice of doctors at lower costs, because so many people are part of this insured group," Obama said.[4]

In addition, Obama's plan would:

- require insurance companies to accept all applicants, including those with already diagnosed illnesses — or "preexisting conditions" — that insurers often decline to cover;
- create a federally regulated national "health insurance exchange" where people could buy coverage from a range of approved private insurers and possibly from a public insurance program as well;
- provide subsidies to help lower-income people buy coverage;
- require all children to have health insurance; and
- require employers except small businesses to either provide "meaningful" coverage to workers or pay a percentage of payroll toward the costs of a public plan.[5]

Points of potential controversy include whether all Americans should be required to buy health coverage.

During the presidential primary campaign, Obama sparred with fellow Democratic candidate Sen. Hillary Rodham Clinton, D-N.Y., who called for a mandate on individuals to buy insurance. Obama disagreed, saying, "my belief is that if we make it affordable, if we provide subsidies to those who can't afford it, they will buy it," and that only children's coverage should be required.[6]

But many analysts, including Daschle, point out that unless coverage is required many people will buy it only after they become sick, making it impossible for health insurance to perform its main task — spreading the costs of care among as many people as possible, not just among those who happen to be sick at a given time.

"The only way we can achieve universal coverage is to require everybody to either purchase private insurance or enroll in a public program," Daschle wrote.[7]

If Obama ends up authorizing a new government-run insurance plan to compete with private insurers for enrollees, as most Democrats favor, the plan could face tough opposition from Republicans.

"Forcing private plans to compete with federal programs, with their price controls and ability to shift costs to taxpayers, will inevitably doom true competition and could ultimately lead to a single-payer, government-run health-care program," said Sen. Michael Enzi, R-Wyo., the top Republican on the HELP Committee. "Any new insurance coverage must be delivered through private health-insurance plans."[8]

Congressional Democrats stand ready to work with the Obama administration to move health-care reform quickly. Two very influential senators, HELP Committee Chairman Sen. Edward Kennedy, D-Mass., and Finance Committee Chairman Sen. Max Baucus, D-Mont., were already crafting health-reform legislation last year and are expected to begin a strong push for legislation soon. But the press of other business and the time-consuming process of gathering support for a specific plan will put off a vote until the end of this year or the beginning of 2010, predicted Rep. Pete Stark, D-Calif., chairman of the House Ways and Means Health Subcommittee. "I don't think we'll do it in the first 100 days," said Stark.[9]

Ironically, the struggling economy, which leaves many more Americans worried about their jobs and therefore their health coverage, may have opened the door for reform by giving business owners, doctors and others a greater stake in getting more people covered, said Henry Aaron, a senior fellow in economic studies at the centrist Brookings Institution. "Before the economic collapse . . . the odds of national reform were nil," but the nation's economic stress makes it somewhat more likely, especially since Congress has been spending large amounts of money on other industries, Aaron said.[10]

Nevertheless, Aaron and some other analysts say the climate for health-care reform may not be much different from that in 1993 when the tide quickly turned against the Clinton administration's attempt at providing universal health care.

The times are "similar," and despite the desire of many for reform, the details will be painful and will spark push-back, Stuart Butler, vice president of the conservative Heritage Foundation, told PBS' "NewsHour." "When you say, 'We've got to make the system efficient by reducing unnecessary costs' . . . that means people's jobs and . . . doctors are going to rebel against that."[11]

— Marcia Clemmitt

---

[1] Quoted in "Daschle: Health Care Flaws Threaten Economic Security," CNNPolitics.com, Jan. 8, 2009, www.cnn.com/2009/POLITICS/01/08/daschle.confirmation.

[2] For background see the following CQ Researcher reports by Marcia Clemmitt: "Universal Coverage," March 30, 2007, pp. 265-288, and "Rising Health Costs," April 7, 2006, pp. 289-312.

[3] Barack Obama, "Modern Health Care for All Americans," The New England Journal of Medicine, Oct. 9, 2008, p. 1537.

[4] Quoted in "In Weak Economy, Obama May Face Obstacles to Health Care Reform," PBS "NewsHour," Nov. 20, 2008, www.pbs.org.

[5] "2008 Presidential Candidate Health Care Proposals: Side-by-Side Summary," health08.org, Kaiser Family Foundation, www.health08.org.

[6] Quoted in Jacob Goldstein, "Clinton and Obama Spar Over Insurance Mandates," The Wall Street Journal Health Blog, Feb. 1, 2008, http://blogs.wsj.com.

[7] Quoted in Teddy Davis, "Obama and Daschle at Odds on Individual Mandates," ABC News blogs, Dec. 11, 2008, http://blogs.abcnews.com.

[8] "Enzi Asks Obama Health Cabinet Nominee Daschle Not to Doom Health-Care Competition," press statement, office of Sen. Mike Enzi, Jan. 8, 2009, http://enzi.senate.gov.

[9] Quoted in Jeffrey Young, "Rep. Stark: No Health Reform Vote in Early '09," The Hill, Dec. 17, 2008, http://thehill.com.

[10] Quoted in Ben Weyl, "Experts Predict a Health Overhaul Despite Troubled Economy," CQ Healthbeat, Dec. 9, 2008.

[11] "In Weak Economy, Obama May Face Obstacles to Health Care Reform," op. cit.

Carolina Sen. John Edwards, who came in second; and Clinton, who finished a disappointing third. Five days later, however, Clinton regained her stride with a 3-percentage point victory over Obama in the first-in-the-nation New Hampshire primary. Edwards' third-place finish kept him in the race, but he dropped out on Jan. 30 after finishing third in primaries in Florida and his birth state of South Carolina.

The one-on-one between Obama and Clinton continued through May. Clinton bested Obama in a series of supposedly "critical" late-season primaries — notably, Ohio and Pennsylvania — even as Obama pulled ahead in delegates thanks to caucus state victories and also-ran proportional-representation winnings from the primaries. He turned the most serious threat to his campaign — his relationship with the sometimes fiery black minister, Jeremiah Wright — into a plus of sorts with a stirring speech on racial justice delivered in Philadelphia on March 18. With Clinton's "electability" arguments unavailing, Obama mathematically clinched the nomination on June 3 as the two split final primaries in Montana and South Dakota. Clinton withdrew four days later, promising to work hard for Obama's election.

With nearly three months before the convention, Obama went to Iraq and Europe to burnish his national security and foreign policy credentials. His 16-month timetable for withdrawal now essentially matched the Iraqi government's own position — weakening a Republican line of attack. An address to a huge and adoring crowd in Berlin underscored Obama's promise to raise U.S. standing in the world. The McCain campaign countered with an ad mocking Obama's celebrity status. On the eve of the convention, Obama picked Biden as his running mate. The selection won praise as sound, if safe. The four-day convention in Denver (Aug. 25-28) went off without a hitch. Obama's acceptance speech drew generally high marks, but some criticism for its length and predictable domestic-policy prescriptions.

McCain countered the next day by picking Alaska Gov. Sarah Palin as his running mate. The surprise selection energized the GOP base but raised questions among observers and voters about his judgment. For the rest of the campaign, the McCain camp tried but failed to find an Obama weak spot. Obama had already survived personal attacks about ties to Rev. Wright, indicted Chicago developer Tony Rezko and one-time radical William Ayers. He had also fended off attacks for breaking his pledge to limit campaign spending by taking public funds. Improved ground conditions in Iraq shifted the contest from national security — McCain's strength — to the economy: Democratic turf. Obama held his own in three debates and used his financial advantage — he raised a record $742 million in all — to engage McCain not only in battleground states but also in supposedly safe GOP states.

By Election Day, the outcome was hardly in doubt. Any remaining uncertainty vanished when Virginia, Republican since 1968, went to Obama early in the evening. By 9:30, one blog had declared Obama the winner. The networks waited until the polls closed on the West Coast — 11 p.m. in the East — to declare Obama to be the 44th president of the United States. In Chicago's Grant Park, tens of thousands of supporters chanted "Yes, we can," as Obama strode on stage.

"If there is anyone out there," Obama began, "who still doubts that America is a place where all things are possible; who still wonders if the dream of our founders is alive in our time; who still questions the power of our democracy, tonight is your answer."[18]

A Team of Centrists?

President-elect Obama began the 76 days between election and inauguration by hitting nearly pitch-perfect notes in his dealings with official Washington — including President

Vice President Biden Brings Foreign-Policy Savvy

"I want to be the last guy in the room on every important decision."

The inauguration of Joseph R. Biden Jr. as the 47th vice president of the United States caps a journey almost as improbable as Barack Obama's. During seven terms as a U.S. senator from Delaware, Biden has never lived in Washington, instead commuting daily by train from Wilmington. In 1972, at age 29, he became the sixth-youngest senator ever elected, leading many to believe the White House was in his future.

But after two failed presidential campaigns — in 1988 and in the last election — Biden seemed fated to remain a Senate lifer.

Along the way he rose to become chairman of the Judiciary Committee and gained national prominence while leading the confirmation hearings of Supreme Court nominees Robert Bork and Clarence Thomas. He had also served twice as chairman of the Foreign Relations Committee.

Obama's limited time in the Senate and lack of international experience led to increased speculation that he would select Biden as his running mate to bridge the gap. "[Joe Biden is] a leader who sees clearly the challenges facing America in a changing world, with our security and standing set back by eight years of failed foreign policy," Obama said in introducing Biden as his selection on Aug. 23, 2008.

But the new president has yet to clarify the specific role Biden will play in the new administration. The appointment of Hillary Rodham Clinton as secretary of State all but ensures that Biden, despite his impressive résumé, will not be the point man on foreign policy as initially expected.

Nor does anyone expect him to emulate former Vice President Dick Cheney's muscular role. Upon taking office in 2001, Cheney demanded — and President George W. Bush approved — a mandate to give him access to "every table and every meeting," expressing his voice in "whatever area the vice president feels he wants to be active in," recalls former White House Chief of Staff Joshua B. Bolten.[1]

Cheney's push to expand presidential war-making authority is arguably his most lasting legacy, but he also served as a gatekeeper for Supreme Court nominees, editor of tax proposals and arbiter of budget appeals.

While most vice presidents arrive eager to expand the influence of their position, Biden faces the unusual conundrum of figuring out how to scale it back. "The only value of power is the effect, the efficacy of its use," he told The New York Times. "And all the power Cheney had did not result in effective outcomes." But without any direct constitutional authority in the executive branch, Biden does not want to return to the days when vice presidents were neither seen nor heard. "I don't think the measure is whether or not I accrete the vestiges of power; it matters whether or not the president listens to me."[2]

And although he says he doesn't seek to wield as much influence as Cheney, many don't expect the loquacious Biden to follow Al Gore either, who in 1992 was assigned a defined portfolio by President Bill Clinton to work on environmental and technology matters. "I think his fundamental role is as a trusted counselor," said Obama senior adviser David Axelrod. "I think that when Obama selected him, he selected him to be a counselor and an adviser on a broad range of issues."[3]

And that's exactly how Biden — who at first balked at accepting the position — wants it. "I don't want to have a portfolio," Biden says. "I don't want to be the guy who handles U.S.-Russian relations or the guy who reinvents government."

"I want to be the last guy in the room on every important decision."

"It's irrelevant what the outside world perceives. What is relevant is whether or not I'm value-added," Biden contends. And very few debate his credentials for the position.

"I'm the most experienced vice president since anybody. Anybody ever serve 36 years as a United States senator?" he asks.[4]

(Continued)

(Continued)

Newly sworn in Vice President Joseph R. Biden, his wife, Jill, and son Beau greet crowds during the Inaugural Parade.

Getty Images/Ethan Miller

But in all likelihood Biden's first move to Washington will surely be his last.

At age 66, he says he has no plans to pursue the presidency, or return to the Senate for that matter, in 2016 — the last full year of a possible second term for Obama. That suggests he'll truly serve Obama's ambitions rather than his own.

"This is in all probability, and hopefully, a worthy capstone in my career," he said.

— Darrell Dela Rosa

[1] Barton Gellman and Jo Becker, " 'A Different Understanding With the President,' " The Washington Post, June 24, 2007, blog.washingtonpost .com/cheney/chapters/chapter_1.

[2] Peter Baker, "Biden Outlines Plans to Do More With Less Power," The New York Times, Jan. 14, 2009, www.nytimes.com/ 2009/01/15/us/ politics/15biden.html?_r=1.

[3] Helene Cooper, "For Biden, No Portfolio but the Role of a Counselor," The New York Times, Nov. 25, 2008, www.nytimes.com/ 2008/11/26/us/ politics/26biden.html.

[4] Baker, op. cit.

Bush and members of Congress — and with the public at large. Beginning with his first post-election session with reporters, Obama sounded both somber but hopeful in confronting what he continually referred to as the worst economic crisis in generations. He completed his selection of Cabinet appointees in record time before taking an end-of-December vacation with his family in Hawaii. Some discordant notes were sounded as Inauguration Day neared in January. But on the eve of the inauguration, polls showed Obama entering the Oval Office with unprecedented levels of personal popularity and hopeful support. (*See graph, p. 280.*)

Acknowledging the severity of the economic crisis, Obama started the announcement of Cabinet-level appointments on Nov. 24 by introducing an economic team that included New York Federal Reserve Bank President Timothy Geithner to be secretary of the Treasury. Geithner had been deeply involved in the Fed's moves in the financial bailout. Obama also named Summers, who had served as deputy undersecretary of the Treasury in the Clinton administration, as special White House assistant for economic policy.

A week later, Obama introduced a national security team that included Hillary Clinton as secretary of State and Gates as holdover Pentagon chief. Clinton accepted the post only after weighing the offer against continuing in the Senate with possibly enhanced visibility and influence. In addition, the appointment required former President Clinton to disclose donors to his post-presidential foundation to try to reduce potential conflicts of interest with his wife's new role.

Along with Gates, Obama also introduced Gen. Jones, a retired Marine commandant and former North Atlantic Treaty Organization supreme commander, as his national security adviser. He also said that he would nominate Holder, a former deputy attorney general, for attorney general; Gov. Janet Napolitano of Arizona for secretary of Homeland Security; and Susan E. Rice, a former assistant secretary of State, for ambassador to the United Nations with Cabinet rank. Holder was in line to be the first African-American to head the Justice Department.

Other Cabinet nominations followed in rapid succession: New Mexico Gov. Bill Richardson, like Clinton one of the contenders for the Democratic nomination, for Commerce; Gen. Eric Shinseki, a critic of Iraq War policies, for Veterans Affairs; and former Senate Democratic Leader Tom Daschle of South Dakota, for Health and Human Services and a new White House office as health reform czar.

Obama picked Shaun Donovan, commissioner of New York City's housing department, for Housing and Urban Development; outgoing Illinois Rep. Ray LaHood, a Republican, for Transportation; and Chicago public schools Commissioner Arne Duncan, a reformer with good relations with Chicago teacher unions, for Education. Steven Chu, a Nobel Prize-winning scientist and an advocate of measures to reduce global warming, was picked for Energy. Sen. Kenneth Salazar, a Colorado Democrat with a moderate record on environmental and land use issues, was tapped for Interior. Former Iowa Gov. Tom Vilsack, who had supported Clinton for the nomination, was chosen for Agriculture. And Rep. Hilda Solis, a California Democrat and daughter of a union family, was designated for Labor.

As Obama prepared to leave for Hawaii, some supporters were griping about the moderate cast of his selections. "We just hoped the political diversity would have been stronger," Tim Carpenter, executive director of Progressive Democrats of America, told Politico.com. But official Washington appeared to be giving him top marks. *The Washington Post* described the future Cabinet as dominated by "practical-minded centrists who have straddled big policy debates rather than staking out the strongest pro-reform positions."[19]

Obama arrived in Washington on Jan. 4 to enroll daughters Malia, 10, and Natasha ("Sasha"), 7, in the private Sidwell Friends School and begin two hectic work weeks before a long weekend of pre-inaugural events. By then, problems had begun to arise, including a corruption scandal over the selection of Obama's successor in the Senate; the withdrawal of one of his Cabinet nominees; and questions about several of his nominees for top posts.

The Senate seat controversy stemmed from a federal investigation of Illinois Gov. Rod Blagojevich that included tape-recorded comments by the Democratic chief executive that were widely depicted as attempting to sell the appointment for political contributions or other favors. In charging Blagojevich with corruption, U.S. Attorney Patrick Fitzgerald specifically cleared Obama of any involvement. But Obama had been forced to answer questions on the issue from Hawaii and had lined up with Senate Democratic Leader Harry Reid in promising not to seat any Blagojevich appointee. When Blagojevich went ahead and appointed former state Comptroller Roland Burris, an African-American, Reid initially resisted but eventually bowed to the fait accompli and welcomed Burris to the Senate.

Richardson had withdrawn from the Commerce post on Jan. 3 after citing a federal probe into a possible "pay for play" scandal in New Mexico.

Two other Cabinet nominees faced critical questions as Senate confirmation hearings got under way. Treasury Secretary-designate Geithner was disclosed to have failed to pay Social Security and Medicare taxes for several years and to have paid back taxes and interest only after being audited. Attorney General-designate Holder faced questions about his role in recommending that President Clinton pardon fugitive financier Marc Rich and in submitting a pardon application for members of the radical Puerto Rican independence movement FALN. Both seemed headed toward confirmation, however.

Current Situation

Moving Quickly

Beginning with his first hours in office, President Obama is moving quickly to put his stamp on government policies by fulfilling campaign promises on such issues as government ethics, secrecy and counterterrorism. Along with the flurry of domestic actions, Obama opened initiatives on the diplomatic front by promising an active U.S. role to promote peace in the Middle East and naming high-level special envoys for the Israeli-Palestinian dispute and the strategically important region of South Asia, including Afghanistan and Pakistan.

In the biggest news of his first days in office, Obama on Jan. 22 signed executive orders to close the Guantánamo prison camp within one year and to prohibit the use of "enhanced" interrogation techniques such as waterboarding by CIA agents or any other U.S. personnel. Human rights groups hailed the actions. "Today is the beginning of the end of that sorry chapter in our nation's history," said Elisa Massimino, executive director and CEO of Human Rights First.

Some Republican lawmakers, however, questioned the moves. "How does it make sense," House GOP Whip Eric Cantor asked, "to close down the Guantánamo facility before there is a clear plan to deal with the terrorists inside its walls?"

An earlier directive, signed late in the day on Jan. 20, ordered Defense Secretary Gates to halt for 120 days any of the military commission proceedings against the remaining 245 detainees at Guantánamo. Separately, Obama directed a review of the case against Ali Saleh Kahlah al-Marri, a U.S. resident and the only person designated as an enemy combatant being held in the U.S.

The ethics and information directives signed on Jan. 21 followed Obama's campaign pledges to limit the "revolving door" between government jobs and lobbyist work and to make government more transparent and accountable.

The new ethics rules bar any executive branch appointees from seeking lobbying jobs during Obama's administration. They also ban gifts from lobbyists to anyone in

Should Congress and the president create a commission to investigate the Bush administration's counterterrorism policies?

YES
Frederick A. O. Schwarz Jr.
Chief Counsel, Brennan Center for Justice, New York University School of Law; co-author, Unchecked and Unbalanced: Presidential Power in a Time of Terror *(New Press, 2008)*

Written for *CQ Researcher*, January 2009

In his inaugural address, President Obama rejected "as false the choice between our safety and our ideals." Throughout our history, seeking safety in times of crisis has often made it tempting to ignore the wise restraints that make us free and to rush into actions that do not serve the nation's long-term interests. (The Alien and Sedition Acts at the dawn of the republic and the herding of Japanese citizens into concentration camps early in World War II are among many historic examples.) After 9/11 we again overreacted to crisis, this time by descending into practices including torture, extraordinary rendition, warrantless wiretapping and indefinite detention. Each breached American values and thus made America less safe.

Our new president is taking steps to reject these actions. And some say this is all that is needed because we need to look forward. Others clamor for criminal prosecutions because to hold our heads high wrongdoers should be held to account.

But, to me, neither of these positions is right. Prosecution is not likely to be productive, and could well be unfair. At the same time, failure to learn more about how we went wrong poses two dangers: First, if we blind our eyes to the truth, we increase the risk of repetition when the next crisis comes.

Second, clearly and fairly assessing and reporting what went wrong — and right — in our reactions to 9/11 will honor America's commitment to openness and the rule of law. Committing ourselves to a full exploration is consistent with the ethos the new president articulated on his first day in office: "The way to make government responsible is to hold it accountable. And the way to make government accountable is to make it transparent."

For these two reasons, I have recommended that the president and Congress appoint an independent, nonpartisan commission to investigate national counterterrorism policies. This is the best way to achieve accountability and an understanding of how to design an effective counterterrorism policy that comports with fundamental values.

Shortly after his reelection in 1864, President Abraham Lincoln nicely articulated the necessity of learning from the past without seeking punishment: "Let us study the incidents of [recent history], as philosophy to learn wisdom from, and none of them as wrongs to be revenged."

NO
David B. Rivkin Jr. and Lee A. Casey
Washington attorneys who served in the Justice Department under Presidents Reagan and George H. W. Bush

Written for *CQ Researcher*, January 2009

A special commission would be both unnecessary and harmful. First, multiple congressional inquiries have already aired and analyzed all of the Bush administration's key legal and policy decisions. Indeed, whether through disclosures, leaks, media and/or congressional investigations, both the process and substance of the administration's war-related decisions have been publicized to an unprecedented extent. If any further inquiry into these policies is necessary, the normal congressional and executive branch investigatory tools are always available, including additional hearings.

Second, a special commission would be fundamentally unfair, beginning — as it would — with the proposition that the Bush policies represent systematic wrongdoing. The Bush policies were based upon well-established case law and reasonable legal extrapolation from the available authorities. Simply because the Supreme Court ultimately decided to change the legal landscape does not mean the Bush administration ignored the law; it did not. Moreover, although there have been many problems and certainly some abuses over the past seven years — Abu Ghraib being a case in point — these have been remarkably rare when compared with past armed conflicts and/or counterterrorism campaigns like the one Britain conducted in Northern Ireland.

A commission would also inevitably involve attacks on career officials in the intelligence community and the departments of Justice and Defense, not merely Bush political appointees. When combined with past investigations, the commission's work would inevitably burden, distract and demoralize the nation's intelligence capabilities. The end result would be the extension of a bureaucratic culture that already favors excessive caution and inaction among our key intelligence and law enforcement officials — the very developments, acknowledged by the 9/11 Commission, as contributing mightily to the analytical, legal and policy failures of 9/11.

Finally, a commission would warp our constitutional fabric and harm civil liberties. While many commissions have operated throughout American history, they have not focused on potential prosecutions. Such a private or quasi-governmental commission would not be constrained by the legal and constitutional limits on Congress and the executive branch, thus raising a host of important constitutional questions.

That the commission's supporters — so determined to vindicate the rights of enemy combatant detainees — seem untroubled by these issues is both ironic and terribly sad.

Will Obama's economic stimulus revive the U.S. economy?

YES
Dean Baker
Co-director, Center for Economic and Policy Research

NO
J. D. Foster
Norman B. Ture Senior Fellow in the Economics of Fiscal Policy, The Heritage Foundation

Written for *CQ Researcher*, January 2009

President Obama's stimulus proposal is a very good start toward rescuing the economy. In assessing the plan, it is vitally important to recognize the seriousness of the downturn. The economy lost an average of more than 500,000 jobs a month in the last three months of 2008. In fact, the actual job loss could have been over 600,000 a month due to the way in which the Labor Department counts jobs in new firms that are not in its survey.

The recent announcements of job loss suggest that the rate of job loss may have accelerated even further. It is possible that we are now losing jobs at the rate of 700,000 a month. This is important, because people must understand the urgency of acting as quickly as possible.

With this in mind, the package being debated does a good job of getting money into the economy quickly. According to the projections of the Congressional Budget Office (CBO), 62 percent of the spending in the package will reach the economy before the end of 2010, with most of the rest coming in 2011. This money will be giving the economy a boost when we need it most.

At this point, there is considerable research on the impact of tax cuts, and the evidence suggests that they do not have nearly as much impact on the economy, primarily because a large portion of any tax cut is saved. According to Martin Feldstein, President Reagan's chief economist, just 10 percent of the tax cuts sent out last spring were spent. The rest was saved. Increased savings can be beneficial to household balance sheets, but savings will not boost the economy right now.

There will also be long-term benefits from President Obama's package. For example, the CBO projected we would save more than $90 billion on medical expenses over the next decade by computerizing medical records, which will be financed through the stimulus. In addition, weatherizing homes and offices and modernizing the electrical grid will substantially reduce our future energy use.

The Obama administration projects that this package will generate close to 4 million jobs, and several independent analysts have arrived at similar numbers. This will not bring the economy back to full employment, but it is still a huge improvement over doing nothing.

The cost of this bill sounds large, but it is important to remember that the need is large. If we were to just do nothing, the economy would continue to spiral downward, with the unemployment rate reaching double-digit levels in the near future.

Written for *CQ Researcher*, January 2009

President Barack Obama promises to create 3.5 million new jobs by the end of 2010, and that vow provides a clear measure by which to judge whether his policies work.

U.S. employment stood at about 113 million people in December 2008, so the Obama jobs pledge will be met if 116.5 million people are working by the end of 2010. Reaching this goal will require effective stimulus policies — and the only fiscal policy that can come close to reaching the goal is to cut marginal tax rates.

Obama's target for jobs creation was chosen carefully. Employment peaked at about 115.8 million jobs in November 2007. Obama's jobs pledge at that time was to create 2.5 million jobs, for a total of 116.5 million private sector jobs.

The November 2008 jobs report showed a half-million jobs lost, so his job-creating target rose by a half-million, affirming the 116.5 million target. Then last month's jobs report showed another half-million jobs lost, and the president raised the target again to its current 3.5 million total.

To stimulate the economy, Obama and congressional Democrats have focused on massive new spending programs. However, the federal budget deficit is likely to exceed $2.5 trillion over the next two years even before any stimulus is added. If deficit spending were truly stimulative, the economy would be at risk of overheating by now, not sliding deeper into recession.

Additional deficit spending won't be any more effective than the first $2 trillion, because government spending doesn't create additional demand in the economy. Deficit spending must be financed by borrowing, so while government spending increases demand, government borrowing reduces demand. Worse, since the government's likely to borrow between $3 trillion and $4 trillion over the next two years, the enormous waves of government debt will likely drive interest rates up. That would only prolong the recession and weaken the recovery.

An effective fiscal stimulus would defer the massive 2011 tax hike (higher tax rates on dividends and capital gains are scheduled to kick in), and also cut individual and corporate tax rates further to reduce the impediments to starting new businesses, hiring, working and investing.

To meet his goal, President Obama should junk his ideology and the wasteful spending that goes with it and focus on cutting marginal tax rates. That's the only way to hit his jobs creation target.

the administration. Good-government groups praised the new policies as the strictest ethics rules ever adopted. Fred Wertheimer, president of the open-government group Democracy 21, called them "a major step in setting a new tone and attitude for Washington."

On information policy, Obama superseded a Bush administration directive promising legal support for agencies seeking to resist disclosure of government records under the Freedom of Information Act. Instead, Obama called on all agencies to release information whenever possible. "For a long time now, there's been too much secrecy in this city," Obama said at a swearing-in ceremony for senior White House staff.

Obama also signed an executive order aimed at greater openness for presidential records following the congressionally established five-year waiting period after any president leaves office. The order supersedes a Bush administration directive in 2001 by giving the incumbent president, not a former president, decision-making authority on whether to invoke executive privilege to prevent release of the former president's records.

On foreign policy, Obama on his first full day in office turned to the fragile cease-fire in Gaza by placing calls to four Mideast leaders: Egyptian President Hosni Mubarak, Israeli Prime Minister Ehud Olmert, Jordanian King Abdullah and Palestinian Authority President Mahmoud Abbas. Obama offered U.S. assistance to try to solidify the ceasefire that had been adopted over the Jan. 17-18 weekend by Israel and Hamas, the ruling party in Gaza.

Israel had begun an offensive against Hamas on Dec. 27 in an effort to halt cross-border rocket attacks into Israel by Hamas supporters. During the transition, Obama had limited himself to a brief statement regretting the loss of life on both sides. White House press secretary Robert Gibbs said Obama used the calls from the Oval Office to pledge U.S. support for consolidating the cease-fire by preventing the smuggling of arms into Hamas from neighboring Egypt. He also promised U.S. support for "a major reconstruction effort for Palestinians in Gaza," Gibbs said.

The next day, Obama took a 10-block ride to the State Department for Hillary Clinton's welcome ceremony as secretary following her 94-2 Senate confirmation on Jan. 21. As part of the event, Clinton announced the appointment of special envoys George Mitchell for the Middle East and Richard Holbrooke for Afghanistan and Pakistan.

In his remarks, Obama renewed support for a two-state solution: Israel and a Palestinian state "living side by side in peace and security." He also promised to refocus U.S. attention on what he called the "perilous" situation in Afghanistan, where he said violence had increased dramatically and a "deadly insurgency" had taken root.

Returning to domestic issues, Obama on Jan. 23 signed — as expected — an order to lift the so-called Mexico City policy prohibiting U.S. aid to any nongovernmental organizations abroad that provide abortion counseling or services. The memorandum instructed Secretary of State Clinton to lift what Obama called the "unwarranted" restrictions. The policy was first put in place by President Ronald Reagan in 1984, rescinded by President Clinton in 1993 and then reinstituted by President Bush in 2001.

After the weekend, Obama reversed another of Bush's policies on Jan. 26 by directing Environmental Protection Agency Administrator Lisa Jackson to reconsider the request by the state of California to adopt automobile emission standards stricter than those set under federal law. In a reversal of past practice, the Bush administration EPA had denied California's waiver request in December 2007. On the same day, Obama instructed Transportation Secretary Ray LaHood to tighten fuel efficiency standards for cars and light trucks beginning with 2011 model cars.

Working With Congress

President Obama is pressing Congress for quick action on an economic stimulus plan even as bipartisan support for a proposal remains elusive. Meanwhile, the new administration is struggling to find ways to make the financial bailout approved before Obama took office more effective in aiding distressed homeowners and unfreezing credit markets.

House Democrats moved ahead with an $825-billion stimulus package after the tax and spending elements won approval in separate, party-line votes by the House Ways and Means Committee on Jan. 22 and the House Appropriations Committee the day before. The full House was scheduled to vote on the package on Jan. 28 after deadline for this issue, but approval was assured given the Democrats' 256-178 majority in the chamber.

Obama used his first weekly address as president on Jan. 24 — now not only broadcast on radio but also posted online as video on YouTube and the White House Web site — to depict his American Recovery and Reinvestment Plan as critical to get the country out of an "unprecedented" economic crisis. The plan, he said, would "jump-start job creation as well as long-term economic growth." Without it, he warned, unemployment could reach double digits, economic output could fall $1 trillion short of capacity and many young Americans could be forced to forgo college or job training.

Without mentioning the tax and spending plan's minimum total cost, Obama detailed a long list of infrastructure improvements to be accomplished in energy, health care, education and transportation. He mentioned a $2,500 college tax credit but did not note other items in the $225 billion in tax breaks included in the plan — either his long-advocated $1,000 tax break for working families or the various business tax cuts added as sweeteners for Republicans.

Republicans, however, remained unconvinced. Replying to Obama's address, House Minority Leader John Boehner called the plan "chock-full of government programs and projects, most of which won't provide immediate relief to our ailing economy." On "Meet the Press" the next day, the Ohio lawmaker again called for more by way of tax cuts, criticized the job-creating potential of Obama's plan and warned of opposition from most House Republicans.

Appearing on another of the Sunday talk shows, McCain told "Fox News Sunday" host Chris Wallace, "I am opposed to most of the provisions in the bill. As it stands now, I would not support it."

On a second front, the principal members of Obama's economic team are assuring Congress of major changes to come in the second stage of the $700-billion financial rescue plan approved last fall. During confirmation hearings, Treasury Secretary-designate Geithner promised the Senate Finance Committee on Jan. 21 to expect "much more substantial

RACE, ETHNICITY, GENDER, AND CLASS

action" to address the problem of troubled banks that has chilled both consumer and corporate credit markets since fall 2008.

Geithner's comments on the financial bailout were overshadowed by sharp questions from Republican senators about the nominee's tax problems while working for the International Monetary Fund. For several years, Geithner failed to pay Social Security and Medicare taxes, which the IMF — as an international institution — does not withhold from employees' pay as domestic employers do. Geithner repeatedly apologized for the mistake and pointed to his payment of back taxes plus interest totaling more than $40,000. In the end, the committee voted 18-5 to recommend confirmation; the full Senate followed suit on Jan. 26 in a 60-34 vote.*

On the bailout, Geithner said he would increase the transparency and accountability of the program once he assumed the virtually unfettered responsibility for dispensing the remaining $350 billion. He acknowledged criticisms that so far the program has benefited large financial institutions but done little for small businesses. He also promised to restrict dividends by companies that receive government help.

With many banks still holding billions in troubled assets on their balance sheets, speculation is increasing in Washington and in financial circles about dramatic action by the government. Possible moves include the creation of a government-run "bad bank" to buy distressed assets from financial institutions or even outright nationalization of one or more banks.

"People continue to be surprised by the poor condition of the banks," says Dean Baker, co-director of the Center for Economic and Policy Research, a liberal think tank in Washington. "Whatever plans they may have made a month ago might be seen as inadequate given the severity of the problem of the banking system."

With the stimulus package on the front burner, however, Obama went to Capitol Hill on Jan. 27 for separate meetings to lobby House and Senate Republicans to support the measure. The closed-door session with the full House GOP conference lasted an hour — slightly longer than scheduled, causing the president to be late for the start of the meeting on the other side of the Capitol with Republican senators.

In between meetings, Obama challenged GOP lawmakers to try to minimize partisan differences. "I don't expect 100 percent agreement from my Republican colleagues, but I do hope we can put politics aside," he said.

For their part, House Republican leaders expressed appreciation for the president's visit and his expressed willingness to compromise. But some renewed their opposition to the proposal in its current form. Rep. Tom Price of Georgia, chairman of the conservative House Republican Study Committee, said the proposal "remains rooted in a liberal, big-government ideology."

Obama's meeting with GOP senators came on the same day that the Senate Finance and Appropriations committees were marking up their versions of the stimulus package. The Senate was expected to vote on the proposal over the weekend, giving the two chambers two weeks to iron out their differences if the bill was to reach Obama's desk before the Presidents' Day recess.

---

* Attorney General-designate Holder, Obama's other controversial Cabinet nominee, was expected to be confirmed by the full Senate on Jan. 29 or 30, after deadline for this issue, following the Senate Judiciary Committee's 17-2 vote on Jan. 28 to recommend confirmation.

Outlook

Peril and Promise

One week after taking office, President Obama is getting high marks from experts on the presidency for carefully stage-managing his first policy initiatives while discreetly moving to set realistic expectations for the months ahead.

"He's started out quite impressively," says Fred Greenstein, professor of politics emeritus at Princeton University in New Jersey and the dean of American scholars on the U.S. presidency. "So far, it's been a striking rollout week."

Other experts agree. "The Obama administration has met expectations for the first week," says Meena Bose, chair of the Peter S. Kalikow Center for the Study of the American Presidency at Hofstra University in Hempstead, N.Y. "There's been virtually no drama, which is an indication of how he intends to run his administration."

"The indications are all positive," says Bruce Buchanan, a professor of political science at the University of Texas in Austin and author of several books on the presidency. Like the others, Buchanan says Obama is holding on to popular support while striving either to win over or to neutralize Republicans on Capitol Hill.

The wider world outside Washington, however, is giving Obama no honeymoon in office. The U.S. economy is continuing to lag, while violence and unrest continue to simmer in three global hot spots: Gaza, Iraq and Afghanistan.

On the economy, Obama has initiated a daily briefing from senior adviser Summers in addition to the daily briefing on foreign policy and national security issues. "Frankly," Obama told congressional leaders on Jan. 23, "the news has not been good." The day before, the Commerce Department had reported that new-home construction fell to its slowest pace since reporting on monthly rates began in 1959. On the same day, new claims for unemployment benefits matched the highest level seen in a quarter-century.[20]

Meanwhile, leading U.S. policy makers were giving downbeat assessments of events in Afghanistan and Iraq. In testimony to the Senate Armed Services Committee, Defense chief Gates warned on Jan. 27 to expect "a long and difficult fight" in Afghanistan. A few days earlier, the outgoing U.S. ambassador to Iraq, Ryan Crocker, warned that what he called "a precipitous withdrawal" could jeopardize the country's stability and revive al Qaeda in Iraq. And special envoy Mitchell left Washington for the Mideast on Jan. 26, just as the fragile cease-fire between Hamas and Israel was jeopardized by the death of an Israeli soldier from a roadside bomb and an Israeli air strike in retaliation.

Obama continues to work at the problems with the same kind of message control that served him well in the election. After reaping a full day's worth of mostly favorable news coverage on the Guantánamo issue, the administration began directing laser-like attention to the economy from Jan. 22 on. For example, the repeal of the Bush administration's ban on funding international groups that perform abortions was announced late on Friday, Jan. 23 — a dead zone for news coverage.

On foreign policy, Obama emphasized the Mitchell and Holbrooke appointments by personally going to the State Department for the announcements. And he underscored the inaugural's outreach to Muslims by granting his first formal television interview as president to the Arabic satellite television network Al Arabiya. Obama called for a new partnership with the Muslim world "based on mutual respect and mutual interest." One of his main tasks, he told the Dubai-based network in an interview aired on Jan. 27, is to communicate that "the Americans are not your enemy."[21]

Obama and his senior aides are also signaling to supporters that some of their agenda items will have to wait. In a pre-inauguration interview with *The Washington Post*, for example, he reiterated his support for a labor-backed bill to make it easier to unionize workers but downgraded it to a post-stimulus agenda item. Similarly, press secretary-designate Gibbs repeated Obama's support for repealing the military's "don't ask, don't tell" policy on homosexuals on the transition's Web site on Jan. 13, but the next day expanded on the answer: "Not everything will get done in the beginning," Gibbs said.[22]

Greenstein and Bose view Obama's inaugural address — which many observers faulted for rhetorical flatness — as a conscious, initial step to lower expectations about the pace of the promised "change we can believe in." Greenstein calls it a "get-down-to-work" address. Obama himself again evoked the inaugural's theme of determination in the face of adversity when he spoke to congressional leaders immediately following the address.

"What's happening today is not about me," Obama said at the joint congressional luncheon on Inauguration Day. "It is about the American people. They understand that we have arrived at a moment of great challenge for our nation, a time of peril, but also extraordinary promise."

"President Obama has done everything he can to tamp down this sense that he somehow walks on water," says Bose. "He has done everything he can to show that he is a man of substance.

"We have to recognize that these challenges aren't going to be met overnight and that we have to have confidence that we're going to meet them," she continues. "Now the question is, 'Can he govern? Can he show results?' "

Notes

1. The text and video of the inaugural address are available on the redesigned White House Web site: www.whitehouse.gov. Some crowd reaction from Christopher O'Brien of CQ Press' College Division.

2. Quoted in Clea Benson, "An Economy in Foreclosure," *CQ Weekly*, Jan. 12, 2009.

3. Quoted in Aamer Madhani, "Will Obama Stick to Timetable?" *Chicago Tribune*, Nov. 6, 2008, p. 11.

4. Quoted in Shailagh Murray and Paul Kane, "Democratic Congress Shows It Will Not Bow to Obama," *The Washington Post*, Jan. 11, 2009, p. A5.

5. Norman Ornstein, "First Steps Toward 'Post-Partisanship' Show Promise," *Roll Call*, Jan. 14, 2009.

6. For a compact, continuously updated biography, see Barack Obama, www.biography.com. Background also drawn from Barack Obama, *Dreams from My Father: A Story of Race and Inheritance* (2004 ed.; originally published 1995). See also David Mendell, *Obama: From Promise to Power* (2007).

7. Quoted in Serge Kovaleski, "Obama's Organizing Years: Guiding Others and Finding Himself," *The New York Times*, July 7, 2008, p. A1.

8. Background drawn from Jody Kantor, "In Law School, Obama Found Political Voice," *The New York Times*, Jan. 28, 2007, sec. 1, p. 1.

9. Background drawn from Janny Scott, "The Story of Obama, Written by Obama," *The New York Times*, May 18, 2008, p. A1.

10. For a story on his mother's influence on Obama, see Amanda Ripley, "A Mother's Story," *Time*, April 21, 2008, p. 36.

11. See David Jackson and Ray Long, "Showing his bare knuckles: In first campaign, Obama revealed hard-edged, uncompromising side in eliminating party rivals," *Chicago Tribune*, April 4, 2007, p. 1; Rick Pearson and Ray Long, "Careful steps, looking ahead: After arriving in Springfield, Barack Obama proved cautious, but it was clear to many he had ambitions beyond the state Senate," *ibid.*, May 3, 2007, p. 1.

12. See Barack Obama, *The Audacity of Hope: Thoughts on Reclaiming the American Dream* (2006), pp. 105-107.

13. See David Mendell, "Obama routs Democratic foes; Ryan tops crowded GOP field," *Chicago Tribune*, March 17, 2004, p. 1.

14. For the full text of the 2,165-word speech, see http://obamaspeeches.com/002-Keynote-Address-at-the-2004-Democratic-National-Convention-Obama-Speech.htm. For Mendell's account, see *Obama, op. cit.*, pp. 272-285. Obama's conversation with Martin Nesbitt may have been reported first in David Bernstein, "The Speech," *Chicago Magazine*, July 2007; the anecdote is briefly repeated in Evan Thomas, *"A Long Time Coming": The Inspiring, Combative 2008 Campaign and the Historic Election of Barack Obama* (2009), p. 6. For the Post's account, see David S. Broder, "Democrats Focus on Healing Divisions," July 28, 2004, p. A1.

15. *CQ's Politics in America 2008* (110th Congress), www.cnn.com/video/#/video/world/2007/01/22/vause.obama.school.cnn.

16. Some background from Thomas, *op. cit.*

17. *Ibid.*, p. 9.

18. Many versions of the speech are posted on YouTube, including a posting of CNN's coverage.

19. Carpenter was quoted in Carrie Budoff Brown and Nia-Milaka Henderson, "Cabinet: Middle-of-the-roaders' dream?" *Politico*, Dec. 19, 2008; Alec MacGillis, "For Obama Cabinet, a Team of Moderates," *The Washington Post*, Dec. 20, 2008, p. A1.

20. See Kelly Evans, "Home Construction at Record Slow Pace," *The Wall Street Journal*, Jan. 23, 2009, p. A3.

21. See Paul Schemm, "Obama tells Arabic network US 'is not your enemy,' " The Associated Press, Jan. 27, 2009.

22. Obama quoted in Dan Eggen and Michael D. Shear, "The Effort to Roll Back Bush Policies Continues," *The Washington Post*, Jan. 27, 2009, p. A4; Gibbs quoted in, "Obama aide: Ending 'don't ask, don't tell' must wait," CNN.com, Jan. 15, 2009.

Bibliography

Books by Barack Obama

Dreams from My Father: A Story of Race and Inheritance (Three Rivers Press, 2004; originally published by Times Books, 1995) is a literate, insightful memoir written in the three years after Obama's graduation from Harvard Law School. The three parts chronicle his "origins" from his birth through college, his three years as a community organizer in Chicago and his two-month pre-law school visit to his father's homeland, Kenya.

The Audacity of Hope: Thoughts on Reclaiming the American Dream (Crown, 2006) is a political manifesto written as Obama considered but had not definitively decided on a presidential campaign. The book opens with a critique of the "bitter partisanship" of current politics and an examination of "common values" that could underline "a new political consensus." Later chapters specifically focus on issues of faith and of race. Includes index.

Change We Can Believe In: Barack Obama's Plan to Renew America's Promise (Three Rivers Press, 2008), which includes a foreword by Obama, outlines steps for "reviving our economy," "investing in our prosperity," "rebuilding America's leadership" and "perfecting our union." Also includes texts of seven speeches from his declaration of candidacy on Feb. 7, 2007, to his July 24, 2008, address in Berlin.

Books About Barack Obama

The only objective, full-length biography is *Obama: From Promise to Power* (Amistad/Harper Collins, 2007) by David Mendell, the *Chicago Tribune* political reporter who began covering Obama in his first race for the U.S. Senate. An updated version was published in 2008 under the title *Obama: The Promise of Change*.

Two critical biographies appeared during the 2008 campaign: David Freddoso, *The Case Against Barack Obama: The Unlikely Rise and Unexamined Agenda of the Media's Favorite Candidate* (Regnery, 2008); and Jerome Corsi, *The Obama Nation: Leftist Politics and the Cult of Personality* (Threshold, 2008). Freddoso, a writer with National Review Online, wrote what one reviewer called a "fact-based critique" depicting Obama as "a fake reformer and a real liberal." Corsi, a conservative author and columnist best known for his book *Unfit for Command* attacking Democratic presidential nominee John Kerry in 2004, came under fierce criticism from the Obama campaign and independent observers for undocumented allegations about Obama's background.

Two post-election books chronicle the 2008 campaign. Evan Thomas, *"A Long Time Coming": The Inspiring, Combative 2008 Campaign and the Historic Election of Barack Obama* (Public Affairs, 2009) is the seventh in *Newsweek*'s quadrennial titles documenting presidential campaigns on the basis of reporting by a team of correspondents, with some reporting specifically not for publication until after the election. Chuck Todd and Sheldon Gawiser, *How Barack Obama Won: A State-by-State Guide to the Historic 2008 Presidential Election* (Vintage, 2009) gives an analytical overview of the campaign and election with detailed voting analyses of every state. A third title, *Obama: The Historic Journey*, is due for publication Feb. 16 by *The New York Times* and Callaway; the author is Jill Abramson, the *Times*' managing editor, in collaboration with the newspaper's reporters and editors.

Other books include John K. Wilson, *Barack Obama: The Improbable Quest* (Paradigm, 2008), an admiring analysis of Obama's political views and philosophy by a lawyer who recalls having been a student in Obama's class on racism and the law at the University of Chicago Law School; Paul Street, *Barack Obama and the Future of American Politics* (Paradigm, 2009), a critical depiction of Obama as a "power-conciliating centrist"; and Jabiri Asim, *What Obama Means: For Our Culture, Our Politics, Our Future* (Morrow, 2009) a depiction of Obama as creating a new style of racial politics — less confrontational than in the past but equally committed to social justice and more productive of results.

Articles

Purdum, Todd, "Raising Obama," *Vanity Fair*, March 2008.
The magazine's national editor, formerly a *New York Times* reporter, provided an insightful portrait of Obama midway through the 2008 primary season.

Von Drehle, David, "Person of the Year: Barack Obama: Why History Can't Wait," *Time*, Dec. 29, 2008.
Time's selection of Obama as person of the year includes an in-depth interview of the president-elect by Managing Editor Richard Stengel, Editor-at-large von Drehle and Time Inc. Editor-in-chief John Huey. The full text is at time.com/obamainterview.

On the Web

The Obama administration unveiled a redesigned White House Web site (www.whitehouse.gov) at 12.01 p.m. on Jan. 20, 2009 — even before President-elect Obama took the oath of office. The "Briefing Room" includes presidential announcements as well as a "Blog" sometimes being updated several times a day. "The Agenda" incorporates Obama's campaign positions, subject by subject. The site includes video of the president's speeches, including the inaugural address as well as the weekly presidential address — previously broadcast only on radio.

For More Information

American Enterprise Institute for Public Policy Research, 1150 17th St., N.W., Washington, DC 20036; (202) 862-5800; www.aei.org. Conservative think tank researching issues on government, economics, politics and social welfare.

Campaign for America's Future, 1825 K St., N.W., Suite 400, Washington, DC 20006; (202) 955-5665; www.ourfuture.org. Advocates progressive policies.

Center for American Progress, 1333 H St., N.W., 10th Floor, Washington, DC 20005; (202) 682-1611; www .americanprogress.org. Left-leaning think tank promoting a government that ensures opportunity for all Americans.

Center for Economic and Policy Research, 1611 Connecticut Ave., N.W., Suite 400, Washington, DC 20009; (202) 293-5380; www.cepr.net. Promotes open debate on key economic and social issues.

Center on Budget and Policy Priorities, 820 First St., N.E., Suite 510, Washington, DC 20002; (202) 408-1080; www.cbpp.org. Policy organization working on issues that affect low- and moderate-income families and individuals.

Concord Coalition, 1011 Arlington Blvd., Suite 300, Arlington, VA 22209; (703) 894-6222; www.concordcoalition.org. Nonpartisan, grassroots organization promoting responsible fiscal policy and spending.

Heritage Foundation, 214 Massachusetts Ave., N.E., Washington, DC 20002; (202) 546-4400; www.heritage.org. Conservative think tank promoting policies based on free enterprise, limited government and individual freedom.

Women's Rights
Are Violence and Discrimination Against Women Declining?

Karen Foerstel

She was 17 years old. The blurry video shows her lying in a dusty road, blood streaming down her face, as several men kick and throw rocks at her. At one point she struggles to sit up, but a man kicks her in the face forcing her back to the ground. Another slams a large, concrete block down onto her head. Scores of onlookers cheer as the blood streams from her battered head.[1]

The April 7, 2007, video was taken in the Kurdish area of northern Iraq on a mobile phone. It shows what appear to be several uniformed police officers standing on the edge of the crowd, watching while others film the violent assault on their phones.

The brutal, public murder of Du'a Khalil Aswad reportedly was organized as an "honor killing" by members of her family — and her uncles and a brother allegedly were among those in the mob who beat her to death. Her crime? She offended her community by falling in love with a man outside her religious sect.[2]

According to the United Nations, an estimated 5,000 women and girls are murdered in honor killings each year, but it was only when the video of Aswad's murder was posted on the Internet that the global media took notice.[3]

Such killings don't only happen in remote villages in developing countries. Police in the United Kingdom estimate that up to 17,000 women are subjected to some kind of "honor"-related violence each year, ranging from forced marriages and physical attacks to murder.[4]

But honor killings are only one type of what the international community calls "gender based violence" (GBV). "It is universal," says Taina Bien-Aimé, executive director of the

From *CQ Researcher*,

May 2008.

Iraqi teenager Du'a Khalil Aswad lies mortally wounded after her "honor killing" by a mob in the Kurdish region of Iraq. No one has been prosecuted for the April 2007 murder, even though a cell-phone video of the incident was posted on the Internet. Aswad's male relatives are believed to have arranged her ritualistic execution because she had dated a boy from outside her religious sect. The United Nations estimates that 5,000 women and girls are murdered in honor killings around the globe each year.

AFP/Getty Images

New York-based women's-rights group Equality Now. "There is not one country in the world where violence against women doesn't exist."

Thousands of women are murdered or attacked around the world each day, frequently with impunity. In Guatemala, where an estimated 3,000 women have been killed over the past seven years, most involving some kind of misogynistic violence, only 1 percent of the perpetrators were convicted.[5] In India, the United Nations estimates that five women are burned to death each day by husbands upset that they did not receive sufficient dowries from their brides.[6] In Asia, nearly 163 million females are "missing" from the population — the result of sex-selective abortions, infanticide or neglect.

And since the 1990s some African countries have seen dramatic upsurges in rapes of very young girls by men who believe having sex with a virgin will protect or cure them from HIV-AIDS. After a 70-year-old man allegedly raped a 3-year-old girl in northern Nigeria's commercial hub city of Kano, Deputy Police Chief Suleiman Abba told reporters in January, "Child rape is becoming rampant in Kano." In the last six months of 2007, he said, 54 cases of child rape had been reported. "In some cases the victims are gang-raped."[7]

Epidemics of sexual violence commonly break out in countries torn apart by war, when perpetrators appear to have no fear of prosecution. Today, in Africa, for instance, UNICEF says there is now a "license to rape" in eastern regions of the Democratic Republic of the Congo, where some human-rights experts estimate that up to a quarter of a million women have been raped and often sexually mutilated with knives, branches or machetes.[8] Several of the Congolese rapists remorselessly bragged to an American film-maker recently about how many women they had gang-raped.[9]

"The sexual violence in Congo is the worst in the world," said John Holmes, the United Nations under secretary general for humanitarian affairs. "The sheer numbers, the wholesale brutality, the culture of impunity — it's appalling."[10]

In some cultures, the female victims themselves are punished. A report by the Human Rights Commission of Pakistan found that a woman is gang-raped every eight hours in that country. Yet, until recently, rape cases could not be prosecuted in Pakistan unless four Muslim men "all of a pious and trustworthy nature" were willing to testify that they witnessed the attack. Without their testimony the victim could be prosecuted for fornication and alleging a false crime, punishable by stoning, lashings or prison.[11] When the law was softened in 2006 to allow judges to decide whether to try rape cases in Islamic courts or criminal courts, where such witnesses are not required, thousands took to the streets to protest the change.[12]

Honor killings are up 400 percent in Pakistan over the last two years, and Pakistani women also live in fear of being blinded or disfigured by "acid attacks" — a common practice in Pakistan and a handful of other countries — in which attackers, usually spurned suitors, throw acid on a woman's face and body.

Only Four Countries Offer Total Equality for Women

Costa Rica, Cuba, Sweden and Norway receive the highest score (9 points) in an annual survey of women's economic, political and social rights. Out of the world's 193 countries, only 26 score 7 points or better, while 28 — predominantly Islamic or Pacific Island countries — score 3 or less. The United States rates 7 points: a perfect 3 on economic rights but only 2 each for political and social rights. To receive 3 points for political rights, women must hold at least 30 percent of the seats in the national legislature. Women hold only 16.6 percent of the seats in the U.S. Congress. The U.S. score of 2 on social rights reflects what the report's authors call "high societal discrimination against women's reproductive rights."

Status of Women's Rights Around the Globe

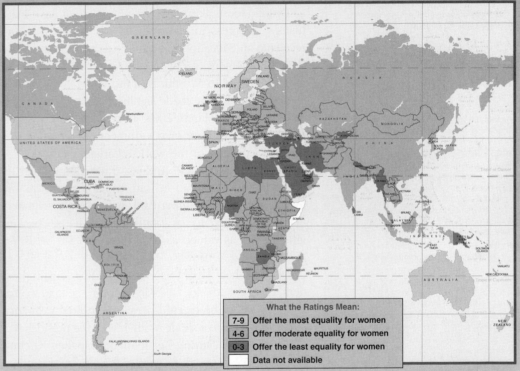

What the Ratings Mean:

7-9	Offer the most equality for women
4-6	Offer moderate equality for women
0-3	Offer the least equality for women
	Data not available

Source: Cingranelli-Richards Human Rights Dataset, http://ciri.binghamton.edu/, based on Amnesty International's annual reports and U.S. State Department annual Country Reports on Human Rights. The database is co-directed by David Louis Cingranelli, a political science professor at Binghamton University, SUNY, and David L. Richards, an assistant political science professor at the University of Memphis.

But statistics on murder and violence are only a part of the disturbing figures on the status of women around the globe. Others include:

- Some 130 million women have undergone female genital mutilation, and another 2 million are at risk every year, primarily in Africa and Yemen.
- Women and girls make up 70 percent of the world's poor and two-thirds of its illiterate.
- Women work two-thirds of the total hours worked by men but earn only 10 percent of the income.

Women's Suffering Is Widespread

More than two decades after the U.N. Decade for Women and 29 years after the U.N. adopted the Convention on the Elimination of All Forms of Discrimination against Women (CEDAW), gender discrimination remains pervasive throughout the world, with widespread negative consequences for society.

According to recent studies on the status of women today:

- Violence against women is pervasive. It impoverishes women, their families, communities and nations by lowering economic productivity and draining resources. It also harms families across generations and reinforces other violence in societies.
- Domestic violence is the most common form of violence against women, with rates ranging from 8 percent in Albania to 49 percent in Ethiopia and Zambia. Domestic violence and rape account for 5 percent of the disease burden for women ages 15 to 44 in developing countries and 19 percent in developed countries.
- Femicide — the murder of women — often involves sexual violence. From 40 to 70 percent of women murdered in Australia, Canada, Israel, South Africa and the United States are killed by husbands or boyfriends. Hundreds of women were abducted, raped and murdered in and around Juárez, Mexico, over the past 15 years, but the crimes have never been solved.
- At least 160 million females, mostly in India and China, are "missing" from the population — the result of sex-selective abortions.
- Rape is being used as a genocidal tool. Hundreds of thousands of women have been raped and sexually mutilated in the ongoing conflict in Eastern Congo. An estimated 250,000 to 500,000 women were raped during the 1994 genocide in Rwanda; up to 50,000 women were raped during the Bosnian conflict in the 1990s. Victims are often left unable to have children and are deserted by their husbands and shunned by their families, plunging the women and their children into poverty.
- Some 130 million girls have been genitally mutilated, mostly in Africa and Yemen, but also in immigrant communities in the West.
- Child rape has been on the increase in the past decade in some African countries, where some men believe having sex with a virgin will protect or cure them from HIV-AIDS. A study at the Red Cross children's hospital in Cape Town, South Africa, found that 3-year-old girls were more likely to be raped than any other age group.
- Two million girls between the ages of 5 and 15 are forced into the commercial sex market each year, many of them trafficked across international borders.
- Sexual harassment is pervasive. From 40 to 50 percent of women in the European Union reported some form of sexual harassment at work; 50 percent of schoolgirls surveyed in Malawi reported sexual harassment at school.
- Women and girls constitute 70 percent of those living on less than a dollar a day and 64 percent of the world's illiterate.
- Women work two-thirds of the total hours worked by men and women but earn only 10 percent of the income.
- Half of the world's food is produced by women, but women own only 1 percent of the world's land.
- More than 1,300 women die each day during pregnancy and childbirth — 99 percent of them in developing countries.

Sources: "Ending violence against women: From words to action," United Nations, October, 2006, www.un.org/womenwatch/ daw/public/VAW_Study/VAW studyE.pdf; www.womankind.org.uk; www.unfp.org; www.oxfam.org.uk; www.ipu.org; www.unicef.org; www.infant-trust.org.uk; "State of the World Population 2000;" http://npr.org; http://asiapacific.amnesty.org; http://news.bbc.co.uk

- Women produce more than half of the world's food but own less than 1 percent of the world's property.
- More than 500,000 women die during pregnancy and childbirth every year — 99 percent of them in developing countries.
- Two million girls between the ages of 5 and 15 are forced into the commercial sex market each year.[13]
- Globally, 10 million more girls than boys do not attend school.[14]

Despite these alarming numbers, women have made historic progress in some areas. The number of girls receiving an education has increased in the past decade. Today 57 percent of children not attending school are girls, compared to two-thirds in the 1990s.[15]

And women have made significant gains in the political arena. As of March, 2008, 14 women are serving as elected heads of state or government, and women now hold 17.8 percent of the world's parliamentary seats — more than ever before.[16] And just three months after the brutal killing of Aswad in Iraq, India swore in its first female president, Pratibha Patil, who vows to eliminate that country's practice of aborting female fetuses because girls are not as valued as boys in India. (*See "At Issue," p. 357.*)[17]

Last October, Argentina elected its first female president, Cristina Fernández de Kirchner,* the second woman in two years to be elected president in South America. Michelle Bachelet, a single mother, won the presidency in Chile in 2006.[18] During her inaugural speech Kirchner admitted, "Perhaps it'll be harder for me, because I'm a woman. It will always be harder for us."[19]

Indeed, while more women than ever now lead national governments, they hold only 4.4 percent of the world's 342 presidential and prime ministerial positions. And in no country do they hold 50 percent or more of the national legislative seats.[20]

"Women make up half the world's population, but they are not represented" at that level, says Swanee Hunt, former U.S. ambassador to Austria and founding director of the Women and Public Policy Program at Harvard's Kennedy School of Government.

---

* Isabel Martínez Perón assumed the presidency of Argentina on the death of her husband, Juan Perón, in 1974 and served until she was deposed in a coup d'etat in 1976; but she was never elected.

Negative Attitudes Toward Women Are Pervasive

Negative attitudes about women are widespread around the globe, among women as well as men. Rural women are more likely than city women to condone domestic abuse if they think it was provoked by a wife's behavior.

| Location | Percentage of women in selected countries who agree that a man has good reason to beat his wife if: | | | | | | Women who agree with: | |
	Wife does not complete housework	Wife disobeys her husband	Wife refuses sex	Wife asks about other women	Husband suspects infidelity	Wife is unfaithful	One or more of the reasons mentioned	None of the reasons mentioned
Bangladesh city	13.8	23.3	9.0	6.6	10.6	51.5	53.3	46.7
Bangladesh province	25.1	38.7	23.3	14.9	24.6	77.6	79.3	20.7
Brazil city	0.8	1.4	0.3	0.3	2.0	8.8	9.4	90.6
Brazil province	4.5	10.9	4.7	2.9	14.1	29.1	33.7	66.3
Ethiopia province	65.8	77.7	45.6	32.2	43.8	79.5	91.1	8.9
Japan city	1.3	1.5	0.4	0.9	2.8	18.5	19.0	81.0
Namibia city	9.7	12.5	3.5	4.3	6.1	9.2	20.5	79.5
Peru city	4.9	7.5	1.7	2.3	13.5	29.7	33.7	66.3
Peru province	43.6	46.2	25.8	26.7	37.9	71.3	78.4	21.6
Samoa	12.1	19.6	7.4	10.1	26.0	69.8	73.3	26.7
Serbia and Montenegro city	0.6	0.97	0.6	0.3	0.9	5.7	6.2	93.8
Thailand city	2.0	0.8	2.8	1.8	5.6	42.9	44.7	55.3
Thailand province	11.9	25.3	7.3	4.4	12.5	64.5	69.5	30.5
Tanzania city	24.1	45.6	31.1	13.8	22.9	51.5	62.5	37.5
Tanzania province	29.1	49.7	41.7	19.8	27.2	55.5	68.2	31.8

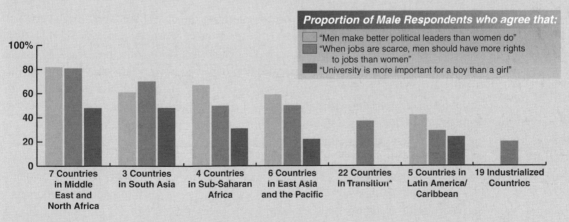

Proportion of Male Respondents who agree that:
- "Men make better political leaders than women do"
- "When jobs are scarce, men should have more rights to jobs than women"
- "University is more important for a boy than a girl"

7 Countries in Middle East and North Africa · 3 Countries in South Asia · 4 Countries in Sub-Saharan Africa · 6 Countries in East Asia and the Pacific · 22 Countries in Transition · 5 Countries in Latin America/Caribbean · 19 Industrialized Countries*

* Countries in transition are generally those that were once part of the Soviet Union.

Sources: World Health Organization, www.who.int/gender/violence/who_multicountry_study/Chapter3-Chapter4.pdf; "World Values Survey," www.worldvaluessruvey.org

While this is "obviously a fairness issue," she says it also affects the kinds of public policies governments pursue. When women comprise higher percentages of officeholders, studies show "distinct differences in legislative outputs," Hunt explains. "There's less

Spain's visibly pregnant new Defense minister, Carme Chacón, reviews troops in Madrid on April 14, 2008. She is the first woman ever to head Spain's armed forces. Women hold nine out of 17 cabinet posts in Spain's socialist government, a reflection of women's entrance into the halls of power around the world.

AP Photo/Bernat Armangue

funding of bombs and bullets and more on human security — not just how to defend territory but also on hospitals and general well-being."

Today's historic numbers of women parliamentarians have resulted partly from gender quotas imposed in nearly 100 countries, which require a certain percentage of women candidates or officeholders.[21]

During the U.N.'s historic Fourth World Conference on Women — held in Beijing in 1995 — 189 governments adopted, among other things, a goal of 30 percent female representation in national legislatures around the world.[22] But today, only 20 countries have reached that goal, and quotas are often attacked as limiting voters' choices and giving women unfair advantages.[23]

Along with increasing female political participation, the 5,000 government representatives at the Beijing conference — one of the largest gatherings in U.N. history — called for improved health care for women, an end to violence against women, equal access to education for girls, promotion of economic independence and other steps to improve the condition of women around the world.[24]

"Let Beijing be the platform from which our global crusade will be carried forward," Gertrude Mongella, U.N. secretary general for the conference, said during closing ceremonies. "The world will hold us accountable for the implementation of the good intentions and decisions arrived at in Beijing."[25]

But more than 10 years later, much of the Beijing Platform still has not been achieved. And many question whether women are any better off today than they were in 1995.

"The picture's mixed," says June Zeitlin, executive director of the Women's Environment & Development Organization (WEDO). "In terms of violence against women, there is far more recognition of what is going on today. There has been some progress with education and girls. But the impact of globalization has exacerbated differences between men and women. The poor have gotten poorer — and they are mostly women."

Liberalized international trade has been a two-edged sword in other ways as well. Corporations have been able to expand their global reach, opening new businesses and factories in developing countries and offering women unprecedented employment and economic opportunities. But the jobs often pay low wages and involve work in dangerous conditions because poor countries anxious to attract foreign investors often are willing to ignore safety and labor protections.[26] And increasingly porous international borders have led to growing numbers of women and girls being forced or sold into prostitution or sexual slavery abroad, often under the pretense that they will be given legitimate jobs overseas.[27]

Numerous international agreements in recent years have pledged to provide women with the same opportunities and protections as men, including the U.N.'s Millennium Development Goals (MDGs) and the Convention on the Elimination of All Forms of Discrimination Against Women (CEDAW). But the MDGs' deadlines for improving the conditions for women have either been missed already or are on track to fail in the coming years.[28] And more than 70 of the 185 countries that ratified CEDAW have filed "reservations," meaning they exempt themselves from certain parts.[29] In fact, there are more reservations against CEDAW than against any other international human-rights treaty in history.[30] The United States remains the only developed country in the world not to have ratified it.[31]

"There has certainly been progress in terms of the rhetoric. But there are still challenges in the disparities in education, disparities in income, disparities in health," says Carla Koppell, director of the Cambridge, Mass.-based Initiative for Inclusive Security, which advocates for greater numbers of women in peace negotiations.

"But women are not just victims," she continues. "They have a very unique and important role to play in solving the problems of the developing world. We need to charge policy makers to match the rhetoric and make it a reality. There is a really wonderful opportunity to use the momentum that does exist. I really think we can."

Amidst the successes and failures surrounding women's issues, here are some of the questions analysts are beginning to ask:

Has globalization been good for women?

Over the last 20 years, trade liberalization has led to a massive increase of goods being produced and exported from developing countries, creating millions of manufacturing jobs and bringing many women into the paid workforce for the first time.

"Women employed in export-oriented manufacturing typically earn more than they would have in traditional sectors," according to a World Bank report. "Further, cash income earned by women may improve their status and bargaining power in the family."[32] The report cited a study of 50 families in Mexico that found "a significant proportion of the women reported an improvement in their 'quality of life,' due mainly to their income from working outside their homes, including in (export-oriented) factory jobs."

But because women in developing nations are generally less educated than men and have little bargaining power, most of these jobs are temporary or part-time, offering no health-care benefits, overtime or sick leave.

Women comprise 85 percent of the factory jobs in the garment industry in Bangladesh and 90 percent in Cambodia. In the cut flower industry, women hold 65 percent of the jobs in Colombia and 87 percent in Zimbabwe. In the fruit industry, women constitute 69 percent of temporary and seasonal workers in South Africa and 52 percent in Chile.[33]

Frequently, women in these jobs have no formal contract with their employers, making them even more vulnerable to poor safety conditions and abuse. One study found that only 46 percent of women garment workers in Bangladesh had an official letter of employment.[34]

"Women are a workforce vital to the global economy, but the jobs women are in often aren't covered by labor protections," says Thalia Kidder, a policy adviser on gender and sustainable livelihoods with U.K.-based Oxfam, a confederation of 12 international aid organizations. Women lack protection because they mostly work as domestics, in home-based businesses and as part-time workers. "In the global economy, many companies look to hire the most powerless people because they cannot demand high wages. There are not a lot of trade treaties that address labor rights."

In addition to recommending that countries embrace free trade, Western institutions like the International Monetary Fund and the World Bank during the 1990s recommended that developing countries adopt so-called structural adjustment economic reforms in order to qualify for certain loans and financial support. Besides opening borders to free trade, the neo-liberal economic regime known as the Washington Consensus advocated privatizing state-owned businesses, balancing budgets and attracting foreign investment.

But according to some studies, those reforms ended up adversely affecting women. For instance, companies in Ecuador were encouraged to make jobs more "flexible" by replacing long-term contracts with temporary, seasonal and hourly positions — while restricting collective bargaining rights.[35] And countries streamlined and privatized government programs such as health care and education, services women depend on most.

Globalization also has led to a shift toward cash crops grown for export, which hurts women farmers, who produce 60 to 80 percent of the food for household consumption in developing countries.[36] Small women farmers are being pushed off their land so crops for exports can be grown, limiting their abilities to produce food for themselves and their families.

While economic globalization has yet to create the economic support needed to help women out of poverty, women's advocates say females have benefited from the broadening of communications between countries prompted by globalization. "It has certainly

Female Peacekeepers Fill Vital Roles

Women bring a different approach to conflict resolution.

The first all-female United Nations peacekeeping force left Liberia in January after a year's mission in the West African country, which is rebuilding itself after 14 years of civil war. Comprised of more than 100 women from India, the force was immediately replaced by a second female team.

"If anyone questioned the ability of women to do tough jobs, then those doubters have been [proven] wrong," said U.N. Special Representative for Liberia Ellen Margrethe Løj, adding that the female peacekeepers inspired many Liberian women to join the national police force.[1]

Women make up half of the world's refugees and have systematically been targeted for rape and sexual abuse during times of war, from the 200,000 "comfort women" who were kept as sex slaves for Japanese soldiers during World War II[2] to the estimated quarter-million women reportedly raped and sexually assaulted during the current conflict in the Democratic Republic of the Congo.[3] But women account for only 5 percent of the world's security-sector jobs, and in many countries they are excluded altogether.[4]

In 2000, the U.N. Security Council unanimously adopted Resolution 1325 calling on governments — and the U.N. itself — to include women in peace building by adopting a variety of measures, including appointing more women as special envoys, involving women in peace negotiations, integrating gender-based policies in peacekeeping missions and increasing the number of women at all decision-making levels.[5]

But while Resolution 1325 was a critical step in bringing women into the peace process, women's groups say more women should be sent on field missions and more data collected on how conflict affects women around the world.[6]

"Women are often viewed as victims, but another way to view them is as the maintainers of society," says Carla Koppell, director of the Cambridge, Mass.-based Initiative for Inclusive Security, which promotes greater numbers of women in peacekeeping and conflict resolution. "There must be a conscious decision to include women. It's a detriment to promote peace without including women."

The first all-female United Nations peacekeeping force practices martial arts in New Delhi as it prepares to be deployed to Liberia in 2006.

AP Photo/Mustafa Quraishi

Women often comprise the majority of post-conflict survivor populations, especially when large numbers of men have either fled or been killed. In the wake of the 1994 Rwandan genocide, for example, women made up 70 percent of the remaining population.

And female peacekeepers and security forces can fill vital roles men often cannot, such as searching Islamic women wearing burkas or working with rape victims who may be reluctant to report the crimes to male soldiers.

"Women bring different experiences and issues to the table," says Koppell. "I've seen it personally in the Darfur and Uganda peace negotiations. Their priorities were quite different. Men were concerned about power- and wealth-sharing. Those are valid, but you get an entirely different dimension from women. Women talked about security on the ground, security of families, security of communities."

In war-torn countries, women have been found to draw on their experiences as mothers to find nonviolent and flexible ways to solve conflict. [7] During peace negotiations in Northern Ireland, for example, male negotiators repeatedly walked out of sessions, leaving a small number of women at the table. The women, left to their own, found areas of common ground and were able to keep discussions moving forward.[8]

"The most important thing is introducing the definition of security from a woman's perspective," said Orzala Ashraf, founder of Kabul-based Humanitarian Assistance for the Women and Children of Afghanistan. "It is not a man in a uniform standing next to a tank armed with a gun. Women have a broader term — human security — the ability to go to school, receive health care, work and have access to justice. Only by improving these areas can threats from insurgents, Taliban, drug lords and warlords be countered."[9]

[1] "Liberia: UN envoy welcomes new batch of female Indian police officers," U.N. News Centre, Feb. 8, 2008, www.un.org/apps/news/story.asp?NewsID=25557&Cr=liberia&Cr1=.

[2] "Japan: Comfort Women," European Speaking Tour press release, Amnesty International, Oct. 31, 2007.

[3] "Film Documents Rape of Women in Congo," "All Things Considered," National Public Radio, April 8, 2008, www.npr.org/templates/story/story.php?storyId=89476111.

[4] "Ninth Annual Colloquium and Policy Forum," Hunt Alternatives Fund, Jan. 22, 2008, www.huntalternatives.org/pages/7650_ninth_annual_colloquium_and_policy_forum.cfm. Also see Elizabeth Eldridge, "Women cite utility in peace efforts," The Washington Times, Jan. 25, 2008, p. A1.

[5] "Inclusive Security, Sustainable Peace: A Toolkit for Advocacy and Action," International Alert and Women Waging Peace, 2004, p. 15, www.huntalternatives.org/download/35_introduction.pdf.

[6] Ibid., p. 17.

[7] Jolynn Shoemaker and Camille Pampell Conaway, "Conflict Prevention and Transformation: Women's Vital Contributions," Inclusive Security: Women Waging Peace and the United Nations Foundation, Feb. 23, 2005, p. 7.

[8] The Initiative for Inclusive Security, www.huntalternatives.org/pages/460_the_vital_role_of_women_in_peace_building.cfm.

[9] Eldridge, op. cit.

improved access to communications and helped human-rights campaigns," says Zeitlin of WEDO. "Less can be done in secret. If there is a woman who is condemned to be stoned to death somewhere, you can almost immediately mobilize a global campaign against it."

Homa Hoodfar, a professor of social anthropology at Concordia University in Montreal, Canada, and a founder of the group Women Living Under Muslim Laws, says women in some of the world's most remote towns and villages regularly e-mail her organization. "Globalization has made the world much smaller," she says. "Women are getting information on TV and the Internet. The fact that domestic violence has become a global issue [shows globalization] provides resources for those objecting locally."

But open borders also have enabled the trafficking of millions of women around the world. An estimated 800,000 people are trafficked across international borders each year — 80 percent of them women and girls — and most are forced into the commercial sex trade. Millions more are trafficked within their own countries.[37] Globalization has sparked a massive migration of women in search of better jobs and lives. About 90 million women — half of the world's migrants and more than ever in history — reside outside their home countries. These migrant women — often unable to speak the local language and without any family connections — are especially susceptible to traffickers who lure them with promises of jobs abroad.[38]

And those who do not get trapped in the sex trade often end up in low-paying or abusive jobs in foreign factories or as domestic maids working under slave-like conditions.

But some experts say the real problem is not migration and globalization but the lack of labor protection. "Nothing is black and white," says Marianne Mollmann, advocacy director for the Women's Rights Division of Human Rights Watch. "Globalization has created different employment opportunities for women. Migration flows have made women vulnerable. But it's a knee-jerk reaction to say that women shouldn't migrate. You can't prevent migration. So where do we need to go?" She suggests including these workers in general labor-law protections that cover all workers.

Mollmann said countries can and should hammer out agreements providing labor and wage protections for domestic workers migrating across borders. With such protections, she said, women could benefit from the jobs and incomes promised by increased migration and globalization.

Should governments impose electoral quotas for women?

In 2003, as Rwanda struggled to rebuild itself after the genocide that killed at least 800,000 Hutus and Tutsis, the country adopted an historic new constitution that, among other things, required that women hold at least 30 percent of posts "in all decision-making organs."[39]

Today — ironically, just across Lake Kivu from the horrors occurring in Eastern Congo — Rwanda's lower house of parliament now leads the world in female representation, with 48.8 percent of the seats held by women.[40]

Before the civil war, Rwandan women never held more than 18 percent of parliament. But after the genocide, the country's population was 70 percent female. Women immediately stepped in to fill the vacuum, becoming the heads of households, community leaders and business owners. Their increased presence in leadership positions eventually led to the new constitutional quotas.[41]

"We see so many post-conflict countries going from military regimes to democracy that are starting from scratch with new constitutions," says Drude Dahlerup, a professor of political science at Sweden's Stockholm University who studies the use of gender quotas. "Today, starting from scratch means including women. It's seen as a sign of modernization and democratization."

Both Iraq and Afghanistan included electoral quotas for women in their new constitutions, and the number of women in political office in sub-Saharan Africa has increased faster than in any other region of the world, primarily through the use of quotas.[42]

But many point out that simply increasing the numbers of women in elected office will not necessarily expand women's rights. "It depends on which women and which positions they represent," says Wendy Harcourt, chair of Women in Development Europe (WIDE), a feminist network in Europe, and editor of *Development*, the journal of the Society for International Development, a global network of individuals and institutions working on development issues. "It's positive, but I don't see yet what it means [in terms of addressing] broader gender issues."

Few Women Head World Governments

Fourteen women currently serve as elected heads of state or government including five who serve as both. Mary McAleese, elected president of Ireland in 1997, is the world's longest-serving head of state. Helen Clark of New Zealand has served as prime minister since 1999, making her the longest-serving female head of government. The world's first elected female head of state was Sirimavo Bandaranaike of Sri Lanka, in 1960.

Current Female Elected Heads of State and Government

Heads of both state and government:

 Gloria Macapagal-Arroyo — President, the Philippines, since 2001; former secretary of Defense (2002) and secretary of Foreign Affairs (2003 and 2006-2007).

 Ellen Johnson-Sirleaf — President, Liberia, since 2006; held finance positions with the government and World Bank.

 Michelle Bachelet Jeria — President, Chile, since 2006; former minister of Health (2000-2002) and minister of Defense (2002-2004).

 Cristina E. Fernández — President, Argentina, since 2007; succeeded her husband, Nestor de Kirchner, as president; former president, Senate Committee on Constitutional Affairs.

Rosa Zafferani — Captain Regent, San Marino, since April 2008; secretary of State of Public Education, University and Cultural Institutions (2004 to 2008); served as captain regent in 1999; San Marino elects two captains regent every six months, who serve as co-heads of both state and government.

Heads of Government:

 Helen Clark — Prime Minister, New Zealand, since 1999; held government posts in foreign affairs, defense, housing and labor.

 Luísa Días Diogo — Prime Minister, Mozambique, since 2004; held several finance posts in Mozambique and the World Bank.

 Angela Merkel — Chancellor, Germany, since 2005; parliamentary leader of Christian Democratic Union Party (2002-2005).

 Yuliya Tymoshenko — Prime Minister, Ukraine, since 2007; chief of government (2005) and designate prime minister (2006).

Zinaida Grecianîi — Prime Minister, Moldova, since March 2008; vice prime minister (2005-2008).

Heads of State:

 Mary McAleese — President, Ireland, since 1997; former director of a television station and Northern Ireland Electricity.

 Tarja Halonen — President, Finland, since 2000; former minister of foreign affairs (1995-2000).

 Pratibha Patil — President, India, since 2007; former governor of Rajasthan state (2004-2007).

 Borjana Kristo — President, Bosnia and Herzegovina, since 2007; minister of Justice of Bosniak-Croat Federation, an entity in Bosnia and Herzegovina (2003-2007).

Source: www.guide2womenleaders.com

While Afghanistan has mandated that women hold at least 27 percent of the government's lower house seats and at least 17 percent of the upper house, their increased representation appears to have done little to improve women's rights.[43] Earlier this year,

Women Still Far from Reaching Political Parity

Although they have made strides in the past decade, women hold only a small minority of the world's leadership and legislative posts (right). Nordic parliaments have the highest rates of female representation — 41.4 percent — compared with only 9 percent in Arab countries (below). However, Arab legislatures have nearly tripled their female representation since 1997, and some countries in Africa have dramatically increased theirs as well: Rwanda, at 48.8 percent, now has the world's highest percentage of women in parliament of any country. The U.S. Congress ranks 70th in the world, with 89 women serving in the 535-member body — or 16.6 percent.

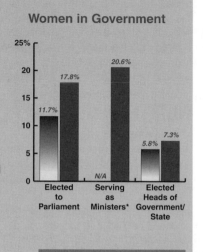

Women in Government

	1997	2008
Elected to Parliament	11.7%	17.8%
Serving as Ministers*	N/A	20.6%
Elected Heads of Government/State	5.8%	7.3%

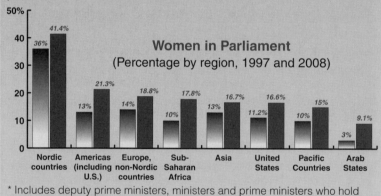

Women in Parliament
(Percentage by region, 1997 and 2008)

	1997	2008
Nordic countries	36%	41.4%
Americas (including U.S.)	13%	21.3%
Europe, non-Nordic countries	14%	18.8%
Sub-Saharan Africa	10%	17.8%
Asia	13%	16.7%
United States	11.2%	16.6%
Pacific Countries	10%	15%
Arab States	3%	9.1%

* Includes deputy prime ministers, ministers and prime ministers who hold ministerial portfolios.

Sources: Interparliamentarian Union, www.ipu.org/wmn-e/world.htm; State of the World's Children 2007, UNICEF, www.unicef.org/sowc07/; "Worldwide Guide to Women in Leadership" database, www.un.org/womenwatch/daw/csw/41sess.htm.

a student journalist was condemned to die under Afghanistan's strict Islamic sharia law after he distributed articles from the Internet on women's rights.[44] And nongovernmental groups in Afghanistan report that Afghan women and girls have begun killing themselves in record numbers, burning themselves alive in order to escape widespread domestic abuse or forced marriages.[45]

Having gender quotas alone doesn't necessarily ensure that women's rights will be broadened, says Hoodfar of Concordia University. It depends on the type of quota a government implements, she argues, pointing out that in Jordan, for example, the government has set aside parliamentary seats for the six women who garner the most votes of any other female candidates in their districts — even if they do not win more votes than male candidates.[46] Many small, conservative tribes that cannot garner enough votes for a male in a countrywide victory are now nominating their sisters and wives in the hope that the lower number of votes needed to elect a woman will get them one of the reserved seats. As a result, many of the women moving into the reserved seats are extremely conservative and actively oppose providing women greater rights and freedoms.

And another kind of quota has been used against women in her home country of Iran, Hoodfar points out. Currently, 64 percent of university students in Iran are women. But the government recently mandated that at least 40 percent of university enrollees be male, forcing many female students out of school, Hoodfar said.

"Before, women didn't want to use quotas for politics because of concern the government may try to use it against women," she says. "But women are beginning to look into it and talk about maybe developing a good system."

Quotas can be enacted by constitutional requirements, such as those enacted in Rwanda, by statute or voluntarily by political parties. Quotas also can vary in their requirements: They can mandate the number of women each party must nominate, how many women must appear on the ballot (and the order in which they appear, so women are not relegated to the bottom of the list), or the number of women who must hold government office. About 40 countries now use gender quotas in national parliamentary elections, while another 50 have major political parties that voluntarily use quotas to determine candidates.

Aside from questions about the effectiveness of quotas, others worry about the fairness of establishing quotas based on gender. "That's something feminists have traditionally opposed," says Harcourt.

"It's true, but it's also not fair the way it is now," says former Ambassador Hunt. "We are where we are today through all kinds of social structures that are not fair. Quotas are the lesser of two evils."

Stockholm University's Dahlerup says quotas are not "discrimination against men but compensation for discrimination against women." Yet quotas are not a panacea for women in politics, she contends. "It's a mistake to think this is a kind of tool that will solve all problems. It doesn't solve problems about financing campaigns, caring for families while being in politics or removing patriarchal attitudes. It would be nice if it wasn't necessary, and hopefully sometime in the future it won't be."

Until that time, however, quotas are a "necessary evil," she says.

Do international treaties improve women's rights?

In recent decades, a variety of international agreements have been signed by countries pledging to improve women's lives, from the 1979 Convention for the Elimination of All Forms of Discrimination Against Women to the Beijing Platform of 1995 to the Millennium Development Goals (MDGs) adopted in 2000. The agreements aimed to provide women with greater access to health, political representation, economic stability and social status. They also focused attention on some of the biggest obstacles facing women.

But despite the fanfare surrounding the launch of those agreements, many experts on women's issues say on-the-ground action has yet to match the rhetoric. "The report is mixed," says Haleh Afshar, a professor of politics and women's studies at the University of York in the United Kingdom and a nonpartisan, appointed member of the House of Lords, known as a crossbench peer. "The biggest problem with Beijing is all these things were stated, but none were funded. Unfortunately, I don't see any money. You don't get the pay, you don't get the job done."

AP Photo/Rajesh Kumar Singh

Women's Work: From Hauling and Churning . . .

Women's work is often back-breaking and monotonous, such as hauling firewood in the western Indian state of Maharashtra (top) and churning yogurt into butter beside Lake Motsobunnyi in Tibet (bottom). Women labor two-thirds of the total hours worked around the globe each year but earn only 10 percent of the income.

National Geographic/Getty Images/Melvyn Goldstein

AP Photo/Sergei Grits

. . . to Gathering and Herding

While many women have gotten factory jobs thanks to globalization of trade, women still comprise 70 percent of the planet's inhabitants living on less than a dollar a day. Women perform a variety of tasks around the world, ranging from gathering flax in Belarus (top) to shepherding goats in central Argentina (bottom).

AFP/Getty Images/Ali Burafi

The Beijing Platform for Action, among other things, called on governments to "adjust budgets to ensure equality of access to public sector expenditures" and even to "reduce, as appropriate, excessive military expenditure" in order to achieve the Platform goals.

But adequate funding has yet to be provided, say women's groups.[47] In a report entitled "Beijing Betrayed," the Women's Environment & Development Organization says female HIV cases outnumber male cases in many parts of the world, gender-related violence remains a pandemic and women still make up the majority of the world's poor — despite pledges in Beijing to reverse these trends.[48]

And funding is not the only obstacle. A 2004 U.N. survey revealed that while many countries have enacted laws in recent years to help protect women from violence and discrimination, long-standing social and cultural traditions block progress. "While constitutions provided for equality between women and men on the one hand, [several countries] recognized and gave precedent to customary law and practice in a number of areas . . . resulting in discrimination against women," the report said. "Several countries noted that statutory, customary and religious law coexist, especially in regard to family, personal status and inheritance and land rights. This perpetuated discrimination against women."[49]

While she worries about the lack of progress on the Beijing Platform, WEDO Executive Director Zeitlin says international agreements are nevertheless critical in raising global awareness on women's issues. "They have a major impact on setting norms and standards," she says. "In many countries, norms and standards are very important in setting goals for women to advocate for. We complain about lack of implementation, but if we didn't have the norms and standards we couldn't complain about a lack of implementation."

Like the Beijing Platform, the MDGs have been criticized for not achieving more. While the U.N. says promoting women's rights is essential to achieving the millennium goals — which aim to improve the lives of all the world's populations by 2015 — only two of the eight specifically address women's issues.[50]

One of the goals calls for countries to "Promote gender equality and empower women." But it sets only one measurable target: "Eliminate gender disparity in primary and secondary education, preferably by 2005, and in all levels of education" by 2015.[51] Some 62 countries failed to reach the 2005 deadline, and many are likely to miss the 2015 deadline as well.[52]

Another MDG calls for a 75 percent reduction in maternal mortality compared to 1990 levels. But according to the human-rights group ActionAid, this goal is the "most off track of all the MDGs." Rates are declining at less than 1 percent a year, and in some countries — such as Sierra Leone, Pakistan and Guatemala — maternal mortality has increased since

1990. If that trend continues, no region in the developing world is expected to reach the goal by 2015.[53]

Activist Peggy Antrobus of Development Alternatives with Women for a New Era (DAWN) — a network of feminists from the Southern Hemisphere, based currently in Calabar, Cross River State, Nigeria — has lambasted the MDGs, quipping that the acronym stands for the "Most Distracting Gimmick."[54] Many feminists argue that the goals are too broad to have any real impact and that the MDGs should have given more attention to women's issues.

But other women say international agreements — and the public debate surrounding them — are vital in promoting gender equality. "It's easy to get disheartened, but Beijing is still the blueprint of where we need to be," says Mollmann of Human Rights Watch. "They are part of a political process, the creation of an international culture. If systematically everyone says [discrimination against women] is a bad thing, states don't want to be hauled out as systematic violators."

Indian women harvest wheat near Bhopal. Women produce half of the food used domestically worldwide and 60 to 80 percent of the household food grown in developing countries.

AP Photo/Prakash Hatvalne

In particular, Mollmann said, CEDAW has made real progress in overcoming discrimination against women. Unlike the Beijing Platform and the MDGs, CEDAW legally obliges countries to comply. Each of the 185 ratifying countries must submit regular reports to the U.N. outlining their progress under the convention. Several countries — including Brazil, Uganda, South Africa and Australia — also have incorporated CEDAW provisions into their constitutions and legal systems.[55]

Still, dozens of ratifying countries have filed official "reservations" against the convention, including Bahrain, Egypt, Kuwait, Morocco and the United Arab Emirates, all of whom say they will comply only within the bounds of Islamic sharia law.[56] And the United States has refused to ratify CEDAW, with or without reservations, largely because of conservatives who say it would, among other things, promote abortion and require the government to pay for such things as child care and maternity leave.

Background

'Structural Defects'

Numerous prehistoric relics suggest that at one time matriarchal societies existed on Earth in which women were in the upper echelons of power. Because early societies did not understand the connection between sexual relations and conception, they believed women were solely responsible for reproduction — which led to the worship of female goddesses.[57]

In more modern times, however, women have generally faced prejudice and discrimination at the hands of a patriarchal society. In about the eighth century B.C. creation stories emerged describing the fall of man due to the weakness of women. The Greeks recounted the story of Pandora who, through her opening of a sealed jar, unleashed death and pain on all of mankind. Meanwhile, similar tales in Judea eventually were recounted in Genesis, with Eve as the culprit.[58]

In ancient Greece, women were treated as children and denied basic rights. They could not leave their houses unchaperoned, were prohibited from being educated or buying or selling land. A father could sell his unmarried daughter into slavery if she lost her virginity before marriage. If a woman was raped, she was outcast and forbidden from participating in public ceremonies or wearing jewelry.[59]

The status of women in early Rome was not much better, although over time women began to assert their voices and slowly gained greater freedoms. Eventually, they were able to own property and divorce their husbands. But early Christian leaders later denounced the legal and social freedom enjoyed by Roman women as a sign of moral decay. In the view of the early church, women were dependent on and subordinate to men.

In the 13th century, the Catholic priest and theologian St. Thomas Aquinas helped set the tone for the subjugation of women in Western society. He said women were created solely to be "man's helpmate" and advocated that men should make use of "a necessary object, woman, who is needed to preserve the species or to provide food and drink."[60]

From the 14th to 17th centuries, misogyny and oppression of women took a step further. As European societies struggled against the Black Plague, the 100 Years War and turmoil between Catholics and Reformers, religious leaders began to blame tragedies, illnesses and other problems on witches. As witch hysteria spread across Europe — instituted by both the religious and non-religious — an estimated 30,000 to 60,000 people were executed for allegedly practicing witchcraft. About 80 percent were females, some as young as 8 years old.[61]

"All wickedness is but little to the wickedness of a woman," Catholic inquisitors wrote in the 1480s. "What else is woman but a foe to friendship, an unescapable punishment, a necessary evil, a natural temptation, a desirable calamity. . . . Women are . . . instruments of Satan, . . . a structural defect rooted in the original creation."[62]

Push for Protections

The Age of Enlightenment and the Industrial Revolution in the 18th and 19th centuries opened up job opportunities for women, released them from domestic confines and provided them with new social freedoms.

In 1792 Mary Wollstonecraft published *A Vindication of the Rights of Women*, which has been hailed as "the feminist declaration of independence." Although the book had been heavily influenced by the French Revolution's notions of equality and universal brotherhood, French revolutionary leaders, ironically, were not sympathetic to feminist causes.[63] In 1789 they had refused to accept a Declaration of the Rights of Women when it was presented at the National Assembly. And Jean Jacques Rousseau, one of the philosophical founders of the revolution, had written in 1762:

"The whole education of women ought to be relative to men. To please them, to be useful to them, to make themselves loved and honored by them, to educate them when young, to care for them when grown, to counsel them, to make life sweet and agreeable to them — these are the duties of women at all times, and what should be taught them from their infancy."[64]

As more and more women began taking jobs outside the home during the 19th century, governments began to pass laws to "protect" them in the workforce and expand their legal rights. The British Mines Act of 1842, for instance, prohibited women from working underground.[65] In 1867, John Stuart Mill, a supporter of women's rights and author of the book *Subjection of Women*, introduced language in the British House of Commons calling for women to be granted the right to vote. It failed.[66]

But by that time governments around the globe had begun enacting laws giving women rights they had been denied for centuries. As a result of the Married Women's Property Act of 1870 and a series of other measures, wives in Britain were finally allowed to own property. In 1893, New Zealand became the first nation to grant full suffrage rights to women, followed over the next two decades by Finland, Norway, Denmark and Iceland. The United States granted women suffrage in 1920.[67]

One of the first international labor conventions, formulated at Berne, Switzerland, in 1906, applied exclusively to women — prohibiting night work for women in industrial occupations. Twelve nations signed on to it. During the second Berne conference in 1913, language was proposed limiting the number of hours women and children could work in industrial jobs, but the outbreak of World War I prevented it from being enacted.[68] In 1924 the U.S. Supreme Court upheld a night-work law for women.[69]

In 1946, public attention to women's issues received a major boost when the United Nations created the Commission on the Status of Women to address urgent problems facing women around the world.[70] During the 1950s, the U.N. adopted several conventions aimed at improving women's lives, including the Convention on the Political Rights of Women, adopted in 1952 to ensure women the right to vote, which has been ratified by 120 countries, and the Convention on the Nationality of Married Women, approved in 1957 to ensure that marriage to an alien does not automatically affect the nationality of the woman.[71] That convention has been ratified by only 73 countries; the United States is not among them.[72]

In 1951 The International Labor Organization (ILO), an agency of the United Nations, adopted the Convention on Equal Remuneration for Men and Women Workers for Work of Equal Value, to promote equal pay for equal work. It has since been ratified by 164 countries, but again, not by the United States.[73] Seven years later, the ILO adopted the Convention on Discrimination in Employment and Occupation to ensure equal opportunity and treatment in employment. It is currently ratified by 166 countries, but not the United States.[74] U.S. opponents to the conventions claim there is no real pay gap between men and women performing the same jobs and that the conventions would impose "comparable worth" requirements, forcing companies to pay equal wages to men and women even if the jobs they performed were different.[75]

In 1965, the Commission on the Status of Women began drafting international standards articulating equal rights for men and women. Two years later, the panel completed the Declaration on the Elimination of Discrimination Against Women, which was adopted by the General Assembly but carried no enforcement power.

The commission later began to discuss language that would hold countries responsible for enforcing the declaration. At the U.N.'s first World Conference on Women in Mexico City in 1975, women from around the world called for creation of such a treaty, and the commission soon began drafting the text.[76]

Women's 'Bill of Rights'

Finally in 1979, after many years of often rancorous debate, the Convention on the Elimination of All Forms of Discrimination Against Women (CEDAW) was adopted by the General Assembly — 130 to none, with 10 abstentions. After the vote, however, several countries said their "yes" votes did not commit the support of their

CHRONOLOGY

1700s-1800s *Age of Enlightenment and Industrial Revolution lead to greater freedoms for women.*

1792 Mary Wollstonecraft publishes *A Vindication of the Rights of Women,* later hailed as "the feminist declaration of independence."

1893 New Zealand becomes first nation to grant women full suffrage.

1920 Tennessee is the 36th state to ratify the 19th Amendment, giving American women the right to vote.

1940s-1980s *International conventions endorse equal rights for women. Global conferences highlight need to improve women's rights.*

1946 U.N. creates Commission on the Status of Women.

1951 U.N. International Labor Organization adopts convention promoting equal pay for equal work, which has been ratified by 164 countries; the United States is not among them.

1952 U.N. adopts convention calling for full women's suffrage.

1960 Sri Lanka elects the world's first female prime minister.

1974 Maria Estela Martínez de Perón of Argentina becomes the world's first woman president, replacing her ailing husband.

1975 U.N. holds first World Conference on Women, in Mexico City, followed by similar conferences every five years. U.N. launches the Decade for Women.

1979 U.N. adopts Convention on the Elimination of All Forms of Discrimination against Women (CEDAW), dubbed the "international bill of rights for women."

1981 CEDAW is ratified — faster than any other human-rights convention.

1990s *Women's rights win historic legal recognition.*

1993 U.N. World Conference on Human Rights in Vienna, Austria, calls for ending all violence, sexual harassment and trafficking of women.

1995 Fourth World Conference on Women in Beijing draws 30,000 people, making it the largest in U.N. history. Beijing Platform outlining steps to grant women equal rights is signed by 189 governments.

1996 International Criminal Tribunal convicts eight Bosnian Serb police and military officers for rape during the Bosnian conflict — the first time sexual assault is prosecuted as a war crime.

1998 International Criminal Tribunal for Rwanda recognizes rape and other forms of sexual violence as genocide.

2000s *Women make political gains, but sexual violence against women increases.*

2000 U.N. calls on governments to include women in peace negotiations.

2006 Ellen Johnson Sirleaf of Liberia, Michelle Bachelet of Chile and Portia Simpson Miller of Jamaica become their countries' first elected female heads of state. . . . Women in Kuwait are allowed to run for parliament, winning two seats.

2007 A woman in Saudi Arabia who was sentenced to 200 lashes after being gang-raped by seven men is pardoned by King Abdullah. Her rapists received sentences ranging from 10 months to five years in prison, and 80 to 1,000 lashes. . . . After failing to recognize any gender-based crimes in its first case involving the Democratic Republic of the Congo, the International Criminal Court hands down charges of "sexual slavery" in its second case involving war crimes in Congo. More than 250,000 women are estimated to have been raped and sexually abused during the country's war.

2008 Turkey lifts 80-year-old ban on women's headscarves in public universities, signaling a drift toward religious fundamentalism. . . . Former housing minister Carme Chacón — 37 and pregnant — is named defense minister of Spain, bringing to nine the number of female cabinet ministers in the Socialist government. . . . Sen. Hillary Rodham Clinton becomes the first U.S. woman to be in a tight race for a major party's presidential nomination.

governments. Brazil's U.N. representative told the assembly, "The signatures and ratifications necessary to make this effective will not come easily."[77]

Despite the prediction, it took less than two years for CEDAW to receive the required number of ratifications to enter it into force — faster than any human-rights convention had ever done before.[78]

Often described as an international bill of rights for women, CEDAW defines discrimination against women as "any distinction, exclusion or restriction made on the basis of sex which has the effect or purpose of impairing or nullifying the recognition, enjoyment or exercise by women, irrespective of their marital status, on a basis of equality of men and women, of human rights and fundamental freedoms in the political, economic, social, cultural, civil or any other field."

Ratifying countries are legally bound to end discrimination against women by incorporating sexual equality into their legal systems, abolishing discriminatory laws against women, taking steps to end trafficking of women and ensuring women equal access to political and public life. Countries must also submit reports at least every four years outlining the steps they have taken to comply with the convention.[79]

CEDAW also grants women reproductive choice — one of the main reasons the United States has not ratified it. The convention requires signatories to guarantee women's rights "to decide freely and responsibly on the number and spacing of their children and to have access to the information, education and means to enable them to exercise these rights."[80]

While CEDAW is seen as a significant tool to stop violence against women, it actually does not directly mention violence. To rectify this, the CEDAW committee charged with monitoring countries' compliance in 1992 specified gender-based violence as a form of discrimination prohibited under the convention.[81]

In 1993 the U.N. took further steps to combat violence against women during the World Conference on Human Rights in Vienna, Austria. The conference called on countries to stop all forms of violence, sexual harassment, exploitation and trafficking of women. It also declared that "violations of the human rights of women in situations of armed conflicts are violations of the fundamental principles of international human rights and humanitarian law."[82]

Shortly afterwards, as fighting broke out in the former Yugoslavia and Rwanda, new legal precedents were set to protect women against violence — and particularly rape — during war. In 1996, the International Criminal Tribunal in the Hague, Netherlands, indicted eight Bosnian Serb police officers in connection with the mass rape of Muslim women during the Bosnian war, marking the first time sexual assault had ever been prosecuted as a war crime.[83]

Two years later, the U.N.'s International Criminal Tribunal for Rwanda convicted a former Rwandan mayor for genocide, crimes against humanity, rape and sexual violence — the first time rape and sexual violence were recognized as acts of genocide.[84]

"Rape is a serious war crime like any other," said Regan Ralph, then executive director of Human Rights Watch's Women's Rights Division, shortly after the conviction. "That's always been true on paper, but now international courts are finally acting on it."[85]

Today, the International Criminal Court has filed charges against several Sudanese officials for rape and other crimes committed in the Darfur region.[86] But others are demanding that the court also prosecute those responsible for the rapes in the Eastern Congo, where women are being targeted as a means of destroying communities in the war-torn country.[87]

Beijing and Beyond

The U.N. World Conference on Women in Mexico City in 1975 produced a 44-page plan of action calling for a decade of special measures to give women equal status and opportunities in law, education, employment, politics and society.[88] The conference also kicked off the U.N.'s Decade for Women and led to creation of the U.N. Development Fund for Women (UNIFEM).[89]

Five years later, the U.N. held its second World Conference on Women in Copenhagen and then celebrated the end of the Decade for Women with the third World Conference in Nairobi in 1985. More than 10,000 representatives from government agencies and NGOs attended the Nairobi event, believed to be the largest gathering on women's issues at the time.[90]

Upon reviewing the progress made on women's issues during the previous 10 years, the U.N. representatives in Nairobi concluded that advances had been extremely limited due to failing economies in developing countries, particularly those in Africa struggling against drought, famine and crippling debt. The conference developed a set of steps needed to improve the status of women during the final 15 years of the 20th century.[91]

Ten years later, women gathered in Beijing in 1995 for the Fourth World Conference, vowing to turn the rhetoric of the earlier women's conferences into action. Delegates from 189 governments and 2,600 NGOs attended. More than 30,000 women and men gathered at a parallel forum organized by NGOs, also in Beijing.[92]

The so-called Beijing Platform that emerged from the conference addressed 12 critical areas facing women, from poverty to inequality in education to inadequate health care to violence. It brought unprecedented attention to women's issues and is still considered by many as the blueprint for true gender equality.

The Beijing Conference also came at the center of a decade that produced historic political gains for women around the world — gains that have continued, albeit at a slow pace, into the new century. The 1990s saw more women entering top political positions than ever before. A record 10 countries elected or appointed women as presidents between 1990 and 2000, including Haiti, Nicaragua, Switzerland and Latvia. Another 17 countries chose women prime ministers.[93]

In 2006 Ellen Johnson Sirleaf of Liberia became Africa's first elected woman president.[94] That same year, Chile elected its first female president, Michelle Bachelet, and Jamaica elected Portia Simpson Miller as its first female prime minister.[95] Also that year, women ran for election in Kuwait for the first time. In Bahrain, a woman was elected to the lower

Women Suffer Most in Natural Disasters

Climate change will make matters worse.

In natural disasters, women suffer death, disease and hunger at higher rates then men. During the devastating 2004 tsunami in Asia, 70 to 80 percent of the dead were women.[1] During cyclone-triggered flooding in Bangladesh that killed 140,000 people in 1991, nearly five times more women between the ages of 20 and 44 died than men.[2]

The smell of death hangs over Banda Aceh, Indonesia, which was virtually destroyed by a tsunami on Dec. 28, 2004. From 70 to 80 percent of the victims were women.

AP Photo

Gender discrimination, cultural biases and lack of awareness of women's needs are part of the problem. For instance, during the 1991 cyclone, Bangladeshi women and their children died in higher numbers because they waited at home for their husbands to return and make evacuation decisions.[3] In addition, flood warnings were conveyed by men to men in public spaces but were rarely communicated to women and children at home.[4]

And during the tsunami, many Indonesian women died because they stayed behind to look for children and other family members. Women clinging to children in floodwaters also tired more quickly and drowned, since most women in the region were never taught to swim or climb trees.[5] In Sri Lanka, many women died because the tsunami hit early on a Sunday morning when they were inside preparing breakfast for their families. Men were generally outside where they had earlier warning of the oncoming floods so they were better able to escape.[6]

Experts now predict global climate change — which is expected to increase the number of natural disasters around the world — will put women in far greater danger than men because natural disasters generally have a disproportionate impact on the world's poor. Since women comprise 70 percent of those living on less than $1 a day, they will be hardest hit by climate changes, according to the Intergovernmental Panel on Climate Change.[7]

"Climate change is not gender-neutral," said Gro Harlem Brundtland, former prime minister of Norway and now special envoy to the U.N. secretary-general on climate change. "[Women are] more dependent for their livelihood on natural resources that are threatened by climate change.... With changes in climate, traditional food sources become more unpredictable and scarce. This exposes women to loss of harvests, often their sole sources of food and income."[8]

Women produce 60 to 80 percent of the food for household consumption in developing countries.[9] As drought, flooding and desertification increase, experts say women and their families will be pushed further into poverty and famine.

Women also suffer more hardship in the aftermath of natural disasters, and their needs are often ignored during relief efforts.

In many Third World countries, for instance, women have no property rights, so when a husband dies during a natural disaster his family frequently confiscates the land from his widow, leaving her homeless and destitute.[10] And because men usually dominate emergency relief and response agencies, women's specific needs, such as contraceptives and sanitary napkins, are often overlooked. After floods in Bangladesh in 1998, adolescent girls reported high rates of rashes and urinary tract infections because they had no clean water, could not wash their menstrual rags properly in private and had no place to hang them to dry.[11]

"In terms of reconstruction, people are not talking about women's needs versus men's needs," says June Zeitlin, executive director of the Women's Environment and Development Organization, a New York City-based international organization that works for women's equality in global policy. "There is a lack of attention to health care after disasters, issues about bearing children, contraception, rape and vulnerability, menstrual needs — things a male programmer is not thinking about. There is broad recognition that disasters have a disproportionate impact on women. But it stops there. They see women as victims, but they don't see women as agents of change."

Women must be brought into discussions on climate change and emergency relief, say Zeitlin and others. Interestingly, she points out, while women are disproportionately affected by environmental changes, they do more than men to protect the environment. Studies show women emit less climate-changing carbon dioxide than men because they recycle more, use resources more efficiently and drive less than men.[12]

(Continued)

"Women's involvement in climate-change decision-making is a human right," said Gerd Johnson-Latham, deputy director of the Swedish Ministry for Foreign Affairs. "If we get more women in decision-making positions, we will have different priorities, and less risk of climate change."[13]

[1] "Tsunami death toll," CNN, Feb. 22, 2005. Also see "Report of High-level Roundtable: How a Changing Climate Impacts Women," Council of Women World Leaders, Women's Environment and Development Organization and Heinrich Boll Foundation, Sept. 21, 2007, p. 21, www.wedo.org/files/Roundtable%20Final%20Report%206%20Nov.pdf.

[2] Ibid.

[3] "Cyclone Jelawat bears down on Japan's Okinawa island," CNN.com, Aug. 7, 2000, http://archives.cnn.com/2000/ASIANOW/east/08/07/asia.weather/index.html.

[4] "Gender and Health in Disasters," World Health Organization, July 2002, www.who.int/gender/other_health/en/genderdisasters.pdf.

[5] "The tsunami's impact on women," Oxfam briefing note, March 5, 2005, p. 2, www.oxfam.org/en/files/bn050326_tsunami_women/download.

[6] "Report of High-level Roundtable," op. cit., p. 5.

[7] "Gender Equality" fact sheet, Oxfam, www.oxfam.org.uk/resources/issues/gender/introduction.html. Also see ibid.

[8] Ibid., p. 4.

[9] "Five years down the road from Beijing: Assessing progress," News and Highlights, Food and Agriculture Organization, June 2, 2000, www.fao.org/News/2000/000602-e.htm.

[10] "Gender and Health in Disasters," op. cit.

[11] Ibid.

[12] "Women and the Environment," U.N. Environment Program, 2004, p. 17, www.unep.org/Documents.Multilingual/Default.asp?DocumentID=468&ArticleID=4488&l=en. Also see "Report of High-level Roundtable," op. cit., p. 7.

[13] Ibid.

house of parliament for the first time.[96] And in 2007, Fernández de Kirchner became the first woman to be elected president of Argentina.

Earlier, a World Bank report had found that government corruption declines as more women are elected into office. The report also cited numerous studies that found women are more likely to exhibit "helping" behavior, vote based on social issues, score higher on "integrity tests," take stronger stances on ethical behavior and behave more generously when faced with economic decisions.[97]

"Increasing the presence of women in government may be valued for its own sake, for reasons of gender equality," the report concluded. "However, our results suggest that there may be extremely important spinoffs stemming from increasing female representation: If women are less likely than men to behave opportunistically, then bringing more women into government may have significant benefits for society in general."[98]

Current Situation

Rise of Fundamentalism

Despite landmark political gains by women since the late 1990s, violence and repression of women continue to be daily occurrences — often linked to the global growth of religious fundamentalism.

In 2007, a 21-year-old woman in Saudi Arabia was sentenced to 200 lashes and ordered jailed for six months after being raped 14 times by a gang of seven men. The Saudi court sentenced the woman — who was 19 at the time of the attack — because she was alone in a car with her former boyfriend when the attack occurred. Under Saudi Arabia's strict Islamic law, it is a crime for a woman to meet in private with a man who is not her husband or relative.[99]

After public outcry from around the world, King Abdullah pardoned the woman in December. A government spokesperson, however, said the king fully supported the verdict but issued the pardon in the "interests of the people."[100]

Another Saudi woman still faces beheading after she was condemned to death for "witchcraft." Among her accusers is a man who claimed she rendered him impotent with her sorcery. Despite international protest, the king has yet to say if he will pardon her.[101]

In Iraq, the rise of religious fundamentalism since the U.S. invasion has led to a jump in the number of women being killed or beaten in so-called honor crimes. Honor killings typically occur when a woman is suspected of unsanctioned sexual behavior — which can range from flirting to "allowing" herself to be raped. Her relatives believe they must murder her to end the family's shame. In the Kurdish region of Iraq, the stoning death of 17-year-old Aswad is not an anomaly. A U.N. mission in October 2007 found that 255 women had been killed in Iraqi Kurdistan in the first six months of 2007 alone — most thought to have been murdered by their communities or families for allegedly committing adultery or entering into a relationship not sanctioned by their families.[102]

The rise of fundamentalism is also sparking a growing debate on the issue of women wearing head scarves, both in Iraq and across the Muslim world. Last August Turkey elected a conservative Muslim president whose wife wears a head scarf, signaling the emergence of a new ruling elite that is more willing to publicly display religious beliefs.[103] Then in February, Turkey's parliament voted to ease an 80-year ban on women wearing head scarves in universities, although a ban on head scarves in other public buildings remains in effect.

"This decision will bring further pressure on women," Nesrin Baytok, a member of parliament, said during debate over the ban. "It will ultimately bring us Hezbollah terror, al Qaeda terror and fundamentalism."[104]

But others said lifting the ban was actually a victory for women. Fatma Benli, a Turkish women's-rights activist and lawyer, said the ban on head scarves in public buildings has forced her to send law partners to argue her cases because she is prohibited from entering court wearing her head scarf. It also discourages religiously conservative women from becoming doctors, lawyers or teachers, she says.[105]

Many women activists are quick to say that it is unfair to condemn Islam for the growing abuse against women. "The problem women have with religion is not the religion but the ways men have interpreted it," says Afshar of the University of York. "What is highly negative is sharia law, which is made by men. Because it's human-made, women can unmake it. The battle now is fighting against unjust laws such as stoning."

She says abuses such as forced marriages and honor killings — usually linked in the Western media to Islamic law — actually go directly against the teachings of the *Koran*. And while the United Nations estimates that some 5,000 women and girls are victims of honor killings each year, millions more are abused and killed in violence unrelated to

AP Photo/Khalid Tanveer

Honor Killings on the Rise

Women in Multan, Pakistan, demonstrate against "honor killings" in 2003 (top). Although Pakistan outlawed such killings years ago, its Human Rights Commission says 1,205 women were killed in the name of family honor in 2007 — a fourfold jump in two years. Nazir Ahmed Sheikh, a Punjabi laborer (bottom), unrepentantly told police in December 2005 how he slit the throats of his four daughters one night as they slept in order to salvage the family's honor. The eldest had married a man of her choice, and Ahmed feared the younger daughters would follow her example.

AP Photo/Human Rights Commission of Pakistan

Islam. Between 10 and 50 percent of all women around the world have been physically abused by an intimate partner in their lifetime, studies show.[106]

"What about the rate of spousal or partner killings in the U.K. or the U.S. that are not called 'honor killings'?" asks Concordia University's Hoodfar. "Then it's only occasional 'crazy people' [committing violence]. But when it's present in Pakistan, Iran or Senegal, these are uncivilized people doing 'honor killings.' "

And Islamic fundamentalism is not the only brand of fundamentalism on the rise. Christian fundamentalism is also growing rapidly. A 2006 Pew Forum on Religion and Public Life poll found that nearly one-third of all Americans feel the Bible should be the basis of law across the United States.[107] Many women's-rights activists say Christian fundamentalism threatens women's rights, particularly with regard to reproductive issues. They also condemn the Vatican's opposition to the use of condoms, pointing out that it prevents women from protecting themselves against HIV.

"If you look at all your religions, none will say it's a good thing to beat up or kill someone. They are all based on human dignity," says Mollmann of Human Rights Watch. "[Bad things] are carried out in the name of religion, but the actual belief system is not killing and maiming women."

In response to the growing number of honor-based killings, attacks and forced marriages in the U.K., Britain's Association of Chief Police Officers has created an honor-based violence unit, and the U.K.'s Home Office is drafting an action plan to improve the response of police and other agencies to such violence. Legislation going into effect later this year will also give U.K. courts greater guidance on dealing with forced marriages.[108]

Evolving Gender Policies

This past February, the U.N. Convention on the Elimination of All Forms of Discrimination Against Women issued a report criticizing Saudi Arabia for its repression of women. Among other things, the report attacked Saudi Arabia's ban on women drivers and its system of male guardianship that denies women equal inheritance, child custody and divorce rights.[109] The criticism came during the panel's regular review of countries that have ratified CEDAW. Each government must submit reports every four years outlining steps taken to comply with the convention.

The United States is one of only eight countries — among them Iran, Sudan and Somalia — that have refused to ratify CEDAW.[110] Last year, 108 members of the U.S. House of Representatives signed on to a resolution calling for the Senate to ratify CEDAW, but it still has not voted on the measure.[111] During a U.N. vote last November on a resolution encouraging governments to meet their obligations under CEDAW, the United States was the lone nay vote against 173 yea votes.[112]

American opponents of CEDAW — largely pro-life Christians and Republicans — say it would enshrine the right to abortion in *Roe v. Wade* and be prohibitively expensive, potentially requiring the U.S. government to provide paid maternity leave and other child-care services to all women.[113] They also oppose requirements that the government modify "social and cultural patterns" to eliminate sexual prejudice and to delete any traces of gender stereotypes in textbooks — such as references to women's lives being primarily in the domestic sector.[114] Many Republicans in Congress also have argued that CEDAW would give too much control over U.S. laws to the United Nations and that it could even require the legalization of prostitution and the abolition of Mother's Day.[115]

The last time the Senate took action on CEDAW was in 2002, when the Senate Foreign Relations Committee, chaired by Democratic Sen. Joseph Biden of Delaware, voted to send the convention to the Senate floor for ratification. The full Senate, however, never took action. A Biden spokesperson says the senator "remains committed" to the treaty and is "looking for an opportune time" to bring it forward again. But Senate ratification requires 67 votes, and there do not appear to be that many votes for approval.

CEDAW proponents say the failure to ratify not only hurts women but also harms the U.S. image abroad. On this issue, "the United States is in the company of Sudan and the Vatican," says Bien-Aimé of Equality Now.

Meanwhile, several countries are enacting laws to comply with CEDAW and improve the status of women. In December, Turkmenistan passed its first national law guaranteeing women equal rights, even though its constitution had addressed women's equality.[116] A royal decree in Saudi Arabia in January ordered an end to a long-time ban on women checking into hotels or renting apartments without male guardians. Hotels can now book rooms to women who show identification, but the hotels must register the women's details with the police.[117] The Saudi government has also said it will lift the ban on women driving by the end of the year.[118]

And in an effort to improve relations with women in Afghanistan, the Canadian military, which has troops stationed in the region, has begun studying the role women play in Afghan society, how they are affected by military operations and how they can assist peacekeeping efforts. "Behind all of these men are women who can help eradicate the problems of the population," said Capt. Michel Larocque, who is working with the study. "Illiteracy, poverty, these things can be improved through women."[119]

Pakistani acid attack survivors Saira Liaqat, right, and Sabra Sultana are among hundreds, and perhaps thousands, of women who are blinded and disfigured after being attacked with acid each year in Pakistan, Bangladesh, India, Cambodia, Malaysia, Uganda and other areas of Africa. Liaqat was attacked at age 18 during an argument over an arranged marriage. Sabra was 15 when she was burned after being married off to an older man who became unsatisfied with the relationship. Only a small percentage of the attacks — often perpetrated by spurned suitors while the women are asleep in their own beds — are prosecuted.

Getty Images/Paula Bronstein

Female farmworkers in Nova Lima, Brazil, protest against the impact of big corporations on the poor in March 2006, reflecting the increasing political activism of women around the globe.

AP Photo/Light Press/Alex de Jesus

In February, during the 52nd session of the Commission on the Status of Women, the United Nations kicked off a new seven-year campaign aimed at ending violence against women. The campaign will work with international agencies, governments and individuals to increase funding for anti-violence campaigns and pressure policy makers around the world to enact legislation to eliminate violence against women.[120]

But women's groups want increased U.N. spending on women's programs and the creation of a single unified agency addressing women's issues, led by an under-secretary general.[121] Currently, four different U.N. agencies address women's issues: the United Nations Development Fund for Women, the International Research and Training Institute for the Advancement of Women (INSTRAW), the Secretary-General's Special Advisor on Gender Issues (OSAGI) and the Division for the Advancement of Women. In 2006, the four agencies received only $65 million — a fraction of the more than $2 billion budget that the U.N.'s children's fund (UNICEF) received that year.[122]

"The four entities that focus on women's rights at the U.N. are greatly under-resourced," says Zeitlin of the Women's Environment & Development Organization. "If the rhetoric everyone is using is true — that investing in women is investing in development — it's a matter of putting your money where your mouth is."

Political Prospects

While the number of women leading world governments is still miniscule compared to their male counterparts, women are achieving political gains that just a few years ago would have been unthinkable.

While for the first time in U.S. history a woman is in a tight race for a major party's nomination as its candidate for president, South America — with two sitting female heads of state — leads the world in woman-led governments. In Brazil, Dilma Rousseff, the female chief of staff to President Luiz Inacio Lula da Silva, is the top contender to take over the presidency when da Silva's term ends in 2010.[123] In Paraguay, Blanca Ovelar was this year's presidential nominee for the country's ruling conservative Colorado Party, but she was defeated on April 20.[124]

And in Europe, Carme Chacón was named defense minister of Spain this past April. She was not only the first woman ever to head the country's armed forces but also was pregnant at the time of her appointment. In all, nine of Spain's 17 cabinet ministers are women.

In March, Pakistan's National Assembly overwhelmingly elected its first female speaker, Fahmida Mirza.[125] And in India, where Patil has become the first woman president, the two major political parties this year pledged to set aside one-third of their parliamentary nominations for women. But many fear the parties will either not keep their pledges or will run women only in contests they are unlikely to win.[126]

There was also disappointment in Iran, where nearly 600 of the 7,000 candidates running for parliament in March were women.[127] Only three won seats in the 290-member house, and they were conservatives who are not expected to promote women's rights.

Should sex-selective abortions be outlawed?

YES Nicholas Eberstadt
*Henry Wendt Chair in Political
Economy, American Enterprise Institute
Member,* President's Council on
Bioethics

NO Marianne Mollmann
*Advocacy Director, Women's Rights
Division, Human Rights Watch*

Written for *CQ Researcher*, January 2009

Written for *CQ Researcher*, January 2009

The practice of sex-selective abortion to permit parents to destroy unwanted female fetuses has become so widespread in the modern world that it is disfiguring the profile of entire countries — transforming (and indeed deforming) the whole human species.

This abomination is now rampant in China, where the latest census reports six boys for every five girls. But it is also prevalent in the Far East, South Korea, Hong Kong, Taiwan and Vietnam, all of which report biologically impossible "sex ratios at birth" (well above the 103-106 baby boys for every 100 girls ordinarily observed in human populations). In the Caucasus, gruesome imbalances exist now in Armenia, Georgia and Azerbaijan; and in India, the state of Punjab tallies 126 little boys for every 100 girls. Even in the United States, the boy-girl sex ratio at birth for Asian-Americans is now several unnatural percentage points above the national average. So sex-selective abortion is taking place under America's nose.

How can we rid the world of this barbaric form of sexism? Simply outlawing sex-selective abortions will be little more than a symbolic gesture, as South Korea's experience has shown: Its sex ratio at birth continued a steady climb for a full decade after just such a national law was passed. As long as abortion is basically available on demand, any legislation to abolish sex-selective abortion will have no impact.

What about more general restrictions on abortion, then? Poll data consistently demonstrate that most Americans do not favor the post-Roe regimen of unconditional abortion. But a return to the pre-Roe status quo, where each state made its own abortion laws, would probably have very little effect on sex-selective abortion in our country. After all, the ethnic communities most tempted by it are concentrated in states where abortion rights would likely be strongest, such as California and New York.

In the final analysis, the extirpation of this scourge will require nothing less than a struggle for the conscience of nations. Here again, South Korea may be illustrative: Its gender imbalances began to decline when the public was shocked into facing this stain on their society by a spontaneous, homegrown civil rights movement.

To eradicate sex-selective abortion, we must convince the world that destroying female fetuses is horribly wrong. We need something akin to the abolitionist movement: a moral campaign waged globally, with victories declared one conscience at a time.

Medical technology today allows parents to test early in pregnancy for fetal abnormalities, hereditary illnesses and even the sex of the fetus, raising horrifying questions about eugenics and population control. In some countries, a growing number of women apparently are terminating pregnancies when they learn the fetus is female. The resulting sex imbalance in countries like China and India is not only disturbing but also leads to further injustices, such as the abduction of girls for forced marriages.

One response has been to criminalize sex-selective abortions. While it is tempting to hope that this could safeguard the gender balance of future generations, criminalization of abortion for whatever reason has led in the past only to underground and unsafe practices. Thus, the criminalization of sex-selective abortion would put the full burden of righting a fundamental wrong — the devaluing of women's lives — on women.

Many women who choose to abort a female fetus face violence and exclusion if they don't produce a boy. Some see the financial burden of raising a girl as detrimental to the survival of the rest of their family. These considerations will not be lessened by banning sex-selective abortion. Unless one addresses the motivation for the practice, it will continue — underground.

So what is the motivation for aborting female fetuses? At the most basic level, it is a financial decision. In no country in the world does women's earning power equal men's. In marginalized communities in developing countries, this is directly linked to survival: Boys may provide more income than girls.

Severe gaps between women's and men's earning power are generally accompanied by severe forms of gender-based discrimination and rigid gender roles. For example, in China, boys are expected to stay in their parental home as they grow up, adding their manpower (and that of a later wife) to the family home. Girls, on the other hand, are expected to join the husbands' parental home. Thus, raising a girl is a net loss, especially if you are only allowed one child.

The solution is to remove the motivation behind sex-selective abortion by advancing women's rights and their economic and social equality. Choosing the blunt instrument of criminal law over promoting the value of women's lives and rights will only serve to place further burdens on marginalized and often vulnerable women.

Several of the tallies are being contested. Twelve other women won enough votes to face run-off elections on April 25; five won.[128]

But in some countries, women running for office face more than just tough campaigns. They are specifically targeted for violence. In Kenya, the greatest campaign expense for female candidates is the round-the-clock security required to protect them against rape, according to Phoebe Asiyo, who served in the Kenyan parliament for more than two decades.[129] During the three months before Kenya's elections last December, an emergency helpdesk established by the Education Centre for Women in Democracy, a nongovernmental organization (NGO) in Nairobi, received 258 reports of attacks against female candidates.[130]

The helpdesk reported the attacks to police, worked with the press to ensure the cases were documented and helped victims obtain medical and emotional support. Attacks included rape, stabbings, threats and physical assaults.[131]

"Women are being attacked because they are women and because it is seen as though they are not fit to bear flags of the popular parties," according to the center's Web site. "Women are also viewed as guilty for invading 'the male territory' and without a license to do so!"[132]

"All women candidates feel threatened," said Nazlin Umar, the sole female presidential candidate last year. "When a case of violence against a woman is reported, we women on the ground think we are next. I think if the government assigned all women candidates with guns…we will at least have an item to protect ourselves when we face danger."[133]

Impunity for Violence

Some African feminists blame women themselves, as well as men, for not doing enough to end traditional attitudes that perpetuate violence against women.

"Women are also to blame for the violence because they are the gatekeepers of patriarchy, because whether educated or not they have different standards for their sons and husbands [than for] their daughters," said Njoki Wainaina, founder of the African Women Development Communication Network (FEMNET). "How do you start telling a boy whose mother trained him only disrespect for girls to honor women in adulthood?"[134]

Indeed, violence against women is widely accepted in many regions of the world and often goes unpunished. A study by the World Health Organization found that 80 percent of women surveyed in rural Egypt believe that a man is justified in beating a woman if she refuses to have sex with him. In Ghana, more women than men — 50 percent compared to 43 percent — felt that a man was justified in beating his wife if she used contraception without his consent.[135] (*See survey results, p. 338.*)

Such attitudes have led to many crimes against women going unpunished, and not just violence committed during wartime. In Guatemala, no one knows why an estimated 3,000 women have been killed over the past seven years — many of them beheaded, sexually mutilated or raped — but theories range from domestic violence to gang activity.[136] Meanwhile, the government in 2006 overturned a law allowing rapists to escape charges if they offered to marry their victims. But Guatemalan law still does not prescribe prison sentences for domestic abuse and prohibits abusers from being charged with assault unless the bruises are still visible after 10 days.[137]

In the Mexican cities of Chihuahua and Juárez, more than 400 women have been murdered over the past 14 years, with many of the bodies mutilated and dumped in the desert. But the crimes are still unsolved, and many human-rights groups, including Amnesty International, blame indifference by Mexican authorities. Now the country's 14-year statute of limitations on murder is forcing prosecutors to close many of the unsolved cases.[138]

Feminists around the world have been working to end dismissive cultural attitudes about domestic violence and other forms of violence against women, such as forced marriage, dowry-related violence, marital rape, sexual harassment and forced abortion, sterilization and prostitution. But it's often an uphill battle.

After a Kenyan police officer beat his wife so badly she was paralyzed and brain damaged — and eventually died — media coverage of the murder spurred a nationwide debate on domestic violence. But it took five years of protests, demonstrations and lobbying by both women's advocates and outraged men to get a family protection bill enacted criminalizing domestic violence. And the bill passed only after legislators removed a provision outlawing marital rape. Similar laws have languished for decades in other African legislatures.[139]

But in Rwanda, where nearly 49 percent of the elected representatives in the lower house are female, gender desks have been established at local police stations, staffed mostly by women trained to help victims of sexual and other violence. In 2006, as a result of improved reporting, investigation and response to rape cases, police referred 1,777 cases for prosecution and convicted 803 men. "What we need now is to expand this approach to more countries," said UNIFEM's director for Central Africa Josephine Odera.[140]

Besides criticizing governments for failing to prosecute gender-based violence, many women's groups also criticize the International Criminal Court (ICC) for not doing enough to bring abusers to justice.

"We have yet to see the investigative approach needed to ensure the prosecution of gender-based crimes," said Brigid Inder, executive director of Women's Initiatives for Gender Justice, a Hague-based group that promotes and monitors women's rights in the international court.[141] Inder's group released a study last November showing that of the 500 victims seeking to participate in ICC proceedings, only 38 percent were women. When the court handed down its first indictments for war crimes in the Democratic Republic of the Congo last year, no charges involving gender-based crimes were brought despite estimates that more than 250,000 women have been raped and sexually abused in the country. After an outcry from women's groups around the world, the ICC included "sexual slavery" among the charges handed down in its second case involving war crimes in Congo.[142]

The Gender Justice report also criticized the court for failing to reach out to female victims. It said the ICC has held only one consultation with women in the last four years (focusing on the Darfur conflict in Sudan) and has failed to develop any strategies to reach out to women victims in Congo.[143]

Outlook

Economic Integration

Women's organizations do not expect — or want — another international conference on the scale of Beijing. Instead, they say, the resources needed to launch such a conference

Seaweed farmer Asia Mohammed Makungu in Zanzibar, Tanzania, grows the sea plants for export to European companies that produce food and cosmetics. Globalized trade has helped women entrepreneurs in many developing countries improve their lives, but critics say it also has created many low-wage, dangerous jobs for women in poor countries that ignore safety and labor protections in order to attract foreign investors.

AP Photo/Karel Prinsloo

would be better used to improve U.N. oversight of women's issues and to implement the promises made at Beijing.

They also fear that the growth of religious fundamentalism and neo-liberal economic policies around the globe have created a political atmosphere that could actually set back women's progress.

"If a Beijing conference happened now, we would not get the type of language or the scope we got 10 years ago," says Bien-Aimé of Equity Now. "There is a conservative movement, a growth in fundamentalists governments — and not just in Muslim countries. We would be very concerned about opening up debate on the principles that have already been established."

Dahlerup of Stockholm University agrees. "It was easier in the 1990s. Many people are afraid of having big conferences now, because there may be a backlash because fundamentalism is so strong," she says. "Neo-liberal trends are also moving the discourse about women toward economics — women have to benefit for the sake of the economic good. That could be very good, but it's a more narrow discourse when every issue needs to be adapted into the economic discourse of a cost-benefit analysis."

For women to continue making gains, most groups say, gender can no longer be treated separately from broader economic, environmental, health or other political issues. While efforts to improve the status of women have historically been addressed in gender-specific legislation or international treaties, women's groups now say women's well-being must now be considered an integral part of all policies.

Women's groups are working to ensure that gender is incorporated into two major international conferences coming up this fall. In September, the Third High-Level Forum on Aid Effectiveness will be hosted in Accra, Ghana, bringing together governments, financial institutions, civil society organizations and others to assess whether assistance provided to poor nations is being put to good use. World leaders will also gather in November in Doha, Qatar, for the International Conference on Financing for Development to discuss how trade, debt relief and financial aid can promote global development.

"Women's groups are pushing for gender to be on the agenda for both conferences," says Zeitlin of WEDO. "It's important because . . . world leaders need to realize that it really does make a difference to invest in women. When it comes to women's rights it's all micro, but the big decisions are made on the macro level."

Despite decades of economic-development strategies promoted by Western nations and global financial institutions such as the World Bank, women in many regions are getting poorer. In Malawi, for example, the percentage of women living in poverty increased by 5 percent between 1995 and 2003.[144] Women and girls make up 70 percent of the world's poorest people, and their wages rise more slowly than men's. They also have fewer property rights around the world.[145] With the growing global food shortage, women — who are the primary family caregivers and produce the majority of crops for home consumption in developing countries — will be especially hard hit.

To help women escape poverty, gain legal rights and improve their social status, developed nations must rethink their broader strategies of engagement with developing countries. And, conversely, female activists say, any efforts aimed at eradicating poverty around the world must specifically address women's issues.

In Africa, for instance, activists have successfully demanded that women's economic and security concerns be addressed as part of the continent-wide development plan known as the New Partnership for Africa's Development (NEPAD). As a result, countries participating in NEPAD's peer review process must now show they are taking measures to promote and protect women's rights. But, according to Augustin Wambo, an agricultural specialist at the NEPAD secretariat, lawmakers now need to back up their pledges with "resources from national budgets" and the "necessary policies and means to support women."[146]

"We have made a lot of progress and will continue making progress," says Zeitlin. "But women's progress doesn't happen in isolation to what's happening in the rest of the world. The environment, the global economy, war, peace — they will all have a major impact on women. Women all over world will not stop making demands and fighting for their rights."

Notes

1. http://ballyblog.wordpress.com/2007/05/04/ warning-uncensored-video-iraqis-stone-girl-to-death-over-loving-wrong-boy/.

2. Abdulhamid Zebari, "Video of Iraqi girl's stoning shown on Internet," Agence France Presse, May 5, 2007.

3. *State of the World Population 2000*, United Nations Population Fund, Sept. 20, 2000, Chapter 3, "Ending Violence against Women and Girls," www.unfpa.org/swp/2000/english/ch03.html.

4. Brian Brady, "A Question of Honour," *The Independent on Sunday*, Feb. 10, 2008, p. 8, www.independent.co.uk/news/uk/home-news/a-question-of-honour-police-say-17000-women-are-victims-every-year-780522.html.

5. Correspondence with Karen Musalo, Clinical Professor of Law and Director of the Center for Gender & Refugee Studies at the University of California Hastings School of Law, April 11, 2008.

6. "Broken Bodies, Broken Dreams: Violence Against Women Exposed," United Nations, July 2006, http://brokendreams.wordpress. com/2006/12/17/dowry-crimes-and-bride-price-abuse/.

7. Various sources: www.womankind.org.uk, www.unfpa.org/gender/docs/studies/summaries/reg_exe_summary.pdf, www.oxfam.org.uk. Also see "Child rape in Kano on the increase," IRIN Humanitarian News and Analysis, United Nations, www.irinnews.org/report.aspx?ReportId=76087.

8. "UNICEF slams 'licence to rape' in African crisis," Agence France-Press, Feb. 12, 2008.

9. "Film Documents Rape of Women in Congo," "All Things Considered," National Public Radio, April 8, 2008, www.npr.org/templates/story/story.php?storyId=89476111.

10. Jeffrey Gettleman, "Rape Epidemic Raises Trauma Of Congo War," *The New York Times*, Oct. 7, 2007, p. A1.

11. Dan McDougall, "Fareeda's fate: rape, prison and 25 lashes," *The Observer*, Sept. 17, 2006, www.guardian.co.uk/world/2006/sep/17/pakistan.theobserver.

12. Zarar Khan, "Thousands rally in Pakistan to demand government withdraw rape law changes," The Associated Press, Dec. 10, 2006.

13. *State of the World Population 2000, op. cit.*

14. Laura Turquet, Patrick Watt, Tom Sharman, "Hit or Miss?" ActionAid, March 7, 2008, p. 10.

15. *Ibid.*, p. 12.

16. "Women in Politics: 2008" map, International Parliamentary Union and United Nations Division for the Advancement of Women, February 2008, www.ipu.org/pdf/publications/wmnmap08_en.pdf.

17. Gavin Rabinowitz, "India's first female president sworn in, promises to empower women," The Associated Press, July 25, 2007. Note: India's first female prime minister was Indira Ghandi in 1966.

18. Monte Reel, "South America Ushers In The Era of La Presidenta; Women Could Soon Lead a Majority of Continent's Population," *The Washington Post*, Oct. 31, 2007, p. A12. For background, see Roland Flamini, "The New Latin America," *CQ Global Researcher*, March 2008, pp. 57-84.

19. Marcela Valente, "Cristina Fernandes Dons Presidential Sash," Inter Press Service, Dec. 10, 2007.

20. "Women in Politics: 2008" map, *op. cit.*

21. *Ibid.*; Global Database of Quotas for Women, International Institute for Democracy and Electoral Assistance and Stockholm University, www.quotaproject.org/country.cfm?SortOrder=Country.

22. "Beijing Betrayed," Women's Environment and Development Organization, March 2005, p. 10, www.wedo.org/files/gmr_pdfs/gmr2005.pdf.

23. "Women in Politics: 2008" map, *op. cit.*

24. Gertrude Mongella, address by the Secretary-General of the 4th World Conference on Women, Sept. 4, 1995, www.un.org/esa/gopher-data/conf/fwcw/conf/una/950904201423.txt. Also see Steven Mufson, "Women's Forum Sets Accord; Dispute on Sexual Freedom Resolved," *The Washington Post*, Sept. 15, 1995, p. A1.

25. "Closing statement," Gertrude Mongella, U.N. Division for the Advancement of Women, Fourth World Conference on Women, www.un.org/esa/gopher-data/conf/fwcw/conf/una/closing.txt.

26. "Trading Away Our Rights," Oxfam International, 2004, p. 9, www.oxfam.org.uk/resources/policy/trade/downloads/trading_rights.pdf.

27. "Trafficking in Persons Report," U.S. Department of State, June 2007, p. 7, www.state.gov/g/tip/rls/tiprpt/2007/.

28. Turquet, *et al.*, *op. cit.*, p. 4.

29. United Nations Division for the Advancement of Women, www.un.org/womenwatch/daw/cedaw/.

30. Geraldine Terry, *Women's Rights* (2007), p. 30.

31. United Nations Division for the Advancement of Women, www.un.org/womenwatch/daw/cedaw/.

32. "The impact of international trade on gender equality," The World Bank PREM notes, May 2004, http://siteresources.worldbank.org/INTGENDER/Resources/premnote86.pdf.

33. Thalia Kidder and Kate Raworth, " 'Good Jobs' and hidden costs: women workers documenting the price of precarious employment," *Gender and Development*, July 2004, p. 13.

34. "Trading Away Our Rights," *op. cit.*

35. Martha Chen, *et al.*, "Progress of the World's Women 2005: Women, Work and Poverty," UNIFEM, p. 17, www.unifem.org/attachments/products/PoWW2005_eng.pdf.

36. Eric Neumayer and Indra de Soys, "Globalization, Women's Economic Rights and Forced Labor," London School of Economics and Norwegian University of Science and Technology, February 2007, p. 8, http://papers.ssrn.com/sol3/papers.cfm?abstract_id=813831. Also see "Five years down the road from Beijing — assessing progress," *News and Highlights*, Food and Agriculture Organization, June 2, 2000, www.fao.org/News/2000/000602-e.htm.

37. "Trafficking in Persons Report," *op. cit.*, p. 13.

38. "World Survey on the Role of Women in Development," United Nations, 2006, p. 1, www.un.org/womenwatch/daw/public/WorldSurvey2004-Women& Migration.pdf.

39. Julie Ballington and Azza Karam, eds., "Women in Parliament: Beyond the Numbers," International Institute for Democracy and Electoral Assistance, 2005, p. 155, www.idea.int/publications/wip2/upload/WiP_inlay.pdf.

40. "Women in Politics: 2008," *op. cit.*

41. Ballington and Karam, *op. cit.*, p. 158.

42. *Ibid.*, p. 161.

43. Global Database of Quotas for Women, *op. cit.*

44. Jerome Starkey, "Afghan government official says that student will not be executed," *The Independent*, Feb. 6, 2008, www.independent.co.uk/news/world/asia/afghan-government-official-says-that-student-will-not-be-executed-778686.html?r=RSS.

45. "Afghan women seek death by fire," BBC, Nov. 15, 2006, http://news.bbc.co.uk/1/hi/world/south_asia/6149144.stm.

46. Global Database for Quotas for Women, *op. cit.*

47. "Beijing Declaration," Fourth World Conference on Women, www.un.org/womenwatch/daw/beijing/beijingdeclaration.html.

48. "Beijing Betrayed," *op. cit.*, pp. 28, 15, 18.

49. "Review of the implementation of the Beijing Platform for Action and the outcome documents of the special session of the General Assembly entitled 'Women 2000: gender equality, development and peace for the twenty-first century,' " United Nations, Dec. 6, 2004, p. 74.

50. "Gender Equality and the Millennium Development Goals," fact sheet, www.mdgender.net/upload/tools/MDGender_leaflet.pdf.

51. *Ibid.*

52. Turquet, *et al.*, *op. cit.*, p. 16.

53. *Ibid.*, pp. 22-24.

54. Terry, *op. cit.*, p. 6.

55. "Inclusive Security, Sustainable Peace: A Toolkit for Advocacy and Action," International Alert and Women Waging Peace, 2004, p. 12, www.huntalternatives.org/download/35_introduction.pdf.

56. "Declarations, Reservations and Objections to CEDAW," www.un.org/womenwatch/daw/cedaw/reservations-country.htm.

57. Merlin Stone, *When God Was a Woman* (1976), pp. 18, 11.

58. Jack Holland, *Misogyny* (2006), p. 12.

59. *Ibid.*, pp. 21-23.

60. Holland, *op. cit.*, p. 112.

61. "Dispelling the myths about so-called witches" press release, Johns Hopkins University, Oct. 7, 2002, www.jhu.edu/news_info/news/home02/oct02/witch.html.

62. The quote is from the *Malleus maleficarum* (*The Hammer of Witches*), and was cited in "Case Study: The European Witch Hunts, c. 1450-1750," *Gendercide Watch*, www.gendercide.org/case_witchhunts.html.

63. Holland, *op. cit.*, p. 179.

64. Cathy J. Cohen, Kathleen B. Jones and Joan C. Tronto, *Women Transforming Politics: An Alternative Reader* (1997), p. 530.

65. *Ibid.*

66. Holland, *op. cit*, p. 201.

67. "Men and Women in Politics: Democracy Still in the Making," IPU Study No. 28, 1997, http://archive.idea.int/women/parl/ch6_table8.htm.

68. "Sex, Equality and Protective Laws," *CQ Researcher*, July 13, 1926.

69. The case was *Radice v. People of State of New York*, 264 U. S. 292. For background, see F. Brewer, "Equal Rights Amendment," *Editorial Research Reports*, April 4, 1946, available at *CQ Researcher Plus Archive*, www.cqpress.com.

70. "Short History of the CEDAW Convention," U.N. Division for the Advancement of Women, www.un.org/womenwatch/daw/cedaw/history.htm.

71. U.N. Women's Watch, www.un.org/womenwatch/asp/user/list.asp-ParentID=11047.htm.

72. United Nations, http://untreaty.un.org/ENGLISH/bible/englishinternetbible/partI/chapterXVI/treaty2.asp.

73. International Labor Organization, www.ilo.org/public/english/support/lib/resource/subject/gender.htm.

74. *Ibid.*

75. For background, see "Gender Pay Gap," *CQ Researcher*, March 14, 2008, pp. 241-264.

76. "Short History of the CEDAW Convention" *op. cit.*

77. "International News," The Associated Press, Dec. 19, 1979.

78. "Short History of the CEDAW Convention" *op. cit.*

79. "Text of the Convention," U.N. Division for the Advancement of Women, www.un.org/womenwatch/daw/cedaw/cedaw.htm.

80. Convention on the Elimination of All Forms of Discrimination against Women, Article 16, www.un.org/womenwatch/daw/cedaw/text/econvention.htm.

81. General Recommendation made by the Committee on the Elimination of Discrimination against Women No. 19, 11th session, 1992, www.un.org/womenwatch/daw/cedaw/recommendations/recomm.htm#recom19.

82. See www.unhchr.ch/huridocda/huridoca.nsf/(Symbol)/A.CONF.157.23.En.

83. Marlise Simons, "For First Time, Court Defines Rape as War Crime," *The New York Times*, June 28, 1996, www.nytimes.com/specials/bosnia/context/0628warcrimes-tribunal.html.

84. Ann Simmons, "U.N. Tribunal Convicts Rwandan Ex-Mayor of Genocide in Slaughter," *Los Angeles Times*, Sept. 3, 1998, p. 20.

85. "Human Rights Watch Applauds Rwanda Rape Verdict," press release, Human Rights Watch, Sept. 2, 1998, http://hrw.org/english/docs/1998/09/02/rwanda1311.htm.

86. Frederic Bichon, "ICC vows to bring Darfur war criminals to justice," Agence France-Presse, Feb. 24, 2008.

87. Rebecca Feeley and Colin Thomas-Jensen, "Getting Serious about Ending Conflict and Sexual Violence in Congo," Enough Project, www.enoughproject.org/reports/congoserious.

88. "Women; Deceived Again?" *The Economist*, July 5, 1975.

89. "International Women's Day — March 8: Points of Interest and Links with UNIFEM," UNIFEM New Zealand Web site, www.unifem.org.nz/IWDPointsofinterest.htm.

90. Joseph Gambardello, "Reporter's Notebook: Women's Conference in Kenya," United Press International, July 13, 1985.

91. "Report of the World Conference to Review and Appraise the Achievements of the United Nations Decade for Women: Equality Development and Peace," United Nations, 1986, paragraph 8, www.un.org/womenwatch/confer/nfls/Nairobi1985report.txt.

92. U.N. Division for the Advancement of Women, www.un.org/womenwatch/daw/followup/background.htm.

93. "Women in Politics," Inter-Parliamentary Union, 2005, pp. 16-17, www.ipu.org/PDF/publications/wmn45-05_en.pdf.

94. "Liberian becomes Africa's first female president," Associated Press, Jan. 16, 2006, www.msnbc.msn.com/id/10865705/.

95. "Women in the Americas: Paths to Political Power," *op. cit.*, p. 2.

96. "The Millennium Development Goals Report 2007," United Nations, 2007, p. 12, www.un.org/millenniumgoals/pdf/mdg2007.pdf.

97. David Dollar, Raymond Fisman, Roberta Gatti, "Are Women Really the 'Fairer' Sex? Corruption and Women in Government," The World Bank, October 1999, p. 1, http://siteresources.worldbank.org/INTGENDER/Resources/wp4.pdf.

98. *Ibid.*

99. Vicky Baker, "Rape victim sentenced to 200 lashes and six months in jail; Saudi woman punished for being alone with a man," *The Guardian*, Nov. 17, 2007, www.guardian.co.uk/world/2007/nov/17/saudiarabia.international.

100. Katherine Zoepf, "Saudi King Pardons Rape Victim Sentenced to Be Lashed, Saudi Paper Reports," *The New*

York Times, Dec. 18, 2007, www.nytimes.com/2007/12/18/world/middleeast/18saudi.html.

101. Sonia Verma, "King Abdullah urged to spare Saudi 'witchcraft' woman's life," *The Times* (Of London), Feb. 16, 2008.

102. Mark Lattimer, "Freedom lost," *The Guardian*, Dec. 13, 2007, p. 6.

103. For background, see Brian Beary, "Future of Turkey," *CQ Global Researcher*, December, 2007, pp. 295-322.

104. Tracy Clark-Flory, "Does freedom to veil hurt women?" *Salon.com*, Feb. 11, 2008.

105. Sabrina Tavernise, "Under a Scarf, a Turkish Lawyer Fighting to Wear It," *The New York Times*, Feb. 9, 2008, www.nytimes.com/2008/02/09/world/europe/09benli.html?pagewanted=1&sq=women&st=nyt&scp=96.

106. Terry, *op. cit.*, p. 122.

107. "Many Americans Uneasy with Mix of Religion and Politics," The Pew Forum on Religion and Public Life, Aug. 24, 2006, http://pewforum.org/docs/index.php?DocID=153.

108. Brady, *op. cit.*

109. "Concluding Observations of the Committee on the Elimination of Discrimination against Women: Saudi Arabia," Committee on the Elimination of Discrimination against Women, 40th Session, Jan. 14-Feb. 1, 2008, p. 3, www2.ohchr.org/english/bodies/cedaw/docs/co/CEDAW.C.SAU.CO.2.pdf.

110. Kambiz Fattahi, "Women's bill 'unites' Iran and US," BBC, July 31, 2007, http://news.bbc.co.uk/2/hi/middle_east/6922749.stm.

111. H. Res. 101, Rep. Lynn Woolsey, http://thomas.loc.gov/cgi-bin/bdquery/z?d110:h.res.00101.

112. "General Assembly Adopts Landmark Text Calling for Moratorium on Death Penalty," States News Service, Dec. 18, 2007, www.un.org/News/Press/docs//2007/ga10678.doc.htm.

113. Mary H. Cooper, "Women and Human Rights," *CQ Researcher*, April 30, 1999, p. 356.

114. Christina Hoff Sommers, "The Case against Ratifying the United Nations Convention on the Elimination of All Forms of Discrimination against Women," testimony before the Senate Foreign Relations Committee, June 13, 2002, www.aei.org/publications/filter.all,pubID.15557/pub_detail.asp.

115. "CEDAW: Pro-United Nations, Not Pro-Woman" press release, U.S. Senate Republican Policy Committee, Sept. 16, 2002, http://rpc.senate.gov/_files/FOREIGNje091602.pdf.

116. "Turkmenistan adopts gender equality law," BBC Worldwide Monitoring, Dec. 19, 2007.

117. Faiza Saleh Ambah, "Saudi Women See a Brighter Road on Rights," *The Washington Post*, Jan. 31, 2008, p. A15, www.washingtonpost.com/wp-dyn/content/article/2008/01/30/AR2008013003805.html.

118. Damien McElroy, "Saudi Arabia to lift ban on women drivers," *The Telegraph*, Jan. 1, 2008.

119. Stephanie Levitz, "Lifting the veils of Afghan women," *The Hamilton Spectator* (Ontario, Canada), Feb. 28, 2008, p. A11.

120. "U.N. Secretary-General Ban Ki-moon Launches Campaign to End Violence against Women," U.N. press release, Feb. 25, 2008, http://endviolence.un.org/press.shtml.

121. "Gender Equality Architecture and U.N. Reforms," the Center for Women's Global Leadership and the Women's Environment and Development Organization, July 17, 2006, www.wedo.org/files/Gender%20Equality%20Architecture%20and%20UN%20Reform0606.pdf.

122. Bojana Stoparic, "New-Improved Women's Agency Vies for U.N. Priority," Women's eNews, March 6, 2008, www.womensenews.org/article.cfm?aid=3517.

123. Reel, *op. cit.*

124. Eliana Raszewski and Bill Faries, "Lugo, Ex Bishop, Wins Paraguay Presidential Election," Bloomberg, April 20, 2008.

125. Zahid Hussain, "Pakistan gets its first woman Speaker," *The Times* (of London), March 20, p. 52.

126. Bhaskar Roy, "Finally, women set to get 33% quota," *Times of India*, Jan. 29, 2008.

127. Massoumeh Torfeh, "Iranian women crucial in Majlis election," BBC, Jan. 30, 2008, http://news.bbc.co.uk/1/hi/world/middle_east/7215272.stm.

128. "Iran women win few seats in parliament," Agence-France Presse, March 18, 2008.

129. Swanee Hunt, "Let Women Rule," *Foreign Affairs*, May-June 2007, p. 109.

130. Kwamboka Oyaro, "A Call to Arm Women Candidates With More Than Speeches," Inter Press Service, Dec. 21, 2007, http://ipsnews.net/news.asp?idnews=40569.

131. Education Centre for Women in Democracy, www.ecwd.org.

132. *Ibid.*

133. Oyaro, *op. cit.*

134. *Ibid.*

135. Mary Kimani, "Taking on violence against women in Africa," *AfricaRenewal*, U.N. Dept. of Public Information, July 2007, p. 4, www.un.org/ecosocdev/geninfo/afrec/vol21no2/212-violence-aganist-women.html.

136. Correspondence with Karen Musalo, Clinical Professor of Law and Director of the Center for Gender & Refugee Studies, University of California Hastings School of Law, April 11, 2008.

137. "Mexico and Guatemala: Stop the Killings of Women," Amnesty International USA Issue Brief, January 2007, www.amnestyusa.org/document.php?lang=e&id=engusa20070130001.

138. Manuel Roig-Franzia, "Waning Hopes in Juarez," *The Washington Post*, May 14, 2007, p. A10.

139. Kimani, *op. cit.*

140. *Ibid.*

141. "Justice slow for female war victims," *The Toronto Star*, March 3, 2008, www.thestar.com/News/GlobalVoices/article/308784p.

142. Speech by Brigid Inder on the Launch of the "Gender Report Card on the International Criminal Court," Dec. 12, 2007, www.iccwomen.org/news/docs/Launch_GRC_2007.pdf

143. "Gender Report Card on the International Criminal Court," Women's Initiatives for Gender Justice, November 2007, p. 32, www.iccwomen.org/publications/resources/docs/GENDER_04-01-2008_FINAL_TO_PRINT.pdf.

144. Turquet, *et al.*, *op. cit.*, p. 8.

145. Oxfam Gender Equality Fact Sheet, www.oxfam.org.uk/resources/issues/gender/introduction.html.

146. Itai Madamombe, "Women push onto Africa's agenda," *AfricaRenewal*, U.N. Dept. of Public Information, July 2007, pp. 8-9.

Bibliography

Books

Holland, Jack, *Misogyny: The World's Oldest Prejudice*, *Constable & Robinson*, 2006.
The late Irish journalist provides vivid details and anecdotes about women's oppression throughout history.

Stone, Merlin, *When God Was a Woman*, *Harcourt Brace Jovanovich*, 1976.
The book contends that before the rise of Judeo-Christian patriarchies women headed the first societies and religions.

Terry, Geraldine, *Women's Rights*, *Pluto Press*, 2007.
A feminist who has worked for Oxfam and other non-governmental organizations outlines major issues facing women today — from violence to globalization to AIDS.

Women and the Environment, *UNEP*, 2004.
The United Nations Environment Programme shows the integral link between women in the developing world and the changing environment.

Articles

Brady, Brian, "A Question of Honour," *The Independent on Sunday*, Feb. 10, 2008, p. 8.
"Honor killings" and related violence against women are on the rise in the United Kingdom.

Kidder, Thalia, and Kate Raworth, " 'Good Jobs' and hidden costs: women workers documenting the price of precarious employment," *Gender and Development*, Vol. 12, No. 2, p. 12, July 2004.

Two trade and gender experts describe the precarious working conditions and job security experienced by food and garment workers.

Reports and Studies

"Beijing Betrayed," *Women's Environment and Development Organization*, March 2005, www.wedo.org/files/gmr_pdfs/gmr2005.pdf.
A women's-rights organization reviews the progress and shortcomings of governments in implementing the commitments made during the Fifth World Congress on Women in Beijing in 1995.

"The Millennium Development Goals Report 2007," *United Nations*, 2007, www.un.org/millenniumgoals/pdf/mdg2007.pdf.
International organizations demonstrate the progress governments have made — or not — in reaching the Millennium Development Goals.

"Trafficking in Persons Report," *U.S. Department of State*, June 2007, www.state.gov/documents/organization/82902.pdf.
This seventh annual report discusses the growing problems of human trafficking around the world.

"The tsunami's impact on women," *Oxfam briefing note*, March 5, 2005, www.oxfam.org/en/files/bn050326_tsunami_women/download.
Looking at how the 2004 tsunami affected women in Indonesia, India and Sri Lanka, Oxfam International

suggests how governments can better address women's issues during future natural disasters.

"Women in Politics," *Inter-Parliamentary Union*, 2005, www.ipu.org/PDF/publications/wmn45-05_en.pdf. The report provides detailed databases of the history of female political representation in governments around the world.

Ballington, Julie, and Azza Karam, "Women in Parliament: Beyond the Numbers," *International Institute for Democracy and Electoral Assistance*, 2005, www.idea .int/publications/wip2/upload/WiP_inlay.pdf. The handbook provides female politicians and candidates information and case studies on how women have overcome obstacles to elected office.

Chen, Martha, Joann Vanek, Francie Lund, James Heintz, Renana Jhabvala and Christine Bonner, "Women, Work and Poverty," *UNIFEM*, 2005, www.unifem.org/attach ments/products/PoWW2005_eng.pdf. The report argues that greater work protection and security is needed to promote women's rights and reduce global poverty.

Larserud, Stina, and Rita Taphorn, "Designing for Equality," *International Institute for Democracy and Electoral Assistance*, 2007, www.idea.int/publications/designing_ for_equality/upload/Idea_Design_low.pdf. The report describes the impact that gender quota systems have on women's representation in elected office.

Raworth, Kate, and Claire Harvey, "Trading Away Our Rights," *Oxfam International*, 2004, www.oxfam.org.uk/ resources/policy/trade/downloads/trading_rights.pdf. Through exhaustive statistics, case studies and interviews, the report paints a grim picture of how trade globalization is affecting women.

Turquet, Laura, Patrick Watt and Tom Sharman, "Hit or Miss?" *ActionAid*, March 7, 2008. The report reviews how governments are doing in achieving the U.N.'s Millennium Development Goals.

For More Information

Equality Now, P.O. Box 20646, Columbus Circle Station, New York, NY 10023; www.equalitynow.org. An international organization working to protect women against violence and promote women's human rights.

Global Database of Quotas for Women; www.quotaproject .org. A joint project of the International Institute for Democracy and Electoral Assistance and Stockholm University providing country-by-country data on electoral quotas for women.

Human Rights Watch, 350 Fifth Ave., 34th floor, New York, NY 10118-3299; (212) 290-4700; www.hrw.org. Investigates and exposes human-rights abuses around the world.

Hunt Alternatives Fund, 625 Mount Auburn St., Cambridge, MA 02138; (617) 995-1900; www.huntalternatives.org. A private foundation that provides grants and technical assistance to promote positive social change; its Initiative for Inclusive Security promotes women in peacekeeping.

Inter-Parliamentary Union, 5, Chemin du Pommier, Case Postale 330, CH-1218 Le Grand-Saconnex, Geneva, Switzerland; +(4122) 919 41 50; www.ipu.org. An organization of parliaments of sovereign states that maintains an extensive database on women serving in parliaments.

Oxfam International, 1100 15th St., N.W., Suite 600, Washington, DC 20005; (202) 496-1170; www.oxfam.org. Confederation of 13 independent nongovernmental organizations working to fight poverty and related social injustice.

U.N. Development Fund for Women (UNIFEM), 304 East 45th St., 15th Floor, New York, NY 10017; (212) 906-6400; www .unifem.org. Provides financial aid and technical support for empowering women and promoting gender equality.

U.N. Division for the Advancement of Women (DAW), 2 UN Plaza, DC2-12th Floor, New York, NY 10017; www .un.org/womenwatch/daw. Formulates policy on gender equality, implements international agreements on women's issues and promotes gender mainstreaming in government activities.

Women's Environment & Development Organization (WEDO), 355 Lexington Ave., 3rd Floor, New York, NY 10017; (212) 973-0325; www.wedo.org. An international organization that works to promote women's equality in global policy.

American Indians

Are They Making Meaningful Progress at Last?

Peter Katel

t's not a fancy gambling palace, like some Indian casinos, but the modest operation run by the Winnebago Tribe of Nebraska may just help the 2,300-member tribe hit the economic jackpot.

Using seed money from the casino, it has launched 12 businesses, including a construction company and an Internet news service. Projected 2006 revenues: $150 million.

"It would be absolutely dumb for us to think that gaming is the future," says tribe member Lance Morgan, the 37-year-old Harvard Law School graduate who runs the holding company for the dozen businesses. "Gaming is just a means to an end — and it's done wonders for our tribal economy."

Indian casinos have revived a myth dating back to the early-20th-century Oklahoma oil boom — that Indians are rolling in dough.[1] While some of the 55 tribes that operate big casinos indeed are raking in big profits, the 331 federally recognized tribes in the lower 48 states, on the whole, endure soul-quenching poverty and despair.

Arizona's 1.8-million-acre San Carlos Apache Reservation is among the poorest. The rural, isolated community of about 13,000 people not only faces devastating unemployment but also a deadly methamphetamine epidemic, tribal Chairwoman Kathleen W. Kitcheyan, told the Senate Indian Affairs Committee in April.

"We suffer from a poverty level of 69 percent, which must be unimaginable to many people in this country, who would equate a situation such as this to one found only in Third World countries," she said. Then, speaking of the drug-related death of one of her own grandsons, she had to choke back sobs.

From *CQ Researcher*,

April 28, 2006.

Jerolyn Fink lives in grand style in the housing center built by Connecticut's Mohegan Tribe using profits from its successful Mohegan Sun casino. Thanks in part to booming casinos, many tribes are making progress, but American Indians still face daunting health and economic problems, and tribal leaders say federal aid remains inadequate.

Getty Images/Mario Tama

"Our statistics are horrific," says Lionel R. Bordeaux, president of Sinte Gleska University, on the Rosebud Sioux Reservation in South Dakota. "We're at the bottom rung of the ladder in all areas, whether it's education levels, economic achievement or political status."[2]

National statistics aren't much better:

- Indian unemployment on reservations nationwide is 49 percent — 10 times the national rate.[3]
- The on-reservation family poverty rate in 2000 was 37 percent — four times the national figure of 9 percent.[4]
- Nearly one in five Indians age 25 or older in tribes without gambling operations had less than a ninth-grade education. But even members of tribes with gambling had a college graduation rate of only 16 percent, about half the national percentage.[5]
- Death rates from alcoholism and tuberculosis among Native Americans are at least 650 percent higher than overall U.S. rates.[6]
- Indian youths commit suicide at nearly triple the rate of young people in general.[7]
- Indians on reservations, especially in the resource-poor Upper Plains and West, are the nation's third-largest group of methamphetamine users.[8]

The immediate prognosis for the nation's 4.4 million Native Americans is bleak, according to the Harvard Project on American Indian Economic Development. "If U.S. and on-reservation Indian per-capita income were to continue to grow at their 1990s' rates," it said, "it would take half a century for the tribes to catch up."[9]

Nonetheless, there has been forward movement in Indian Country, though it is measured in modest steps. Among the marks of recent progress:

- Per-capita income rose 20 percent on reservations, to $7,942, (and 36 percent in tribes with casinos, to $9,771), in contrast to an 11 percent overall U.S. growth rate.[10]
- Unemployment has dropped by up to 5 percent on reservations and in other predominantly Indian areas.[11]
- Child poverty in non-gaming tribes dropped from 55 percent of the child population to 44 percent (but the Indian rate is still more than double the 17 percent average nationwide).[12]

More than two centuries of court decisions, treaties and laws have created a complicated system of coexistence between tribes and the rest of the country. On one level, tribes are sovereign entities that enjoy a government-to-government relationship with Washington. But the sovereignty is qualified. In the words of an 1831 Supreme Court decision that is a bedrock of Indian law, tribes are "domestic dependent nations."[13]

The blend of autonomy and dependence grows out of the Indians' reliance on Washington for sheer survival, says Robert A. Williams Jr., a law professor at the University of Arizona and a member of North Carolina's Lumbee Tribe. "Indians insisted in their treaties that the Great White Father protect us from these racial maniacs in the states — where racial discrimination was most developed — and guarantee us a right to education, a right to water, a territorial base, a homeland," he says. "Tribes sold an awful lot of land in return for a trust relationship to keep the tribes going."

Today, the practical meaning of the relationship with Washington is that American Indians on reservations, and to some extent those elsewhere, depend entirely or partly on federal funding for health, education and other needs. Tribes with casinos and other businesses lessen their reliance on federal dollars.

Unlike other local governments, tribes don't have a tax base whose revenues they share with state governments. Federal spending on Indian programs of all kinds nationwide currently amounts to about $11 billion, James Cason, associate deputy secretary of the Interior, told the Senate Indian Affairs Committee in February.

But the abysmal conditions under which many American Indians live make it all too clear that isn't enough, Indians say. "This is always a discussion at our tribal leaders' meetings," says Cecilia Fire Thunder, president of the Oglala Sioux Tribe in Pine Ridge, S.D. "The biggest job that tribal leaders have is to see that the government lives up to its responsibilities to our people. It's a battle that never ends."

Indeed, a decades-old class-action suit alleges systematic mismanagement of billions of dollars in Indian-owned assets by the Interior Department — a case that has prompted withering criticism of the department by the judge (see p. 134).

Government officials insist that, despite orders to cut spending, they've been able to keep providing essential services. Charles Grim, director of the Indian Health Service, told the Indian Affairs Committee, "In a deficit-reduction year, it's a very strong budget and one that does keep pace with inflationary and population-growth increases."

In any event, from the tribes' point of view, they lack the political muscle to force major increases. "The big problem is the Indians are about 1 percent of the national population," says Joseph Kalt, co-director of the Harvard Project. "The voice is so tiny."

Conditions on Reservations Improved

Socioeconomic conditions improved more on reservations with gambling than on those without gaming during the 1990s, although non-gaming reservations also improved substantially, especially compared to the U.S. population. Some experts attribute the progress among non-gaming tribes to an increase in self-governance on many reservations.

Socioeconomic Changes on Reservations, 1990-2000*
(shown as a percentage or percentage points)

	Non-Gaming	Gaming	U.S.
Real per-capita income	+21.0%	+36.0%	+11.0%
Median household income	+14.0%	+35.0%	+4.0%
Family poverty	-6.9	-11.8	-0.8
Child poverty	-8.1	-11.6	-1.7
Deep poverty	-1.4	-3.4	-0.4
Public assistance	+0.7	-1.6	+0.3
Unemployment	-1.8	-4.8	-0.5
Labor force participation	-1.6	+1.6	-1.3
Overcrowded homes	-1.3	-0.1	+1.1
Homes lacking complete plumbing	-4.6	-3.3	-0.1
Homes lacking complete kitchen	+1.3	-0.6	+0.2
College graduates	+1.7	+2.6	+4.2
High school or equivalency only	-0.3	+1.8	-1.4
Less than 9th-grade education	-5.5	-6.3	-2.8

* The reservation population of the Navajo Nation, which did not have gambling in the 1990s, was not included because it is so large (175,000 in 2000) that it tends to pull down Indian averages when it is included.

Source: Jonathan B. Taylor and Joseph P. Kalt, "Cabazon, The Indian Gaming Regulatory Act, and the Socioeconomic Consequences of American Indian Governmental Gaming: A Ten-Year Review, American Indians on Reservations: A Databook of Socioeconomic Change Between the 1990 and 2000 Censuses," Harvard Project on American Indian Economic Development, January 2005

Revenues From Casinos Almost Doubled

Revenue from Indian gaming operations nearly doubled to $19.4 billion from 2000-2004. The number of Indian casinos increased from 311 to 367 during the period.

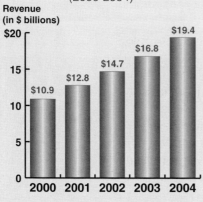

Indian Gaming Revenues
(2000-2004)

Revenue
(in $ billions)

Source: Indian Gaming Commission

Faced with that grim political reality, Indians are trying to make better use of scarce federal dollars through a federally sponsored "self-governance" movement. Leaders of the movement say tribes can deliver higher-quality services more efficiently when they control their own budgets. Traditionally, federal agencies operate programs on reservations, such as law enforcement or medical services.

But since the 1990s, dozens of tribes have stepped up control of their own affairs both by building their own businesses and by signing self-governance "compacts" with the federal government. Compacts provide tribes with large chunks of money, or block grants, rather than individual grants for each service. Then, with minimal federal oversight, the tribes develop their own budgets and run all or most services.

The self-governance trend gathered steam during the same time that Indian-owned casinos began booming. For many tribes, the gambling business provided a revenue stream that didn't flow from Washington.

According to economist Alan Meister, 228 tribes in 30 states operated 367 high-stakes bingo halls or casinos in 2004, earning an estimated $19.6 billion.[14]

The gambling houses operate under the 1988 Indian Gaming Regulatory Act (IGRA), which was made possible by a U.S. Supreme Court ruling upholding tribes' rights to govern their own activities.[15] A handful of tribes are doing so well that $80 million from six tribes in 2000-2003 helped fuel the scandal surrounding one-time Washington super-lobbyist Jack Abramoff, whose clients were among the most successful casino tribes.[16]

If the Abramoff scandal contributed to the notion of widespread Indian wealth, one reason may be the misimpression that tribes don't pay taxes on their gambling earnings. In fact, under the IGRA, federal, state and local governments took in $6.3 billion in gambling-generated tax revenues in 2004, with 67 percent going to the federal government. In addition, tribes paid out some $889 million in 2004 to state and local governments in order to get gambling operations approved.[17]

The spread of casinos has prompted some cities and counties, along with citizens' groups and even some casino-operating tribes, to resist casino-expansion plans.

The opposition to expansion is another reason tribal entrepreneur Morgan doesn't think gaming is a good long-range bet for Indians' future. His vision involves full tribal control of the Indians' main asset — their land. He argues for ending the "trust status" under which tribes can't buy or sell reservation property — a relic of 19th-century protection against rapacious state governments.

Indian Country needs a better business climate, Morgan says, and the availability of land as collateral for investments would be a big step in that direction. "America has a wonderful economic system, probably the best in the world, but the reservation tends to be an economic black hole."

As Indians seek to improve their lives, here are some of the issues being debated:

Is the federal government neglecting Native Americans?

There is wide agreement that the federal government bears overwhelming responsibility for Indians' welfare, but U.S. and tribal officials disagree over the adequacy of the aid Indians receive. Sen. John McCain, R-Ariz., chairman of the Senate Indian Affairs Committee, and Vice Chairman Byron L. Dorgan, D-N.D., have been leading the fight for more aid to Indians. "We have a full-blown crisis . . . particularly dealing with children and elderly, with respect to housing, education and health care," Dorgan told the committee on Feb. 14. He characterized administration proposals as nothing more than "nibbling around the edges on these issues . . . making a few adjustments here or there.' "

Administration officials respond that given the severe federal deficit, they are focusing on protecting vital programs. "As we went through and prioritized our budget, we basically looked at all of the programs that were secondary and tertiary programs, and they were the first ones on the block to give tradeoffs for our core programs in maintaining the integrity of those," Interior's Cason told the committee.

For Indians on isolated reservations, says Bordeaux of the Rosebud Sioux, there's little alternative to federal money. He compares tribes' present circumstances to those after the buffalo had been killed off, and an Army general told the Indians to eat beef, which made them sick. "The general told them, 'Either that, or you eat the grass on which you stand.'"

But David B. Vickers, president of Upstate Citizens for Equality, in Union Springs, N.Y., which opposes Indian land claims and casino applications, argues that accusations of federal neglect are inaccurate and skirt the real problem. The central issue is that the constitutional system is based on individual rights, not tribal rights, he says. "Indians are major recipients of welfare now. They're eligible. They don't need a tribe or leader; all they have to do is apply like anybody else."

Pat Ragsdale, director of the Bureau of Indian Affairs (BIA), acknowledges that Dorgan's and McCain's criticisms echo a 2003 U.S. Commission on Civil Rights report, which also called underfunding of Indian aid a crisis. "The government is failing to live up to its trust responsibility to Native peoples," the commission concluded. "Efforts to bring Native Americans up to the standards of other Americans have failed in part because of a lack of sustained funding. The failure manifests itself in massive and escalating unmet needs."[18]

"Nobody in this government disputes the report, in general," says Ragsdale, a Cherokee. "Some of our tribal communities are in real critical shape, and others are prospering."

The commission found, for example, that in 2003 the Indian Health Service appropriation amounted to $2,533 per capita — below even the $3,803 per capita appropriated for federal prisoners.

Concern over funding for Indian programs in 2007 centers largely on health and education. Although 90 percent of Indian students attend state-operated public schools, their schools get federal aid because tribes don't pay property taxes, which typically fund public schools. The remaining 10 percent of Indian students attend schools operated by the BIA or by tribes themselves under BIA contracts.

Controversial Whiteclay, Neb., sells millions of cans of beer annually to residents of the nearby Pine Ridge Reservation in South Dakota. Alcohol abuse and unemployment continue to plague the American Indian community.

AP Photo/William Lauer

"There is not a congressman or senator who would send his own children or grandchildren to our schools," said Ryan Wilson, president of the National Indian Education Association, citing "crumbling buildings and outdated structures with lead in the pipes and mold on the walls."[19]

Cason told the Indian Affairs Committee the administration is proposing a $49 million cut, from $157.4 million to $108.1 million, in school construction and repair in 2007. He also said that only 10 of 37 dilapidated schools funded for replacement by 2006 have been completed, with another 19 scheduled to finish in 2007. Likewise, he said the department is also behind on 45 school improvement projects.

McCain questioned whether BIA schools and public schools with large Indian enrollments would be able to meet the requirements set by the national No Child Left Behind Law.[20] Yes, replied Darla Marburger, deputy assistant secretary of Education for policy. "For the first time, we'll be providing money to . . . take a look at how students are achieving in ways that they can tailor their programs to better meet the needs of students." Overall, the Department of Education would spend about $1 billion on Indian education under the administration's proposed budget for 2007, or $6 million less than in 2006.

McCain and Dorgan are also among those concerned about administration plans to eliminate the Indian Health Service's $32.7 million urban program, which this year made medical and counseling services available to some 430,000 off-reservation Indians at 41 medical facilities in cities around the nation. (*See sidebar, p. 126.*) The administration argues that the services were available through other programs, but McCain and Dorgan noted that "no evaluation or evidence has been provided to support this contention."[21]

Indian Health Service spokesman Thomas Sweeney, a member of the Citizen Potawatomi Nation of Oklahoma, says only 72,703 Indians used urban health centers in 2004 and that expansion of another federal program would pick up the slack.[22]

In Seattle, elimination of the urban program would cut $4 million from the city's Indian Health Board budget, says Executive Director Ralph Forquera. "Why pick on a $33 million appropriation?" he asks. In his skeptical view, the proposal reflects another "unspoken" termination program. You take a sub-population — urban Indians — and eliminate funding, then [you target] tribes under 1,000 members, and there are a lot of them. Little by little, you pick apart the system."

The IHS's Grim told the Senate committee on Feb. 14 the cuts were designed to protect funding that "can be used most effectively to improve the health status of American Indian and Alaskan Native people."

Have casinos benefited Indians?

Over the past two decades, Indian casinos have become powerful economic engines for many tribal economies. But the enthusiasm for casinos is not unanimous.

"If you're looking at casinos in terms of how they've actually raised the status of Indian people, they've been an abysmal failure," says Ted Jojola, a professor of planning at the University of New Mexico and a member of Isleta Pueblo, near Albuquerque. "But in terms of augmenting the original federal trust-responsibility areas — education, health, tribal government — they've been a spectacular success. Successful gaming tribes have ploughed the money either into diversifying their economies or they've augmented funds that would have come to them anyway."

Tribes with casinos near big population centers are flourishing. The Coushatta Tribe's casino near Lake Charles, La., generates $300 million a year, enough to provide about $40,000 to every member.[23] And the fabled Foxwoods Resort Casino south of Norwich, Conn., operated by the Mashantucket Pequot Tribe, together with Connecticut's other big casino, the Mohegan Tribe's Mohegan Sun, grossed $2.2 billion just from gambling in 2004.[24]

There are only about 830 Coushattas, so their benefits also include free health care, education and favorable terms on home purchases.[25] The once poverty-stricken Mashantuckets have created Connecticut's most extensive welfare-to-work program, open to both tribe members and non-members. In 1997-2000, the program helped 150 welfare recipients find jobs.[26]

Most tribes don't enjoy success on that scale. Among the nation's 367 Indian gambling operations, only 15 grossed $250 million or more in 2004 (another 40 earned $100 million to $250 million); 94 earned less than $3 million and 57 earned $3 million to $10 million.[27]

"We have a small casino that provides close to $3 million to the tribal nation as a whole," says Bordeaux, on the Rosebud Sioux Reservation. The revenue has been channeled into the tribe's Head Start program, an emergency home-repair fund and other projects. W. Ron Allen, chairman of the Jamestown S'Klallam Tribe in Sequim, Wash., says his tribe's small casino has raised living standards so much that some two-dozen students a year go to college, instead of one or two.

Efforts to open additional casinos are creating conflicts between tribes that operate competing casinos, as well as with some of their non-Indian neighbors. Convicted lobbyist Abramoff, for example, was paid millions of dollars by tribes seeking to block other tribal casinos.[28]

Some non-Indian communities also oppose casino expansion. "We firmly believe a large, generally unregulated casino will fundamentally change the character of our community forever," said Liz Thomas, a member of Tax Payers of Michigan Against Casinos, which opposes a casino planned by the Pokagon Band of Potawotami Indians Tribe in the Lake Michigan town of New Buffalo, where Thomas and her husband operate a small resort.

"People are OK with Donald Trump making millions of dollars individually," says Joseph Podlasek, executive director of the American Indian Center of Chicago, "but if a race of people is trying to become self-sufficient, now that's not respectable."

Nevertheless, some American Indians have mixed feelings about the casino route to economic development. "I don't think anyone would have picked casinos" for that purpose, says the University of Arizona's Williams. "Am I ambivalent about it? Absolutely. But I'm not ambivalent about a new fire station, or Kevlar vests for tribal police fighting meth gangs."

"There's no question that some of the money has been used for worthwhile purposes," concedes Guy Clark, a Corrales, N.M., dentist who chairs the National Coalition Against Legalized Gambling. But, he adds, "If you do a cost-benefit analysis, the cost is much greater than the benefit." Restaurants and other businesses, for example, lose customers who often gamble away their extra money.

Even some Indian leaders whose tribes profit from casinos raise caution flags, especially about per-capita payments. For Nebraska's Winnebagos, payments amount to just a few hundred dollars, says CEO Morgan. What bothers him are dividends "that are just big enough that you don't have to work or get educated — say, $20,000 to $40,000."

But there's no denying the impact casinos can have. At a January public hearing on the Oneida Indian Nation's attempt to put 17,000 acres of upstate New York land into tax-free "trust" status, hundreds of the 4,500 employees of the tribe's Turning Stone Resort and Casino, near Utica, showed up in support. "When I was a kid, people worked for General Motors, General Electric, Carrier and Oneida Ltd.," said casino Human Resources Director Mark Mancini. "Today, people work for the Oneida Indian Nation and their enterprises."[29]

For tribes that can't build independent economies any other way, casinos are appealing. The 225,000-member Navajo Nation, the biggest U.S. tribe, twice rejected gaming before finally approving it in 2004.[30] "We need that infusion of jobs and revenue, and people realize that," said Duane Yazzie, president of the Navajos' Shiprock, N.M., chapter.[31]

But the Navajos face stiff competition from dozens of casinos already in operation near the vast Navajo reservation, which spreads across parts of Arizona, New Mexico and Utah and is larger than the state of West Virginia.

Would money alone solve American Indians' problems?

No one in Indian Country (or on Capitol Hill) denies the importance of federal funding to American Indians' future, but some Indians say it isn't the only answer.

"We are largely on our own because of limited financial assistance from the federal government," said Joseph A. Garcia, president of the National Congress of American Indians, in his recent "State of Indian Nations" speech.[32]

Fifty-two tribal officials and Indian program directors expressed similar sentiments in March before the House Appropriations Subcommittee on the Interior. Pleading their case before lawmakers who routinely consider billion-dollar weapons systems and other big projects, the tribal leaders sounded like small-town county commissioners as they urged lawmakers to increase or restore small but vital grants for basic health, education and welfare services.

"In our ICWA [Indian Child Welfare Act] program, currently we have a budget of $79,000 a year," said Harold Frazier, chairman of the Cheyenne River Sioux, in South Dakota. "We receive over 1,300 requests for assistance annually from 11 states and eight counties in South Dakota. We cannot give the type of attention to these requests that they deserve. Therefore, we are requesting $558,000."

To university President Bordeaux, federal funding is vital because his desolate reservation has few other options for economic survival. "What's missing is money," he says.

Money is crucial to improving Indians' health, says Dr. Joycelyn Dorscher, director of the Center of American Indian and Minority Health at the University of Minnesota-Duluth.

Especially costly are programs to combat diabetes and other chronic diseases, says Dorscher, a Chippewa. While health programs have to be carefully designed to fit Indian cultural patterns, she says, "Everything comes down to time or money in the grand scheme of things."

But with funding from Washington never certain from year to year, says the Harvard Project's Kalt, "The key to economic development has not been federal funding" but rather "tribes' ability to run their own affairs."

For tribes without self-government compacts, growing demands for services and shrinking funding from Washington make keeping the dollars flowing the highest priority. "We're always afraid of more cutbacks," says Oglala Sioux President Fire Thunder.

But an Indian education leader with decades of federal budgetary negotiations acknowledges that problems go beyond funding shortfalls. "If you ask students why they dropped out, they say, 'I don't see a future for myself,' " says David Beaulieu, director of Arizona State University's Center for Indian Education. "Educators need to tie the purposes of schooling to the broad-based purposes of society. We're more successful when we tie education to the meaning of life."

The University of Arizona's Williams says a tribe's success and failure may be tied more to the way its government is organized than to how much funding it gets.

Williams says the first priority of tribes still using old-style constitutions should be reorganization, because they feature a weak executive elected by a tribal council. "That's what the BIA was used to," he explains. "It could play off factions and families, and the economic system would be based on patronage and taking care of your own family." Under such a system, he adds, "there's not going to be any long-term strategic planning going on."[33]

Yet other needs exist as well, says the American Indian Center's Podlasek. "It's so difficult for us to find a place to do a traditional ceremony," he says. "We had a traditional healer in town last month, and he wanted to build a sweat lodge. We actually had to go to Indiana. Doing it in the city wasn't even an option."

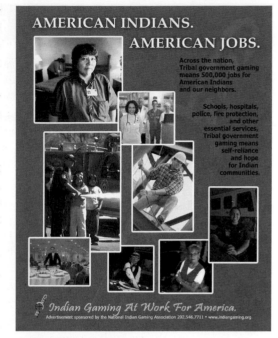

A National Indian Gaming Association advertisement touts the benefits of tribal gaming operations to American Indian communities. Some 228 tribes in 30 states operated 367 high-stakes bingo halls or casinos in 2004.

National Indian Gaming Association

Background

Conquered Homelands

Relations between Indian and non-Indian civilizations in the Americas began with the Spanish Conquistadors' explorations of the 1500s, followed by the French and British. By turns the three powers alternated policies of enslavement, peaceful coexistence and all-out warfare against the Indians.[34]

1800s *United States expands westward, pushing Indians off most of their original lands, sometimes creating new reservations for them.*

1830 President Andrew Jackson signs the Indian Removal Act, forcing the Cherokees to move from Georgia to Oklahoma.

1832 Supreme Court issues the last of three decisions defining Indians' legal status as wards of the government.

1871 Congress makes its treaties with tribes easier to alter, enabling non-Indians to take Indian lands when natural resources are discovered.

Dec. 29, 1890 U.S. soldiers massacre at least 150 Plains Indians, mostly women and children, at Wounded Knee, S.D.

1900-1950s *Congress and the executive branch undertake major shifts in Indian policy, first strengthening tribal governments then trying to force cultural assimilation.*

1924 Indians are granted U.S. citizenship.

1934 Indian Reorganization Act authorizes expansion of reservations and strengthening of tribal governments.

1953 Congress endorses full assimilation of Indians into American society, including "relocation" from reservations to cities.

1960s-1980s *In the radical spirit of the era, Native Americans demand respect for their traditions and an end to discrimination; federal government concedes more power to tribal governments, allows gambling on tribal lands.*

1969 American Indian Movement (AIM) seizes Alcatraz Island in San Francisco Bay to dramatize claims of injustice.

July 7, 1970 President Richard M. Nixon vows support for Indian self-government.

Feb. 27, 1973 AIM members occupy the town of Wounded Knee on the Pine Ridge, S.D., Sioux Reservation, for two months; two Indians die and an FBI agent is wounded.

1988 Indian Gaming Regulatory Act allows tribes to operate casinos under agreements with states.

1990s *Indian-owned casinos boom; tribal governments push to expand self-rule and reduce Bureau of Indian Affairs (BIA) supervision.*

1994 President Bill Clinton signs law making experimental self-governance compacts permanent.

March 27, 1996 U.S. Supreme Court rules states can't be forced to negotiate casino compacts, thus encouraging tribes to make revenue-sharing deals with states as the price of approval.

June 10, 1996 Elouise Cobell, a member of the Blackfeet Tribe in Montana, charges Interior Department mismanagement of Indian trust funds cheated Indians out of billions of dollars. The case is still pending.

Nov. 3, 1998 California voters uphold tribes' rights to run casinos; state Supreme Court later invalidates the provision, but it is revived by a 1999 compact between the tribes and the state.

2000s *Indian advocates decry low funding levels, and sovereignty battles continue; lobbying scandal spotlights Indian gambling profits.*

2000 Tribal Self-Governance Demonstration Project becomes permanent.

2003 U.S. Commission on Civil Rights calls underfunding for Indians a crisis, saying federal government spends less for Indian health care than for any other group, including prison inmates.

Feb. 22, 2004 *Washington Post* reports on Washington lobbyist Jack Abramoff's deals with casino tribes.

March 29, 2005 U.S. Supreme Court blocks tax exemptions for Oneida Nation of New York on newly purchased land simply because it once owned the property.

April 5, 2006 Tribal and BIA officials testify in Congress that methamphetamine addiction is ravaging reservations.

By 1830, with the Europeans largely gone, white settlers moved westward into Georgia, Mississippi and Alabama. Unwilling to share the rich frontier land, they pushed the Indians out. President Andrew Jackson backed the strategy, and Congress enacted it into the Indian Removal Act of 1830, which called for moving the region's five big tribes into the Oklahoma Territory.

If the law didn't make clear where Indians stood with the government, the treatment of Mississippi's Choctaws provided chilling evidence. Under a separate treaty, Choctaws who refused to head for Oklahoma could remain at home, become citizens and receive land. In practice, none of that was allowed, and Indians who stayed in Mississippi lived marginal existences.

Georgia simplified the claiming of Cherokee lands by effectively ending Cherokee self-rule. The so-called "Georgia Guard" reinforced the point by beating and jailing Indians. Jackson encouraged Georgia's actions, and when Indians protested, he said he couldn't interfere. The lawsuit filed by the Cherokees eventually reached the Supreme Court.

Chief Justice John Marshall's 1831 majority opinion, *Cherokee Nation v. Georgia*, would cast a long shadow over Indians' rights, along with two other decisions, issued in 1823 and 1832. "Almost all Indian policy is the progeny of the conflicting views of Jackson and Marshall," wrote W. Dale Mason, a political scientist at the University of New Mexico.[35]

In concluding that the court couldn't stop Georgia's actions, Marshall defined the relationship between Indians and the U.S. government. While Marshall wrote that Indians didn't constitute a foreign state, he noted that they owned the land they occupied until they made a "voluntary cession." Marshall concluded the various tribes were "domestic dependent nations." In practical terms, "Their relations to the United States resembles that of a ward to his guardian."[36]

Having rejected the Cherokees' argument, the University of Arizona's Williams writes, the court "provided no effective judicial remedy for Indian tribes to protect their basic human rights to property, self-government, and cultural survival under U.S. law."[37]

Along with the *Cherokee* case, the other two opinions that make up the so-called Marshall Trilogy are *Johnson v. M'Intosh* (also known as *Johnson v. McIntosh*), and *Worcester v. State of Georgia*.[38]

In *Johnson*, Marshall wrote that the European empires that "discovered" America became its owners and had "an exclusive right to extinguish the Indian title of occupancy, either by purchase or by conquest. The tribes of Indians inhabiting this country were fierce savages. . . . To leave them in possession of their country was to leave the country a wilderness."[39]

However, Marshall used the 1832 *Worcester* opinion to define the limits of state authority over Indian tribes, holding that the newcomers couldn't simply eject Indians.

"The Cherokee nation . . . is a distinct community occupying its own territory . . . in which the laws of Georgia can have no force," Marshall wrote. Georgia's conviction and sentencing of a missionary for not swearing allegiance to the state "interferes forcibly with the relations established between the United States and the Cherokee nation."[40] That is, the federal government — not states — held the reins of power over tribes.

According to legend, Jackson remarked: "John Marshall has made his decision — now let him enforce it." Between Jackson's disregard of the Supreme Court and white settlers' later manipulation of the legal system to vacate Indian lands, the end result was the dispossession of Indian lands.

Forced Assimilation

The expulsions of the Native Americans continued in the Western territories — especially after the Civil War. "I instructed Captain Barry, if possible to exterminate the whole

Budget Cuts Target Health Clinics

When Lita Pepion, a health consultant and a member of the Blackfeet Nation, learned that her 22-year-old-niece had been struggling with heroin abuse, she urged her to seek treatment at the local Urban Indian Clinic in Billings, Mont.

But the young woman had so much trouble getting an appointment that she gave up. Only recently, says Pepion, did she overcome her addiction on her own.

The clinic is one of 34 federally funded, Indian-controlled clinics that contract with the Indian Health Service (IHS) to serve urban Indians. But President Bush's 2007 budget would kill the $33-million program, eliminating most of the clinics' funding.

Indians in cities will still be able to get health care through several providers, including the federal Health Centers program, says Office of Management and Budget spokesman Richard Walker. The proposed budget would increase funding for the centers by nearly $2 billion, IHS Director Charles W. Grim told the Senate Indian Affairs Committee on Feb. 14, 2006.[1]

But Joycelyn Dorscher, president of the Association of American Indian Physicians, says the IHS clinics do a great job and that, "It's very important that people from diverse backgrounds have physicians like themselves."

Others, however, including Pepion, say the clinics are poorly managed and lack direction. Ralph Forquera, director of the Seattle-based Urban Indian Health Institute, says that while the clinics "have made great strides medically, a lack of resources has resulted in services from unqualified professionals." In addition, he says, "we have not been as successful in dealing with lifestyle changes and mental health problems."

Many Indian health experts oppose the cuts because Indians in both urban areas and on reservations have more health problems than the general population, including 126 percent more chronic liver disease and cirrhosis, 54 percent more diabetes and 178 percent more alcohol-related deaths.[2]

Indian health specialists blame the Indians' higher disease rates on history, lifestyle and genetics — not just on poverty. "You don't see exactly the same things happening to other poor minority groups," says Dorscher, a North Dakota Chippewa, so "there's something different" going on among Indians.

In the view of Donna Keeler, executive director of the South Dakota Urban Indian Health program and an Eastern Shoshone, historical trauma affects the physical wellness of patients in her state's three urban Indian clinics.

Native Americans in downtown Salt Lake City, Utah, demonstrate on April 21, 2006, against the elimination of funding for Urban Indian Health Clinics.

AP Photo/Salt Lake Tribune

Susette Schwartz, CEO of the Hunter Urban Indian Clinic in Wichita, Kan., agrees. She attributes Indians' high rates of mental health and alcohol/substance abuse to their long history of government maltreatment. Many Indian children in the 19th and early 20th centuries, she points out, were taken from their parents and sent to government boarding schools where speaking native languages was prohibited. "Taking away the culture and language years ago," says Schwartz, as well as the government's role in "taking their children and sterilizing their women" in the 1970s, all contributed to Indians' behavioral health issues.

Keeler also believes Indians' low incomes cause their unhealthy lifestyles. Many eat high-fat, high-starch foods because they are cheaper, Pepion says. Growing up on a reservation, she recalls, "We didn't eat a lot of vegetables because we couldn't afford them."

Opponents of the funding cuts for urban Indian health centers also cite a recent letter to President Bush from Daniel R. Hawkins Jr., vice president for federal, state and local government for the National Association of Community Health Centers. He said the urban Indian clinics and community health centers are complementary, not duplicative.

While Pepion does not believe funding should be cut entirely, she concedes that alternative health-care services are often "better equipped than the urban Indian clinics." And if American Indians want to assimilate into the larger society, they can't have everything culturally separate, she adds. "The only way that I was able to assimilate into an urban society was to make myself do those things that were uncomfortable for me," she says.

But Schwartz believes a great benefit of the urban clinics are their Indian employees, "who are culturally competent and sensitive and incorporate Native American-specific cultural ideas." Because of their history of cultural abuse, it takes a long time for Native Americans to trust non-Indian health providers, says Schwartz. "They're not just going to go to a health center down the road."

Dorscher and Schwartz also say the budget cuts could lead to more urban Indians ending up in costly emergency rooms because of their reluctance to trust the community health centers. "Ultimately, it would become more expensive to cut the prevention and primary care programs than it would be to maintain them," Dorscher says.

— Melissa J. Hipolit

[1] Prepared testimony of Director of Indian Health Service Dr. Charles W. Grim before the Senate Committee on Indian Affairs, Feb. 14, 2006.

[2] Urban Indian Health Institute, "The Health Status of Urban American Indians and Alaska Natives," March 16, 2004, p. v.

village," Lt. Col. George Green wrote of his participation in an 1869 campaign against the White Mountain Apaches in Arizona and New Mexico. "There seems to be no settled policy, but a general policy to kill them wherever found."[41]

Some military men and civilians didn't go along. But whether by brute force or by persuasion, Indians were pushed off lands that non-Indians wanted. One strategy was to settle the Indians on reservations guarded by military posts. The strategy grew into a general policy for segregating Indians on these remote tracts.

Even after the Indians were herded onto lands that no one else wanted, the government didn't respect reservation boundaries. They were reconfigured as soon as non-Indians saw something valuable, such as mineral wealth.

The strategy of elastic reservation boundaries led to the belief — or rationalization — that reservations served no useful purposes for Indians themselves. That doctrine led to a policy enshrined in an 1887 law to convert reservations to individual landholdings. Well-meaning advocates of the plan saw it as a way to inculcate notions of private property and Euro-American culture in general.

All tribal land was to be divided into 160-acre allotments, one for each Indian household. The parcels wouldn't become individual property, though, for 25 years.

Indian consent wasn't required. In some cases, government agents tried persuading Indians to join in; in others, the divvying-up proceeded even with many Indians opposed. In Arizona, however, the government backed off from breaking up the lands of the long-settled Hopis, who resisted attempts to break up their territory. The vast Navajo Nation in

Disease Toll Higher Among Indians

American Indians served by the Indian Health Service (IHS) — mainly low-income or uninsured — die at substantially higher rates than the general population from liver disease, diabetes, tuberculosis, pneumonia and influenza as well as from homicide, suicide and injuries. However, Indians' death rates from Alzheimer's disease or breast cancer are lower.

Health Status of American Indians*
Compared to General Population
(deaths per 100,000 population)

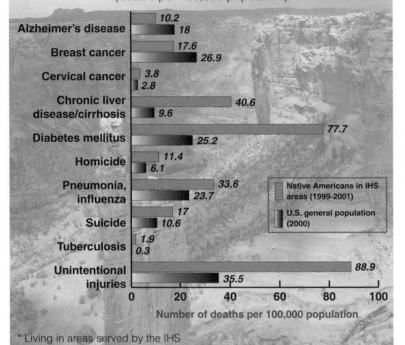

	Native Americans in IHS areas (1999-2001)	U.S. general population (2000)
Alzheimer's disease	10.2	18
Breast cancer	17.6	26.9
Cervical cancer	3.8	2.8
Chronic liver disease/cirrhosis	40.6	9.6
Diabetes mellitus	77.7	25.2
Homicide	11.4	6.1
Pneumonia, influenza	33.6	23.7
Suicide	17	10.6
Tuberculosis	1.9	0.3
Unintentional injuries	88.9	35.5

Number of deaths per 100,000 population

* Living in areas served by the IHS

Source: "Indian Health Service: Health Care Services Are Not Always Available to Native Americans," Government Accountability Office, August 2005

Background image: Canyon de Chelly, Navajo Nation, Arizona (Navajo Tourism)

Arizona, Utah and New Mexico was also left intact.

While widely reviled, the "forced assimilation" policy left a benign legacy for the affected Indians: the grant of citizenship. Beyond that, the era's Indians were restricted to unproductive lands, and with little means of support many fell prey to alcoholism and disease.

The bleak period ended with President Franklin D. Roosevelt. In his first term he appointed a defender of Indian culture, John Collier, as commissioner of Indian affairs. Collier pushed for the Indian Reorganization Act of 1934, which ended the allotment program, financed purchases of new Indian lands and authorized the organization of tribal governments that enjoyed control over revenues.

Termination

After World War II, a new, anti-Indian mood swept Washington, partly in response to pressure from states where non-Indians eyed Indian land.

Collier resigned in 1945 after years of conflict over what critics called his antagonism to missionaries proselytizing among the Indians and his sympathies toward the tribes. The 1950 appointment of Dillon S. Myer—fresh from supervising the wartime internment of Japanese-Americans—clearly reflected the new attitude. Myer showed little interest in what Indians themselves thought of the new policy of shrinking tribal land holdings. "I realize that it will not be possible always to obtain Indian cooperation. . . . We must proceed, even though [this] may be lacking."[42]

Congress hadn't authorized a sweeping repeal of earlier policy. But the introduction of dozens of bills in the late 1940s to sell Indian land or liquidate some reservation holdings entirely showed which way the winds were blowing. And in 1953, a House Concurrent Resolution declared Congress' policy to be ending Indians' "status as wards of the United States, and to grant them all of the rights and privileges pertaining to American citizenship." A separate law granted state

RACE, ETHNICITY, GENDER, AND CLASS

jurisdiction over Indian reservations in five Midwestern and Western states and extended the same authority to other states that wanted to claim it.[43]

The following year, Congress "terminated" formal recognition and territorial sovereignty of six tribes. Four years later, after public opposition began building (spurred in part by religious organizations), Congress abandoned termination. In the meantime, however, Indians had lost 1.6 million acres.

At the same time, though, the federal government maintained an associated policy — relocation. The BIA persuaded Indians to move to cities — Chicago, Denver and Los Angeles were the main destinations — and opened job-placement and housing-aid programs. The BIA placed Indians far from their reservations to keep them from returning. By 1970, the BIA estimated that 40 percent of all Indians lived in cities, of which one-third had been relocated by the bureau; the rest moved on their own.[44]

Activism

Starting in the late 1960s, the winds of change blowing through American society were felt as deeply in Indian Country as anywhere. Two books played a crucial role. In 1969, Vine Deloria Jr., member of a renowned family of Indian intellectuals from Oklahoma, published his landmark history, *Custer Died For Your Sins*, which portrayed American history from the Indians' viewpoint. The following year, Dee Brown's *Bury My Heart at Wounded Knee* described the settling of the West also from an Indian point of view. The books astonished many non-Indians. Among young Indians, the volumes reflected and spurred on a growing political activism.

It was in this climate that the newly formed American Indian Movement (AIM) took over Alcatraz Island, the former federal prison site in San Francisco Bay (where rebellious Indians had been held during the Indian Wars), to publicize demands to honor treaties and respect Native Americans' dignity. The takeover lasted from Nov. 20, 1969, to June 11, 1971, when U.S. marshals removed the occupiers.[45]

A second AIM-government confrontation took the form of a one-week takeover of BIA headquarters in Washington in November 1972 by some 500 AIM members protesting what they called broken treaty obligations. Protesters charged that government services to Indians were inadequate in general, with urban Indians neglected virtually completely.

Another protest occurred on Feb. 27, 1973, when 200 AIM members occupied the village of Wounded Knee on the Oglala Sioux's Pine Ridge Reservation in South Dakota. U.S. soldiers had massacred at least 150 Indians at Wounded Knee in 1890. AIM was protesting what it called the corrupt tribal government. And a weak, involuntary manslaughter charge against a non-Indian who had allegedly killed an Indian near the reservation had renewed Indian anger at discriminatory treatment by police and judges.

Native American children and adults in the Chicago area keep in touch with their cultural roots at the American Indian Center. About two-thirds of the nation's Indians live in urban areas.

American Indian Center/Warren Perlstein

The occupation soon turned into a full-blown siege, with the reservation surrounded by troops and federal law-enforcement officers. During several firefights two AIM members were killed, and an FBI agent was wounded. The occupation ended on May 8, 1973.

Self-Determination

Amid the surging Indian activism, the federal government was trying to make up for the past by encouraging tribal self-determination.[46]

In 1975, Congress passed the Indian Self-Determination and Education Assistance Act, which channeled federal contracts and grants directly to tribes, reducing the BIA role and effectively putting Indian communities in direct charge of schools, health, housing and other programs.

And to assure Indians that the era of sudden reversals in federal policy had ended, the House in 1988 passed a resolution reaffirming the "constitutionally recognized government-to-government relationship with Indian tribes." Separate legislation set up a "self-governance demonstration project" in which eligible tribes would sign "compacts" to run their own governments with block grants from the federal government.[47]

By 1993, 28 tribes had negotiated compacts with the Interior Department. And in 1994, President Bill Clinton signed legislation that made self-governance a permanent option.

For the general public, the meaning of newly strengthened Indian sovereignty could be summed up with one word: casinos. In 1988, Congress enacted legislation regulating tribal gaming operations. That move followed a Supreme Court ruling (*California v. Cabazon*) that authorized tribes to run gambling operations. But tribes could not offer a form of gambling specifically barred by the state.

The law set up three categories of gambling operations: Class I, traditional Indian games, controlled exclusively by tribes; Class II, including bingo, lotto, pull tabs and some card games, which are allowed on tribal lands in states that allow the games elsewhere; and Class III, which takes in casino games such as slot machines, roulette and blackjack, which can be offered only under agreements with state governments that set out the size and types of the proposed casinos.

Limits that the Indian Gaming Regulatory Act put on Indian sovereignty were tightened further by a 1996 Supreme Court decision that the Seminole Tribe couldn't sue Florida to force negotiation of a casino compact. The decision essentially forced tribes nationwide to make revenue-sharing deals with states in return for approval of casinos.[48]

Meanwhile, particularly on reservations from Minnesota to the Pacific Northwest, a plague of methamphetamine addiction and manufacturing is leaving a trail of death and shattered lives. By 2002, Darrell Hillaire, chairman of the Lummi Nation, near Bellingham, Wash., said that members convicted of dealing meth would be expelled from the tribe.[49]

But the Lummis couldn't stop the spread of the scourge on other reservations. National Congress of American Indians President Garcia said early in 2006: "Meth-amphetamine is a poison taking Indian lives, destroying Indian families, and razing entire communities."[50]

Current Situation

Self-Government

Some Indian leaders are advocating more power for tribal governments as the best way to improve the quality of life on reservations.

Under the Tribal Self-Governance Demonstration Project, made permanent in 1994, tribes can replace program-by-program grants by entering into "compacts" with the federal government, under which they receive a single grant for a variety of services. Some 231 tribes and Alaskan Native villages have compacts to administer a total of about $341 million in programs. Of the Indian communities now living under compacts, 72 are in the lower 48 states.[51]

Under a set of separate compacts, the Indian Health Service has turned over clinics, hospitals and health programs to some 300 tribes and Alaskan villages, 70 of them non-Alaskan tribes.

The self-governance model has proved especially appropriate in Alaska, where the majority of the native population of 120,000 is concentrated in 229 villages, many of them remote, and compact in size, hence well-suited to managing their own affairs, experts say.

Another advantage of Alaska villages is the experience they acquired through the 1971 Alaska Native Claims Settlement Act, which granted a total of $962 million to Alaska natives born on or before Dec. 18, 1971, in exchange for giving up their claims to millions of acres of land. Villages formed regional corporations to manage the assets. In addition all Alaska residents receive an annual dividend ($946 in 2005) from natural-resource royalty income.[52]

"The emergence of tribal authority is unprecedented in Indian Country's history," says Allen, of the Jamestown S'Klallam Tribe, one of the originators of the self-governance model. "Why not take the resources you have available and use them as efficiently as you can — more efficiently than currently being administered?"[53]

But the poorer and more populous tribes of the Great Plains and the Southwest have turned down the self-governance model. "They can't afford to do it," says Michael LaPointe, chief of staff to President Rodney Bordeaux of the Rosebud Sioux Tribe. "When you have a lot of poverty and not a lot of economic activity to generate tribal resources to supplement the unfunded mandates, it becomes impossible."

In contrast with the Jameston S'Klallam's tiny membership of 585 people, there are some 24,000 people on the Rosebud Siouxs' million-acre reservation. The tribe does operate law enforcement, ambulances and other services under contracts with the government. But it can't afford to do any more, LaPointe says.

A combined effect of the gambling boom and the growing adoption of the self-governance model is that much of the tension has gone out of the traditionally strained relationship between the BIA and tribes. "BIA people are getting pushed out as decision-makers," Kalt says. Some strains remain, to be sure. Allen says he senses a growing reluctance by the BIA to let go of tribes. "They use the argument that that the BIA doesn't have the money [for block grants]," he says.

BIA Director Ragsdale acknowledges that tougher financial-accounting requirements sparked by a lawsuit over Interior Department handling of Indian trust funds are slowing the compact-approval process. (*See "Trust Settlement" on p. 134.*) But, he adds, "We're not trying to hinder self-governance."

Limits on Gambling

Several legislative efforts to limit Indian gaming are pending. Separate bills by Sen. McCain and House Resources Committee Chairman Richard Pombo, R-Calif., would restrict tribes' ability to acquire new land for casinos in more favorable locations.

More proposals are in the pipeline. Jemez Pueblo of New Mexico wants to build a casino near the town of Anthony, though the pueblo is 300 miles away.[54]

In eastern Oregon, the Warm Springs Tribe is proposing an off-reservation casino at the Columbia River Gorge. And in Washington state, the Cowlitz and Mohegan tribes are planning an off-reservation casino near Portland.[55] The process has been dubbed "reservation shopping."

Under the Indian Gaming Regulatory Act of 1988, a tribe can acquire off-reservation land for casinos when it is:

- granted as part of a land claim settlement;
- granted to a newly recognized tribe as its reservation;
- restored to a tribe whose tribal recognition is also restored; or
- granted to a recognized tribe that had no reservation when the act took effect.

The most hotly debated exemption allows the secretary of the Interior to grant an off-reservation acquisition that benefits the tribe without harming the community near the proposed casino location. Both Pombo and McCain would repeal the loophole created by this so-called "two-part test." Under Pombo's bill, tribes acquiring land under the other exemptions would have to have solid historic and recent ties to the property. Communities, state governors and state legislatures would have to approve the establishment of new casinos, and tribes would reimburse communities for the effects of casinos on transportation, law enforcement and other public services.

McCain's bill would impose fewer restrictions than Pombo's. But McCain would give the National Indian Gaming Commission final say over all contracts with outside suppliers of goods and services.

The bill would also ensure the commission's control over big-time gambling — a concern that arose from a 2005 decision by the U.S. Court of Appeals for the District of Columbia that limited the agency's jurisdiction over a Colorado tribe. The commission has been worrying that applying that decision nationwide would eliminate federal supervision of casinos.

McCain told a March 8 Senate Indian Affairs Committee hearing that the two-part test "is fostering opposition to all Indian gaming."[56]

If the senator had been aiming to soften tribal opposition to his bill, he didn't make much headway. "We believe that it grows out of anecdotal, anti-Indian press reports on Indian gaming, the overblown issue of off-reservation gaming, and a 'pin-the-blame-on-the-victim' reaction to the Abramoff scandal," Ron His Horse Is Thunder, chairman of the Standing Rock Sioux Tribe of North Dakota and South Dakota, told the committee. He argued that the bill would amount to unconstitutional meddling with Indian sovereignty.

But the idea of restricting "reservation-shopping" appeals to tribes facing competition from other tribes. Cheryle A. Kennedy, chairwoman of the Confederated Tribes of the Grand Ronde Community of Oregon, said her tribe's Spirit Mountain Casino could be hurt by the Warm Springs Tribes' proposed project or by the Cowlitz and Mohegan project.[57]

Urban Indians: Invisible and Unheard

Two-thirds of the nation's 4.4 million American Indians live in towns and cities, but they're hard to find.[1] "Indians who move into metropolitan areas are scattered; they're not in a centralized geographical area," says New Mexico Secretary of Labor Conroy Chino. "You don't have that cohesive community where there's a sense of culture and language, as in Chinatown or Koreatown in Los Angeles."

Chino's interest is professional as well as personal. In his former career as a television journalist in Albuquerque, Chino, a member of the Acoma Pueblo, wrote an independent documentary about urban Indians. His subjects range from a city-loving San Franciscan who vacations in Hawaii to city-dwellers who return to their reservations every vacation they get. Their lives diverge sharply from what University of Arizona anthropologist Susan Lobo calls a "presumption that everything Indian is rural and long, long ago."[2]

Indian society began urbanizing in 1951, when the Bureau of Indian Affairs (BIA) started urging reservation dwellers to move to cities where — it was hoped — they would blend into the American "melting pot" and find more economic opportunity and a better standard of living.[3]

But many found the urban environment oppressive and the government assistance less generous than promised. About 100,000 Indians were relocated between 1951 and 1973, when the program wound down; unable to fit in, many fell into alcoholism and despair.[4]

Still, a small, urban Indian middle class has developed over time, partly because the BIA began systematically hiring Indians in its offices. Indians keep such a low profile, however, that the Census Bureau has a hard time finding them. Lobo, who consulted for the bureau in 1990, recalls that the agency's policy at the time was to register any household where no one answered the door as being in the same ethnic group as the neighbors. That strategy worked with urban ethnic groups who tended to cluster together, Lobo says, but not with Native Americans because theirs was a "dispersed population."

By the 2000 census that problem was resolved, but another one cropped up. "American Indians are ingenious at keeping expenses down — by couch-surfing, for instance," Lobo says. "There's a floating population that doesn't get counted because they weren't living in a standard residence."

But other urban Indians live conventional, middle-class lives, sometimes even while technically living on Indian land. "I am highly educated, a professor in the university, and my gainful employment is in the city of Albuquerque," says Ted Jojola, a professor of planning at the University of New Mexico (and a member of the Census Bureau's advisory committee on Indian population). "My community [Isleta Pueblo] is seven minutes south of Albuquerque. The reservation has become an urban amenity to me."

Some might see a home on Indian land near the city as a refuge from discrimination. "There have been years where you couldn't reveal you were native if you wanted to get a job," says Joseph Podlasek, executive director of the American Indian Center of Chicago.

(Continued)

(Continued)

Joycelyn Dorscher, president of the Association of American Indian Physicians, recalls a painful experience several years ago when she rushed her 6-year-old daughter to a hospital emergency room in Minneapolis-St. Paul, suspecting appendicitis. The young intern assigned to the case saw an Indian single mother with a sick child and apparently assumed that the daughter was suffering from neglect. "She told me if I didn't sit down and shut up, my daughter would go into the [child-protective] system," recalls Dorscher, who at the time was a third-year medical student.

Even Chino, whose mainstream credentials include an M.A. from Princeton, feels alienated at times from non-Indian city dwellers. He notes that Albuquerque officials ignored Indians' objections to a statue honoring Juan de Oñate, the 16th-century conqueror who established Spanish rule in what is now New Mexico. "Though native people protested and tried to show why this is not a good idea," Chino says, "the city went ahead and funded it."[5]

In the long run, Chino hopes a growing presence of Indian professionals — "we're not all silversmiths, or weavers" — will create more acceptance of urban Indians and more aid to combat high Indian dropout rates and other problems. "While people like having Indians in New Mexico and like visitors to get a feel for the last bastion of native culture," he says, "they're not doing that much for the urban Indian community, though we're paying taxes, too."

---

[1] Urban Indians were 64 percent of the population in 2000, according to the U.S. Census Bureau. For background, see, "We the People: American Indians and Alaska Natives in the United States," U.S. Census Bureau, 2000, p. 14, www.census.gov/prod/2006pubs/censr-28.pdf.

[2] "Looking Toward Home," *Native American Public Telecommunications*, 2003, www.visionmaker.org.

[3] Donald L. Fixico, *The Urban Indian Experience in America* (2000), pp. 9-11.

[4] *Ibid.*, pp. 22-25.

[5] Oñate is especially disliked at Acoma, Chino's birthplace, where the conqueror had the feet of some two-dozen Acoma men cut off in 1599 after Spanish soldiers were killed there. For background, see Wren Propp, "A Giant of Ambivalence," *Albuquerque Journal*, Jan. 25, 2004, p. A1; Brenda Norrell, "Pueblos Decry War Criminal," *Indian Country Today*, June 25, 2004.

Pombo's bill would require the approval of new casinos by tribes that already have gambling houses up and running within 75 miles of a proposed new one.

The House Resources Committee heard another view from Indian Country at an April 5 hearing. Jacquie Davis-Van Huss, tribal secretary of the North Fork Rancheria of the Mono Indians of California, said Pombo's approval clause would doom her tribe's plans. "This provision is anti-competitive," she testified. "It effectively provides the power to veto another tribe's gaming project simply to protect market share."

Trust Settlement

McCain's committee is also grappling with efforts to settle a decade-old lawsuit that has exposed longstanding federal mismanagement of trust funds. In 1999, U.S. District Judge Royce Lamberth said evidence showed "fiscal and governmental irresponsibility in its purest form."[58]

The alternative to settlement, McCain and Dorgan told the Budget Committee, is for the case to drag on through the courts. Congressional resolution of the conflict could also spare the Interior Department further grief from Lamberth. In a February ruling, he said

Should tribes open casinos on newly acquired land?

YES   Ernest L. Stevens, Jr.
*Chairman, National Indian
Gaming Association*

NO   State Rep. Fulton Sheen, R-Plainwell
Michigan House of Representatives

From statement before U.S. House Committee on Resources, Nov. 9, 2005

Indian gaming is the Native American success story. Where there were no jobs, now there are 553,000 jobs. Where our people had only an eighth-grade education on average, tribal governments are building schools and funding college scholarships. Where the United States and boarding schools sought to suppress our languages, tribal schools are now teaching their native language. Where our people suffer epidemic diabetes, heart disease and premature death, our tribes are building hospitals, health clinics and wellness centers.

Historically, the United States signed treaties guaranteeing Indian lands as permanent homes, and then a few years later, went to war to take our lands. This left our people to live in poverty, often on desolate lands, while others mined for gold or pumped oil from the lands that were taken from us.

Indian gaming is an exercise of our inherent right to self-government. Today, for over 60 percent of Indian tribes in the lower 48 states, Indian gaming offers new hope and a chance for a better life for our children.

Too many lands were taken from Indian tribes, leaving some tribes landless or with no useful lands. To take account of historical mistreatment, the Indian Gaming Regulatory Act (IGRA), provided several exceptions to the rule that Indian tribes should conduct Indian gaming on lands held on Oct. 17, 1988.

Accordingly, land is restored to an Indian tribe in trust status when the tribe is restored to federal recognition. For federally recognized tribes that did not have reservation land on the date IGRA was enacted, land is put into trust. Or, a tribe may apply to the secretary of the Interior. The secretary consults with state and local officials and nearby Indian tribes to determine whether an acquisition of land in trust for gaming would be in the tribe's "best interest" and "not detrimental to the surrounding community."

Now, legislation would require "newly recognized, restored, or landless tribes" to apply to have land taken in trust through a five-part process. Subjecting tribes to this new and cumbersome process discounts the fact that the United States mistreated these tribes by ignoring and neglecting them, taking all of their lands or allowing their lands to be stolen by others.

We believe that Congress should restore these tribes to a portion of their historical lands and that these lands should be held on the same basis as other Indian lands.

From statement to U.S. House Committee on Resources, April 5, 2006

The rampant proliferation of tribal gaming is running roughshod over states' rights and local control and is jeopardizing everything from my own neighborhood to — as the Jack Abramoff scandal has demonstrated — the very integrity of our federal political system.

In 1988, Congress passed the Indian Gaming Regulatory Act (IGRA) in an effort to control the development of Native American casinos and, in particular, to make sure that the states had a meaningful role in the development of any casinos within their borders. At that time, Native American gambling accounted for less than 1 percent of the nation's gambling industry, grossing approximately $100 million in revenue.

Since that time, the Native American casino business has exploded into an $18.5 billion industry that controls 25 percent of gaming industry revenue. Despite this unbridled growth, IGRA and the land-in-trust process remain basically unchanged.

When Congress originally enacted IGRA, the general rule was that casino gambling would not take place on newly acquired trust land. I believe Congress passed this general rule to prevent precisely what we see happening: a mad and largely unregulated land rush pushed by casino developers eager to cash in on a profitable revenue stream that is not burdened by the same tax rates or regulations that other businesses have to incur. "Reservation shopping" is an activity that must be stopped. And that is just one component of the full legislative overhaul that is needed.

IGRA and its associated land-in-trust process is broken, open to manipulation by special interests and in desperate need of immediate reform. It has unfairly and inappropriately fostered an industry that creates enormous wealth for a few select individuals and Las Vegas interests at the expense of taxpaying families, small businesses, manufacturing jobs and local governments.

Our research shows that while local and state governments receive some revenue-sharing percentages from tribal gaming, the dollars pale in comparison to the overall new costs to government and social-service agencies from increased infrastructure demands, traffic, bankruptcies, crime, divorce and general gambling-related ills.

I do not think this is what Congress had in mind. Somewhere along the way, the good intentions of Congress have been hijacked, and it is time for this body to reassert control over this process. It is imperative that Congress take swift and decisive steps today to get its arms around this issue before more jobs are lost and more families are put at risk.

Harvard Law School graduate Lance Morgan, a member of Nebraska's Winnebago Tribe, used seed money from his tribe's small casino to create several thriving businesses. He urges other tribes to use their casino profits to diversify. "Gaming is just a means to an end," he says.

Ho-Chunk, Inc.

Interior's refusal to make payments owed to Indians was "an obscenity that harkens back to the darkest days of United States-Indian relations."[59]

Five months later, Lamberth suggested that Congress, not the courts, may be the proper setting for the conflict. "Interior's unremitting neglect and mismanagement of the Indian trust has left it in such a shambles that recovery may prove impossible."[60]

The court case has its roots in the 1887 policy of allotting land to Indians in an effort to break up reservations. Since then, the Interior Department has been responsible for managing payments made to landholders, which later included tribes, for mining and other natural-resource extraction on Indian-owned land.

But for decades, Indians weren't receiving what they were owed. On June 10, 1996, Elouise Cobell, an organizer of the Blackfeet National Bank, the first Indian-owned national bank on a reservation, sued the Interior Department charging that she and all other trust fee recipients had been cheated for decades out of money that Interior was responsible for managing. "Lands and resources — in many cases the only source of income for some of our nation's poorest and most vulnerable citizens — have been grossly mismanaged," Cobell told the Indian Affairs Committee on March 1.

The mismanagement is beyond dispute, said John Bickerman, who was appointed to broker a settlement. Essentially, Bickerman told the Senate Indian Affairs Committee on March 28, "Money was not collected; money was not properly deposited; and money was not properly disbursed."

As of 2005, Interior is responsible for trust payments involving 126,079 tracts of land owned by 223,245 individuals — or, 2.3 million "ownership interests" on some 12 million acres, Cason and Ross Swimmer, a special trustee, told the committee.

Bickerman said a settlement amount of $27.5 billion proposed by the Indian plaintiffs was "without foundation." But the Interior Department proposed a settlement of $500 million based on "arbitrary and false assumptions," he added. Both sides agree that some $13 billion should have been paid to individual Indians over the life of the trust, but they disagree over how much was actually paid.

Supreme Court Ruling

Powerful repercussions are expected from the Supreme Court's latest decision in a centuries-long string of rulings involving competing claims to land by Indians and non-Indians.

In 2005, the high court said the Oneida Indian Nation of New York could not quit paying taxes on 10 parcels of land it owns north of Utica.[61]

After buying the parcels in 1997 and 1998, the tribe refused to pay property taxes, arguing that the land was former tribal property now restored to tribal ownership, and thereby tax-exempt.[62]

The court, in an opinion written by Ruth Bader Ginsburg, concluded that though the tribe used to own the land, the property right was too old to revive. "Rekindling the embers of sovereignty that long ago grew cold" is out of the question, Ginsburg wrote. She invoked the legal doctrine of "laches," in which a party who waits too long to assert his rights loses them.[63]

Lawyers on both sides of Indian law cases expect the case to affect lower-court rulings throughout the country. "The court has opened the cookie jar," Williams of the University of Arizona argues. "Does laches only apply to claims of sovereignty over reacquired land? If a decision favoring Indians is going to inconvenience too many white people, then laches applies — I swear that's what it says." Tribes litigating fishing rights, water rights and other assets are likely to suffer in court as a result, he argues.

In fact, only three months after the high court decision, the 2nd U.S. Circuit Court of Appeals in New York invoked laches in rejecting a claim by the Cayuga Tribe. Vickers of Upstate Citizens for Equality says that if the 2nd Circuit "thinks that laches forbids the Cayugas from making a claim because the Supreme Court said so, you're going to find other courts saying so."

In Washington, Alexandra Page, an attorney with the Indian Law Resource Center, agrees. "There are tribes in the West who have boundary disputes on their reservations; there are water-law cases where you've got people looking back at what happened years ago, so the Supreme Court decision could have significant practical impact. The danger is that those with an interest in limiting Indian rights will do everything they can to expand the decision and use it in other circumstances."

Outlook

Who Is an Indian?

If advocates of Indian self-governance are correct, the number of tribes running their own affairs with minimal federal supervision will keep on growing. "The requests for workshops are coming in steadily," says Cyndi Holmes, self-governance coordinator of the Jamestown S'Klallam Tribe.

Others say that growth, now at a rate of about three tribes a year, may be nearing its upper limit. "When you look at the options for tribes to do self-governance, economics really drives whether they can," says LaPointe of the Rosebud Sioux, whose tribal government doesn't expect to adopt the model in the foreseeable future.

But the longstanding problems of rural and isolated reservations are not the only dimension of Indian life. People stereotypically viewed as tied to the land have become increasingly urban over the past several decades, and the view from Indian Country is that the trend will continue.

That doesn't mean reservations will empty out or lose their cultural importance. "Urban Indian is not a lifelong label," says Susan Lobo, an anthropologist at the University of Arizona. "Indian people, like everyone else, can move around. They're still American Indians."

For Indians, as for all other peoples, moving around leads to intermarriage. Matthew Snipp, a Stanford University sociologist who is half Cherokee and half Oklahoma Choctaw,

notes that Indians have long married within and outside Indian society. But the consequences of intermarriage are different for Indians than for, say, Jews or Italians.

The Indian place in American society grows out of the government-to-government
relationship between Washington and tribes. And most tribes define their members by
what's known as the "blood quantum" — their degree of tribal ancestry.

"I look at it as you're kind of USDA-approved," says Podlasek of the American Indian
Center. "Why is no other race measured that way?"

Podlasek is especially sensitive to the issue. His father was Polish-American, and
his mother was Ojibway. His own wife is Indian, but from another tribe. "My kids
can be on the tribal rolls, but their kids won't be able to enroll, unless they went
back to my tribe or to their mother's tribe to marry — depending on what their partners' blood quantum is. In generations, you could say that, by government standards,
there are no more native people."

Snipp traces the blood-quantum policy to a 1932 decision by the Indian Affairs
Commission, which voted to make one-quarter descent the minimum standard. The
commissioners were concerned, Snipp says, reading from the commission's report, that
thousands of people "more white than Indian" were receiving "shares in tribal estates and
other benefits." Tribes are no longer bound by that decision, but the requirement —
originally inserted at BIA insistence — remains in many tribal constitutions.

On the Indian side, concern over collective survival is historically well-founded. Historian
Elizabeth Shoemaker of the University of Connecticut at Storrs calculated that the Indian
population of what is now the continental United States plummeted from a top estimate
of 5.5 million in 1492 to a mere 237,000 in 1900. Indian life expectancy didn't begin to
rise significantly until after 1940.[64]

Now, Indians are worrying about the survival of Indian civilization at a time when
Indians' physical survival has never been more assured.

Even as these existential worries trouble some Indian leaders, the living conditions that
most Indians endure also pose long-term concerns.

Conroy Chino, New Mexico's Labor secretary and a member of Acoma Pueblo, says
continuation of the educational disaster in Indian Country is dooming young people to
live on the margins. "I'm out there attracting companies to come to New Mexico, and
these kids aren't going to qualify for those good jobs."

Nevertheless, below most non-Indians' radar screen, the Indian professional class is
growing. "When I got my Ph.D. in 1973, I think I was the 15th in the country," says
Beaulieu of Arizona State University's Center for Indian Education. "Now we have all kinds
of Ph.D.s, teachers with certification, lawyers." And Beaulieu says he has seen the difference that Indian professionals make in his home state of Minnesota. "You're beginning to
see an educated middle class in the reservation community, and realizing that they're
volunteering to perform lots of services."

In Albuquerque, the University of New Mexico's Jojola commutes to campus from Isleta
Pueblo. Chairman of an advisory committee on Indians to the U.S. Census Bureau, Jojola
shares concerns about use of "blood quantum" as the sole determinant of Indian identity.
"A lot of people are saying that language, culture and residence should also be considered," he says.

That standard would implicitly recognize what many Indians call the single biggest
reason that American Indians have outlasted the efforts of those who wanted to exterminate

or to assimilate them. "In our spirituality we remain strong," says Bordeaux of the Rosebud Sioux. "That's our godsend and our lifeline."

Notes

1. For background, see "The Administration of Indian Affairs," *Editorial Research Reports 1929* (Vol. II), at *CQ Researcher Plus Archive*, CQ Electronic Library, http://library.cqpress.com.

2. For background see Phil Two Eagle, "Rosebud Sioux Tribe, Demographics," March 25, 2003, www.rosebudsiouxtribe-nsn.gov/demographics.

3. "American Indian Population and Labor Force Report 2003," p. ii, Bureau of Indian Affairs, cited in John McCain, chairman, Senate Indian Affairs Committee, Byron L. Dorgan, vice chairman, letter to Senate Budget Committee, March 2, 2006, http://indian.senate.gov/public/_files/Budget5.pdf.

4. Jonathan B. Taylor and Joseph P. Kalt, "American Indians on Reservations: A Databook of Socioeconomic Change Between the 1990 and 2000 Censuses," Harvard Project on American Indian Economic Development, January 2005, pp. 8-13; www.ksg.harvard.edu/hpaied/pubs/pub_151.htm. These data exclude the Navajo Tribe, whose on-reservation population of about 175,000 is 12 times that of the next-largest tribe, thus distorting comparisons, Taylor and Kalt write.

5. *Ibid.*, p. 41.

6. McCain and Dorgan, *op. cit.*

7. "Injury Mortality Among American Indian and Alaska Native Youth, United States, 1989-1998," *Morbidity and Mortality Weekly Report*, Centers for Disease Control and Prevention, Aug. 1, 2003, www.cdc.gov/mmwr/preview/mmwrhtml/mm5230a2.htm#top.

8. Robert McSwain, deputy director, Indian Health Service, testimony before Senate Indian Affairs Committee, April 5, 2006.

9. *Ibid.*, p. xii.

10. Taylor and Kalt, *op. cit.*

11. *Ibid.*, pp. 28-30.

12. *Ibid.*, pp. 22-24.

13. The decision is *Cherokee Nation v. Georgia*, 30 U.S. 1 (1831), http://supreme.justia.com/us/30/1/case.html.

14. Alan Meister, "Indian Gaming industry Report," Analysis Group, 2006, p. 2. Publicly available data can be obtained at, "Indian Gaming Facts," www.indiangaming.org/library/indian-gaming-facts; "Gaming Revenues, 2000-2004," National Indian Gaming Commission, www.nigc.gov/TribalData/GamingRevenues20042000/tabid/549/Default.aspx.

15. The ruling is *California v. Cabazon Band of Mission Indians*, 480 U.S. 202 (1987), http://supreme.justia.com/us/480/202/case.html.

16. For background, see Susan Schmidt and James V. Grimaldi, "The Rise and Steep Fall of Jack Abramoff," *The Washington Post*, Dec. 29, 2005, p. A1. On March 29, Abramoff was sentenced in Miami to 70 months in prison after pleading to fraud, tax evasion and conspiracy to bribe public officials in charges growing out of a Florida business deal. He is cooperating with the Justice Department in its Washington-based political-corruption investigation. For background see Peter Katel, "Lobbying Boom," *CQ Researcher*, July 22, 2005, pp. 613-636.

17. Meister, *op. cit.*, pp. 27-28. For additional background, see John Cochran, "A Piece of the Action," *CQ Weekly*, May 9, 2005, p. 1208.

18. For background, see, "A Quiet Crisis: Federal Funding and Unmet Needs in Indian Country," U.S. Commission on Civil Rights, July, 2003, pp. 32, 113. www.usccr.gov/pubs/na0703/na0731.pdf.

19. Ryan Wilson, "State of Indian Education Address," Feb. 13, 2006, www.niea.org/history/SOIEAddress06.pdf.

20. For background see, Barbara Mantel, "No Child Left Behind," *CQ Researcher*, May 27, 2005, pp. 469-492.

21. McCain and Dorgan, *op. cit.*, pp. 14-15.

22. According to the Health and Human Services Department's budget proposal, recommended funding of $2 billion for the health centers would allow them to serve 150,000 Indian patients, among a total of 8.8 million patients. For background, see "Budget in Brief, Fiscal Year 2007," Department of Health and Human Services, p. 26, www.hhs.gov/budget/07budget/2007BudgetInBrief.pdf.

23. Peter Whoriskey, "A Tribe Takes a Grim Satisfaction in Abramoff's Fall," *The Washington Post*, Jan. 7, 2006, p. A1.

24. Meister, *op. cit.*, p. 15.

25. Whoriskey, *op. cit.*

26. For background see Fred Carstensen, *et al.*, "The Economic Impact of the Mashantucket Pequot Tribal National Operations on Connecticut," Connecticut Center for Economic Analysis, University of Connecticut, Nov. 28, 2000, pp. 1-3.

27. "Gambling Revenues 2004-2000," National Indian Gaming Commission, www.nigc.gov/TribalData/GamingRevenues20042000/tabid/549/Default.aspx.

28. Schmidt and Grimaldi, *op. cit.*

29. Alaina Potrikus, "2nd Land Hearing Packed," *The Post-Standard* (Syracuse, N.Y.), Jan. 12, 2006, p. B1.

30. For background see "Profile of the Navajo Nation," Navajo Nation Council, www.navajonationcouncil.org/profile.

31. Leslie Linthicum, "Navajos Cautious About Opening Casinos," *Albuquerque Journal*, Dec. 12, 2004, p. B1.

32. For background, see "Fourth Annual State of Indian Nations," Feb. 2, 2006, www.ncai.org/News_Archive.18.0.

33. For background see Theodore H. Haas, *The Indian and the Law* (1949), p. 2; thorpe.ou.edu/cohen/tribalgovtpam2pt1&2.htm#Tribal%20Power%20Today.

34. Except where otherwise noted, material in this section is drawn from Angie Debo, *A History of the Indians of the United States* (1970); see also, Mary H. Cooper, "Native Americans' Future," *CQ Researcher*, July 12, 1996, pp. 603-621.

35. W. Dale Mason, "Indian Gaming: Tribal Sovereignty and American Politics," 2000, p. 13.

36. *Cherokee Nation v. Georgia*, *op. cit.*, 30 U.S.1, http://supct.law.cornell.edu/supct/html/historics/USSC_CR_0030_0001_ZO.html.

37. Robert A. Williams Jr., *Like a Loaded Weapon: the Rehnquist Court, Indians Rights, and the Legal History of Racism in America* (2005), p. 63.

38. *Johnson v. M'Intosh*, 21 U.S. 543 (1823), www.Justia.us/us21543/case.html; *Worcester v. State of Ga.*, 31 U.S. 515 (1832), www.justia.us/us/31/515/case.html.

39. *Johnson v. M'Intosh*, *op. cit.*

40. *Worcester v. State of Ga.*, *op. cit.*

41. Quoted in Debo, *op. cit.*, pp. 219-220.

42. Quoted in *ibid.*, p. 303.

43. The specified states were Wisconsin, Minnesota (except Red Lake), Nebraska, California and Oregon (except the land of several tribes at Warm Springs). For background, see Debo, *op. cit.*, pp. 304-311.

44. Cited in Debo, *op. cit.*, p. 344.

45. For background see Troy R. Johnson, *The Occupation of Alcatraz Island: Indian Self-Determination and the Rise of Indian Activism* (1996).

46. For background, see Mary H. Cooper, "Native Americans' Future," *CQ Researcher*, July 12, 1996, pp. 603-621.

47. For background see "History of the Tribal Self-Governance Initiative," Self-Governance Tribal Consortium, www.tribalselfgov.org/Red%20Book/SG_New_Partnership.asp.

48. Cochran, *op. cit.*

49. For background see Paul Shukovsky, "Lummi Leader's Had It With Drugs, Sick of Substance Abuse Ravaging the Tribe," *Seattle Post-Intelligencer*, March 16, 2002, p. A1.

50. "Fourth Annual State of Indian Nations," *op. cit.*

51. Many Alaskan villages have joined collective compacts, so the total number of these agreements is 91.

52. For background see Alexandra J. McClanahan, "Alaska Native Claims Settlement Act (ANCSA)," Cook Inlet Region Inc., http://litsite.alaska.edu/aktraditions/ancsa.html; "The Permanent Fund Dividend," Alaska Permanent Fund Corporation, 2005, www.apfc.org/alaska/dividendprgrm.cfm?s=4.

53. For background see Eric Henson and Jonathan B. Taylor, "Native America at the New Millennium," Harvard Project on American Indian Development, Native Nations Institute, First Nations Development Institute, 2002, pp. 14-16, www.ksg.harvard.edu/hpaied/pubs/pub_004.htm.

54. Michael Coleman, "Jemez Casino Proposal At Risk," *Albuquerque Journal*, March 10, 2006, p. A1; Jeff Jones, "AG Warns Against Off-Reservation Casino," *Albuquerque Journal*, June 18, 2005, p. A1.

55. For background see testimony, "Off-Reservation Indian Gaming," House Resources Committee, Nov. 9, 2005, http://resourcescommittee.house.gov/archives/109/full/110905.htm.

56. Jerry Reynolds, "Gaming regulatory act to lose its 'two-part test,'" *Indian Country Today*, March 8, 2006.

57. Testimony before House Resources Committee, Nov. 9, 2005.

58. Matt Kelley, "Government asks for secrecy on its lawyers' role in concealing document shredding," The Associated Press, Nov. 2, 2000.

59. "Memorandum and Order," Civil Action No. 96-1285 (RCL), Feb. 7, 2005, www.indiantrust.com/index.cfm?FuseAction=PDFTypes.Home&PDFType_id=1&IsRecent=1.

60. "Memorandum Opinion," Civil Action 96-1285 (RCL), July 12, 2005, www.indiantrust.com/index.cfm?FuseAction=PDFTypes.Home&PDFType_id=1&IsRecent=1.

61. Glenn Coin, "Supreme Court: Oneidas Too Late; Sherrill Declares Victory, Wants Taxes," *The Post-Standard* (Syracuse), March 30, 2005, p. A1.

62. *Ibid.*

63. *City of Sherrill, New York, v. Oneida Indian Nation of New York*, Supreme Court of the United States, 544 U.S._(2005), pp. 1-2, 6, 14, 21.

64. Elizabeth Shoemaker, *American Indian Population Recovery in the Twentieth Century* (1999), pp. 1-13.

Bibliography

Books

Alexie, Sherman, *The Toughest Indian in the World*, *Grove Press*, 2000.
In a short-story collection, an author and screenwriter draws on his own background as a Spokane/Coeur d'Alene Indian to describe reservation and urban Indian life in loving but unsentimental detail.

Debo, Angie, *A History of the Indians of the United States*, *University of Oklahoma Press*, 1970.
A pioneering historian and champion of Indian rights provides one of the leading narrative histories of the first five centuries of Indian and non-Indian coexistence and conflict.

Deloria, Vine Jr., *Custer Died For Your Sins: An Indian Manifesto*, *University of Oklahoma Press*, 1988.
First published in 1969, this angry book gave many non-Indians a look at how the United States appeared through Indians' eyes and spurred many young Native Americans into political activism.

Mason, W. Dale, *Indian Gaming: Tribal Sovereignty and American Politics*, *University of Oklahoma Press*, 2000.
A University of New Mexico political scientist provides the essential background on the birth and early explosive growth of Indian-owned gambling operations.

Williams, Robert A., *Like a Loaded Weapon: The Rehnquist Court, Indians Rights, and the Legal History of Racism in America*, *University of Minnesota Press*, 2005.
A professor of law and American Indian Studies at the University of Arizona and tribal appeals court judge delivers a detailed and angry analysis of the history of U.S. court decisions affecting Indians.

Articles

Bartlett, Donald L., and James B. Steele, "Playing the Political Slots; How Indian Casino Interests Have Learned the Art of Buying Influence in Washington," *Time*, Dec. 23, 2002, p. 52.
In a prescient article that preceded the Jack Abramoff lobbying scandal, veteran investigative journalists examine the political effects of some tribes' newfound wealth.

Harden, Blaine, "Walking the Land with Pride Again; A Revolution in Indian Country Spawns Wealth and Optimism," *The Washington Post*, Sept. 19, 2004, p. A1.
Improved conditions in many sectors of Indian America have spawned a change in outlook, despite remaining hardships.

Morgan, Lance, "Ending the Curse of Trust Land," *Indian Country Today*, March 18, 2005, www.indiancountry.com/content.cfm?id=1096410559.

A lawyer and pioneering tribal entrepreneur lays out his vision of a revamped legal-political system in which Indians would own their tribal land outright, with federal supervision ended.

Robbins, Ted, "Tribal cultures, nutrition clash on fry bread," "All Things Considered," *National Public Radio*, Oct. 26, 2005, transcript available at www.npr.org/templates/story/story.php?storyId= 4975889.
Indian health educators have tried to lower Native Americans' consumption of a beloved but medically disastrous treat.

Thompson, Ginger, "As a Sculpture Takes Shape in New Mexico, Opposition Takes Shape in the U.S.," *The New York Times*, Jan. 17, 2002, p. A12.
Indian outrage has clashed with Latino pride over a statue celebrating the ruthless Spanish conqueror of present-day New Mexico.

Wagner, Dennis, "Tribes Across Country Confront Horrors of Meth," *The Arizona Republic*, March 31, 2006, p. A1.
Methamphetamine use and manufacturing have become the scourge of Indian Country.

Reports and Studies

"Indian Health Service: Health Care Services Are Not Always Available to Native Americans," *Government Accountability Office*, August 2005.
Congress' investigative arm concludes that financial shortfalls combined with dismal reservation conditions, including scarce transportation, are stunting medical care for many American Indians.

"Strengthening the Circle: Interior Indian Affairs Highlights, 2001-2004," *Department of the Interior* (undated).
The Bush administration sums up its first term's accomplishments in Indian Country.

Cornell, Stephen, *et al.*, "Seizing the Future: Why Some Native Nations Do and Others Don't," *Native Nations Institute, Udall Center for Studies in Public Policy, University of Arizona, Harvard Project on American Indian Economic Development, John F. Kennedy School of Government, Harvard University*, 2005.
The authors argue that the key to development lies in a tribe's redefinition of itself from object of government attention to independent power.

For More Information

Committee on Indian Affairs, U.S. Senate, 838 Hart Office Building, Washington, DC 20510; (202) 224-2251; http://indian.senate.gov/public. A valuable source of information on developments affecting Indian Country.

Harvard Project on American Indian Economic Development, John F. Kennedy School of Government, 79 John F. Kennedy St., Cambridge, MA 02138; (617) 495-1480; www.ksg.harvard.edu/hpaied. Explores strategies for Indian advancement.

Indian Health Service, The Reyes Building, 801 Thompson Ave., Suite 400, Rockville, MD 20852; (301) 443-1083; www.ihs.gov. One of the most important federal agencies in Indian Country; provides a wide variety of medical and administrative information.

National Coalition Against Legalized Gambling, 100 Maryland Ave., N.E., Room 311, Washington, DC 20002; (800) 664-2680; www.ncalg.org. Provides anti-gambling material that touches on tribe-owned operations.

National Indian Education Association, 110 Maryland Ave., N.E., Suite 104, Washington, DC 20002; (202) 544-7290; www.niea.org/welcome. Primary organization and lobbying voice for Indian educators.

National Indian Gaming Association, 224 Second St., S.E., Washington, DC 20003; (202) 546-7711; www.indiangaming.org. Trade association and lobbying arm of the tribal casino industry.

Self-Governance Communication and Education Tribal Consortium, 1768 Iowa Business Center, Bellingham, WA 98229; (360) 752-2270; www.tribalselfgov.org. Organizational hub of Indian self-governance movement; provides a wide variety of news and data.

Upstate Citizens for Equality, P.O. Box 24, Union Springs, NY 13160; http://upstate-citizens.org. Opposes tribal land-claim litigation.

References

Aberson, Christopher, Shoemaker, Carl, & Tomolillo, Christina. 2004. "Implicit Bias and Contact: The Role of Interethnic Friendships." *Journal of Social Psychology,* 144:335–347.

Abrahamson, Harold. 1980. "Assimilation and Pluralism." In Stephan Thernstrom, Ann Orlov, & Oscar Handlin (Eds.), *Harvard Encyclopedia of American Ethnic Groups* (pp. 150–160). Cambridge, MA: Harvard University Press.

Acuna, Rodolfo. 1988. *Occupied America* (3rd ed.). New York: Harper & Row.

————. 1999. *Occupied America* (4th ed.). New York: Harper & Row.

Adarand Constructors, Inc. v. Pena, 515 U.S. 200 (1995).

Adorno, T. W., Frenkel-Brunswick, E., Levinson, D., & Sanford, N. 1950. *The Authoritarian Personality.* New York: Harper & Row.

"The African Diaspora." n.d. *Slave Trade and African American Ancestry.* Retrieved December 4, 2007, from http://www .homestead.com/wysinger/mapofafricadiaspora.html.

Agbayani-Siewert, Pauline, & Revilla, Linda. 1995. "Filipino Americans." In Pyong Gap Min (Ed.), *Asian Americans: Contemporary Issues and Trends* (pp. 134–168). Thousands Oaks, CA: Sage.

Aizenman, N. C. 2006. "Immigration Debate Wakes a 'Sleeping Latino Giant.'" *Washington Post,* April 6, p. A1.

Alba, Richard. 1985. *Italian Americans: Into the Twilight of Ethnicity.* Englewood Cliffs, NJ: Prentice Hall.

————. 1990. *Ethnic Identity: The Transformation of White America.* New Haven, CT: Yale University Press.

————. 1995. "Assimilation's Quiet Tide." *The Public Interest,* 119:3–19.

Alba, Richard, Logan, John, Lutz, Amy, & Stults, Brian. 2002. "Only English by the Third Generation? Loss and Preservation of the Mother Tongue Among the Grandchildren of Contemporary Immigrants." *Demography,* 39: 467–484.

Alba, Richard, & Nee, Victor. 1997. "Rethinking Assimilation Theory for a New Era of Immigration." *International Migration Review,* 31:826–875.

————. 2003. *Remaking the American Mainstream: Assimilation and Contemporary Immigration.* Cambridge, MA: Harvard University Press.

Aleiss, Angela. 2005. *Making the White Man's Indian: Native Americans and Hollywood Movies.* Westport, CT: Praeger.

Allport, Gordon. 1954. *The Nature of Prejudice.* Reading, MA: Addison-Wesley.

Almquist, Elizabeth M. 1979. "Black Women and the Pursuit of Equality." In Jo Freeman (Ed.), *Women: A Feminist Perspective* (pp. 430–450). Palo Alto, CA: Mayfield.

Altemeyer, Bob. 2004. "Highly Dominating, Highly Authoritarian Personalities." *Journal of Social Psychology,* 144:421–448.

Alvarez, Rodolfo. 1973. "The Psycho-historical and Socioeconomic Development of the Chicano Community in the United States." *Social Science Quarterly,* 53:920–942.

American Indian Higher Education Consortium. 2001. *Building Strong Communities: Tribal Colleges as Engaged Institutions.* Retrieved December 12, 2004, from http://www.ihep.com/Pubs/PDF/Communities.pdf.

American Sociological Association. 2003. *The Importance of Collecting Data and Doing Scientific Research on Race.* Retrieved June 19, 2007, from http://www2.asanet.org/media/asa_race_statement .pdf.

Amott, Teresa, & Matthaei, Julie. 1991. *Race, Gender, and Work: A Multicultural History of Women in the United States.* Boston: South End.

Andersen, Margaret L. 1993. *Thinking About Women: Sociological Perspectives on Sex and Gender* (3rd ed.). New York: Macmillan.

Anti-Defamation League. 2000. *Anti-Semitism in the United States.* Retrieved July 12, 2002, from http://www.adl.org/backgrounders/Anti_Semitism_us.html.

Anton, Mike. 2001. "After the Attack: The Psychic Toll." *Los Angeles Times,* September 22, A26.

Arab American Anti-Discrimination Committee. 2002. *ADC Fact Sheet: The Condition of Arab Americans Post 9/11.* Retrieved June 22, 2002, from http://www.adc.org/terror_attack/9-11aftermath .pdf.

Aronson, E., & Patnoe, S. 1997. *The Jigsaw Classroom: Building Cooperation in the Classroom* (2nd ed.). New York: Addison Wesley Longman.

Aronson, Eliot, & Gonzalez, Alex. 1988. "Desegregation, Jigsaw, and the Mexican-American Experience." In Phyllis Katz & Dalmas Taylor (Eds.), *Eliminating Racism: Profiles in Controversy* (pp. 301–314). New York: Plenum Press.

Ashmore, Richard, & DelBoca, Frances. 1976. "Psychological Approaches to Understanding Group Conflict." In Phyllis Katz (Ed.), *Towards the Elimination of Racism* (pp. 73–123). New York: Pergamon.

"Asia: Original Sin, Australia's Aborigines." 2007. *Economist,* June 2, p. 67.

Australian Bureau of Statistics. 2002. "Australian Social Trends 2002, Population, National Summary Tables." Retrieved July 5, 2002, from http://www.abs.gov.au.

Australian Human Rights and Equal Opportunity Commission. 1997. *Bringing Them Home: Report of the National Inquiry Into the Separation of Aboriginal and Torres Strait Islander Children From Their Families.* Retrieved July 5, 2002, from http://www.austlii.edu.au/au/special/rsjproject/rsjlibrary/hreoc/stolen/.

"Average Years of Schooling of Adults by Country." n.d. Retrieved March 21, 2008, from http://www.nationmaster.com/red/graph/edu_ave_yea_of_sch_of_adu-education-average-years-schooling-adults&ob=ws.

Avery, Robert, & Rendall, Michael. 2002. "Lifetime Inheritances of Three Generations of Whites and Blacks." *American Journal of Sociology,* 107:1300–1346.

Baca Zinn, Maxine, & Dill, Bonnie Thornton. 1994. *Women of Color in U.S. Society.* Philadelphia: Temple University Press.

Baca Zinn, Maxine, & Eitzen, D. Stanley. 1990. *Diversity in Families.* New York: HarperCollins.

Bames, Robert. 2007. "Divided Court Limits Use of Race by School Districts." *Washington Post,* June 29, p. A1.

Barreto, Manuela, & Ellemers, Naomi. 2005. "The Perils of Political Correctness: Men's and Women's Responses to Old-Fashioned and Modern Sexist Views." *Social Psychology Quarterly,* 68:75–88.

Barringer, Herbert, Takeuchi, David, & Levin, Michael. 1995. *Asians and Pacific Islanders in the United States.* New York: Russell Sage Foundation.

Barringer, Herbert, Takeuchi, David, & Xenos, Peter. 1990. "Education, Occupational Prestige, and Income of Asian Americans." *Sociology of Education,* 63:27–43.

Bean, Frank, & Stevens, Gillian. 2003. *America's Newcomers and the Dynamics of Diversity.* New York: Russell Sage Foundation.

Beaton, Anne, Tougas, Francine, & Joly, Stephane. 1996. "Neosexism Among Male Managers: Is It a Matter of Numbers?" *Journal of Applied Social Psychology,* 26:2189–2204.

Becerra, Rosina. 1988. "The Mexican American Family." In Charles H. Mindel, Robert W. Habenstein, & Roosevelt Wright Jr., *Ethnic Families in America: Patterns and Variations* (3rd ed., pp. 141–172). New York: Elsevier.

Beck, E. M., & Clark, Timothy. 2002. "Strangers, Community Miscreants, or Locals: Who Were the Black Victims of Mob Violence?" *Historical Methods,* 35(2):77–84.

Beck, E. M., & Tolnay, Stewart. 1990. "The Killing Fields of the Deep South: The Market for Cotton and the Lynching of Blacks, 1882–1930." *American Sociological Review,* 55:526–539.

Beinart, William. 1994. *Twentieth-Century South Africa.* New York: Oxford University Press.

Bell, Daniel. 1973. *The Coming of Post-industrial Society.* New York: Basic Books.

Bell, Derrick. 1992. *Race, Racism, and American Law* (3rd ed.). Boston: Little, Brown.

Benedict, Ruth. 1946. *The Chrysanthemum and the Sword: Patterns of Japanese Culture.* Boston: Houghton Mifflin.

Benjamin, Lois. 2005. *The Black Elite.* Lanham, MD: Rowman & Littlefield.

Berkowitz, Leonard. 1978. "Whatever Happened to the Frustration-Aggression Hypothesis?" *American Behavioral Scientist,* 21:691–708.

Bird, Elizabeth. 1999. "Gendered Construction of the American Indian in Popular Media." *Journal of Communication,* 49:60–83.

Biskupic, Joan. 1989. "House Approves Entitlement for Japanese-Americans." *Congressional Quarterly Weekly Report,* October 28, p. 2879.

Black-Gutman, D., & Hickson, F. 1996. "The Relationship Between Racial Attitudes and Social-Cognitive Development in Children: An Australian Study." *Developmental Psychology,* 32:448–457.

Blassingame, John W. 1972. *The Slave Community: Plantation Life in the Antebellum South.* New York: Oxford University Press.

Blau, Peter M., & Duncan, Otis Dudley. 1967. *The American Occupational Structure.* New York: Wiley.

Blauner, Robert. 1972. *Racial Oppression in America.* New York: Harper & Row.

Blessing, Patrick. 1980. "Irish." In Stephan Thernstrom, Ann Orlov, & Oscar Handlin (Eds.), *Harvard Encyclopedia of American Ethnic Groups* (pp. 524–545). Cambridge, MA: Harvard University Press.

Bluestone, Barry, & Harrison, Bennet. 1982. *The Deindustrialization of America.* New York: Basic Books.

Blumer, Herbert. 1965. "Industrialization and Race Relations." In Guy Hunter (Ed.), *Industrialization and Race Relations: A Symposium* (pp. 200–253). London: Oxford University Press.

Bobo, Lawrence. 1988. "Group Conflict, Prejudice, and the Paradox of Contemporary Racial Attitudes." In Phyllis Katz & Dalmar Taylor (Eds.), *Eliminating Racism: Profiles in Controversy* (pp. 85–114). New York: Plenum Press.

_____. 2001. "Racial Attitudes and Relations at the Close of the Twentieth Century." In N. Smelser, W. Wilson, & F. Mitchell (Eds.), *America Becoming: Racial Trends and Their Consequences* (Vol. 1, pp. 264–301). Washington, DC: National Academy Press.

Bodnar, John. 1985. *The Transplanted.* Bloomington: Indiana University Press.

Bogardus, Emory. 1933. "A Social Distance Scale." *Sociology and Social Research,* 17:265–271.

Bonacich, Edna. 1972. "A Theory of Ethnic Antagonism: The Split Labor Market." *American Sociological Review,* 37:547–559.

Bonacich, Edna, & Modell, John. 1980. *The Economic Basis of Ethnic Solidarity: Small Business in the Japanese American Community.* Berkeley: University of California Press.

Bonilla-Silva, Eduardo. 2001. *White Supremacy and Racism in the Post–Civil Rights Era.* Boulder, CO: Lynne Riener.

_____. 2006. *Racism Without Racists* (2nd ed.). Lanham, MD: Rowman & Littlefield.

Booth, Alan, Granger, Douglas, Mazur, Alan, & Kivligham, Katie. 2006. "Testosterone and Social Behavior." *Social Forces,* 86:167–191.

Bordewich, Fergus. 1996. *Killing the White Man's Indian.* New York: Doubleday.

Borjas, George. 1999. *Heaven's Door: Immigration Policy and the American Economy.* Princeton, NJ: Princeton University Press.

Boswell, Terry. 1986. "A Split Labor Market Analysis of Discrimination Against Chinese Immigrants, 1850–1882." *American Sociological Review,* 51:352–371.

Bouvier, Leon F., & Gardner, Robert W. 1986. "Immigration to the U.S.: The Unfinished Story." *Population Bulletin,* November, p. 41.

Brace, Matthew. 2001. "A Nation Divided." *Geographical,* 73:14–20.

Brittingham, Angela, & de la Cruz, C. Patricia. 2004. *Ancestry: 2000.* Retrieved June 29, 2007, from http://www.census.gov/prod/2004pubs/c2kbr-35.pdf.

Brody, David. 1980. "Labor." In Stephan Thernstrom, Ann Orlov, & Oscar Handlin (Eds.), *Harvard Encyclopedia of American Ethnic Groups* (pp. 609–618). Cambridge, MA: Harvard University Press.

Brooks, Roy L. (Ed.). 1999. *When Sorry Isn't Enough: The Controversy Over Apologies and Reparations for Human Injustice.* New York: New York University Press.

Brown, Dee. 1970. *Bury My Heart at Wounded Knee.* New York: Holt, Rinehart & Winston.

Brown, Kendrick T., Brown, Tony N., Jackson, James S., Sellers, Robert M., & Manuel, Warde J. 2003. "Teammates on and off the Field? Contact With Black Teammates and the Racial Attitudes of White Student Athletes." *Journal of Applied Social Psychology,* 33:1379–1404.

Brown, Rupert. 1995. *Prejudice: Its Social Psychology.* Cambridge, MA: Blackwell.

Browne, Irene. (Ed.). 1999. *Latinas and African American Women at Work: Race, Gender, and Economic Inequality.* New York: Russell Sage Foundation.

Brown v. Board of Education of Topeka, 247 U.S. 483 (1954).

Buraku Liberation League. 2001. *Discrimination Against Buraku People.* Retrieved July 10, 2002, from http://www.blhrri.org/index_e.htm.

Buriel, Raymond. 1993. "Acculturation, Respect for Cultural Differences, and Biculturalism Among Three Generations of Mexican American and Euro-American School Children." *Journal of Genetic Psychology,* 154:531–544.

Burns, Peter, & Gimpel, James. 2000. "Economic Insecurity, Prejudicial Stereotypes, and Public Opinion on Immigration Policy." *Political Science Quarterly,* 115:201–205.

Camarillo, Albert, & Bonilla, Frank. 2001. "Hispanics in a Multicultural Society: A New American Dilemma?" In N. Smelser, W. Wilson, & F. Mitchell (Eds.), *America Becoming: Racial Trends and Their Consequences* (Vol. 2, pp. 103–134). Washington, DC: National Academy Press.

Camarota, Steven. 2002. *Immigrants in the United States, 2002.* Center for Immigration Studies. Retrieved February 15, 2005, from http://www.cis.org/articles/2002/back1302.html.

———. 2007. *Immigration Is Hurting the U.S. Worker.* Center for Immigration Studies. Retrieved March 15, 2008, from http://www.cis.org/articles/2007/sacoped071107.html.

Cameron, James. 2001. "Social Identity, Modern Sexism, and Perceptions of Personal and Group Discrimination by Women and Men." *Sex Roles,* 45:743–766.

Cancio, S., Evans, T., & Maume, D. 1996. "Reconsidering the Declining Significance of Race: Racial Differences in Early Career Wages." American Sociological Review, 61:541–556.

Central Statistics Office, Ireland. 2006. *Population and Migration Estimates, April 2006.* Retrieved July 9, 2007, from http://www.cso.ie/releasespublications/documents/population/current/popmig.pdf.

Chan, Sucheng. 1990. "European and Asian Immigrants Into the United States in Comparative Perspective, 1820s to 1920s." In Virginia Yans-McLaughlin (Ed.), *Immigration Reconsidered: History, Sociology, and Politics* (pp. 37–75). New York: Oxford University Press.

Charles, Camille. 2003. "The Dynamics of Racial Residential Segregation." *Annual Review of Sociology,* 29:167–207.

Cheng, Susan M., & Ho, T. Linh. 2003. *A Portrait of Race and Ethnicity in Hawaii: An Analysis of Social and Economic Outcomes of Hawaii's People.* Honolulu, HI: Pacific American Research Center. Retrieved April 15, 2005, from http://www.thepaf.org/Research/Portrait_I.pdf.

Chirot, Daniel. 1994. *How Societies Change.* Thousand Oaks, CA: Pine Forge Press.

Cho, Sumi. 1993. "Korean Americans vs. African Americans: Conflict and Construction." In Robert Gooding-Williams (Ed.), *Reading Rodney King, Reading Urban Uprising* (pp. 196–211). New York: Routledge & Kegan Paul.

Churchill, Ward. 1985. "Resisting Relocation: Dine and Hopis Fight to Keep Their Land." *Dollars and Sense,* December, pp. 112–115.

Civil Rights Act of 1964, Pub. L. 88-352, § 42 U.S.C. 2000 (1964).

Clark, M. L., & Person, Willie. 1982. "Racial Stereotypes Revisited." *International Journal of Intercultural Relations,* 6:381–392.

Cofer, Judith Ortiz. 1995. "The Myth of the Latin Woman: I Just Met a Girl Named Maria." In *The Latin Deli: Prose and Poetry* (pp. 148–154). Athens: University of Georgia Press.

Cohen, Adam, & Taylor, Elizabeth. 2000. *American Pharaoh, Mayor Richard J. Daley: His Battle for Chicago and the Nation.* New York: Little, Brown.

Cohen, Steven M. 1985. *The 1984 National Survey of American Jews: Political and Social Outlooks.* New York: American Jewish Committee.

Conot, Robert. 1967. *Rivers of Blood, Years of Darkness.* New York: Bantam.

Conzen, Kathleen N. 1980. "Germans." In Stephan Thernstrom, Ann Orlov, & Oscar Handlin (Eds.), *Harvard Encyclopedia of American Ethnic Groups* (pp. 405–425). Cambridge, MA: Harvard University Press.

Cornell, Stephen. 1987. "American Indians, American Dreams, and the Meaning of Success." *American Indian Culture and Research Journal,* 11:59–71.

———. 1988. *The Return of the Native: American Indian Political Resurgence.* New York: Oxford University Press.

———. 1990. "Land, Labor, and Group Formation: Blacks and Indians in the United States." *Ethnic and Racial Studies,* 13:368–388.

———. 2006. *What Makes First Nations Enterprises Successful? Lessons From the Harvard Project.* Tucson, AZ: Native Nations Institute for Leadership, Management, and Policy.

Cornell, Stephen, & Kalt, Joseph. 1998. *Sovereignty and Nation-Building: The Development Challenge in Indian Country Today.* Cambridge, MA: Harvard Project on American Indian Economic Development. Retrieved August 22, 2007, from http://sparky.harvard.edu/hpaied/docs/CornellKalt%20Sov-NB.pdf.

———. 2000. "Where's the Glue? Institutional and Cultural Foundations of American Indian Economic Development." *Journal of Socio-economics,* 29:443–470.

Cornell, Stephen, Kalt, Joseph, Krepps, Matthew, & Taylor, Johnathan. 1998. *American Indian Gaming Policy and Its Socio-economic Effects: A Report to the National Impact Gambling Study Commission.* Cambridge, MA: Economics Resource Group.

Cortes, Carlos. 1980. "Mexicans." In Stephan Thernstrom, Ann Orlov, & Oscar Handlin (Eds.), *Harvard Encyclopedia of American Ethnic Groups* (pp. 697–719). Cambridge, MA: Harvard University Press.

Cose, Ellis. 1993. *The Rage of a Privileged Class.* New York: HarperCollins.

Cowan, Gloria. 2005. "Interracial Interactions at Racially Diverse University Campuses." *Journal of Social Psychology,* 145:49–63.

Cox, Oliver. 1948. *Caste, Class, and Race: A Study in Social Dynamics.* New York: Modern Reader Paperbacks.

Crow Dog, Mary. 1990. *Lakota Woman.* New York: HarperCollins.

Curtin, Philip. 1990. *The Rise and Fall of the Plantation Complex.* New York: Cambridge University Press.

D'Alessio, Stewart, Stolzenberg, Lisa, & Eitle, David. 2002. "The Effect of Racial Threat on Interracial and Intraracial Crimes." *Social Science Research,* 31:392–408.

Damico, Sandra, & Sparks, Christopher. 1986. "Cross-Group Contact Opportunities: Impact on Interpersonal Relationships in Desegregated Middle Schools." *Sociology of Education,* 59:113–123.

D'Angelo, Raymond. 2001. *The American Civil Rights Movement: Readings and Interpretations.* New York: McGraw-Hill.

Debo, Angie. 1970. *A History of the Indians of the United States.* Norman: University of Oklahoma Press.

Degler, Carl. 1971. *Neither Black nor White: Slavery and Race Relations in Brazil and the United States.* New York: Macmillan.

de la Cruz, Patricia, & Brittingham, Angela. 2003. *The Arab Population: 2000.* Retrieved March 19, 2008, from http://www.census.gov/prod/2003pubs/c2kbr-23.pdfhttp://www.census.gov/prod/2003pubs/c2kbr-23.pdf.

Deloria, Vine. 1969. *Custer Died for Your Sins.* New York: Macmillan.

———. 1970. *We Talk, You Listen.* New York: Macmillan.

———. 1995. *Red Earth, White Lies.* New York: Scribner's.

Del Pinal, Jorge, & Singer, Audrey. 1997. "Generations of Diversity: Latinos in the United States." *Population Bulletin,* 52 (3):1–48. Washington, DC: Population Reference Bureau.

DeNavas, Carmen, Proctor, Bernadette, & Mills, Robert. 2004. *Income, Poverty, and Health Insurance Coverage in the United States: 2003.* Washington, DC: U.S. Government Printing Office.

DeNavas-Walt, Carmen, Proctor, Bernadette, & Lee, Cheryl. 2006. *Income, Poverty and Health Insurance Coverage in the United States: 2005.* Washington, DC: U.S. Government Printing Office. Retrieved March 15, 2008, from http://www.census.gov/prod/2006pubs/p60-231.pdf.

Deutsch, Morton, & Collins, Mary Ann. 1951. *Interracial Housing: A Psychological Evaluation of a Social Experiment.* Minneapolis: University of Minnesota Press.

Devine, Patricia, & Elliot, Andrew. 1995. "Are Racial Stereotypes Really Fading? The Princeton Trilogy Revisited." *Personality and Social Psychology Bulletin,* 21:1139–1150.

Dinnerstein, Leonard. 1977. "The East European Jewish Immigration." In Leonard Dinnerstein & Frederic C. Jaher (Eds.), *Uncertain Americans* (pp. 216–231). New York: Oxford University Press.

Dixon, Jeffrey. 2006. "The Ties That Don't Bind: Towards Reconciling Group Threat and Contact Theories of Prejudice." *Social Forces,* 84:2179–2204.

Dixon, Jeffrey, & Rosenbaum, Michael. 2004. "Nice to Know You? Testing Contact, Cultural, and Group Threat Theories of Anti-Black and Anti-Hispanic Stereotypes." *Social Science Quarterly,* 85:257–280.

Dollard, John, Miller, Neal E., Doob, Leonard W., Mowrer, O. H., & Sears, Robert R. (with Ford, Clellan S., Hovland, Carl Iver, & Sollenberger, Richard T.). 1939. *Frustration and Aggression.* New Haven, CT: Yale University Press.

"Dominicans Saved From Sea Tell of Attacks and Deaths of Thirst." 2004. *New York Times,* August 12, p. A13.

D'Orso, Michael. 1996. *Like Judgement Day: The Ruin and Redemption of a Town Called Rosewood.* New York: Putnam.

Doyle, Anna Beth, & Aboud, Frances E. 1995. "A Longitudinal Study of White Children's Racial Prejudice as a Socio-cognitive Development." *Merrill-Palmer Quarterly,* 41:209–228.

Drake, Richard. 1860. *Revelations of a Slave Smuggler.* New York: Robert M. Dewitt.

Du Bois, W. E. B. 1961. *The Souls of Black Folk.* Greenwich, CT: Fawcett.

Duleep, Harriet O. 1988. *Economic Status of Americans of Asian Descent.* Washington, DC: U.S. Commission on Civil Rights.

Eichenwald, Kurt. 1996. "Texaco to Make Record Payment in Bias Lawsuit." *New York Times,* November 16, p. 1.

Elkins, Stanley. 1959. *Slavery: A Problem in American Institutional and Intellectual Life.* New York: Universal Library.

Ellison, Christopher, & Powers, Daniel. 1994. "The Contact Hypothesis and Racial Attitudes Among Black Americans." *Social Science Quarterly,* 75:385–400.

Ellsworth, Scott. 1982. *Death in a Promised Land: The Tulsa Race Riot of 1921.* Baton Rouge: Louisiana State University Press.

Entine, Jon. 2000. *Taboo: Why Black Athletes Dominate Sports and Why We're Afraid to Talk About It.* New York: Public Affairs.

Espinosa, Kristin, & Massey, Douglas. 1997. "Determinants of English Proficiency Among Mexican Migrants to the United States." *International Migration Review,* 31:28–51.

Espiritu, Yen. 1996. "Colonial Oppression, Labour Importation, and Group Formation: Filipinos in the United States." *Ethnic and Racial Studies,* 19:29–49.

———. 1997. *Asian American Women and Men.* Thousand Oaks, CA: Sage.

Essien-Udom, E. U. 1962. *Black Nationalism.* Chicago: University of Chicago Press.

"Europe: The Integration Dilemma: Minorities in Germany." 2007. *Economist,* July 19, p. 39.

Evans, Sara M. 1979. *Personal Politics.* New York: Knopf.

———. 1989. *Born for Liberty: A History of Women in America.* New York: Free Press.

Evans, William, & Topoleski, Julie. 2002. *The Social and Economic Impact of Native American Casinos.* Retrieved December 5, 2004, from http://www.bsos.umd.edu/econ/evans/wpapers/evans_topoleski_casinos.pdf.

Fanning, Bryan. 2003. *Racism and Social Change in the Republic of Ireland.* Manchester, UK: Manchester University Press.

Farley, John. 2000. *Majority-Minority Relations* (4th ed.). Englewood Cliffs, NJ: Prentice Hall.

Farley, Reynolds. 1996. *The New American Reality.* New York: Russell Sage Foundation.

Faux, Jeff. 2004. "NAFTA at 10: Where Do We Go From Here?" *Nation,* February 2, pp. 11–14.

Feagin, Joe. 2001. *Racist America: Roots, Current Realities, and Future Reparations.* New York: Routledge.

Feagin, Joe R., & Feagin, Clairece Booher. 1986. *Discrimination American Style: Institutional Racism and Sexism.* Malabar, FL: Robert E. Krieger.

Feagin, Joe, & O'Brien, Eileen. 2004. *White Men on Race: Power, Privilege, and the Shaping of Cultural Consciousness*. Boston: Beacon Press.

Feagin, Joe R., & Vera, Hernan. 1995. *White Racism: The Basics*. New York: Routledge.

Fears, Darryl. 2007a. "Hate Crime Reporting Uneven." *Washington Post,* November 20, p. A3.

———. 2007b. "La. Town Fells White Tree, But Tension Runs Deep." *Washington Post,* August 4, p. A3.

Federal Bureau of Investigation. 2004. *Hate Crime Statistics*. Retrieved October 24, 2004, from http://www.fbi.gov/ucr/hatecrime202.pdf.

———. 2006. *Hate Crime Statistics, 2005*. Retrieved from http://www.fbi.gov/ucr/hc2005/table1.htm.

———. 2007. *Hate Crime*. Retrieved December 2, 2007, from http://www.fbi.gov/hq/cid/civilrights/hate.htm.

Firefighters Local Union No. 1784 v. Stotts, 467 U.S. 561 (1984).

Fitzpatrick, Joseph P. 1976. "The Puerto Rican Family." In Charles H. Mindel & Robert W. Habenstein (Eds.), *Ethnic Families in America* (pp. 173–195). New York: Elsevier.

———. 1980. "Puerto Ricans." In Stephan Thernstrom, Ann Orlov, & Oscar Handlin (Eds.), *Harvard Encyclopedia of American Ethnic Groups* (pp. 858–867). Cambridge, MA: Harvard University Press.

——— 1987. *Puerto Rican Americans: The Meaning of Migration to the Mainland* (2nd ed.). Englewood Cliffs, NJ: Prentice Hall.

Foner, Nancy. 2005. *In a New Land: A Comparative View of Immigration*. New York: NYU Press.

Fong, Eric, & Markham, William. 1991. "Immigration, Ethnicity, and Conflict: The California Chinese, 1849–1882." *Sociological Inquiry,* 61:471–490.

Fong, Timothy. 2002. *The Contemporary Asian American Experience* (2nd ed.). Upper Saddle River, NJ: Prentice Hall.

Fonte, John. 2004. "How to Make an American." *American Enterprise,* 15(6):4–5.

Forbes, H. D. 1997. *Ethnic Conflict: Commerce, Culture and the Contact Hypothesis*. New Haven, CT: Yale University Press.

Forner, Philip S. 1980. *Women and the American Labor Movement: From World War I to the Present*. New York: Free Press.

Franklin, John Hope. 1967. *From Slavery to Freedom* (3rd ed.). New York: Knopf.

Franklin, John Hope, & Moss, Alfred. 1994. *From Slavery to Freedom* (7th ed.). New York: McGraw-Hill.

Frazier, E. Franklin. 1957. *Black Bourgeoisie: The Rise of a New Middle Class*. New York: Free Press.

Fry, Richard. 2007. *The Changing Racial and Ethnic Composition of U.S. Public Schools*. Pew Research. Retrieved October 18, 2007, from http://pewhispanic.org/files/reports/79.pdf.

Fukuyama, Francis. 2004. *Identity Crisis: Why We Shouldn't Worry About Mexican Immigration*. Retrieved April 2, 2005, from http://slate.msn.com/id/2101756/#continuearticle.

Gabe, Thomas, Falk, Gene, & McCarthy, Maggie. 2005. *Hurricane Katrina: Social-Demographic Characteristics of Impacted Areas*. Congressional Research Service, U.S. Congress. Retrieved June 21, 2007, from http://www.gnocdc.org/reports/crsrept.pdf.

Gallagher, Charles. 2001. *Playing the Ethnic Card: How Ethnic Narratives Maintain Racial Privilege*. Paper presented at the Annual Meetings of the Southern Sociological Society, April 4–7, Atlanta, GA.

Gallup Organization. 2007. "Americans Overwhelmingly Favor Interracial Dating." Retrieved December 5, 2007, from http://www.amren.com/mtnews/archives/2005/10/gallup_american.php.

Gallup Poll. 2006. "Race Relations." Retrieved May 17, 2007, from http://www.galluppoll.com/content/default.aspx?ci=1687&pg=4.

Gans, Herbert. 1979. "Symbolic Ethnicity: The Future of Ethnic Groups and Cultures in America." *Ethnic and Racial Studies,* 2:1–20.

Garcia, Maria Cristina. 1996. *Havana USA: Cuban Exiles and Cuban Americans in South Florida, 1959–1994*. Berkeley: University of California Press.

Garvey, Marcus. 1969. *Philosophy and Opinions of Marcus Garvey* (Vols. 1–2, Amy Jacques Garvey, Ed.). New York: Atheneum.

———. 1977. *Philosophy and Opinions of Marcus Garvey* (Vol. 3, Amy Jacques Garvey & E. U. Essien-Udom, Eds.). London: Frank Cass.

Genovese, Eugene D. 1974. *Roll, Jordan, Roll: The World the Slaves Made*. New York: Pantheon.

Gerth, Hans, & Mills, C. Wright. (Eds.). 1946. *From Max Weber: Essays in Sociology*. New York: Oxford University Press.

Geschwender, James A. 1978. *Racial Stratification in America*. Dubuque, IA: William C. Brown.

Giago, T. 1992. "I Hope the Redskins Lose." *Newsweek,* January 27, p. 8.

Gladwell, Malcolm. 1995. "Personal Experience, the Primary Gauge." *Washington Post,* October 8, p. A26.

Glaeser, Edward, & Vigdor, Jacob. 2001. *Racial Segregation in the 2000 Census: Promising News*. Washington, DC: Brookings Institution.

Glazer, Nathan, & Moynihan, Daniel. 1970. *Beyond the Melting Pot* (2nd ed.). Cambridge: MIT Press.

Gleason, Philip. 1980. "American Identity and Americanization." In Stephan Thernstrom, Ann Orlov, & Oscar Handlin (Eds.), *Harvard Encyclopedia of American Ethnic Groups* (pp. 31–57). Cambridge, MA: Harvard University Press.

Glick, Peter, & Fiske, Susan. 1996. "The Ambivalent Sexism Inventory: Differentiating Hostile and Benevolent Sexism." *Journal of Personality and Social Psychology,* 70:491–512.

Glick, Peter, Fiske, Susan, Mladinic, Saiz, Antonio, Jose L., Abrams, Dominic, et al. 2000. "Beyond Prejudice as Simple Antipathy: Hostile and Benevolent Sexism Across Cultures." *Journal of Personality and Social Psychology,* 79:763–775.

Goldstein, Amy, & Suro, Robert. 2000. "A Journey on Stages: Assimilation's Pull Is Still Strong but Its Pace Varies." *Washington Post,* January 16, p. A1.

Goldstein, Sidney, & Goldscheider, Calvin. 1968. *Jewish Americans: Three Generations in a Jewish Community*. Englewood Cliffs, NJ: Prentice Hall.

Gooding-Williams, Robert. 1964. *Assimilation in American Life*. New York: Oxford University Press.

———. 1993. *Reading Rodney King, Reading Urban Uprising*. New York: Routledge & Kegan Paul.

Gordon, M. M. (1964). *Assimilation in American Life: The Role of Race, Religion and National Origins*. New York: Oxford University Press.

Goren, Arthur. 1980. "Jews." In Stephan Thernstrom, Ann Orlov, & Oscar Handlin (Eds.), *Harvard Encyclopedia of American Ethnic Groups* (pp. 571–598). Cambridge, MA: Harvard University Press.

Gratz v. Bollinger, 539 U.S. 244 (2003).

Gray, David J. 1991. "Shadow of the Past: The Rise and Fall of Prejudice in an American City." *American Journal of Economics and Sociology,* 50:33–39.

Grebler, Leo, Moore, Joan W., & Guzman, Ralph C. 1970. *The Mexican American People.* New York: Free Press.

Greeley, Andrew M. 1974. *Ethnicity in the United States: A Preliminary Reconnaissance.* New York: Wiley.

Green, Donald. 1999. "Native Americans." In Antony Dworkin and Rosalind Dworkin (Eds.), *The Minority Report* (pp. 255–277). Orlando, FL: Harcourt-Brace.

Grutter v. Bollinger, 539 U.S. 306 (2003).

Guilbault, Rose Del Castillo. 1993. "Americanization Is Tough on Macho." In Dolores La Guardia and Hans Guth (Eds.), *American Voices* (pp. 163–165). Mountain View, CA: Mayfield.

Gutman, Herbert. 1976. *The Black Family in Slavery and Freedom, 1750–1925.* New York: Vintage.

Hacker, Andrew. 1992. *Two Nations: Black and White, Separate, Hostile, Unequal.* New York: Scribner's.

Hamer, Fannie Lou. 1967. *To Praise Our Bridges: An Autobiography of Fannie Lou Hamer.* Jackson, MS: KIPCO.

Handlin, Oscar. 1951. *The Uprooted.* New York: Grosset & Dunlap.

Hansen, Marcus Lee. 1952. "The Third Generation in America." *Commentary,* 14:493–500.

Hanson, Jeffery, & Rouse, Linda. 1987. "Dimensions of Native American Stereotyping." *American Indian Culture and Research Journal,* 11:33–58.

Harjo, Suzan. 1996. "Now and Then: Native Peoples in the United States." *Dissent,* 43:58–60.

Hartley, E. L. 1946. *Problems in Prejudice.* New York: Kings Crown.

Hartman, Andrew. 2005. "Language as Oppression: The English-Only Movement in the United States." *Poverty & Race,* 14:1–8.

Hawkins, Hugh. 1962. *Booker T. Washington and His Critics: The Problem of Negro Leadership.* Boston: D. C. Heath.

Heaton, Tim, Chadwick, Bruce, & Jacobson, Cardell. 2000. *Statistical Handbook on Racial Groups in the United States.* Phoenix, AZ: Oryx.

Heer, David M. 1996. *Immigration in America's Future.* Boulder, CO: Westview Press.

Herberg, Will. 1960. *Protestant-Catholic-Jew: An Essay in American Religious Sociology.* New York: Anchor.

Herrnstein, Richard, & Murray, Charles. 1994. *The Bell Curve.* New York: Free Press.

Higham, John. 1963. *Strangers in the Land: Patterns of American Nativism, 1860–1925.* New York: Atheneum.

Hill-Collins, Patricia. 1991. *Black Feminist Thought.* New York: Routledge.

Hirschman, Charles. 1983. "America's Melting Pot Reconsidered." *Annual Review of Sociology,* 9:397–423.

Hirschman, Charles & Wong, Morrison. 1984. "Socioeconomic Gains of Asian Americans, Blacks, and Hispanics: 1960-1976." *American Journal of Sociology,* 90:584–607.

Hirschman, Charles, & Wong, Morrison. 1986. "The Extraordinary Educational Attainment of Asian-Americans: A Search for Historical Evidence and Explanations." *Social Forces,* 65:1–27.

Hoefer, Michael, Rytina, Nancy, & Campbell, Christopher. 2007. *Estimates of the Unauthorized Immigrant Population Residing in the United States: January, 2006.* Department of Homeland Security. Retrieved October 11, 2007, from http://www.dhs.gov/xlibrary/assets/statistics/publications/ill_pe_2006.pdf.

hooks, bell. 1996. *Bone Black.* New York: Henry Holt.

Hostetler, John. 1980. *Amish Society.* Baltimore: Johns Hopkins University Press.

Hovland, Carl I., & Sears, Robert R. 1940. "Minor Studies of Aggression: Correlation of Lynchings and Economic Indices." *Journal of Psychology,* 9:301–310.

"How to Tell Your Friends From the Japs." 1941. *Time,* October–December, p. 33.

Hoxie, Frederick. 1984. *A Final Promise: The Campaign to Assimilate the Indian, 1880–1920.* Lincoln: University of Nebraska Press.

Hraba, Joseph. 1979. *American Ethnicity.* Itasca, IL: F. E. Peacock.

———. 1994. *American Ethnicity* (2nd ed.). Itasca, IL: F. E. Peacock.

Hughes, Michael, & Thomas, Melvin. 1998. "The Continuing Significance of Race Revisited: A Study of Race, Class and Quality of Life in America, 1972 to 1996." *American Sociological Review,* 63:785–803.

Huntington, Samuel. 2004. *Who Are We: The Challenges to America's National Identity.* New York: Simon & Schuster.

Hurh, Won Moo. 1998. *The Korean Americans.* Westport, CT: Greenwood.

Hyman, Herbert, & Sheatsley, Paul. 1964. "Attitudes Toward Desegregation." *Scientific American,* 211:16–23.

Ibish, Hussein. (Ed.). 2003. *Report on Hate Crimes and Discrimination Against Arab Americans: The Post–September 11 Backlash.* Washington, DC: American-Arab Anti-Discrimination Committee. Retrieved February 14, 2005, from http://www.adc.org/hatecrimes/pdf/2003_report_web.pdf.

Iceland, John, Weinberg, Donald, & Steinmetz, Erika. 2002. *Racial and Ethnic Residential Segregation in the United States: 1980–2000.* U.S. Census Bureau, Series CENSR-3. Washington, DC: U.S. Government Printing Office. Retrieved August 17, 2006, from http://www.census.gov/prod/2002pubs/censr-3.pdf.

"Immigrants as a Percentage of State Population (Most Recent) by Country." n.d. Retrieved July 9, 2007, http://www.nationmaster.com/red/graph/imm_imm_pop_imm_as_per_of_sta_pop-immigrant-population-immigrants-percentage-state&ob=ws.

Institute for Social Research. 1996. *World Values Survey.* Ann Arbor, MI: Inter-university Consortium for Political and Social Research.

Instituto Brasileiro do Geografica e Estatistica. 1999. "Distribution of the Resident Population, by Major Regions, Urban or Rural Situation, Sex, Skin Color or Race." Retrieved July 17, 2002, from http://www.ibge.gov.br/english/estatistica/populacao/trabalhoerendimento/pnad99/sintese/tab1_2_b_1999.shtm.

Ivey, Steve. 2005. "White House Blind to Poverty in U.S." *Chicago Tribune,* September 22, p. 1.

Jackman, Mary. 1973. "Education and Prejudice or Education and Response Set." *American Sociological Review,* 40:327–339.

_____. 1978. "General and Applied Tolerance: Does Education Increase Commitment to Racial Integration?" *American Journal of Political Science,* 22:302–324.

_____. 1981. "Education and Policy Commitment to Racial Integration." *American Journal of Political Science,* 25:256–259.

Jackman, Mary, & Muha, M. 1984. "Education and Intergroup Attitudes: Moral Enlightenment, Superficial Democratic Commitment, or Ideological Refinement?" *American Sociological Review,* 49:751–769.

Jackson, Beverly. 2000. *Splendid Slippers: A Thousand Years of an Erotic Tradition.* Berkeley, CA: Ten Speed Press.

Jacobs, David, & Wood, Katherine. 1999. "Interracial Conflict and Interracial Homicide: Do Political and Economic Rivalries Explain White Killings of Blacks or Black Killings of Whites?" *American Journal of Sociology,* 105:157–180.

Jacobs, Harriet. 1987. *Incidents in the Life of a Slave Girl, Written by Herself* (Jean Yellin, Ed.). Cambridge, MA: Harvard University Press.

Jacoby, Russell, & Glauberman, Naomi. 1995. *The Bell Curve Debate.* New York: Random House.

Jibou, Robert M. 1988. "Ethnic Hegemony and the Japanese of California." *American Sociological Review,* 53:353–367.

Joe, Jennie, & Miller, Dorothy. 1994. "Cultural Survival and Contemporary American Indian Women in the City." In Maxine Zinn & Bonnie T. Dill (Eds.), *Women of Color in U.S. Society* (pp. 185–202). Philadelphia: Temple University Press.

Jones, James. 1997. *Prejudice and Racism* (2nd ed.). New York: McGraw-Hill.

Jones, Jeffrey. 2001. *Racial or Ethnic Labels Make Little Difference to Blacks, Hispanics.* Retrieved July 5, 2002, from http://www.gallup.com/poll/releases/pr010911.asp.

Jordan, Winthrop. 1968. *White Over Black: American Attitudes Towards the Negro: 1550–1812.* Chapel Hill: University of North Carolina Press.

Josephy, Alvin M. 1968. *The Indian Heritage of America.* New York: Knopf.

Kallen, Horace M. 1915a. "Democracy Versus the Melting Pot." *Nation,* February 18, pp. 190–194.

_____. 1915b. "Democracy Versus the Melting Pot." *Nation,* February 25, pp. 217–222.

Karlins, Marvin, Coffman, Thomas, & Walters, Gary. 1969. "On the Fading of Social Stereotypes: Studies in Three Generations of College Students." *Journal of Personality and Social Psychology,* 13:1–16.

Kasarda, John D. 1989. "Urban Industrial Transition and the Underclass." *Annals of the American Academy,* 501:26–47.

Katz, Phyllis. 1976. "The Acquisition of Racial Attitudes in Children." In Phyllis Katz (Ed.), *Towards the Elimination of Racism* (pp. 125–154). New York: Pergamon.

Katz, Phyllis, & Taylor, Dalmas. (Eds.). 1988. *Eliminating Racism: Profiles in Controversy.* New York: Plenum Press.

Kennedy, Randall. 2001. "Racial Trends in the Administration of Criminal Justice." In N. Smelser, W. Wilson, & F. Mitchell (Eds.), *America Becoming: Racial Trends and Their Consequences* (Vol. 2, pp. 1–20). Washington, DC: National Academy Press.

Kennedy, Ruby Jo. 1944. "Single or Triple Melting Pot: Intermarriage Trends in New Haven, 1870–1940." *American Journal of Sociology,* 49:331–339.

_____. 1952. "Single or Triple Melting Pot? Inter-marriage Trends in New Haven, 1870–1950." *American Journal of Sociology,* 58:56–59.

Kephart, William, & Zellner, William. 1994. *Extraordinary Groups.* New York: St. Martin's.

Killian, Lewis. 1975. *The Impossible Revolution, Phase 2: Black Power and the American Dream.* New York: Random House.

Kim, Kwang Chung, Hurh, Won Moo, & Fernandez, Marilyn. 1989. "Intra-group Differences in Business Participation: Three Asian Immigrant Groups." *International Migration Review,* 23:73–95.

Kinder, Donald R., & Sears, David O. 1981. "Prejudice and Politics: Symbolic Racism Versus Racial Threats to the Good Life." *Journal of Personality and Social Psychology,* 40:414–431.

King, C. Richard, Staurowsky, Ellen J., Baca, Lawrence, Davis, Laurel R., & Pewewardy, Cornel. 2002. "Of Polls and Race Prejudice: Sports Illustrated's Errant 'Indian Wars.'" *Journal of Sport and Social Issues,* 26: 381–403.

King, Martin Luther, Jr. 1958. *Stride Toward Freedom: The Montgomery Story.* New York: Harper & Row.

_____. 1963. *Why We Can't Wait.* New York: Mentor.

_____. 1968. *Where Do We Go From Here: Chaos or Community?* New York: Harper & Row.

King, Robert D. 1997. "Should English Be the Law?" *The Atlantic Monthly,* 279:55–62.

Kitano, Harry H. L. 1976. *Japanese Americans.* Englewood Cliffs, NJ: Prentice Hall.

_____. 1980. "Japanese." In Stephan Thernstrom, Ann Orlov, & Oscar Handlin (Eds.), *Harvard Encyclopedia of American Ethnic Groups* (pp. 561–571). Cambridge, MA: Harvard University Press.

Kitano, Harry, & Daniels, Roger. 1988. *Asian Americans: Emerging Minorities.* Englewood Cliffs, NJ: Prentice Hall.

_____. 1995. *Asian Americans: Emerging Minorities* (2nd ed.). Englewood Cliffs, NJ: Prentice Hall.

_____. 2001. *Asian Americans: Emerging Minorities* (3rd ed.). Upper Saddle River, NJ: Prentice Hall.

Kleg, M., & Yamamoto, K. 1998. "As the World Turns: Ethno-racial Distances After 70 Years." *Social Science Journal,* 35:183–191.

Kluegel, James R., & Smith, Eliot R. 1982. "Whites' Beliefs About Blacks' Opportunities." *American Sociological Review,* 47:518–532.

Kochhar, Rakesh. 2004. *The Wealth of Hispanic Households.* Washington, DC: Pew Hispanic Center. Retrieved February 15, 2004, from http://www.pewhispanic.org/site/docs/pdf/The%20Wealth%200f%20Hispanic%20Households.pdf.

Kraybill, Donald B., & Bowman, Carl F. 2001. *On the Backroad to Heaven: Old Order Hutterites, Mennonites, Amish, and Brethren.* Baltimore: Johns Hopkins University Press.

Kritz, Mary, & Girak, Douglas. 2004. *The American People: Immigration and a Changing America.* New York: Russell Sage Foundation.

Krysan, Maria, & Farley, Reynolds. 2002. "The Residential Preferences of Blacks: Do They Explain Persistent Segregation?" *Social Forces,* 80:937–981.

Kuperman, Diane. 2001. "Stuck at the Gates of Paradise." *UNESCO Courier,* September, pp. 24–26.

Kwong, Peter. 1987. *The New Chinatown.* New York: Hill & Wang.

Labaton, Stephen. 1994. "Denny's Restaurants to Pay $54 Million in Race Bias Suits." *New York Times,* May 25, p. A1.

Lacy, Dan. 1972. *The White Use of Blacks in America.* New York: McGraw-Hill.

Lai, H. M. 1980. "Chinese." In Stephan Thernstrom, Ann Orlov, & Oscar Handlin (Eds.), *Harvard Encyclopedia of American Ethnic Groups* (pp. 217–234). Cambridge, MA: Harvard University Press.

Lame Deer, John (Fire), & Erdoes, Richard. 1972. "Listening to the Air." In *Lame Deer, Seeker of Visions* (pp. 119–121). New York: Simon & Schuster.

Lamont-Brown, Raymond. 1993. "The Burakumin: Japan's Underclass." *Contemporary Review,* 263:136–140.

Landale, Nancy, & Oropesa, R. S. 2002. "White, Black, or Puerto Rican? Racial Self-Identification Among Mainland and Island Puerto Ricans." *Social Forces,* 81:231–254.

Lapchick, Joseph. 2006. *2005 Racial and Gender Report Card.* Institute for Diversity and Ethics in Sport. Retrieved February 29, 2008, from http://www.bus.ucf.edu/sport/cgi-bin/site/sitew .cgi?page=/ides/index.htx.

LaPiere, Robert. 1934. "Attitudes vs. Actions." *Social Forces,* 13:230–237.

Lavelle, Kristin, & Feagin, Joe. 2006. "Hurricane Katrina: The Race and Class Debate." *Monthly Review,* 58:52–66.

Lee, Sharon. 1998. "Asian Americans: Diverse and Growing." *Population Bulletin,* 53(2):1–40. Washington, DC: Population Reference Bureau.

Lee, Sharon, & Edmonston, Barry. 2005. *New Marriages, New Families: U.S. Racial and Hispanic Intermarriage.* Washington, DC: Population Reference Bureau. Retrieved March 13, 2008, from http://www.prb.org/pdf05/60.2NewMarriages.pdf.

Lee, Sharon, & Fernandez, Marilyn. 1998. "Trends in Asian American Racial/Ethnic Intermarriage: A Comparison of 1980 and 1990 Census Data." *Sociological Perspectives,* 41:323–343.

Lee, Sharon M., & Yamanaka, Keiko. 1990. "Patterns of Asian American Intermarriage and Marital Assimilation." *Journal of Comparative Family Studies,* 21:287–305.

Lenski, Gerhard. 1984. *Power and Privilege: A Theory of Stratification.* Chapel Hill: University of North Carolina Press.

Lenski, Gerhard, Nolan, Patrick, & Lenski, Jean. 1995. *Human Societies: An Introduction to Macrosociology* (7th ed.). New York: McGraw-Hill.

Levin, Jack, & McDevitt, Jack. 1993. *Hate Crimes: The Rising Tide of Bigotry and Bloodshed.* New York: Plenum Press.

Levine, Lawrence. 1977. *Black Culture and Black Consciousness.* New York: Oxford University Press.

Levy, Jacques. 1975. *Cesar Chavez: Autobiography of La Causa.* New York: Norton.

Lewis, Oscar. 1959. *Five Families: Mexican Case Studies in the Culture of Poverty.* New York: Basic Books.

_____. 1965. *La Vida: A Puerto Rican Family in the Culture of Poverty.* New York: Random House.

_____. 1966. "The Culture of Poverty." *Scientific American,* October, pp. 19–25.

Lewis Mumford Center. 2001. *Ethnic Diversity Grows, Neighborhood Integration Lags Behind.* Retrieved July 2, 2002, from http://mumford1.dyndns.org/cen2000/report.html.

Lieberson, Stanley. 1980. *A Piece of the Pie: Blacks and White Immigrants Since 1880.* Berkeley: University of California Press.

Lieberson, Stanley, & Waters, Mary C. 1988. *From Many Strands.* New York: Russell Sage Foundation.

Light, Ivan, & Bonacich, Edna. 1988. *Immigrant Entrepreneurs: Koreans in Los Angeles, 1965–1982.* Berkeley: University of California Press.

Lincoln, C. Eric. 1961. *The Black Muslims in America.* Boston: Beacon Press.

Ling, Huping. 2000. "Family and Marriage of Late-Nineteenth and Early-Twentieth Century Chinese Immigrant Women." *Journal of American Ethnic History,* 9:43–65.

"Literacy, Total Population by Group." n.d. Retrieved March 21, 2008, from http://www.nationmaster.com/graph/edu_lit_tot_pop-education-literacy-total-population.

Livingstone, David. 1874. *The Last Journals of David Livingstone, in Central Africa, From 1865 to His Death* (Horace Waller, Ed.). John Murray: London.

Locust, Carol. 1990. "Wounding the Spirit: Discrimination and Traditional American Indian Belief Systems." In Gail Thomas (Ed.), *U.S. Race Relations in the 1980s and 1990s: Challenges and Alternatives* (pp. 219–232). New York: Hemisphere.

Logan, John. n.d. *The Impact of Katrina: Race and Class in Storm-Damaged Neighborhoods.* Retrieved February 29, 2008, from http://www.s4.brown.edu/katrina/report .pdf.

Logan, John, Alba, Richard, & McNulty, Thomas. 1994. "Ethnic Economies in Metropolitan Regions: Miami and Beyond." *Social Forces,* 72:691–724.

Lopata, Helena Znaniecki. 1976. *Polish Americans.* Englewood Cliffs, NJ: Prentice Hall.

Lopez, Ian F. Haney. 2006. "Colorblind to the Reality of Race in America." *Chronicle of Higher Education,* 53(11):B6.

_____. 2006. *White by Law: The Legal Construction of Race.* New York: NYU Press.

Lurie, Nancy Oestrich. 1982. "The American Indian: Historical Background." In Norman Yetman & C. Hoy Steele (Eds.), *Majority and Minority* (3rd ed., pp. 131–144). Boston: Allyn & Bacon.

Lyman, Stanford. 1974. *Chinese Americans.* New York: Random House.

Malcolm X. 1964. *The Autobiography of Malcolm X.* New York: Grove.

Malik, Kenan. 2000. "Yes, Nature Does Help to Explain African Sporting Success. If You Think That's Racist, Your Idea of Race Is Wrong." *New Statesman,* September 18, pp. 13–18.

Mangiafico, Luciano. 1988. *Contemporary American Immigrants.* New York: Praeger.

Mannix, Daniel P. 1962. *Black Cargoes: A History of the Atlantic Slave Trade.* New York: Viking Press.

Marable, Manning. 2001. "An Idea Whose Time Has Come. . . . Whites Have an Obligation to Recognize Slavery's Legacy." *Newsweek,* August 27, p. 22.

Marcelli, Enrico, & Heer, David. 1998. "The Unauthorized Mexican Immigrant Population and Welfare in Los Angeles County: A Comparative Statistical Analysis." *Sociological Perspectives,* 41:279–303.

Margolis, Richard. 1989. "If We Won, Why Aren't We Smiling?" In Charles Willie (Ed.), *Round Two of the Willie/Wilson Debate* (2nd ed., pp. 95–100). Dix Hills, NY: General Hall.

Marks, Jonathan. 2000. "Review of Taboo: Why Black Athletes Dominate Sports and Why We're Afraid to Talk About It." *Human Biology,* 72:1074.

Martin, Philip, & Midgley, Elizabeth. 1999. "Immigration to the United States." *Population Bulletin,* 54(2): 1–44. Washington, DC: Population Reference Bureau.

Martin, Phillip, & Widgren, Jonas. 2002. *International Migration: Facing the Challenge.* Washington, DC: Population Reference Bureau.

Marvasti, Amir, & McKinney, Karyn. 2004. *Middle Eastern Lives in America.* Lanham, MD: Rowman & Littlefield.

Marx, Karl, & Engels, Friedrich. 1967. *The Communist Manifesto.* Baltimore: Penguin. (Original work published 1848)

Massarik, Fred, & Chenkin, Alvin. 1973. "United States National Jewish Population Study: A First Report." In *American Jewish Committee, American Jewish Year Book, 1973* (pp. 264–306). New York: American Jewish Committee.

Massey, Douglas. 1995. "The New Immigration and Ethnicity in the United States." *Population and Development Review,* 21:631–652.

———. 2000. "Housing Discrimination 101." *Population Today,* 28: 1, 4.

Massey, Douglas, & Denton, Nancy. 1993. *American Apartheid.* Cambridge, MA: Harvard University Press.

Massey, Douglas, & Singer, Audrey. 1995. "New Estimates of Undocumented Mexican Migration to the United States and the Probability of Apprehension." *Demography,* 32:203–213.

Mauer, Marc, & Huling, Tracy. 2000. "Young Black Americans and the Criminal Justice System." In Jerome Skolnick & Elliot Currie (Eds.), *Crisis in American Institutions* (11th ed., pp. 417–424). New York: Allyn & Bacon.

Mazzuca, Josephine. 2004. *For Most Americans, Friendship Is Colorblind.* Retrieved September 17, 2004, from http://www.gallup.com.

McConahay, John B. 1986. "Modern Racism, Ambivalence, and the Modern Racism Scale." In John F. Dovidio & Samuel Gartner (Eds.), *Prejudice, Discrimination and Racism* (pp. 91–125). Orlando, FL: Academic Press.

McDowell, Amber. 2004. "Cracker Barrel Settles Lawsuit; Black Customers, Workers Reported Discrimination." *Washington Post,* September 10, p. E1.

McLaren, Lauren. 2003. "Anti-immigrant Prejudice in Europe: Contact, Threat Perception, and Preferences for the Exclusion of Migrants." *Social Forces,* 81:909–936.

McLemore, S. Dale. 1973. "The Origins of Mexican American Subordination in Texas." *Social Science Quarterly,* 53:656–679.

McNickle, D'Arcy. 1973. *Native American Tribalism: Indian Survivals and Renewals.* New York: Oxford University Press.

McPherson, Miller, Smith-Lovin, Lynn, & Brashears, Matthew. 2006. "Social Isolation in America: Changes in Core Discussion Networks Over Two Decades." *Social Forces,* 71:353–375.

McWhorter, John. 2001. "Blood Money: An Analysis of Slavery Reparations." *American Enterprise,* 12:18.

McWilliams, Carey. 1961. *North From Mexico: The Spanish-Speaking People of the United States.* New York: Monthly Review Press.

Medoff, Marshall. 1999. "Allocation of Time and Hateful Behavior: A Theoretical and Positive Analysis of Hate and Hate Crimes." *American Journal of Economics and Sociology,* 58:959–973.

Merton, Robert. 1968. *Social Theory and Social Structure.* New York: Free Press.

Miller, Neal, & Bugleski, R. 1948. "Minor Studies of Aggression: The Influence of Frustrations Imposed by the Ingroup on Attitudes Expressed Towards Outgroups." *Journal of Psychology,* 25:437–442.

Miller, Norman, & Brewer, Marilyn. (Eds.). 1984. *Groups in Contact: The Psychology of Desegregation.* Orlando, FL: Academic Press.

Min, Pyong Gap. (Ed.). 1995. *Asian Americans: Contemporary Trends and Issues.* Thousand Oaks, CA: Sage.

Mindel, Charles, Habenstein, Robert, & Wright, Roosevelt. (Eds.). *Ethnic Families in America: Patterns and Variations* (3rd ed., pp. 141–159). New York: Elsevier.

Mirandé, Alfredo. 1985. *The Chicano Experience: An Alternative Perspective.* Notre Dame, IN: University of Notre Dame Press.

Mirandé, Alfredo, & Enriquez, Evangelica. 1979. *La Chicana: The Mexican-American Women.* Chicago: University of Chicago Press.

Moore, Joan W. 1970. *Mexican Americans.* Englewood Cliffs, NJ: Prentice Hall.

Moore, Joan W., & Pachon, Harry. 1985. *Hispanics in the United States.* Englewood Cliffs, NJ: Prentice Hall.

Moore, Joan, & Pinderhughes, Raquel. 1993. *In the Barrios: Latinos and the Underclass Debate.* New York: Sage.

Moquin, Wayne, & Van Doren, Charles. (Eds.). 1971. *A Documentary History of Mexican Americans.* New York: Bantam.

Moraes, Lisa de. 2005. "Kanya West's Torrent of Criticism, Live on NBC." *Washington Post,* September 3, p. C1.

Morawska, Ewa. 1990. "The Sociology and Historiography of Immigration." In Virginia Yans-McLaughlin (Ed.), *Immigration Reconsidered: History, Sociology, and Politics* (pp. 187–238). New York: Oxford University Press.

Morgan, Edmund. 1975. *American Slavery, American Freedom.* New York: Norton.

Morin, Richard. 1995. "A Distorted Image of Minorities." *Washington Post,* October 8, pp. A1, A26.

Morin, Richard, & Cottman, Michael. 2001. "Discrimination's Lingering Sting." *Washington Post,* June 22, p. A1.

Morris, Aldon D. 1984. *The Origins of the Civil Rights Movement.* New York: Free Press.

Morris, Edward. 2005. "'Tuck in That Shirt!' Race, Class, Gender and Discipline in an Urban School." *Sociological Perspectives,* 48:25–48.

Moynihan, Daniel. 1965. *The Negro Family: The Case for National Action.* Washington, DC: U.S. Department of Labor.

Mujica, Mauro. 2003. "Official English Legislation: Myths and Realities." *Human Events,* 59:24.

Myrdal, Gunnar. 1962. *An American Dilemma: The Negro Problem and Modern Democracy.* New York: Harper & Row. (Original work published 1944)

Nabakov, Peter. (Ed.). 1999. *Native American Testimony* (Rev. ed.). New York: Penguin.

National Academy of Sciences. 1997. *The New Americans: Economic, Demographic, and Fiscal Effects of Immigration*. Retrieved January 12, 2005, from http://books.nap.edu/execsumm_pdf/5779.pdf.

National Advisory Commission. 1968. *Report of the National Advisory Commission on Civil Disorders*. New York: Bantam Books.

National Council on Crime and Delinquency. 2007. *And Justice for Some: Differential Treatment of Youth of Color in the Justice System*. Retrieved March 12, 2008, from http://www.nccd-crc.org/nccd/pubs/2007jan_justice_for_some.pdf.

National Indian Gaming Commission. 2004. *Annual Account, 2004*. Retrieved August 29, 2007, from http://www.nigc.gov/LinkClick.aspx?link=reading_room%2fbiennial_reports%2fnigc_2004_annual_report.pdf&tabid=118&mid=753.

_____. 2007. "Growth in Indian Gaming. 1995–2006." Retrieved March 13, 2008, from http://www.nigc.gov/Portals/0/NIGC%20Uploads/Tribal%20Data/19962006revenues.pdf.

_____. n.d. *Gaming Revenue Reports*. Retrieved August 29, 2007, from http://www.nigc.gov/Default.aspx?tabid=67/.

National Opinion Research Council. 1972–2007. *General Social Survey*. Chicago: Author.

National Origins Act, Pub. L. 139, Chapter 190, § 43 Stat. 153 (1924).

National Public Radio. 2004. *Immigration Survey*. Retrieved February 15, 2005, from http://www.npr.org/templates/story/story.php?storyId=4062605.

Neissen, Jan, Schibel, Yongmi, & Thompson, Cressida. (Eds.). 2005. *Current Immigration Debates in Europe: Ireland*. Brussels, Belgium: Migration Policy Group. Retrieved March 8, 2008, from http://www.migpolgroup.com/multiattachments/3006/DocumentName/EMD_Ireland_2005.pdf.

Nelli, Humbert S. 1980. "Italians." In Stephan Thernstrom, Ann Orlov, & Oscar Handlin (Eds.), *Harvard Encyclopedia of American Ethnic Groups* (pp. 545–560). Cambridge, MA: Harvard University Press.

Nishi, Setsuko. 1995. "Japanese Americans." In Pyong Gap Min (Ed.), *Asian Americans: Contemporary Trends and Issues* (pp. 95–133). Thousand Oaks, CA: Sage.

Noel, Donald. 1968. "A Theory of the Origin of Ethnic Stratification." *Social Problems,* 16:157–172.

Nolan, Patrick, & Lenski, Gerhard. 2004. *Human Societies*. Boulder, CO: Paradigm.

Novak, Michael. 1973. *The Rise of the Unmeltable Ethnics: Politics and Culture in the 1970s*. New York: Collier.

Ogunwole, Stella. 2002. *The American Indian and Alaska Native Population*. 2000. Accessed on March 13, 2008, from http://www.census.gov/prod/2002pubs/c2kbr01-15.pdf.

_____. 2006. *We the People: American Indians and Alaska Natives in the United States*. Accessed March 13, 2008, from http://www.census.gov/prod/2006pubs/censr-28.pdf.

O'Hare, William, Pollard, Kelvin, Mann, Taynia, & Kent, Mary. 1991. *African Americans in the 1990s*. Washington, DC: Population Reference Bureau.

Oliver, Melvin, & Shapiro, Thomas. 2001. "Wealth and Racial Stratification." In N. Smelser, W. Wilson, & F. Mitchell (Eds.), *America Becoming: Racial Trends and Their Consequences* (Vol. 1, pp. 222–251). Washington, DC: National Academy Press.

_____. 2006. *Black Wealth, White Wealth* (2nd ed.). New York: Taylor & Francis.

Olson, James, & Wilson, R. 1984. *Native Americans in the Twentieth Century*. Provo, UT: Brigham Young University Press.

Omi, Michael, & Winant, Howard. 1986. *Racial Formation in the United States From the 1960s to the 1980s*. New York: Routledge & Kegan Paul.

O'Neil, Dennis. n.d. *Human Biological Adaptability*. San Marcos, CA: Behavioral Sciences Department, Palomar College. Retrieved February 25, 2008, from http://anthro.palomar.edu/adapt/adapt_4.htm.

Orfield, Gary. 2001. *Schools More Separate: Consequences of a Decade of Resegregation*. Cambridge, MA: Harvard University, The Civil Rights Project. Retrieved June 28, 2002, from http://www.law.harvard.edu/civilrights.

Orfield, Gary, & Lee, Chungmei. 2006. *Racial Transformation and the Changing Nature of Segregation*. Cambridge, MA: The Civil Rights Project at Harvard University. Retrieved March 12, 2008, from http://www.civilrightsproject.ucla.edu/research/deseg/Racial_Transformation.pdf.

Organization for Economic Co-operation and Development. 2008. "International Migration Data 2007." Retrieved from http://www.oecd.org/document/3/0,3343,en_2825_494553_39336771_1_1_1_1,00.html.

Orreniou, Pia. 2001. "Illegal Immigration and Enforcement Along the U.S.-Mexico Border: An Overview." *Economic & Financial Review,* January 1, pp. 2–11.

Osofsky, Gilbert. 1969. *Puttin' On Ole Massa*. New York: Harper & Row.

O'Sullivan, Eoin. 2003. *Migration and Housing in Ireland: Report to the European Observatory on Homelessness*. Retrieved February 14, 2005, from http://www.feantsa.org/files/national_reports/ireland/ireland_migration_2002.pdf.

Oswalt, Wendell, & Neely, Sharlotte. 1996. *This Land Was Theirs*. Mountain View, CA: Mayfield.

Parish, Peter J. 1989. *Slavery: History and Historians*. New York: Harper & Row.

Park, Robert E., & Burgess, Ernest W. 1924. *Introduction to the Science of Society*. Chicago: University of Chicago Press.

Parke, Ross, & Buriel, Raymond. 2002. "Socialization Concerns in African American, American Indian, Asian American, and Latino Families." In Nijole Benokraitis (Ed.), *Contemporary Ethnic Families in the United States* (pp. 211–218). Upper Saddle Brook, NJ: Prentice Hall.

Parrado, Emilio, & Zenteno, Rene. 2001. "Economic Restructuring, Financial Crises, and Women's Work in Mexico." *Social Problems,* 48:456–477.

Parrillo, Vincent. 2003. *Strangers to These Shores* (7th ed.). Boston: Allyn & Bacon.

Pego, David. 1998. "To Educate a Nation: Native American Tribe Hopes to Bring Higher Education to an Arizona Reservation." *Black Issues in Higher Education,* 15:60–63.

Perez, Lisandro. 1980. "Cubans." In Stephan Thernstrom, Ann Orlov, & Oscar Handlin (Eds.), *Harvard Encyclopedia of American Ethnic Groups* (pp. 256–261). Cambridge, MA: Harvard University Press.

Perlman, Joel. 2005. *Italians Then, Mexicans Now*. New York: Russell Sage Foundation.

Petersen, Williams. 1971. *Japanese Americans*. New York: Random House.

Peterson, Mark. 1995. "Leading Cuban-American Entrepreneurs: The Process of Developing Motives, Abilities, and Resources." *Human Relations*, 48:1193–1216.

Pettigrew, Thomas. 1958. "Personality and Sociocultural Factors in Intergroup Attitudes: A Cross-National Comparison." *Journal of Conflict Resolution*, 2:29–42.

———. 1971. *Racially Separate or Together?* New York: McGraw-Hill.

———. 1980. "Prejudice." In Stephan Thernstrom, Ann Orlov, & Oscar Handlin (Eds.), *Harvard Encyclopedia of American Ethnic Groups* (pp. 820–829). Cambridge, MA: Harvard University Press.

———. 1997. "Generalized Intergroup Contact Effects on Prejudice." *Personality and Social Psychology Bulletin*, 23:175–185.

———. 1998. "Intergroup Contact Theory." *Annual Review of Psychology*, 49:65–85.

Pettit, Becky, & Western, Bruce. 2004. "Mass Imprisonment and the Life Course: Race and Class Inequality in U.S. Incarceration." *American Sociological Review*, 69:151–169.

Pew Charitable Trust. 2008. *One in a Hundred: Behind Bars in the United States*. Retrieved March 12, 2008, from http://www.pewtrusts.org/uploadedFiles/wwwpewtrustsorg/Reports/sentencing_and_corrections/one_in_100.pdf.

Pew Hispanic Center. 2004. *Assimilation and Language*. Retrieved January 21, 2007, from http://pewhispanic.org/files/factsheets/11.pdf.

———. 2005. *Hispanics: A People in Motion*. Washington, DC: Pew Hispanic Center. Retrieved March 16, 2008, from http://pewhispanic.org/files/reports/40.pdf.

———. 2006. *The State of American Public Opinion on Immigration in Spring 2006: A Review of Major Surveys*. Retrieved March 16, 2008, from http://www.pewhispanic.org/files/factsheets/18.pdf.

———. 2007. *The Latino Electorate: An Analysis of the 2006 Election*. Retrieved October 20, 2007, from http://pewhispanic.org/files/factsheets/34.pdf.

Pew Research Center. 2006a. *Hispanic Attitudes Toward Learning English*. Retrieved October 18, 2007, from http://pewhispanic.org/files/factsheets/20.pdf.

———. 2006b. *The State of American Public Opinion on Immigration in Spring 2006*. Retrieved December 7, 2007, from http://pewhispanic.org/factsheets/factsheet.php?FactsheetID=18.

———. 2007. *Muslim Americans: Middle Class and Mostly Mainstream*. Retrieved December 8, 2007, from http://pewresearch.org/assets/pdf/muslim americans.pdf.

Phillips, Ulrich B. 1918. *American Negro Slavery*. New York: Appleton.

Piersen, William D. 1996. *From Africa to America: African American History From the Colonial Era to the Early Republic, 1526–1790*. New York: Twayne.

Pilger, John. 2000. "Australia Is the Only Developed Country Whose Government Has Been Condemned as Racist by the United Nations." *New Statesman*, 129:17.

Pincus, Fred. 2003. *Reverse Discrimination: Dismantling the Myth*. Boulder, CO: Lynne Reiner.

Pitt, Leonard. 1970. *The Decline of the Californios: A Social History of the Spanish-Speaking Californians, 1846–1890*. Berkeley: University of California Press.

Plessy v. Ferguson, 163 U.S. 537 (1896).

Pollard, Kelvin, & O'Hare, William. 1999. "America's Racial and Ethnic Minorities." *Population Bulletin*, 54(3):29–39. Washington, DC: Population Reference Bureau.

Polner, Murray. 1993. "Asian Americans Say They Are Treated Like Foreigners." *New York Times*, March 7, p. 1.

Popp, Danielle, Donavan, Roxanne, Crawford, Mary, Marsh, Kerry, & Peele, Melanie. 2003. "Gender, Race, and Speech Style Stereotypes." *Sex Roles*, 48(7/8):317–325.

Population Reference Bureau. 2007a. "World Population Data Sheet." Retrieved February 13, 2008, from http://www.prb.org.

———. 2007b. "World Population Highlights." Retrieved February 13, 2008, from http://www.prb.org.

Portes, Alejandro. 1990. "From South of the Border: Hispanic Minorities in the United States." In Virginia Yans-McLaughlin (Ed.), *Immigration Reconsidered* (pp. 160–184). New York: Oxford University Press.

Portes, Alejandro, & Bach, Robert L. 1985. *Latin Journey: Cuban and Mexican Immigrants in the United States*. Berkeley: University of California Press.

Portes, Alejandro, & Manning, Robert. 1986. "The Immigrant Enclave: Theory and Empirical Examples." In Susan Olzak & Joanne Nagel (Eds.), *Competitive Ethnic Relations* (pp. 47–68). New York: Academic Press.

Portes, Alejandro, & Rumbaut, Rubén. 1996. *Immigrant America: A Portrait* (2nd ed.). Berkeley: University of California Press.

———. 2001. *Legacies: The Story of the Immigrant Second Generation*. New York: Russell Sage Foundation.

———. (2001). *Ethnicities: Children of Immigrants in America*. New York: Russell Sage Foundation.

Portes, Alejandro, & Zhou, Min. 1992. "Gaining the Upper Hand: Economic Mobility Among Immigrant and Domestic Minorities." *Ethnic and Racial Studies*, 15:491–518.

———. 1993. "The New Second Generation: Segmented Assimilation and Its Variants." In *Annals of the American Academy of Political and Social Science*, November, pp. 74–96.

Posadas, Barbara. 1999. *The Filipino Americans*. Westport, CT: Greenwood Press.

Potter, George. 1973. *To the Golden Door: The Story of the Irish in Ireland and America*. Westport, CT: Greenwood Press.

Poulan, Richard. 2003. "Globalization and the Sex Trade: Trafficking and the Commodification of Women and Children." *Canadian Women Studies*, 22:38–43.

Powers, Daniel, & Ellison, Christopher. 1995. "Interracial Contact and Black Racial Attitudes: The Contact Hypothesis and Selectivity Bias." *Social Forces*, 74:205–226.

Powlishta, K., Serbin, L., Doyle, A., & White, D. 1994. "Gender, Ethnic, and Body-Type Biases: The Generality of Prejudice in Childhood." *Developmental Psychology*, 30:526–537.

Price, S. L., & Woo, Andrea. 2002. "The Indian Wars: The Campaign Against Indian Nicknames and Mascots Presumes That They Offend Native Americans—But Do They? We Took a Poll, and You Won't Believe the Results" (Special report). *Sports Illustrated*, March 4, pp. 66–73.

Prosise, Theodore O., & Johnson, Ann. 2004. "Law Enforcement and Crime on Cops and World's Wildest Police Videos: Anecdotal Form and the Justification of Racial Profiling." *Western Journal of Communication*, 68(1):72–92.

Puzo, Mario. 1993. "Choosing a Dream: Italians in Hell's Kitchen." In W. Brown & A. Ling (Eds.), *Visions of America* (pp. 56–57). New York: Persea.

Quillian, Lincoln, & Campbell, Mary. 2003. "Beyond Black and White: The Present and Future of Multiracial Friendship Segregation." *American Sociological Review,* 68:540–567.

Quindlen, Anna. 2007. "Newcomers by Numbers." *Newsweek,* August 20, p. 90.

Rader, Benjamin G. 1983. *American Sports: From the Age of Folk Games to the Age of Spectators.* Englewood Cliffs, NJ: Prentice Hall.

Rawick, George P. 1972. *From Sundown to Sunup: The Making of the Black Community.* Westport, CT: Greenwood Press.

Raymer, Patricia. 1974. "Wisconsin's Menominees: Indians on a Seesaw." *National Geographic,* August, pp. 228–251.

Read, Jen'nan Ghazal. 2004. "Cultural Influences on Immigrant Women's Labor Force Participation: The Arab-American Case." *International Migration Review,* 38:52–77.

Reich, Michael. 1986. "The Political-Economic Effects of Racism." In Richard Edwards, Michael Reich, & Thomas Weisskopf (Eds.), *The Capitalist System: A Radical Analysis of American Society* (3rd ed., pp. 381–388). Englewood Cliffs, NJ: Prentice Hall.

"Religion Statistics, Protestantism by Country, Percent Protestants by Country." n.d. Retrieved March 21, 2008, from http://www.nationmaster.com/red/graph/rel_pro_by_cou_pro_pro-religion-protestantism-country-protestants-protestant&ob=ws/.

Rifkin, Jeremy. 1996. *The End of Work: The Decline of the Global Labor Force and the Dawn of the Post-market Era.* New York: Putnam.

Robertson, Claire. 1996. "Africa and the Americas? Slavery and Women, the Family, and the Gender Division of Labor." In David Gaspar & Darlene Hine (Eds.), *More Than Chattel: Black Women and Slavery in the Americas* (pp. 4–40). Bloomington: Indiana University Press.

Robinson, Randall. 2001. *The Debt: What America Owes to Blacks.* New York: Plume.

Rodriguez, Clara. 1989. *Puerto Ricans: Born in the USA.* Boston: Unwin-Hyman.

Rodriguez, Clara, & Cordero-Guzman, Hector. 1992. "Placing Race in Context." *Ethnic and Racial Studies,* 15:523–542.

Rodriguez, Luis. 1993. *Always Running: La Vida Loca.* New York: Touchstone Books.

Rosenfield, Michael. 2002. "Measures of Assimilation in the Marriage Market: Mexican Americans 1970–1990." *Journal of Marriage and the Family,* 64:152–163.

Rouse, Linda, & Hanson, Jeffery. 1991. "American Indian Stereotyping, Resource Competition, and Status-Based Prejudice." *American Indian Culture and Research Journal,* 15:1–17.

Royster, Deirdre. 2003. *Race and the Invisible Hand: How White Networks Exclude Black Men From Blue Collar Jobs.* Berkeley:University of California Press.

———. 2007. *White Like Me Black Me.* Unpublished manuscript.

Rumbaut, Rubén. 1991. "Passage to America: Perspectives on the New Immigration." In Alan Wolfe (Ed.), *America at Century's End* (pp. 208–244). Berkeley: University of California Press.

———. 1995. "Vietnamese, Laotian, and Cambodian Americans." In Pyong Gap Min (Ed.), *Asian Americans: Contemporary Issues and Trends* (pp. 232–270). Thousand Oaks, CA: Sage.

———. 1996 "Origins and Destinies: Immigration, Race, and Ethnicity in Comtemporary America." In S. Pedraza & R. G. Rumbaut (Eds.), *Origins and Destinies: Immigration, Race, and Ethnicity in America* (pp. 21–42). Belmont, CA: Wadsworth.

Rumbaut, Rubén, & Portes, Alejandro. 2001. *Ethnicities: Children of Immigrants in America.* New York: Russell Sage Foundation.

Russell, James W. 1994. *After the Fifth Sun: Class and Race in North America.* Englewood Cliffs, NJ: Prentice Hall.

Saenz, Rogelio. 1999. "Mexican Americans." In Antony Dworkin & Rosalind Dworkin (Eds.), *The Minority Report* (pp. 209–229). Orlando, FL: Harcourt Brace.

———. 2005. *The Social and Economic Isolation of Urban African Americans.* Population Reference Bureau. Retrieved August 8, 2007, from http://prb.org/Articles/2005/TheSocialandEconomicIsolation ofUrbanAfricanAmericans.aspx.

Sanchirico, Andrew. 1991. "The Importance of Small Business Ownership in Chinese American Educational Achievement." *Sociology of Education,* 64:293–304.

Schafer, John, & Navarro, Joe. 2004. "The Seven Stage Hate Model: The Psychopathology of Hate Groups." *The FBI Law Enforcement Bulletin,* 72:1–9

Schlesinger, Arthur M., Jr. 1992. *The Disuniting of America: Reflections on a Multicultural Society.* New York: Norton.

Schoener, Allon. 1967. *Portal to America: The Lower East Side, 1870–1925.* New York: Holt, Rinehart & Winston.

Schumann, Howard, Steeh, Charlotte, & Bobo, Lawrence. 1997. *Racial Attitudes in America: Trends and Interpretations.* Cambridge, MA: Harvard University Press.

Sears, David. 1988. "Symbolic Racism." In Phyllis Katz & Dalmas Taylor (Eds.), *Eliminating Racism: Profiles in Controversy* (pp. 53–84). New York: Plenum Press.

Sears, David, & Henry, P. J. 2003. "The Origins of Modern Racism." *Journal of Personality and Social Psychology,* 85:259–275.

See, Katherine O'Sullivan, & Wilson, William J. 1988. "Race and Ethnicity." In Neil Smelser (Ed.), *Handbook of Sociology* (pp. 223–242). Newbury Park, CA: Sage.

Selzer, Michael. 1972. *"Kike": Anti-Semitism in America.* New York: Meridian.

Selznik, G. J., & Steinberg, S. 1969. *The Tenacity of Prejudice.* New York: Harper & Row.

Shannon, William V. 1964. *The American Irish.* New York: Macmillan.

Shapiro, Thomas. 2004. *The Hidden Cost of Being African American.* New York: Oxford University Press.

Sheet Metal Workers v. EEOC, 478 U.S. 421 (1986).

Shelton, B. A., & John, D. 1996. "The Division of Household Labor." *Annual Review of Sociology,* 22:299–322.

Sherif, Muzafer, Harvey, O. J., White, B. Jack, Hood, William, & Sherif, Carolyn. 1961. *Intergroup Conflict and Cooperation: The Robber's Cave Experiment.* Norman, OK: University Book Exchange.

Sheth, Manju. 1995. "Asian Indian Americans." In Pyong Gap Min (Ed.), *Asian American: Contemporary Issues and Trends* (pp. 168–198). Thousand Oaks, CA: Sage.

Shim, Doobo. 1998. "From Yellow Peril Through Model Minority to Renewed Yellow Peril (Asians in Popular Media)." *Journal of Communication Inquiry,* 22:385–410.

Shinagawa, Larry, & Pang, Gin Yong. 1996. "Asian American Panethnicity and Intermarriage." *Amerasia Journal,* 22:127–153.

Sigelman, Lee, & Welch, Susan. 1993. "The Contact Hypothesis Revisited: Black-White Interaction and Positive Racial Attitudes." *Social Forces,* 71:781–795.

Simon, Julian. 1989. *The Economic Consequences of Immigration*. Cambridge, MA: Blackwell.

Simpson, George, & Yinger, Milton. 1985. *Racial and Cultural Minorities: An Analysis of Prejudice and Discrimination*. New York: Plenum Press.

Sklare, Marshall. 1971. *America's Jews*. New York: Random House.

Smedley, Audrey. 1999. *Race in North America: Origins and Evolution of Worldview* (2nd ed.). Boulder, CO: Westview Press.

Smelser, N., Wilson, W., & Mitchell, F. (Eds.). 2001. *America Becoming: Racial Trends and Their Consequences* (2 vols.). Washington, DC: National Academy Press.

Smith, Christopher B. 1994. "Back to the Future: The Intergroup Contact Hypothesis Revisited." *Sociological Inquiry,* 64:438–455.

Smith, James, & Edmonston, Barry. (Eds.). 1997. *The New Americans: Economic, Demographic, and Fiscal Effects of Immigration*. Washington, DC: National Academy Press.

Smith, Kevin, & Seelbach, Wayne. 1987. "Education and Intergroup Attitudes: More on the Jackman and Muha Thesis." *Sociological Spectrum,* 7:157–170.

Smith, Tom, & Dempsey, Glenn. 1983. "The Polls: Ethnic Social Distance and Prejudice." *Public Opinion Quarterly,* 47:584–600.

Smith, Vern. 2001. "Debating the Wages of Slavery." *Newsweek,* August 27, pp. 20–25.

Snipp, C. Matthew. 1989. *American Indians: The First of This Land*. New York: Russell Sage Foundation.

————. 1992. "Sociological Perspectives on American Indians." *Annual Review of Sociology,* 18:351–371.

————. 1996. "The First Americans: American Indians." In S. Pedraza & R. G. Rumbaut (Eds.), *Origins and Destinies: Immigration, Race, and Ethnicity in America* (pp. 390–403). Belmont, CA: Wadsworth.

"A Sorry Tale." 2000. *The Economist,* 356:12.

Southern Poverty Law Center. 2007. "Active U.S. Hate Groups in 2006." Retrieved March 25, 2008, from http://www.splcenter.org/intel/map/hate.jsp.

Spicer, Edward H. 1980. "American Indians." In Stephan Thernstrom, Ann Orlov, & Oscar Handlin (Eds.), *Harvard Encyclopedia of American Ethnic Groups* (pp. 58–122). Cambridge, MA: Harvard University Press.

Spickard, Paul. 1996. *Japanese Americans: The Formation and Transformations of an Ethnic Group*. New York: Twayne.

Spilde, Kate. 2001. "The Economic Development Journey of Indian Nations." Retrieved July 5, 2002, from http://indiangaming.org/library/newsletters/index.html.

Stampp, Kenneth. 1956. *The Peculiar Institution: Slavery in the Antebellum South*. New York: Random House.

Staples, Robert. 1988. "The Black American Family." In Charles Mindel, Robert Habenstein, & Roosevelt Wright (Eds.), *Ethnic Families in America* (3rd ed., pp. 303–324). New York: Elsevier.

Steinberg, Stephen. 1981. *The Ethnic Myth: Race, Ethnicity, and Class in America*. New York: Atheneum.

Stember, C. H. 1961. *Education and Attitude Change*. New York: Institute of Human Relations Press.

Stepick, Alex, Stepick, Carol Dutton, Eugene, Emmanuel, Teed, Deborah, & Labissiere, Yves. 2001. "Shifting Identities and Intergenerational Conflict: Growing Up Haitian in Miami." In Rubén Rumbaut & Alejandro Portes (Eds.), *Ethnicities: Children of Immigrants in America* (pp. 229–266). Berkeley: University of California Press.

Stoddard, Ellwyn. 1973. *Mexican Americans*. New York: Random House.

Stoll, Michael. 2004. *African Americans and the Color Line*. New York: Russell Sage Foundation:

Strolovitch, Dara, Warren, Dorian, & Frymer, Paul. 2006. *Katrina's Political Roots and Divisions: Race, Class, and Federalism in American Politics*. Retrieved June 20, 2007, from http://understandingkatrina.ssrc.org.

Stuckey, Sterling. 1987. *Slave Culture: Nationalist Theory and the Foundations of Black America*. New York: Harper & Row.

Sung, Betty Lee. 1990. "Chinese American Intermarriage." *Journal of Comparative Family Studies,* 21:337–352.

Swaine, Thomas, & Nishimoto, Richard S. 1946. *The Spoilage*. Berkeley: University of California Press. Retrieved February 11, 2005, from http://www.geocities.com/Athens/8420/kurihara.html.

Swim, Janet, & Cohen, Laurie. 1997. "Overt, Covert, and Subtle Sexism: A Comparison Between the Attitudes Toward Women and Modern Sexism Scales." *Psychology of Women Quarterly,* 21:103–119.

Swim, Janet, Mallett, Robyn, & Stangor, Charles. 2004. "Understanding Subtle Sexism: Detection and Use of Sexist Language." *Sex Roles,* 51:117–128.

Takaki, Ronald. 1993. *A Different Mirror: A History of Multicultural America*. Boston: Little, Brown.

Taylor, Jared, & Whitney, Glayde. 1999. "Crime and Racial Profiling by U.S. Police: Is There an Empirical Basis?" *Journal of Social, Political and Economic Studies,* 24:485–516.

————. 2002. "Racial Profiling: Is There an Empirical Basis?" *Mankind Quarterly,* 42:285–313.

Taylor, Jonathan, & Kalt, Joseph. 2005. *American Indians on Reservations: A Databook of Socioeconomic Change Between the 1990 and 2000 Censuses*. Harvard University: The Harvard Project on American Indian Economic Development. Retrieved March 13, 2008, from http://www.hks.harvard.edu/hpaied/pubs/documents/AmericanIndiansonReservationsADatabookof SocioeconomicChange.pdf.

Telles, Edward. 2004. *Race in Another America: The Significance of Skin Color in Brazil*. Princeton, NJ: Princeton University Press.

Telles, Edward, & Ortiz, Vilma. 2008. *Generations of Exclusion: Mexican Americans, Assimilation, and Race*. New York: Russell Sage Foundation.

Terkel, Studs. 1992. *Race*. New York: New Press.

Thernstrom, Stephan, & Thernstrom, Abigail. 1997. *America in Black and White*. New York: Simon & Schuster.

Thomas, Melvin. 1993. "Race, Class, and Personal Income: An Empirical Test of the Declining Significance of Race Thesis, 1968–1988." *Social Problems,* 40:328–342.

Thornton, Russell. 2001. "Trends Among American Indians in the United States." In N. Smelser, W. Wilson, & F. Mitchell (Eds.), *America Becoming: Racial Trends and Their Consequences* (Vol. 1, pp. 135–169). Washington, DC: National Academy Press.

Tilly, Charles. 1990. "Transplanted Networks." In Virginia Yans-McLaughlin (Ed.), *Immigration Reconsidered: History, Sociology, and Politics* (pp. 79–95). New York: Oxford University Press.

Tougas, Francine, Rupert, Ann, & Joly, Stephane. 1995. "Neosexism: Plus Ça Change, Plus C'est Pareil." *Personality & Social Psychology Bulletin,* 21:842–850.

Trevanian. 2005. *The Crazy Ladies of Pearl Street*. New York: Crown Books.

Tsai, Shih-Shan Henry. 1986. *The Chinese Experience in America*. Bloomington: Indiana University Press.

Udry, Richard. 2000. "Biological Limits of Gender Construction." *American Sociological Review*, 65:443–457.

"Unemployment Rate (Most Recent) by Country." n.d. Retrieved March 21, 2008, from http://www.nationmaster.com/red/graph/lab_une_rat-labor-unemployment-rate&ob=ws.

United Nations. 2006. *The Millennium Development Goals Report 2006*. Retrieved August 8, 2007, from http://mdgs.un.org/unsd/mdg/Resources/Static/Products/Progress2006/MDGReport2006.pdf.

United Steelworkers of America, AFL-CIO-CLC v. Weber, 443 U.S. 193 (1979).

U.S. Bureau of Indian Affairs. 1991. *American Indians Today: Answers to Your Questions*. Washington, DC: U.S. Department of the Interior.

———. 1997. *1997 Labor Market Information on the Indian Labor Force*. Retrieved May 17, 2002, from http://www.doi.gov/bia/Labor/97LFRCovFinal.pdf.

U.S. Bureau of the Census. 1978. *Statistical Abstract of the United States, 1977*. Washington, DC: Government Printing Office.

———. 1979. *Current Population Survey*. Washington, DC: Government Printing Office.

———. 1990. "Summary File 3." Retrieved March 15, 2008, from http://factfinder.census.gov/servlet/DatasetMainPageServlet?_program=DEC&_submenuId=datasets_1&_lang=en.

———. 1997. *Statistical Abstract of the United States, 1996*. Washington, DC: Government Printing Office.

———. 2000a. "American Indian and Alaska Native Summary File." Retrieved March 13, 2008, from http://factfinder.census.gov/servlet/DatasetMainPageServlet?_program=DEC&_submenuId=datasets_1&_lang=en.

———. 2000b. "Black or African American: Maps for People Indicating One Race, Black or African American." Retrieved March 13, 2008, from http://www.census.gov/population/cen2000/atlas/censr01-106.pdf.

———. 2000c. "National Population Projections." Retrieved May 15, 2007, from http://www.census.gov/population/projections/nation/summary/np-t5-h.pdf.

———. 2000d. "Number of People, Hispanic or Latino Origin, All Races." Retrieved March 17, 2008, from http://www.census.gov/population/cen2000/atlas/censr01-111.pdf.

———. 2000e. "Number of People, 2000, One Race: Asian." Retrieved March 17, 2008, from http://www.census.gov/population/cen2000/atlas/censr01-108.pdf.

———. 2000f. "Summary File 4." Retrieved February 29, 2008, from http://factfinder.census.gov/servlet/DatasetMainPageServlet?_program=DEC&_submenuId=datasets_1&_lang=en.

———. 2001. "Profiles of General Demographic Characteristics, 2000, Florida." Retrieved March 16, 2008, from http://www.census.gov/prod/cen2000/dp1/2kh12.pdf.

———. 2002. *Statistical Abstract of the United States, 2001* (121st ed.). Washington, DC: Government Printing Office.

———. 2004a. *Ancestry 2000*. Retrieved February 27, 2008, from http://www.census.gov/prod/2004pubs/c2kbr-35.pdf.

———. 2004b. "Population by Region, Sex, and Hispanic Origin Type, With Percent Distribution by Hispanic Origin Type, 2004." Retrieved March 16, 2008, from http://www.census.gov/population/socdemo/hispanic/ASEC2004/2004CPS_tab19.2.pdf.

———. 2005. *Statistical Abstract of the United States, 2005*. Washington, DC: Government Printing Office.

———. 2006. "Estimates of the Population by Race Alone or in Combination and Hispanic or Latino Origin for the United States and States." Retrieved March 11, 2008, from http://www.census.gov/Press-Release/www/2006/cb06-123table1.xls.

———. 2007a. "American Community Survey, 2006." Retrieved March 11, 2008, from http://factfinder.census.gov/servlet/DatasetMainPageServlet?_program=ACS&_submenuId=datasets_2&_lang=en&_ts=.

———. 2007b. *Statistical Abstract of the United States, 2007*. Washington, DC: Government Printing Office. Retrieved March 15, 2008, from http://www.census.gov/compendia/statab/past_years.html.

———. 2007c. "Table P 36, Full-Time, Year-Round All Workers by Median Income and Race and Sex: 1955 to 2005." Retrieved March 10, 2008, from http://www.census.gov/hhes/www/income/histinc/p36w.html (Whites); http://www.census.gov/hhes/www/income/histinc/p36b.html (Blacks).

———. 2008. "1990 Summary Tape File 3." Retrieved March 7, 2008, from http://factfinder.census.gov/servlet/DatasetMainPageServlet?_program=DEC&_tabId=DEC2&_submenuId=datasets_1&_lang=en&_ts=222966429406.

U.S. Commission on Civil Rights. 1976. *Puerto Ricans in the Continental United States: An Uncertain Future*. Washington, DC: Government Printing Office.

———. 1992. *Civil Rights Issues Facing Asian Americans in the 1990s*. Washington, DC: Government Printing Office.

U.S. Department of Homeland Security. 2003. *Yearbook of Immigration Statistics, 2002*. Washington, DC: Government Printing Office.

———. 2005. *Yearbook of Immigration Statistics*. Washington, DC: Government Printing Office. Retrieved November 24, 2007, from http://www.dhs.gov/xlibrary/assets/statistics/yearbook/2006/OIS_2006_Yearbook.pdf.

———. 2006. *Yearbook of Immigration Statistics, 2005*. Washington, DC: Government Printing Office.

———. 2007. *Yearbook of Immigration Statistics, 2006*. Washington, DC: Government Printing Office. Retrieved November 24, 2007, from http://www.dhs.gov/ximgtn/statistics/publications/yearbook.shtm.

U.S. Immigration and Naturalization Service. 1993. *Statistical Yearbook of the Immigration and Naturalization Service, 1992*. Washington, DC: Government Printing Office.

"Utah Supreme Court Rules That Non-Indian Members of Native American Church Can Use Peyote in Church Ceremonies." 2004. *New York Times*, June 23, p. A20.

Valentine, Sean, & Mosley, Gordon. 2000. "Acculturation and Sex-Role Attitudes Among Mexican Americans: A Longitudinal Analysis." *Hispanic Journal of Behavioral Sciences*, 22:104–204.

Van Ausdale, Debra, & Feagin, Joe. 2001. *The First R: How Children Learn Race and Racism*. Lanham, MD: Rowman & Littlefield.

van den Berghe, Pierre L. 1967. *Race and Racism: A Comparative Perspective*. New York: Wiley.

———. 1981. *The Ethnic Phenomenon*. New York: Elsevier.

Vigilant, Linda. 1997. "Race and Biology." In Winston Van Horne (Ed.), *Global Convulsions: Race, Ethnicity, and Nationalism at the End of the Twentieth Century* (pp. 23–47). Albany: SUNY.

Vincent, Theodore G. 1976. *Black Power and the Garvey Movement.* San Francisco: Ramparts.

Vinje, David. 1996. "Native American Economic Development on Selected Reservations: A Comparative Analysis." *American Journal of Economics and Sociology,* 55:427–442.

Voting Rights Act, 42 U.S.C. § 1971 (1965).

Wagley, Charles, & Harris, Marvin. 1958. *Minorities in the New World: Six Case Studies.* New York: Columbia University Press.

"Ward Connerly: Interview." 2003. *American Enterprise,* April/May, pp. 18–22.

Washington, Booker T. 1965. *Up From Slavery.* New York: Dell.

Waters, Mary. 1990. *Ethnic Options.* Berkeley: University of California Press.

_____. 1996. "Optional Ethnicities: For Whites Only?" In Sylvia Pedraza & Ruben Rumbaut (Eds.), *Origins and Destinies: Immigration, Race, and Ethnicity in America* (pp. 449–452). Belmont, CA: Wadsworth.

Wax, Murray. 1971. *Indian Americans: Unity and Diversity.* Englewood Cliffs, NJ: Prentice Hall.

Weeks, Philip. 1988. *The American Indian Experience.* Arlington Heights, IL: Forum Press.

Weil, Frederick. 1985. "The Variable Effects of Education on Liberal Attitudes: A Comparative-Historical Analysis of Anti-Semitism Using Public Opinion Survey Data." *American Sociological Review,* 50:458–474.

Weitz, Rose, & Gordon, Leonard. 1993. "Images of Black Women Among Anglo College Students." *Sex Roles,* 28:19–34.

Weitzer, Ronald, & Tuch, Steven. 2005. "Racially Biased Policing: Determinants of Citizen Perceptions." *Social Forces,* 83:1009–1030.

Wellner, Alison. 2007. *U.S. Attitudes Toward Interracial Dating Are Liberalizing.* Population Reference Bureau. Retrieved December 5, 2007, from http://www.prb.org/Articles/2005/USAttitudesTowardInterracialDatingAreLiberalizing.aspx.

White, Deborah Gray. 1985. *Ar'n't I a Woman? Female Slaves in the Plantation South.* New York: Norton.

Whiting, Robert. 1990. *You Gotta Have Wa.* New York: Macmillan.

Wilkens, Roger. 1992. "L.A.: Images in the Flames—Looking Back in Anger: 27 Years After Watts, Our Nation Remains Divided by Racism." *Washington Post,* May 3, p. C1.

Williams, Gregory. 1995. *Life on the Color Line.* New York: Dutton.

Williams, Juan. 1987. *Eyes on the Prize. America's Civil Rights Years, 1954–1965.* New York: Penguin.

Williams, R. 1964. *Strangers Next Door.* Englewood Cliffs, NJ: Prentice Hall.

Willie, Charles. (Ed.). 1989. *Round Two of the Willie/Wilson Debate* (2nd ed.). Dix Hills, NY: General Hall.

Wilson, George. 1997. "Payoffs to Power Among Males in the Middle Class: Has Race Declined in Its Significance?" *Sociological Quarterly,* 38:607–623.

Wilson, William J. 1973. *Power, Racism, and Privilege: Race Relations in Theoretical and Sociohistorical Perspectives.* New York: Free Press.

_____. 1980. *The Declining Significance of Race* (2nd ed.). Chicago: University of Chicago Press.

_____. 1987. *The Truly Disadvantaged: The Inner City, the Underclass, and Public Policy.* Chicago: University of Chicago Press.

_____. 1996. *When Work Disappears.* New York: Knopf.

Wirth, Louis. 1945. "The Problem of Minority Groups." In Ralph Linton (Ed.), *The Science of Man in the World* (pp. 347–372). New York: Columbia University Press.

Wittig, M., & Grant-Thompson, S. 1998. "The Utility of Allport's Conditions of Intergroup Contact for Predicting Perceptions of Improved Racial Attitudes and Beliefs." *Journal of Social Issues,* 54:795–812.

Wolfenstein, Eugene V. 1993. *The Victims of Democracy: Malcolm X.* New York: Guilford Press.

Wong, Jade Snow. 1993. "Fifth Chinese Daughter." In Dolores LaGuardia & Hans Guth (Eds.), *American Voices* (pp. 48–55). Palo Alto, CA: Mayfield.

Wong, Morrison. 1995. "Chinese Americans." In Pyong Gap Min (Ed.), *Asian Americans: Contemporary Trends and Issues* (pp. 58–94). Thousand Oaks, CA: Sage.

Wood, Peter, & Chesser, Michele. 1994. "Black Stereotyping in a University Population." *Sociological Focus,* 27:17–34.

Woodrum, Eric. 1979. *Japanese Americans: A Test of the Assimilation Success Story.* Paper presented at the Southern Sociological Society, April, Atlanta, GA.

Woodward, C. Vann. 1974. *The Strange Career of Jim Crow* (3rd ed.). New York: Oxford University Press.

Worsnop, Richard. 1992. "Native Americans." *CQ Researcher,* May 8, pp. 387–407.

Wright, Richard. 1940. *Native Son.* New York: Harper & Brothers.

_____. 1945. *Black Boy: A Record of Childhood and Youth.* New York: Harper & Brothers.

_____. 1988. *12 Million Black Voices.* New York: Thunder's Mouth Press.

Wyman, Mark. 1993. *Round Trip to America.* Ithaca, NY: Cornell University Press.

Xie, Yu, & Goyette, Kimberly. 2004. *A Demographic Portrait of Asian Americans.* New York: Russell Sage Foundation.

Yamato, Alexander. 1994. "Racial Antagonism and the Formation of Segmented Labor Markets: Japanese Americans and Their Exclusion From the Work Force." *Humboldt Journal of Social Relations,* 20:31–63.

Yancey, George. 1999. "An Examination of the Effects of Residential and Church Integration on Racial Attitudes of Whites." *Sociological Perspectives,* 42:279–294.

_____. 2007. *Interracial Contact and Social Change.* Boulder, CO: Lynne Rienner.

Yinger, J. Milton. 1985. "Ethnicity." *Annual Review of Sociology,* 11:151–180.

Zhou, Min. 1992. *Chinatown.* Philadelphia: Temple University Press.

Zhou, Min, & Bankston, Carl. 1998. *Growing Up American: How Vietnamese Children Adapt to Life in the United States.* New York: Russell Sage Foundation.

Zhou, Min, & Logan, John R. 1989. "Returns on Human Capital in Ethnic Enclaves: New York City's Chinatown." *American Sociological Review,* 54:809–820.

Glossary and Index

Numbers in brackets refer to the chapter in which the term is introduced.

Abolitionism [4] The movement to abolish slavery in the South, 216–217

Aboud, F. E., 119

Abrahamson, H., 50

Acculturation [2] The process by which one group (generally a minority or immigrant group) learns the culture of another group (generally the dominant group), 53 (exhibit), 54

    African Americans, contemporary experience of, 175–176, 215

    American Indians, coercive acculturation, 305, 306–307, 324–325, 325 (exhibit)

    chains of immigration and, 68–69

    cultural pluralism and, 58

    enclave/middleman minorities and, 59

    ethnicity and, 83

    European immigrant groups and, 72–81, 170, 171

    Hispanic Americans, contemporary experience of, 384–386, 384–385 (exhibits)

    human capital theory and, 55

    literacy and, 85

    slavery, impact on slaves, 178–179

    structural pluralism, 58–59

    See also Assimilation; Pluralism

Activism:

    American Indians and, 312–313, 342

    dual criminal justice system and, 265

    Mexican American protest/Chicano movement, 364–367

    minority group activism, social change and, 234

    nonviolent direct action, 252–254, 259, 367

    public sociology assignments and, 1–7

    sports mascots, activism against, 342

Acuna, R., 365, 366

Adarand Constructors, Inc. v. Pena (1995), 233

Affective prejudice [1] The emotional or "feeling" dimension of individual prejudice. The prejudiced individual attaches negative emotions to other groups, 34, 109–110

    authoritarian personality theory and, 110

    childhood prejudice and, 119

    scapegoat hypothesis and, 109–110

    See also Discrimination; Prejudice

Affirmative action [5] Affirmative action programs are designed to counter the effects of institutional discrimination and the legacy of minority group inequality, 90, 137, 137 (exhibit), 233–234, 236, 267, 271, 289, 293

Affluence, 55

    See also Income; Wealth

African Americans, 15

    African nations, immigration quotas and, 71

    Black Protest movement and, 214–215

    blended individuals and, 30

    culture, effects of slavery on, 192–194

    de jure segregation and, 205–209

    disadvantage of, 92

    disenfranchisement of, 40, 208

    geographic distribution of, 86, 86 (exhibit), 87

    industrialization, impact of, 204–214

    institutional discrimination and, 35–36

    job opportunities, discrimination and, 16, 16 (exhibit)

    lynching of, 109–110, 208

    mass migration of, 209–213, 209–210 (exhibits)

    minority group status, dimensions of, 175–180, 178 (exhibit)

    modern racism and, 136–138, 137 (exhibit)

    Northern communities of, 210, 212–213

    political power of, 210, 254

    racial profiling and, 148–151, 266

    recent immigrants from Africa, 13, 476–478, 476–477 (exhibits)

    reconstruction and, 204–205

    reparations and, 235–238

    stereotypes of, 111–112, 111 (exhibit)

    urban underclass and, 270

    white ethnic groups, competition with, 210–211, 214

    See also African Americans/contemporary life; American populations; Dominant-minority relations/ industrialization; Dominant-minority relations/ preindustrial America; Hate groups; Jim Crow system; Slavery

African Americans/contemporary life, 249–250, 288–289, 335–336

    acculturation process and, 175–176, 507–508

    black middle class, 267–269, 268 (exhibit), 271

    Black Power movement, 256–258, 276, 289

    black protest movement and, 253–254, 259

    color-blind racism and, 271, 275, 289–293

    criminal justice system and, 264–266

    de facto segregation and, 255–256

    de jure segregation, end of, 250–251

    discrimination and, 274–275

    economic resources and, 254–255, 256, 275, 284–286, 285–287 (exhibits)

citizenship restrictions and, 171, 411, 416
  gender roles and, 409–410
  immigration quota system and, 71
  kinship relations and, 408
  origins/cultures of, 407–410
  prejudice against, 115, 122–123
  public shame/humiliation and, 409
  saving face and, 409
  See also American populations; Asian Americans/contemporary
    life; Pacific Islanders
Asian Americans/contemporary life, 405–407, 406–409 (exhibits), 423–424
  acculturation and, 429, 430 (exhibit)
  Asian Indian community, 425
  assimilation and pluralism and, 429–440, 508
  Chinese American community, development of, 410–415,
    412 (exhibit)
  collectivistic societal practices and, 408–409
  colonized racial minority groups and, 442–443
  Confucian moral system and, 408
  contact situations, development of communities, 410–423
  contemporary immigration from Asia, 424–428
  diverse experience and, 424–425
  educational opportunities and, 433–435, 434–436 (exhibits),
    442–443
  face work and, 409
  Filipino American community, 427
  gender roles and, 409–410
  intermarriage, incidence of, 439, 440 (exhibit)
  invisible minorities and, 413, 414, 448–449
  Japanese American community, development of,
    412 (exhibit), 416–423
  Korean American community, 425–427
  language acculturation and, 427, 430 (exhibits)
  model minority status and, 415, 447
  origins/cultures and, 407–410
  patriarchal values and, 410
  political power and, 435–436
  prejudice/discrimination and, 428–429
  primary structural assimilation and, 439, 440 (exhibit)
  residential patterns and, 431–433, 431–433 (exhibits)
  secondary structural assimilation and, 431–440
  success in America, cultural/structural explanations, 440–447
  Vietnamese American community, 427–428
  white ethnics and, 441
  See also American Community Survey (ACS); Asian Americans;
    Pacific Islanders
Asian Indians, 59, 406 (exhibit), 407–409 (exhibits)
  contemporary immigration of, 424, 425
  job opportunities/income status and, 436–438,
    437–439 (exhibits)
  language ability of, 410, 430 (exhibit)
  See also Asian Americans; Asian Americans/contemporary life
Assimilation [2] The process by which formerly distinct and separate
    groups merge and become one group, 49–50, 94–95, 507–509
  acculturation/cultural assimilation, 51, 53 (exhibit), 54
  Anglo-conformity and, 51, 54, 55, 57
  Black Power movement and, 256, 258

blended populations and, 55
  Gordon's stages of assimilation, 53–54, 53 (exhibit)
  human capital theory and, 55
  immigrant groups, patterns of assimilation and, 72–81, 74 (exhibit)
  individual subprocesses of, 54
  integration/structural assimilation, 53 (exhibit), 54, 72–74,
    74 (exhibit)
  intermarriage/marital assimilation, 53 (exhibit), 54
  melting pot metaphor, 50–51, 83, 97, 100, 507, 512
  Northern/Western Protestant Europeans and, 65
  Park's race relations cycle and, 52–53
  Red Power and, 315
  reverse assimilation and, 54, 57
  segmented assimilation, 93, 97, 486–489, 488 (exhibits)
  slavery, impact on slaves, 178–179
  sojourners and, 85
  termination policy, American Indians and, 310
  three-generation pace of, 487
  traditional theoretical foundation of, 51–55, 273
  triple melting pot and, 83
  types of, 50–51
  See also European immigrants; Group systems; Immigrant
    groups; New Americans; Pluralism; Structural assimilation;
    White ethnic groups
Aukica, M., 98–99
Australian Human Rights and Equal Opportunity Commission, 338
Australian Aborigines, 338–339
Authoritarian personality theory, 110, 117

Baca, L., 341–343
Bach, R. L., 376, 377
Barrios, 393
Bean, F., 482, 483, 487, 488, 489
Bibb, H., 176–177
Biological principles of race, 23–25, 222
Biskupic, J., 422
Black Americans. *See* African Americans; African Americans/contemporary
    life; Black Power movement; Black protest movement
Black belt, 86, 86 (exhibit)
Black Codes, 207
Black liberation movement, 259
Black Nationalism, 256, 257, 258, 289
Black Panthers, 59
Black Power movement [6] A coalition of African American groups that
    rose to prominence in the 1960s. Some central themes of the
    movement were black nationalism, autonomy for African American
    communities, and pride in race and African heritage, 90, 256–258,
    276, 289, 365
Black protest movement [6], 214–215, 220, 253–254, 259
  See also Civil rights movement
Black Separatists, 5
Blaming the victim, 136
Blassingame, J. W., 180
Blau, P. M., 55
Blauner, R., 170, 305, 441
Blauner hypothesis [4] Minority groups created by colonization will
    experience more intense prejudice, racism, and discrimination than

second generation of, 414–415
success of, 415, 445–447
tongs/Tong Wars and, 413
See also Asian Americans; Asian Americans/
contemporary life
Chinese Consolidated Benevolent Association (CCBA), 414
Chinese Exclusion Act of 1882, 60, 411, 416, 425, 428, 504
Cho, S., 427
Citizenship process, 171, 396–397, 416
Civil Rights Act of 1964, 254
Civil rights movement [6] The effort of African Americans in the 1950s
and 1960s to win the rights they were entitled to under the U.S.
Constitution, 29, 40, 210, 237, 251
Brown v. Board of Education of Topeka,
251–252
freedom riders and, 253
legislation for civil rights, 254, 267
Montgomery boycott, 253
nonviolent direct action protest and, 252–254
Plessy v. Ferguson, 251
southern civil rights movement and, 255
success/limitations of, 254–255
tactics in, 253, 254
See also African-Americans/contemporary life; Black Power
movement
Civil War, 204, 206, 256, 267
Clark, M. L., 112
Class. *See* Social class
Classification of populations, 13
biological/genetic principles and, 23–25
skin color distribution and, 21–22, 22 (exhibit)
Western traditions and, 23
See also Minority groups; Race
Clinton, H. R., 282
Clinton, W. J., 284
Coal extraction, 65
Cofer, J. O., 372–373
Coffman, T., 111
Cognitive prejudice [1] The "thinking" dimension of individual prejudice.
The prejudiced individual thinks about other groups in terms of
stereotypes, 33, 110
childhood prejudice and, 119
selective perception and, 110–111
stereotyping and, 110–113
See also Discrimination; Prejudice
Cohen, A., 256
Cohen, L., 138
Collectivistic society, 303, 309, 324, 408–409
Collins, M. A., 132
Colombians, 379, 379 (exhibit), 381, 388, 389
assimilation process and, 395
economic conditions for, 391, 391–394 (exhibits), 392, 492
See also Hispanic Americans; Hispanic Americans/
contemporary life; South America
Colonization:
English colonies, 190, 191
French colonies, 190–191

Hawaiian culture and, 184–185, 185 (exhibits)
language as wedge, 101
power/affluence, white minority group and, 14
Puerto Rico and, 352–353
Spanish colonies, 190, 191
Western perspectives on race and, 23, 32
Colonized minority groups [4] Groups whose initial contact with the
dominant group was through conquest or colonization,
80, 101, 170, 171, 172, 178, 179, 339, 503–504
African Americans, 364
Asian Americans, 442–443
Mexican Americans, 352, 353–354, 363, 364–365, 386
Puerto Ricans, 386
Color-blind racism [3], 136, 271, 275, 289–293
See also Modern racism
Color-blind racism
Commerce:
Jewish immigrants and, 67–68, 70
See also Job opportunities; Labor markets; Manufacturing
occupations
Communism, 71
Community Schools, Inc. v. Seattle School District (2007), 234
Community Service Organization (Los Angeles), 365
Competition [4] A situation in which two or more parties struggle for
control of some scarce resource:
African Americans vs. white ethnic groups, 210–211,
214, 222
Chinese-Anglo contact and, 411
contact situation, group competition/power and, 503–505
education, status attainment and, 55
European immigrants, dispersal of, 64
fluid competitive group relations, 227, 228 (exhibit)
group competition, prejudice and, 115–117
intergroup inequalities and, 169, 170, 171, 172 (exhibit), 224
race relations cycle and, 52–53
rigid competitive group relations, 203, 221–222, 227,
228 (exhibit), 411
white ethnicity, resurgence of, 90
Conflict theory, xvi, 116–117
Confucianism, 407, 408, 445
Connerly, W., 290–291
Contact hypothesis. *See* Dominant-minority relations/preindustrial
America; Equal status contact hypothesis
Contemporary intergroup relations, 243–244
assimilation/pluralism and, 275–287, 277–282 (exhibits),
285–287 (exhibits)
Black Nationalism and, 256, 257, 258
Black Power movement and, 256–258
civil rights movement and, 251–255
criminal justice system and, 264–266
de facto segregation and, 255–256
de jure segregation and, 250–251
post-1960s, black-white relations, 263–287
prejudice/discrimination and, 274–275
social class, increasing inequality and,
266–272
urban unrest, 256

institutional discrimination and, 175

labor supply problem, labor-intensive work and, 167–168

Mexican Americans, minority status of, 186–189, 189–191, 194–195

Noel hypothesis and, 168–170, 169 (exhibit), 171–172, 172 (exhibit), 182, 188–189

paternalistic relations and, 172–174

prejudice/racism and, 175, 178, 178 (exhibit)

slavery, origins of, 164–168, 166 (exhibit), 171–172, 172 (exhibit)

Spanish colonization efforts and, 190, 191

See also Dominant-minority relations/industrialization

Dominicans, 379, 379 (exhibit), 380, 386

assimilation process and, 395, 487

economic conditions for, 391, 391–394 (exhibits), 392, 492

See also Hispanic Americans; Hispanic Americans/ contemporary life

Doob, L. W., 109

Doyle, A. B., 119

Driving while black (DWB), 266

Drug abuse, 237, 265, 266

Dubois, W. E. B., 19, 215, 235

Duleep, H. O., 416

Duncan, O. D., 55

Duvalier dictatorship, 464

Eastern European immigrants:

American culture, preference hierarchy and, 82

blue-collar social class and, 83–84

Jewish immigrants, ethnic enclaves and, 66–68

laborer class and, 65–66, 73–74, 74 (exhibit)

women workers and, 85

See also European immigrants; Jewish Americans; White ethnic groups

East Indians. *See* Asian Indians

Economic opportunity:

African Americans, contemporary experience of, 254–255, 256, 275, 284–286, 285–287 (exhibits)

American Indians, contemporary experience of, 318–319, 318–319 (exhibits), 331–334, 332–334 (exhibits)

black middle class and, 267–269, 268 (exhibit)

bounded solidarity and, 446

deindustrialization and, 202–203

enclave economies, 67, 68, 71

hate crimes, social class and, 146

Hispanic Americans, contemporary experience of, 390–393, 391–394 (exhibits)

industrial economy and, 203

political machinery and, 75–77

spoils system and, 75

structural mobility, contemporary industrialization and, 81

sweatshops, 361, 435

urban poverty and, 269–270

white ethnic groups and, 87, 88 (exhibit)

See also Education opportunities; Income; Job opportunities; Labor market

Education opportunities:

African American opportunities, 279–281, 279–282 (exhibits)

American Indian opportunities, 329–330, 330–331 (exhibits)

Asian American opportunities, 433–435, 434–436 (exhibits)

assimilation, generational patterns of, 73–74, 74 (exhibit), 81

bilingual education, 57

boarding schools, American Indians and, 305, 306–307

community colleges, proliferation of, 330

dropout rates, 281

employment requirements and, 224–225

German Americans and, 65

Hispanic American opportunities, 387–389, 388–389 (exhibits)

immigrants, Americanization of, 51, 67–68

Indian Self-Determination and Education Assistance Act and, 312

Jewish Americans and, 67–68

job market, upward mobility and, 81

Mexican American school segregation, 364

New Orleans, racial differentials and, 40, 41 (exhibit)

postindustrial society and, 40

prejudice, education effects on, 127–130, 128–129 (exhibits)

quota systems and, 68

racial gap and, 281, 281–282 (exhibits)

school integration, 279–281, 279–282 (exhibits)

status attainment theory and, 55

stratification and, 19

white ethnic groups and, 87, 88 (exhibit)

Eitzen, D. S., 364

Elkins, S., 178, 192–193

Ellis, C. P., 144

Emancipation, 216

Enclave minority group [2] A group that establishes its own neighborhood and relies on a set of interconnected businesses for economic survival, 59, 171

chains of immigration and, 68–69, 360, 387

Chinese Americans and, 67, 413–414

contemporary stream of immigrants and, 479

Cuban Americans and, 67, 375–377, 479

Eastern European Jewish immigrants, 66–68

Japanese Americans and, 417

Jewish Americans and, 66–68, 479

Korean Americans and, 426

Enemy groups, 115–116

Enforceable trust, 446

Engels, F., 116

English colonization efforts, 190, 191

English Language Unity Act of 2003, 98

English-only policy, 57, 98–101

Enriquez, E., 367

Entinc, J., 42, 43

Entrepreneurship:

Asian Americans and, 446

Jewish immigrants and, 67–68

Equal opportunity policy, 236

Equal status contact hypothesis [3] A theory of prejudice reduction asserting that equal status and cooperative contacts between groups will tend to reduce prejudice, 131

stereotypes of, 111 (exhibit), 112
symbolic ethnicity and, 90–91
women immigrant workers, 84
See also European immigrants

Jacobs, H., 176, 177
Jacobson, C., 209
Jamaicans, 464–465 (exhibits), 466
Japanese Americans, 235, 406–407, 406–409 (exhibits), 416, 423–424
    agriculture and, 417
    amae and, 444
    anti-Japanese campaign, 416–417
    enryo and, 444
    ethnic enclaves and, 417
    gaman/gambotte and, 444–445
    gender roles and, 422
    group harmony and, 409
    intermarriage, incidence of, 439, 440 (exhibit)
    invisible minority of, 448–449
    Issei, 417, 419
    job opportunities/income status and, 436–438,
        437–439 (exhibits)
    land ownership and, 416–417
    language acculturation and, 429, 430 (exhibit)
    Little Tokyo, 69, 423
    military service of, 418, 422
    Nisei, 417–418, 419, 422–423
    post-World War II era and, 422–423
    public shame/humiliation and, 409
    relocation camps and, 235, 418–422
    reparations and, 235, 422
    Sansei, 419, 423
    second generation of, 416, 417–418
    success of, 444–445
    Yonsei, 423
Jena (Louisiana), 265
Jewish Americans, 15, 82
    anti-immigrant sentiment and, 69–71
    anti-Semitism and, 70–71, 115
    commercial enterprises, enclave economy and, 67, 68, 71
    educated/acculturated succeeding generation and, 67–68
    group cohesion and, 67
    higher education, quotas in, 68
    Jewish immigrants, ethnic enclaves and, 66–68
    religion and, 82–83
    religious persecution and, 84, 85
    stereotypes of, 111, 111 (exhibit), 112
    women immigrants, 84–85
Jibou, R. M., 416, 417
Jigsaw method [3] A learning technique that requires cooperation among students, 133, 135
Jim Crow system [5], 205–209, 210, 214, 215, 222, 232, 236, 504
    Black Power movement and, 258
    contemporary experience of, 250–252, 256
    cultural domination and, 276
    southern childhood, female experience, 260–261
    See also De jure segregation

Job opportunities:
    African Americans, contemporary experience of, 284–286,
        285–286 (exhibits)
    American Indians, contemporary experience of, 331–334,
        332–334 (exhibits)
    Asian Americans, contemporary experience of, 436–438,
        437–439 (exhibits)
    current immigration trends and, 491–492
    discrimination and, 16, 16 (exhibit), 34
    European immigrants, 60–61, 60 (exhibit), 69
    Hispanic Americans, contemporary experience of, 390–393,
        391–394 (exhibits)
    immigrants, Americanization and, 51, 54
    Puerto Ricans and, 368–370
    racial oppression and, 40
    segmented job market, 271
    stratification and, 20
    structural mobility, contemporary industrialization and, 81
    See also Income; Labor-intensive work; Labor markets;
        Occupations
Joe, J., 311
Johnson, A., 148, 149–150
Johnson, L. B., 254
Joly, S., 138
Jones, J., 110
Jonyers, J., 283
Josephy, A. M., 303, 310
Justice norm, 123, 126

Kallen, H. M., 55, 57
Kalt, J., 312, 316, 317, 331
Karlins, M., 111
Katz, P., 119
Kennedy, J. F., 284
Kennedy, R., 266
Kennedy, R. J., 82
Kent, M., 281, 283
King, C. R., 341–343
King, M. L., Jr., 253, 254, 367
King, R., 264, 265
Kitano, H. H. L., 184, 412, 415, 416, 417, 418, 423, 425, 426, 427, 428,
    444–445
Kivligham, K., 33
Kleg, M., 121
Kochhar, R., 267
Korean Americans, 59, 226, 406–409 (exhibits), 424, 425–427, 430 (exhibit)
    intermarriage, incidence of, 439, 440 (exhibit)
    job opportunities/income status and, 436–438,
        437–439 (exhibits)
    See also Asian Americans; Asian Americans/contemporary life
Korean War, 226, 425
Krepps, M., 316
Kritz, M., 426
Krysan, M., 279
Ku Klux Klan (KKK), 5, 71, 130, 140, 141, 208, 252
Kuperman, D., 263
Kurihara, J., 420–421

Labissiere, Y., 464, 465, 466

Labor-intensive work [4] A form of work in which the bulk of the effort is provided by human beings working by hand. Machines and other labor-saving devices are rare or absent, 61

    infrastructure construction and, 65

    Mexican American day laborers, 188–189

    plantation system, 167

    slavery and, 40, 167–168, 175

    unskilled/semi-skilled laborers, 65–66

    white indentured servants and, 167

Labor markets:

    child labor, 85

    deindustrialization and, 224

    division of labor, 221

    dual labor market, 225–226

    education, upward mobility and, 81

    foreign-born labor force, 61

    German Americans and, 64–65

    guest workers, 382

    immigrant laborers, 65–66, 491–492

    indentured servitude and, 166–167, 171–172, 172 (exhibit)

    Mexican American laborers, 188–189, 358, 359–360, 361–362, 364, 365

    occupational specialization and, 221–222

    primary labor market, 225

    Puerto Ricans and, 369–370

    secondary labor market, 226

    segmented job market, African Americans and, 271

    service sector jobs, 202, 216, 222–224, 224 (exhibit)

    split labor market situations, 117, 365, 392, 411

    structural mobility and, 81

    urban underclass and, 270

    white-collar jobs, 222–224, 224 (exhibit)

    white ethnic working class, 84, 90

    women immigrants and, 84–85

    See also Income; Job opportunities; Occupations; Split labor market; Stratification

Labor strikes, 115, 251, 367

Labor unions, 78–79, 117, 207, 211, 365, 366–367

Lai, H. M., 413, 414, 415, 428

Lame Deer, J., 326–327

Lamont-Brown, R., 448

Land ownership, 416

Language, 53, 54

    colonization and, 101

    cultural pluralism and, 58

    English-only policies, 57, 98–101

    language acculturation, American Indians and, 324, 325 (exhibit)

    language acculturation, Asian Americans, 427, 430 (exhibit)

    language acculturation, Hispanic Americans and, 384–385, 384–385 (exhibits)

    language acculturation, slaves and, 179

    second-generation immigrants and, 67–68, 72

Laotians, 406, 424, 428

Lapchick, J., 42

LaPiere, R., 122, 123

Latinos, 353

    See also Central America; Cuban Americans; Hispanic Americans; Hispanic Americans/contemporary life; Mexican Americans; Puerto Ricans; South America

Lavelle, K., 38, 39

Law. *See* Government policy

League of United Latin American Citizens (LULAC), 364

Lee, S. M., 412, 436, 439

Lenski, G., 17, 19

Lesbians. *See* Gays/lesbians

Level of development [1] The stage of evolution of society. The stages discussed in this text relate to agrarian and industrial subsistence technology, 19

Levin, J., 146

Lewis, O., 354

Life chances, 20, 27

Limited English proficient (LEP), 99

Lindbergh, C., 71

Literacy tests, 208

Locust, C., 303

Logan, J., 38, 384

Lopata, H. Z., 79

Lopez, I. F. H., 291–293

Lopez, J., 367

Lower East Side (New York City), 67

Lurie, N. O., 172

Lutz, A., 384

Lyman, S., 408, 411, 413, 428

Lynchings, 109–110, 208

Machismo [8] A cultural value stressing male dominance, virility, and honor, 354, 356–357

Malcolm X, 257

Malik, K., 43–44

Mandela, N., 221

Mann Act, 29

Mann, T., 281, 283

Manning, R., 67, 374, 377

Manufacturing (secondary) occupations [5] Occupations involving the transformation of raw materials into finished products ready for the marketplace. An example is an assembly line worker in an automobile plant, 223, 224, 224 (exhibit)

    assembly line work, 221

    deindustrialization and, 202

    hate crimes, social class and, 146

    industrial laborers, 65, 66, 73–74

    mechanization and, 66

    offshoring/job migration, 269

    specialization and, 221

    women immigrants and, 84

Manzanar, 419

Maquiladoras, 231, 361

Marable, M., 235, 236–237

Marielitos [8] Refugees from Cuba who arrived in the United States in 1980, 374

Marital assimilation [2] Intermarriage between members of different groups, 53 (exhibit), 54

patterns of, 73–74, 74 (exhibit)
See also Marriage
Marriage:
African Americans, contemporary experience of, 286–287
American Indians, contemporary experience of, 334, 335 (exhibit)
arranged marriages, 65, 72, 408
Asian Americans, contemporary experience of, 439, 440 (exhibit)
Emancipation and, 216
European immigrants, intermarriage among, 82–83, 87, 91
Hispanic Americans, contemporary experience of, 394
interracial marriages, 16, 28–30, 287
marital assimilation, 53 (exhibit), 54, 91
minority groups and, 14, 16
mixed marriages, 28–30, 73
Marshall, T., 252
Martin, P., 484
Marvasti, A., 474–475
Marx, K., 17, 18, 20, 116
Marxism, 17
bourgeoisie, 18
Cuban revolution, 374
group competition, prejudice and, 116–117
inequality in society and, 17–18
means of production, 18
proletariat, 18
See also Cuban Americans; Social class; Stratification
Massey, D., 278, 486, 487, 489
Matrilineal society, 183
Matrix of domination, 31, 114
Matthaei, J., 79, 179, 183, 216, 259, 304, 360, 364, 367, 409, 415, 422, 423, 427
Mauer, M., 266
Maume, D., 271
Mazur, A., 33
Mbeke, T. M., 221
McDevitt, J., 146
McKinney, K., 474–475
McLaren, L., 134, 135
McNickle, D., 310
McWhorter, J., 235, 237–238
McWilliams, C., 383
Means of production [1] A Marxist term that refers to the materials, tools, resources, and organizations by which the society produces and distributes goods and services, 18
Mechanization, 66
Mediterranean peoples, 23
Medoff, M., 146
Melting pot [2] A type of assimilation in which all groups contribute in roughly equal amounts to the creation of a new culture and society, 50–51, 83, 97, 100, 507, 512
Meredith v. Jefferson County, Kentucky, Board of Education (2007), 234
Merton, R., 113
Mestizo [4] A person of mixed white and Native American ancestry, 190
Mexican-American Legal Defense Fund, 398

Mexican Americans, 64, 164, 353–354, 367–368
American government immigration policy, 358–363
ancestries of, 352
Arizona/New Mexico and, 187
assimilation and, 386, 487
Blauner hypothesis and, 188–189
California and, 187
Chicanismo and, 365
Chicano movement and, 365–367
colonized status of, 352, 353–354, 363–364, 394–395
cultural patterns of, 354–355
culture of poverty and, 354
disadvantage of, 92
economic conditions for, 391, 391–394 (exhibits), 392, 488–489, 492
family ties and, 355
geographic distribution of, 86, 86 (exhibit), 87
illegal immigration, 359 (exhibit), 360, 361–363
immigration patterns of, 355, 355 (exhibit), 358–363, 359 (exhibit), 368
labor pool and, 188–189, 358, 359–360, 361–362, 364, 365
machismo, 354, 356–357
maquiladoras, 231, 361
Mexican economy, globalization of, 361–362
minority status, dimensions of, 186–189
Noel hypothesis and, 188–189
Operation Wetback and, 360
political power of, 365, 366–367
protest/resistance and, 364–367
repatriation campaign and, 358–359
segregation experience of, 364
Texas and, 186–187
See also Hispanic Americans; Hispanic Americans/ contemporary life
Mexican nationals, 61
Mexican Revolution, 359 (exhibit)
Middle Easterners, 110, 466–468, 468–469 (exhibits)
cultural dimensions of, 468–469
Detroit, Michigan case example, 472–473
residential patterns of, 469–470, 470 (exhibit)
September 11th terrorist attack and, 470–471, 474–475
See also American Community Survey (ACS); Immigrant groups; New Americans
Middleman minority groups [2] Groups that rely on small businesses, dispersed throughout a community, for economic survival, 59, 171
Migration:
African American, Northward migration of, 209–213, 209–210 (exhibits)
forced migration/expulsion, 59–60
Puerto Ricans and, 368–370
pull and, 358, 368–370
push and, 358, 368–370
repatriation policy and, 244, 358–359
See also Immigrant groups
Miller, D., 311
Miller, N. E., 109
Mills, C. W., 76

Min, P. G., 410, 426, 427

Parke, R., 303

Parks, R., 253

Parrillo, V., 121

Past-in-present institutional discrimination [5] Patterns of inequality or unequal treatment in the present that are caused by some pattern of discrimination in the past, 233, 268, 269, 442

Paternalism [4] A form of dominant-minority relations often associated with plantation-based, labor-intensive, agrarian technology. In paternalistic relations, minority groups are extremely unequal and highly controlled. Rates of overt conflict are low, 172–174, 203, 228 (exhibit), 304–305, 501

Patriarchy [1] Male dominance. In a patriarchal society, men have more power than women do, 31, 84, 178, 189, 304, 410

Patriotic Renewalists, 397

Pearl Harbor, 418

Pennsylvania Dutch communities, 58

Perez, L., 374

Personal experiences. *See* Narrative portraits

Personality development:

authoritarian personality theory, 110

individual traits, 55, 272

prejudice and, 117

Person, W., 112

Petersen, W., 416

Pettigrew, T., 110, 112, 118, 131

Pettit, B., 266

Pew Charitable Trust, 266

Pew Hispanic Center, 354, 362, 385, 390, 492

Pewewardy, C., 341–343

Philippines. *See* Filipinos

Phillips, U. B., 178

Piersen, W. D., 192, 193

Plantation system [4] A labor-intensive form of agriculture that requires large tracts of land and a large, cheap labor force. This was a dominant form of agricultural production in the American South before the Civil War, 167

paternalism and, 172–174

See also Racism; Slavery

Plessy v. Ferguson (1896), 208, 251

Pluralism [2] A situation in which groups have separate identities, cultures, and organizational structures, 49–50, 55–57, 509–511

African Americans, contemporary experience of, 275–287, 277–282 (exhibits), 285–287 (exhibits)

American Indians, contemporary experience of, 324–335, 508

American society and, 57, 58–59

Asian Americans, contemporary experience of, 429–440, 508

Black Power movement and, 258

Catholicism, practice of, 70

chains of immigration and, 68–69

cultural pluralism, 58

enclave minorities and, 59

ethnic revival and, 54, 57, 89–90

Hispanic Americans, contemporary experience of, 384–395, 508

integration, equality and, 57

middleman minorities and, 59

multiculturalism and, 57–58

Red Power and, 315

structural pluralism, 58–59, 289

types of, 58–59

See also Assimilation; Cultural pluralism; Group systems; Immigrant groups

Policy. *See* Government policy

Polish Americans:

anti-immigrant sentiment and, 69–71

Little Warsaw and, 69, 87

religious institution and, 79

See also Eastern European immigrants

Polish National Catholic Church, 79

Political power:

African Americans, contemporary experience of, 282–284

American Indians, contemporary experience of, 330–331

Asian Americans, contemporary experience of, 435–436

Hispanic Americans, contemporary experience of, 389–390

Irish political power, 75–77

Mexican Americans, contemporary experience of, 365, 366–367

Poll taxes, 208

Pollard, K., 210, 281, 283, 331, 426

Populism, 207

Portes, A., 67, 93, 363, 369, 374, 375, 376, 377, 378, 444, 445–447

Postindustrial society, 19, 40, 217

See also Dominant-minority relations/industrialization; Dominant-minority relations/postindustrial society

Poverty. *See* American Community Survey (ACS); Economic opportunity; Income; Urban underclass

Powderly, T., 78

Powell, C., 282

Power [1] The ability to achieve goals even in the face of opposition from others, 19

European power, 22

group competition, prejudice and, 116–117

See also Dominant-minority relations; Political power; Power dynamics

Power dynamics:

colonized minority groups, 14

contact situation, group competition/power and, 503–505

differential in power, 122, 169, 170, 171–172, 303, 411

equal status contact hypothesis, 130–135, 134 (exhibit)

paternalistic relations and, 172–174

rigid-competitive group system and, 203, 221–222, 227, 228 (exhibit), 411

stratification and, 19, 20

See also Dominant group; Dominant-minority relations; Minority groups; Paternalism; Political power

Preindustrial society. *See* Dominant-minority relations/preindustrial America

Prejudice [1] The tendency of individuals to think and feel negatively toward others, xvi, 33–34, 34 (exhibit), 107–109

affective prejudice, 34, 109–110, 119

African Americans, contemporary experience of, 286–287

American Indians, contemporary experience of, 322–324

American stereotypes and, 111–112, 111 (exhibit)

anti-immigration prejudice, 69–71, 117

Asian Americans, contemporary experience of, 428–429

authoritarian personality theory and, 110, 117

consolidation process and, 22
historic white supremacy attitudes and, 27
human evolution and, 21–22
interracial marriages, 16
markers of group membership, 15, 23
mixed-race individuals, 13, 22, 26, 28–30
prejudice and, 113–114
pure races, elimination of, 22
racial identity, fluid nature of, 26–27
skin color, distribution of, 21–22, 22 (exhibit), 23
social class and, 270–272
social construction of, 25, 26–27
sports performance and, 42–44
two-race model, 262
Western traditions and, 23
See also Assimilation; Group systems; Immigrant groups;
　Minority groups; Race relations cycle; Racial inequalities;
　Racism
Race relations cycle [2] A concept associated with Robert Park, who
　believed that relations between different groups would go through
　predictable cycles, from conflict to eventual assimilation, 52–53, 93
Racial inequalities, xvi
Black Power movement and, 256–258
Black protest movement and, 214–215
de facto segregation and, 255–256
disadvantage, minority groups and, 14, 15
discrimination/access to education and, 137
interracial marriage and, 16, 28–30
job opportunities and, 16, 16 (exhibit)
modern racist attitudes and, 285
structural racism, 236–237
See also Hurricane Katrina; Race; Racism; Slavery; Stratification
Racial minority groups [1] Minority groups identified primarily by physical
　characteristics such as skin color (e.g., Asian Americans), 15
affirmative action, 90
colonized racial minorities, 80
contemporary immigrants and, 92–93
cultural pluralism and, 90
disadvantages/dilemmas of, 92
distinctions among, 57
melting pot process and, 51
white ethnic groups and, 90, 92
See also Race; Racial inequalities; Racism
Racial Privacy Initiative, 290–291
Racial profiling, 148–151, 266
Racism [1] A belief system that asserts the inferiority of a group, xvi, 36
anti-immigration sentiment and, 69–71
apartheid, 218–221, 219 (exhibit)
Black Power movement and, 256–257
color-blind racism, 136, 271, 275, 289–293
English-only movement and, 99–101
exploitation and, 175
ideological racism, 34–35
immigrant tales and, 92
immigration quota system and, 71
Jim Crow system, 205–209

miscegenation and, 16, 30
modern racism, prejudice and, 136–138, 137 (exhibit), 274–275
one-drop rule, 28, 262
racial hatred, dynamics of, 144–145
racial profiling, 148–151, 266
redlining, 278
slavery and, 175, 178, 178 (exhibit)
split labor market theory and, 117
See also Civil rights movement; Hate groups; Urban underclass
Railroad construction, 411
Rationality, 222
Reagan, R., 271
Reconstruction [5] The period of Southern race relations following the Civil
　War. Reconstruction lasted from 1865 until the 1880s and witnessed
　many racial reforms, all of which were reversed during de jure
　segregation, or the Jim Crow era, 204–205, 216, 237, 251
Redlining, 278
Red Power movement, 313–315, 365
Red tape, 222
Relationships. *See* Dominant-minority relations; Social relationships
Religion, 53
anti-Catholic sentiment, 69, 70
anti-Semitism and, 70–71
Asian religions, 407
Catholic immigrants, 76–77, 79–80, 82–83
cultural pluralism and, 58
ethclass and, 83
ethnicity and, 83
European immigrants, 60–61, 61 (exhibit), 63–65, 82–83
Jewish immigrants and, 70–71, 82–83
mixed marriages and, 28
patriarchal society and, 31
Protestant immigrants, 63–65, 70, 77, 82–83
social mobility and, 79–80
structural pluralism and, 58
triple melting pot and, 83
Relocation camps [9] The camps in which Japanese Americans were held
　during World War II, 235, 418–422
Relocation policy for American Indians, 309–311, 316 (exhibit)
Reparations, 235–238, 422
Repatriation [8] A government campaign begun during the Great
　Depression of the 1930s to deport illegal immigrants back to Mexico.
　The campaign also caused legal immigrants and native-born
　Mexican Americans to leave the United States, 244, 358–359
Republican Party, 284
Reservations, 182, 304–305, 311, 316 (exhibit)
gaming/economic development and, 320–321, 320 (exhibit),
　322(exhibit)
industry, development of, 317–319
See also American Indians; American Indians/contemporary life
Residential patterns:
African Americans, contemporary life, 276–279, 277–278 (exhibits)
American Indians, contemporary life, 328–329, 328–329 (exhibits)
Asian Americans, 431–433, 431–433 (exhibits)
Hispanic Americans, contemporary life, 386–387,
　386–388 (exhibits)

Resistance. *See* Activism; Black protest movement; Chicano movement; Mexican Americans; Nonviolent direct action; Red Power; Revolution

Resource distribution:

local government and, 75

natural resources, American Indian control of, 315–317

stratification and, 17, 20

white ethnicity, resurgence of, 90

Responsibility of individuals, 136, 137

Revolution [2] A minority group goal. A revolutionary group wishes to change places with the dominant group or create a new social order, perhaps in alliance with other groups, 59

Rice, C., 282

Rigid competitive group system [5] A system of group relations in which the dominant group Seeks to exclude minority groups or limit their ability to compete for scarce resources such as jobs, 203, 221–222, 227, 228 (exhibit), 411

See also Competition; De jure segregation

Robber's Cave experiment, 115–116, 132, 254

Robertson, C., 180

Rodriguez, C., 370, 394

Rodriguez, L., 94, 95

Roman Catholicism. *See* Catholic immigrants

Roosevelt, F. D., 251, 308, 418, 419

Roosevelt, T., 396397

Royster, D., 26, 27, 271

Rumbaut, R., 93, 360, 376, 378

Rupert, A., 138

Rural areas:

European immigration and, 64

Japanese Americans and, 416

Mexican agriculture, 361

Puerto Ricans and, 368–369

Russell, J. W., 190, 191

Saenz, R., 269

Salvadorans, 379, 379 (exhibit), 381, 388

assimilation process and, 395

economic conditions for, 391–394 (exhibits), 482

See also Hispanic Americans; Hispanic Americans/contemporary life

Sansei [9] Third-generation Japanese Americans, 419, 423

Saving face, 409

Scapegoat hypothesis [3] A theory of prejudice that posits that under certain conditions, people will express their aggressions against substitute targets. When other groups are chosen as substitute targets, prejudice increases, 109–110, 146–147

Schlesinger, A. M., Jr., 51

School populations:

diversity in, 2–3

school integration, 279–281, 279–282 (exhibits)

See also Education opportunities

Sears, R. R., 109

Secondary labor market [5] The segment of the labor market that includes low-paying, low-skilled, insecure jobs, 226, 478–479, 483

Secondary occupations [5], 223, 224 (exhibit)

See also Manufacturing (secondary) occupations

Scondary sector of the social structure [2] Relationships and organizations that are public, task oriented, and impersonal. Organizations in the secondary sector can be large, 53, 53 (exhibit), 54

Secondary structural assimilation. *See* Structural assimilation

Segmented assimilation [2] The idea that assimilation in the United States is now fragmented and can have a number of outcomes in addition to eventual entry into mainstream society, 93, 97

argument against, 487–489, 488 (exhibits)

argument in favor of, 486–487

contemporary assimilation and, 486

See also Assimilation; New Americans

Segregation, 34, 216

African American residential patterns and, 276–279, 277–278 (exhibits)

American Indian residential patterns and, 328–329, 328–329 (exhibits)

apartheid social structure, 218–221219 (exhibit)

Brown v. Board of Education of Topeka, 251–252

de facto segregation, 255–256

de jure segregation, 40, 205–209, 250–251

dissimilarity index, 278, 278 (exhibit)

Hispanic Americans, education of, 387, 388 (exhibit)

Mexican American experience of, 364

occupational segregation, 229, 231

school segregation/integration, 279–281, 279–282 (exhibits)

white flight and, 278–279

See also Civil rights movement; Discrimination; Dominant-minority relations/industrialization; Racism

Selective perception [3] The tendency to *See* only what one expects to *See.* Associated with stereotyping in individual prejudice, 110–111

Self-conscious social units, 14, 15–16

Self-determination. *See* Indian Self-Determination and Education Assistance Act of 1975

Self-fulfilling prophecy, 118

Separatism [2] A minority group goal. A separatist group wishes to sever all ties with the dominant group, 59, 89

September 11, 2001, 110, 122, 147, 456, 470–471, 474–475

Service (tertiary) occupations [5] Jobs that involve providing services. Examples include retail clerk, janitor, and schoolteacher, 202, 216, 222–224, 224 (exhibit)

Seven Degrees of Social Distance, 120

Sexism, 138–140, 139 (exhibit), 259

Sexual harassment, 140, 230, 231–232

Shapiro, T., 267, 275

Sharecropping [5] A system of farming often used in the South during de jure segregation. The sharecropper (often black), or tenant, worked the land, which was actually owned by someone else (usually white), in return for a share of the profits at harvest time. The landowner supplied a place to live and credit for food and clothing, 207, 216, 250

Sheet Metal Workers v. EEOC (1986), 233

Sherif, C., 115, 132

Sherif, M., 115, 132

Sigelman, L., 132

Simpson, G., 112, 118

Skin color, 15
    adaptive coloring, 22
    distribution of, 21–22, 22 (exhibit)
    race, distinguishing marker for, 23, 25
    social construction of race and, 25
    See also Minority groups; Race; Racism
Skinheads, 5, 71, 140, 141
Slavery, 21, 23, 40, 60, 61
    African American culture, effects of slavery on, 192–194
    American Indians and, 167–168, 171–172, 172 (exhibit)
    assimilation/acculturation, impact of slavery and, 178–179
    Blauner hypothesis and, 172
    caste-like barriers and, 172, 173
    chattel slavery, 173
    Christianity and, 116
    differential in power and, 171–172, 175
    gender relations and, 179–180
    indentured servants and, 166–167, 171–172, 172 (exhibit)
    labor-intensive work, plantation system and, 167–168, 172–174
    language acculturation and, 179
    laws/regulations and, 167, 173
    minority group status, dimensions of, 175–180, 178 (exhibit)
    Noel hypothesis and, 171–172, 172 (exhibit)
    origins of, 164–168, 166 (exhibit), 171–172, 172 (exhibit)
    paternalistic relations and, 172–174
    plantation system and, 167
    prejudice and, 115, 116, 175, 178, 178 (exhibit)
    resistance/accommodation, traditions of, 174
    runaway slaves and, 174
    school for civilization and, 178
    slave life, narrative portrait of, 176–177
    slave rebellion and, 174
    South Africa, settlement of, 219
    See also Dominant-minority relations/industrialization;
        Dominant-minority relations/preindustrial America
Smedley, A., 167, 175
Smith, T., 121
Snipp, C. M., 301, 310, 311, 312, 317, 323, 334
Social capital, 446
Social class [1] A group of people who command similar amounts
    of valued goods and services, such as income, property,
    and education, 17
    black middle class, 267–269, 268 (exhibit)
    bourgeoisie, 18
    enclave immigrants and, 67–68
    ethclass and, 83
    hate crimes and, 146
    increasing inequality in, 266–272
    middle class success and, 272
    minority groups and, 20, 40
    open class systems, 227
    prejudice and, 113–114
    prestige and, 18
    proletariat, 18
    race and, 270–272
    social mobility and, 20, 55, 66, 72–73

structural integration and, 83–84
structural mobility and, 81
urban underclass, 270
vulnerability and, 39
white ethnic working class, 84, 90
See also Ethnic succession; Social structure; Stratification
Social construction [1] A perception shared by members of a society
    or group that reflects habitual routines or institutionalized social
    processes. Social constructions (such as race or stereotypes) become
    real to the people who share them:
    race and, 25, 28
    racial identity, case example of, 26–27
Social distance [3] The degree of intimacy to which a person is willing to
    admit members of other groups, 120–122, 121 (exhibit), 383, 428–429
Social mobility [1] Movement from one social class to another,
    20, 55, 66, 72, 100, 368
Social relationships, 53
    chains of immigration and, 68–69, 360
    enclave/middleman minorities and, 59
    Jewish immigrants and, 67–68
    Norwegian immigrants and, 64
    racial exclusion, closed networks and, 271–272
    See also Assimilation; Dominant-minority relations;
        Group systems; Pluralism
Social structure [2] The networks of social relationships, groups,
    organizations, communities, and institutions that organize the work
    of a society and connect individuals to each other and to the larger
    society, 53
    ascribed status and, 14, 16
    equal status contact hypothesis and:
    immigrants, social marginality and, 72
    individual traits, human capital theory and, 55
    industrialization and, 61–62
    minorities, disadvantage/inequality and, 14, 15, 20
    minority groups, self-conscious social units of, 14, 15–16
    primary sector of, 53, 53 (exhibit), 54
    privileged position, perpetuation of, 20
    secondary sector of, 53, 53 (exhibit), 54
    self-conscious social units, 14, 15–16
    social distance and, 120–122, 121 (exhibit)
    structural assimilation and, 53 (exhibit), 54
    structural mobility and, 81
    See also American society; Group systems; Noel
        hypothesis; Pluralism; Social class; Social
        construction; Stratification
Socialization [3] The process of physical, psychological, and social
    development by which a person learns his or her culture:
    gender roles and, 32–33
    ideological racism and, 34–35
    prejudice and, 117, 119, 122, 175
    second generation immigrants and, 72–73
    See also Assimilation; Dominant-minority relations
Societal evolution, 19
Sociology, 17, 81, 92–93
    prejudice, sociological approach to, 147–148
    See also Public sociology

Taylor, E., 256
Taylor, J., 148, 150–151, 312, 316, 331
Technology:
    capital-intensive technology, 62
    deindustrialization and, 202–203
    industrialization and, 61–62
    information-based society, 19, 146, 202, 501
    mechanization of manufacturing and, 66
    postindustrial society and, 19
    subsistence technology, 19, 22, 61, 81, 500–503
Teed, D., 464, 465, 466
Telles, E., 487
Tenant farming, 207
Terkel, S., 144, 145
Termination policy for Native Americans [7] A policy by which all special
    relationships between the federal government and American Indians
    would be abolished, 309–311, 313, 316 (exhibit)
Terrorist attacks:
    Ku Klux Klan and, 208
    September 11, 2001, 110, 122, 147, 456, 470–471, 474–475
    USA Patriot Act and, 471
    war on terrorism, xvi
Tertiary occupations [5] *See* service (tertiary) occupations, 202, 216, 222–
    224, 224 (exhibit)
Textile mills, 84
Thernstrom, A., 286
Thernstrom, S., 286
Third-generation interest principle, 89
Thomas, T., 265
Thoreau, H. D., 253
Thornton, R., 302
Tijerina, R. L., 366
Tong Wars, 413
Tongs [9] Secret societies in Chinatowns that sometimes fought with other
    Chinese American groups over control of resources, 413
Tougas, F., 138
Trail of Broken Treaties, 314
Transcontinental railroad, 411
Trevanian, 124
Triangle Shirtwaist Company fire, 79
Trigueña identity, 370
Triple melting pot [2] The idea that structural assimilation for European
    immigrants took place within the context of the three major
    American religions, 83
Truman, H., 250
Trust, 446
Tsai, S. -S. H., 411, 413
Turner, N., 174
Two-race model, 262–263

Underclass. *See* Urban underclass
Undocumented immigrants, 359 (exhibit), 360, 361–363, 479, 484–485, 492
Union movement. *See* Labor unions
United Farm Workers, 366, 367
United Mine Workers, 79
United Nations Committee on the Elimination of Racial Discrimination, 339
United States Citizenship and Immigration Services (USCIS), 396

United Steelworkers of America, AFL-CIO v. Weber (1979), 233
Universal Negro Improvement Association, 215
Urban areas:
    African Americans, mass migration of, 209–210,
        209–210 (exhibits)
    colonized racial minorities and, 80
    Eastern European Jewish immigrants and, 67–68
    ethnic neighborhoods, 75
    German immigrants and, 64
    political machines and, 75–77
    racial unrest/riots, 256
    spoils system and, 75
    white ethnic groups and, 90
    working class neighborhoods, 90
    See also Urbanization; Urban underclass
Urbanization, 62, 217, 254
Urban underclass [6] The urban lower classes, consisting largely of African
    Americans and other minority groups of color, which have been
    more or less permanently barred from the mainstream economy and
    the primary labor market, 270, 503
    American Indians and, 310–311, 311 (exhibit), 331, 337
    colonized racial minorities and, 80
    de jure segregation and, 270
    enclave minorities, locus of control and, 376
    family institution, culture of poverty and, 272–274,
        273–274 (exhibits)
    Hispanic Americans, 393
    immigrant laborers and, 61, 65
    urban poverty, African Americans and, 269–270
USA Patriot Act of 2001, 471
U.S. Bureau of the Census. *See* American Community Survey (ACS)
U.S. society. *See* American society

Van Doren, C., 366
Vicious cycle of prejudice [3] A process in which a condition is assumed to
    be true and forces are then set in motion to create and perpetuate
    that condition, 118–119, 118 (exhibit), 175
Victimization:
    blaming the victim, 136
    English-only movement and, 99–100
    racial/class pattern of, 38, 265, 266
Victims of Crime Act, 235
Vietnamese, 406–409 (exhibits), 410, 424, 425, 427–428, 430 (exhibit),
    440 (exhibit), 483, 487
Vietnam War, 258, 427–428
Violence:
    Black Power movement and, 257–258
    domestic violence, 231–232
    Italian immigrant victims of, 69–70
    post-1960s black-white relations and, 263–266
Voting rights, 40, 204, 206, 207
    disenfranchisement measures, 208, 254, 283
    First Reconstruction and, 237
    Northern United States and, 210
    universal suffrage, 216–217
Voting Rights Act of 1965, 254, 283
Vulnerability, 39

Wagley, C., 14
Walters, G., 111
War Relocation Authority, 419
War on terrorism, xvi
Washington, B. T., 214, 215
Wax, M., 181, 305
Wealth:
    black middle class and, 267, 268 (exhibit)
    definition of, 267
    labor market, changing structure of, 224
    racial oppression and, 236, 237
    stratification and, 18, 20
    wealth transmission, 236
    See also Income
Weber, M., 18, 19
Weeks, P., 313
Weinberg, D., 329, 388, 433
Welch, S., 132
Welfare rights, 482–483, 492
Western, B., 266
Western European immigrant groups, 63–65, 71, 73, 82
    See also European immigrants; White ethnic groups
White American population:
    Black Power movement and, 256–258
    diversity in minority groups and, 12–13, 12 (exhibit)
    European Americans and, 90–92
    immigrant assimilation, generational patterns of, 73–74, 74 (exhibit)
    job opportunities, discrimination and, 16, 16 (exhibit)
    middle-class values/lifestyles and, 13
    White ethnicity and, 57
    See also African Americans; African Americans/ contemporary life; American Indians/contemporary life; American populations; American society; White ethnic groups
White Anglo-Saxon Protestants (WASPs), 73–74, 74 (exhibit)
White Aryan Resistance (WAR), 140
White, B. J., 115, 132
White Citizens' Councils, 252
White, D. G., 179, 180, 192, 194
White ethnic groups:
    African Americans, competition with, 210–211, 214
    American individualism and, 92
    Asian Americans and, 441
    ethnic revival and, 89–90
    European immigrants, 60–61, 60 (exhibit)
    geographical distribution, contemporary descendants and, 86–87, 86 (exhibit)
    hate crimes and, 146
    immigrant tales and, 91–92
    indentured servants, 167, 171–172, 172 (exhibit)

integration/equality and, 87, 88 (exhibits)
intermarriage rates and, 87, 91
labor movement and, 78
minority groups of color and, 90
political/economic dimensions of, 90
political party machinery and, 75–77
religious institution and, 79–80
structural mobility, integration and, 81
symbolic ethnicity and, 90–91
third generation interest principle and, 89
working class status of, 84, 90
See also American Community Survey (ACS); European immigrants
White flight, 278–279
White supremacy attitudes, 27, 34, 99
White-collar jobs, 222–224, 224 (exhibit)
Whiting, R., 409
Whitney, G., 148, 150–151
Widgren, J., 484
Wilder, D., 282
Wilson, G., 173, 175
Wilson, R., 314, 315
Wilson, W. J., 35, 209, 251, 252, 270, 271
Women:
    European immigrants and, 84–85
    female-headed households, 272–274, 273–274 (exhibits)
    labor movement and, 78–79
    minority status and, 14, 16, 20, 31, 32
    women workers, 79, 84–85
    See also Gender roles
Wong, J. S., 412, 415, 506
Wong, M., 443
Woo, A., 340–341
Wood, P., 112
Woodward, C. V., 131, 206
Work. *See* Income; Job opportunities; Labor-intensive work; Labor markets; Occupations; Plantation system; Sharecropping
World War I, 226, 256
World War II, 226, 234, 235, 251, 254, 282, 310, 312, 359, 365, 415, 416, 428, 504
Wounded Knee (South Dakota), 314
Wright, R., 212–213

Yamamoto, K., 121
Yamanaka, K., 439
Yinger, J. M., 54
Yinger, M., 112, 118
Yonsei [9] Fourth-generation Japanese Americans, 423

Zhou, M., 414, 444, 445–447
Zinn, M. B., 364

Supporting researchers for more than 40 years

Research methods have always been at the core of SAGE's publishing program. Founder Sara Miller McCune published SAGE's first methods book, *Public Policy Evaluation*, in 1970. Soon after, she launched the *Quantitative Applications in the Social Sciences* series—affectionately known as the "little green books."

Always at the forefront of developing and supporting new approaches in methods, SAGE published early groundbreaking texts and journals in the fields of qualitative methods and evaluation.

Today, more than 40 years and two million little green books later, SAGE continues to push the boundaries with a growing list of more than 1,200 research methods books, journals, and reference works across the social, behavioral, and health sciences. Its imprints—Pine Forge Press, home of innovative textbooks in sociology, and Corwin, publisher of PreK–12 resources for teachers and administrators—broaden SAGE's range of offerings in methods. SAGE further extended its impact in 2008 when it acquired CQ Press and its best-selling and highly respected political science research methods list.

From qualitative, quantitative, and mixed methods to evaluation, SAGE is the essential resource for academics and practitioners looking for the latest methods by leading scholars.

For more information, visit **www.sagepub.com**.

A Timeline of Group Relations in the United States, 1940–2008

	1940	1945	1950	1955	1960	1965	1970

AFRICAN AMERICANS

- **1941** March on Washington
- **1947** Jackie Robinson first black in major league baseball
- **1948** U.S. armed forces integrated
- **1954** *Brown v. Topeka Board of Education*
- **1955** Montgomery bus boycott
- **1963** Protest in Birmingham; March on Washington
- **1964** Civil Rights Act
- **1965** Voting Rights Act; Malcolm X assassinated; Riots in Watts and elsewhere
- **1968** Martin Luther King assassinated

BLACK POWER MOVEMENTS RISES TO PROMINENCE

← CIVIL RIGHTS MOVEMENT → ← URBAN UNREST & RIOTS →

NATIVE AMERICANS

- **1944** NCAI
- **1946** Indian Claims Commission
- **1953** Termination Policy
- **1961** NIYC founded
- **1965** Fish-in in Washington
- **1968** AIM founded
- **1969** Alcatraz occupied
- **1972** Trail of Broken Treaties
- **1973** Wounded Knee occupied

RED POWER MOVEMENT RISES TO PROMINENCE

← URBANIZATION → ← PAN-TRIBALISM GROWS →

HISPANIC AMERICANS

- **1942** Zoot Suit Riots, Los Angeles; Bracero Program
- **1946** Community Services Organization and American GI Forum founded
- Operation Wetback begins
- Number of Puerto Ricans on the mainland triples
- Revolution in Cuba
- **1963** Alianza de Mercedes founded
- **1965** Crusade for Justice founded Chávez's grape boycott
- Immigration from South and Central America and the Caribbean increases in rate and diversity
- **1973** Election victory for La Raza Unida, Crysyal City, Texas

← MIGRATION OF PUERTO RICANS TO MAINLAND INCREASES →

IMMIGRATION FROM CUBA
CHICANO MOVEMENT RISES TO PROMINENCE ←

ASIAN AMERICANS

- **1941** Internment camps
- Declining societal prejudice and upward mobility for educated Chinese and Japanese Americans
- "Bipolar" occupational profiles
- Immigration from Asia increases in rate and diversity ←

WHITE ETHNIC AMERICANS

- Most groups well into a third generation
- Continuing assimilation/ethnicity and religion intermixed
- Ethnic resurgence

	1940	1945	1950	1955	1960	1965	1970

U.S. Society

- **1944** Roosevelt reelected
- **1948** Truman elected
- **1952** Eisenhower elected
- **1956** Eisenhower reelected
- **1960** Kennedy elected
- **1963** Kennedy assassinated
- **1964** Johnson elected
- **1968** Nixon elected
- **1972** Nixon reelected

← Economic Growth and Prosperity → ← Vietnam War →

← Baby Boom → ← Antiwar Movement →